Communications
in Computer and Information Science 1485

More information about this series at http://www.springer.com/series/7899

Teresa Guarda · Filipe Portela ·
Manuel Filipe Santos (Eds.)

Advanced Research in Technologies, Information, Innovation and Sustainability

First International Conference, ARTIIS 2021
La Libertad, Ecuador, November 25–27, 2021
Proceedings

 Springer

Editors
Teresa Guarda ⓘ
Universidad Estatal Península de Santa Elena
La Libertad, Ecuador

Filipe Portela ⓘ
Universidade do Minho
Guimarães, Portugal

Manuel Filipe Santos ⓘ
Universidade do Minho
Guimarães, Portugal

ISSN 1865-0929   ISSN 1865-0937 (electronic)
Communications in Computer and Information Science
ISBN 978-3-030-90240-7   ISBN 978-3-030-90241-4 (eBook)
https://doi.org/10.1007/978-3-030-90241-4

This Springer imprint is published by the registered company Springer Nature Switzerland AG
The registered company address is: Gewerbestrasse 11, 6330 Cham, Switzerland

Preface

New digital evolution and transformation trends are enabling communication and ubiquitous computing between global citizens, industry, organizations, networked machines, and physical objects, providing a promising vision of the future integrating the real world of knowledge agents and things with the virtual world of information.

The current reality and the future of computing and communications are supported by a dynamic technological evolution in many fields, from wireless sensors and networks to nanotechnology.

Due to its broad impact in many fields, it has rapidly gained global attention from academia, governments, industry, and the general public. This change in the network of agencies profoundly modifies the landscape of human activity, particularly as regards knowledge acquisition and production, offering new possibilities but also challenges that need to be explored and assessed.

This book contains a selection of papers accepted for presentation and discussion at the International Conference on Advanced Research in Technologies, Information, Innovation, and Sustainability (ARTIIS 2021).

ARTIIS is an international forum for researchers and practitioners to present and discuss the most recent innovations, trends, results, experiences, and concerns from the perspectives of technologies, information, innovation, and sustainability.

The first edition of ARTIIS was realized this year, and it was a success. We received 155 contributions from authors in 37 countries around the world. The acceptance rate was 35.48%, with 53 regular papers and 2 short papers selected for presentation at the conference.

This conference had the support of the CIST Research and Innovation Center of Universidad Estatal Peninsula de Santa Elena, Ecuador, and the Algoritmi Research Center of the University of Minho, Portugal. It was realized in a hybrid format, taking place both taking place both online and in person at the Santa Elena Peninsula, Salinas, Ecuador, during November 25–27, 2021.

The Program Committee was composed of a multidisciplinary group of more than 122 experts from 25 countries, with the responsibility of evaluating, in a 'double-blind review' process, the chapters received for each of the main themes proposed for the conference: Computing Solutions, Data Intelligence, Ethics, Security, and Privacy and Sustainability.

- Computing Solutions addresses the development of applications and platforms involving computing for some area of knowledge or society. It includes topics like networks, pervasive computing, gamification, and software engineering.
- Data Intelligence focuses on data (e.g., text, images) acquisition and processing using smart techniques or tools. It includes topics like computing intelligence, artificial intelligence, data science, and computer vision.

- Ethics, Security, and Privacy considers a more strict and secure area of information systems where the end-user is the main concern. Vulnerabilities, data privacy, and cybersecurity are the main subjects of this topic.
- Sustainability explores a new type of computing which is more green, connected, efficient, and sustainable. Topics like immersive technology, smart cities, and sustainable infrastructure are part of this chapter.

The papers accepted are published in this volume in the Communications in Computer and Information Science series (CCIS), which is indexed in DBLP, Google Scholar, EI-Compendex, SCImago, and Scopus. CCIS volumes are also submitted for inclusion in ISI Proceedings.

ARTIIS 2021 included several special sessions held in parallel with the conference. These special sessions were as follows: ACMaSDA 2021 – Applications of Computational Mathematics to Simulation and Data Analysis; CICITE 2021 – Challenges and the Impact of Communication and Information Technologies on Education; ISHMC 2021 – Intelligent Systems for Health and Medical Care; IWEBTM 2021 – International Workshop on Economics, Business, and Technology Management; IWET 2021 – International Workshop on Electronic and Telecommunications; TechDiComM 2021 – Technological Strategies on Digital Communication and Marketing; and RTNT 2021 – Boost Tourism using New Technologies.

We acknowledge all of those who contributed to this book: authors, organizing chairs, the steering committee, the Program Committee, special sessions chairs, and editors. We deeply appreciate their involvement and support, which were crucial for the success of the International Conference on Advanced Research in Technologies, Information, Innovation, and Sustainability (ARTIIS 2021).

The success of this first edition gives us a lot of confidence to continue the work. So, we hope to see you in the second edition in 2022.

November 2021

Teresa Guarda
Filipe Portela
Manuel Filipe Santos

Organization

Honorary Chair

Brij Bhooshan Gupta   NIT Kurukshetra, India

General Chairs

Teresa Guarda   Universidad Estatal Peninsula de Santa Elena, Ecuador

Filipe Portela   University of Minho, Portugal

Program Committee Chairs

Teresa Guarda   Universidad Estatal Peninsula de Santa Elena, Ecuador

Filipe Portela   University of Minho, Portugal

Manuel Filipe Santos   University of Minho, Portugal

Organizing Chairs

Maria Fernanda Augusto   Universidad Estatal Peninsula de Santa Elena, Ecuador

Marcelo Leon   Universidad Tecnológica Empresarial de Guayaquil, Ecuador

Jose Maria Diaz-Nafria   Universidad a Distancia de Madrid, Spain

Isabel Lopes   Instituto Politécnico de Bragança, Portugal

Domingos Martinho   ISLA Santarem, Portugal

Sajid Anwar   Institute of Management Sciences, Pakistan

Steering Committee

Wolfgang Hofkirchner   Technische Universität Wien, Austria

Valentina Lenarduzz   LUT University, Finland

Bruno Sousa   University of Coimbra, Portugal

Ricardo Vardasca   ISLA Santarem, Portugal

Workshops Committee

Sajid Anwar   Institute of Management Sciences, Pakistan

Jose Maria Diaz-Nafria   Universidad a Distancia de Madrid, Spain

Teresa Guarda   Universidad Estatal Peninsula de Santa Elena, Ecuador

Program Committee

Abreu, Maria José	Universidade do Minho, Portugal
Alanis Garza, Arnulfo	Instituto Tecnologico de Tijuana, Mexico
Alcaraz, Cristina	Universidad de Malaga, Spain
Aljuboori, Abbas	University of Information Technology and Communications, Iraq
Almeida, Sofia	Universidade Europeia, Portugal
Alvarez, Francisco	Universidad Autónoma de Aguascalientes, Mexico
Alves, Victor	University of Minho, Portugal
Andrade, António	Universidade Católica Portuguesa, Portugal
Anselma, Luca	Università di Torino, Italy
Anwar, Sajid	Institute of Management Sciences, Pakistan
Arcos, Claudio	Fundación San Francisco Global, Ecuador
Augusto, Maria Fernanda	Universidad Estatal Peninsula de Santa Elena, Ecuador
Azevedo, Ana	Instituto Politécnico do Porto, Portugal
Bacca Acosta, Jorge Luis	University of Girona, Spain
Balaji G, Naveen	University of KwaZulu-Natal, South Africa
Balsa, Carlos	Instituto Politécnico de Bragança, Portugal
Bandurova, Inna	Oxford Brookes University, UK
Baras, Karolina	Universidade da Madeira, Portugal
Belli, Simone	Universidad Complutense de Madrid, Spain
Biloborodova, Tetiana	Volodymyr Dahl East Ukrainian National University, Ukraine
Caballero Morales, Santiago Omar	Universidad Popular Autónoma del Estado de Puebla, Mexico
Cano-Olivos, Patricia	Universidad Popular Autónoma del Estado de Puebla, Mexico
Casillas Martín, Sonia	Universidad de Salamanca, Spain
Cortez, Paulo	University of Minho, Portugal
Costa, Ângelo	Universidade do Minho, Portugal
Díaz-Nafría, José María	Universidad a Distancia de Madrid, Spain
Dourado, Antonio	University of Coimbra, Portugal
Duarte, Júlio	University of Minho, Portugal
Dutta, Kamlesh	National Institute of Technology, Hamirpur, India
Fajardo-Flores, Silvia	Universidad de Colima, Mexico
Fernandes, António	Instituto Politécnico de Bragança, Portugal
Fernandes, Paula Odete	Instituto Politécnico de Bragança, Portugal
Filipe Santos, Manuel	University of Minho, Portugal
Flores, Jose	Universidad Popular Autónoma del Estado de Puebla, Mexico
Gago, Pedro	Polytechnic Institute of Leiria, Portugal
Gatica, Gustavo	Universidad Andrés Bello, Chile

Gomes, Luis	Universidade dos Açores, Portugal
Gomes, Raphael	Instituto Federal de Goiás, Brazil
Guarda, Teresa	Universidad Estatal Península de Santa Elena, Ecuador
Guarnizo Marin, Jose	Universidad Santo Tomás, Colombia
Guerra, Helia	University of the Azores, Portugal
Gupta, Nishu	Vaagdevi College of Engineering, India
Härer, Felix	University of Fribourg, Switzerland
Hornink, Gabriel	Federal University of Alfenas, Brazil
Hossian, Alejandro	Universidad Tecnológica Nacional, Argentina
Ilarri, Sergio	University of Zaragoza, Spain
Khan, Fakhri	Institute of Management Sciences, Pakistan
Khattak, Asad	Zayed University, United Arab Emirates
Kirsch-Pinheiro, Manuele	Université Paris 1 Panthéon-Sorbonne, France
Lancheros-Cuesta, Diana	Universidad de la Salle, Colombia
Lenarduzzi, Valentina	LUT University, Finland
Leon, Marcelo	Universidad Tecnológica Empresarial de Guayaquil, Ecuador
Lopes, Arminda	Madeira Interactive Technologies Institute, Portugal
Lopes, Frederico	Universidade Federal do Rio Grande do Norte, Brazil
Lopes, Isabel	Instituto Politécnico de Bragança, Portugal
Machado, José	University of Minho, Portugal
Marques, Nuno	NOVA School of Science and Technology, Portugal
Martinho, Domingos	ISLA Santarém, Portugal
Martinho, Ricardo	Polytechnic Institute of Leiria, Portugal
Maskeliunas, Rytis	Kaunas University of Technology, Lithuania
Mura, Ivan	Duke Kunshan University, China
Novais, Paulo	University of Minho, Portugal
Oliveira, Pedro	Instituto Politécnico de Bragança, Portugal
Paiva, Sara	Instituto Politécnico de Viana do Castelo, Portugal
Panagiotakis, Spyros	Hellenic Mediterranean University, Greece
Peixoto, Hugo	Universidade do Minho, Portugal
Pereira, Javier	Universidad Tecnologica de Chile, Chile
Pereira, Robson	Instituto Militar, Brazil
Pérez-Montoro, Mario	Universidad de Barcelona, Spain
Pinto, Filipe	Polytechnic Institute of Leiria, Portugal
Pinto, Mario	Instituto Politécnico do Porto, Portugal
Pinto, Mónica	Universidad de Malaga, Spain
Polkowski, Zdzislaw	Jan Wyzykowski University, Poland
Pombo, Nuno	University of Beira Interior, Portugal
Portela, Filipe	Universidade do Minho, Portugal
Queirós, Ricardo	Instituto Politécnico do Porto, Portugal

Quintela, Helder	Instituto Politécnico Cávado do Ave, Portugal
Ribeiro, Maria Isabel	Instituto Politécnico Bragança, Portugal
Riboni, Daniele	University of Cagliari, Italy
Rufino, José	Polytechnic Institute of Braganca, Portugal
Rusu, Eugen	Dunarea de Jos University of Galati, Romania
Sá, Jorge	University of Minho, Portugal
Semaan, F. S.	Universidade Federal Fluminense, Brazil
Shah, Babar	Zayed University, United Arab Emirates
Sharma, Manik	DAV University, India
Simões, Alberto	Instituto Politécnico Cávado do Ave, Portugal
Sousa, Bruno	University of Coimbra, Portugal
Sousa, Maria	CIEO, Portugal
Stavrakis, Modestos	University of the Aegean, Greece
Swacha, Jakub	University of Szczecin, Poland
Tchernykh, Andrei	CICESE Research Center, Mexico
Teh, Phoey Lee	Sunway University, Malaysia
Vardasca, Ricardo	ISLA Santarém, Portugal
Verdezoto, Nervo	Cardiff University, UK
Vicente, Henrique	Universidade de Évora, Portugal
Vieira de Castro, António	Instituto Politécnico do Porto, Portugal
Wei, Ran	Dalian University of Technology, China
Zolotas, Athanasios	University of York, UK

Sponsors

Universidad Estatal Peninsula de Santa Elena, Ecuador

Universidade do Minho, Portugal

ISLA Santarem, Portugal

Universidad Tecnológica Empresarial de Guayaquil, Ecuador

Institute of Management Sciences, Pakistan

BITrum Interdisciplinary Research Group

UNIAG, Portugal

Universidad a Distancia de Madrid, Spain

Instituto de Investigación Científica y Desarrollo Tecnológico

Contents

Computing Solutions

Computing Solutions

Dental Image Segmentation by Clustering Methods

Carlos Balsa[1]([envelope]) [iD], Cláudio Alves[1], Ronan Guivarch[2] [iD], and Sandrine Mouysset[3] [iD]

[1] Research Centre in Digitalization and Intelligent Robotics (CeDRI), Instituto Politécnico de Bragança, Bragança, Portugal
{balsa,claudioalves}@ipb.pt
[2] Université de Toulouse - INP - IRIT, Toulouse, France
Ronan.Guivarch@irit.fr
[3] Université de Toulouse, UPS - IRIT, Toulouse, France
Sandrine.Mouysset@irit.fr

Abstract. Segmentation of dental radiography allows the identification of human individuals but also could be used for the development of more effective diagnostic, monitoring, and evaluation of appropriate treatment plans. In practice, dark background and bones tissues are not distinguished with contour extraction methods on dental images. So we propose to first apply the k-means method and then extract the contours on the clustering result. We present an initialization of the k centroids based on the grey scale histograms, a weighted norm that includes both grey scale and geometrical information, and tests it on dental X-ray images. Then we describe a promising parallel clustering method based on kernel affinity.

Keywords: Image segmentation · Dental radiography · k-means · Norms · Spectral clustering

1 Introduction

Dental radiography is the most common way to get image of teeth. The X-ray images contain many information that can be extracted through techniques of digital image processing where the most important procedure is image segmentation. Image-processing procedure are used in computer applications such as human identification systems or assisting in clinical aspects like dental diagnosis systems and dental treatment systems [16].

The dental X-ray is a valuable tool in forensic odontology which is a branch of forensics concerned with identifying human individuals based on their dental feature prior and after death. Unlike other biometric identifiers, the teeth are not affected by the early decomposition of body tissues after death. For this reason, teeth are specially used as biometric identifiers of human cadaver under adverse circumstances encountered in mass disasters (tsunamis, airplane crashes,...) or when identification takes place a long time after the death [18].

The use of dental biometry in forensic identification requires a *ante-mortem* and *post-mortem* radiography that are both segmented and compared for identification of undefined victims [3]. The comparison on the contour (or shape) of corresponding individual tooth would require reliable segmentation technique that can extract the morphology of each individual tooth from gum, bone and other body tissues [18].

© Springer Nature Switzerland AG 2021
T. Guarda et al. (Eds.): ARTIIS 2021, CCIS 1485, pp. 3–17, 2021.
https://doi.org/10.1007/978-3-030-90241-4_1

Segmentation of dental radiography allows also the development of more effective diagnostic, monitoring and evaluation of appropriate treatment plans. In oral surgery, the segmentation is used to set up digitalized dental casts used in the simulation and the planning of orthodontic interventions [7]. It enables also a non-destructive evaluation that suits the simulation of endodontics, orthodontics, and other dental treatments [5]. Dental image-segmentation is also used to aid in determining areas of lesion especially the lesions below the cortical plate that are difficult to observe by the human eye [8].

Despite the diversity and quantity of applications, computer aided dental X-rays analysis is a challenging task if we want it to be automatic, or even semi-automatic. According to Shuo Li and co-authors [8], the challenging of dental X-rays analysis results from four characteristics: (1) poor image modalities: noise, low contrast, and sampling artifacts; (2) complicated topology; (3) arbitrary teeth orientation; and (4) lack of clear lines of demarcation between regions of interest.

Usually, dental image segmentation aims to achieve the two-dimensional contour (or shape) of the tooth or of some internal micro-structures. The automatic execution of these tasks involves the choice of the method according to the characteristics of the image. Each image point of a digital image, also called pixel, is characterized by a vector $x \in \mathbb{R}^p$ that is one-dimensional ($p = 1$) and corresponds to the grey intensity in grey scale images. This vector is three-dimensional ($p = 3$) and corresponds to the intensity of Red, Green and Blue in RGB scale images. The images used in this work are in grey scale ($p = 1$) because they result from dental radiography.

The segmentation techniques, most commonly used, can be classified into two broad categories: (1) techniques based on the homogeneity of the region, over the individualizing of the regions that satisfy a given criterion, and (2) techniques based on the detection of edges (borders) of a region, which allow tracing the boundaries between regions with different characteristics.

The methods belonging to the first category are looking for points with similar intensity values [6]. In this category, the clustering technique aims at partitioning a data set by bringing together similar elements in subsets, called clusters [12]. The similarity depends on the distance between each couple of data points and a reduced distance indicates that they are more similar.

Among the clustering techniques, k-means method [10] is a well-known method that partitions the dataset in exactly k clusters. This is achieved in a sequence of steps. In each step the cluster's centroid (arithmetic vector mean) is computed. The minimum distance between each data point and the clusters' different centroids will decide the formation of new clusters. The algorithm presents a rather fast convergence, but one cannot guarantee that the algorithm finds the global minimum [4] and, because during the initialization, the first centroids are chosen randomly, the results can be different for one run to another. To overcome this drawback, we propose to exploit the pick and valleys from the grey scale histogram of distribution. We apply the Otsu thresholding method [14] which lead to define the initial centroids as the distinct thresholds. The k-means algorithm based on a local procedure will converged in few steps.

We propose in this paper a process using a sequence of simple steps, with few supervision, in order to improve the dental image segmentation and contour detection but also that is more robust and no subject to random initialization. We propose a weighted norm which includes both grey scale and geometrical informations of the dental X-ray to observe if the geometrical information will improve the partitioning result.

This paper is organised as follows: in Sect. 2 we describe the dental images selected and the results of contour extraction with no treatment. In Sect. 3, we present the *k*-means algorithm, how we improve its robustness, and experimental results. Section 4 mentions a parallel approach to deal with the limitations we reach when the size of the images increases. Finally we conclude and describe future work in Sect. 5.

2 Contour Extraction on Dental Images

In this section, the dental X-ray images are firstly described. Then, the contour detections methods are presented, tested and thus, reveal some limits.

2.1 Data Description

We select four images shown in Fig. 1 to test the algorithms. These images come from typical dental X-rays made by two Portuguese dentists and were kindly provided by them for the realization of this work. Image **rx1** is a typical image, while the three others have some particularities. The image **rx2** has very high tonalities, **rx3** is an image with high definition and **rx4** represents a devitalized tooth with fillings in the nerve channels and inside of the crown.

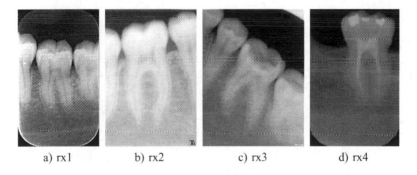

a) rx1   b) rx2   c) rx3   d) rx4

Fig. 1. Test images.

The **rx1** image has 612×366 pixels, **rx2** has 768×512 pixels, **rx3** has 1600×1200 and **rx4** has 1536×1023 pixels. All images are in grey scale with tonality values that ranges from 0 to 255, where 0 corresponds to black and 255 to white. We can present the number of pixels with the same intensity level in a histogram. The Fig. 2 contains this grey scale histogram corresponding to each test image.

In all histograms of Fig. 2 one can see a large number of pixels with very low tonality. These pixels are part of the dark background of the image.

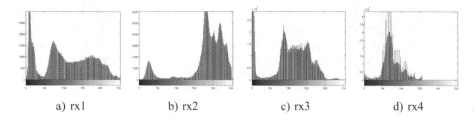

a) rx1   b) rx2   c) rx3   d) rx4

Fig. 2. Grey scale histograms.

If we shift the scale to the right we find another high frequency of tonality corresponding to the bone tissue. Its value range varies from image to image and depends from the X-ray process, especially in light intensity. For the images **rx1**, **rx3** and **rx4** the tonality of the bone tissue is between 50 and 100 and for **rx2** is between 250 and 200. The difference is due to the fact that **rx2** is much brighter than the other images.

Continuing to shift to the right, we found another peak frequency which corresponds essentially to the tooth region. This peak may be more or less close to the peak corresponding to the bone. For instance, the two peaks are close in **rx2** and **rx4** while they are more distant in **rx1** and **rx3**. We also observed that between the two tonality values, corresponding to bone and tooth, there are values with high frequencies, making hard the distinction between the two regions. In the right part of the **rx4** histogram there are several smaller peaks that indicate the existence of small regions with light colour, probably due to filling material in the tooth.

2.2   Contour Detection Methods

The methods that we have used in this work to detect the contour of the teeth are also known as edge detection methods and are included in the function `edge` of the Matlab Image Processing Toolbox (IPT). These methods detect the points corresponding to the meaningful discontinuities in the intensity values. Such discontinuities are detected by using the gradient or the Laplacian of the intensity function of the image. These approaches correspond to search points with high values of the gradient function or zero crossing points of the Laplacian function. We present here a short survey of the main edge detectors methods.

If the function $f(x,y)$ gives the grey intensity value for each point with coordinate (x,y), the corresponding gradient function will be defined by the following vector:

$$\nabla f = \begin{bmatrix} g_x \\ g_y \end{bmatrix} = \begin{bmatrix} \frac{\partial f}{\partial x} \\ \frac{\partial f}{\partial y} \end{bmatrix} \tag{1}$$

The magnitude of this vector is given by the corresponding norm $\|\nabla f\|$. To simplify the computations, the magnitude is sometimes computed using approximated standard norms. The magnitude of the gradient has the same behaviour as the derivatives. It is zero in regions of constant intensity and its value changes proportionally to the degree of intensity variation in regions with different grey tonalities. When the gradient vector is non zero at coordinate (x, y), it points always in the direction of the maximum variation of the intensity function $f(x, y)$. The maximum rate of change occurs at the angle:

$$\alpha(x, y) = \tan^{-1}\left(\frac{g_x}{g_y}\right) \tag{2}$$

The main differences between edge detection methods are how to estimate the derivatives $\partial f/\partial x$ and $\partial f/\partial y$. Since the domain is digital (discrete), derivatives in a point with coordinate (x, y) are approached by finite differences.

In the **Roberts method** [17] the derivatives are computed taking into account sets of 2×2 points

$$g_x \approx f(x+1, y+1) - f(x, y)$$
$$g_y \approx f(x+1, y) - f(x, y+1) \tag{3}$$

The Roberts contour detector is the simplest and the oldest method used to detect edges. It is mainly used to detect diagonal edges. However, its efficiency is limited because it uses a small number of points to detect the variation of intensity.

In the **Prewitt method** [15] the first derivatives in a point with coordinate (x, y) are computed taking into account the set of 3×3 neighbouring points. This approach includes the nature of the data on opposite sides of the center point, with coordinate (x, y), and thus carry more information regarding the direction of an edge [6].

The **Sobel method** [19] is similar to the Prewitt method. There are only small differences in the coefficients used to approach the first derivatives. It uses a weight of 2 in the center coefficient which provides better noise-suppression and consequently image smoothing [6].

All the previous edge detector methods are based on a specified thresholding of $\|\nabla f\|$. The **Canny method** [2] has a slightly different approach. The gradient is computed using the derivatives of a Gaussian filter, instead of computing the gradient directly from the intensity function $f(x, y)$. This filter is defined by the Gaussian function

$$G(x, y) - \exp\left(-\frac{x^2 + y^2}{2\sigma^2}\right) \tag{4}$$

where σ is the standard deviation. After, the image is smoothed using the Gaussian filter, to reduce the noise, the magnitude of the gradient and the edge direction, equation (2) are computed at each point in order to find all the edges. The determined edge points are classified as strong or weak edges according to the position of the gradient magnitude comparatively to two different thresholds T_1 and T_2, previously fixed. The Canny method returns the strong edges and weak edges that are connected with them.

Another approach to detect points with meaningful changes in the intensity values is based on the idea of finding the zeros of the second derivatives. This idea is exploited in the **LoG method** [11] that consists in computing Laplacian of filtered image. The Laplacian of the Gaussian function (Eq. (4)) is

$$\nabla^2 G(x, y) = \left[\frac{x^2 + y^2 - 2\sigma^2}{\sigma^4}\right] \exp\left(-\frac{x^2 + y^2}{2\sigma^2}\right) \tag{5}$$

The expression in Eq. (5) is called the *Laplacian of a Gaussian* (LoG). The convolution of the intensity function of the image $f(x,y)$ with the LoG filter $\nabla^2 G(x,y)$ has two effects. The first is that the image is smoothed (the noise is reduced), the second is that the Laplacian is computed, which yields a double-edge image. The localization of the edges is achieved by finding the zeros crossings between the double edges.

Edge detectors that are based on the same concept as LoG method but where the convolution is carried out using a specific filter function different from the Gaussian are called **zero-crossing detectors** [6].

2.3   Limits of Contour Detection on Dental Images

We test these methods with the four dental images using MATLAB toolbox. The function to detect contours is the function edge. We choose to use edge with no adjustment of the threshold parameter; we remind that our goal is to have an automatic process, so we no not want to tune this parameter.

The results are similar with the four examples and can be divided in two categories. At first category the results where there is too many edges (canny, log, zerocross) (see Fig. 3, on each figure the edges are printed in red over the original image **rx3**). At second category results where there is not enough edges (prewitt, roberts, sobel) (see Fig. 4).

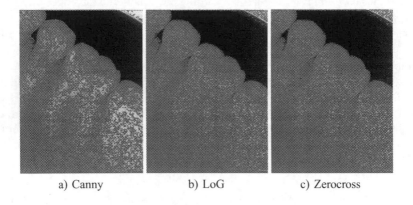

a) Canny   b) LoG   c) Zerocross

Fig. 3. Results with too many edges

In both situations, the results are unusable. Dark background and bones tissues are not distinguished with contour extraction on dental images. We present in the next section how a segmentation of the images before the edge detection can be useful.

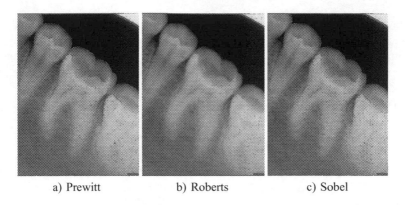

| a) Prewitt | b) Roberts | c) Sobel |

Fig. 4. Results with not enough edges

3 Image Segmentation with Clustering Techniques

In the following, k-means, one of the most important clustering method, is presented. Then an initialization based on the dental images and a weighted norm which includes the geometrical coordinates are proposed and then tested on images.

3.1 k-means Algorithm

We are concerned with n data observations $S = \{x_i, i = 1..n\} \in \mathbb{R}^p$ that we want to classify in k clusters, where k is predetermined. We organize the data as lines in a matrix $X \in \mathbb{R}^{n \times p}$. To describe the k-means method as proposed in [4], we denote a partition of vectors $x_1, \ldots, x_n$ in k clusters as $\prod = \{\pi_1, \ldots, \pi_k\}$ where $\pi_j = \{q : x_q \in \text{cluster} j\}$ defines the set of vectors in cluster j. The centroid (arithmetic mean) of the cluster j is:

$$m_j = \frac{1}{|\pi_j|} \sum_{\ell \in \pi_j} x_\ell \tag{6}$$

where $|\pi_j|$ is the number of elements in cluster j. The sum of the squared distance, in a given norm, between the data points and the j cluster's centroid is known as the *coherence*:

$$E_j = \sum_{q \in \pi_j} \left\| x_q - m_j \right\|^2 \tag{7}$$

The closer the vectors are to the centroid, the smaller the value of E_j. The quality of a clustering process can be measured as the *overall coherence*:

$$E(m_1, .., m_k) = \sum_{j=1}^{k} E_j \tag{8}$$

The k-means is considered as an optimization method because it seeks a partition process that minimizes $E(m_1, .., m_k)$ and, consequently, finds an optimal coherence. The problem of minimizing the *overall coherence* is NP-hard and, therefore, very difficult to achieve. The basic algorithm for k-means clustering is an iterative two-step heuristic procedure. Firstly, each vector is assigned to its closest group. After that, new centroids are computed using the assigned vectors. In the following version of k-means algorithm, proposed by [4], these steps are iterated until the changes in the *overall coherence* are lower than a certain tolerance.

Algorithm 1. The k-means algorithm

---

1. Start with k initial centroid vectors $m_j^{(0)}$ for $j = 1, \ldots, k$. Compute $E(m_1^{(0)}, \ldots, m_k^{(0)})$. Put $t = 1$.
2. For each vector x_i find the closest centroid. If the closest centroid is m_p^{t-1} assign x_i to $\pi_p^{(t)}$.
3. Compute the centroids $m_j^{(t)}$ for $j = 1, \ldots, k$ of the new partitioning $\Pi^{(t)}$.
4. If $\left| E(m_1^{(t)}, \ldots, m_k^{(t)}) - E(m_0^{(t-1)}, \ldots, m_k^{(t-1)}) \right| <$ tol, stop; Otherwise $t = t + 1$ and go to step 2.

Since it is a heuristic algorithm there is no guarantee that k-means will converge to the global minimum. A deterministic version of k-means, called Global k-means [1,9], is a variant of k-means that does not depend on any initial positions for the cluster center and with the local search of k-means at each step, it provides excellent results in terms of the mean square clustering error criterion or overall coherence E. But with images with high dimension, the computational complexity and the memory cost are too important when using Matlab.

3.2 Initialization

The k-means algorithm based in a local search procedure suffers from its sensitivity with initial conditions on the centroids. To avoid this issue, it is common to run it multiple times, with different starting conditions choosing the solution with the smaller $E(m_1, \ldots, m_k)$ but it is still not robust as we can see in Fig. 5 where we present the results of two runs of k-means on images **rx2** and **rx3** ($k = 4$) with the same input parameters.

We propose to exploit the histograms of dental images (cf. Fig. 2) to define the initialization of the centroids. We use a thresholding method, called Otsu's method [14], to fix initial centroids with respect to the grey scaled distribution of the image. Peaks and valleys of the image histogram are exploited for choosing the appropriate value for the thresholds T_1 and T_2. Global thresholding, using multiple thresholds T_1, T_2, create an image G from the data image I such that:

$$G(i,j) = \begin{cases} a & \text{if } I(i,j) > T_2 \\ b & \text{if } T_1 \leq I(i,j) \leq T_2 \\ c & \text{if } I(i,j) < T_1. \end{cases} \tag{9}$$

Otsu's multiple thresholding, as k-means, is based on the interclass variance max-imization in the sense that well thresholded classes have well discriminated intensity values. Each centroid will represent a threshold from the Otsu method.

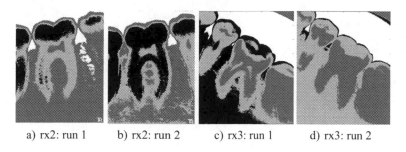

a) rx2: run 1   b) rx2: run 2   c) rx3: run 1   d) rx3: run 2

Fig. 5. Two results of k-means on **rx2** and **rx3**

As the k-means algorithm is based in a local search procedure, Otsu's method conditions the segmentation in an optimized way. The minimization of the overall coherence E with this initialization permits extracting more information in the clusters specially when the dental X-ray presents some difficulty as shown in Fig. 1 with the depth of **rx3** and the restoration materials of **rx4**.

3.3 About the Norms

When dealing with grey-scale images, one have the possibility to use different norms to measure the distance among the elements of a data set in segmentation algorithms.

Let us consider an image I of size $l \times m$ and denote a pixel p as a triplet (i, j, I_{ij}) where (i, j) are the coordinates of the pixel in I and I_{ij} its grey intensity.

Norms where only the grey intensity I_{ij} is taking into account can be considered. For instance MATLAB k-means function permits us to choose between the L_1-norm (called City-Block norm) or the L_2-norm (or Euclidian norm). The distance between two pixels $p = (i, j, I_{ij})$ and $p' = (i', j', I_{i'j'})$ is then computed by

$$d_1(p, p') = |I_{ij} - I_{i'j'}| \tag{10}$$

for the L_1-norm and

$$d_2(p, p') = \|I_{ij} - I_{i'j'}\|_2 \tag{11}$$

for the L_2-norm. In practice, the clustering results with either the L_1 or L_2 norm are exactly the same. So in the following, we will show the resulting segmentation with norm d_1.

But one may consider norms where the geometry of the image is also taking into account. Then, the resulting clusters of the segmentation algorithms will group pixels with close grey intensity but also that are close to each others in the image. Norms that include both grey intensity and geometry can be defined with a weight on each part. In the experiments, we use the following norm to compute the distance between two pixels p and p':

$$d_G(p, p') = \alpha \left(\left(\frac{i - i'}{l} \right)^2 + \left(\frac{j - j'}{m} \right)^2 \right)^{\frac{1}{2}} + \beta \left| \frac{I_{ij} - I_{i'j'}}{256} \right| \tag{12}$$

12   C. Balsa et al.

3.4   Experimental Results

The analysis of histograms (Fig. 2) allowed us to identify three main grey tonality, corresponding to the three main regions of the images: tooth, bone and dark background. Based on this observation we apply the k-means method to separate the image pixels into three clusters for **rx1** and is plotted Fig. 6. As expected, the three clusters correspond mainly to the principal image areas, namely the tooth, bone tissue and the dark background. Cluster 1 includes most of the teeth as well as the small pieces of bone tissue that are lighter. Cluster 2 includes most of the bone tissue as well as the most shaded parts of the tooth, particularly the crown and the pulp cavity. Cluster 3 includes only the background image around the crown. This last area can be used to define the contour of the tooth crown.

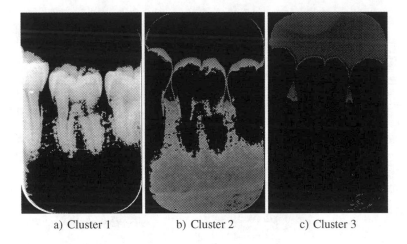

a) Cluster 1   b) Cluster 2   c) Cluster 3

Fig. 6. Segmentation of **rx1** by k-means in 3 clusters.

In the following, we apply the Sobel method (unless mentioned) for the contour detection on the clustering results from k-means for all the test images (we observe that after segmentation, the results are roughly the same regardless of the edge detection method used). We plot on the original image the detected contours in red color in Fig. 7 for results with the norm d_1 and norm d_G. The parameters α and β of the norm d_G are 0.05 and 0.95 (the results are very sensitive to these values and the geometric part has to be small).

The results obtained by classifying into 3 clusters **rx1** show that the contours which separate the clusters 2 and 3 fail to perfectly separate the bone from the tooth. This is due to the similarity between tonalities in both parts of the image. All pixels with similar tonality values are included in the same cluster, regardless of their position in the image.

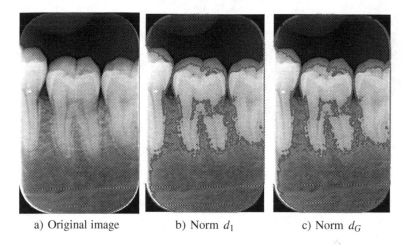

a) Original image   b) Norm d_1 c) Norm d_G

Fig. 7. Results with image **rx1** ($k = 3$)

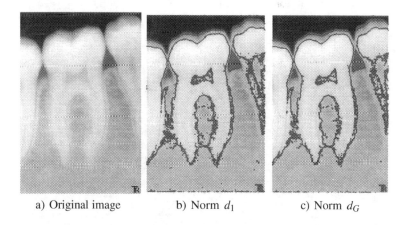

a) Original image   b) Norm d_1 c) Norm d_G

Fig. 8. Results with image **rx2** ($k = 3$).

The contours resulting from the clustering of **rx2** in three clusters are shown in Fig. 8. It is noted that although **rx2** having tonalities of tooth and bone regions very close (see Fig. 2b), the division into three regions permits separate much of the tooth from the bone tissue. The contour of the first and the second clusters contain a large part of respectively the tooth and the bone. As had already been observed for **rx1**, the segmentation of the tooth fails especially around the roots where small lighter areas of bone are affected to the bone region. It fails also in the top of the crown and in the pulp cavity due to darker tonalities of the pixels in these area. The use of norm d_G suppresses some noise around the contours of the tooth.

Image **rx3** presents a different angle of incidence of the rays. Figure 9 shows the four regions resulting from the segmentation of the image **rx3** by k-means method. Compared with previous images, the separation between the tooth and bone tissue in

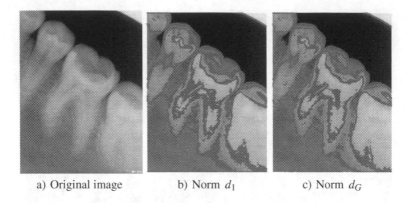

a) Original image   b) Norm d_1 c) Norm d_G

Fig. 9. Results with image **rx3** ($k = 4$).

the root zone is well achieved. This may be due to the high resolution of the image resulting in a smoother variation in the tonalities of grey, which better differentiate the various structures resulting from the X-ray. The use of geometrical distance filters some noise around the root canals.

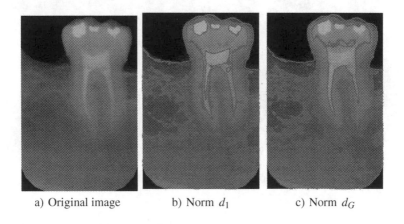

a) Original image   b) Norm d_1 c) Norm d_G

Fig. 10. Results with image **rx4** ($k = 6$).

The tooth shown in the image **rx4** is devitalized. As it includes material restoration, the image is segmented in six clusters and the detected contours are plotted in Fig. 11. This result shows that k-means is appropriate to isolate the morphology of dental restorations for the norm d_1 (or d_2) (Fig. 10b) whereas the filling of root canals and crown restoration materials are included in the cluster associated with the tooth when the segmentation is made in tree clusters (Fig. 10c).

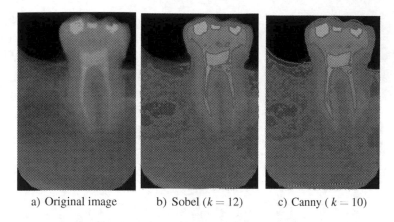

a) Original image   b) Sobel ($k = 12$)   c) Canny ($k = 10$)

Fig. 11. Results with image **rx4** with sobel and canny filter.

Results on image **rx4** with the norm d_G for $k = 6$ show that the crown restoration material is not captured although it is done with norm d_1. So we try higher values of k to evaluate when those parts are detected. We obtain the value $k = 12$ (see Fig. 11) with Sobel method. If we use now the Canny method, $k = 10$ is sufficient to detect those restorations but we observe some noise at the bottom of the image. In fact, we find the behaviour of the edge detection methods mentioned in Sect. 2.3 but with some good results in the interesting parts of the image.

4   Parallel Spectral Clustering

The k-means algorithm with Euclidean measure could only create linearly separated clusters. But kernel affinity, for example Gaussian affinity defined by Eq. (4), are useful when considering non-convex shaped subsets of points.

Spectral clustering aims at selecting dominant eigenvectors of a parametrized Gaussian affinity matrix in order to build an embedding space in which the clustering is made. The drawback of clustering method is that the complete affinity matrix should be computed. And the memory cost and the computational complexity lead to adapt this method for parallelization with a divide and conquer strategy [13] in a FORTRAN code with MPI parallel environment.

By exploiting the topology of images, clustering can be made on subdomains by breaking up the data set into data subsets with respect to their geometrical coordinates in a straightforward way. With an appropriate Gaussian affinity parameter [12] and a method to determine the number of clusters, each processor applies independently the spectral clustering on a subset of data points and provides a local partition on this data subsets. Based on these local partitions, a grouping step ensures the connection between subsets of data and determines a global partition.

At the grouping level, spectral clustering algorithm is made on a subset with geometrical coordinates close to the boundaries of the previous subdomains. This partitioning will connect together clusters which belong to different subdomains thanks to a transitive relation.

As the image is divided in data subset according to the geometrical coordinates, we use the geometrical norm defined by Eq. (12). Figure 12 presents a first result of parallel sprectral clustering followed by edge detection on dental image **rx1**. The results are promising and permits us to continue this work with images of high dimension/precision.

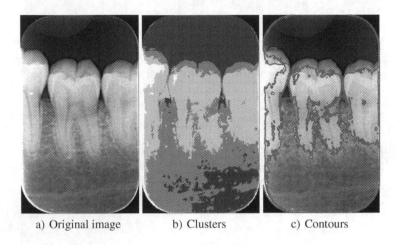

a) Original image   b) Clusters   c) Contours

Fig. 12. Results with parallel sprectral clustering.

5   Conclusion

The successful of the segmentation depends largely on the target image. If the goal is to obtain the contour of the tooth, the existence of shaded areas, especially in the periphery, make this task difficult. Care must also be taken to position and calibrate the equipment to provide the best angle of incidence for the rays. It should be taken also care in positioning and calibrating the equipment in a manner to provide the best angle of incidence of the rays. This process is responsible for the homogeneity of the regions in each of the different structures.

The k-means method allows to split the image into several parts depending on the tonality of grey. This method adapts well to the problem of segmentation of dental images where there are three dominants tonalities. The clustering into three clusters allows to divide the image into three regions: the tooth, the bone and the dark background. With the use of a larger number of clusters it is possible to isolate other structures inside the tooth, for example, the materials used in dental treatments. With an optimal initialization of the centroids and the possibility of using a geometrical norm k-means offers different segmentations which lead to detect more precisions in the contours with classical methods such as Sobel or Canny methods.

We present in this paper a sequence of simple steps to improve the robustness of k-means method with very few input parameters, essentially the number of clusters which value could be fixed by an analysis of grey scale histograms. We mention the spectral clustering method, that is a promising method when considering images with high dimension and/or precision. To be able to process theses images, parallel methods, parallel spectral clustering but also a parallel Global k-means, are necessary and it is in this direction that our future work will lead.

References

1. Agrawal, A., Gupta, H.: Global K-means (gkm) clustering algorithm: a survey. Int. J. Comput. Appl. **79**, 20–24 (2013)
2. Canny, J.: A computational approach to edge detection. In: Readings in Computer Vision, pp. 184–203. Elsevier (1987)
3. Dighe, S., Shriram, R.: Preprocessing, segmentation and matching of dental radiographs used in dental biometrics. Int. J. Sci. Appl. Info. Technol. **1**(2), 52–56 (2012)
4. Eldén, L.: Matrix Methods in Data Mining and Pattern Recognition. Society for Industrial and Applied Mathematics, Philadelphia (2007)
5. Gao, H., Hossain, M.J., Chae, O., Chen, J.X.: Visualization of tooth for non destructive evaluation. In: Advanced Nondestructive Evaluation II. World Scientific Publishing Company, August 2008
6. Gonzalez, R.C., Woods, R.E.: Digital Image Processing. Pearson Education, London (2008)
7. Kronfeld, T., Brunner, D., Brunnett, G.: Snake-based segmentation of teeth from virtual dental casts. Comput. Aided Des. Appl. **7**(2), 221–233 (2010)
8. Li, S., Fevens, T., Krzyżak, A., Jin, C., Li, S.: Semi-automatic computer aided lesion detection in dental x-rays using variational level set. Pattern Recogn. **40**(10), 2861–2873 (2007)
9. Likas, A., Vlassis, N., Verbeek, J.J.: The global k-means clustering algorithm. Pattern Recogn. **36**(2), 451–461 (2003)
10. MacQueen, J.: Some methods for classification and analysis of multivariate observations. In: Le Cam, L.M., Neyman, J. (eds.) Proceedings of the Fifth Berkeley Symposium on Mathematical Statistics and Probability, vol. 1, pp. 281–297. University of California Press (1967)
11. Marr, D., Hildreth, E.: Theory of edge detection. Proc. Roy. Soc. London. Ser. B. Biol. Sci. **207**(1167), 187–217 (1980)
12. Mouysset, S., Noailles, J., Ruiz, D.: Using a global parameter for gaussian affinity matrices in spectral clustering. In: Palma, J.M.L.M., Amestoy, P.R., Daydé, M., Mattoso, M., Lopes, J.C. (eds.) VECPAR 2008. LNCS, vol. 5336, pp. 378–390. Springer, Heidelberg (2008). https://doi.org/10.1007/978-3-540-92859-1_34
13. Mouysset, S., Noailles, J., Ruiz, D., Guivarch, R.: On a strategy for spectral clustering with parallel computation. In: Palma, J.M.L.M., Daydé, M., Marques, O., Lopes, J.C. (eds.) VECPAR 2010. LNCS, vol. 6449, pp. 408–420. Springer, Heidelberg (2011). https://doi.org/10.1007/978-3-642-19328-6_37
14. Otsu, N.: A threshold selection method from gray-level histograms. IEEE Trans. Syst. Man Cybernet. **9**(1), 62–66 (1979)
15. Prewitt, J.: Object enhancement and extraction. In: Lipkin, B., Rosenfeld, A. (eds.) Picture Processing and Psychopictorics, pp. 75–149. Academic Press, New York (1970)
16. Rad, A., Rahim, M.S.M., Rehman, A., Altameem, A., Saba, T.: Evaluation of current dental radiographs segmentation approaches in computer-aided applications. IETE Tech. Rev. **30**(3), 210 (2013)
17. Roberts, L.: Machine perception of three-dimensional solids. In: Tippett, J.T., et al. (eds.) Optical and Electro-Optical Information Processing, May 1965
18. Said, E., Fahmy, G.F., Nassar, D., Ammar, H.: Dental x-ray image segmentation. In: Jain, A.K., Ratha, N.K. (eds.) Biometric Technology for Human Identification. SPIE August 2004
19. Sobel, I.E.: Camera models and machine perception. Ph.D. dissertation, Stanford University, Stanford (1970)

glossaLAB: Enabling the Co-creation of Interdisciplinary Knowledge Through the Reviving of Long-Term Conceptual Elucidation

José María Díaz-Nafría[1,2,3]([✉]) [ID], Antonio Jesús Muñóz-Montoro[1] [ID],
Isaac Seoane[1] [ID], Javier Bravo-Agapito[4] [ID], Gerhard Chroust[4] [ID],
Modestos Stavrakis[3,5] [ID], and Teresa Guarda[2,6,7] [ID]

[1] Madrid Open University, Madrid, Spain
{josemaria.diaz.n,antoniojesus.munoz.m,isaac.seoane}@udima.es
[2] BITrum-Research Group, León, Spain
[3] Institute for a Global Sustainable Information Society, Vienna, Austria
[4] Universidad Complutense de Madrid, Madrid, Spain
javier.bravo@ucm.es, gerhard.chroust@jku.at
[5] University of the Aegean, Mytilene, Greece
modestos@aegean.gr
[6] Universidad Estatal Peninsula de Santa Elena, La Libertad, Ecuador
[7] CIST – Centro de Investigación en Sistemas y Telecomunicaciones, Universidad Estatal
Peninsula de Santa Elena, La Libertad, Ecuador

Abstract. As we have discussed in previous works, glossaLAB project is devoted to the integration of an extensive encyclopedic corpus into a system of *interdisciplinary glossaries* -whose concept has been described thoroughly-. By that means, glossaLAB intends to offer a platform for the co-creation of interdisciplinary and transdisciplinary knowledge that revives sound endeavours to strengthen the capacity of systems science and information studies -including a panoply of related disciplines- based on the clarification of concepts, theories, metaphors and problems addressed by these disciplines. To this purpose, the first step consists in the transference of contents from the original non-standard formats -mostly focused on a particular way of presentation- to an interoperable coding through which the content can be delivered to multiple platforms, and particularly to the elucidation platform, based on MediaWiki technology in which the co-creation of contents is to be continued. The magnitude of the corpus -over six thousand articles in a hypertext of more than one hundred thousand links- requires the automation of the process. We describe the process developed to make the content interoperable and to deploy it into the glossaLAB platform set up for the continuation of the elucidation process. Furthermore, glossaLAB is devised as a federated system of interdisciplinary glossaries which evolve autonomously but cooperate in the development of a network of transdisciplinary concepts whose performance is intended to grow over time. This organisation also serves to the qualification of the integration of knowledge achieved through the elucidation process based on a bi-dimensional measurement of the diversity of the co-created knowledge and the effectiveness of the integration achieved.

© Springer Nature Switzerland AG 2021
T. Guarda et al. (Eds.): ARTIIS 2021, CCIS 1485, pp. 18–33, 2021.
https://doi.org/10.1007/978-3-030-90241-4_2

Keywords: Knowledge organization · Interdisciplinarity · Transdisciplinarity · Knowledge integration · Systems science · Information studies

1 Introduction

"We will evermore need good models of complex situations, that cannot anymore be understood, evaluated and amended by the exclusive use of our present linear and reductionist models. Some examples of such situations are: underdevelopment; the universal squandering of resources; the worldwide spread of unemployment; the hothouse effect [...]" (C. François [13], p. 11)

Throughout the 20th century, the need to break down the walls that separate the specialities in which knowledge is forged has become progressively more clear [3, 6]. Specialization as a privileged mode of knowledge production was the architect of great achievements of modernity; however, it has accumulated problems that are imperceptible to the specialised gaze. In the 21st century, we know that global challenges such as climate and ecological balances, peace, poverty… – even when we are just addressing local issues – require considering the many factors that participate in the solution. For this, it is necessary to study reality and to confront it in a multi-perspectivistic and synthetic manner, beyond the analytical view that has fostered the development of "linear and reductionist models", woven in the looms of specialised disciplines since the beginning of modernity. This necessity has motivated that educational and scientific policies have focused for decades on building interdisciplinary and transdisciplinary scientific-technical strategies, particularly promoted from international institutions [8–12, 14, 20, 21].

However, despite the effort done in the last decades, we still lack well-established frameworks enabling, on the one hand, the articulation of disciplinary knowledge across institutional and cognitive barriers, on the other, the assessment of the quality of interdisciplinarity [12, 19]. Referring to Transdisciplinary Research (TDR) Belcher et al. [1] have stressed the relevance of the latter void because it reinforces the former void: "The lack of a standard and broadly applicable framework for the evaluation of quality in TDR is perceived to cause an implicit or explicit devaluation of high-quality TDR or may prevent quality TDR from being done." (*ibid*: p. 14). Many endeavours, aimed at fortifying TDR, focus on improving methodologies; others on developing evaluation means.

1.1 glossaLAB Project

The glossaLAB project [6] intends to contribute to both horns of the dilemma of strengthening the establishment of transdisciplinarity; supporting, on one side, the enhancement of transdisciplinary performance; on the other, offering tools for the assessment of such performance in the process of knowledge co-creation. This objective materialises in the development of an open online platform, capable to facilitate and evaluate the cooperative elucidation of concepts, theories, metaphors and problems in the study of systems and information from specific applications to the most overarching abstractions in a federated system of *interdisciplinary-glossaries* (ID-G) (where the concept of *interdisciplinary-glossaries*, which be abbreviated as ID-G from now on, has been defined in [3, 5]. The highest level of this ID-G system is occupied by the *Encyclopedia of Systems Science and Cybernetics Online* (ESSCO) and the lowest level by a set of ID-G, focused on problem-oriented projects [6].

For the on-setting of ESSCO, one of the most remarkable objectives of the project is making inter-operable the encyclopedic corpus of Charles François's *International Encyclopedia of Systems and Cybernetics* (IESC) [13], whose praiseworthy contents crystalised an elucidation work of decades. In addition, two other encyclopedic ventures enrich the initial corpus from which ESSCO departs, namely, the *Principia Cybernetica*, devoted to cybernetics and systems theory [15], and *glossariumBITri*, devoted to the interdisciplinary study of information and constituting the first instance of the concept of ID-G as a framework for knowledge co-creation and integration assessment [7]. The elucidation purpose to which these encyclopedic projects served come alive again, by making their contents interoperable and available on the glossaLAB platform, not only to be read but also to be further developed.

The value of the elucidation in the study of systems and information for the strengthening of trans- and inter-disciplinarity has a double reason: (i) the capacity of systems science at large to underpin transdisciplinarity, as stressed since the 1970s and recalled on numerous occasions: "systems theory examined the abstract organisation of phenomena, independent of their substance, type, or spatial or temporal scale of existence ... [It gave] rise to the idea of an abstract structural unity of scientific knowledge against the background of... progressive fragmentation..." ([21]: p.17); [17]; (ii) the proliferation of systems approaches and systems-related disciplines has interfered in the capacity of systems sciences to facilitate the integration of scientific knowledge [2, 16], as claimed by Klir at relatively early times: "The comparison of individual conceptual frameworks used in individual approaches to general systems theory appears to be very difficult. A metatheory must be used to decide whether one concept is identical to, is different from, or is a proper subset of a concept drawn from another theory." [18].

Thus systems concepts facilitate the breaking down of cognitive barriers, but at the same time require the decrease of the epistemic apparent complexity to improve its *intensional performance,* and the increase of the *referencing capacity* to expand its applicability. GlossaLAB project intends to contribute to this goal [6].

Figure 1 schematizes the main purposes of the project. The encyclopedic corpus is shown on the left and the glossaLAB platform on the right, while the transference process is represented through the flow diagram in between. The focus on increasing the interoperability of contents is also represented in the bidirectional passage to other formats shown on the lower part. The project as a whole embraces three layers [6]: at the *technical layer*, glossaLAB aims at developing a platform for knowledge integration based on the elucidation of concepts, metaphors, theories and problems, including the semantically-operative recompilation of aforementioned encyclopedic contents. At the *theoretical layer*, the project pursues the increase of the "intensional performance" of the contents recompiled, and the elucidation of new concepts. Finally, at the *meta-theoretical layer*, glossaLAB is committed to evaluating the knowledge integration achieved through the co-creation process based on (a) the diversity of the disciplines involved and (b) the integration properties of the conceptual network deployed through the elucidation process.

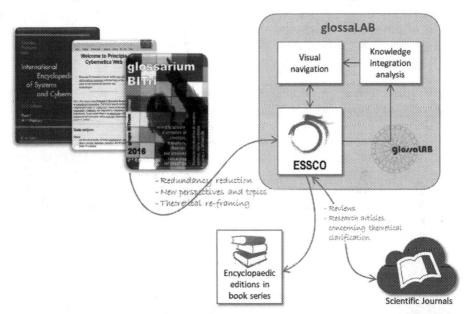

Fig. 1. Overview of glossaLAB project: (i) recompiling encyclopedic corpus; (ii) re-elaborating and increasing contents: improving intentional and extensional performance; (iii) facilitating content co-creation, navigation and integration analysis; (iv) multiplying outputs and impacts.Making the encyclopedic corpus interoperable

We will focus this article on the technical layer as regards (i) the conversion of the encyclopedic corpus into interoperable formats; (ii) its transference to the glossaLAB platform; (iii) the creation of the platform based on MediaWiki technology to articulate the federated system of ID-G referred above with the following capacities: a) enabling the interdisciplinary peer-reviewed co-creation of contents (applying different quality controls depending on the collection to which the contribution is proposed); b) assessing the achievements of knowledge integration; c) facilitating semantic navigation, and d) extracting contents to different formats.

Due to the volume of the corpus –which involves over six thousand articles to be incorporated into a hypertext of more than one hundred thousand links– the challenge of (i) and (ii) concerns the automation of the related endeavours, as we will see in Sect. 2. The architecture of glossaLAB as a system of federated ID-G will be discussed in Sect. 3, while the design of the network infrastructure that supports the platform will be addressed in Sect. 4.

2   Making the Encyclopedic Corpus Interoperable

As regards the aforementioned purpose of making the encyclopedic corpus interoperable and accessible through the glossaLAB platform, the process was divided into two main undertakings: (i) the re-codification of the contents in their original format to a standardised one; (ii) the re-codification from the standard format into the formats required for its proper handling in the glossaLAB platform, which is engined by MediaWiki technology.

The problem is significantly different for the first and largest encyclopedic corpus involved and the others since the former one is originally coded in an editorial-specific format, oriented towards paper printing, while the latter is already available online in html code. Thus we will focus the following description of the transference endeavour on the François' encyclopedia (IESC) since it is the one that has no trivial solution.

Figure 2 represents the basic processes involved in the conversion of the original IESC contents into an interoperable form and its dumping into the glossaLAB platform, for which the intermediate milestone is represented by the attainment of the codification in LaTex of the original corpus. Where LaText was selected in virtue of: availability of macros for conversion; ease conversion to other standard formats (XML, html, RTF, PostScript...) using open source tools; ability to represent the metadata contained in the original source; and direct conversion to pdf for the creation of book editions.

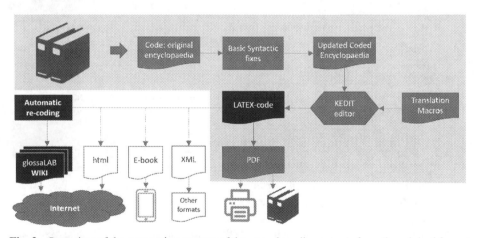

Fig. 2. Overview of the conversion process of the encyclopedic contents from the original format to LaTex and from this to the glossaLAB platform and other interoperable formats.

2.1   From Source Format to LaTex

Figure 3 shows, for the sake of illustration, the first article of IESC -as printed- and its basic components which are codified using the printout-oriented code of the encyclopedia's editor, De Gruyter. This codes permits the identification of the following basic elements: Term identifier; Term name; Original chategorisation within a set of 5 categories; Paragraphs that constitute the content of the clarification; Auhors whose conceptions are being considered and whose related works are being referenced in the bibliography; In-text references; Links to other terms (or voice).

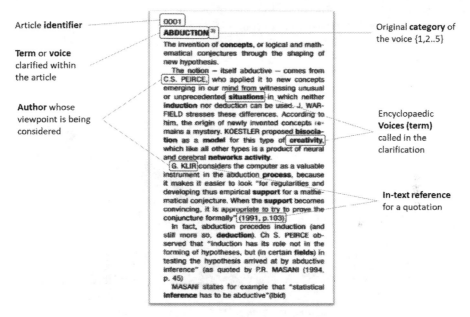

Fig. 3. The original organization of an encyclopedic article from IESC.

For the conversion, schematized in Fig. 2, it was necessary to recognize the syntactic structure of the document both by using provided tags (see Fig. 3) and by the typographical properties of the document (e.g. "all names are written in upper case", "all terms are printed in bold type").

The conversion into the LaTex-format was done by a KEDIT routine which performed multiple passes over the original text, successively replacing original constructs with the new (converted) constructs (see Fig. 2). In many cases, the sequence of steps was essential since later passes assumed certain changes performed by the previous passes. Of considerable help was the 'regular expression feature' of KEDIT, which enabled the identification and conversion of syntactical structures through the localisation of patterns defined by sequences of characters. In its simplest form it has the following format:

```
c reg /ABC{?*}DEF/GHI &1 JKL / * *
```

having the effect that a string of arbitrary characters "?*" which is preceded by "ABC" and followed by "DEF" is converted to "GHI(string between ABC and DEF) JKL", where ABC, DEF, GHI and JKL are arbitrary strings and "?*" denotes a variable'wildcat', whose value is used for "&". Numerous specifications are available and much more complicated examples (with several variables, etc.) are also allowed.

Figure 4 shows the final file structure of the encyclopedia converted to LaTex format. As it can be seen, the encyclopedia is composed of.sty files,.tex files and.jpg files. The.sty files are supplementary files that increase the functionality of the LaTex code. The.tex files contain the content of the encyclopaedia in plain text together with a set of LaTex instructions and commands required for compilation. Finally, the.jpg files are the original encyclopaedia figures. All these files are organised in a set of folders to facilitate their management.

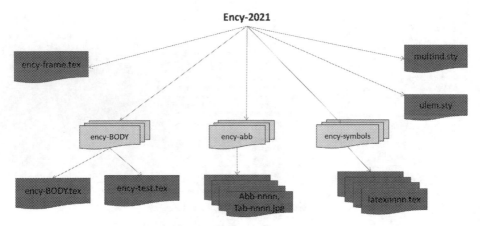

Fig. 4. The file structure of the encyclopedia converted to LaTex.

2.2 From LaTex to MediaWiki Format

The Reconstruction of the Original Hypertext into MediaWiki Formats. Once the encyclopedia has been processed in LaTex format, we develop an application to transfer the LaTex content to a format compatible with MediaWiki. Due to the large size of the encyclopedia, this application is necessary as it would be unfeasible to manually include all encyclopedia terms in MediaWiki. Different platforms were evaluated for the development of the application, deciding the use of MATLAB as it allows the creation of very versatile data structures, which eases the automated analysis of the encyclopedic contents and the subsequent reconstruction of its implicit hypertextual structure in the MediaWiki platform, even including enhanced features.

The application developed takes as input a file in LaTex format and makes an analysis of its regular expressions, which enables the identification of all the terms within the encyclopedia and its constitutive components. It subsequently creates a rich data structure. In this way, for each term in the encyclopedia, the application extracts: the authors referred to, the content, the original categorization of the term, and the other terms which are originally referred to in the article (corresponding to the implicit hypertextual structure of the encyclopedia). Then, a text file including this information is generated in MediaWiki format. This will allow the automatic inclusion of all encyclopedia contents and its implicit hypertext structure into the MediaWiki platform.

Figure 5 illustrates the basic hypertextual structure of IESC encyclopedic content, basically composed by the following elements: the voices (terms) defined in the articles and the links existing among them; the authors whose work discussed within the articles is being referred to in each author's page; the media files composed by figures and tables, which may also include links to authors, voices and media. The numbers reflected in the lower right side of the blocks (representing the sets of voices and authors) are the number of elements of each set for the IESC edition of 2004 [13].

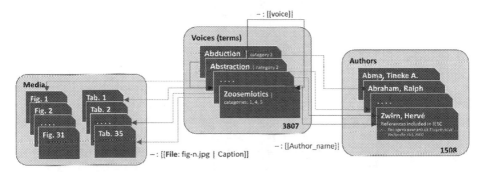

Fig. 5. Content architecture within the MediaWiki platform

It should be noted that the tool created for the reconstruction of the original hypertext allows a detailed analysis of the encyclopedia content thanks to the data structure created, which makes it possible to carry out a deeper analysis of its network structure (co-occurrence matrices, distance measures, cluster analysis, etc.), as needed to fulfil the metatheoretical objectives of the project concerning the analysis of knowledge integration [6].

The Dump of the Reconstructed Contents into the GlossaLAB Platform. The previous step generates thousands of text files that must be dumped into the glossaLAB platform, provided that these files contain the information in the wiki format, which re-codes the metadata inherited from the original corpus. By these means, we enable the deployment of the hypertext in the new platform which reproduces the original hypertext with enhanced features.

For this purpose, we have designed an ad-hoc computer program to feed the platform automatically. This program uses a maintenance script of MediaWiki. The kernel of this program is based on two scripts of the Mediawiki: edit.php and importTextFiles.php. The first one adds wiki content to a site page in Mediawiki, whilst the second one creates a site page with wiki content. For example, if the encyclopedic contents of the term "Abstraction" are to be dumped, these scripts are used as follows:

$$\text{php edit.php -s ``Quick edit'' -m Abstraction < abstraction.txt} \quad (1)$$

$$\text{php importTextFiles.php -s ``Creating a site page'' abstraction.txt} \quad (2)$$

In case the content of the abstraction.txt file to the already existing site page "Abstraction" the code in (1) is executed, while for creating the site page "Abstraction" with the content of abstraction.txt executing the code in (2) is more appropriate. However, the code in (1) can also create a site page if this page is not in the Mediawiki.

Once the contents of IESC are dumped into the glossaLAB platform, the structure illustrated in Fig. 5 corresponds to: a file per media element; a page per voice; and a page per author. The categorisation devised, as explained in the next section, enables the integration of the encyclopedic corpus into the more complex federated system of ID-G that enables: on the one hand, the coexistence and cooperation between autonomous clarification endeavours; on the other, the analysis of the integration of knowledge achieved, as well as the other features referred to at the end of Sect. 1.1.

3   Interdisciplinary Content Architecture

System of Federated ID-G. As mentioned above, glossaLAB is conceived as a system of federated *Interdisciplary Glossaries* (ID-G), illustrated in Fig. 6. These ID-G evolve autonomously but cooperate in the development of a network of transdisciplinary concepts whose *intensional* and *extensional performance* [6] is intended to grow over time. Since the scope, abstraction level and quality criteria of each ID-G are different, we distinguish different levels of abstraction. The more abstract (and usually more qualified) the contents are, the higher they are located. The lowest level is composed of problem-oriented ID-G (the illustration shows some project-specific ID-G, named with the prefix gL- and a suffix characterising the target project), while ESSCO occupies the highest level of abstraction, responding also to a high-quality level. Below the lowest visible level (i.e. publically accessible) there is a fundamental ground of proposals where the knowledge co-creation is carried out through content proposals and interdisciplinary discussion. The vertical dynamics corresponds to the building up of the transdisciplinary conceptual framework composed by a network of concepts sufficiently abstract. The blue vertical arrows represent the escalation between levels, provided that the contribution involved satisfies the quality and abstraction criteria.

For the sake of a better understanding of the vertical dynamics, we can illustrate the process with the hypothetical history of a contribution that starts being proposed to a problem-oriented ID-G and success scaling up all the way up until the maximal level:

Step 1) A contribution is proposed to gL.edu in the context of a seminar in the field of information studies.
Step 2) A set of **interdisciplinary peers** from different knowledge fields -having access to the proposal- **discuss** and enrich the contents proposed.
Step 3) According to the **quality criteria** of gL.edu (which may be different to other ID-G) the proposal is made public.
Step 4) The **curator** of the article, considering the quality and generality of the article and eventually enhancing its content, deems it appropriate for glossariumBITri and launches a proposal.
Step 5) The article is discussed by a designated set of peers from different knowledge fields giving place to some improvements and the acceptance of being published within the **collection** of glossariumBITri;

Step 6) The voice is enriched over time with other contributions and its curator deems it is qualified to become a contribution to ESSCO.
Step 7) The contribution is discussed by a designated panel that brings about some amendments and accepts it for publication within the collection of ESSCO.

In this example, the escalation has gone through three revisions in order to show a case with the longest run, but the process from the proposal layer to the highest level can be done in a single leap if the proposal is submitted to ESSCO from the onset.

In the previous example, key elements of the federated system of subsidiary ID-G have been highlighted. Some functional components of the platform enable its implementation, as *categories, namespaces, page curation* utilities, *discussion* pages (which constitute basic components of the MediaWiki distribution), among which it is the category tree devised for glossaLAB that more clearly reveals the design of the platform for the implementation of the federated system described above.

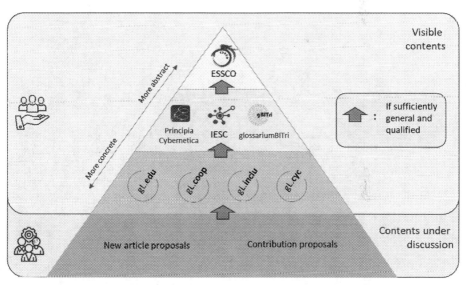

Fig. 6. GlossaLAB as a federated system of ID-G. The more abstract and qualified contents are located at the higher level, being ESSCO at the top, while the lowest level is composed of problem-oriented elucidations.

GlossaLAB Category Tree. Figure 7 shows the category tree (until a certain granularity level) devised for the articulation of the platform as a system of subsidiary ID-G, which responds to the basic objectives of enabling: a) the cooperative development of transdisciplinary knowledge, and b) the assessment of its achievements. As we can observe at the lowest level, the basic categories are *authors, sources, knowledge domains* and *collections*. It is important to note they are not exclusive categories. Indeed, we can speak of an author who is a contributor to one of the sources; is characterised by their expertise in several knowledge domains and is a curator of a collection. All in all, the categorisation depicted in Fig. 7 enables:

1. The organization of the participation of **users** adequately classified by knowledge domains, including the acknowledging of authorship and curation responsibility.
2. The integration of **sources** attributing adequate credits and facilitating the continuation of their respective long-term endeavours.
3. The categorization of **knowledge domains** (KD), whose design (only partially shown in the illustration comprising KD main categories but none of the 67 subcategories that cover all UDC range) has been discussed in previous works [3, 6]. This categorisation constitutes a key element for a) the articulation of the interdisciplinary methodology (designation of discussion panels); b) the evaluation of knowledge integration;

The subsidiary organization of ID-G and **collections** we have discussed above, where a collection is composed of the articles published according to its own quality criteria, as it were in the example given above: glossaLAB.edu; glossariumBITri and ESSCO.

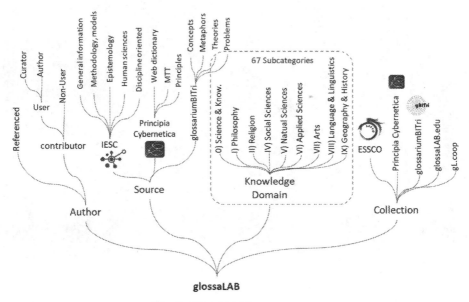

Fig. 7. GlossaLAB's category tree.

4   System Infrastructure

Another fundamental factor supporting the deployment of the platform concerns its network infrastructure. In the short- and mid-terms, service has to be continuously and securely provided for both developments of the platform functionalities, and the co-creation and accessibility of the knowledge base. In the long-term, the continuity of these services needs to be provided, though integrated into a network of open-data labs backed up by a worldwide distributed infrastructure that constitutes the infrastructural support of the PRIMER initiative [4].

4.1 Current Network Architecture

The computer network system that supports the glossaLAB infrastructure is based on a distributed architecture that allows public and private access to the mandatory set of services needed to deploy the collaborative cloud platform. The current architecture, represented in Fig. 8, is deployed on a set of redundant servers provided within the cloud infrastructure hosted by the Faculty of Systems and Telecommunications (FACSISTEL) at State University of Santa Elena Peninsula (UPSE, Ecuador). The core set of servers provided are operating Linux based servers with Debian like distribution installed.

These servers are securely accessible from the web thanks to a firewall system, offering private access for administration, development and debugging to the project staff, and also allowing access to the general public willing to consult contents or participate in the knowledge co-creation. Within the set of glossaLAB servers represented in Fig. 8, there is, on the one hand, a group of replicated servers for further development of platform functionalities -only accessible to glossaLAB teams-; on the other, a set of production servers from where the most stable current version of the system is provided for public access. In the current stage, each functional wiki system is interlinked to a twin system constituting a wiki-farm that supports knowledge co-creation in both English (EN) and Spanish (ES). In future stages, additional wikis may be included in these wiki farms to support further languages. As shown in the illustration, each wiki system requires a backup subsystem to protect it against possible malfunctions or data loss.

With these settings, MediaWiki basic functionality offers to glossaLAB users secure front-end access from any internet connection, using any web browser and any kind of device; where the current URL -to be masked by a shorter one- is: http://facsistel.upse.edu.ec:89/glossalab-en for access to the English wiki.

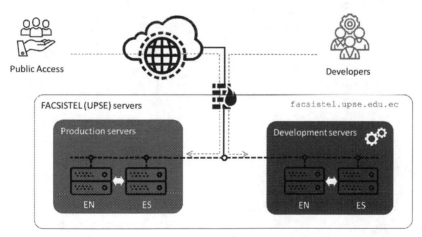

Fig. 8 Current glossaLAB's network architecture of glossaLAB, distinguishing production and development sub-platforms, for public and developers access respectively.

4.2 Long-Term Structure

As mentioned above and according to the objectives of the PRIMER initiative, described in [4], glossaLAB platform is to be included in the long term as part of a computer network of open data lab. The architecture of the proposed infrastructure, represented in Fig. 9, consists primarily of an intensive computing facility located in Mexico; and a storage area network (SAN) facility hosted throughout different Ecuadorian locations: Urcuqui where cogLAB and glossaLAB shall be hosted; Quito hosting incLAB; Santa Elena hosting coopLAB, and Cuenca hosting biciLAB. Secondarily, two supercoputing centers, Quinde I (in Ecuador) and Calendula (in Spain), will offer auto-scaling extensional capacity for backing up the primary computing and storage capacity whenever it is overloaded.

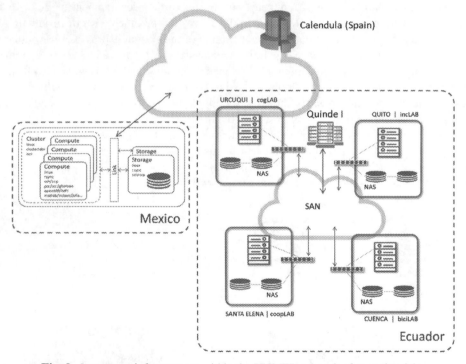

Fig. 9. Long-term infrastructure within the PRIMER network of open data labs.

The storage systems involved will handle large volumes of data that need to be securely stored, managed and backed up with redundancy as a central requirement across the different locations. In order to centralise the management of the storage capacity and server network, a storage area network will be implemented on top of network-attached storage (NAS) servers (Spain, Mexico & Ecuador) and a cluster of computing servers responsible for the computing-intensive applications (Mexico). The primary focus here is to increase the effectiveness of the intensive applications in terms of data and processing as well as to provide continuous availability of the data, protection and security. The

SAN provides a number of benefits at a low level (block) network access to actual storage. These include: a) continuous availability of the actual application, fault tolerance and reliable service delivery by providing multiple paths to the data, b) enhanced application performance by providing off-load storage functions or segregate networks, c) quality services in terms of storage utilisation (backup and online recovery, storage virtualisation, cluster support), d) system scalability by providing isolation capabilities that allow non-disruptive server/peripheral expansion, e) better bandwidth handling and QOS that avoids bottlenecks found in traditional LAN storage servers (bandwidth, latency, queue depth), f) storage virtualization by abstracting logical storage from physical storage, and g) enhanced overall planning by providing improved management, development, adaptability, and affordability.

5 Conclusions

Coping with global challenges requires the establishment of sound interdisciplinary settings capable to integrate the knowledge produced in multiple disciplines and to evaluate the quality of such integration [1, 8–12, 14, 19–21]. Since knowledge integration is ultimately reflected in the conceptual network, interdisciplinary glossaries (ID-G) –one of glossaLAB's pillars– offers a means to intensify such integration, as well as a proxy to evaluate the integration achieved [3, 5, 6]. The second pillar of glossaLAB is constituted by the encyclopedic corpus to be revived, which offers an excellent platform to leverage the general study of systems and information as a transdisciplinary conceptual framework for the articulation of integrative approaches [16, 21]. However, the lack of interoperability and extension of the sources employed (Fig. 1) requires the deployment of an automatic re-codification. We have discussed a successful way to achieve this purpose using LaTex as an intermediate code that facilitates the creation of outputs in different formats and platforms, and particularly into the codes required for the articulation of the corpus into a large elucidation endeavour using MediaWiki technology.

The system of federated ID-G devised (Fig. 6) poses a novel approach that makes possible the symbiotic development of problem-oriented elucidations and the continuous enrichment of the encyclopedic contents in which the transdisciplinary conceptual network is forged. The articulation of contents using the category tree designed (Fig. 7) provides an innovative solution to build-up such system of federated ID-G from the level of real-world problems all the way up until the most abstract concepts, increasing the intensional and extensional performance of the transdisciplinary conceptual framework deployed and its assessment [6]. The network infrastructure conceived offers reliable support to deploy the capacity of glossaLAB immersed in a broad context of education, innovation and research addressing challenges of global relevance.

References

1. Belcher, B.M., Rasmussen, K.E., Kemshaw, M.R., Zornes, D.A.: Defining and assessing research quality in a transdisciplinary context. Res. Eval. **25**(1), 1–17 (2016). https://doi.org/10.1093/reseval/rvv025. Accessed 15 July 2021

2. Castellani, B.: Map of the complexity sciences. In: Art & Science Factory, Kent State University, Ohio (2018). http://www.art-sciencefactory.com. Accessed 9 July 2021
3. Díaz-Nafría, J.M., Burgin, M., Rodriguez-Bravo, B.: Knowledge structures and conceptual networks for evaluation of knowledge integration. In: Dodig-Crnkovic, G., Burgin, M. (eds.) Philosophy and Methodology of Information: The Study of Information in the Transdisciplinary Perspective, pp. 457–489. WORLD SCIENTIFIC (2019). https://doi.org/10.1142/978 9813277526_0021
4. Díaz- Nafría, J.M., et al.: PRIMER initiative: promoting interdisciplinary methodologies in education and research. CEUR-WS, **2486**, pp. 168–182 (2019). http://ceur-ws.org/Vol-2486/ icaiw_edusynergies_4.pdf. Accessed 15 July 2021
5. Díaz-Nafría, J.M., Guarda, T., Coronel, I.: A network theoretical approach to assess knowledge integration in information studies. In: Rocha, Á., Guarda, T. (eds.) MICRADS 2018. SIST, vol. 94, pp. 360–371. Springer, Cham (2018). https://doi.org/10.1007/978-3-319-78605-6_31
6. Díaz-Nafría, J.M., et al.: glossaLAB: co-creating interdisciplinary knowledge. In: Florez, H., Leon, M., Diaz-Nafria, J.M., Belli, S. (eds.) ICAI 2019. CCIS, vol. 1051, pp. 423–437. Springer, Cham (2019). https://doi.org/10.1007/978-3-030-32475-9_31
7. Díaz-Nafría, J.M., Salto, F., Pérez-Montoro, M.: glossariumBITri: Interdisciplinary Elucidation of Concepts, Metaphors, Theories and Problems Concerning Information. UPSE-BITrum, Libertad, Ecuador/León, Spain (2016). https://goo.gl/QnJpQ4. Accessed 1 Aug 2019. http://glossarium.bitrum.unileon.es/glossary. Accessed 1 Aug 2019
8. DEA-FBE: Thinking Across Disciplines – Interdisciplinarity in Research and Education. Danish Business Research Academy (DEA) & Danish Forum for Business Education (FBE), Copenhagen (2008). http://cordis.europa.eu/news/rcn/118314_en.html. Accessed 1 Dec 2017
9. EC: New societal challenges for the European Union – New Challenges for Social Sciences and Humanities. Thinking across boundaries – Modernising European Research. Publication Office of the EU, Luxembourg (2009). https://tinyurl.com/yju93wkh. Accessed 1 June 2021
10. EC: Communication from the Commission: Horizon 2020 - The Framework Programme for Research and Innovation. COM/2011/0808 final, European Commission, Brussels (2011). http://eur-lex.europa.eu/legal-content/EN/TXT/?uri=CELEX:52011D C0808. Accessed 1 June 2021
11. EURAB: Interdisciplinarity In Research. Final Report. European Commission - European Research Advisory Board (EURAB). European Commission, Brussels (2004). https://tinyurl. com/yz6f6m6p. Accessed 1 June 2019
12. EURAB: The new renaissance: will it happen? innovating Europe out of the crisis. Third and final report of the European research area board. Brussels: European commission- European Research Area Board. European Commission, Brussels (2012). http://ec.europa.eu/research/ erab/pdf/3rd-erab-final-report_en.pdf. Accessed 1 June 2019
13. François, C.: Internacional enciclopaedia of systems and cybernetics. K.G. Saur, Munich (2004)
14. Hainaut, L.: d': Interdisciplinarity in General Education. UNESCO, Paris (1986)
15. Heylighen, F.; Joslyn, C.; Turchin, V. (eds.): Principia Cybernetica Web. Principia Cybernetica Project, Brussels (2016). http://cleamc11.vub.ac.be/REFERPCP.html. Accessed 1 June 2019
16. Hieronymi, A.: Understanding systems science: a visual and integrative approach. Syst. Res. Behav. Sci. **30**, 580–595 (2013)
17. Jantsch, E.: Inter- and transdisciplinary university: a systems approach to education and innovation. High Educ. **1**, 7–37 (1972). https://doi.org/10.1007/BF01956879
18. Klir, G.J. (ed.): Trend in General Systems Theory. John Wiley & Sons, New York (1972)
19. McLeish, T., Strang, V.: Evaluating interdisciplinary research: the elephant in the peer-reviewers' room. Palgrave Commun. **2**, 16055 (2016). https://doi.org/10.1057/palcomms.201 6.55

20. NAS: Facilitating Interdisciplinary Research. National Academy of Sciences (NAS), National Academy of Engineering (NAE) and Institute of Medicine (IM), The National Academies Press, Washington (2005). https://www.nap.edu/catalog/11153/facilitating-interdisciplinary-research. Accessed 1 June 2019
21. OECD: Addressing societal challenges using transdisciplinary research. In: OECD Science, Technology and Industry Policy Papers, No. **88**, OECD Publishing, Paris (2020). https://doi.org/10.1787/0ca0ca45-en.

Evaluation of Quality of Service in VoIP Traffic Using the E Model

Yohanna Daza Alava[1]($\boxtimes$) ⓘ, Dannyll Michellc Zambrano[2] ⓘ,
Emilio Cedeño Palma[2] ⓘ, Leonardo Chancay Garcia[2] ⓘ, and Marely Cruz Felipe[2] ⓘ

[1] Instituto de Postgrado, Universidad Técnica de Manabí, Portoviejo, Ecuador
`ydaza6005@utm.edu.ec`
[2] Facultad de Ciencias Informáticas, Universidad Técnica de Manabí, Portoviejo, Ecuador
`{michellc.zambrano,emilio.cedeno,leonardo.chancay,`
`marely.cruz}@utm.edu.ec`

Abstract. Real-time applications such as Voice over IP (VoIP) are very sensitive to variables such as jitter, delay and packet loss. The Quality of Service (QoS) together with the available bandwidth allows to have a quality service, which added to the Quality of User Experience (QoE) provides a way to evaluate the communication. In this work we evaluate the variables delay, jitter and packet loss in VoIP application, together with the QoE (R factor and MOS) of the user using the E model. The variables of delay, jitter and packet loss were measured in three scenarios where the channel was saturated and the bandwidth was limited, to determine the relationship between two QoS variables: delay and jitter with respect to the R factor. Finally, the QoS and QoE that allows early detection of quality degradation in a VoIP call was evaluated, taking into account factors such as bandwidth and codec.

Keywords: Voice over IP · Delay · Packet loss · Jitter · R-factor · MOS

1 Introduction

The growth of traffic generated by real-time applications, the reduction of technology costs and the need to provide a better telecommunications service, has led to the migration to new technologies used in WAN networks. As a result, conventional network technologies are expected to become obsolete, and an analysis is needed to consider the network technology that will optimize WAN services and thus improve the transmission of data, voice and video in real time, in a convergent environment.

For an optimal choice of WAN technology, it is important to know the type of traffic to be transmitted over the links, e.g. the integration of voice and data in a single network infrastructure ensuring that its transport is performed with an excellent quality of service (QoS), so it should be considered that the network traffic must support a low tolerance in terms of latency, packet loss, variable delays or jitter, because information is transmitted in real time as the voice. The conceptualization of quality of service has evolved and is now complemented by customer participation, which is determined by the quality of

© Springer Nature Switzerland AG 2021
T. Guarda et al. (Eds.): ARTIIS 2021, CCIS 1485, pp. 34–43, 2021.
https://doi.org/10.1007/978-3-030-90241-4_3

experience (QoE), understood as the overall acceptability of an application or service, as subjectively perceived by the end user.

In general terms of quality, a quality VoIP call depends among other factors on delay, jitter and packet loss. In [1] QoS parameters for VoIP such as jitter are analyzed using multifractal and Markov models postulating new ways of modeling. However, in [2] they analyze VoIP using the MOS elicitation methodology, preamble on the E-model and develop a non-intrusive model for the Opus codec. Finally, in [3] they have the simplified case of the E-model, specifically predictions using PESQ MOS for four codec types and based on user experience.

Regarding VoIP quality improvement, in [4] the authors evaluate the network performance using simulation tools. Based on the findings, the existing network is redesigned to ensure the deployment of a new service and provide more capacity for future expansion.

In WLAN environments there are problems due to the fact that the displacements interrupt the wireless signal, having to consider additional factors such as CPU needs, network bandwidth, among others [5]. To attack this problem some works [6] use the ASNC (Adaptive Source Network-rate Control) scheme which aims to minimize packet loss based on the MOS and R-factor [6].

A new protocol for VoIP transmissions is presented in [7]. The authors propose an objective QoS metric based on the R factor based on the E model. One of the objectives of this metric is to define a flexibility index to maximize the number of acceptable VoIP calls. The study is performed in distributed wireless networks in hostile environments. Other works [7–10] propose the variables delay, jitter and packet loss as metrics to evaluate VoIP performance. The evaluations of these metrics are made from the user's experience, so the relationship between the performance parameters of the codecs and other elements that make up VoIP with the QoS and QoE associated with the user must be established.

In general, all these concepts are the basis for what is called "traffic engineering", which aims to analyze traffic in order to offer better and more predictable services, by supporting dedicated bandwidth, improving packet loss characteristics, avoiding and managing network congestion, organizing and prioritizing traffic.

In this work the interest is given in the measurements, and characterization of jitter, delay and packet loss parameters that characterize the QoS for VoIP communication over a WAN network, together with the analysis using the non-intrusive predictive technique of the ITU-T E-model [11].

2   Materials and Methods

VoIP is the sending of voice packets over an IP (Internet Protocol) based network. In IP networks by packet switching, each packet is sent independently, has its own IP header, and will be sent separately by the routers (nodes). In a VoIP call there are protocols which allow voice traffic over a WAN network, including the Cloud. [10].

The transport protocol used for VoIP is RTP together with the Real Time Control Protocol (RTCP) which provides control services and other functionalities. RTP does not offer guarantees on the quality of service or on the delay of data delivery, so it needs the support of lower-level layers. In real-time data transmission it is essential that delay, packet loss and jitter parameters are within values considered normal for good call quality, which is why the RTP protocol uses the RTCP protocol for control [10]. All VoIP packets are composed of two components: voice samples and IP/UDP/RTP headers [15].

It is important in a network to implement QoS policies for VoIP traffic to ensure good voice quality when network resources are congested [17]. There are a number of factors that can affect the quality of VoIP service as perceived by the end user. Some of the common factors include delay, jitter and packet loss. QoS problems in VoIP stem from two main factors:

1. the Internet (including the Cloud) is a packet-switched based system and therefore information does not always travel the same path. This produces effects such as packet loss or jitter.
2. VoIP communications take place in real time, which causes effects such as echo, packet loss and delay to be very annoying and detrimental and must be avoided.

In addition, the type of codec used must be taken into account as it influences the delay and jitter buffer. The function of the jitter buffer is to temporarily store VoIP packets, as a resource to minimize jitter and discard packets that arrive too late.

For this work, the parameters of the ITU-T G114 recommendation (International Telecommunication Union, 2017) [12] for VoIP shown in Table 1.

Table 1. ITU-T G114 reference values [12].

Parameters	Value
Maximum jitter (ms)	30
Average jitter (ms)	25
Maximum delay (ms)	150
Packet loss %	1

2.1 Bandwidth and Codec

It is necessary to know the voice codec bandwidth calculations and features to modify or conserve bandwidth when using VoIP. One of the most important factors to consider when building VoIP networks is proper channel capacity planning [17].

For VoIP packet calculations, a 40-byte header is used, of which 20 bytes correspond to the IP protocol, 8 bytes to the UDP protocol (User Datagram Protocol) and 12 bytes to the RTP protocol [15]. It should be noted that voice communication is analog, while the data network is digital. The transformation of the analog signal to a digital signal is performed by means of an analog-to-digital conversion, which is a function of the codec.

ITU-T G.711 is a digital coding standard for representing an audio signal at human voice frequencies, using 8-bit resolution words, with a rate of 8000 samples per second.

Therefore, the G.711 encoder whose characteristics are displayed in Table 2 provides a data stream of 64 Kbit/s [16].

To achieve an optimized signal to noise ratio for human speech signals, a compression method is used before encoding the signal (level compression should not be confused with digital data compression) [16].

Table 2. ITU-T G 711 codec characteristics [15]

Parameters	Value
Speed (kbps)	64
MOS	4.1
VoIP Header Size (ms)	20
VoIP Header Size (Bytes)	160
Packets per second (PPS)	50
Ethernet Bandwidth (Kbps)	87.2

2.2 Traffic Model – E Model

VoIP communication quality measurements can be performed using both objective and subjective methods. MOS, defined in International Telecommunication Union, 2017 [13], is the most commonly used subjective technique.

Objective measurement techniques can be classified as intrusive or non-intrusive, intrusive methods are more accurate, but are usually not suitable for monitoring real-time traffic, as they need reference data and injection of polling traffic into the network. Non-intrusive techniques do not need reference data and can be used to monitor and/or predict voice quality directly from the network and system performance metrics, e.g., packet loss, delay, jitter and codec.

The ITU-T E-Model is a computational model that can be used to non-intrusively predict voice quality. It allows the estimation of the expected voice quality, based on some parameters such as codec, quantization distortion, QoS variables [14].

According to the equipment degradation factor method, the fundamental principle of the E-model is based on a concept given in the description of the "OPINE Model". The result of any calculation with the E-model in a first stage is a transmission rating factor called "R-factor", which combines all relevant transmission parameters for the considered connection. This R-factor is expressed by the equation: [13]

$$R = R_0 - I_s - I_d - I_{e-eff} + A \qquad (1)$$

Where Ro represents in principle the basic signal to noise ratio, including noise sources such as circuit noise and ambient noise; Is is a combination of all impairments occurring more or less simultaneously with the speech signal; Id represents impairments caused by delay; Ie-eff is the effective impairment factor and represents impairments caused by low bit rate codecs, including also impairments due to randomly distributed packet losses; A is the advantage factor and allows to compensate for impairment factors when the user benefits from other types of accesses.

A MOS score for a conversational situation on the 1–5 scale of the R factor can be obtained using the equations: [14]

$$R < 0 : MOS_{CQE} = 1$$

$$0 < R < 100 : MOS_{CQE} = 1 + 0,035R + R(R - 60) * (100 - R) * 7 \times 10^6 \quad (2)$$

$$R > 100 : MOS_{CQE} = 4,5$$

In some cases, transmission planners may not be familiar with the use of quality measures such as the R-factor. Table 3 presents the relationship between the R-factor value and user satisfaction.

Table 3. Relationship between R factor and user satisfaction [11].

R factor (lower limit)	MOS CQE (lower limit)	User satisfaction
90	4.34	Very satisfied
80	4.03	Satisfied
70	3.6	Some users dissatisfied
60	3.2	Many users dissatisfied
50	2.58	Almost all users dissatisfied

2.3 Procedure and Method Evaluation

A WAN network was configured through which a real-time application is transmitted in the case of analysis is Voice over IP between two common LANs. The codec used is G 711.

The call was made from the VoIP1 client to the VoIP2 client, passing through the VoIP PBX with a duration of 5.9 min, which examined 17690 RTP packets, based on the number of packets that must be transmitted every second to deliver the bit rate of the G711 codec, as shown in Table 2.

For all scenarios, regression was performed to visualize the relationship between the independent variables (cause) "delay" and "jitter", with respect to the dependent variable R factor (effect).

Equation (2) was used to obtain the MOS value. The R factor value was calculated using Eq. (1), considering the G 711 codec and the packet loss value in percentage in each scenario.

In the first scenario there is an ideal channel without saturation, a normal call was established between VoIP1 and VoIP 2 clients.

In the second scenario, the channel was saturated with injected packets. A call was established between VoIP1 and VoIP 2 clients.

In scenario 3, the channel bandwidth was saturated and limited. The network was saturated with RTP injected packets. At the server, the channel bandwidth was limited to 500 Kbps and a low priority for VoIP. A call was established between VoIP1 and VoIP 2 clients.

3 Results and Discussion

For scenario 1, the values are normal in a channel without saturation, unlike scenario 2 where the highest values are presented (Fig. 1). These values in scenario 2 were to be expected since the channel was saturated with packets. The maximum jitter value of scenario 2, shown in Table 4, is close to the reference limits, Table 4. The values in scenario 3 went up due to channel saturation.

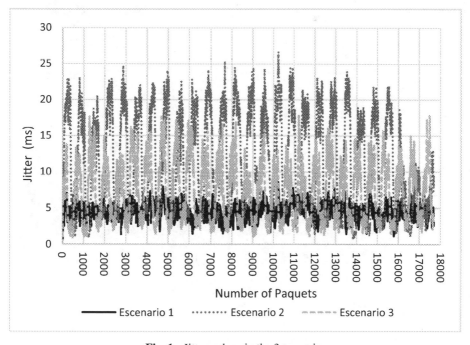

Fig. 1. Jitter values in the 3 scenarios

For scenario 2 (Fig. 1), it can be seen that the jitter values begin to decrease from about packet 16000 onwards, due to the decrease in packet injection. For scenario 3, from about packet 16500 onwards, the jitter increases (peak values) as more RTP packets are injected.

Table 4. Parameter results in calls

Results	Maximum jitter (ms)	Average jitter (ms)	Maximum delay (ms)	Packet loss %	Bandwidth (kbps)
Scenario 1	8.58	4.5	40.14	0	80.62
Scenario 2	26.64	11.67	111.87	0.2	80.78
Scenario 3	17.89	7.31	111.62	0.63	80.92

See (Fig. 2) the delay values for the three scenarios evaluated. For scenario 1, the delay values are those expected in a channel without saturation, as shown in Table 4.

Scenario 2 shows the highest peak delay values (Fig. 2), due to the higher number of packets in the network due to channel saturation. The delay started to decrease from about packet 16000 onwards, due to the decrease in packet injection.

For scenario 3 (Fig. 2), the delay values remain within the limits of the reference values in Table 1, from about packet 16500 onwards, the delay increases (peak values) as more RTP packets are injected.

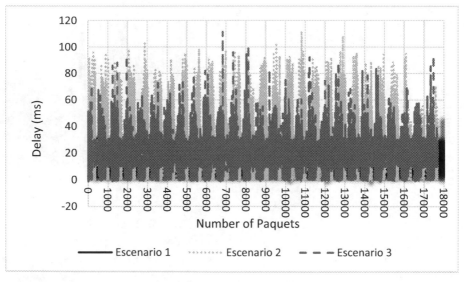

Fig. 2. Delay values in the 3 scenarios

See (Fig. 3) MOS values for the three scenarios, with expected results. Scenario 3 has the lowest values, due to the higher channel saturation and bandwidth limitation.

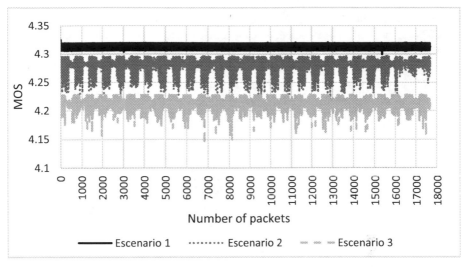

Fig. 3. MOS values in the 3 scenarios

Table 5 shows the average, maximum and minimum values for the three scenarios, which are between 4.03 and 4.34 at the level of a "satisfied" communication, according to Table 3 regarding User Satisfaction.

Table 5. Values MOS

Results	Scenario 1	Scenario 2	Scenario 3
Average	4.31	4.28	4.21
Minimum	4.30	4.22	4.14
Maximum	4.33	4.30	4.23

RTP packet loss in scenario 3 is higher compared to the other scenarios, due to bandwidth limitation and RTP packet injection. (Table 4). In scenario 1 there is no RTP packet loss because it is not saturated, but once the channel starts to be injected packets start to saturate and the RTP packet loss starts to increase, as it happened in scenario 2.

An important factor to analyze is the bandwidth. Table 4 shows the values obtained in kbps for the three scenarios, which are within the expected values according to Table 2 due to the use of the G 711 codec.

When the independent variables (cause) delay and jitter were regressed against the dependent variable R factor (effect) in the three scenarios, a multiple linear regression of the type $y = a + b \times 1 + c \times 2$ was obtained, where $\times 1$ is the Delay variable and $\times 2$ is the Jitter variable.

$$R - factor = a + b * Delay + c * Jitter \qquad (3)$$

Table 6 shows the values of the coefficients a, b and c of the equation type $y = a + b \times 1 + c \times 2$. From the values of a, b and c it is observed that the R factor and implicitly the MOS depend mostly on the delay variable, noting that the coefficient "c" tends to 0 for this particular case study, due to the G 711 codec.

In scenario 3, by saturating the channel and limiting the bandwidth, there is an echo due to the greater injection of RTP packets in the channel.

Table 6. Regression factor F values with respect to delay and jitter variables

	Scenario 1	Scenario 2	Scenario 3
a	89.4432	88.32	85.953882
b (Delay)	−0.024	−0.024	−0.024
c (Jitter)	−2.15E-16	−7.176E-18	1.902E-17

4 Conclusions

Since voice is quite predictive and if isolated packets are lost, they can be recomposed at reception in a very optimal way, the percentage of packet loss did not exceed 1%. The use of the G 711 codec, which does not use compression, was a great help.

The bandwidth for VoIP communication did not exceed the limit value in the three scenarios, staying within the normal range for the G 711 codec, because the bandwidth is strongly related to the codec.

When the channel was limited, priority was given to RTP packets, and when the channel was saturated with packets, an echo was heard due to the delay, so priority mechanisms are necessary to guarantee QoS in VoIP conversations.

By monitoring VoIP systems the MOS during a call can be calculated and reported, this gives the possibility to detect poor performance. In experimental networks such as the one implemented the MOS is only measured when two users make a call, it is preferable to generate traffic in addition to limiting the channel bandwidth (scenarios 2 and 3), and measure delay, jitter and packet loss. This allows early detection of VoIP quality degradation without waiting for the user to make a call and be affected.

Future work could perform several VoIP calls from terminals with wireless connectivity and evaluate the QoS parameters, applying the E-model to obtain a traffic model.

This research could be carried out in simulators with calls from clients using different types of codec, e.g. G 729 that uses voice compression, and establish the influence of jitter and delay variables in calls with lower bandwidth.

References

1. Toral, H., Pathan, A., Ramirez, J.C.: Accurate modeling of VoIP traffic QoS parameters in current and future networks with multifractal and Markov models. Math. Comput. Modell. **57**(11), 2832–2845 (2013)

2. Triyason, T., Kanthamanon, P.: E-Model parameters estimation for VoIP with non-ITU codec speech quality prediction. In: Meesad, P., Boonkrong, S., Unger, H. (eds.) Recent Advances in Information and Communication Technology 2016. Advances in Intelligent Systems and Computing, vol 463, p. 13. Springer, Cham (2016). https://doi.org/10.1007/978-3-319-404 15-8

3. Assem, H., Malone, D., Dunne, J., O'Sullivan, P.: Monitoring VoIP call quality using improved simplified E-model. In: International Conference on Computing, Networking and Communications (ICNC), p. 13 (2013)

4. Hussaina, T.Y, Habib, S.: Assessing and redesigning enterprise networks through NS-2 to support VoIP. In: Procedia Computer Science, vol. 5, p. 742–748 (2011)

5. Gámez, J., Palomares, J., Olivares, J.: Estudio e implantación de sistemas VOIP en entornos industriales. In: Transfer Program 2008. Junta de Andalucía (2008)

6. Zheng, J., Mao, S., Midkiff, S.F., Zhu, H. (eds.): ADHOCNETS 2009. LNICSSITE, vol. 28. Springer, Heidelberg (2010). https://doi.org/10.1007/978-3-642-11723-7

7. De Rango, F., Fazio, P., Scarcello, F., Conte, F.: A new distributed application and network layer protocol for VoIP in mobile Ad Hoc networks. IEEE Trans. Mob. Comput. **13**(10), 2185–2198 (2014)

8. Charonyktakis, P., Plakia, M., Tsamardinos, I., Papadopouli, M.: On user-centric modular QoE prediction for VoIP based on machine-learning algorithms. IEEE Trans. Mob. Comput. **15**(6), 1443–1456 (2016)

9. Seytnazarov, S., Kim, Y.T.: QoS-Aware adaptive A-MPDU aggregation scheduler for voice traffic in aggregation-enabled high throughput WLANs. IEEE Trans. Mob. Comput. **16**(10), 2862–2875 (2017)

10. Zambrano, D.: Estudio de las características de nuevas arquitecturas web basadas en Webrtc alojada en la nube y factible implementación para aplicaciones de voz sobre IP (VoIP), PUCE - Pontificia Universidad Católica del Ecuador, p. 65 (2016)

11. Internacional Telecomunication Union. The E-Model, a computational model for use in transmission planning. https://www.itu.int/rec/T-REC-G.107. Accessed 20 January 2020

12. Internacional Telecomunication Union: T recommendation G.114: one-way transmission time. https://www.itu.int/rec/T-REC-G.114. Accessed 20 January 2020

13. Internacional Telecomunication Union. Mean Opinion Score (MOS) terminology. https://www.itu.int/rec/T-REC-P.800.1. Accessed 20 January 2020

14. Garroppo, R.G., Giordano, S., Iacono, D., Tavanti, L.: Experimental and simulation analysis of a WiMAX system in an emergency marine scenario. Comput. Commun. **34**(7), 847–861 (2011)

15. CISCO: Voice Over IP - per call bandwidth consumption. https://www.cisco.com/c/en/us/sup port/docs/voice/voice-quality/7934-bwidth-consume.html. Accessed 30 January 2020

16. Internacional Telecomunication Union: G.711: Modulación por impulsos codificados (MIC) de frecuencias vocales. https://www.itu.int/rec/T-REC-G.711/es. Accessed 30 January 2020

17. Cruz, M., Pinargote, M., Zambrano, D.: Evaluation of QoS solutions for local area networks. In: Revista Ibérica de Sistemas e Tecnologias de Informação; Lousada N.º E29, pp. 27–40 (2020)

Multi-agent System for the Area of Medical Emergencies for Health Surveillance (MAS-AMeHs)

Jorge Bautista[1]([✉]), Arnulfo Alanis[2], Efraín Patiño[3], and Fabiola Hernandez-Leal[2]

[1] Master's Program in Information Technology, Department of Systems and Computing, National Technology of Mexico, Campus Tijuana, Calzada del Tecnológico S/N, Fracionamiento Tomas Aquino, 22414 Tijuana, B.C., Mexico
jorge.bautista@tectijuana.edu.mx
[2] Department of Systems and Computing, National Technology of Mexico, Campus Tijuana, Calzada del Tecnológico S/N, Fraccionamiento Tomas Aquino, 22414 Tijuana, B.C., Mexico
{alanis,fabiola.hernandez}@tectijuana.edu.mx
[3] School of Medicine, Autonomous University of Baja California, Tijuana, B.C., Mexico
efrain.patio@uabc.edu.mx

Abstract. In this paper, it is proposed an APK that works in conjunction with an emergency triage system that may help both patients and doctors using IoT. The classification system implemented on this work reads the data provided by the user (oxygen saturation, hearth rate) on the app, this will be processed, as the results are given in real time and classified on an emergency color system (green, yellow, orange and red) the doctor would be notified instantly, allow him to be up to date with its patient's condition and help him get a better analysis and have a mor exact diagnose, this being beneficial for both patient and doctor.

Keywords: Classification · Triage · Oxygen saturation · Multi-Agents

1 Introduction

The health industry has been rapidly evolving throughout the years upon the population's changing needs. Specially nowadays with the rise of the COVID-19 pandemic, there is high demand for methods that can monitor a patient's physiological parameters such as temperature, oxygen, and PH. However, to achieve this, evolving challenges need to be addressed.

Technology is one of the most reliable tools to check the level of these parameters on the human body with devices that are portable and can be used at one's convenience. These function with the Internet of Health Thing (IoTH), also known as mobile health, which focuses on using information and communication devices and technologies in the health field [1].

The use of this kind of devices that allow the population to check their physiological levels anytime and anywhere offer a higher life expectancy for older adults [2]. Additionally, patients of different age groups can develop a healthier life by attending their health necessities and thus preventing many diseases through constant monitoring.

T. Guarda et al. (Eds.): ARTIIS 2021, CCIS 1485, pp. 44–55, 2021.
https://doi.org/10.1007/978-3-030-90241-4_4

These devices may be used along with applications that can capture and interpret the data in ways that can assist both patients and doctors since the information can be used to their convenience.

Common tools used in this regard are oximeters, devices that provide real-time estimates of arterial oxygen saturation, and thermometers, which provide estimate body temperatures. Both parameters are correlated with COVID-19 symptoms thus constant monitoring is fundamental.

In this paper we present a multiagent classification system that analyses the blood oxygen saturation (SpO2), heart rate (HR), body temperature, and PH to assess the risk of a patient based on Mexico's Emergency Triage.

2 Emergency Triage

Triage is a set of values, which considers selecting, categorizing and prioritizing da-ta. If we focus on the medical area, it supports or helps to be able to have a determination of the values for medical care, this will allow to evaluate and have a categorization and selection of users (patients), considering their clinical situation and prognosis [3].

Three objectives are considered: A) the identification of the users (patients), according to their vital risk situation, B) to have a prioritization value according to their level or degree of classification, C) to decide of the corresponding area for the care of the users (patients), D) to provide information of the assistance process, E) to keep a good order and follow-up of the users (patients) [4]. And depending on the situation that arises will be the one to be used.

For this research, the Triage of the Mexican Institute of Social Security (IMSS) is used, which is indicated in Table 1, and all values are validated.

Table 1. Emergency triage

	Red	Orange	Yellow	Green
Situation	Resuscitation	Very serious	Serious	Not serious
Attention	immediate	< 10 min	< 30 min	120 min
SpO2 (%)	< 80	80–89	90–94	> 95%
HR (BPM)	> 130 bpm	120–130 or < 40	111–120 or 40–49	50 – 120

2.1 Pulse Oximeter

Pulse oximetry is one of the various techniques used to measure physiological parameters, in this specific case is to measure oxygen saturation (SpO2) and heart rate in non-invasively manner, it is a very common method used clinically in all types of patients [5].

2.2 Oxygen Saturation

What we describe as "saturated" on oxygen is when the hemoglobin molecule carries up to four oxygen molecules, this hemoglobin saturation should be 100%. A person with healthy lungs and low to sea level breathing air should always have an arterial oxygen saturation between 95% and 100% [6].

2.3 Heart Rate

Heart rate is one of the easiest vital signs to read. This is convenient since the data contains important forecast information to prevent future heart related diseases in adults. The number of beats per minute (bpm) should be between 60 and 90 according to several studies, but the American Heart Association differs with a max bpm of 100. However, these standards are believed to not be completely representative of the real world [7, 8].

3 Internet of Things (IoT)

Nowadays, Internet of Things, or IoT, is widely used in a variety of applications becoming important for daily life activities. IoT is the interaction of devices through a network, this has allowed a more friendly ecosystem between smart devices, making them interact with each other in a more efficient way.

As IoT has grown on different fields and how user interacts in a more friendly way with a bast variety of smart devices, it has also found his way into helping in the medical field, as it became a very powerful tool as it helps with diagnose and a constant monitoring of patients [11].

3.1 Internet of Health Thing (IoTH)

A particular branch that greatly benefits from the Internet of Things is healthcare. IoT technology can be used as a monitoring system for patients and in mobile applications to detect medical issues based on the patterns of the user. Smartphones have become such a fundamental part in everyday lives that is easy to gain constant data and mine it to gain automatic control of the individual's personalized healthcare. IoT healthcare can be very efficient and helpful but there are also several issues. Cloud computing can handle the data providing flexibility, service integration, parallel processing, but also security problems Security is one of the major issues with IoT healthcare. The data can be corrupted by external sources thus it is necessary to have a "privacy-preserving IoT system". IoT based healthcare needs to address "accuracy, computational time, and current difficulties". Another drawback of the cloud data center is its very large energy consumption which at the same time increases its cost. However, a monitoring system requires low latency so there is no chance of losing data as well as low energy consumption [11].

3.2   IoT Healthcare Architecture and Applications

Using IoT, sensors are placed in patients to obtain data that is connected to control devices and health-monitoring units. The data can be stored in the cloud which helps to manage and secure it. At the same time, the cloud is beneficial since it provides flexibility, both patients and doctors can access it remotely. Keeping the data secure is fundamental since there can be a loss of integrity. To encrypt the data from the sensor to the cloud center can be complex. To reduce this, a cloud novel framework is proposed to manage the data, this one provides a Software as a Service (SaaS), which is a hybrid cloud environment [11].

3.3   Cloud Integration

The data obtained from the monitoring of the mobile application can be stored in the cloud platform. This one provides "flexibility, scalability, and more resources to process the data". Using this technology, a better experience in healthcare can be provided to the patients since the different medical processes are integrated and more accurate diagnosis provided [10].

3.4   Big Data

Big data technology is used to store huge quantities of data. The merge of big data and the cloud has influenced how remote healthcare is carried out. For example, Amazon Elastic MapReduce (EMR). EMR loads the data using Apace pig, which is used to extend the scalable feature [10].

3.5   Security

Security is the main concern in IoT healthcare since the sensor data can be corrupted by outside sources compromising the patient's personal information. A recent security method in IoT is IDP, which optimizes the data access time, resource utilization, and reduces the energy consumption. This can be achieved through an algorithm called Non-dominated Sorting Genetic Algorithm II [10].

3.6   Challenges

IoT has been adopted in different types of applications and provide distinct support for the healthcare system such as patient monitoring, a smart home system for the diabetic patient [10].

4   Methodology

The present work is based on an Emergency Triage's system created previously [3].

The multi-agent system will support the classification of data such as oxygen saturation, temperature, heart rate. The methodology is composed of five stages.

The system is divided into three intelligent agents, which help to collect the data (data collection agent), classify it (classification agent) and manipulating inputs trough the APK (Multiagent monitoring system), as shown in Fig. 1.

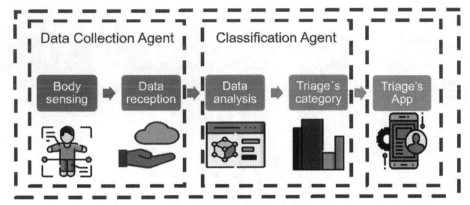

Fig. 1. Methodology.

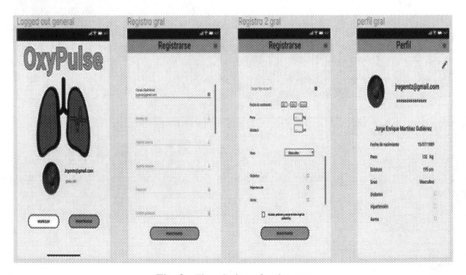

Fig. 2. First designs for the app.

For the APK development a flowchart was designed, and it was decided the tools to be utilized; it would be created using Android Studio and Firebase for our data storage, also it was work based on the SCRUM methodology.

As the development continued, the initial designs for the app focused on being very user friendly, the thought on this was that the easier and the less screens the app had the easier would be for the user to get used to regular usage of this tool, as it will be very easy to learn.

Fig. 3. First designs for the app.

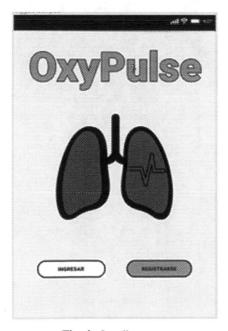

Fig. 4. Landing page.

In Fig. 2 and 3 the app only consists of 8 main screens, which takes care of:

- Login.
- Register Page.
- User profile.
- Physiological parameters capture page.
- User record.

It was also decided that the app's UI would be separated into 2, one for the main user (in this case patient) and one for the doctor.

Figure 4 displays the first screen which both patients and doctors can see. It contains two different buttons, one to log in to the app and another one to create a new account if needed.

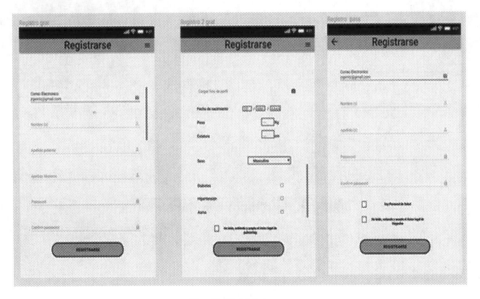

Fig. 5. Register page.

It was decided that the Register page would only apply to the main user, the patient, since doctors would be registered directly in the app. In Fig. 5 we capture vital information from the user such as age, gender, record of diseases, etc.

Once the user is registered, the app can be successfully accessed from the Login page using the patient's e-mail and password as presented in Fig. 6.

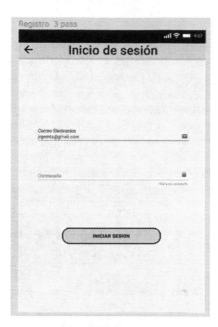

Fig. 6. Login page.

5 Experimental Stage

The participants for capture readings were 4 people that continuously used the pulse oximeter and were in mostly calm conditions, as they were watching TV or listening to music.

Something important was the processing of the data once it is captured, confusion matrices were used because it can calculate the matrix, accuracy, precision and recall, also it allows the data accuracy to be obtained through different metrics [12].

Once the data was captured and processed, the next step was getting the APK ready for testing, the development was done through the scrum methodology and was made in android studio.

As the development for the app finalized the data obtained was implemented on the APK, so the test can be done using our already existing information and adjustments can be made depending on these results.

6   Results

The app was a success on the matter that it was correctly implemented with the triage system, as it was able to both process the data, send it to our database and finally give a correct result on the UI.

Some of the challenges that it encountered was to be user friendly and very intuitive to use as it continued to grow. It kept the idea of being simplistic, not a flashy app but only showing the necessary information to the user and validating the fields as it can only write what is required.

As for the triage is concerned, the implementation in app for both oxygen saturation and heart rate were correct and classified on their correct scenarios most of the time.

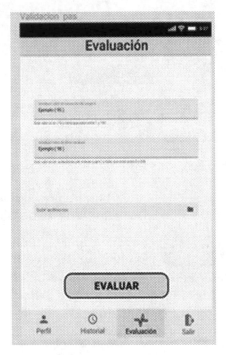

Fig. 7. Evaluation page.

Fig. 8. Results page. (Color figure online)

In Figs. 7 and 8 the process of capturing the data is at display. first, we let the user take the measurements, on this example both oxygen saturation and heart rate. Once the information is recorded and processed, the results can be accessed in the Results page. These ones will be displayed using a color-coded scheme: green for normal levels, yellow for prevention, and red for urgent care needed.

As for Fig. 9 both user (doctors and patients) can see a record from past readings, allowing them to keep track of how they have progress. For the Doctor it allows him to see all his patients, selecting one of them shows all their readings.

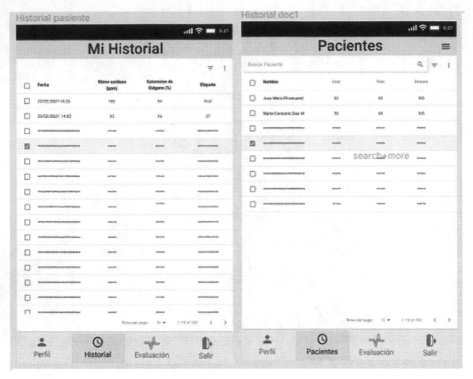

Fig. 9. Patient and doctor records.

7   Conclusions and Discussions

The classification system gives very good results and its potential for future improvements is still very much wide open. The system continues to grow and give more tools to use in the analysis of physiological parameters that could help not only to attend patients with diseases but to help in the prevention of this for other users.

Although the system has been adding more parameters to read constantly, it still has potential to keep adding features, both in more physiological parameters to read, but also as a user experience in the APK that was designed, adding features for both users and doctors that would utilize this tool.

As the infrastructure for the app is easy to use and can be used anywhere anytime, this system does not give an official analysis or detection of a disease, it is meant to be used only as a tool for the doctor to give him the information necessary for a complete diagnosis.

Future work will continue with the improvement of the APK, adding features to continue to be user friendly but most importantly, to be migrated to another platform so it can also be used on iOS devices, and continue with the implementation of both temperature and PH on the triage.

References

1. Da Costa, C.A., Pasluosta, C.F., Eskofier, B., da Silva, D.B., da Rosa Righi, R.: Internet of health things: toward intelligent vital signs monitoring in hospital wards. Artif. Intell. Med. **89**, 61–69 (2018). https://doi.org/10.1016/j.artmed.2018.05.005
2. Alaoui, M., Lewkowicz, M.: Practical issues related to the implication of elderlies in the design process – The case of a living lab approach for designing and evaluating social TV services. IRBM. **36**, 259–265 (2015). https://doi.org/10.1016/J.IRBM.2015.06.002
3. IMSS: Unidad 4: Evacuación de Áreas Críticas Tema 2: Triage
4. García-Regalado, J.F., Arellano-Hernández, N., Loría-Castellanos, J.: Triage hospitalario. Revisión de la literatura y experiencia en México. Prensa Med. Argent. **102**, 233–241 (2016)
5. Bhogal, A.S., Mani, A.R.: Pattern analysis of oxygen saturation variability in healthy individuals: entropy of pulse oximetry signals carries information about mean oxygen saturation. Front. Physiol. **8**, 1–9 (2017). https://doi.org/10.3389/fphys.2017.00555
6. Pulse Oximeter. American Thoracic Society. Patient Information Series (2011). https://www.thoracic.org/patients/patient-resources/resources/pulse-oximetry.pdf
7. World Health Organization: Pulse Oximetry Training Manual. Lifebox
8. Avram, R., et al.: Real-world heart rate norms in the health eHeart study. NPJ Digit. Med. **2**, 58 (2019). https://doi.org/10.1038/s41746-019-0134-9
9. Yunda, L., Pacheco, D., Millan, J.: A Web-based fuzzy inference system based tool for cardiovascular disease risk assessment. Nova **13**(24), 7 (2015)
10. Kulkarni, A., Chong, D., Batarseh, F.A.: Foundations of data imbalance and solutions for a data democracy. In: data democracy, pp. 83–106. Elsevier (2020)
11. Selvaraj, S., Sundaravaradhan, S.: Challenges and opportunities in IoT healthcare systems: a systematic review. SN Appl. Sci. **2**(1), 1–8 (2019)
12. Hernandez-Leal, F., Alanis, A., Patiño, E., Jimenez, S.: Multiagent emergency triage classification system for health monitoring. In: Jezic, G., Chen-Burger, J., Kusek, M., Sperka, R., Howlett, R.J., Jain, L.C. (eds.) Agents and Multi-Agent Systems: Technologies and Applications 2021. SIST, vol. 241, pp. 361–370. Springer, Singapore (2021). https://doi.org/10.1007/978-981-16-2994-5_30

A Non-invasive Method for Premature Sudden Cardiac Death Detection: A Proposal Framework

Nancy Betancourt[1,2](✉), Marco Flores-Calero[3], and Carlos Almeida[4]

[1] Escuela Politécnica Nacional, Departamento de Ciencias de la Computación, Ladrón de Guevara, P.O.Box 17–01-2759, Quito E11-253, Ecuador
[2] Departamento de Ciencias Exactas, Universidad de las Fuerzas Armadas - ESPE, Av. General Rumiñahui s/n, Sangolquí, Ecuador
ncbetancourt@espe.edu.ec
[3] Departamento de Eléctrica Electrónica y Telecomunicaciones, Universidad de las Fuerzas Armadas - ESPE, Av. General Rumiñahui s/n, Sangolquí, Ecuador
mjflores@espe.edu.ec
[4] Departamento de Matemática, Escuela Politécnica Nacional, Ladrón de Guevara, E11-253 Quito, Ecuador
carlos.almeidar@epn.edu.ec

Abstract. Sudden Cardiac Death is considered one of the main cause of mortality worldwide. The incomprehensible nature of this cardiac disease increases the necessity to develop new methods to predict this pathology. According to the literature review, several methods to predict SCD have been developed using Heart Rate Variability (HRV) and T-wave alternans (TWA). HRV has been extensively studied and it is considered as index in the cardiovascular risk stratification. On the other hand, T-wave alternans has been considered an important, non-invasive, very promising indicator to stratify the risk of sudden cardiac death. In this context, based on HRV and TWA as a risk stratification indices, this article proposes a research framework to stratify and predict the Sudden Cardiac Death (SCD) disease using non-invasive methods, by mixing elements of the HRV and TWA approaches, thus producing an hybrid approach.

Keywords: ECG · SCD · HRV · TWA · Prediction

1 Introduction

Sudden cardiac death (SCD) is defined as the natural death caused by cardiac disease occurring at most one hour after symptoms appear or within twenty four hours in a person without any precondition that seems fatal [1]. SCD is a leading cause of cardiovascular mortality [2–4] producing nine million deaths worldwide according to the World Health Organization [5]. It is estimated that 400,000 deaths per year are caused by SCD in the United States [6,7]. Only 1–2% of patients can survive when SCD occurs outside of a hospital [6]. Most patients are identified only after they have experienced severe hearth diseases

© Springer Nature Switzerland AG 2021
T. Guarda et al. (Eds.): ARTIIS 2021, CCIS 1485, pp. 56–69, 2021.
https://doi.org/10.1007/978-3-030-90241-4_5

such as ischemia, infarction, ventricular conduction abnormalities, or potassium abnormalities [7–9]. However, these patients represent 2% to 3% of the total SCD victims [3]. According to the literature, Ventricular Fibrillation (VF) and Ventricular Tachycarida (VT) are the primary causes that can produce SCD [10–12], representing aproximately 20% of SCD episodes [13]. In Ecuador, heart ischemic diseases mortality is about 13.5% of the total deaths recorded in year 2020 [14]. An important standard clinical procedure for investigation of cardiac abnormalities is the Electrocardiogram (ECG) [15]. ECG reflects the electrical activity of the heart, which is composed of two phases called depolarization and repolarization (contraction and relaxation, respectively) [4,15]. Each beat corresponds to an electrical wave that crosses the different structures of the heart. These waves are knowing as P wave, Q, R and S (QRS complex) and T wave (Fig. 1). The study of their morphology, intervals, waves, amplitude and other feature allows to propose new approaches. In recent years, new methods to stratify and predict the SCD risk have been developed [3,11,17–21]. There are different algorithms implemented in the literature for computing the risk stratification indices [17]. However, this work is focused in two indices: Heart Rate Variability (HRV) and T-Wave Alternans (TWA) [7,11,18,19,22].

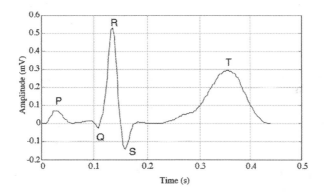

Fig. 1. ECG for one normal heartbeat showing typical amplitudes and time durations for the P, QRS, and T waves [16].

HRV measures and analyzes the temporal variation between sets of consecutive cardiac beats. The instantaneous HRV signal is calculated from the R-R intervals recorded by an ECG signal. Analysis of Heart Rate Variability has provided a non-invasive method to predict SCD [11]. HRV is probably the mostly analyzed index in the cardiovascular risk stratification technical literature, and an important number of models and methods have been developed for this purpose [1]. The methods can be grouped under time-domain, frequency-domain and Non-Linear methods.

The T-wave represents ventricular repolarization in the ECG. The changes in the shape or amplitude of the T wave is known as T-wave alternan (TWA) [15,23]. These magnitudes are typically in the order of microvolts so it is difficult to detect the alternation. TWA is a heart rate dependent phenomenon that has proven to be a non-invasive indicator to stratify cardiac risks [6,24]. Alternans can be seen in any segment of ECG waveform including QRS, ST, and T wave. Different approaches have been proposed for automatic TWA analysis, like: Spectral Methods (SM), Modified Moving Average methods (MMA), Complex Demodulation methods (CD) and Statistical Test methods (ST) [23]. In this document we will focus on the results of the methods SM and MMA due to the following reasons: according to the literature the SM and MMA are the most used methods [25]. Also, the SM method has been included in medical equipment such as CH2000 and Heartwave II (Cambridge Heart Inc, Bedford, MA), and MMA is implemented in the ambulatory MARS systems [1].

The incomprehensible nature of SCD disease increases the urgency to develop new methods to estimate and predict this pathology, which leads to a more effective prevention [26]. The early identification of SCD risk factors is an unresolved problem in clinical cardiology [12].

Based on HRV and TWA as risk stratification indices, this work presents a proposal research framework to stratify and predict SCD. The rest of the paper is divided in the following parts. Section two presents the methodology used to carry out the literature review. Section three shows the related works of SCD prediction. Section four shows the proposal research framework. Discussion is presented in section five. The conclusions and future works are presented in the last section.

2   Methodology of Literature Review

To carry out the proposal research, a Literature Review (LR) was undertaken based on the guidelines proposed by Kitchenham [27]. The LR is divided in three phases: (1) planning of the review, (2) development of the review and (3) reporting the analysis of the results. In the review planning stage, the inclusion criteria were established taking into account the references since 2001 in the English language. The next sources listed were used in the literature review of relevant research: Scopus, Web of Science, IEEE Xplore, Library Digital ACM and Springer.

In order to select the studies related to SCD prediction, the development stage of the review was been performed. The search chains and the related terms, allowed an exhaustive review, improving the search in the sources selected. Table 1 shows the chains of search. The search results returned around 60 related jobs, of which 20 papers were relevant in relation to the study topic, to conduct the literature review. Finally, in the results analysis stage, three domains were defined that allow grouping the results and discussion: i) Sudden cardiac death ii) Heart Rate Variability, and iii) T wave alternans.

3   Related Works

The schema of Fig. 2 represents the different stages that have been considered in this paper for analysing the SCD prediction methods that exists in the literature.

Table 1. Boolean Search Chains

Search chains	Related terms	Boolean chains
Sudden Cardiac Death (SCD)	ECG	ALL("sudden cardiac death" AND "ECG") OR ("SCD" AND "ECG")
	Preprocessing	ALL("sudden cardiac death" AND "preprocessinng") OR ("SCD" AND "preprocessing")
	Feature extraction	ALL("sudden cardiac death" AND "feature extractions") OR ("SCD" AND "feature extractions")
	Detection	ALL("sudden cardiac death" AND "detection") OR ("SCD" AND "detection")
Heart Rate Variability (HRV)	ECG	ALL("heart rate variability" AND "ECG") OR ("HRV" AND "ECG")
	Preprocessing	ALL("heart rate variability" AND "preprocessing") OR ("HRV" AND "preprocessing")
	Feature extraction	ALL("heart rate variability" AND "feature extractions") OR ("HRV" AND "feature extractions")
	Detection	ALL("heart rate variability" AND "detection") OR ("HRV" AND "detection")
T wave alternans (TWA)	ECG	ALL("T wave alternans" AND "ECG") OR ALL ("TWA" AND "ECG")
	Preprocessing	ALL("T wave alternans" AND "preprocessing") OR ALL("TWA" AND "preprocessing")
	Feature extraction	ALL("T wave alternans" AND "feature extractions") OR ALL("TWA" AND "feature extraction")
	Detection	ALL("T wave alternans" AND "detection") OR ALL("TWA" AND "detection")

The first stage in the block diagram refers to the databases that have been used in the methods analysed. The preprocessing stage shows the denoising techniques applied, the feature extraction stage presents the selected linear or nonlinear features used to predict SCD and, finally, the classification stage shows the techniques used in the selected papers to differentiate between ECG signal of normal subject (**Ho**) from those susceptible to SCD (**H1**). The process analysis was carried out for each risk stratification index (HRV and TWA) using the diagram above presented.

Fig. 2. Process used to analyse SCD methods of the literature review.

3.1 Databases

The MIT-BIH Normal Sinus Rhythm Database (NSRDB) [28] and Sudden Cardiac Death Holter Database (SCDHDB) [29] were used in the methods proposed by Acharya et al. [10], Fujita et al. [19], Sanchez et al. [13], Devi et al. [12], Ebrahimzadeh et al. [11], and Lai et al. [24] to predict SCD using HRV.

NSRDB includes 18 long-term ECG recordings of subjects referred to the Arrhythmia Laboratory at Boston's Beth Israel Hospital (now the Beth Israel Deaconess Medical Center). Subjects included in this database were found to have had no significant arrhythmias; they include 5 men, aged 26 to 45, and 13 women, aged 20 to 50 128 Hz sampling rate.

SCDHDB includes 18 patients with underlying sinus rhythm (4 with intermittent pacing), 1 who was continuously paced, and 4 with atrial fibrillation. All patients had a sustained ventricular tachyarrhythmia, and most had an actual cardiac arrest. In total 23 patients with SCD (ages ranging from 18 to 89 years 256 Hz sampling rate).

To evaluate the method proposed by Makikallio et al. [30], the authors used a random sample of 480 people, aged 65 or older, living in the city of Turku, Finland. The data was sampled digitally (with 256 Hz frequency) and transferred to a computer for analysis of HR variability.

On the other hand, Rosenbaum et al.[31] (SM) used the data obtained of 83 patitents, with a sampling rate 500 Hz. Nearing et al. [32] (MMA) used simulated ECG signals, with a sampling rate 500 Hz.

3.2 Preprocessing

An unavoidable problem when recording the signal is the presence of disturbances or unwished signals that can alter the original signal. The power line interference (higher frequency noise) and the baseline wander (lower frequency noise) are the two of more frequent noises that are present in ECG [33, 34]. These types of noise considerably alter the signal, preventing the identification of the start and end of the waves. In order to minimize changes in the morphology of the signal wich do not have cardiac origin, it is necessary to use techniques of denoising [35].

In the work proposed by Acharya et al. [10] and Fujita et al. [19] wavelet based denoising using daubechies 6 (db6) mother wavelet was used. The method proposed by Sanchez et al. [13], a low-pass finite impulse response (FIR) filter was implemented to sample the signal. In the paper presented by Devi et al. [12] the signals are filtered using fast fourier transformation for the removal of baseline wandering noise and notch filter for removal of power line interference. The ECG signals in the work proposed by Ebrahimzadeh et al. [11] would pass through a moving-average filter so that the baseline wander is eliminated; also, a notch filter will then be utilized to remove power-line frequency. The baseline drift and the noise of each ECG fragment were removed by using a median filter and a band-pass filter (0.5–100 Hz), respectively, in the method proposed by Lai et al. [24].

In the work of Rosenbaum et al. [31] (SM) ECG recording were amplified and filtered. Nearing et al. [32] (non linear- MMA) used a low-pass filtering to remove high-frequency. This was accomplished using an eighth-order digital Butterworth filter with a corner frequency 50 Hz. The baseline wander was estimated based on isoelectric points in each ECG beat by calculating a cubic spline and was subtracted from the ECG signal. In the last two methods analised, the authors do not give details of the preprocessing stage.

3.3   Feature Extraction

To predict SCD using HRV, the nonlinear methods as Fractal Dimension (FD), Hurst's exponent (H), Detrended Fluctuation Analysis (DFA), Correlation Dimension (CD), Approximate Entropy (ApproxEnt) and Sample Entropy (SampEnt) are used to extract the features from the non-stationary complex ECG signals [10, 19]. Table 2 presents the feature extraction of the proposed methods.

On the other hand, in TWA methods, the feature extraction in the paper [31] is carried out segmenting the signal and using fixed window to extract QRS complex, ST segment and T waves; after that the features are aligned using QRS complex. In the work of [32] the ST-T segment is obtained, but this process is not specified.

Table 2. A summary of the feature extraction in the proposed methods

Author	Feature extraction	Features ranking selection
Acharya et al. [10]	Nonlinear features	Student's t-test
Fujita et al. [19]	Nonlinear features	Student's t-test
Sanchez et al. [13]	Homogeneity analysis is used for feature extraction.	ANOVA test
Devi et al. [12]	Nonlinear features, time domain features	Statistical analysis using Kruskal–Wallis test
Ebrahimzadeh et al. [11]	Nonlinear features	Student's t-test
Lai et al. [24]	Arrhythmic risk markers	Student's t-test

3.4   Classification

The features described in Table 2 are ranked based on the t-value and used as input to the classifiers to find the minimum number of features needed to obtain the highest performance. The main goal of classification is to select the best classifier that results in a highest accuracy in classifying the ECG signals belonging to normal and SCD subjects, with the minimum number of significant features. The methods for markers classification used in the literature are: Decision Tree (DT), K-Nearest Neighbor (KNN), Support Vector Machine (SVM), Enhanced Probabilistic Neural Network (EPNN), Multilayer Perceptron (MLP), Mixture of Expert classifier (ME), Naive Bayes (NB) and Random Forest (RF). Table 3 shows the methods used in the classification stage. In the case of TWA, to distinguish between the ECG signal of a normal subject from those susceptible to sudden cardiac death, the following process is performed by the authors. The main steps of the SM methodology [31] are: (1) Selection of 128 equally spaced points in the ST-T complex of a 128-beat ECG stream. (2) Each selection has its spectrum computed by the Fourier Transform, in a total of 128 spectra. (3) all 128 spectrum are averaged to create a composite spectrum; from this composite spectrum, the alternans power is computed as the power at 0.5 cpb minus the average noise power measured; the correspondent TWA amplitude is the square root of the alternans power.

Table 3. Methods used for markers classification using HRV

Paper	Classification methods
[10]	DT, KNN, SVM
[19]	DT, KNN, SVM
[13]	EPNN
[12]	DT, KNN, SVM
[11]	MLP, KNN, SVM, ME
[24]	DT, KNN, SVM, NB, RF

In paper [32] the even ECG beats in the sequence are assigned to group A and the odd ECG beats to group B. Modified moving average beats are continuously calculated. To measure T-wave alternans, the maximum absolute value of the difference between the A and B modified moving average computed beats is determined within the ST segment and T-wave region, from the J point to the end of the T wave.

3.5 Results of Literature Review

Table 4 presents a summarized information about review focused on HRV. According to the results, the method developed by Lai et al. [24] shows the best percentage of accuracy and the major time of SCD prediction. However, the authors tested the proposed method in a small patient data with 28 SCD and 18 normal patients.

Table 4. A summary of the proposed methods (Not Specified NS)

Author	Length of signal	Accuracy	Sens.	Spec.
Acharya et al.[10]	4 min before SCD	92.11%	92.5%	91.6%
Fujita et al.[19]	4 min before SCD	94.7%	95%	94.4%
Sanchez et al.[13]	20 min before SCD	95.8%	NS	NS
Ebrahimzadeh et al.[11]	13 min before SCD	90.18%	NS	NS
Lai et al. [24]	30 min before SCD	99.49%	99.75%	99.04%

In the case of TWA results, the MMA method [32] can be applied in stress tests and ambulatory tests; however, the exact values of the thresholds have not yet been defined to calculate the maximum alternating magnitude, resulting in the classification of the tests being around 75% of accuracy. On the other hand, SM [36] is a method that requires a stable heart rate of 105–110 beats per minute over a period, using a specialized exercise protocol, pharmacological agents or atrial pacing. Due to these restrictions, approximately 20–40% of the tests are classified as "indeterminate", either due to factors related to the patient such as the inability to reach the target heart rate, excessive ventricu-lar ectopia, atrial fibrillation or technical problems as noise in the recording.

3.6 Discussion

The methods analyzed in this section present different scenarios. In each stage (preprocessing, feature extraction and detection), different strategies have been proposed by the authors to predict SCD. Hence, considering the analysis conducted, two frameworks have been developed to show the processes that have been identified to predict sudden cardiac death.

In Fig. 3 four stages were identified (preprocessing, fidutial points detections, feature extractions and classification). Each stage depends on results of the previous stages, i.e. noise elimination, complex QRS detection, RR intervals detection, feature extraction (using time domain methods, frequency domain methods or non linear methods); finally classification is carry out using supervised methods (KNN, SVM, MLP, NN) to decide the presence of SCD or not.

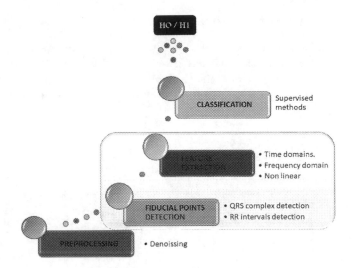

Fig. 3. Framework that shows the different stages that have been performed to predict SCD using HRV

Figure 4 presents the three principal stages detected to carry out the SCD detection using TWA (preprocessing, data reduction and analysis). In the preprocessing stage, the subprocess denoising is carried out first; after that, QRS complex is detected and segmentation is the last process described. The data reduction stage is a process where the ectopic beats are eliminated. To decide between hypotesis $H0$ or $H1$ a global detection statistic Z_l is computed, where, l represents $l-th$ beat located in the analysis window, and $\lambda(l)$ is the threshold. These values are compared: if $Z_l > \lambda(l)$ then $H1$ holds, otherwise $H0$ holds.

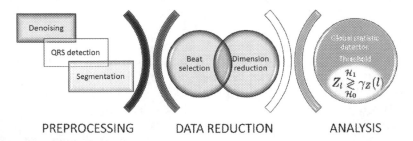

Fig. 4. Framework that presents the process carried out to predict SCD using TWA

4   Research Proposal

Based on the frameworks above identified we now present our proposal for a new method to predict SCD. In the diagram shown on Fig. 5, three stage are detected:

– Preprocessing
– Feature extraction
– Classification

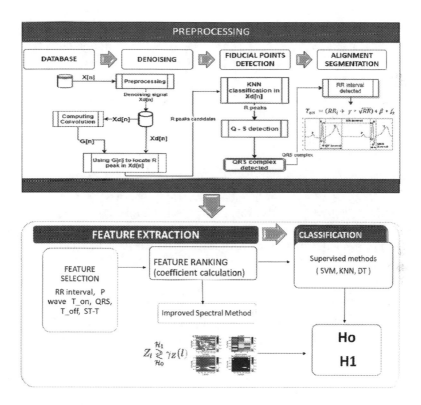

Fig. 5. Framework of proposed method to predict SCD

4.1   Preprocessing

In this stage, four tasks are identified: database, denoissing, fidutial points detection, alignment/segmentation.

Database. Raw signals $X[n]$ are selected of the physionet database (TWADB, ADB, NSRDB, QTDB).

Denoising. In order to improve the signal $X[n]$, Discrete Wavelet Transform (DWT) will be applied to eliminate intrinsic noise [35,37]. This technique allows to compute the filtering coefficients that would using by Inverse Wavelet Transform (DWT) to obtain the denoising signal $Xd[n]$.

Computing Convolution. In this stage, a convolution G[n] is computed. Using G[n], we detect a set of max points (R peaks candidates). A threshold is necessary to eliminate the other waves (P, T). The output of this process is a set of R peaks candidates located in Xd[n].

Fidutial Points Detection. A KNN classifier is used to locate R peaks in Xd[n]. Using R peaks, Q and S peaks are located (QRS complex detected). This process allows to eliminate R peaks candidates falsely detected.

Alignment-Segmentation. In this stage, RR intervals are detected to segment the waves that are inside the ECG signal.

4.2   Feature Extractions

This process is carried out in two stages. The first one is the feature selection where the specific waves, intervals and segments are selected. The ST-T segment will be analysed to compute the variability and the alternance on the T wave. In the second stage, the best coefficients are selected using a set of statistical methods. These coefficients allow to improve the spectral method to calculate Ho' or $H1'$.

4.3   Classification

Using the coefficients, a set the supervised method as SVM and DT will be used to detect SCD, i.e. compute Ho or $H1$. Finally, a comparison will be carry out between Ho and Ho' or $H1$ and $H1'$ to select the best and improve the results.

5   Conclusions

This paper presents a new research proposal to create a non-invasive method for premature Sudden Cardiac Death detection. To achieve this goal, a literature review was carried out. This review allowed to gain insight into the main works developed in this field. Hence, we were able to identify the different stages carried out in the different approaches and elaborated two representative frameworks to predict SCD using HRV and TWA. HRV was initially promising but was later shown not be predictive of arrhythmic mortality [1]. There is still debate regarding the best timing for performance of HRV measurements [24]. On the other hand, according to the literature, it can be seen that the proposed methods for TWA analysis are based on two of the most used methods (MMA and SM), the accuracy improves but only in certain cases and under certains conditions, which complicates a comparison between methods since the same database or the same sample size is not used. Also, these proposed techniques are rarely used in clinical practice, due to its limited diagnostic accuracy or the lack of standard procedures to implement the computational process.

In this context, it is important to develop hybrid methods that allow to integrate the advantages of two risk stratification indices (HRV and TWA) for SCD prediction. So, the work presented in this paper puts forward a new research proposal framework to predict SCD. It is also intended to answer the following research questions: Is it possible to predict the SCD from the ECG signal analysis using HRV?, Is the information contained in the T wave sufficient for generating an effective method for SCD detection?, Is it possible to create a new hybrid method using the best features of TWA and HRV that allow detect SCD? To answer these questions, we will be used the current computational power and the new AI techniques to develop new efficient techniques for improving efficiency in SCD detection.

References

1. Gimeno-Blanes, F.J., Blanco-Velasco, M., Barquero-Pérez, Ó., García-Alberola, A , Rojo-álvarez, J.L.: Sudden cardiac risk stratification with electrocardiographic indices - a review on computational processing, technology transfer, and scientific evidence. Front. Physiol. **7**, 1–17 (2016)
2. Narayan, S., Botteron, G., Smith, J.: T-wave alternans spectral magnitude is sensitive to electrocardiographic beat alignment strategy. In: Computers in Cardiology, vol. 24, no. 2, pp. 593–596 (1997)
3. Pham, Q., Quan, K.J., Rosenbaum, D.S.: T-wave alternans: marker, mechanism, and methodology for predicting sudden cardiac death. J. Electrocardiol. 36(Suppl.), 75–81 (2003)
4. Monasterio, V., Clifford, G.D., Laguna, P., Martí Nez, J.P.: A multilead scheme based on periodic component analysis for T-wave alternans analysis in the ECG. Ann. Biomed. Eng. **38**(8), 2532–2541 (2010)
5. The top 10 causes of death
6. Shen, T.W., Tsao, Y.T.: An improved spectral method of detecting and quantifying T-wave Alternans for SCD risk evaluation. Comput. Cardiol. **35**, 609–612 (2008)
7. Ghoraani, B., Krishnan, S., Selvaraj, R.J., Chauhan, V.S.: T wave alternans evaluation using adaptive time-frequency signal analysis and non-negative matrix factorization. Med. Eng. Phys. **33**(6), 700–711 (2011)
8. Valverde, E., Arini, P.: Study of T-wave spectral variance during acute myocardial ischemia. In: 2012 Computing in Cardiology, pp. 653–656 (2012)
9. Murukesan, L., Murugappan, M., Iqbal, M.: Sudden cardiac death prediction using ECG signal derivative (Heart rate variability): a review, pp. 8–10 (2013)
10. Acharya, U.R., et al.: An integrated index for detection of sudden cardiac death using discrete wavelet transform and nonlinear features. Knowl. Based Syst. **83**, 145–158 (2015)
11. Ebrahimzadeh, E., et al.: An optimal strategy for prediction of sudden cardiac death through a pioneering feature-selection approach from HRV signal. Comput. Methods Programs Biomed. **169**, 19–36 (2019)

12. Devi, R., Tyagi, H.K., Kumar, D.: A novel multi-class approach for early-stage prediction of sudden cardiac death. Biocybern. Biomed. Eng. **39**(3), 586–598 (2019)
13. Amezquita-Sanchez, J.P., Valtierra-Rodriguez, M., Adeli, H., Perez-Ramirez, C.A.: A novel wavelet transform-homogeneity model for sudden cardiac death prediction using ECG signals. J. Med. Syst. **42**(10), 1–15 (2018). https://doi.org/10.1007/s10916-018-1031-5
14. Instituto Nacional de Estadística y Censo: Estadísticas Vitales: Registro estadístico de Defunciones Generales de 2020, pp. 1–32 (2020)
15. Irshad, A., Bakhshi, A.D., Bashir, S.: A bayesian filtering application for T -wave altemans analysis. In: 12th International Bhurban Conference on Applied Sciences & Technology (IBCAST), Islamabad, Pakistan, pp. 222–227, 13th - 17th, January (2015)
16. Tompkins, W.J.: Biomedical Digital Signal Processing: C-language Examples and Laboratory Experiments for the IBM PC. Prentice Hall, Hauptbd (2000)
17. Goldberger, J.J., et al.: American heart association/American college of cardiology foundation/heart rhythm society scientific statement on noninvasive risk stratification techniques for identifying patients at risk for sudden cardiac death. A scientific statement from the american heart association council on clinical cardiology committee on electrocardiography and arrhythmias and council on epidemiology and prevention. Heart Rhythm **5**(10) (2008)
18. Demidova, N.M., et al.: T wave alternans in experimental myocardial infarction: Time course and predictive value for the assessment of myocardial damage. J. Electrocardiol. **46**(3), 263–269 (2013)
19. Fujita, H., et al.: Sudden cardiac death (SCD) prediction based on nonlinear heart rate variability features and SCD index. Appl. Soft Comput. Journal. **43**, 510–519 (2016)
20. Liu, J., et al.: Improvement in sudden cardiac death risk prediction by the enhanced American college of cardiology/American heart association strategy in Chinese patients with hypertrophic cardiomyopathy. Heart Rhythm **17**(10), 1658–1663 (2020)
21. Parsi, A., Byrne, D., Glavin, M., Jones, E.: Heart rate variability feature selection method for automated prediction of sudden cardiac death. Biomed. Sig. Process. Control **65**(January 2020), 102310 (2021)
22. Verrier, R.L., Kumar, K., Nearing, B.D.: Basis for sudden cardiac death prediction by T-wave alternans from an integrative physiology perspective. Heart Rhythm **6**(3), 416–422 (2009)
23. Martínez, J.P., Olmos, S.: Methodological principles of T wave alternans analysis: a unified framework. IEEE Trans. Biomed. Eng, **52**(4), 599–613 (2005)
24. Lai, D., Zhang, Y., Zhang, X., Su, Y., Bin Heyat, M.B.: An automated strategy for early risk identification of sudden cardiac death by using machine learning approach on measurable arrhythmic risk markers. IEEE Access **7**, 94701–94716 (2019)
25. Betancourt, N., Almeida, C., Flores-Calero, M.: T wave alternans analysis in ECG signal: a survey of the principal approaches. In: Rocha, Á., Ferrás, C., Paredes, M. (eds.) Inf. Technol. Syst., pp. 417–426. Springer International Publishing, Cham (2019)
26. Chugh, S.S.: Early identification of risk factors for sudden cardiac death. Nat. Rev. Cardiol. **7**(6), 318 (2010)
27. Kitchenham, B.: Procedures for performing systematic reviews (2004)

28. Goldberger, A.L., et al.: Physiobank, physiotoolkit, and physionet: components of a new research resource for complex physiologic signals. Circulation **101**(23), e215–e220 (2000)
29. Greenwald, S.D.: The development and analysis of a ventricular fibrillation detector. PhD thesis, Massachusetts Institute of Technology (1986)
30. Mäkikallio, T.H., et al.: Prediction of sudden cardiac death by fractal analysis of heart rate variability in elderly subjects. J. Am. Coll. Cardiol. **37**(5), 1395–1402 (2001)
31. Rosenbaum, D.S., Jackson, L.E., Smith, J.M., Garan, H., Ruskin, J.N., Cohen, R.J.: Electrical alternans and vulnerability to ventricular arrhythmias. N. Engl. J. Med. **330**(4), 235–241 (1994)
32. Nearing, B.D., Verrier, R.L.: Modified moving average analysis of t-wave alternans to predict ventricular fibrillation with high accuracy. J. Appl. Physiol. **92**(2), 541–549 (2002)
33. AlMahamdy, M., Riley, H.B.: Performance study of different denoising methods for ECG signals. Procedia Comput. Sci. **37**, 325–332 (2014)
34. Biswas, U., Hasan, K.R., Sana, B., Maniruzzaman, M.: Denoising ECG signal using different wavelet families and comparison with other techniques. In: 2nd International Conference on Electrical Engineering and Information and Communication Technology, iCEEiCT 2015, pp. 21–23, May 2015
35. Betancourt, N., Flores-Calero, M., Almeida, C.: ECG denoising by using FIR and IIR filtering techniques: an experimental study. In: ACM International Conference Proceeding Series, pp. 111–117 (2019)
36. Smith, J.M., Clancy, E.A., Valeri, C.R., Ruskin, J.N., Cohen, R.J.: Electrical alternans and cardiac electrical instability. Circulation **77**(1), 110–121 (1988)
37. Strasser, F., Muma, M., Zoubir, A.M.: Motion artifact removal in ECG signals using multi-resolution thresholding. In: European Signal Processing Conference (Eusipco), pp. 899–903 (2012)

Towards Portuguese Sign Language Identification Using Deep Learning

Ismael Costa⬤, Domingos Martinho⬤, and Ricardo Vardasca(✉)⬤

ISLA Santarém, Largo Cândido dos Reis, 2000-241 Santarém, Portugal
{domingos.martinho,ricardo.vardasca}@islasantarem.pt

Abstract. In Portugal there are above 80,000 people with hearing impairment with the need to communicate through the sign language. Equal opportunities and social inclusion are the major concerns of the current society. It is aim of this research to create and evaluate a Deep Learning model that using a dataset with images of characters in Portuguese sign language can identify the gesture of a user, recognizing it. For model training, 5826 representative samples of the characters 'C', 'I', 'L', 'U' and 'Y' in Portuguese sign language. The Deep Learning model is based on a convolutional neural network. The model evaluated using the sample allowed for an accuracy of 98.5%, which is considered as a satisfactory result. However, there are two gaps: the existence of datasets with the totality of the alphabet in the Portuguese sign language and with the various representations of movement that each word has at the layout of letters. Using the proposed model with more complete datasets would allow to develop more inclusive user interfaces and equal opportunities for users with auditory difficulties.

Keywords: Deep learning · Inclusion user interfaces · Portuguese sign language

1 Introduction

One of the greatest current challenges is the digital transformation, which must be inclusive and must promote the integration of all individuals without any discrimination. In Portugal, there are about 83,000 people with reference to hearing loss (0.8% of the resident population) [1]. Hearing loss has a negative social and economic impact on people, families, and communities. Individuals with hearing difficulties or who have been deaf throughout life are distinct from congenital deaf people, as they have learned a language and can overcome their difficulty through video subtitles. Congenital deaf people have enormous difficulty in understand the written form, so any method-based text-only is inappropriate.

To help congenital deaf people, sign language was created and developed, the first proposal for a gesture dictionary corresponding to alphabet letters was proposed in XVII century for the Spanish language [2]. After which several dictionaries were created and developed. for different languages, where word creation is in addition to being letter-based, these are completed with hand movements and facial expressions.

© Springer Nature Switzerland AG 2021
T. Guarda et al. (Eds.): ARTIIS 2021, CCIS 1485, pp. 70–80, 2021.
https://doi.org/10.1007/978-3-030-90241-4_6

Among the existing sign languages, the most used dictionary worldwide is the American Sign Language (ASL), which is also the one that is more easily found in an image database that can be used for digital processing of sign language. The static example of the correspondence of the gesture to the letter in the ASL dictionary is shown in Fig. 1.

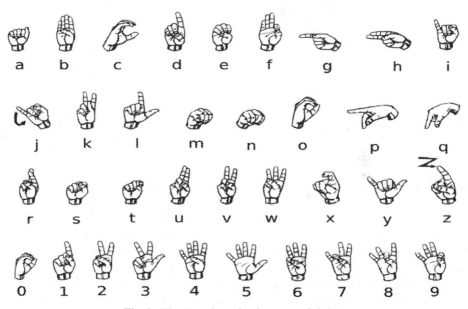

Fig. 1. The American sign language alphabet.

In the 19th century, by order of King João VI, the Institute for the Deaf and Blind (Instituto de Surdos-Mudos e Cegos) was founded in Casa Pia and the Swedish specialist Pär Aron Borg was invited to coordinate it. This was fundamental for the teaching of deaf people in Portugal and allowed them to communicate through an alphabet and a sign language of Swedish origin, a teaching method that was adopted in Portugal and had Borg as its creator [3]. Since 1997, the Portuguese Sign Language (PSL) has been enshrined in the Constitution of the Portuguese Republic, being one of the first countries to legislate a sign language [4]. The alphabet of the PSL is shown in Fig. 2.

It is aim of this research to create and evaluate a Deep Learning model that using a dataset with images of characters in Portuguese sign language can identify the gesture of a user, recognizing it.

The background related to this work is present in the next chapter. In Sect. 3 is presented the methodology used in development of the proposed solution, the results are described in Sect. 4, followed by the last chapter with the presentation of discussion, conclusion, and further work.

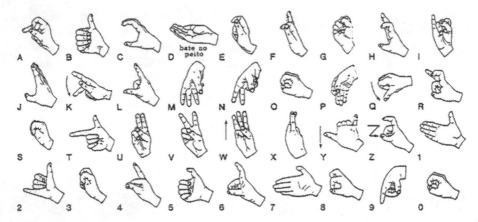

Fig. 2. The Portuguese sign language alphabet.

2 Background

The sign language gestures can be segmented in images using a global thresholding algorithm (in a binary image), infrared illumination based (camera provides a distance), software based (color separation), HSV (hue, saturation, lightness) brightness factor matching and Binary Large OBject method [5].

The feature extraction can be achieved through Edge Detection using HSV brightness matching, palm point detection, center of region detection, dimensionality reduction, scale-invariant feature transform technique and leap motion [5].

The classification techniques available for sign classification are Hidden Markov Models (HMM) (statistical model designed using Bayes network), Machine learning algorithms (Artificial Neural Network, k-Nearest Neighbors, Support Vector Machine) and deep learning techniques such as Convolutional Neural Network (CNN) [5].

Before the application of deep learning in sign language classification and detection it has also been performed through machine learning, which is less powerful than deep learning but faster.

The Portuguese sign language (PSL) signs were isolated and classified with machine learning methods using data gathered with a Microsoft Kinect and data gloves, the obtained accuracy results were 87.3% with Random Trees, 96.6% with Boost Cascade, 80.4% with Artificial Neural Networks, 98.2% with K-Nearest Neighbors, 96.8% with Naive Bayes and 100% with Support Vector Machine [6].

A dataset consisting of 2524 images with 70 images per category. Each of the 36 categories represented a different character of American Sign Language (ASL). All images were augmented to create a dataset of 14781 images, 75% were used for training and remaining 25% for test. The model of training was based in the VGG16 CNN architecture with 4 epochs, the average training accuracy was of 95.54%, being the digit 0 that who presented the worst accuracy. The validation accuracy after the 4 epochs was of 94.68 in predicting the given image gesture [7].

Previous approaches for classifying American sign language were: using real time video input with HMM and Euclidean distance achieved 90% accuracy [8], static images input for Histogram of Orientation Gradient (HOG), Histogram of Boundary Description (HBD) and the Histogram of Edge Frequency (HOEF) with SVM reached 98.1% accuracy [9], real time video input for PCA and fuzzy logic obtained 91% accuracy [10] and real time video input for HMM and ANN with error back propagation algorithm achieved 91% accuracy [11].

With a dataset of 41258 training and 2728 testing samples. Each sample provides a RGB image (320 × 320 pixels), Depth map (320 × 320 pixels), Segmentation masks (320 × 320 pixels) for the classes: background, person, three classes for each finger and one for each palm, 21 Key points for each hand with their uv coordinates in the image frame. The pre-trained model based in a SqueezeNet model processed the images by dividing every pixel by 255 and then resizing the image to 244 × 244. The results of the squeezing process are concatenated and separated in two groups of 4 convulsions each being one single and other of 3 × 3 filters, being finally concatenated for the output. From the tests a maximum training accuracy of 87.47% is attained. The validation accuracy attained is 83.29% [12].

A model of CNN based in a convolutional layer of 16 filters (2 × 2) reducing spatial dimensions to 32 × 32 with added max pooling filters (increased to 5 × 5), a dropout rate of 20% and a SoftMax classifier for producing the output. All 1000 images of ASL of 26 characters and 10 digits were resized to 50 × 50 pixels and the total number of epochs used to train the network is 50 with a batch size of 500. For chars an accuracy of 90.04% was achieved in 4.31 s, characters 'A', 'C' and 'D' presented highest accuracy (100%), and 'Z' the lowest (67.78%). The digits obtained 93.44% accuracy in 3.93 s in real-time recognition, the best (100%) was reached by the digit '5' and the worst (83.33%) by the '8' digit [13].

Using the Modified National Institute of Standards and Technology database (MNIST) database of American Sign Language with 60000 images spread by 24-character classes, 'J' and 'Z' were excluded because they require motion. Principal Component Analysis (PCA) was used for sign identification with a custom CNN model with 11 layers: 4 Convolutional layers, 3 Pooling (Max) layers, 2 Dense Connected, 1 Flatten and 1 Dropout layer. A Rectified Linear Unit (ReLu) activation function was used to avoid negativities. The training dataset consists of 27455 images with 784 (28 × 28) features, on average each letter class has 1000 images, the validation set consists of 7172 images with 784 (28 × 28) features. A dropout layer with a given probability of 20% is included to avoid model overfitting as it drops out 20% of the hidden and visible units from these densely connected layers. The final training of model from scratch produces a considerably high level of 99% accurateness on the training set. The output is taken from the SoftMax Layer with 24 class classification. The model was trained to minimize loss by usage of cross entropy ADAM, for 10 epochs on a batch size of 128. The model was trained with a learning rate of 0.001 with 0 decay. The validation accuracy of the model is greater than 93% and only 6 epochs were required for a stable result. For further research it is suggested that the images should be segmented using the OpenCV library [14].

Two modified pre-trained AlexNet and VGG16 based CNN models have been proposed for gesture recognition and classification using a ASL dataset with 36 classes, characters and digits, 70 images per class (2520 images). The methodology consisted of pre-processing (image resize, data augmentation, dataset split into training and test), feature extraction with a pre-trained CNN architecture and classification with SVM until the accuracy achieves the desired value. Using a 70% training and 30% test sets, the AlexNet showed troubles in achieving 100% accuracy with digits '0' and '6' and with 'E', 'M', 'O', 'U', 'W' and 'Z' characters. The VGG16 model also not classified 100% accurately the digits '0', '2', '6' and '9' and the chars 'I', 'K', 'M', 'S', 'T', 'W' and 'X'. the VGG16 model (99.82%) performed badly when compared with the AlexNet model (99.76%). In terms of training time the AlexNet model took 5.83 min when VGG16 model took 88 min [15].

A research on ASL recognition comparing the deep learning approaches AlexNet and model E on a dataset of 3000 × 29 100 × 100 pixel images of hand gesture language, found that the model E presented a training accuracy of 19.38% and validation accuracy of 30.94%, whereas the AlexNet model showed a training accuracy of 2.50% and validation accuracy of 3.28% with 50 epochs. Another important aspect was that the AlexNet requires 1.72 h while model E takes 0.71 h in training the model [16].

A total of 61.614 images were collected for 28 classes, comprised of 26 alphabets, including 'J' and 'Z', as well as two classes for space and delete. All the images were scaled to 224 × 224 pixels, and then, normalized to be fed to the VGG_Net architecture. A 70% training and 30% test sets were chosen. An accuracy of 98.53% was obtained for the training set, and 98.84% for the validation set in real-time. In terms of accuracy, the highest (99.95%) was obtained for the character 'L' and the lowest (97.31%) was obtained was for the character 'M' [17].

3   Methodology

From the related research, it can be observed that there is no freely available images dataset of the PSL, which has an impact on the development of research in the area and implementation of machine learning and deep learning solutions.

The development of a solution that allows the interpretation of sign language must be performed at several steps, initially each character and digit must be identified individually and statically, then the dynamic identification of characters that presupposes motion, and finally the recognition of the construction of words combined with a grammar and semantics.

Since there is no Portuguese sign language dataset, there was a need to adapt an existing dataset including the characters that are common to another sign language dictionary, in this case the American, which is the one that offered more freely accessible datasets.

As dataset for this research, an adaptation of the original dataset published on the Kaggle platform provided by "tecperson" [18] was used. The sign language dataset is presented in this work following the comma separated value (CSV) format, labeled with the written language characters and the monochromatic hue values of the pixels that make up the image. The standardized format of the classic MNIST dataset contains 28 × 28 pixel images with grayscale values 0–255.

From the original 24-character American Sign Language reference dataset only the characters common to PSL were considered (Fig. 3). For the learning and assessment process, 5 labels (0–4) corresponding to the common characters between LGA and LGP were used: 0 – 'C', 1 – 'I', 2 – 'L', 3 – 'U' and 4 – 'Y'. The dataset considered for the 3 sign language symbols has 5826 samples.

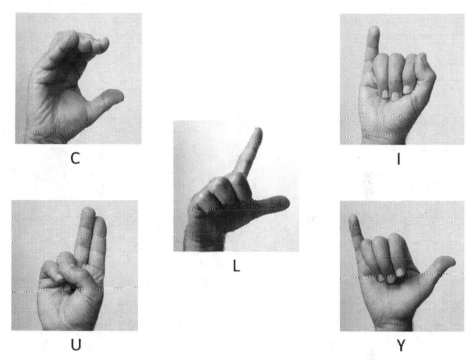

Fig. 3. Examples of images of selected characters for the dataset of this research.

3.1 Deep Learning Model

The algorithm of the deep learning classification model based on a CNN was carried out based on 2 different configurations and 2 evaluation methods. The code proposed in this work was adapted from the original code developed by Wan [19].

For the training operation of the algorithm, convulsion layers (Conv2d) were used, applying a 2D convolution over an input signal composed of several input layers. Subsequently, grouping layers (MaxPool2d) were applied by applying a maximum 2D grouping to an input signal composed of several input layers. Repeated new convulsive layers and then applied a linear transformation to the input data.

To optimize the model, in order to allow it to achieve the state of maximum precision, given the resource constraints, such as time, computing capacity, memory, etc., the stochastic gradient descent (SGD) optimization technique was used, which is made available through the "torch.optim" package.

The Cross-entropy loss technique was used in this work as a learning optimizer, this technique is very common in classification tasks both in Machine Learning and in Deep Learning [20].

The model will achieve a very satisfactory performance when the loss value (Cross entropy loss) is less than 0.02. When this value is less than 0.00, the algorithm will be in its perfect learning state.

The infrastructure of the learning model used in the implementation of this research is shown in Fig. 4. In that the features are the amount of grey value intensity, C – Convolutions, S – Subsampling.

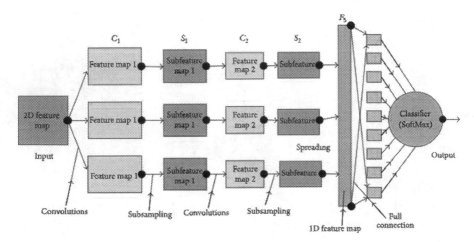

Fig. 4. The infrastructure of the classification model used in this research.

For the development and testing of the model, the programming language Python v.3.8 and the artificial vision library OpenCV v.4.4 were used.

A dataset composed of LGP images representative of the characters 'C', 'I', 'L', 'U' and Y" with a total of 5,826 samples was used to train the model. For this process, 12 iterations (epocs) were considered because this number of iterations presents a loss value = 0.0035 (loss) calculated by the average of 10 executions. As this value is less than 0.02, the performance of the model is considered very satisfactory.

For the model evaluation process, a set of 1,405 different samples from the samples used in the training process was considered. The performance evaluation of the model was carried out in two phases. All training samples (5,826 samples) were considered, and an evaluation performed using a pre-trained model available in the PyTorch library, a second evaluation performed based on the ONNX Runtime inference accelerator method [21].

In the last phase, the process of evaluating the model in real time is carried out by collecting the user's video image by the device's camera. In this real-time evaluation, the user must present a PSL gesture corresponding to one of the selected characters and check in the user interface whether the model is able to identify the correct character through the interpreted image. During the process of translating the PSL character read in real time, the model will search for a list of possible Portuguese characters. When the character is found in the list, it is displayed in the user interface.

4   Results

The verification of the number of executions necessary in training the model is shown in Fig. 5, 10 runs are satisfactory.

```
[0,      0] loss: 3.184757
[1,      0] loss: 1.029089
[2,      0] loss: 0.353557
[3,      0] loss: 0.411881
[4,      0] loss: 0.019408
[5,      0] loss: 0.017968
[6,      0] loss: 0.003132
[7,      0] loss: 0.107467
[8,      0] loss: 0.003781
[9,      0] loss: 0.052442
[10,     0] loss: 0.010813
[11,     0] loss: 0.000543
```

Fig. 5. Results of loss values (loss) at each iteration (epoch).

The accuracy of the training and validation of the model using the training and validation sets is shown in Fig. 6, the implementation using the PyTorch library presents a value more for training but lower for validation, however in both cases the accuracy is higher than 88.5%.

```
========== PyTorch ==========
Training accuracy: 99.8
Validation accuracy: 99.0
========== ONNX ==========
Training accuracy: 99.9
Validation accuracy: 98.6
```

Fig. 6. Model evaluations with dataset using PyTorch and ONNX methods.

An example of the execution of a PSL gesture with recognition of the respective characters is shown in Figs. 7 and 8, the gesture corresponding to the characters 'L' and 'C' was correctly identified.

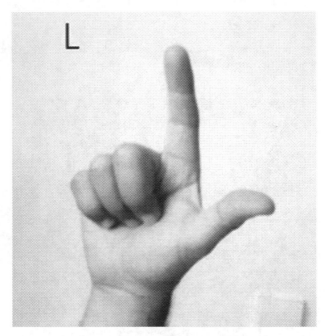

Fig. 7. Real-time PSL 'L' character recognition model evaluation user interface.

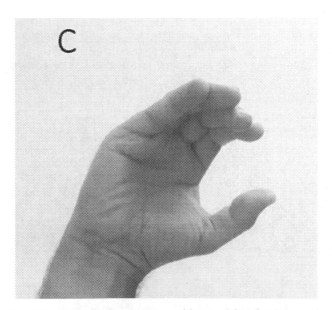

Fig. 8. Real-time PSL 'C' character recognition model evaluation user interface.

5 Discussion and Conclusion

The major barrier for the development of this research was the absence of a freely available PSL characters image dataset, to overcome this limitation a ASL characters image dataset [18] was used, selecting only the images that have correspondence between PSL and ASL.

This manuscript only covers the first phase in PSL recognition, it is the first step towards a more comprehensive investigation.

The PSL character classification results presented by this investigation using the developed deep learning model surpass most results presented by machine learning classifiers with data collected by smart gloves and Microsoft Kinetic system [6].

It is important to verify that the results of classification in training and validation presented by this simple and fast implementation surpass the results of other more complex implementations applied to ASL [11–13].

No entanto fica aquém dos resultados de outras implementações de mais complexas aplicadas à ASL usando VGG_Net e AlexNet [15–17], mas requer menor capacidade computacional.

For the best knowledge of the authors of this investigation, this is the first attempt to apply a low-complexity deep learning model to the identification of PSL characters.

It is concluded that the model demonstrated a high efficiency even considering the learning using a reduced number of samples. The proposed solution based on image collection using a commonly used webcam will be viable given the easy accessibility that this medium will have for most users.

For future work, it is proposed the development of a dataset that includes all PSL characters and digits, even those with motion, which will allow an evaluation of the model's effectiveness in translating the PSL more complete. The proposed deep learning model should also be tested for dynamic PSL words identification, even if for that purpose a grammar and lexicon are required to be developed.

This work was a first step towards the creation of fully integrative user interface for deaf people, which not only should be capable of recognize their communication gestures, as should provide them responses in the same language through the usage of an animated avatar also using a deep learning method, or even in a more advanced development be an important aid for PSL learning for subjects in need of it.

References

1. Gonçalves, C.: Enquadramento familiar das pessoas com deficiência: Uma análise exploratória dos resultados dos Censos 2001. Revista de Estudos Demográficos **33**, 69–94 (2003)
2. Bonet, J.P.: Reduction de las letras, y arte para enseñar a ablar los mudos. Por Francisco Abarca de Angulo (1930)
3. Olsson, C.G.: Omsorg och kontroll. En handikapphistorisk studie 1750–1930. Umeå: Umeå universitet (2010)
4. Correia, M.D.F.S., Coelho, O., Magalhães, A., Benvenuto, A.: Learning/teaching philosophy in sign language as a cultural issue. J. Educ Cult. Soci. **4**(1), 9–19 (2013)

5. Safeel, M., Sukumar, T., Shashank, K.S., Arman, M.D., Shashidhar, R., Puneeth, S.B.: Sign language recognition techniques-a review. In: 2020 IEEE International Conference for Innovation in Technology (INOCON), pp. 1–9 (2020)

6. Escudeiro, P., et al.: Virtual sign–a real time bidirectional translator of portuguese sign language. Procedia Comput. Sci. **67**, 252–262 (2015)

7. Masood, S., Thuwal, H.C., Srivastava, A.: American sign language character recognition using convolution neural network. In: Satapathy, S.C., Bhateja, V., Das, S. (eds.) Smart Computing and Informatics. SIST, vol. 78, pp. 403–412. Springer, Singapore (2018). https://doi.org/10. 1007/978-981-10-5547-8_42

8. Nandy, A., Prasad, J.S., Mondal, S., Chakraborty, P., Nandi, G.C.: Recognition of isolated indian sign language gesture in real time. : Information Processing and Management, pp. 102–107 (2010). https://doi.org/10.1007/978-3-642-12214-9_18

9. Lilha, H., Shivmurthy, D.: Analysis of pixel level features in recognition of real life dual-handed sign language data set. In: Recent Trends in Information Systems (ReTIS), pp. 246–251 (2011)

10. Kishore, P.V.V., Kumar, P.R.: A video based indian sign language recognition system (INSLR) using wavelet transform and fuzzy logic. Int. J. Eng. Technol. **4**(5), 537 (2012)

11. Kishore, P.V.V., Prasad, M.V.D., Kumar, D.A., Sastry, A.S.C.S.: Optical flow hand tracking and active contour hand shape features for continuous sign language recognition with artificial neural networks. In: IEEE 6th International Conference on Advanced Computing (IACC), pp. 346–351 (2016)

12. Kasukurthi, N., Rokad, B., Bidani, S., Dennisan, D.: American sign language alphabet recognition using deep learning. CoRR (2019). https://arxiv.org/abs/1905.05487. Accessed 15 July 2021

13. Tolentino, L.K.S., Juan, R.O.S., Thio-ac, A.C., Pamahoy, M.A.B., Forteza, J.R.R., Garcia, X.J.O.: Static sign language recognition using deep learning. Int. J. Mach. Learn. Comput. **9**(6), 821–827 (2019)

14. Sabeenian, R.S., Sai Bharathwaj, S., Mohamed Aadhil, M.: Sign language recognition using deep learning and computer vision. J. Adv. Res. Dyn. Contr. Syst. **12**(05-Special Issue), 964–968 (2020)

15. Barbhuiya, A.A., Karsh, R.K., Jain, R.: CNN based feature extraction and classification for sign language. Multimedia Tools Appl. **80**(2), 3051–3069 (2020)

16. Pratama, Y., Marbun, E., Parapat, Y., Manullang, A.: Deep convolutional neural network for hand sign language recognition using model E. Bull. Electr. Eng. Inf. **9**(5), 1873–1881 (2020)

17. Kadhim, R.A., Khamees, M.: A real-time american sign language recognition system using convolutional neural network for real datasets. TEM J. **9**(3), 937 (2020)

18. Tecperson: Kaggle datasets: sign language MNIST. drop-in replacement for MNIST for hand gesture recognition tasks. https://www.kaggle.com/datamunge/sign-language-mnist. Accessed 15 July 2021 (2020)

19. Wan, A.: How to build a neural network to translate sign language into english. https://github. com/alvinwan/sign-language-translator. Accessed 15 July 2021 (2019)

20. Wang, B.: Loss functions in machine learning. https://medium.com/swlh/cross-entropy-loss-in-pytorch-c010faf97bab. Accessed 15 July 2021

21. Verucchi, M., et al.: A systematic assessment of embedded neural networks for object detection. In: 2020 25th IEEE International Conference on Emerging Technologies and Factory Automation (ETFA), 1, pp. 937–944 (2020)

Evaluation of Manets Metrics for AODV and DSDV Protocols in VoIP Communications Using OMNeT++

Yohanna Daza Alava[1]($\boxtimes$) (iD), Dannyll Michellc Zambrano[2] (iD), and Jimmy Manuel Zambrano Acosta[1] (iD)

[1] Instituto de Postgrado, Universidad Técnica de Manabí, Portoviejo, Ecuador
{ydaza6005,jimmy.zambrano}@utm.edu.ec
[2] Facultad de Ciencias Informáticas, Universidad Técnica de Manabí, Portoviejo, Ecuador
michellc.zambrano@utm.edu.ec

Abstract. A MANET presents solutions to wireless connections without the need to use a network infrastructure for its implementation, they dynamically create a network at any time and place, thus providing mobility to the nodes so that the packets reach their destination, so it is necessary that all nodes can fulfill the role of transmitter, receiver or routers.

The objective of this work is to implement a MANET in a disaster area to analyze the performance of routing protocols and determine which one provides the best communication conditions taking into account the metrics to be evaluated in this type of scenarios.

This work compares the approach of a proactive protocol with a reactive protocol. The methodology was based on a descriptive analysis of the AODV and DSDV protocols, where the flow of UDP packets in real time was evaluated using metrics such as latency, packet loss and energy consumption referred to Quality of Services (QoS) in a simulation environment implemented in Omnet++, these were executed with 30, 40 and 50 nodes over a randomly generated traffic pattern and a mobility pattern of nodes with different transmission speeds of 12, 24 and 36 Mbps.

As a result, it was determined that the AODV Protocol presents better performance during real-time streaming transmission. Therefore, under the conditions of the proposed scenario, it is more efficient to use this Reactive protocol.

Keywords: MANET · AODV · DSDV · QoS · VoIP

1 Introduction

A Mobile Ad-Hoc Network (MANET) is a temporary network formed by a set of mobile nodes without infrastructure support. This network is self-configurable with a dynamic topology that allows communication between user terminals temporarily assembled without relying on a conventional communication infrastructure, here the nodes play the role of transmitter, receiver or routers; it also allows to easily add and remove devices to the network [1].

© Springer Nature Switzerland AG 2021
T. Guarda et al. (Eds.): ARTIIS 2021, CCIS 1485, pp. 81–92, 2021.
https://doi.org/10.1007/978-3-030-90241-4_7

MANETs are a type of multi-hop wireless network because by having mobile nodes they are dynamically interconnected and related to maintain network connectivity. In addition, they can be deployed quickly in unexpected conditions, for example, in a disaster, when it is difficult to immediately build a new fixed infrastructure [2, 3].

To provide communication within the network, routing protocols are used to find routes between mobile nodes, allowing packets to be sent through other nodes to their destination. Also, MANET routing protocols are considered bandwidth and energy constrained mainly because that ad-hoc multi-hop relies on each mobile node in the network to act as a router and packet forwarder. Among the routing protocols offered by this type of networks are Proactive, Reactive and Hybrid protocols [4].

Proactive protocols use a table to keep all routes updated, nodes can easily obtain routing information and establish a session in a simple way. There are several proactive protocols including DSDV (Destination Sequence Distance Vector), CGSR (Cluster-head Gateway Switch Routing), OLSR (Optimized Link State Routing), Scalable Routing using the HEAT protocol, BATMAN (Better Approach to Mobile AdHoc Networking), DREAM (Distance Routing Effect Algorithm for Mobility), among others [5, 6].

Reactive search for routes only when necessary or when a node wants to find a path to a destination node, it must initiate a route discovery process. Once a suitable path is found, it is maintained until the route is no longer required. The main reactive protocols include AODV (AdHoc On Demand distance Vector routing), DSR (Dynamic Source Routing), TORA (Temporally Ordered Routing Algorithm), LQSR (Link Quality Source Routing), among others [5, 6].

The AODV protocol is a reactive protocol that searches for a route when a network node requires it, it is a protocol that requires little bandwidth because it sends packets only when necessary, although it causes a high latency in the network [7]. This IP routing protocol allows sending nodes to find and maintain routes to receiving nodes, the protocol searches for possible routes when there is a request and follows the shortest route (for messages), e.g. the one that responds first, keeping the routes active until it is not needed [8].

The DSDV protocol is based on the Bellman-Ford distribution (BDF) algorithm, which compared to the link-state update method is computationally more efficient and requires much less storage space [5]. In this algorithm, neighboring nodes periodically exchange (proactive protocol) their complete routing tables with neighbors to estimate how far away the other non-neighboring nodes are. Although DSDV provides only one route for each destination (it does not allow storing secondary routes), it always chooses the route with the fastest support in the number of hops to this destination [8].

In [9] the authors analyze the importance of rapid deployment networks and the provision of adequate emergency services in the post-disaster scenario is presented. Also, the network parameters that are very important in these environments, such as routing overhead, energy efficiency, topological changes, bandwidth utilization for multimedia applications, etc., have not been extensively investigated.

In [10] solutions are presented that have proposed to address disaster-prone areas based on Ad-Hoc paradigms such as MANET, Vehicular Ad-Hoc Network (VANET), etc. In addition, they presented the open challenges of ad hoc networking paradigms for information exchange in disaster-prone areas, but did not focus on issues related to rapid and temporary installation, terminal probability, and mobility in disaster-prone areas.

In [11] showed solutions based on MANET and Delay Tolerant Networking (DTN) are discussed in the post-disaster scenario. However, the results do not include any guide to analyze the protocol based on network parameters, including delay, packet delivery ratio, power, etc., (which is one of the objectives of this paper).

In [12] the authors have examined the implications of cognitive radio technologies and the requirements for these networks in the post-disaster scenario are presented. Cognitive radio communication technologies are considered an effective tool in the post-disaster setting due to the capacity for self-organization in the disaster environment. Besides, that study not include network architecture and routing models involved in a disaster environment.

In [13] a comparative study of legacy-based public safety nets and long-term evolution in disaster-prone areas is presented. It also includes the experimental study based on Software Defined Radio (SDR), this is a radiocommunication system implemented using components such as modulators, demodulators, amplifiers, etc. Furthermore, the authors did not consider the assessment and design issues associated with public safety nets in the disaster setting.

In [14] showed wireless technologies used by the public safety organization in an emergency scenario are discussed with a particular focus on the US and Europe. Fragmentation of the public safety wireless communications system could cause interoperability issues that adversely affect the disaster environment. The document also does not discuss the system requirements for disaster prevention and resource management in the disaster scenario. To address the shortcomings of the existing survey documents discussed above, we studied various routing protocols based on MANETs or a combination of MANETs to build an efficient Disaster Area Network (DAN) in the post-disaster environment. Likewise, this work presents a simulation of routing protocols in MANET networks in disaster areas, mainly in terms of the network layer.

A disaster area network with the different protocols and architectures discussed in the previous paragraphs has its own advantages and disadvantages. Choosing the right network architecture with the right protocol is a difficult task and should take into account factors such as the size of the network, the lifespan of the network, the types of data to be transmitted, the topology, and the mobility models, etc. The size of the network affects the performance of routing protocols in a disaster zone. When the network is small, routing protocols can generally work efficiently without being interrupted. When the size of the network increases, an increasing number of nodes participate in the operation of the network, generating a large number of air packets on the network that require high bandwidth. The low overhead protocols described in [15–17] are suitable for a large network. Power limitation is an important factor for wireless networks in disaster areas. From a routing protocol point of view, the message header is directly related to power consumption. The higher the number of transmitted messages, the higher the power consumption. Due to the mobile nature of nodes, a node's battery is difficult to replace. We need to extend the life of the network to use it efficiently by keeping the nodes up and running for as long as possible. The energy-efficient routing protocols presented in [16] vary the lifetime by keeping the mobile nodes alive for a longer period of time. Also the energy efficiency protocols presented in [15] and in [16] try to reduce total energy consumption using interconnection patterns and self-stabilization paradigm respectively. The downside of using energy efficient routing protocols is that the delay and delivery ratio can be affected due to the breakdown of active paths, as few paths are discovered during the route discovery phase. Topology and mobility are other important factors for the disaster zone network [18, 19].

This work examines some variables of the quality of service such as packet lost, latency and power consumption in MANET that use the routing protocols AODV and DSDV, analyzing the advantages and disadvantages of using these protocols in disaster scenarios through a simulated environment, to determine which is the most appropriate and that allows stable and rapid communication.

2   Materials and Methods

The tests developed to analyze the performance of routing protocols become complex and costly, for this reason it is proposed to use OMNET++ (Object Oriented Networks Modular Discrete Event Simulator) to create a simulation environment as close as possible to reality, making it possible to perform the necessary variations, taking a reactive protocol and a proactive protocol for the analysis. All the nodes of the network are configured in such a way that they can send or receive information packets, and the nodes will also be available to be part of the route selected by the protocol. The nodes will be randomly distributed throughout the simulation scenario.

In this research, different simulation environments have been proposed in a defined area, knowing that in a disaster area there is an increasing number of nodes in the network, the following parameters and metrics were established, the simulations were executed with 30, 40 and 50 nodes on a randomly generated traffic pattern and a node mobility pattern with transmission speeds of 12, 24 and 36 Mbps, the result obtained is the average value of these simulations executed 20 times.

Table 1 shows the parameters for the simulated environments, where the number of nodes and the transmission speeds were detailed previously; the simulation time will be 180 s taking into account that a conversation in a hostile environment does not exceed 3 min, the packet size is 512 bytes, the area of the simulated environment in this investigation is 160,000 m^2 (400 m * 400 m), human speed was determined by the results obtained in the study [20], in which walking consists of traveling 89.7 m in one minute. This is why a node displacement speed of 1.4 m/s was taken as a simulation parameter; This speed was obtained by converting 89.7 meter per minute to meters per second.

Choosing a routing protocol in MANET is decided based on the performance parameters that will define the QoS (Quality of Service). In this research, the performance of the MANET routing protocol is evaluated based on the following metrics: packet loss, latency, and power consumption.

The present study uses UDP packet streaming (User Datagram Protocol) for the transmission of VoIP, using the AODV and DSDV protocols in simulated environments with the OMNeT++ software that is used to model any system that can be simulated with discrete events.

Table 1. Simulation environment parameters.

Parameters	Values/Features
Number of nodes	30/40/50
Simulation Time (s)	180
Package Size (bytes)	512
Environment Size (m * m)	400 * 400
Type of traffic / rate	Constant Bit Rate (CBR)/4 packets/s
Pedestrian Speed (m/s)	1.4 m/s
Transmission Rate (Mbps)	12/24/36
Simulation / Operating System	OMNET++ 5.4.1/Windows 10 Pro 64 bits

3 Results and Discussion

The results of the simulation in OMNET++, respect to the percentage of packet lost that occurs in the AODV and DSDV protocols for the three node densities (30, 40 and 50) with a transmission speed of 12 Mbps, at first glance, it can be said that the DSDV protocol has a higher percentage of data loss in the three scenarios, compared to the AODV protocol. (Fig. 1).

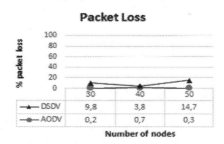

Fig. 1. Results with transmission rate 12 Mbps.

The percentage of packet loss that occurs in the AODV and DSDV protocols with three different numbers of nodes (30, 40 and 50) and with a Transmission Speed of 24 Mbps, with a similarity in the percentage of losses but a little lower than the previous figure, the DSDV protocol has a higher percentage of losses compared to the AODV (Fig. 2).

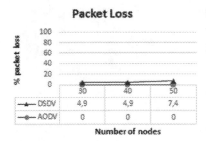

Fig. 2. Results with transmission rate 12 Mbps

The analysis of packet lost is carried out using a Transmission Speed of 36 Mbps, where as there is a greater width, the percentage of losses has decreased in the case of the DSDV protocol, but still greater than the percentage that shows the AODV protocol (Fig. 3).

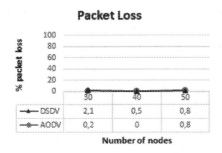

Fig. 3. Results with transmission rate 36 Mbps

Another of the metrics analyzed in this research was latency. The latency comparisons in networks are made through variations in the number of hops, the smaller the number of hops in the network, the greater the consistency be-tween the simulated and real results. The latency values in each protocol were then analyzed.

See (Fig. 4), it is possible to verify the value obtained from the latency in milliseconds (ms) of both protocols at a transmission speed of 12 Mbps. We can see when simulating 30 nodes, there is a latency of 734 ms in AODV and 638 ms with DSDV; When the nodes were increased to 40, it was observed that in both protocols there was an increase in latency, giving 758 ms in AODV and 698 ms in DSDV. And finally, simulating 50 nodes, the latency was decreased by 662 ms and 634 ms.

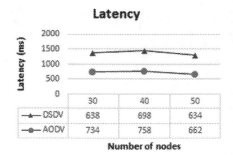

Fig. 4. Results with transmission rate 12 Mbps

The latency values based on the number of nodes for each protocol and at a speed of 24 Mbps. Using the 30 nodes, the latency in AODV is 672 ms and in DSDV it is 688 ms; with 40 nodes, it was observed that in both protocols there was a 730 ms increase in AODV and 694 ms in DSDV. And using 50 AODV nodes had an increase of 762 ms and in DSDV the latency was decreased by 600 ms. (Fig. 5).

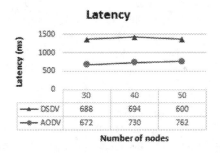

Fig. 5. Results with transmission rate 24 Mbps

Increasing the transmission speed to 36 Mbps, see (Fig. 6), these values represent the latency in both protocols. With a node count of 30, the AODV protocol has a latency of 712 ms and DSDV has 642 ms. With 40 nodes, both protocols had an increase, 734 ms in AODV and 760 ms in DSDV. And finally with 50 AODV nodes it maintains the latency with 734 ms and in DSDV the latency dropped to 700 ms.

In a MANET network, the nodes that make up this network are usually powered by battery banks, which have a limited capacity, so it is convenient to optimize energy consumption. See (Fig. 7) the energy consumption in milli watts (mw) in the sender node is shown with the different numbers of nodes at a transmission speed of 12 Mbps. With 30 nodes the energy consumption in AODV is 15152 mw and in DSDV is 141240 mw; with 40 nodes in AODV it consumes 16084 mw and in DSDV the consumption is 230427 mw and finally with 50 nodes the consumption is 14025 mw for AODV and 339327 mw for DSDV.

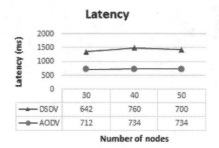

Fig. 6. Results with transmission rate 36 Mbps

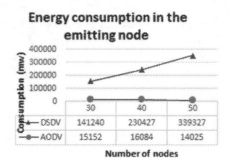

Fig. 7. Results with transmission rate 12 Mbps

Energy consumption values (Fig. 8) are shown in the emitting node with a transmission speed of 24 Mbps. With 30 nodes in AODV the consumption is 14522 mw while in DSDV the value increases to 138150 mw; The same happens with 40 nodes in AODV, consumption is 14916 mw and in DSDV it is 243015 mw and when increasing the nodes to 50 this value increases considerably, going from 15402 mw in AODV to 342291 mw in DSDV.

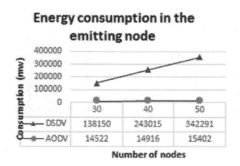

Fig. 8. Results with transmission rate 24 Mbps

Energy consumption in the emitting node with a bandwidth of 36 Mbps and when simulating 30 nodes, the energy consumption in AODV is 14686 mw and in DSDV it is 141654 mw; By increasing the number of nodes to 40 in AODV the consumption is 14834 mw and in DSDV it is 241695 mw and finally with 50 nodes the consumption is 15672 mw for AODV and 339565 mw for DSDV. (Fig. 9).

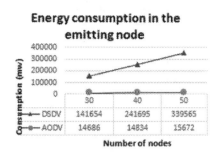

Fig. 9. Results with transmission rate 36 Mbps

Energy consumption will be evaluated in the receiver node, (Fig. 10) the energy consumption is observed in milli watts (mw) at a transmission speed of 12 Mbps. With 30 nodes the energy consumption in AODV it is 15064 mw and in DSDV it is 132970 mw; with 40 nodes in AODV it consumes 15598 mw and in DSDV the consumption is 217218 mw and finally with 50 nodes the consumption is 13764 mw for AODV and 310311 mw for DSDV.

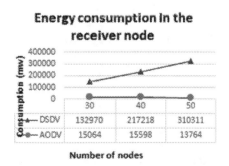

Fig. 10. Results with transmission rate 12 Mbps

See (Fig. 11) with 24 Mbps in the receiving node it is observed that with 30 nodes in AODV the consumption is 14039 mw while in DSDV the value increases to 138238 mw; with 40 nodes in AODV the consumption is 14842 mw and in DSDV it is 219393 mw and when increasing the nodes to 50 this value is from 15392 mw in AODV to 304530 mw in DSDV.

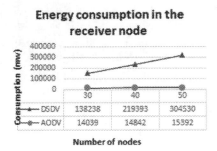

Fig. 11. Results with transmission rate 24 Mbps

With 30 nodes the energy consumption in AODV is 14478 mw and in DSDV it is 133166 mw; with 40 nodes in AODV the consumption is 14812 mw and in DSDV it is 215044 mw and with 50 nodes the consumption is 15148 mw for AODV and 343510 mw for DSDV. (Fig. 12).

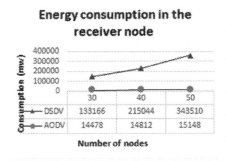

Fig. 12. Results with transmission rate 36 Mbps

4   Conclusions

MANETs bring benefits to the community in disaster areas due to their decentralized architecture and make it easier for many devices to communicate with each other, without the need for infrastructure. Their routing protocols facilitate the structure of these networks and one of the challenges they face is the evaluation and design in which they operate at low data rates and respond to dynamic changes in topology due to node mobility.

Different values of transmission speed 12, 24 and 36 Mbps, and evaluating the AODV and DSDV protocols, the three environments that have been simulated in OMNET++ are analyzed according to the number of nodes, the AODV Protocol has a lower percentage of packet loss during the transmission of the same, as well as latency and energy consumption in the nodes because this protocol does not maintain the routes for each node but as they transmit such data, they discover the path to follow to ensure communication.

The DSDV protocol has a higher percentage of packet loss, due to the fact that routing tables are maintained for each node in the network. As the nodes are in motion, many changes are generated in the routes, which causes a greater loss of data in transmission.

Reactive protocols optimize power consumption, while proactive protocols using route tables produce a large number of signaling packets resulting in high power consumption.

References

1. Ponsam, J.G. Srinivasan, D.R.: A survey on manet security challenges, attacks and its countermeasures 3(1), p. 6 (2014)
2. Goyal, P., Parmar, V., Rishi, R.: MANET: vulnerabilities, challenges, attacks, Application. 11, p. 6 (2011)
3. Mohammed, S.A.: An enhancement process for reducing energy consumption in wireless sensor network. Int. J. Emerg. Trends Eng. Res. 8(6), 2765–2769 (2020). https://doi.org/10.30534/ijeter/2020/89862020
4. Sandoval Salguero, R.: Análisis comparativo de protocolos de enrutamiento para redes Ad-hoc móviles heterogéneas y homogéneas (2020). http://repositorio.ucsg.edu.ec/handle/3317/15046. Accessed 17 Apr. 2021
5. Roshan, R., Mishra, S., Meher, C. P.: A Comparison between the AODV and DSDV routing protocols for mobile ad-hoc network using NS2. In: 6th International Conference on Computing for Sustainable Global Development (IndiaCom), pp. 286–289 (2019)
6. Chaw, E.E.: Análisis de los protocolos de enrutamiento para las redes móviles Ad-Hoc con el simulador NS-3. (2019). http://repositorio.ucsg.edu.ec/handle/3317/12730. Accessed 17 Apr. 2021
7. Chamba Macas, F.: Implementación de protocolos de enrutamiento reactivo y proactivos para redes inalámbricas móviles Ad-hoc (2017). http://repositorio.ucsg.edu.ec/handle/3317/8343. Accessed: 16 Apr. 2021
8. Raffelsberger, C. Hellwagner, H.: Evaluation of MANET routing protocols in a realistic emergency response scenario. In: Proceedings of the 10th International Workshop on Intelligent Solutions in Embedded Systems, pp. 88–92 (2012). https://ieeexplore.ieee.org/abstract/document/6273588/metrics#metrics
9. Miranda, K., Molinaro, A., Razafindralambo, T.: A survey on rapidly deployable solutions for post-disaster networks. IEEE Commun. Mag. 54(4), 117–123 (2016). https://doi.org/10.1109/MCOM.2016.7452275
10. Nakamura, D., Uchida, N., Asahi, H., Takahata, K., Hashimoto, K., Shibata, Y.: Wide area disaster information network and its resource management system. In: en 17th International Conference on Advanced Information Networking and Applications, 2003, AINA 2003, pp. 146–149 (2003). https://doi.org/10.1109/AINA.2003.1192858
11. del Pilar Salamanca, M., Camargo, J.: A survey on IEEE 802.11-based MANETs and DTNs for survivor communication in disaster scenarios. In: 2016 IEEE Global Humanitarian Technology Conference (GHTC), pp. 197–204 (2016). https://doi.org/10.1109/GHTC.2016.7857280.
12. Ghafoor, S., Sutton, P., Sreenan, C., Brown, K.: Cognitive radio for disaster response networks: survey, potential, and challenges. IEEE Wirel. Commun. 21(5), 70–80 (2014). https://doi.org/10.1109/MWC.2014.6940435
13. Kumbhar, A., Koohifar, F., Güvenç, İ., Mueller, B.: A survey on legacy and emerging technologies for public safety communications. IEEE Commun. Surv. Tutor., 19(1), 97–124 (2017). https://doi.org/10.1109/COMST.2016.2612223

14. Baldini, G., Karanasios, S., Allen, D., Vergari, F.: Survey of wireless communication tech-
    nologies for public safety. IEEE Commun. Surv. Tutor., **16**(2), pp. 619–641 (2014). https://
    doi.org/10.1109/SURV.2013.082713.00034.
15. Uddin, M.Y.S., Ahmadi, H., Abdelzaher, T., Kravets, R.: A low-energy, multi-copy inter-
    contact routing protocol for disaster response networks. In: 6th Annual IEEE Communications
    Society Conference on Sensor, Mesh and Ad Hoc Communications and Networks, SECON
    2009, Rome, Italy (2009). https://doi.org/10.1109/SAHCN.2009.5168904
16. Tiwari, V.K., Malviya, D.A.K.: An energy efficient multicast routing protocol for MANET. Int.
    J. Eng. Comput. Sci., **5**(11), http://www.ijecs.in/index.php/ijecs/article/view/3077. Accessed
    26 July 2020. Art. n.o 11, 2016
17. Roy, S., Garcia-Luna-Aceves, J.J.: Node-centric hybrid routing for ad hoc networks. In:
    International Mobility and Wireless Access Workshop, pp. 63–71 (2002). https://doi.org/10.
    1109/MOBWAC.2002.1166954
18. Aschenbruck, N., de Waal, C., Martini, P.: Distribution of nodes in disaster area scenarios
    and its impact on topology control strategies. In: IEEE INFOCOM Workshops 2008, pp. 1–6
    (2008). https://doi.org/10.1109/INFOCOM.2008.4544598
19. Gyoda, K., Nguyen, N.H., Okada, K., Takizawa, O.: Analysis of Ad Hoc network performance
    in emergency communication models. In: 22nd International Conference on Advanced Infor-
    mation Networking and Applications - Workshops (AINA workshops 2008), pp. 1083–1088
    (2008). https://doi.org/10.1109/WAINA.2008.93
20. Studenski, S.: Gait speed and survival in older adults. JAMA **305**(1), 50 (2011). https://doi.
    org/10.1001/jama.2010.1923

Evaluation of LoRa Technology for Aquaculture Pool Monitoring

Cristhian Alava-Troya[1]([✉]) [iD] and Jorge Parraga-Alava[2]([✉]) [iD]

[1] Instituto de Posgrado, Universidad Técnica de Manabí, Avenida Jose María Urbina, Portoviejo, Ecuador
calava9376@utm.edu.ec

[2] Facultad de Ciencias Informáticas, Universidad Técnica de Manabí, Avenida Jose María Urbina, Portoviejo, Ecuador
jorge.parraga@usach.cl

Abstract. Low Power Wide Area Networks (LPWAN) have emerged as ideal tools for environmental monitoring and smart metering. This paper is based on the design of a wireless sensor network using LoRaWAN technology to monitor water temperature in aquaculture pools. The setting for this research was the facilities of the Luis Arboleda Martíncz Technological Institute, in the city of Manta. To implement the monitoring system, a methodology consisting of four stages is established: analysis of the environment, selection of equipment, implementation of the system, and tests and measurements. The LoRa technology was evaluated by determining coverage maps, graphs on the signal strength and signal-noise ratio, the tests were carried out in interior environments, exterior with buildings, and exterior open to the sea. This article discusses the performance of LoRa and presents the results of the evaluation based on field tests with the equipment, checking the effectiveness of LoRa in environmental monitoring applications in the studied scenarios.

Keywords: Lora · LoRaWAN · Aquaculture · Sensors

1 Introduction

The LoRa technology is widely used in the IoT (Internet of Things) that refers to connecting objects to the cloud, also known as the Internet. LoRaWAN is a wireless transmission technology, similar to those generally known as WiFi, Bluetooth and others [1], but what makes it different from the previous ones is that it works at a much lower wave frequency. In telecommunications, it has been shown that low-frequency waves have the quality of being able to travel long distances without affecting the data that is transmitted. The amount of data that this protocol usually carries is small information from sensors, so the results are networks with low energy consumption [2]. These LoRa solutions are found in many areas of daily life, including the monitoring of environmental variables.

© Springer Nature Switzerland AG 2021
T. Guarda et al. (Eds.): ARTIIS 2021, CCIS 1485, pp. 93–105, 2021.
https://doi.org/10.1007/978-3-030-90241-4_8

There are new trends in communications such as the Internet of Things, also known as IoT [3], which makes extensive use of low-consumption networks called Low Power Wide Area Network (LPWAN), which is used because they effectively meet the connectivity requirements in large areas, have a great capacity for the integration of equipment and minimum use of energy, ideal for connecting devices such as sensors for their use in monitoring variables [4].

There are other technologies from which you can draw resources, such as Bluetooth and ZigBee, but compared to LoRa these end up being short-range. For this reason, LoRa stands out in the implementation of LPWAN environments thanks to its wide coverage, because the end nodes are regularly low cost and simple to implement their topology, which is generally of the star type [5].

LoRaWAN has achieved a high deployment in industrial sensorization and all kinds of environmental parameter measurement projects in different situations. In the measurement of environmental variables, different scenarios can occur, currently, there are studies on the performance of LoRaWAN in agricultural environments, there are also investigations on the behavior of this technology in large cities and urbanized areas where there are regularly buildings, houses, vehicular traffic, and others items to test LoRaWAN performance.

The results obtained in the research entitled "On the Use of LoRaWAN for Indoor Industrial IoT Application" confirm that LoRaWAN can be considered as a strongly viable opportunity for the monitoring of environmental variables [6], since it is capable of providing high reliability and punctuality while ensuring very low energy consumption. The efficiency of this type of sensor network in open areas without obstacles is very high, however, the behavior of this technology in mixed environments is not clear. In the article entitled "LoRaWAN Range Extender for Industrial IoT", the authors state that LoRaWAN promises long-range environments with many obstacles but can suffer from coverage problems. Also, the inverse relationship between data rates and range can be unacceptable for many applications [7]. In the research work called "Using LoRa for industrial wireless networks" LoRa technology for the implementation of industrial wireless networks suitable for sensors and actuators of the Industry 4.0 era is analyzed [8]. After a brief overview of LoRa and LoRaWAN, the document addresses the discussion on the use of LoRa for industrial applications compared to traditional industrial wireless systems. The cited research analysis clarifies that the LoRa protocol offers great benefits for environmental measurement environments that are becoming more and more familiar with the Internet of Things, but the reference is also made to the limitations that this technology may have in places where there are obstacles or noise that are reflected in low coverage levels.

In aquaculture pools, it is important to know about variables such as water temperature, salinity, turbidity, dissolved oxygen, hydrogen potential, among others, for which the implementation of wireless sensor networks is recommended [9], where the using LoRaWAN offers vast advantages in these types of scenarios.

This research investigates the benefits and impediments of LoRaWAN in mixed environments, where the network transmits data on land, interior, exterior, and sea surfaces in the same setting, as happens regularly in aquaculture pools.

2 Methodology

A methodology is determined based on similar research on the implementation of wire-lessly connected sensor networks. The methodology defined for this work consists of four stages: environmental analysis, equipment selection, system implementation, and tests and measurements.

Environment Analysis. To implement a wireless sensor network with a high level of efficiency, it is important to know the geographical area where the monitoring system is located. At this stage, the distance between the sensors and the walkway is determined, the physical space where the equipment is located, whether indoors or outdoors. In this way, the best method is chosen to make a stable connection of the wireless link.

Equipment Selection. In this stage, the analysis of the equipment available on the market, its technical characteristics, its coverage ranges, battery life, and other details for the implementation of the system is carried out.

System Implementation. At this stage, the electronic components are installed on-site, the LoRaWAN gateway is configured, which is responsible for sending all the information to a cloud server for further processing and analysis of the information collected by sensors.

Tests and Measurements. This stage describes the tests carried out to control coverage, signal intensity, and other important indicators within a sensor network. After conducting inspections, satellite distance measurements, and line-of-sight checks, the experiments were carried out. This stage includes the verification of the technical specifications on coverage and the ability to transmit information from the sensor network.

3 Results

A physical inspection was carried out at the installation site, the geography of the site was identified, the distance from the pools is around 500 m to the gateway. It was possible to measure this distance using Google map satellites. It was identified that the measurements were to be carried out in mixed environments (land and sea). A star logic scheme typical of a LoRaWAN sensor network was incorporated.

The equipment selected for implementation is the LoRaWAN LG308 gateway that allows the LoRa wireless network to be connected to an IP network via WiFi, Ethernet or cellular [10], and the LHT65 temperature and humidity detector that was previously coated to protect it from water, this module has a shielded sensor connected to a cable that allows it to be submerged in liquids [11]. The topology and the selected equipment are observed in Fig. 1.

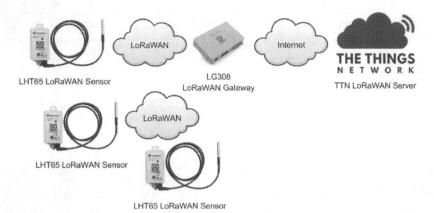

Fig. 1. Topology of a LoRaWAN sensor network.

The gateway was configured in the allowed band of 915 MHz and it was connected to the internet, to synchronize it with The Things Network TTN Server, a solution for LoRa networks. As a second step, the integration with Cayenne My Devices was programmed, as it provides a friendly interface to display sensor data, allowing its users to access to view the data recorded by the system through apps or from any browser, as can be viewed in Fig. 2.

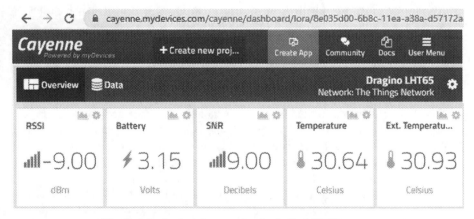

Fig. 2. Monitoring data sent by the LoRa LHT65 sensor.

The equipment used for the experiment does not provide information on the transmission delay, nor the RTT payload lengths. The uplink payload includes a total of 11 bytes and contains the sensor identifier, sensor model, and logged data. Uplink packets are sent every 10 min by default. The downlink payload has a total of 24 bytes. The optimal parameters selected for the gateway configuration are shown in Table 1.

Table 1. Parameters set in the LG308 gateway.

Lora radio	Frecuency	Bandwitdh	Coding rate (CR)	Spreading factor (SF)
Tx	903.9–904.6 MHz	125 kbits	5	7
Rx	904.6–905.3 MHz	125 kbits	5	7

Frequency. The frequency from 903.9 MHz to 905.3 MHz was set in the gateway, which corresponds to channel two in the Frequency Sub Band configuration. This channel is chosen because in the South American region it is determined that LoRa works in the US902–928 range, complying with the regulations.

Bandwidth. The optimal bandwidth with the established configuration is 125 kbits, which ensures a bit rate of up to 5.5 kbps/s, however, this bandwidth can be affected by low signal power, noise, and distance. The computers used to occupy a maximum of 24 bytes, so the network cannot be saturated.

Coding Rate (CR). This parameter refers to the proportion of transmitted bits that actually carry information, a CR value was set at 5 that better favors network performance.

Spreading Factor (SF). Compared to a higher spreading factor, a lower spreading factor provides a higher bit rate for fixed bandwidth and a scramble rate of 5. SF7 was set as it provides a higher bit rate than the others.

3.1 Experiments

Three experiments were carried out, which aimed to determine the coverage, the signal strength, the signal-noise ratio, and the packet losses in three different scenarios: exterior with barriers, interior, exterior in open spaces to the sea. The experiments are detailed below.

Outdoor LoRa Coverage with Barriers. The first experiment aims to analyse the effectiveness of LoRa in open spaces with barriers and was based on the placement of the gateway at a height of 4 m, ensuring that its repeater antenna surpasses the top of some buildings. It proceeded to send data to the gateway and record shipments on scales of 10 m until reaching 100 m, from then on reading was taken every 100 m, this procedure was carried out in a 360-degree radius. In this way, the heat map shown in Fig. 3 was generated.

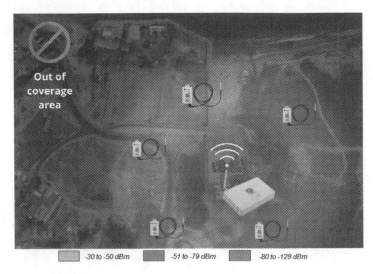

Fig. 3. LoRa outdoor coverage with barriers.

LoRa Coverage in Closed Spaces. Figure 4 shows the Lora coverage indoors. One of the most common examples in these interior environments are offices that are mostly made up of walls and other barriers.

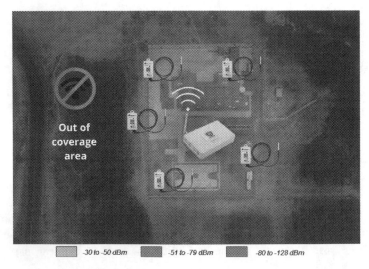

Fig. 4. LoRa coverage in closed spaces.

With this background, the gateway was placed inside a building, and the internet connection was made, such as in the previous scenario, readings were taken with the same distance scales in meters.

It was found that the coverage of the LoRaWAN equipment was clearly affected by the barriers, that is, the walls of the building, in such a way that the signal power levels dropped considerably when encountering the first obstacle, and in the same way too as more barriers were added. By that, the graph is reduced only to the Institute's facilities, where it can be seen that very close to the gateway the highest concentration of the signal, and in the surroundings, there are levels between −70 and 80-dBm, which as the distance increases, these power levels tend to lower even more.

LoRa Coverage in Open Spaces to the Sea. The third experiment aims to determine the efficiency of LoRa in open spaces to the sea, under that, the gateway was placed at a height of 6 m in an open area within the facilities that have a direct line of sight to the sea.

The heat map indicates that the signal strength values are very good at 600 m out to sea, around −70 dBm. Similarly, in the vicinity, the signal levels are similar, except in areas where there are elevations in between that are higher than the gateway.

This provides evidence of the effectiveness of Lora in these types of environments, where the Gateway is high enough and there are no major obstacles. That is why, it is observed in Fig. 5 that the coverage has an acceptable level in the vicinity of the sea.

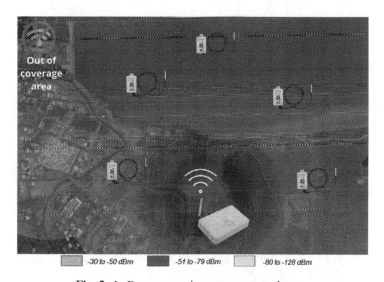

Fig. 5. LoRa coverage in open spaces to the sea.

Received Signal Strength Indicators (RSSI). To understand the effectiveness of LoRa technology, we performed three types of measurements to determine important information about coverage and signal quality, as a first experiment we placed the gateway at a height of 2 m outside. At the same time, the signal strength readings of the RSSI (Received Signal Strength Indicator) began making scales of 100 m. These data were sent to the gateway and this, in turn, through a connection to the cloud, sent them to the TTN (The Things Network) server for registration, treatment, and visualization on the IoT platform called Cayenne.

The results shown by the platform indicate that indeed the LoRaWAN protocol enjoys excellent signal strength in open spaces where it was found that at distances greater than 500 m the SRRI was maintained at −75 dBm.

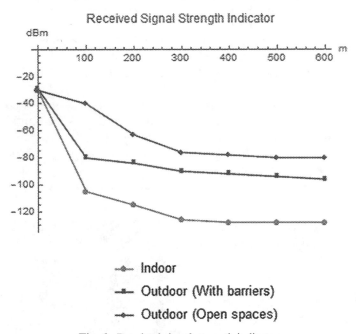

Fig. 6. Received signal strength indicator.

Figure 6 shows that at a distance of 500 m the RSSI levels begin to fall in a slow and sustained manner, so this makes us understand that there is an optimal range for sending information that covers a radius of 1–2 km. It should be noted that these measurements are made using a gateway with a 70 dBm gain antenna. In the second scenario, a drop in signal power is clearly noticeable at 100 m, this is because this line refers to the Outdoor environment with obstacles, and it is just when the walls are placed between the sensor and the gateway when producing these abrupt signal losses, where the signal power is placed by −80 dBm. Once these obstacles are overcome, the signal is maintained until reaching −90 dBm at a distance of 600 m.

For the third case study (indoor environments) the signal drop is more noticeable, where the signal drops to −105 dBm at 100 m, and there is much difficulty in sending the information. As we argued previously, it is evident that the walls inside the offices considerably attenuate the signal, so it is only recommended to use this technology in interior environments where there are not many barriers. After 300 m, the signal stagnates at −128 dBm, with this it is impossible to communicate with the main gateway, so the sensor network would not be operational, or at least the node (s) at those distances they will not be able to send their data to the cloud.

Signal Noise Ratio. SNR is defined as the ratio between the power of the transmitted signal and the power of the noise that corrupts it. This margin is measured in decibels. The SNR "single number ratio" or simplified noise reduction, indicates the average value of isolation or protection at various frequencies. An SNR value of 35 dB, for example, indicates that noise of 100 dB reduces it to 65 dB. The third experiment aims to determine the efficiency of LoRa in open spaces to the sea, under that, the gateway was placed at a height of 6 m in an open area within the facilities that have a direct line of sight to the sea. SNR tests were performed in the three scenarios described above, taking data from the signal-to-noise ratio on 100-m scales. The results obtained can be verified in Fig. 7.

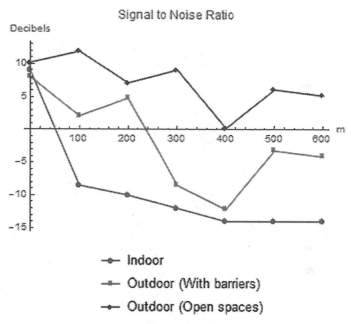

Fig. 7. Signal-to-noise ratio indicator.

To understand what happens with the SNR in the three scenarios studied, it must be taken into account that there are several obstacles between the equipment with which the respective tests were carried out. In the study area, there are walls the size of 8 m high, tall palm trees and there are also small internal walls for the division of the operational offices of the workshops where the students of the Institute normally do aquaculture practices. Figure 7 shows in general for the three scenarios that between 200 and 500 m the difference between signal and noise begins to become larger, which directly influences the amount of power received by Dragino's LG308 gateway, it is presumed That is because we are in a highly populated and industrialized area where they can make all kinds of wireless signals in the spectrum. In the Indoor environment, the line indicates that the SNR is below −10 Decibels; this is because at distances of 200 m onwards the communication between the sensor and the gateway became practically null. It can be argued that in this sector, as it is an urban area, the signals are more prone to noise and this directly influences the quality of the transmission.

A More In-depth Look at RSSI. The purpose of this last experiment is to better understand what happens in the three scenarios proposed utilizing a smaller scale, which is why readings have been taken at intervals of 10 m until reaching the 60 m that surround the gateway. It can be seen that for open spaces without barriers, the signal strength degrades in a very low way, almost imperceptible in the first 60 m, as can be seen in Fig. 8.

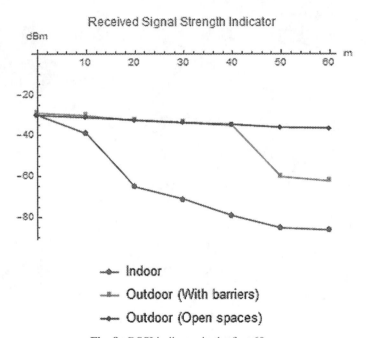

Fig. 8. RSSI indicator in the first 60 m.

This does not happen in an Outdoor environment with barriers, since a drop in signal strength is clearly noticeable at 40 m, which coincides with the location of the walls about the gateway, thus suggesting that these are the reason for power loss. In the indoor environment, the loss of the signal is noticeable at 10 m; this is influenced by the walls near the gateway, such as the power drops that at 60 m the RSSI indicator is around − 80 decibels.

Table 2. Summary of LoRa performance in the proposed scenarios.

Analized Indicators	Scenarios		
	Interiors	Exteriors with barriers	Exteriors open to the sea
SRRI at 60 m	−83 dBm. *Regular*	−59 dBm. *Optimal*	−31 dBm. *Optimal*
SNR at 60 m	−3 dBm. *Regular*	4 dBm. *Optimal*	12 dBm. *Optimal*
Losses at 60 m	30%. *Regular*	5%. *Optimal*	0%. *Optimal*
SRRI at 200 m	−110 dBm. *Pessimal*	−80 dBm. *Regular*	−59 dBm. *Optimal*
SNR at 200 m	−10 dBm. *Regular*	5 dBm. *Optimal*	7 dBm. *Optimal*
Losses at 200 m	95%. *Pessimal*	20%. *Regular*	5%. *Optimal*
SRRI at 600 m	−120 dBm. *Pessimal*	−84 dBm. *Regular*	−64 dBm. *Optimal*
SNR at 600 m	−13 dBm. *Pessimal*	−4 dBm. *Regular*	5 dBm. *Optimal*
Losses at 600 m	100%. *Pessimal*	30%. *Regular*	7%. *Regular*

Table 2 refers to the performance of LoRa in the three experimentation scenarios, the SRRI (Received Signal Strength Indicator), the SNR (Signal Noise Relation), and the packet losses in scales of 60, 200, and 600 m are analyzed. The values were placed in decibels and percentages, three evaluations were defined about the measured variables and their effect on the quality of the link, where *Optimal* refers to the fact that the measured value ensures excellent communication between the gateway and the node, *Regular* refers to the fact that the value taken guarantees a stable communication level with moderate errors and *Pessimal* indicates that the value obtained a response to an unstable or null connection.

4   Discussions

The aforementioned experiments show that LoRaWAN technology works favorably in open spaces, reaching long transmission distances, a situation that does not happen in environments where there are elements that avoid communication.

This research has shown that the LoRaWAN equipment analyzed in this document reliably sends information −93 dBm in open spaces up to 600 m. Similarly, it was found that walls or obstacles cause the signal to drop considerably. It must be taken into account that the gateway only has a small omnidirectional antenna, similar to those of Wi-Fi access points and that for the tests it was only given height in the stage without barriers, for the other experiments the gateway only rose to a distance of 2 m.

The Luis Arboleda Martínez Institute was chosen since its facilities have what is necessary to be located in a mixed environment, since there are workshops, offices, spaces open to the sea, etc. In the sector, there are high elevations, so in the scenarios, with barriers, the reliable RSSI values a radius of approximately 200 m, in addition to the obstacles, the signal could also be affected by pedestrian and river traffic in this zone. To compare the three environments studied Fig. 9 was generated.

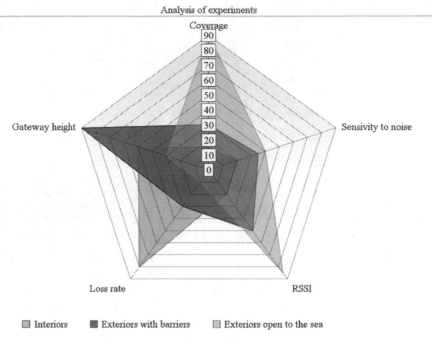

Fig. 9. General analysis of the different experiments.

5   Conclusions

Temperature monitoring in aquaculture pools is performed efficiently by a LoRaWAN based sensor network, outdoors with open spaces to the sea at distances of around 600 m.

For the experiments, a frequency of 903.9 to 105.3 MHz, a coding rate (CR) of 5, and a spreading factor of FS7 were determined, which provided a eficient bandwidth. With these parameters, the signal strength and coverage indicators of LoRa in open spaces to the sea were optimal, however, the same does not happen in open spaces with nearby buildings or in closed spaces with the gateway located indoors.

The packet loss rate in indoor environments is accentuated in relation to the number of barriers located between the gateway and the node. In open spaces to the sea, the rate of packet loss is very low, however, in open spaces with nearby buildings, there are higher packet losses if the gateway does not have enough height.

If an aquaculture pool is located in a land area, it is advisable to locate the gateway close to it, taking into account the barriers that can affect the coverage, on the contrary, if the pool is located offshore, it is only necessary to give enough height to the gateway.

It is concluded that the performance of LoRa depends on several factors such as coding rate, spreading factor, type of environment, be it interior or exterior, the elevation of the gateway, types of obstacles in the signal path, elevations of land, trees, buildings, as well as the distances between the gateway and the node.

References

1. Neumann, P., Montavont, J., Noël, T.: Indoor deployment of low-power wide area networks (LPWAN): a LoRaWAN case study. In: IEEE 12th International Conference on Wireless and Mobile Computing, Networking and Communications (WiMob), pp. 1–8 (2016)
2. Lim, J., Lee, J., Kim, D., Kim, J.: Performance analysis of LoRa(Long Range) according to the distances in indoor and outdoor spaces. J. KIISE **44**(7), 733–741 (2017)
3. Zorbas, D., Abdelfadeel, K., Kotzanikolaou, P., Pesch, D.: TS-LoRa: time-slotted LoRaWAN for the industrial Internet of Things. Comput. Commun. **153**, 1–10 (2020)
4. Sisinni, E., Carvalho, D.F., Ferrari, P., Flammini, A., Silva, D.R.C., Da Silva, I.M.D.: Enhanced flexible LoRaWAN node for industrial IoT. In: 14th IEEE International Workshop on Factory Communication Systems (WFCS), pp. 1–4 (2018)
5. Leonardi, L., Battaglia, F., Patti, G., Bello, L.L.: Industrial LoRa: a novel medium access strategy for LoRa in industry 4.0 applications. In: IECON 2018 - 44th Annual Conference of the IEEE Industrial Electronics Society, pp. 4141–4146 (2018)
6. Luvisotto, M., Tramarin, F., Vangelista, L., Vitturi, S.: On the use of LoRaWAN for indoor industrial IoT applications. Wirel. Commun. Mob. Comput. **2018**, e3982646 (2018)
7. Sisinni, E., et al.: LoRaWAN range extender for industrial IoT. IEEE Trans. Ind. Inform. **16**(8), 5607–5616 (2020)
8. Rizzi, M., Ferrari, P., Flammini, A., Sisinni, E., Gidlund, M.: Using LoRa for industrial wireless networks. In: IEEE 13th International Workshop on Factory Communication Systems (WFCS), pp. 1–4 (2017)
9. Flores Mollo, S., Aracena Pizarro, D., Flores Mollo, S., Aracena Pizarro, D.: Remote monitoring system of aquaculture in tanks for shrimp breeding. Ingeniare Rev. Chil. Ing. **26**, 55–64 (2018)
10. LG308 Indoor LoRaWAN Gateway. https://www.dragino.com/products/lora-lorawan-gateway/item/140-lg308.html. Accessed 03 May 2021
11. LHT65 LoRaWAN Temperature and Humidity Sensor. https://www.dragino.com/products/temperature-humidity-sensor/item/151-lht65.html. Accessed 04 May 2021

Utility Evaluation of Software Product: An Industry Implementation

Antonio Quiña-Mera[1,2]([✉]) [iD], Jordy Taez Granda[1], Pablo Landeta-López[3] [iD], Franklin Montaluisa Yugla[4], and Cathy Guevara-Vega[1,2] [iD]

[1] Engineering in Applied Sciences Faculty, Department of Software, Universidad Técnica del Norte, Ibarra, Ecuador
{aquina,jmtaezg,cguevara}@utn.edu.ec
[2] Network Science Research Group E-CIER, Ibarra, Ecuador
[3] Engineering in Applied Sciences Faculty, Department of Information Technology - Online, Universidad Técnica del Norte, Ibarra, Ecuador
palandeta@utn.edu.ec
[4] Department of Software Engineering, Universidad de Las Fuerzas Armadas ESPE, Latacunga, Ecuador
fjmontaluisa@espe.edu.ec

Abstract. Evaluating the utility of a software product is necessary because it allows organizational processes to function properly and for end users to be satisfied. At this way, we decided to automate the management process in the planning, register and monitoring of activities in the development and quality areas of a technology development company. We figured out that this process has limitations due to the use of multiple tools such as software and applications that work in isolation, which complicates the orderly and systematized work and activities of the team. In this study we evaluated the utility of quality in use over a software implementation called "ITE CHECK ONE" that automated that process. In the evaluation we used five utility metrics based on the ISO/IEC 25010 and ISO/IEC 25022 standards; the artifacts used in the evaluation are available in a public link on Zenodo. The results show that the utility of the software reached 90.28% by users. We conclude that the evaluation process answers the research question and reveals characteristics of possible improvements in the evaluated software.

Keywords: Quality in use · Utility evaluation · ISO/IEC 25010 · ISO/IEC 25022 · SOA · Software engineering

1 Introduction

Currently, utility as a sub-characteristic of satisfaction in quality in use is essential for the development of a software product. Software evaluation is an important step in determining customer or end-user satisfaction and requirements [7].

During the management process in the planning, registering, and monitoring of activities at the development and quality area, the use of various heterogeneous and low-quality digital and computer tools is evidenced [12] like Microsoft Excel, Planner,

© Springer Nature Switzerland AG 2021
T. Guarda et al. (Eds.): ARTIIS 2021, CCIS 1485, pp. 106–117, 2021.
https://doi.org/10.1007/978-3-030-90241-4_9

ProofHub, Toggl Plan, nTask, Teamwork, Workzone [15]. For software development teams, the use of these tools creates problems such as file duplication, document clutter and information with low quality [2].

However, these problems cannot be solved by focusing only on the process and classical planning techniques. It requires a holistic approach that also considers the business environment social aspects, such as corporate strategies, organizational policies, negotiations, and cooperation to finally do the process automation [1].

To be part of this digital transformation, we feel the need to develop a software that allows to automate the management process about the planning, registering, and monitoring of activities in the development and quality area, which we call "ITE CHECK ONE", this being our greatest motivation.

According to the above, we based this study on the Design Science Research (DSR) approach [13] that helps evaluate criteria of value and usefulness of the software product. We posed the question Does ITE CHECK ONE software implementation useful?. The research aims to answer the research question by evaluating the quality-in-use of ITE CHECK ONE software implementation in an organization, using the ISO/IEC 25010 [17] and ISO/IEC 25022 [16] which exposes the model and metrics necessary to measure the quality in use of the software product. The software's implementation was carried out at the company in Ecuador.

The rest of the paper is structured as follows: Sect. 2: Research Design: we establish the research activities based on DSR, theoretical foundation, and artifact design and build (software implementation). Section 3: Results: Evaluation of quality-in-use results of the software artifact. Section 4: Discussion: discussion of the research. Section 5: Conclusions and future work.

2 Research Design

For the research methodology we follow the Design Science Research guide (DSR) [13], see Table 1.

Table 1. Research design methodology.

Activity	Components	Paper section
Problem diagnosis	Problem; Objective Population and sample	Introduction Research design
Theoretical foundation	SOA architecture; SCRUM Framework; ISO/IEC 25010; ISO/IEC 25022	Research design
Artefact design: "ITE CHECK ONE" Software implementation	Requirements; Design (Process and Architecture); Development and Deployment; and satisfaction survey	Research design
Evaluation of the software artifact	Evaluation of the quality-in-use	Results

2.1 Population and Sample

The research was developed in a company involved to the development of business software in Ecuador. The study population was 29 people from the development area; composed by three people who developed the "ITE CHECK ONE" software (a Product Owner, a Scrum Master, and a programmer). The remaining 26 people were: 6 leaders, 1 consultant, and 19 developers, who used the pro- posed software and through a survey evaluated the utility sub-characteristic of quality satisfaction in use characteristic of software product using the model of the ISO/IEC 25010 standard and the metrics of the ISO/IEC 25022 standard.

2.2 Theoretical Foundation

SOA Architecture. The Service-Oriented Architecture (SOA) is an architectural design for software development based on a business or service model [18]. The main function is the integration of different types of services and give agility to the business model [3]. The services can be used to develop other applications or join a services group that communicate information with each other without depending on their location or technology [10].

SCRUM Framework. Scrum ensures the effectiveness of product and work management techniques to continually improve the product, team, and work environment [8]. Scrum is composed of the following elements: work team, events, artifacts, and associated rules. Each element has a specific purpose within the process. The roles involved in the Scrum process are Product Owner, Scrum Master, and Development Team [14]. Scrum life cycle is divided into three phases [19]: Pregame (system definition and requirements update), Development (iterations and delivery of product releases) and Postgame (product delivery); the practices for each phase are:

- Pre-game: Vision, User Stories, Product Backlog.
- Development: Sprint, Sprint Planning Meeting, Sprint Backlog, Daily SCRUM Meeting, Impediments List, Burn Down Chart, Increase, Sprint Review Meeting, and Sprint Retrospective Meeting.
- Post-game: Project Closing Meeting.

ISO/IEC 25022 Standard. The ISO/IEC 25000 standards family guides the evaluation of internal, external, and in-use quality of software products through models, metrics and processes using quality requirements specification [20]. In this research, the following was applied: the model of the ISO/IEC 25010 standard and the evaluation metrics of the utility sub-characteristic which belong to quality in use satisfaction characteristic of the ISO/IEC 25022 standard. The ISO/IEC 25022 standard has five characteristics: effectiveness, efficiency, satisfaction, freedom from risk, and context coverage.

2.3   Software Artifact Design and Implementation

In this activity three tasks are established: definition of functional requirements [9], software design, software product implementation and deployment.

Definition of Functional Requirements. To obtain the functional requirements, a planning meeting was done with the Product Owner and the development team. In this meeting, 11 user stories were defined which were considered in the Product Backlog for the development of the software. The user roles that used the software were as follows:

– Consultant: User who establishes the Sprint framework and should review all the progress of the teams.
– Scrum Master: Team Leader who distributes activities to programmers and monitors team performance.
– Developer: Team member who tracks progress through tasks in assigned activities.

Software Design. Based on SOA architecture for software design. Technological tools were previously established by the Product Owner considering the technological infrastructure of the company where the developed software was implemented (see Fig. 1).

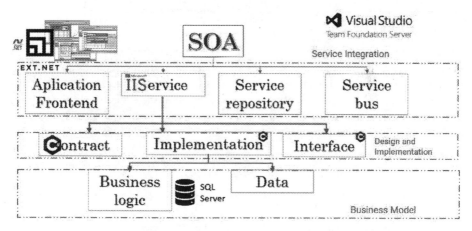

Fig. 1. Technological components of the "ITE CHECK ONE" software architecture.

Table 2 shows the architecture components and tools used in the design of software "ITE CHECK ONE".

Table 2. Architecture components and tools of "ITE CHECK ONE" software.

Component	Tool	Description
Database	Microsoft SQL Server	It is a relational database management system. The development language used is Transact-SQL [21]
Services layer	Entity Framework	It is a set of technologies in ADO.NET supporting the development of data-driven software applications [22]
	C#	Multi-paradigm programming language developed and standardized for.NET [23]
	Microsoft.NET WCF	It is the messaging platform that takes part of.NET 3.0 Platform API [24]
Application layer	Microsoft EXT. NET	It is a library for web development in C # and Asp.Net language, easy to use. Allows the design of web applications optimizing the use of Microsoft Visual Studio IDE [25]

Implementation and Deployment of the Software. During the software development, researchers analyzed and defined the documents and information of the management process in the planning, registering, and monitoring of activities in the development and quality area of the technological department of the company. We use the scrum framework in an iterative and incremental process; the iteration called sprint lasted two weeks. Each Sprint consisted of a planning meeting of the user stories described in the technical work tasks, a review meeting of the software product increment, and a retrospective meeting to carry out a continuous improvement of the execution of the project. Table 3 shows the summary of activities and the results obtained in each execution and development phase of the project.

Table 3. Summary of development and implementation activities.

Phase	Sprint (duration)	Deliverables
Pre-game	Sprint 0 (40 h)	– Requirements: 11 user stories; Product Backlog – Architecture Design: Process Diagram; Software Architecture; Initial Database Diagram
Game	Sprint 1 (40 h) Sprint 2 (40 h)	– Software Product Increment 1 – Software Product Increment 2
Post-game	Sprint 3 (40 h)	– Satisfaction survey – Deployment of the software product – Delivery-Receipt Act

Definition of Software Quality-in-Use Metrics. After completing the design, development, and implementation of the software "ITE CHECK ONE" we validated the utility of the software artifact through the quality-in-use metrics of ISO/IEC 25010 and ISO/IEC 25022 with the following activities: 1) Definition of the quality-in-use model y 2) Measurement and evaluation of the quality-in-use model.

Definition of the Quality-in-Use Model. To define the quality-in-use model, it is necessary that the Product Owner and the Scrum Master to assign the level of importance and the percentage value of quality to the sub-characteristics and characteristics established in the metrics of ISO/IEC 25010 and ISO/IEC 25022. For the present investigation, utility sub characteristic considers 100% of the expected value of the quality model. Table 4 shows the evaluation metrics.

Measurement and Evaluation of the Quality-in-Use Model. To evaluate the five metrics of the quality-in-use utility sub-characteristic, three methods were applied, see Table 4. For Satisfaction with characteristic metric, a semi-structured survey of 15 questions was applied to 26 of 29 people in the population. Five questions were applied to evaluate the solution to the problem and the remaining 10 questions to evaluate the utility sub-characteristic. The survey questions were based on the SUMI satisfaction questionnaires [4] and SUS [5] and an acceptance range was established through a score from 1 to 100, see Table 5. In addition, the Likert scale [11] was used for its assessment. The survey form is enabled in [27]. For the metrics Directional use and Use of functions, observation method was applied. For the metrics Proportion of users complaining and proportion of user complaints about a particular feature, the method of listing complaints in a registry was applied.

Table 4. Summary of development and implementation activities.

Metric	Description	Measurement function	Method
Satisfaction with features	User satisfaction with the system characteristics	$X = \Sigma Ai$ Ai = Answer to a question related to a specific characteristic	Survey
Discretionary use	The proportion of potential users who choose to use the system	$X = A/B$ A = Number of users using the system B = Number of potential users who could have used the system	Counting and observing user behavior

(continued)

Table 4. (*continued*)

Metric	Description	Measurement function	Method
Using functions	The proportion of an identified set of system users who use a subset or role in the system	X = A/B A = Number of users using the system subset B = Number of identified users of the system	Counting and observing user behavior
Proportion of users complaining	The proportion of users who have complaints	X = A/B A = Number of users complaining B = Number of users using the system	Measure user behavior by list of records
Proportion of user complaints about a particular feature	The proportion of user complaints about a particular characteristic	X = A/B A = Number of user complaints for a particular characteristic B = Total number of user complaints about features	Measure user behavior by list of records

Table 5. SUS-based acceptance range for utility sub-characteristic metric evaluation.

Category	Scale	Score range
A	Outstanding	$80.3 < X \leq 100$
B	Correct	$68 < X \leq 80.3$
C	Suitable	$51 < X \leq 68$
D	Failed	$0 < X \leq 51$

3   Results

This section presents the results of the statistical analysis to obtain the survey reliability and the results of the utility sub-characteristic of the software "ITE CHECK ONE".

3.1   Results of Statistical Analysis

To verify the survey reliability, the results obtained were processed and executed through statistical tests using the R programming language [26] through RStudio. We applied the Exploratory Factor Analysis (EFA) and maximum likelihood. In addition, we performed the Cronbach's Alpha analysis through exploratory factor analysis, and it was evidenced that the information obtained through the survey is consistent and satisfaction averages can be obtained from these data. Initially, for the additivity assumption, we obtained the bivariate correlation matrix for all possible combinations of questions, we observed that there is a possible relationship between the first two questions and the last three. Subsequently, to verify the assumptions of normality and linearity, we run a false regression analysis based on the standardized residuals obtained for the quantiles ×2.

The regression histogram made from the quantiles allowed us to verify that the frequencies were distributed with a normal trend centered between −2 to 2. In the same way, the assumption of linearity was verified with a linear trend of the increasing quantiles in the interval from −2 to 2, (see Fig. 2).

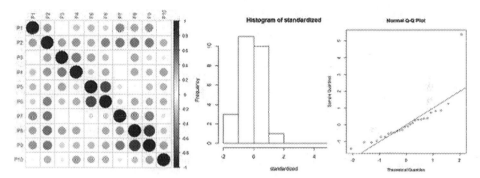

Fig. 2. Correlation matrix, normality assumption and survey linearity.

The exploratory factor analysis carried out showed that the saturation value (ML) was greater than 0.2 and verified the relationship that each question in the questionnaire has with the others. This allowed grouping and evaluating them, (see Fig. 3). The source code in R language of the present statistical analysis is enabled in appointment [27].

```
Factor Analysis using method =  ml
Call: fa(r = noout, nfactors = 2, rotate = "oblimin", fm = "ml")
Standardized loadings (pattern matrix) based upon correlation matrix
       ML1    ML2   h2    u2  com
P1     0.33  0.23 0.20 0.802 1.8
P2     0.50  0.27 0.38 0.619 1.5
P3     0.33  0.32 0.26 0.740 2.0
P4     0.33  0.16 0.16 0.841 1.4
P5    -0.08  1.01 1.00 0.005 1.0
P6     0.26  0.68 0.61 0.394 1.3
P7     0.40  0.08 0.18 0.817 1.1
P8     1.02 -0.12 1.00 0.005 1.0
P9     0.78  0.16 0.69 0.309 1.1
P10    0.20  0.28 0.15 0.852 1.8

                        ML1   ML2
SS loadings            2.63  1.99
Proportion Var         0.26  0.20
Cumulative Var         0.26  0.46
Proportion Explained   0.57  0.43
Cumulative Proportion  0.57  1.00
```

Fig. 3. Standardized correlation matrix of the survey.

The average SUS score for the case of the 26 users had a value of 87.88, which, being in a range above 80, is outstanding. In addition, the statistical average with a value of 90.27 for the metric "Satisfaction with characteristic" obtained through the analysis of Cronbach's Alpha supports the score mentioned before, see Table 6. In this way it is shown that the application is useful for the particular use case of the users.

Table 6. Score and average result for characteristic satisfaction based on SUS.

Average Score (SUS)	87.88
Standardized average (p)	90.27324
Median	92.05
D.S	9.67
Max. Lim	99.94
Min. Lim	80.60
Quintile Value	16
Q1 Q2 Q3 Q4 Q5	$20 \leq p \geq 36$ $36 \leq p \geq 52$ $52 \leq p \geq 68$ $68 \leq p \geq 84$ $84 \leq p \geq 100$

Table 7 shows the results obtained for the five-evaluation metrics in Utility after applying the evaluation methods defined in Table 4.

Table 7. Utility evaluation metrics.

Metrics	Value (%)
Satisfaction with features	87.88
Discretionary use	100
Using functions	80.20
Proportion of users complaining	7.7
Proportion of user complaints about a particular feature	10
Average of the total percentage of evaluation in software Utility	**90.28**

4 Discussion

The study from Miguel P. [6] in 2014 indicates the importance of applying the ISO/IEC 25010 standard to evaluate a software product and identifies some characteristics in the software life cycle that should be evaluated through quality of software in use, such as the transferability of the software. We consider that our study, in addition to using the ISO/IEC 25010 standard, applies the ISO/IEC 25022 standard to evaluate the usefulness of a software product, this complements the evaluation of the quality in use. We note that the tools used in the development of the proposed software are free versions, especially of the Ext.Net Framework. This is a limitation since it can only be used for the development of simple applications with basic implementations for administrative purposes such as handling forms and CRUD operations of entities in databases. In addition, is important to involve a larger number of end users or, in the absence of end users, dual experts to evaluate the software product. The authors believe it is necessary to mention that the artifacts such as requirements, design and the development environment of the proposed software were developed in Spanish. We consider that the same environment should be used in Spanish for the next software implementation but not in another language because we do not know if the translation of the artifacts into another language affects the validity of the research.

5   Conclusions and Future Work

We conducted this study based on the Design Science Research approach to answer the research question: Does ITE CHECK ONE software implementation useful?. The method to answer this question consisted of establishing, designing, developing, implementing, and validating the software artifact "ITE CHECK ONE". We performed the validation of the artifact evaluating the utility sub- characteristic of the quality in use applying the metrics of the ISO/IEC 25010 and ISO/IEC 25022 standards. Through software implementation, we automated the management process in the planning, registering, and monitoring of activities in the development and quality area of the company.

The implementation of the proposed software helped 26 people (6 leaders, 1 consultant, and 19 developers) with the work planning to the objectives fulfillment established by the company. The use of "ITE CHECK ONE" helped to reduce the use of Excel, duplicate files, and disorganization in folders for work tracking of the software teams members. In this way, the quality of information in work activities management was increased.

Finally, the Utility of the software "ITE CHECK ONE" was 90.28%. We conclude and answer the research question saying that the implementation of "ITE CHECK ONE" is useful and works for what it was created.

As future work, we propose that after six months, the use of the developed software be monitored and measure if the percentage of profit has improved. In addition, perform a complementary version of the job tracking process in a mobile application, which would give users the facility to update and monitor the information at any time.

References

1. Kir, H., Erdogan, N.: A knowledge-intensive adaptive business process management framework. Inf. Syst. **95**(1), 101639 (2021)

2. Niazi, M., et al.: Challenges of project management in global software development: a client-vendor analysis. Inf. Softw. Technol. **80**(1), 1–19 (2016)
3. Welke, R., Hirschheim, R., Schwarz, A.: Service-oriented architecture maturity. Comput. J. **44**(2), 61–67 (2011)
4. Azizi, R., Zakerian, S., Rahgozar, M.: Determining reliability and validity of the Persian version of software usability measurements inventory (SUMI) questionnaire. Int. J. Occup. Hyg. **5**(1), 31–34 (2013)
5. Brooke, J.: SUS: a quick and dirty usability scale. Usabil. Eval. Ind. 189 (1995)
6. Miguel, J.P., Mauricio, D., Rodriguez, G.: A review of software quality models for the evaluation of software products. Int. J. Softw. Eng. Appl. **5**(6), 31–53 (2014)
7. Guevara-Vega, C., Hernández-Rojas, J., Botto-Tobar, M., García-Santillán, I., Basantes Andrade, A., Quiña-Mera, A.: Automation of the municipal inspection process in Ecuador applying mobile-D for android. In: Botto-Tobar, M., León-Acurio, J., Díaz Cadena, A., Montiel Díaz, P. (eds.) ICAETT 2019. AISC, vol. 1066, pp. 155–166. Springer, Cham (2020). https://doi.org/10.1007/978-3-030-32022-5_15
8. Quiña-Mera, A., Chamorro Andrade, L., Montaluisa Yugla, J., Chicaiza Angamarca, D., Guevara-Vega, C.P.: Improving software project management by applying agile methodologies: a case study. In: Botto-Tobar, M., Montes León, S., Camacho, O., Chávez, D., Torres-Carrión, P., Zambrano Vizuete, M. (eds.) ICAT 2020. CCIS, vol. 1388, pp. 672–685. Springer, Cham (2021). https://doi.org/10.1007/978-3-030-71503-8_52
9. Guevara-Vega, C.P., Guzmán-Chamorro, E.D., Guevara-Vega, V.A., Andrade, A.V.B., Quiña-Mera, J.A.: Functional requirement management automation and the impact on software projects: case study in Ecuador. In: Rocha, Á., Ferrás, C., Paredes, M. (eds.) ICITS 2019. AISC, vol. 918, pp. 317–324. Springer, Cham (2019). https://doi.org/10.1007/978-3-030-11890-7_31
10. Rosen, M., Lublinsky, B., Smith, K., Balcer, M.: Applied SOA: Service-Oriented Architecture and Design Strategies, 1st edn. Wiley, Indianapolis (2012)
11. Likert, R.: A technique for the measurement of attitudes. Archiv. Psychol. **22**, 11–20 (1932)
12. Morten, E., Pernille, B.: Routine and standardization in global software development. In: Proceedings of the 18th International Conference on Supporting Group Work (GROUP 2014), pp. 12–23. Association for Computing Machinery, New York (2014)
13. Hevner, A., Chatterjee, S.: Design science research in information systems. In: Design Research in Information Systems. Integrated Series in Information Systems, vol 22. Springer, Boston (2010)
14. Srivastava, A., Bhardwaj, S., Saraswat, S.: SCRUM model for agile methodology. In: Proceeding - IEEE International Conference on Computing. Communication and Automation (ICCCA), 2017, pp. 864–869. IEEE, India (2017)
15. Best Project Management Tools & Software for 2021. https://www.proofhub.com/articles/top-project-management-tools-list. Accessed 02 June 2021
16. ISO/IEC 25022. NTE INEN-ISO/IEC 25022 International Organization for Standardization, "ISO/IEC 25022". https://www.iso.org/standard/35746.html. Accessed 02 June 2021
17. ISO/IEC 25010. NTE INEN-ISO/IEC 25010 International Organization for Standardization, "ISO/IEC 25010". https://www.iso.org/standard/35733.html. Accessed 03 June 2021
18. SOA Architecture. Service-Oriented Architecture. https://www.ibm.com/cloud/learn/soa. Accessed 03 June 2021
19. The Scrum Guide. The Definitive Guide to Scrum: The Rules of the Game. https://scrumguides.org/docs/scrumguide/v2020/2020-Scrum-Guide-US.pdf,#zoom=100. Accessed 03 June 2021
20. ISO/IEC 25000. NTE INEN-ISO/IEC 25000 International Organization for Standardization, "ISO/IEC 25000". https://www.iso.org/standard/64764.html. Accessed 04 June 2021

21. Microsoft SQL Server. What is SQL Server? https://www.sqlservertutorial.net/getting-sta rted/what-is-sql-server/. Accessed 05 June 2021
22. Entity Framework. What is Entity Framework? https://www.entityframeworktutorial.net/ what-is-entityframework.aspx. Accessed 05 June 2021
23. C#. Programming Language. https://docs.microsoft.com/en-us/dotnet/csharp/language-ref erence/language-specification/introduction. Accessed 05 June 2021
24. Microsoft .NET WCF. Develop Service-Oriented Applications with WCF. https://docs.mic rosoft.com/en-us/dotnet/framework/wcf/. Accessed 05 June 2021
25. Microsoft EXT. NET. https://ext.net/download/. Accessed 05 June 2021
26. R Language. The R Project for Statistical Computing. https://www.r-project.org/. Accessed 07 June 2021
27. Anonymous. Supplemental Material - Utility evaluation of software product: An Industry Implementation. Zenodo. https://doi.org/10.5281/zenodo.4950275. Accessed 14 June 2021

An Algorithm for Automatic QRS Delineation Based on ECG-gradient Signal

Nancy Betancourt[1,2,4(✉)], Marco Flores-Calero[3,4], and Carlos Almeida[2,4]

[1] Departamento de Ciencias de la Computación, Escuela Politécnica Nacional, Ladrón de Guevara, E11-253 P.O.Box 17–01-2759, Quito, Ecuador
[2] Departamento de Ciencias Exactas, Universidad de las Fuerzas Armadas - ESPE, Av. General Rumiñahui s/n, Sangolquí, Ecuador
ncbetancourt@espe.edu.ec
[3] Departamento de Eléctrica Electrónica y Telecomunicaciones, Universidad de las Fuerzas Armadas - ESPE, Av. General Rumiñahui s/n, Sangolquí, Ecuador
mjflores@espe.edu.ec
[4] Departamento de Matemática, Escuela Politécnica Nacional, Ladrón de Guevara, E11-253 Quito, Ecuador
carlos.almeidar@epn.edu.ec

Abstract. In this work, an algorithm based on digital signal processing and machine learning is developed for QRS complexes detection in ECG signals. The algorithm for locating the complexes uses a gradient signal and the KNN classification method. In the first step, an efficient process for denoising signals using Stationary Wavelet Transform (SWT), Discrete Wavelet Transform (DWT), and a combination of filtering thresholds is developed. In the second stage, the phase of fiducial points detection is carry out, the gradient of the signal is computed for being used as a feature for the detection of the R-peak. Therefore, a KNN classification method is used in order to separate R-peaks and non R-peaks. The algorithm computes a set of thresholds to recalculate the R-peaks positions that has been omitted or falsely detected due to the ECG wave forms. Finally, the each R peak permits locate Q and S peaks. The results indicate that the algorithm correctly detects 99.7% of the QRS complexes for the MIT-BIH Arrhythmia database and the 99.8% using the QT Database. The average processing-time that the algorithm takes to process a signal from the denoising stage to fiducial points detection is 4.95 s.

Keywords: ECG · QRS complex · Detection · Segmentation · Delineation · Denoising

1 Introduction

The electrocardiography represents an clinical procedure for finding cardiac abnormalities [1,2]. The electrocardiogram (ECG) is a bio-signal that reflects

T. Guarda et al. (Eds.): ARTIIS 2021, CCIS 1485, pp. 118–129, 2021.
https://doi.org/10.1007/978-3-030-90241-4_10

the electrical activity of the heart. One cycle of the ECG represents the depolarization and repolarization of the atrium and the ventricle (contraction and
relaxation, respectively) which occurs for every heartbeat [3,4]. Each beat corresponds to an electrical wave that crosses the different structures of the heart
giving rise to the different waves of the ECG known as P wave, Q, R and S waves
(QRS complex) and T wave (Fig. 1).

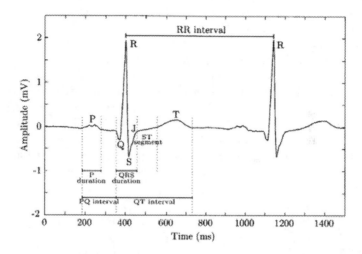

Fig. 1. Wave definitions of the cardiac cycle and important wave durations and intervals
[3].

The analysis of specific segments of the ECG is a common non-invasive technique for the diagnosis of cardiovascular diseases. In this sense, the accurate
identification of specific points in the ECG could help to improve results in a
clinical application such as heart arrhythmia [5–7]. The ECG segmentation process can be performed manually and may offer reliable results when it is done
by expert clinicians. However, this method is tedious and time consuming. So,
many researchers have been interested in automatic ECG segmentation. Signal processing techniques and computing systems are tools that allow to develop
automatic methods for segmentation and interpretation of the ECG. In this context, it is important to develop efficient algorithms that allow accurate detection
of EGC fiducial points. The first step for this segmentation process is to delineate the QRS complex, which means to detect the onset, the peak, and the
offset of the waves. An accurate delineation of the complex will allow to delineate other components like P and T waves, RR and QT intervals, ST segments,
or any other morphological parameters. However, ECG automatic segmentation
is a hard task due to different aspects such as the difficulty to identify the small
amplitude of the P wave, this due to interferences arising from the movement of
electrodes or muscle noise. The P and T waves can be biphasic, this increase the
difficulty to an accurately determination of their onsets and offsets. Otherwise,

some ECG cycles may not contain some waves or segments, for example, the P wave may be missing. Some techniques have been proposed for feature extraction on the ECG, some of them are based on wavelet transforms and techniques using machine learning approaches [8–13]. This paper is focused on the delineation of QRS complex. Before executing the segmentation process the algorithm applies some techniques of denoising such as: Stationary Wavelet Transform (SWT), Inverse Stationary Wavelet Transform (ISWT) and Discrete Wavelet Transform (DWT) [14]. After that, a gradient signal function is calculated in order to locate R peaks in the signal. Subsequently, an algorithm based on K-Nearest Neighbors (KNN) is applied to eliminate false R peaks. A set of thresholds is calculated for detecting peaks Q and S. In addition, these thresholds allow to the signal to be segmented. The computational time for the overall process is also reported.

The ECG arrhythmia recordings employed in this study are derived from the MIT-BIH Arrhythmia database [15], which is a complete system distributing information since 1980 and can be accessed from the PhysioBank. Furthermore, a set of signals from QT Database has been used to evaluate the algorithm. Section 2 describes a new methodology for automatic QRS delineation. Section 3 shows the results in graphical and tabulated form while in Sect. 4 conclusion based on results are discussed.

2   Methodology

The proposed algorithm is based on two steps (Fig. 2). In the first step, the ECG signal is pre-processed in order to highlight their relevant features. In the second step, the algorithm identifies and locates the QRS complex.

2.1   ECG Signal Pre-processing

Before detecting fiducial points some techniques for ECG denoising are applied. The power line interference (higher frequency noise) and the baseline wander (lower frequency noise) are the types of noise that considerably alter the signal, this kind of noise does no permit the identification of the start and end of the waves inside the ECG. In order to improve the signal and eliminate the noise, it is necessary to use denoising techniques. The algorithm start with the Stationary Wavelet Transform (SWT) a tool used for non-stationary signals, such as ECG. The implementation of the SWT is based on the work of [14]. In this work a simplest mother wavelet is used (Haar wavelet), and the order of SWT is $M = 3$. After that, the Inverse Stationary Wavelet Transform (ISWT) is calculated. This process permit detecting specified signal components like motion artifacts and outliers as well as QRS complexes. To eliminate the intrinsic noise Discrete Wavelet Transform (DWT) is used, a set of thresholds is calculated to obtain the filtering coefficient. These coefficient are used to obtain the denoising signal using Inverse Wavelet Transform (IDTW) (Fig. 3).

2.2   Fiducial Points Location

For the ECG segmentation, the gradient of the signal has been used as a feature for R-peak detection. The KNN algorithm locates the R peak, after that the algorithm computes thresholds to recalculate the R points positions that were omitted or falsely detected due to the ECG waves form. Finally, the R point permits to locate the Q and S points.

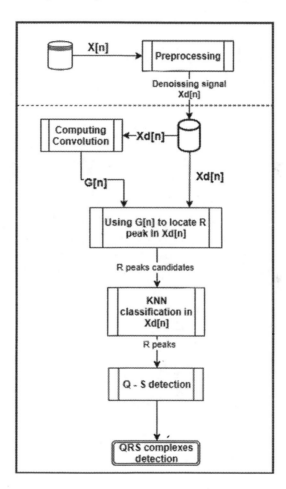

Fig. 2. Fiducial peaks location: General schema for QRS complexes detection based on ECG- gradient and KNN.

Gradient Signal. A discrete convolution technique is used in order to compute the gradient signal. The discrete convolution of Xd and V is given by:

$$G[n] = \sum_{m=-\infty}^{\infty} Xd[n-m]V[m] \tag{1}$$

where Xd is the input signal, V is the impulse response and G is output signal. In this case, Xd is the denoising ECG signal and V is the kernel given by $[1, -1]$.

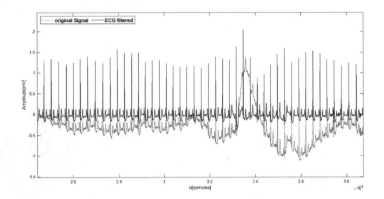

Fig. 3. Example of SWT signal filtering: MIT-DB record 101 (female, age 75).

The QRS complex is a part of the ECG whose amplitude value is higher with respect to the other waves, such as T, P, ST-interval and PR-interval. The convolution calculation helps to locate a higher gradient value compared to the other waves inside the ECG. [16]. In this context, the maximum points detected in the gradient curve is used to detect the R-peak in the ECG signal (Fig. 4).

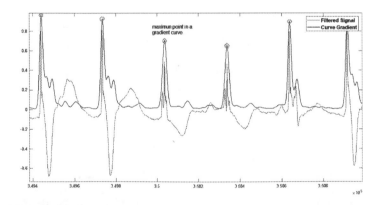

Fig. 4. Gradient signal computed by equation (1) to detect maximun points: MIT-BIH record 107 m.

KNN Algorithm for R-Peak Classification. The k-nearest neighbors (KNN) algorithm is a supervised machine learning algorithm that can be used to solve classification and regression problems [16]. According to the stage above described, the maximun points in the gradient signal G allows to detect the R-peak candidates. However, the algorithm detects peaks that do not correspond to a correct R-peak position, as we can see in Fig. 5. To overcome this drawback, a KNN classification algorithm is developed. Using the results presented by Saini et al. [16], to train the KNN algorithm this work uses five-fold cross-validation, and the optimal K value is 3 with Euclidean distance.

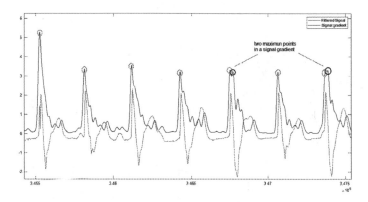

Fig. 5. Maximun points detected over gradient signal. KNN algorithm is used to classify and eliminate wrong maximum points detected. MIT-BIH record 107 m.

R-Peak Detection. Let R' be a point with the greatest amplitude in gradient signal G after use KNN classification algorithm. Using R' peak and the threshold computed by standard deviation, the method construct a window of size u to detect the final R-peak on $Xd[n]$ signal (see Fig. 6).

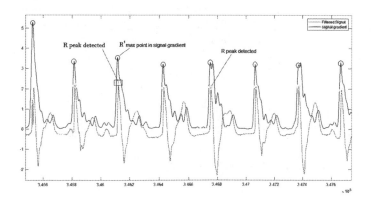

Fig. 6. R peak detection. MIT-BIH record 107 m.

Q and S Point Detection. Using R peak, the method defines a window and explore the signal searching Q and S points. Finally the QRS complex is detected (Fig. 7).

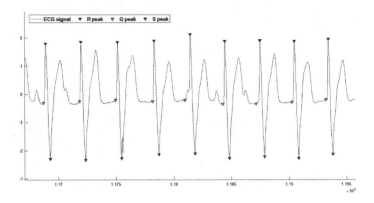

Fig. 7. QRS complex detected. MIT-BIH record 107 m.

3   Results and Validation

3.1   Description of the Databases

The databases used for the validation of the algorithm and the QRS complex detection are: MIT-BIH Arrhythmia (MIT-DB) and QT Database (QTDB) [15, 17,18].

The MIT-DB contains recordings that correspond at 48 patients, each record has a duration of 30 min, there are in total 24 h of ECG data. In this database there are also files with annotations that have bben developed by two expert cardiologists. These information allow to identify the onset and offset of the waves into the ECG. The MIT-BIH database contains approximately 110,000 beats [15]. In this work, 109494 beats have been processed.

The algorithm has been evaluated using 49 recording of the QT Database. Table 1 shows the composition of the database that has been used in this work.

3.2   Evaluation Metrics for QRS Complex

Three metrics are used for evaluation: detection rate, sensitivity, and specificity.

$$\text{Detection rate, } D_r = \frac{(\text{Peaks} - \text{FN})}{\text{Peaks}} \tag{2}$$

$$\text{Sensitivity, } S_e = \frac{TP}{(TP + FN)} \tag{3}$$

$$\text{Specificity, } S_p = \frac{TP}{(TP + FP)} \tag{4}$$

Table 1. Distribution of the 49 records in QTDB. Source [17]

Database	Records
MIT-BIH Arrhythmia Database	15
MIT-BIH ST Change Database	6
MIT-BIH Supraventricular Arrhythmia Database	12
MIT-BIH Normal Sinus Rhythm Database	10
MIT-BIH Long-Term ECG Database	4
Sudden Death	2
Total	49

3.3 Performance Evaluation and Discussion

Table 2 show the results obtained in this work. The proposed algorithm has processed 53397 beats, 110 FN, 94 FP. According to the equations (2)–(4) are: the detection rate is 99.80%, Sensitivity (Se) is 99.79% and the specificity is 99.82%.

Therefore, the proposed method has been validated using the MIT-BIH Arrhythmia databases. The algorithm is applied to channel I of 48 recording with a duration of 30 min, 109494 beats have been processed and validated. The detection has been considered as true positive (TP) if the proposed method detects the QRS complex, false negative (FN) if the algorithm does not detect the QRS complex and false positive (FP) if the method detects a false QRS complex and this is considered as positive. Further, time from preprocessing stage to fiducial points detection is showed (Time (s)). Table 3 contains 8 columns, the first one shows the number of signal processed; in the second column, the number of beats in the signal is shown according MIT-BIH arrhythmia DB; third, fourth and fifth columns show the TP, FP, FN respectively. In the next columns, the percentage rate and time of process of each signal is shown. The proposed method has processed 109,494 beats and it has produced 273 FN beats and 129 FP beats. The detection failure is 405 beats. (A total of 48 signals was processed, however, the Table 3 shows only 10 records due to the number pages limitations.)

Hence, according to the equations (2)–(4) the detection rate is 99.76%, the S_e is 99.67% and the S_p is 99.73%.

The average processing time is 4.15 seconds, by using a laptop DELL Inspiron N4050, Core i5 2.40 GhZ with 8 GB RAM.

In order to evaluate the performance of the proposed algorithm, it has been compared with two well-known methods. The first one is Pan Tompkins algorithm [19], that is a referent in the literature to detect the fiducial points. The second one is the method proposed by Saini et al. [16] that allows detect the points of interest using a KNN approach.

In this work a convolution was calculated, a gradient curve $G[n]$ was used to detect maximun points inside $G[n]$, this process allow to detect R peaks

Table 2. Results of evaluating the proposed method using MIT-BIH QTDB

Data	Peaks	Detected peaks	TP	FP	FN	Se (%)	Sp (%)
sel30m	1019	1009	1009	10	0	99	100
sel100m	1134	1134	1134	0	0	100	100
sel102m	1088	1088	1088	0	0	100	100
sel103m	1048	1048	1048	0	0	100	100
sel104m	1113	1109	1109	4	0	99,6	100
sel114m	870	865	865	5	0	99,4	100
sel116m	1186	1186	1186	0	0	100	100
sel117m	766	766	766	0	0	100	100
sel123m	756	756	756	0	0	100	100
sel14046m	1260	1260	1260	0	0	100	100
sel14157m	1092	1085	1083	9	2	99,2	99,8
sel14172m	663	663	663	0	0	100	100
sel15814m	1036	1037	1036	0	1	100	99,9
sel16265m	1031	1031	1031	0	0	100	100
sel16272m	851	851	851	0	0	100	100
sel16273m	1112	1112	1112	0	0	100	100
sel16420m	1063	1063	1063	0	0	100	100
sel16483m	1087	1087	1087	0	0	100	100
sel16539m	922	922	922	0	0	100	100
sel16773m	1008	1008	1008	0	0	100	100
sel16786m	925	925	925	0	0	100	100
sel16795m	761	761	761	0	0	100	100
sel17152m	1628	1628	1628	0	0	100	100
sel17453m	1047	1047	1047	0	0	100	100
sel213m	1642	1642	1640	0	2	100	99,9
sel221m	1240	1250	1238	2	9	99,8	99,3
sel223m	1037	1309	1305	2	2	99,8	99,8
sel230m	1077	1077	1077	0	0	100	100
sel231m	731	731	731	0	0	100	100
sel232m	863	866	863	0	3	100	99,7
sel233m	1533	1531	1529	4	15	99,7	99
sel301m	1352	1351	1335	7	9	99,5	99,3
sel302m	1501	1499	1495	2	4	99,9	99,7
sel306m	1039	1039	1039	0	0	100	100
sel307m	854	854	853	1	1	99,9	99,9
sel308m	1291	1296	1264	6	32	99,5	97,53
sel310m	2011	2011	2011	0	0	100	100
sel803m	1026	1026	1026	0	0	100	100
sel808m	904	903	903	1	0	99,9	100
sel811m	704	704	704	0	0	100	100
sel820m	1159	1159	1159	0	0	100	100
sel821m	1558	1558	1558	0	0	100	100
sel840m	1179	1180	1179	0	1	100	99,9
sel847m	804	804	798	7	6	99,2	99,3
sel853m	1115	1113	1113	2	0	99,8	100
sel872m	990	990	990	0	0	100	100
sel873m	859	859	859	0	0	100	100
sel883m	893	893	893	0	0	100	100
sel891m	1353	1311	1304	48	7	96,44	99,46
Total	53181	53397	53304	110	94	99,79	99,82

Table 3. Some results of evaluating the proposed method using MIT-BIH Arrhythmia DB

Data	Peaks	Detected peaks	TP	FP	FN	Rate%	Time(s)
101	1865	1865	1865	0	0	100	3.81
107	2137	2137	2137	0	0	100	3.58
111	2124	2124	2124	0	0	100	3.87
114	1879	1881	1876	3	3	99.8	3.07
200	2601	2608	2598	3	10	99.6	5.83
203	2980	2973	2973	0	7	99.76	5.72
210	2650	2630	2623	7	27	98.9	6.12
213	3251	3246	3246	0	5	99.8	3.37
217	2208	2222	2208	14	0	100	5.79
230	2256	2256	2256	0	0	100	5.03
Total	109494	109350	109221	129	273	99.76	4.15

Table 4. Comparison of the performance of the proposed method with other algorithms for the MIT-BIH database and QT database.

Database (Annotations)	QRS detector	Paper	Detection rate (%)
MIT-BIH Arrhyt. (109,809 beats)	A real-time QRS detection based upon digital analysis of slope, amplitude and width	[19]	99.30
MIT-BIH Arrhyt. (109,966 beats)	QRS detection using K-Nearest Neighbor algorithm (KNN) and evaluation on standard ECG databases	[16]	99.81
MIT-BIH Arrhyt. (109,494 beats)	Proposed method	–	99.76
QTDB (86741 beats)	An improved QRS complex detection method having low computational load	[20]	99.8
QTDB (53181 beats)	Proposed method	–	99.8

candidates in a ECG signal $X[n]$. The KNN approach is used to eliminate maximun point falsely detected in $G[n]$. After that, the R peaks are located using a window of size u in $X[n]$, this innovation improves the detection rate.

The proposed method works properly as a QRS detector for the employed databases, and it provides a satisfying high performance in difficult distorted records of MIT-BIH.

4   Conclusion and Future Works

In this paper, a new algorithm, based on digital signal processing and machine learning, to detect the complex QRS was presented. The algorithm is based on two steps. The first one is the phase of denoising, which allowed to enhance the signal to obtain the relevant sections. The second phase was the QRS point locations, to achieve this, a gradient signal was calculated to improve the R point detection. Despite obtaining a detection rate of 99.76% and 99, 80% (Arrhythmia DB and QTDB respectively) (see Table 4), it is necessary to improve the degree of detection of the interest points. In this sense, a second phase our work will focus on overcome the detection rate of the QRS complex and detect T and P waves using others Machine Learning techniques that allow to overcome the results obtained. Further, in our work the processing time from the denoising stage to fiducial point detection stage is calculated for each signal. In average, the processing-time is 4.95 s. This advanced method will be helpful for future health systems based on computer automated diagnostic. As future work, the European ST-T database and Sudden death database included in the QTDB will be used for test our algorithm.

References

1. Blanco-Velasco, M., Cruz-Roldán, F., Godino-Llorente, J.I., Barner, K.E.: Nonlinear trend estimation of the ventricular repolarization segment for T-wave alternans detection. IEEE Trans. Biomed. Eng. **57**(10), 2402–2412 (2010)
2. Nemati, S., Abdala, O., Monasterio, V., Yim-Yeh, S., Malhotra, A., Clifford, G.D.: A nonparametric surrogate-based test of significance for T-wave alternans detection. IEEE Trans. Biomed. Eng. **58**(5), 1356–1364 (2011)
3. Sörnmo, L., Laguna, P.: Bioelectrical Signal Processing in Cardiac and Neurological Applications, vol. 8. Academic Press, Cambridge (2005)
4. Iravanian, S., Kanu, U.B., Christini, D.J.: A class of monte-carlo-based statistical algorithms for efficient detection of repolarization alternans. IEEE Trans. Biomed. Eng. **59**(7), 1882–1891 (2012)
5. Irshad, A., Bakhshi, A.D., Bashir, S.: Department of electrical engineering, College of electrical and mechanical engineering, national University of science and technology, Islamabad, Pakistan. Department of electrical engineering, University of engineering and technology, Lahore, Pakista, pp. 222–227 (2015)
6. Madeiro, J.P., Cortez, P.C., Marques, J.A., Seisdedos, C.R., Sobrinho, C.R.: An innovative approach of QRS segmentation based on first-derivative, hilbert and wavelet transforms. Med. Eng. Phys. **34**(9), 1236–1246 (2012)
7. Pham, Q., Quan, K.J., Rosenbaum, D.S.: T-Wave alternans: marker, mechanism, and methodology for predicting sudden cardiac death. J. Electrocardiol. **36**(Suppl.), 75–81 (2003)

8. Sanamdikar, S.T.: Extraction of different features of ECG signal for detection of cardiac arrhythmias by using wavelet transformation Db 6. In: 2017 International Conference on Energy, Communication, Data Analytics and Soft Computing (ICECDS), pp. 2407–2412 (2017)

9. Sharma, L.D., Sunkaria, R.K.: A robust QRS detection using novel pre-processing techniques and kurtosis based enhanced efficiency. Measurement **87**, 194–204 (2016)

10. Nannaparaju, V., Narasimman, S.: Detection of T-wave alternans in ECGs by wavelet analysis. Procedia Mat. Sci. **10**(2014), 307–313 (2015)

11. Li, Z., Ni, J., Gu, X.: A denoising framework for ECG signal preprocessing. In: Proceedings - 6th International Conference on Internet Computing for Science and Engineering, ICICSE 2012, pp. 176–179 (2012)

12. Noohi, M., Sadr, A.: T wave detection by correlation method in the ECG signal. In: 2010 The 2nd International Conference on Computer and Automation Engineering (ICCAE), vol. 5, pp. 550–552 (2010)

13. Martinez, J.P., Almeida, R., Olmos, S., Rocha, A.P., Laguna, P.: A wavelet-based ECG delineator: evaluation on standard databases. IEEE Trans. Biomed. Eng. **51**(4), 570–581 (2004)

14. Strasser, F., Muma, M., Zoubir, A.M.: Motion artifact removal in ECG signals using multi-resolution thresholding. In: European Signal Processing Conference (Eusipco), pp. 899–903 (2012)

15. Moody, G.B., Mark, R.G.: The impact of the MIT-BIH arrhythmia database. IEEE Eng. Med. Biol. Mag. **20**(3), 45–50 (2001)

16. Saini, I., Singh, D., Khosla, A.: QRS detection using k-nearest neighbor algorithm (KNN) and evaluation on standard ECG databases. J. Adv. Res. **4**(4), 331–344 (2013)

17. Laguna, P., Mark, R.G., Goldberg, A., Moody, G.B.: A database for evaluation of algorithms for measurement of QT and other waveform intervals in the ECG. In: Computers in cardiology 1997, pp. 673–676. IEEE (1997)

18. Goldberger, A.L., et al.: Physiobank, physiotoolkit, and physionet: components of a new research resource for complex physiologic signals. Circulation **101**(23), e215–e220 (2000)

19. Pan, J., Tompkins, W.J.: Pan tomkins 1985 - QRS detection.pdf. IEEE Trans. Biomed. Eng. **32**(3), 230–236 (1985)

20. Yakut, Ö., Bolat, E.D.: An improved QRS complex detection method having low computational load. Biomed. Sig. Process. Control **42**, 230–241 (2018)

English Assessment Online Tool International Test of English Proficiency as an External Assessment Strategy in the PINE Career at UPSE University

Carolina Lituma Briones[1], Kléber Loor Zambrano[1(✉)], and Vanessa González Lainez[2]

[1] Universidad Estatal Península de Santa Elena, La Libertad, Ecuador
kloor@upse.edu.ec
[2] Universidad de La Rioja, Quito, Ecuador
vgonzalez@upse.edu.ec

Abstract. The evaluation of the level of English according to the standards established by the common European framework of reference is reflected in the redesign of the pedagogy of national and foreign languages of the UPSE the online application of the International Examination of Proficiency in English or International Test of English Proficiency (ITEP) carried out by the Continuing Education Center in conjunction with the National and Foreign Language Pedagogy Career of the Santa Elena Peninsula State University in 2019 and 2020. The objective of this study was to determine the level of English of the students of the National and Foreign Language Pedagogy Career of the UPSE according to the common European framework of reference through an online exam in the ITEP in the teaching-learning process English assessment online tool ITEP as an external assessment strategy. To measure the level of English language skills in the national and foreign language pedagogy at the Peninsula de Santa Elena state university, this research aims to describe the processes planned and executed to carry out this online assessment and at the same time present the results obtained. So that they become essential inputs for decision-making and actions that allow meeting the professional profile embodied in this academic unit.

Keywords: Skills · English · Learning

1 Introduction

The higher education institutions HEI in Ecuador are aimed at guiding strategies that guarantee to be effective in an academic environment that is currently more internationalized, with high quality standards marked by the predominance of the English language. Connected with international collaboration, scientific research, and other university processes.

According to this context, higher education institutions HEI face great challenges related to the improvement of the third and fourth level career plans, planning of research

T. Guarda et al. (Eds.): ARTIIS 2021, CCIS 1485, pp. 130–141, 2021.
https://doi.org/10.1007/978-3-030-90241-4_11

agendas and establishing adequate mechanisms linked to society; before these challenges, it is essential to have competitive human resources, inter-institutional relationships that guarantee collaboration and mutual benefit. All this requires more and more mastery and frequent use of the English language, both at the level of students, teachers and managers; for this reason, the importance of perfecting the process of teaching this language in any institution of higher education.

In accordance with the above, the Santa Elena Peninsula State University is a prestigious institution of the Ecuadorian higher education system, evidenced by its accreditation by the Council for the Assurance of the Quality of Higher Education - CACES, which it officially received on 28 October 2020, after complying with the quality parameters required by this body.

In order to provide students with the required level in English, courses and modules have been carried out with an exit profile of a high intermediate level (B2), in accordance with the guidelines of the Common European Framework of reference, which are developed by Career Pedagogy of National and Foreign Languages.

The Faculty of Education Sciences and Languages has the Pedagogy of National and Foreign Languages career whose mission is to train competent professionals in English Language Pedagogy who apply research, linking and teaching in a critical and interdisciplinary way for the integral formation of the human being. For this reason, the International English Proficiency Exam or ITEP is applied to the students of this career, this test assesses the level of English from the beginner level to the advanced level.

1.1 Problem Statement

Students of the Pedagogy of National Languages of the UPSE must take eight semesters to obtain their degree, however their level of English has not been measured through an external evaluation. The lack of a clear proposal that investigates the evaluation of curricular English online, and the lack of feedback on the student's performance in terms of their linguistic competence, make a study that addresses this situation necessary to determine their real level of English, which is so important for their future professional development. However, there is little information about the online learning assessment research [1]. This lack of research is also presented in the Faculty of Educational Sciences and Idioms of the UPSE where there is no way to accredit the linguistic competence of English online through the international exam.

Derived from the above, a review of the theses of the undergraduate and master's program of the Faculty of Education Sciences and Languages of the UPSE was carried out, where it was found that the themes are oriented to teaching, methodology, translation, didactics, linguistics, discourse studies, professional development, and evaluation among others (UPSE 2019). The theses focused on evaluation and accreditation, review strategies and methods, and suggest forms of instruction to improve the numerical performance of students' linguistic competence take a standardized international English test [2].

1.2 Research Question

What is the level of English of the students of the National and Foreign Language Pedagogy Career of the UPSE according to the common European framework of reference through an online exam in the ITEP in the teaching-learning process that validates its development professional?

1.3 General Objective

Determine the level of English of the students of the National and Foreign Language Pedagogy Career of the UPSE according to the common European framework of reference through an online exam in the ITEP in the teaching-learning process.

2 Literature Revies

2.1 The Evaluation Process

The day-to-day life of a person is framed by the decisions and actions that he executes, from this it follows that each action carried out has consequences; this cycle repeats itself throughout the life of the human being. Decisions require a conscious or unconscious evaluation of the situations that arise, from going to study, to work, bathing, shopping, playing, driving, and activities that are not directly physiological, but rather complement the quality of life of the patient person [3]. These examples reflect mostly unconscious evaluations, whereas those we have in an educational institution are mostly conscious. The evaluation process will be approached starting with a descriptive search of what evaluation is.

A common approach that institutions make in their pedagogical models is to want to plan, organize and measure everything that happens in the teaching-learning process; without considering unpredictable human-type factors [4]. Despite this pedagogical ambition, the planning and evaluation processes provide a broad panorama of the educational activity and help to establish the most convenient ways to achieve the proposed objectives. There are different interpretations of what can be defined as evaluation, here are some positions.

In a general and broad way, evaluation is understood as, "the process by which it is tried to judge the degree to which learning was achieved" [5]. This definition is ambiguous and can be confused with qualification, accreditation, test or exam. Three didactic approaches that support it are also considered in the evaluation of learning: traditional didactics, educational technology, and critical didactics.

From traditional didactics or education, evaluating is, "the application of exams, which aim to check if the knowledge transmitted by the teacher was acquired" [5]. Another perspective linked to online evaluation of learning is related to educational technology, in this regard evaluation is defined as, "the objective quantification or measurement of learning [5]. From critical didactics [5] defines evaluation as, a comprehensive academic process of the learner that informs about their knowledge, skills, attitudes, habits (…) as an activity that within the teaching-learning process allows obtaining data that offers the opportunity to correct errors, save obstacles, highlighting successes, that is,, that allow the educational task to be improved"(p. 65). This last definition highlights the accompaniment to the process, either by modifying or improving it, from a competency assessment perspective, defines assessment as:

A formative and summative process through which it is identified to what extent the students have developed a better performance in solving the problems that are presented to them and that will be presented to them throughout their lives, using the knowledge, skills of the thinking, skills and attitudes that will allow them to have the competencies required to do so (p. 85). This last definition of evaluation gives a more holistic interpretation of the act of evaluating since it provides different elements. The types of process involved, formative and summative, the purpose of the evaluation framed in the solution of problems, and the acquisition of competences are mentioned. Higher education in Ecuador as a pedagogical model gives continuity to the previous school level of upper secondary education, and therefore is marked by the development of competencies In the UPSE, competences are linked to social constructivism, and the way of evaluating such knowledge and processes is done considering this last approach to the definition of evaluation.

2.2   English Assessment

A first definition of language assessment is given by the Common European Framework [6] "assessment of the degree of linguistic command that the user has" (p. 176). It is understood that the user is the person who uses the language in its oral or written form, and also the fact that all tests are forms of evaluation. However, this is not an inclusive definition that considers or specifies neither the ways nor the resources to arrive at such an assessment. In the assessment of language proficiency, not only language proficiency is included, but the type and quality of the student's speech also influence. Another perspective of language assessment concerns the purposes of assessment [7]. Categorizes the types of language tests according to the information they provide, and groups them into four types: language proficiency, achievement, diagnostic and level tests. This distribution also considers aspects of an objective, subjective, direct, indirect, discrete, integrating, norm-referenced and criteria-referenced type. These items and categories are explained below.

2.3   Types of English Assessment Tests

The evaluation that is carried out through written tests or exams is called testing in English, and in Spanish it will be adjusted to the test. This type of measurement is used in different areas of academic, sports, cultural and social life [3], 35 refers to the use of tests in sports doping, in psychometric tests in the area of psychology, the standards that provide institutions with a score of the cognitive abilities of new students, and others related to the measurement of knowledge and skills. In the area of languages, some of the most frequently used tests have been identified and grouped: aptitude or command of the language, aptitude or academic achievement, diagnosis, level, and criteria.

2.4 Online Exam

The comparison between the inconveniences and the benefits of the use of technology in the training of professionals in universities, is moving away when in the member countries of the OECD there are more and more graduates of semi-schooled and virtual modalities [8]. In addition, a trend is seen in the increase of online learning; notwithstanding this demand, there is still latent research on the evaluation of this learning, and especially on its quality assurance. An online test has the characteristic of being objective in terms of its graduation since it is programmed to meet certain conditions in the selection of the correct answer options. This electronic evaluation tool must meet certain characteristics agreed by one or more participants who agree on a content and a consensus is reached which will be reflected in a timely manner on the day of the exam. On the other hand, the format adopted will depend on the software used for its preparation and integration of 39 parts of the test [9]. In addition, language specialists who develop an online exam should also consider the following debatable elements in the use of technology for the assessment of language proficiency: - The effects of technology on language assessment: the attitudes of the student in terms of anxiety and motivation. - The deviation of the degree of linguistic competence with the use of technologies. - The impact on the use of technology when measuring the construct of linguistic ability. - The impact of technology with the nature of the assessment tasks. - The technology limits to grading answers automatically as opposed to grading answers by a teacher [10]. Despite these observations and the detractors of online exams, the use of technology in the evaluation of languages is increasing given its evolution and the demand for its use, mainly by the students born in this century. In sum, the online English assessment involves more aspects than the simple writing of reagents to make up an electronic test. The English teacher and the area teacher academy should consider aspects of learning assessment as a process,

3   International English Proficiency Exam or ITEP

ITEP International was founded in 2002 by international educators, the ITEP location is already being used by several academic institutions in the United States, Mexico and Canada; each can reach a broader group of students and partners through exposure in ITEP online marketing and promotional materials and at hundreds of test center locations around the world.

The ITEP placement is designed to fit the specific needs of any Intensive English Program (IEP). The test is delivered online and includes tasks aimed at beginning to advanced levels of English proficiency to suit various levels of programs. As with all other ITEP exams, the ITEP placement is aligned with the Common European Framework of Reference (CEFR), and the score reports provide a level designation from A1 to C2.

It is important to emphasize that ITEP is recognized by the Evaluation of Academic Credentials Institute (ACEI) and ACCET, it is internationally approved and accepted as an international examination of English.

Characteristics of the ITEP

We should mention several features of the International English Proficiency Exam such as the following: convenient because of the on-demand programming available at your facilities and why ITEP placement is also available on paper; fast because ITEP placement is not timed, with an average completion time of 60 min, that is, the results are available immediately; practical because the data of the people who take the exam, photos and samples are available to you online at any time;

Placement Test

This diagnostic test is designed for any English program, including intensive English courses, the test can be done online or in writing, this test assesses the level of English from beginner to advanced level. It is important to mention that this test assesses grammar, listening comprehension, vocabulary and reading comprehension.

ITEP Location Structure

In each section, test takers will find content and questions directed at different levels of proficiency.

- A. A grammar - a part
  Part 1. Fifteen multiple-choice fill-in-the-blank questions that test the examinee's familiarity with a key characteristic of.
  English structure; questions range from beginner to advanced.
- B. Listen: three parts
  Part 1. Five short conversations from beginner to intermediate level, each followed by at least one question.
  Part 2. Two longer intermediate level dialogues followed by multiple questions.
  Part 3. A two to three minute lecture, followed by five multiple choice questions.
- C. Vocabulary - two parts
  Part 1. Six multiple-choice questions to fill in the blanks.
  Part 2. Four multiple-choice questions that test the examinee's familiarity with synonyms.
- D. Reading - three parts
  Part 1. A low-intermediate level passage (120 words) followed by four multiple-choice questions.
  Part 2. An intermediate level passage (160 words) followed by four multiple-choice questions.
  Part 3. A higher-level passage (450 words) followed by six multiple-choice questions.
- E Writing - a part
  Part 1. Optional writing Section (100 words); the answer is provided on the score report, but it is not graded by ITEP.

4 Legal Framework

The Undersecretariat of Educational Professional Development requests the reform of article 7 of the Ministerial Agreement MINEDUC-MINEDUC-2017-00065-A of July 20, 2017, amended with Agreement No. MINEDUC-MINEDUC-2018-00004-A of January 16 of 2018, including in the table of the list of certificates to accredit the level of English according to the Common European Framework of Reference for Languages (MCE) the International Test Of English Proficiency (ITEP Academic) exam, to evaluate the level of knowledge of the language of English foreign language teachers [11].

5 Career of Pedagogy of National and Foreign Languages of the Santa Elena Peninsula State University

The mission of PINE's career is to train competent professionals in English Language Pedagogy who critically and interdisciplinary apply research, linking and teaching for the integral formation of the human being, promoting respect and strengthening inter-culturality. Likewise, it has the vision of becoming the benchmark career of pedagogical, technological, scientific and innovative training of future professionals of the English Language within the framework of equal opportunities and multi-interculturality for the construction of an inclusive society, based on the human values.

The professional profile of the PINE career mentions that the four basic skills of the English language must be managed, apply methods and techniques of teaching the English language to achieve the comprehensive training of the student in different environments and levels of education, use computer resources and technologies effectively in the teaching-learning processes of the English language promoting personal and collective critical thinking, developing a culture of research for professional training through work project designs, essays, scientific articles, in the search for solutions to problems of society, use the English language as a tool in other areas of training at a national and international level, develop ethical principles and values, that contribute to achieving good living by demonstrating critical, inter - multi - multicultural thinking, integrating the ancestral and contemporary knowledge of Ecuador and English-speaking countries, promoting interculturality and internationalization of the Career and evaluating with criteria of reliability and without bias Under international standards for language teaching in different educational contexts, based on these guidelines, the ITEP exam was applied to students of the PINE career. Integrates the ancestral and contemporary knowledge of Ecuador and English-speaking countries promoting interculturality and the internationalization of the Career and evaluate with criteria of reliability and without bias under international standards for the teaching of languages in different educational contexts, based on to these guidelines, the ITEP exam was applied to the students of the PINE career. Integrates the ancestral and contemporary knowledge of Ecuador and English-speaking countries promoting interculturality and the internationalization of the Career and evaluate with criteria of reliability and without bias under international standards for the teaching of languages in different educational contexts, based on to these guidelines, the ITEP exam was applied to the students of the PINE career.

6   ITEP Exam Results for PINE Students

Through the management carried out by the Director of the Center for Continuing Education and through the Language Center of the UPSE, the ITEP exam was carried out to the students of the Pedagogy of National and Foreign Languages, to evaluate the level of English from the beginner level to advanced level. The exam in question was carried out on 274 students of the PINE career, carried out on December 6, 2019, and February 21, 2020. The exam was carried out in the Networks and CISCO laboratory of the UPSE.

6.1   The Test Results Given to PINE Students Reflect the Following

In the leveling course the exam was carried out on 31 students, of which 25 of them have the A1 level, 4 students have the A2 level and only 2 students have the B1 level, as can be seen in the following Table 1.

In the course 1/1 Day of the PINE career, 44 students took the exam, of which 27 have the A1 level, 13 the A2 level and 4 students the B1 level, below it is detailed in the following Table 1.

In the course 2/1 in the evening of the PINE career, the exam was carried out on 22 students, 16 students have the A1 level, 3 students the A2 level and 3 students the B1 level.

In the 2/2 Evening course 33 students of the PINE career took the exam, 27 of them have the A1 level, 4 the A2 level, and 1 student the B1 and B2 level respectively, below it is detailed in the following Table 1.

In the course 3/1 of the daytime shift of the PINE career, 23 students took the exam, 9 of them have the A1 level, 6 students the A2 level, 6 students the B1 level, 1 student the B2 level and 1 students meet the C1 level.

In the course 3/2 of the day during the daytime course of PINE, 22 students took the exam, 6 of them have the A1 level, 8 students the A2 level, 7 students the B1 level, 1 student the B2 level.

In the course 4/1 of the Afternoon session of the PINE career, 32 students took the exam, 12 of them have the A1 level, 9 students the A2 level, 10 students the B1 level, 1 student the B2 level.

In the course 4/2 of the daytime race of PINE, 27 students took the exam, 10 of them have the A1 level, 8 students the A2 level, 7 students the B1 level, 1 student the B2 level and 1 students meet the C1 level.

In the course 5/1 of the daytime of the PINE career, 24 students took the exam, 6 of them have the A1 level, 5 students the A2 level, 7 students the B1 level, 4 students the B2 level and 2 students meet the C1 level (Table 1).

Table 1. Examination results of the leveling course

Leveling									
CEFR level	1/1	1/1 Day	2/1 Evening	2/2 Evening	3/1 Day	3/2 Day	4/1 Evening	4/2 Evening	5/1 Day
A1	25	27	16	27	9	9	12	10	6
A2	4	13	3	4	6	6	9	8	5
B1	2	4	3	1	6	6	10	7	7
B2	0	0	0	1	1	1	1	1	4
C1	0	0	0	0	1	1	0	1	2
Total	**31**	**44**	**22**	**33**	**23**	**23**	**32**	**27**	**24**

These were the results of the i-TEP Prep Plus (Placement Test) exams administered at the Santa Elena Peninsula State University, below it is specified in a general way at what level are the students of the Pedagogy of National and Foreign Languages career to the Faculty of Education Sciences and Languages.

Table 2. PINE race exam results

English level pine	
A1	146
A2	63
B1	51
B2	10
C1	4
Total students	**274**

Representing these data in a percentage and graphic way, we can indicate that 53% of the students of the Pedagogy of National and Foreign Languages career have the A1 level, followed by 23% with the A2 level, 19% with the B1 level, EL 4% with level B2 and with a minimum percentage of 1% with level C1 (Table 2, Fig. 1).

In the results of the International Examination of Competences in English or ITEP, an average of each area that was taken in the exam is presented, that is, in the area of grammar (Grammar) it was measured: articles of grammar and prepositions, grammatical conjunctions, grammar that expresses quantity, grammatical parts of speech, grammatical pronouns, grammatical sentence structure and forms of grammatical verbs, these areas were scored with a maximum range of 100 points, as we can see the highest average is in the area of grammatical pronouns with an average of 90.77 and the lowest average is in the area of the grammatical parts of speech with 33.91. Table 3 indicate the percentage of each area related to grammar.

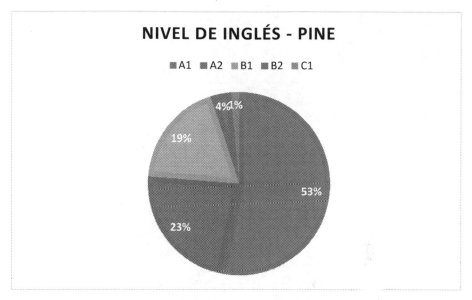

Fig. 1. PINE career exam results

Table 3. Results of the grammar area of the PINE career

Grammar	Average
Grammar articles & prepositions	62.94
Grammar conjunctions	53.94
Grammar expressing quantity	34.31
Grammar parts of speech	33.91
Grammar pronouns	90.77
Grammar sentence structure	36.33

In the area of listening (Listening) several aspects were evaluated such as: listening to capture details, listening to connection content, listening to determine the purpose, listening to the main idea and listening making implications; As we can see, the highest average is in listening to the main idea with 43.35% and the lowest percentage is in the area of listening to determine the purpose, Table 4 indicates the percentage of each area related to listening.

In the area of reading (Reading), several aspects were evaluated such as: reading detail, reading the main idea, reading sequence, synthesis reading and vocabulary reading; As we can see, the area with the highest average is vocabulary reading with 49.29% and the lowest average is the area of reading detail with 35.39%, below a table is presented where it indicates the percentage of each area related to read (Table 5).

Table 4. Results of the grammar area of the PINE career

Listening	Average
Listening catching details	37.75
Listening connecting content	29.45
Listening determining the purpose	23.04
Listening main idea	43.35
Listening making implications	33.52

Table 5. Results of the grammar area of the PINE career

Reading	Average
Reading detail	35.39
Reading main idea	41.54
Reading sequencing	41.13
Reading synthesis	46.61
reading vocabulary	49.29

It is important to mention that the area of writing (Writing) and speech (Speaking) were also evaluated.

7 Conclusions

The application of the ITEP exam allowed to determine the level of English that the students of the Pedagogy of National and Foreign Languages have, in addition to analyzing and establishing study strategies by the teachers who teach their classes to this group of students. The results allow us to clearly see the reality regarding the English level of the students in terms of receptive or productive abilities and it was determined that they are heterogeneous and are not related to the semester of study. The Pine Career has these essential inputs for decision-making and actions that allow meeting the professional profile set out in this academic unit.

Mastery of the English language is achieved thanks to the articulation of each of its skills such as: listening, reading, writing, speaking. These four skills form a system where each of them has its uniqueness and specificity for learning. Therefore, each skill presents evaluation indicators that are evaluated individually in the first instance and then articulated with each other through the evaluation of reception skills such as listening and reading and production skills such as speaking and writing; being articulate in your assessment will ensure language proficiency.

8   Recommendations

Continuous assessment must become an integral part of the curriculum of the Pedagogy of National and Foreign Languages career of the UPSE, so that students can be reinforced in the different areas where there are difficulties and guide students in a process reflection on the level of English they currently have.

For the improvement of the teaching of the English language at the Santa Elena Peninsula State University, with emphasis on the processes of teaching, research and connection with society, ICTs and a high level of technological component are required in the teaching of languages, the teaching of Online languages, integration with other entities related to the teaching of the English language, international certifications in language teaching and receiving exams with international certifications.

It is important to socialize with the teachers of the Pine Race, other forms of evaluation that go beyond quantitative measurement. The use of rubrics, part of the qualitative assessment, as an example, provides another way to view student progress. To achieve this combination, it is necessary that teachers and students join their efforts to achieve the proposed learning. Pine's Career Director should be the guiding element to analyze whether teachers meet the proposed standards.

References

1. Quesada. Evaluación del aprendizaje en la educación a distancia en línea. RED: Revista de Educación a distancia. No. 6 (2006)
2. Amador. Analyzing scores obtained by LEMO and LEI undergraduate students in the TOEFL: perceptions and performance (2014)
3. McNamara: Language Testing. Oxford University Press, New York (2000)
4. Bachman, L.P.: Language Testing in Practice. Oxford University Press, England (1996)
5. Morán, M.P.: Propuesta de Evaluación y Acreditación en el Proceso de Enseñanza-Aprendizaje desde una Perspectiva Grupal, p. 61. México, Perfiles Educativos (2012)
6. CEFR. https://rm.coe.int/common-european-framework (2001). [En línea]. https://rm.coe.int/common-european-framework-of-reference-for-languages-learning-teaching/16809ea0d4
7. Hughes: Testing for Language Teachers, 2nd edn. Cambridge University Press, Cambridge (2003)
8. Salvat, B.G.: Evolución y Retos de la Educación Virtual (2011)
9. Douglas: Assessing Languages for Specific Purposes. Cambridge University Press, United Kingdom (2000)
10. Dorrego, E.: Educación a Distancia y Evaluación del Aprendizaje. RED (2006)
11. iTEP Academic. iTEP (2018). [En línea]. https://itepecuador.ec/
12. C. P. o. g. Practices. https://www.cambridgeenglish.org (2011). [En línea]. https://www.cambridgeenglish.org/Images/126011-using-cefr-principles-of-good-practice.pdf

Software Frameworks that Improve HCI Focused on Cognitive Cities. A Systematic Literature Review

Gema Giler-Velásquez⬚, Bryan Marcillo-Delgado⬚, Mónica Vaca-Cardenas⬚, and Leticia Vaca-Cardenas⁽✉⁾ ⬚

Universidad Técnica de Manabí, Portoviejo 130105, Ecuador
leticia.vaca@utm.edu.ec

Abstract. Due to the technological advances, the reference frameworks to carry out web and mobile applications primarily focus on improving Human-Computer Interaction (HCI). This document compiles a series of current trends both in framework and in developing systems that enhance HCI in the new paradigm of cognitive cities. For this, a Systematics Literature Review (SLR) methodology has been applied, based on an exhaustive search in Scientific libraries of the Informatics field. This research presents new frameworks that improve HCI in medicine, education, and urban planning; based on the development of Cognitive Cities.

Keywords: HCI · Cognitive cities · Framework · Smart cities · Machine learning

1 Introduction

The interaction with computer systems has currently evolved considerably. A field of great study is the HCI, which seeks to improve the interaction between man and computer. HCI's problems focused only on how users without technical education interacted with word processing software, spreadsheets, and database applications; however, over time, many other topics of particular interest to the HCI community have been included, such as empirical research, artifact growth, and contributions to theory and methodology [1]. Thanks to the fact that the HCI is carried out in the research of multiple disciplines, it is essential to update standards and expectations in related fields.

In the study reported by [2], it is stated that we live in a time of change, with emphasis on the care provided by professionals to people who are expected to participate in decision-making actively. Technically, this change is supported by new health technologies and information resources.

The enormous success of computing technologies has brought tremendous benefits for individuals, families, communities, businesses, and government, transforming human life significantly for the better [3]. As a result, Human-Computer Interaction (HCI) has been researched, practiced, and taught worldwide in various contexts [4]. For example, [5] presents HCIDL, a modeling language organized in a model-based engineering. This proposal is intended to model multiobjective, multimodal plastic interaction interfaces

© Springer Nature Switzerland AG 2021
T. Guarda et al. (Eds.): ARTIIS 2021, CCIS 1485, pp. 142–157, 2021.
https://doi.org/10.1007/978-3-030-90241-4_12

using user interface description languages. By combining plasticity and multimodality, HCIDL improves the usability of user interfaces through adaptive behavior by providing end-users with an interaction set adapted to terminal input/output and an optimal design.

Art and Human-Computer Interaction (HCI) are compatible with each other, addressing interconnected components in both interaction, creativity, affect, and presence [6]. Furthermore, interactive art has become a standard part of life due to the many ways that the computer and the Internet have made it easy [7].

On the other hand, the most common techniques of Machine Learning (ML) and Artificial Intelligence (AI), according to [8], have achieved outstanding performance and an important impact on clinical research to achieve precision medicine, as well as improving healthcare workflows. However, the heterogeneity and uncertainty inherent in health information sources pose new challenges for physicians in their decision-making tasks. Artificial intelligence (AI) developments bring much comfort to people especially, for people with disabilities. Artificial intelligence techniques with advanced computer interface design (HCI) will provide much more help in real life [9].

Human-computer interaction analyzes a series of multifactorial decisions and situations that are influenced by the corresponding feedback. Cognitive modeling provides a method to understand and explain how these dynamic decisions are made [10]. It demonstrates how cognitive modeling allows flexible simulation of decision-making in dynamic environments for different individual strategies.

HCI helps designers, analysts, and users identify system needs from text style, fonts, layout, graphics, and color. At the same time, usability confirms whether the system is efficient, effective, safe, helpful, easy to learn, easy to remember, and easy to use and evaluate, to obtain user satisfaction.

In this sense, this research aims to collect and analyze bibliographic information to simplify the investigation regarding Software Frameworks that improve HCI in the new paradigm of cognitive cities.

2 Background

Currently, with the rapid development of technology, developed countries have given great importance to HCI research. Being a multidisciplinary subject brings together the experience of computing with various sciences to understand and facilitate interaction between users and computers. In this section, some relevant concepts for this study are summarized.

2.1 HCI

Making an analogy with human life, HCI covers all aspects of it, from birth to death; since, HCI has gone through all kinds of computing, from device ecology to nanotechnology [11]. Not surprisingly, the role of theory in HCI has also vastly expanded since the early days of scientific testing to include other functions such as describing, explaining, criticizing, and as a basis for generating new didactic designs. In just a few decades, the astonishing growth of interactive systems has transformed the world [12], allowing people to connect with family and friends, obtain medical advice, conduct business, and organize political movements. The remarkably rapid spread of human-computer interaction (HCI) research has brought profound changes that enrich people's lives. As stated by [13], the quality of HCI lies in the idea that the software must be defined under the integral participation of the end-user (person who will use the system) and in the construction and determination of each phase of the software. Since the most crucial criterion for the acceptance of the final product resides in interpreting the mental model of these users when carrying out their processes daily to replicate them in the software later, to achieve their immediate acceptance, with little or no need for training.

2.2 Framework

The term framework is defined as "a set of tools, libraries, conventions and good practices that aim to encapsulate repetitive tasks in easily reusable generic modules" [14]. In such a way, a framework is a set of components that helps pure languages develop applications or systems. A framework is considered an incomplete generic and configurable application. We can add what we need to make from a framework into an application. Additionally, a framework is an MVC (Model-View-Controller) paradigm. [15] states that the model represents the information and business rules, the view contains the elements of the user interface and texts, forms, and the controller is the one that manages the communication between the view and the business logic.

2.3 Cognitive Cities

Everything is connected to the Internet in modern cities, and the amount of data available online is growing dramatically. Humans face two main challenges: i) extracting valuable knowledge from Big Data and ii) being part of the equation as active actors in the Internet of things. Fuzzy smart systems are currently used in many applications in the context of smart cities. Now is the time to address the effective interaction between smart systems and citizens to move from Smart to Cognitive Cities [16]. Smart cities use data and technology to improve efficiency and sustainability, enhancing the quality of life and the experience of working in the city [17]. Based on the advances in cognitive computing, cognitive cities expand the concept of smart cities by introducing cognition and learning [18]. Citizens as sensors is a new paradigm that transforms the idea of efficiency implemented in a "smart city" into the notion of resilience oriented to "cognitive cities" [19].

3   Methodology

The methodology used in this research is a systematic review of the scientific literature (SLR) [20], produced by searching scientific repositories where studies and applications of frameworks were obtained that favor HCI focused on cognitive cities. The scientific SLR review was developed in the following order:

1. The keywords were defined
2. The research questions were established

3. The repositories were chosen
4. Search phrases were defined by combining the keywords.
5. Articles were selected.
6. Relevant information was reported.

1. The defined keywords were: HCI, Frameworks, Frameworks and HCI, HCI in cognitive cities.
2. With them, two research questions were established:

   a. RQ1: What are the existing frameworks that favor HCI?
   b. RQ2: What studies have been conducted on HCI focused on Cognitive Cities?

3. Then, the bibliographic repositories were chosen:

   c. ScienceDirect
   d. IEEE Explore.
   e. Scholar Google
   f. Oxford academy

4. The number of articles detailed in Fig. 1 was found when applying the keywords in the search:

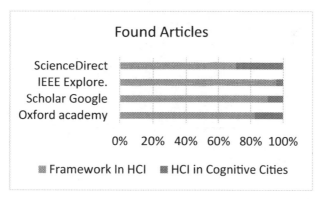

Fig. 1. Found articles and repositories

5. The first article selection filter was applied; this was to choose articles published between 2015–2020. Those articles related to the framework that seek an improvement in the HCI and that focus on cognitive cities were filtered. Therefore, the following search string was defined, which allowed a more precise filter in the investigation:

   (((("All metadata": FRAME) AND "All metadata": HCI) OR "All metadata": COGNITIVE CITIES) AND "All metadata": HCI).

Table 1. Found items.

Science direct	IEEE explore	Google scholar	Oxford academy
226	150	200	145

6. In the selection process, relevance was taken into consideration based on the title, the abstract, and the findings. After analyzing each article, those that answered the research questions were selected and separated. As a final result, 41 articles that fulfilled the specifications were obtained. For question 1, 19 articles were chosen in relation to frameworks or applications focused on HCI. Twenty six most relevant articles on studies carried out in HCI in the new paradigm of cognitive cities were chosen to answer question 2. Finally, the most pertinent information was classified and organized, which is reported in the following section (Table 1).

4 Results and Discussion

4.1 Results

Table 2 reflects the classification of the chosen articles, which argued and answered the research questions, broken down by repository and the question that each one answers.

Table 2. Articles

Repositories	Research questions	
	RQ1	RQ2
ScienceDirect	[21–27]	[24–38]
ScienceDirect	[21–27]	[24–38]
IEEE Explore	[39–42]	[43–47]
Oxford Academy	[48–51]	[52–56]
Google Scholar	[57–60]	[61]

RQ1: Current Trends and Frameworks Focused on Improving HCI
This field is fascinating and broad due to all the research involved in having a system development framework that is intuitive to the human being, regardless of their intellectual characteristics, since the system must fit each need. Goncalves et al. [62] conducted a literary exploration and interviewed 20 HCI researchers to define which HCI approaches they should employ to develop an interactive system. They concluded that the most significant agreement among the researchers was for the HCI approaches

that support the verification and validation phases and the use of functional frameworks in some activities of the last stages of software development (technical solution and product integration).

Due to technological advances over time, HCI must be refined as it has a complex role in communication methods [63], as in the study carried out by [48]. Therefore, this study explores the role and ethical obligation of human-computer interaction (HCI) researchers who operate and design sensitive environments.

Several framework developments focused on HCI were found, which are mentioned in Table 3.

Table 3. xxx.

Article title	Contribution
A framework for negotiating ethics in sensitive settings: Hospice as a case study [48]	Framework for exploring ethical dilemmas in HCI research
"Designing for Coping" [49]	It is a framework for situating concerns in HCI design, which consists of four factors: malleability, direct manipulability, meta-manipulability, and social manipulability
"An iterative, interdisciplinary, collaborative framework for developing and evaluating digital behavior change interventions" [50]	It is a framework for DBCI (digital behavior change interventions): an interactive, interdisciplinary and collaborative framework that combines the science of behavior, human-centered design, and data science
"Audiovisual perception-based multimodal HCI," [40]	It is an HCI framework based on multiple modalities. The hotspot can be determined based on various characteristics, including looking, pointing, and speaking in a non-contact and useless manner
"Conceptual Framework for Evaluating Intuitive Interaction Based on Image Schemas" [51]	It is a framework for evaluating the intuitive interaction from image schemes. The framework comprises four phases: objective identification, image schema extraction, analysis, and evaluation. It quantifies the intuitive interaction by comparing the image schemes expected by the designer of a product with those used by its users
"A framework for dynamic hand Gesture Recognition using keyframes extraction," [41]	User-independent framework for dynamic hand gesture recognition in which a novel algorithm for keyframe extraction is proposed
"An Multi-client Web-based Interactive HCI for Interactive Supercomputing," [42]	It is a ubiquitous web-based interface that allows sharing the simulation in progress simultaneously among multiple users, based on developing a framework for interactive supercomputing

(continued)

Table 3. (*continued*)

Article title	Contribution
"A framework for human interaction with mobiquitous services in a smart environment," [24]	It is a framework for modeling the interaction between humans and computers once specific technologies are selected and used
"Technology and the Givens of Existence: Toward an Existential Inquiry Framework in HCI Research" [58]	Existential Research Framework at HCI. The envisioned framework is intended to complement current approaches in HCI by explicitly focusing on the existential aspects of technology design and use
"Reliability Management Framework and Recommender System for Hyper-converged Infrastructured Data Centers" [39]	It is a hierarchical framework for measuring the reliability of HCI data centers. This framework measures the reliability of networks, storage, and computational resources based on their availability, interruption, and inactivity time with the help of neural networks
"Empowerment in HCI - A Survey and framework" [59]	It is a framework that serves as a lens to analyze the notions of empowerment in current HCI research
"Human-computer interaction and international public policymaking: A framework for understanding and taking future actions" [57]	Discussion framework to understand the role of human-computer interaction (HCI) in the formulation of public policies
"Development of a Conceptual Framework for Improving Safety for Pedestrians Using Smartphones While Walking: Challenges and Research Needs," [21]	It is a framework used to evaluate and improve the safety of pedestrians using smartphones while walking in critical environments
"A foundational framework for smart sustainable city development: Theoretical, disciplinary, and discursive dimensions and their synergies," [25]	It is a framework for the strategic development of smart and sustainable cities based on scientific principles, theories, academic disciplines, and discourses used to guide urban actors in their practice towards sustainability and analyze its impact
"A framework for data-driven adaptive GUI generation based on DICOM" [22]	It is a framework for the generation of GUI (graphical user interface) based on data of medical diagnostic software
BCI Framework Based on Games to Teach People with Cognitive and Motor Limitations [23]	It is a framework BCI (Brain-Computer Interface) to process brain signals resulting from imagination processes used together with games to teach or improve people's autonomy with physical disabilities

(*continued*)

Table 3. (*continued*)

Article title	Contribution
A pedagogical framework and a transdisciplinary design approach to innovate HCI education [60]	It is an Apple Framework as a pedagogical tool and a transdisciplinary design approach to innovate HCI education. Students do not work for a client but rather work together with urban stakeholders to better frame the problem and address societal challenges
"A framework for collecting inclusive design data for the UK population," [26]	It is a framework to capture the capacity and measurements of the psychological, social, and economic context in product designs
The digital transformation of business models in the creative industries: A holistic framework an emerging trends,"[27]	It is a holistic business framework used to analyze empirical evidence from creative industries

To answer question RQ1, articles that are based on improving HCI were selected, such as [48], which has been developed to address ethics within HCI; [39, 59] measure the reliability within the HCI and [57] understand the role of the HCI in public policy. Articles [40, 41, 49–51, 58], are HCI frameworks that seek to capture human interaction without contact. In the field of cognitive cities, frameworks [21, 24, 25, 42], seek the development of smart cities based on HCI. Apple [60] was found which is a framework that innovates HCI education. In the area of medicine frameworks [22, 23] seek to improve and contribute to people's health with the help of systems that are efficiently oriented to HCI. Finally, we have articles [26, 27], which use frameworks oriented to HCI to measure, improve, and help decision-making for the design of marketing strategies.

RQ2: HCI in Cognitive Cities
Currently, the concepts of cognitive cities or smart cities are booming. In this broad framework, a vision of technological citizenship is sought, which efficiently uses each city's space. Table 4 details the development of ideas that benefit human beings in a cognitive city.

Table 4. HCI in cognitive cities

Article title	Contribution
"A framework for human interaction with mobiquitous services in a smart environment," [24]	It provides conceptual help to design, analyze and implement human interaction with mobiquitous services and applications (convergence strategy of mobile and ubiquitous technologies) in smart environments

(*continued*)

Table 4. (*continued*)

Article title	Contribution
"A foundational framework for smart sustainable city development: Theoretical, disciplinary, and discursive dimensions and their synergies," [25]	It researches and analyzes how to advance and sustain the contribution of sustainable urban forms to the city development goals with the support of ubiquitous computing ICT
"My.Eskwela: Designing an enterprise learning management system to increase social network and reduce cognitive load [28]	Design of an enterprise learning management system to increase social networks and reduce cognitive load
"Creating design guidelines for building city dashboards from a user's perspectives," [29]	Design guidelines for building city control panels from a user's perspective. It is claimed that city dashboards are increasingly becoming an urban governance and management tool in cognitive cities
"A computational cognitive modeling approach to understand and design mobile crowdsourcing for campus safety reporting," [30]	Mobile crowdsourcing design for campus safety reporting demonstrates the value of applying a computational cognitive modeling approach to address the HCI research questions more broadly
"When we talk about older people in HCI, who are we talking about? Towards a 'turn to community in the design of technologies for a growing ageing population," [31]	It states that technologies created' for older people should be designed to meet the communities' situated and dynamic needs/interests to which they belong. Findings and other epistemological discourses located in HCI were obtained to introduce a different perspective, a turn to the community in the design of technologies for a growing aging population
"Intelligent technologies to optimize performance: Augmenting cognitive capacity and supporting self-regulation of critical thinking skills in decision-making," [32]	Intelligent system that can optimize cognitive performance and, through self-regulation, help students develop critical thinking. Provides an example that highlights the information-rich context of work, environment, and the role of self-regulation at work in association with technology to achieve maximum performance
"Hybrid video surveillance systems using P300 based computational cognitive threat signature library," [33]	Threat signature library using cognitive technology that improves the intelligence of CIBMS (Comprehensive Integrated Border Management System) to reduce human effort by using cognitive science through the application of Brain-Computer Interface (BCI)

(*continued*)

Table 4. (*continued*)

Article title	Contribution
"Communicating the user state: Introducing cognition-aware computing in industrial settings," [34]	Development of cognition-aware computing in industrial settings, through the introduction of a sensitive workplace. The final objective of the study is a proposal for an online detection system for deviations in user state, ultimately avoiding operator errors and improving the work experience
"Improving 3D em data segmentation by joint optimization over boundary evidence and biological priors," [43]	An automated neuron segmentation algorithm for isotropic 3D electron microscopy data is presented
"A Low-Cost Pupil Center Localization Algorithm Based on Maximized Integral Voting of Circular Hollow Kernels" [54]	It is a low-cost pupil center localization algorithm, where pupil center localization is a fundamental requirement for robust eye-tracking systems. This research presents a computationally inexpensive algorithm with high precision in terms of performance and processing speed
"Development of HCI management software for automatic medical analyzers," [44]	A management software for AMAs, (automatic medical analyzers) was developed as the biochemical analyzer and hematology analyzer. It was composed of management software and control systems, which simplify the design process and make its maintenance and operation more convenient
"Designing technology for spatial needs: Routines, control and social competences of people with autism," [35]	Its a cognitive approach to urbanism. The authors explore how autistic individuals conceptualize and experience the spaces they inhabit
"A proposed effective framework for elderly with dementia using data mining," [45]	Intelligent techniques that meet the specific needs of patients with cognitive deficits and evaluate interaction changes based on the patient's behavior at different stages of the disease
"Stakeholder Attitudes Toward and Values Embedded in a Sensor-Enhanced Personal Emergency Response System" [53]	It is an application of a sensor-enhanced medical alert system or a personal emergency response system (PER), proposed from the perspective of care recipients (users) and care providers. The data was collected in the context of a field test of a PER system that admits both user-initiated alerts and automatic alerts of fall detection
"Design of human-centered augmented reality for managing chronic health conditions," [61]	It shows how AR (Augmented Reality) could be applied to help older patients beyond the current healthcare technologies

(*continued*)

Table 4. (*continued*)

Article title	Contribution
"A Non-contact Framework based on Thermal and Visual Imaging for Classification of Affective States during HCI," [46]	It presents a non-contact system based on twin channels of visual and thermal image sequences to record the affective states of an individual during Human-Computer Interaction (HCI)
"Gaze estimation using EEG signals for HCI in augmented and virtual reality headsets," [47]	Approximate gaze estimation using EEG sensors with applications in element selection for HCI or rendered foveed for VR/AR devices
"Strategies for intuitive interaction in public urban spaces," [52]	Design of strategies for intuitive interaction in public urban spaces, based on applications that have been developed over the years, in contrast to similar efforts elsewhere
"ISAB: Integrated Indoor Navigation System for the Blind" [55]	It presents an innovative approach to the specific challenge of indoor navigation of blind people. It uses a multi-level solution with the help of an intuitive smartphone interface. In addition, it uses a set of different communication technologies to help users reach an object with high precision
"CIT: Integrated cognitive computing and cognitive agent technologies based cognitive architecture for human-like functionality in artificial systems," [36]	It exposes a novel cognitive architecture that combines cognitive computing and cognitive agent technologies to perform human-like functionality
"A framework for collecting inclusive design data for the UK population," [26]	It gives strategies behind specific inclusive design research to set the foundation for measuring inclusion in product designs
"Cognitive outcomes of brand heritage: A signaling perspective," [37]	It shows that the brand's heritage improves the brand's perceived quality and generates a surcharge for established companies
"The digital transformation of business models in the creative industries: A holistic framework and emerging trends," [27]	It examines how digital technologies facilitate business model innovations in the creative industries
"Survey on biometry for cognitive automotive systems," [38]	Biometric systems used for high-tech security access, law enforcement, and/or business transactions
"Enabling Smart City With Intelligent Congestion Control Using Hops With a Hybrid Computational Approach" [56]	Congestion-free traffic has been one of the main objectives of the last decade. This study proposed a model with a hybrid computational approach in which the current signal incorporates the information from associative signals. It will help improve traffic flow and reduce traffic congestion

The chosen articles promote cognitive cities' development and aim to improve HCI, answering the research question RQ2. This Research question was chosen because it is desired to acquire inventions that are included in the cognitive development of a city, and in the course of the investigation, projects that favor intelligent environments were found [24–33, 36, 43, 46, 47, 55].

Systems that help improve people's quality of life within inclusive public spaces [25, 29, 34, 35, 52, 56] within a cognitive city, additionally public security [30], and education [54]. Likewise, research that seeks improvements in the area of health [44, 45, 53, 61]. In a cognitive city, the use of technology is sought to improve all aspects of life in a community.

Findings were made of projects that contribute to the development of business management [28] to achieve a cognitive city, such as business models [27], design inclusion [26], brand inheritance [37] and trade security [38].

5 Conclusions

This research generates a compendium of technological advances to significantly improve the interaction of people with computers (HCI), where the communication that is promoted is more intuitive and friendly. In addition, projects, research, and applications mentioned in this research will allow the constitution of cognitive cities.

In response to current trends in frameworks that improve HCI, the found frameworks are of different types: backend, frontend, or simply theoretical ones. They were chosen because the meaning of having a framework is to receive a basis for the development of an application or system, and the selected ones are oriented toward improving HCI.

The field of study of HCI is very extensive and multidisciplinary, related to different areas of knowledge. Based on what it is analyzed in this document, the selected advances contribute to the growth and improvement of Human-Computer Interaction, and HCI-oriented frameworks enrich human intuition and allow the development of user-friendly interfaces. Work should be done to achieve the development of a cognitive city to improve people's life quality, in which new technologies applied to HCI are promoted.

This bibliographic review is part of a research project that aims to develop a framework of web and mobile applications that favor HCI in the new paradigm of Cognitive cities; it will constitute the theoretical support in its development.

References

1. Lazar, J., Feng, J.H., Hochheiser, H.: Introduction to HCI research. In: Research Methods in Human Computer Interaction (2017)
2. Blandford, A.: HCI for health and wellbeing: challenges and opportunities. Int. J. Hum. Comput. Stud. **131**, 41–51 (2019). https://doi.org/10.1016/j.ijhcs.2019.06.007
3. Shneiderman, B.: Encounters with HCI pioneers: a personal history and photo journal. Synth. Lect. Human-Center. Inf. (2019). https://doi.org/10.2200/s00889ed1v01y201812hci041
4. Gomes Guimaraes, T., Oliveira Prates, R.: HCI education in Brazil in the light of curricula guidelines. In: Proceedings - 2018 44th Latin American Computing Conference, CLEI 2018, Oct. 2018, pp. 784–793. https://doi.org/10.1109/CLEI.2018.00099

5. Gaouar, L., Benamar, A., Le Goaer, O., Biennier, F.: HCIDL: human-computer interface description language for multi-target, multimodal, plastic user interfaces. Futur. Comput. Inf. J. (2018). https://doi.org/10.1016/j.fcij.2018.02.001

6. Jeon, M., Fiebrink, R., Edmonds, E.A., Herath, D.: From rituals to magic: interactive art and HCI of the past, present, and future. Int. J. Hum. Comput. Stud. **131**, 108–119 (2019). https://doi.org/10.1016/j.ijhcs.2019.06.005

7. Edmonds, E.: The art of interaction: what HCI can learn from interactive art. Synth. Lect. Human-Center. Inf. **11**(1), i–73 (2018). https://doi.org/10.2200/s00825ed1v01y201802hci039

8. Rundo, L., Pirrone, R., Vitabile, S., Sala, E., Gambino, O.: Recent advances of HCI in decision-making tasks for optimized clinical workflows and precision medicine. J. Biomed. Inform. (2020). https://doi.org/10.1016/j.jbi.2020.103479

9. Ding, I.J., Lin, Z.Y.: A service robot design with an advanced HCI scheme for the person with disabilities. In: Proceedings of the 2017 IEEE International Conference on Information, Communication and Engineering: Information and Innovation for Modern Technology, ICICE 2017, Oct 2018, pp. 531–534. https://doi.org/10.1109/ICICE.2017.8479297

10. Zhang, Z., Russwinkel, N., Prezenski, S.: Modeling individual strategies in dynamic decision-making with ACT-R: a task toward decision-making assistance in HCI. Procedia Comp. Sci. **145**, 668–674 (2018). https://doi.org/10.1016/j.procs.2018.11.064

11. Rogers, Y.: HCI theory: classical, modern, and contemporary. Synth. Lect. Human-Center. Inf. **5**(2), 1–129 (2012). https://doi.org/10.2200/s00418ed1v01y201205hci014

12. Shneiderman, B.: Revisiting the astonishing growth of human–computer interaction research. Computer (Long. Beach. Calif.) **50**(10), 8–11 (2017). https://doi.org/10.1109/MC.2017.3641625

13. Toledo, G.T., Pimentel, J.J.A., Acevedo, F.A., Rodriguez, E.W.M.: Aprendizaje Basado en Proyectos Dentro de un Curso Universitario de Interacción Humano Computadora Learning Based on Projects Within a University Course of (2019). https://redib.org/Record/oai_articulo1770944-aprendizaje-basado-en-proyectos-dentro-de-un-curso-universitario-de-interacción-humano-computadora--learning-based-projects-within-a-university-course-human-computer-interaction. Accessed 30 Mar 2021

14. Samaniego Larrea, M.J.: Estudio Comparativo de Productividad de Frameworks PHP Orientados a objetos para Desarrollar el Sistema de Seguimiento de Incidentes de la infraestructura de Red en la ESPOCH. Escuela Superior Politécnica de Chimborazo (2015)

15. Vilcaguano Zumba, M.I., Tierra Llamuca, J.M.: Análisis comparativo del rendimiento de los framework YII y CODEIGNITER. Caso práctico: Junta General de Usuarios de Riego Chambo - Guano (2015). http://dspace.espoch.edu.ec/handle/123456789/3777

16. Jose, C.M., Alonso, M., Castiello, C.: "Linguistic Descriptions for Cognitive Cities: an Illustrative Use Case | Centro Singular de Investigación en Tecnoloxías Intelixentes - CiTIUS." https://citius.usc.es/investigacion/publicacions/listado/linguistic-descriptions-cognitive-cities-illustrative-use-case. Accessed 30 Mar 2021

17. Albino, V., Berardi, U., Dangelico, R.M.: Smart cities: definitions, dimensions, performance, and initiatives. J. Urban Technol. **22**(1), 3–21 (2015). https://doi.org/10.1080/10630732.2014.942092

18. Psaltoglou, A.: Archi-DOCT: La revista electrónica de investigación doctoral en arquitectura. http://www.archidoct.net/issue11.html. Accessed 30 Mar 2021

19. Recalde, L., Meza, J., Terán, L.: Cognitive systems for urban planning: a literature review. In: Santos, H., Pereira, G.V., Budde, M., Lopes, S.F., Nikolic, P. (eds.) SmartCity 360 2019. LNICSSITE, vol. 323, pp. 249–270. Springer, Cham (2020). https://doi.org/10.1007/978-3-030-51005-3_22

20. Ferreras Fernández, T.: Revisión sistemática de la literatura (SLR) y Mapping (2018). https://moodle2.usal.es/pluginfile.php/1167207/mod_resource/content/1/SLR_y_m apping_clase_presentacion.pdf
21. Kong, X., Xiong, S., Zhu, Z., Zheng, S., Long, G.: Development of a conceptual framework for improving safety for pedestrians using smartphones while walking: challenges and research needs. Procedia Manuf. **3**, 3636–3643 (2015). https://doi.org/10.1016/j.promfg.2015.07.749
22. Gambino, O., Rundo, L., Cannella, V., Vitabile, S., Pirrone, R.: A framework for data-driven adaptive GUI generation based on DICOM. J. Biomed. Inform. **88**, 37–52 (2018). https://doi.org/10.1016/j.jbi.2018.10.009
23. Cecílio, J., Andrade, J., Martins, P., Castelo-Branco, M., Furtado, P.: BCI framework based on games to teach people with cognitive and motor limitations. Procedia Comp. Sci. **83**, 74–81 (2016). https://doi.org/10.1016/j.procs.2016.04.101
24. Volpentesta, A.P.: A framework for human interaction with mobiquitous services in a smart environment. Comput. Human Behav. **50**, 177–185 (2015). https://doi.org/10.1016/j.chb.2015.04.003
25. Bibri, S.E.: A foundational framework for smart sustainable city development: theoretical, disciplinary, and discursive dimensions and their synergies. Sustain. Cities Soc. **38**, 758–794 (2018). https://doi.org/10.1016/j.scs.2017.12.032
26. Langdon, P., Johnson, D., Huppert, F., Clarkson, P.J.: A framework for collecting inclusive design data for the UK population. Appl. Ergon. **46**, 318–324 (2015). https://doi.org/10.1016/j.apergo.2013.03.011
27. Li, F.: The digital transformation of business models in the creative industries: a holistic framework and emerging trends. Technovation **92–93**, 102012 (2020). https://doi.org/10.1016/j.technovation.2017.12.004
28. Llantos, O.E., Estuar, M.R.J.E.: My.Eskwela: designing an enterprise learning management system to increase social network and reduce cognitive load. Procedia Comp. Sci. **138**, 595–602 (2018). https://doi.org/10.1016/j.procs.2018.10.080
29. Young, G.W., Kitchin, R.: Creating design guidelines for building city dashboards from a user's perspectives. Int. J. Hum. Comput. Stud. **140**, 102429 (2020). https://doi.org/10.1016/j.ijhcs.2020.102429
30. Huang, Y., White, C., Xia, H., Wang, Y.: A computational cognitive modeling approach to understand and design mobile crowdsourcing for campus safety reporting. Int. J. Hum. Comput. Stud. **102**, 27–40 (2017). https://doi.org/10.1016/j.ijhcs.2016.11.003
31. Righi, V., Sayago, S., Blat, J.: When we talk about older people in HCI, who are we talking about? Towards a 'turn to community' in the design of technologies for a growing ageing population. Int. J. Hum. Comput. Stud. **108**, 15–31 (2017). https://doi.org/10.1016/j.ijhcs.2017.06.005
32. Kitsantas, A., Baylor, A.L., Hiller, S.E.: Intelligent technologies to optimize performance: augmenting cognitive capacity and supporting self-regulation of critical thinking skills in decision-making. Cogn. Syst. Res. **58**, 387–397 (2019). https://doi.org/10.1016/j.cogsys.2019.09.003
33. Jotheeswaran, J., Singh, A., Pippal, S.: Hybrid video surveillance systems using P300 based computational cognitive threat signature library. Procedia Comp. Sci. **145**, 512–519 (2018). https://doi.org/10.1016/j.procs.2018.11.115
34. Mijović, P., et al.: Communicating the user state: introducing cognition-aware computing in industrial settings. Saf. Sci. **119**, 375–384 (2019). https://doi.org/10.1016/j.ssci.2017.12.024
35. Rapp, A., Cena, F., Castaldo, R., Keller, R., Tirassa, M.: Designing technology for spatial needs: routines, control and social competences of people with autism. Int. J. Hum. Comput. Stud. **120**, 49–65 (2018). https://doi.org/10.1016/j.ijhcs.2018.07.005

36. Chandiok, A., Chaturvedi, D.K.: CIT: Integrated cognitive computing and cognitive agent technologies based cognitive architecture for human-like functionality in artificial systems. Biol. Inspired Cogn. Archit. **26**, 55–79 (2018). https://doi.org/10.1016/j.bica.2018.07.020

37. Pecot, F., Merchant, A., Valette-Florence, P., De Barnier, V.: Cognitive outcomes of brand heritage: a signaling perspective. J. Bus. Res. **85**, 304–316 (2018). https://doi.org/10.1016/j.jbusres.2018.01.016

38. Lozoya-Santos, J.D.J., Sepúlveda-Arróniz, V., Tudon-Martinez, J.C., Ramirez-Mendoza, R.A.: Survey on biometry for cognitive automotive systems. Cogn. Syst. Res. **55**, 175–191 (2019). https://doi.org/10.1016/j.cogsys.2019.01.007

39. Nasir, A., Alyas, T., Asif, M., Akhtar, M.N.: Reliability management framework and recommender system for hyper-converged infrastructured data centers. In: 2020 3rd International Conference on Computing, Mathematics and Engineering Technologies: Idea to Innovation for Building the Knowledge Economy, iCoMET 2020, Jan 2020, pp. 1–6. https://doi.org/10.1109/iCoMET48670.2020.9074136

40. Yang, S., Guan, Y.: Audio–visual perception-based multimodal HCI. J. Eng. **2018**(4), 190–198 (2018). https://doi.org/10.1049/joe.2017.0333

41. Pathak, B., Jalal, A.S., Agrawal, S.C., Bhatnagar, C.: A framework for dynamic hand Gesture Recognition using key frames extraction. In: 2015 5th National Conference on Computer Vision, Pattern Recognition, Image Processing and Graphics, NCVPRIPG 2015, Jun 2016, pp. 1–4. https://doi.org/10.1109/NCVPRIPG.2015.7490038.

42. Yamamoto, Y., Arakawa, F., Fujii, A., Fukuma, S., Mori, S.I.: An multi-client web-based interactive HCI for interactive supercomputing. In: Proceedings - 20th IEEE/ACIS International Conference on Software Engineering, Artificial Intelligence, Networking and Parallel/Distributed Computing, SNPD 2019, Jul 2019, pp. 461–465. https://doi.org/10.1109/SNPD.2019.8935648

43. Krasowski, N., Beier, T., Knott, G.W., Koethe, U., Hamprecht, F.A., Kreshuk, A.: Improving 3D em data segmentation by joint optimization over boundary evidence and biological priors. In: Proceedings - International Symposium on Biomedical Imaging, Jul 2015, vol. 2015–July, pp. 536–539. https://doi.org/10.1109/ISBI.2015.7163929

44. Huang, W., Fang, F., Ma, X., Dong, Z., Xu, X.: Development of HCI management software for automatic medical analyzers. In: Proceedings of the 2015 10th IEEE Conference on Industrial Electronics and Applications, ICIEA 2015, Nov 2015, pp. 2030–2035. https://doi.org/10.1109/ICIEA.2015.7334447

45. Shohieb, S.M., El-Rashidy, N.M.: A proposed effective framework for elderly with dementia using data mining. In: 2018 International Seminar on Research of Information Technology and Intelligent Systems, ISRITI 2018, Nov 2018, pp. 685–689. https://doi.org/10.1109/ISRITI.2018.8864331

46. Nayak, S., Panda, S.K., Uttarkabat, S.: A Non-contact Framework based on Thermal and Visual Imaging for Classification of Affective States during HCI (2020). https://doi.org/10.1109/ICOEI48184.2020.9142883

47. Montenegro, J.M.F., Argyriou, V.: Gaze estimation using EEG signals for HCI in augmented and virtual reality headsets. In: Proceedings - International Conference on Pattern Recognition, Jan 2016, pp. 1159–1164. https://doi.org/10.1109/ICPR.2016.7899793

48. Ferguson, R., Crist, E., Moffatt, K.: A framework for negotiating ethics in sensitive settings: hospice as a case study: Table 1. Interact. Comput. **29**(1), 10–26 (2017). https://doi.org/10.1093/iwc/iww018

49. Heyer, C.: Designing for coping. Interact. Comput. **30**(6), 492–506 (2018). https://doi.org/10.1093/iwc/iwy025

50. Sucala, M., Ezeanochie, N.P., Cole-Lewis, H., Turgiss, J.: An iterative, interdisciplinary, collaborative framework for developing and evaluating digital behavior change interventions. Transl. Behav. Med. **10**(6), 1538–1548 (2020). https://doi.org/10.1093/tbm/ibz109

51. Kess Asikhia, O., Setchi, R., Hicks, Y., Walters, A.: Conceptual framework for evaluating intu-
    itive interaction based on image schemas. Interact. Comput. **27**(3), 287–310 (2015). https://
    doi.org/10.1093/iwc/iwu050
52. Hespanhol, L., Tomitsch, M.: Strategies for intuitive interaction in public urban spaces.
    Interact. Comput. **27**(3), 311–326 (2015). https://doi.org/10.1093/iwc/iwu051
53. Dahl, Y., et al.: Stakeholder attitudes toward and values embedded in a sensor-enhanced
    personal emergency response system. Interact. Comput. **28**(5), 598–611 (2016). https://doi.
    org/10.1093/iwc/iwv036
54. Ince, I.F., Erdem, Y.S., Bulut, F., Sharif, M.H.: A low-cost pupil center localization algorithm
    based on maximized integral voting of circular Hollow Kernels. Comput. J. **59**(3), 1001–1015
    (2019). https://doi.org/10.1093/comjnl/bxy102
55. Doush, I.A., Alshatnawi, S., Al-Tamimi, A.K., Alhasan, B., Hamasha, S.: ISAB: integrated
    indoor navigation system for the blind. Interact. Comput. **29**(2), 181–202 (2017). https://doi.
    org/10.1093/iwc/iww016
56. Abbas, S., Khan, M.A., Athar, A., Shan, S.A., Saeed, A., Alyas, T.: Enabling smart city with
    intelligent congestion control using hops with a hybrid computational approach. Comput. J.
    (2020). https://doi.org/10.1093/comjnl/bxaa068
57. Lazar, J., et al.: Human-computer interaction and international public policymaking: a frame-
    work for understanding and taking future actions. Found. Trends Human-Comput. Interact.
    9(2), 69–149 (2015). https://doi.org/10.1561/1100000062
58. Kaptelinin, V.: Technology and the givens of existence: toward an existential inquiry frame-
    work in HCI research. In: Conference on Human Factors in Computing Systems - Proceedings,
    Apr 2018, vol. 2018–April. https://doi.org/10.1145/3173574.3173844
59. Schneider, H., Eiband, M., Ullrich, D., Butz, A.: Empowerment in HCI - a survey and frame-
    work. In: Conference on Human Factors in Computing Systems - Proceedings, Apr. 2018,
    vol. 2018–April. https://doi.org/10.1145/3173574.3173818
60. Mulder, I.: A pedagogical framework and a transdisciplinary design approach to innovate
    HCI education, pp. 68–70, 1377. Accessed 21 May 2021. [Online]. http://pure.tudelft.nl/ws/
    portalfiles/portal/5506483/A_pedagogical_framework.pdf
61. McLaughlin, A.C., Matalenas, L.A., Coleman, M.G.: Design of human centered augmented
    reality for managing chronic health conditions. In: Aging, Technology and Health, pp. 261–
    296. Elsevier, Amsterdam (2018)
62. Gonçalves, T.G., Loslever, P., de Oliveira, K.M., Kolski, C.: Investigating agreement among
    HCI researchers about human-computer interaction in CMMI-DEV model: a case study.
    Interact. Comput. **32**(1), 81–100 (2020). https://doi.org/10.1093/iwc/iwaa006
63. Vaca-Cardenas, L., Avila-Pesantez, D., Vaca-Cardenas, M., Meza, J.: Trends and challenges of
    HCI in the new paradigm of cognitive cities (2020). https://doi.org/10.1109/ICEDEG48599.
    2020.9096845

Planning a Virtual Tour to a Research Center as an Educational Resource

Ana Sofia Nogueira[1,3](✉) (iD), Joana Fernandes[1,3] (iD), António Vieira de Castro[2,3] (iD), and Sílvia Araújo[1,3] (iD)

[1] University of Minho, 4710-057 Braga, Portugal
sofia.1998@live.com.pt, saraujo@ilch.uminho.pt
[2] ISEP - P.Porto, 4200-072 Porto, Portugal
avc@isep.ipp.pt
[3] Research Group - SIIS, Braga, Portugal

Abstract. This paper aims to explain how virtual tours are an important resource that can bring students closer to science, by allowing them to visit research centers and laboratories – not only from their country, but also internationally – without requiring their physical presence. This technology enables them to see places they would not be able to visit because of either distance or other impediments, but also spaces that even in a physical visit they wouldn't be able to enter, such as the cleanroom, which are highly monitored and controlled environments that can only be seen from the outside on a normal school visit. A virtual tour allows the students to see up close what goes on inside these rooms as well as the equipment used there, while also having access to more information than they would on a physical visit. This form of remote visit combined with the potential of gamification as a pedagogical strategy can be an innovative way to teach science and engage students.

We will explore the processes of developing a gamified and interactive 360° virtual tour for a research center, as an educational tool for students that communicates science in a strategic, enjoyable, and interactive way. For this purpose, the virtual tour created will be of the International Iberian Nanotechnology Laboratory [INL], leading international organization in Europe in the fields of nanotechnology and nanoscience.

Keywords: Virtual tour · Interactive tour · Educational tool · Gamification · Strategic science communication

1 Contextualization

Education has always been fundamental so that future generations can put into practice the knowledge acquired by their predecessors. The practices have varied over the years evolving in methodological terms, however, a huge technological evolution and the widespread use of the internet in recent years has significantly altered the way of teaching and learning. This allowed for a more digital and interactive experience for students to showcase their full potential in new learning environments.

© Springer Nature Switzerland AG 2021
T. Guarda et al. (Eds.): ARTIIS 2021, CCIS 1485, pp. 158–168, 2021.
https://doi.org/10.1007/978-3-030-90241-4_13

1.1 The Importance of Educational Visits

According to Shakil et al. [1], a field trip or excursion is a journey by a group of people to a place away from their normal environment. The purpose of the trip is usually observation for education, non-experimental research or to provide students with experience outside their everyday activities. Field trips give them a chance to get out of the classroom and experience something new, which is necessary for their educational level.

Educational visits allow students to have real-world contact and different experiences, as well as increase student interest, knowledge, and motivation [2].

Many researchers have investigated knowledge gain and learning that occurred during field trips. Normally, as referred by Nadelson & Jordan [3], students who directly participate during a field experience generate a more positive attitude towards the core subject of the trip.

1.2 The Problem

We identified that in Portugal, there is still little affluence to higher education in scientific and technological areas. This fact may be related to the lack of interest of students in these areas, or due to the difficulty in the core subjects to access these degrees [4].

For this reason, we placed our target audience in the 8th and 11th grades since it's in this age gap that the students will have to make decisions regarding their academic future.

1.3 Our Goals

As a main goal, we expect to be able to successfully map out relevant areas previously selected of the INL and, from there, create a virtual tour of the building.

Moreover, we will be interviewing the scientists that work at the institute to acquire information about their areas of research and about each laboratory/division, that will later be gamified into the virtual tour in the form of hotspots, – which will be turned into either interactive videos, text, images, videos, quizzes, or other game-based elements – that enable the users to further explore their surroundings while making the tour more interactive.

As a consequential goal or outcome, we expect our target audience – mainly teenagers from 8th to 11th grades – to expand their interest in science by learning it in a nonconventional and entertaining way, while also making a real research center and its scientists more easily approachable to them.

Through science communication we hope to awaken, in the younger audiences, one or more of the personal responses to science or, as it's referred to in [5], the vowel analogy: Awareness, Enjoyment, Interest, Opinion, and Understanding, as well as Interaction, or activities of contact, and Action, seen as behavior or attitudes [6]. Using specifically strategic science communication as a tool, we aim to present science as a popular and attractive subject, thus drawing students to scientific fields of study, in particular the INL.

2   Methodology

The virtual tour we intend to make will be based on the research center focused on nanotechnology, the INL. This virtual field trip, aimed at young students, has the potential to become a powerful educational tool with activities that allow the transmission of scientific knowledge to the tour's participants.

2.1   The INL

The International Iberian Nanotechnology Laboratory [INL][1] is a leading international organization in Europe in the fields of nanotechnology and nanoscience and it was founded by the governments of Portugal and Spain.

Created in 2008 in Braga, Portugal, this intergovernmental organization fosters inter-disciplinary research, develops a variety of projects based on pioneer research focused on six main areas that complement each other: Environment, Health, Energy, Food, Information and Communication Technology and Future Emerging Technologies.

Scientists and engineers from all over the world – about 40 countries – work in a highly interdisciplinary environment and strive to make INL become a world-wide hub for the deployment of nanotechnology addressing society's grand challenges [7].

2.2   Description of a Physical Visit to INL

The INL hosts restricted visits to its premises, aimed to increase and foster public engagement, communicate science, and promote their work and research. They take place on pre-selected dates, throughout the school year [from October to June] and have a total duration of 2 h.

These visits are intended for students of universities and high schools where the field of study is science and technology from the 10th to 12nd grade. The requests for these visits must be made at least one month in advance and the students need to be at least 15 years old to attend them.

The tours obey the following script:

1. Cleanroom side corridor;
2. Staircase to level -2;
3. High Accuracy laboratory;
4. Staircase to level 0;
5. Walk through P0 Main Open Space Corridor and Stop at the middle lobby;
6. Staircase Area B level 0 to level 1;
7. Walk through P1 open space along PI labs;
8. Bio Labs facility;
9. Staircase Area C level 1 to level 0.

Information about the INL, their research and each laboratory are explained to the visitors while they are taking the tour.

---

[1] More information at https://inl.int/.

2.3   Limitations of a Physical Visit

We identified five main problems with the physical visits to INL:

- Starting with the fact that visits are limited to students older than fifteen years old and attending courses in scientific areas.
- Since there are some facilities that are not accessible to the general public they cannot be visited by students. Such spaces include the cleanroom, due to the high-level control of air circulation, and some of the underground laboratories.
- Another limitation identified was the fact that researchers from each of the areas developed in the laboratory are not always on the premises, so that they can explain to visiting students something about a given research area.
- Distance also has its part in the limitations of face-to-face visits, since, for various reasons, it is not always possible for a student, or even a researcher interested in INL as a research place to develop their work, to move to the laboratory.
- Finally, one of the main impulses for this project is the current pandemic situation has prevented many visits from being made, following the rules of the various confinements and social distance.

With the virtual tour, we are trying to create a solution for these problems and limitations, so that the laboratory can be accessed by everyone everywhere at any time.

2.4   Workflow

Before we started to build the virtual tour, we followed four main steps as presented in Fig. 1 below:

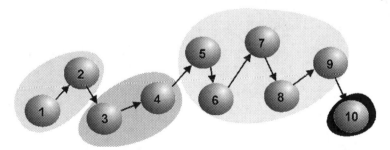

Fig. 1. Planning of the work methodology. (Color figure online)

The grey area represents the planning phase, composed of two main steps:

1. Identifying the problem;
2. Preliminary meetings with INL and dealing with bureaucratic matters;
   The yellow area represents the state of the art:
3. Analysis of similar virtual tours;

4. Identification of technological tools and software to develop the tour;
   The green area represents the steps of the development of the tour:
5. Identification of places of interest for the virtual tour;
6. Capture of photos, videos, and editing;
7. Creation of interactive content;
8. Assembly of the virtual tour;
9. Export of the virtual tour for online distribution.

Finally, the pink area is the phase of tests and validations.

3 Planning and Developing the Virtual Tour

3.1 Bureaucratic Issues and Initial Planning

Given the nature of this project and the fact that it involves an international organization, it was necessary to carry out a series of preliminary meetings with the INL's communications department to identify the possibility of carrying out this visit, explain our objectives and the purposes of our study, and obtain the necessary authorizations.

Throughout these preliminary meetings, the department also provided us with fundamental elements for the planning of the visit, such as the maps of the building, the usual routes in the *in situ* visits and detailed information about the laboratories mentioned in these visits.

After analyzing the information acquired at the meetings, we began to plan the visit and define the educational content that is going to be produced to integrate it. With the help of a representative from the INL communications department, we also proceeded to select the spaces to be mapped out.

3.2 Laboratories and Information

On the table below [Table 1], we list and describe the labs selected to integrate our virtual tour.

Table 1. Table of content of selected INL labs.

Laboratories	Content
Cleanroom [level 0]	High degree of air purity, temperature and pressure; Mostly focused on ICT research; Dressing room equipped with special "clean suits" and a air chamber; Separated into bays, and each bay is dedicated to a specific process; Lithography bay; Bio-bay: a space for biologists to work under cleanroom conditions
High Accuracy Lab [level -2]	Transmission Electron Microscopy [TEM], a tool for structural characterization of materials; X-Ray Photoelectron Spectroscopy [XPS]; Fourier Transform Infra-Red spectroscopy [FTIR system]

(continued)

Table 1. (*continued*)

Laboratories	Content
Dry Labs	Dry labs equipped with compressed air, cooling water and vacuum lines; Small Magnetic Resonance Imaging [MRI] machine; Raman spectroscopy microscope; Hyperthermia
Wet Labs	Water Quality: water monitoring systems, biosensors lab, and the zebrafish room
Central Bio	Molecular biology: detection of nucleic acid; Microbiology

As referred before, the cleanroom is not accessible on physical tours, but we were allowed to integrate it in our visit, which will allow the users to visit this space that we consider an advantage from a live tour.

3.3 Tools and Software

By analyzing similar projects and conducting online research, we narrowed down some software that seemed most fitting for this project. We were mainly looking for software that were free to use and allowed the most customization and gamification possible through its features.

We found the most suitable tool to be *Lapentor*[2], since it offers unlimited free use and freedom for publishing the virtual tour in self or cloud hosting. It enables many customization features: stylish themes, 9 types of interactive hotspots [directional sound, video, link, scene connectors, photo, note, article, lens flare and distorted media], 21 functional plugins and intentional view [to control what should be seen in the virtual tour]. For the treatment of the images, *Nadir Patch*[3] offers free cloud-based tools for patching and stitching 360 photos.

3.4 Initial Preparation of the 360 Photos

Using the Samsung Gear 360 camera[4], we were able to collect all the images necessary for the virtual tour (Fig. 2).

---

[2] Available on https://lapentor.com/.

[3] Available on https://nadirpatch.com/.

[4] Information available on https://www.samsung.com/global/galaxy/gear-360/.

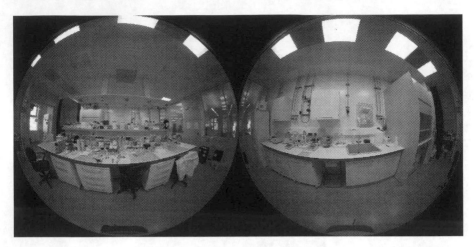

Fig. 2. 360 Photo before stitching.

To stitch the photos together, we used the "Gear 360 Stitching" feature in *Nadir Patch*. We simply uploaded the image we intended to stitch and downloaded the respective equirectangular projection.

Since the tripod that held the camera is noticeable in the bottom of the pictures, we also had to use the "Sphere patching tool" feature. We uploaded the equirectangular projection and a circular logo of the INL, adjusted the size and angle of the logo in order for it to cover the whole tripod, and created the final image (Fig. 3).

Fig. 3. Equirectangular projection of the 360 photo with the INL's logo patched at the bottom.

After all the images are stitched and patched, it is time to upload them into *Lapentor* and start creating the virtual tour (Fig. 4).

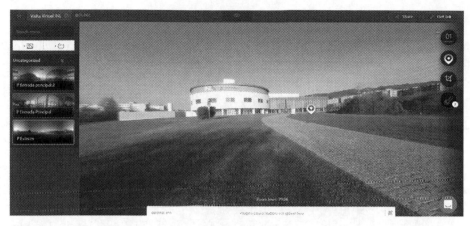

Fig. 4. Editing screen of *Lapentor* with a stitched image of the exterior of INL.

4 Material to Be Integrated into the Visit

Since one of our goals is to make the students more committed to their learning and attentive to the information provided on the tour, we have selected some material to be integrated into the visit. This information will be collected through resources that already exist, as well as interviews with the scientists of INL, that will provide data about the laboratories and the projects developed there.

4.1 Gamification

The term "gamification" first appeared in 2008 and had its origin in the digital media industry but did not gain widespread recognition until approximately 2010 [8]. Despite the term's relatively recent coinage, there seems to be a general agreement about its meaning. Gamification has been defined as the use of game design elements [mechanics, techniques, aesthetics, etc.] in non-game contexts such as finance, health, and education [8]. As referred to by Kapp [9], the goal of incorporating these game design elements into teaching are to motivate students to act, focus on problem solving, promote learning and obtain the motivation that games attain. The author also explains that these elements aim at a greater commitment in the students' own learning, due to issues specific to human psychology, such as the taste for challenges, and desire for recognition and reward.

By incorporating gamification into the virtual tour, it's hoped to obtain the same degree of involvement and motivation in students that would normally be caused by a game. Hence, combining 360° photography and simulated environments with gamification and adaptive learning design can trigger the virtual tour's user's curiosity, resulting in heightened stimulation and a richer and more unique experience, while gaining a deeper understanding of science.

4.2 Gamification Content

In an effort to incorporate didactic and pedagogical content into the virtual visit, a large portion of this project will be the production of interactive content, as well as the adaptation of content that already exists and has been carried out in other projects.

The content we are planning to incorporate on the virtual tour is:

- Timeline of INL's projects

  We will develop a timeline of the projects and research developed in the laboratory, so both students and other audiences will have a clearer perception of the work done in the field of nanotechnology and nanoscience.
- Glossary of scientific terms

  We will proceed to the realization of a glossary of terms related to nanotechnology and nanoscience. This glossary will consist of terms obtained from other pre-existing glossaries on the subject, as well as terms used by the scientists during their interviews, so that we can present students with a learning tool that is as comprehensive as possible.
- Photo gallery of scientists

  The idea of making a gallery with some of the INL scientists and researchers came from the need to make the image of the scientist more approachable to the public, to make people realize that they're not so different from us, and to demystify certain stereotypes.
- Interactive videos

  Using $H5P^5$, a free and open-source content collaboration framework that enables users to easily create and share interactive content, we will enrich the videos we collect from the scientist's interviews, – and others already existent – with questions, true or false, drag and drop, etc. With this, we hope to captivate the student's attention to details and the overall information in the videos and engage them to answer correctly to the questions and get the maximum scores.
- Quizzes

  Much like the interactive videos, the quizzes intend to create a greater involvement and motivation in students by providing a sense of challenge and reward. These quizzes will be created using software such as *Quizziz*[6], *H5P* or *Kahoot*[7].
- Information hotspots

  Information hotspots are the most commonly used forms of gamification in every virtual tour, as it is a feature available in almost all virtual tour creation software. The hotspots allow the tour's creator to easily share information with the user in the form of images, text, audio or video. These hotspots will allow us to insert extra information about the laboratories and its equipment.
- Podcast

  The podcast "NanoCast - Communicating Science with an Accent" [10] was developed as part of the PortLingE academic project in partnership between the INL and the Institute of Arts and Humanities of the University of Minho. In 15 tracks, 15 INL scientists from different nationalities offer insight into their work at the laboratory and

[5] Available on https://h5p.org/.
[6] Available on https://quizizz.com/.
[7] Available on https://kahoot.com/.

answer a few questions in their native tongue. The intimate nature of the questions humanizes scientists and brings them a little closer to younger people, and this is one of the reasons why we will incorporate the podcast in our virtual tour.

5   Validation of the Results

As a method of evaluating the tour's results, we will assess our target audience's scientific literacy by presenting a sample of them with two questionnaires on the matter: one to be answered in an earlier stage of the project, and the second to be answered after their first experience with the virtual tour.

The first questionnaire will enlighten us on their perception of science and gamification in education. The second will let us know if our virtual tour served its purpose as a strategic science communication tool and as a substitute for physical educational visits; and will also give us feedback on the user experience and insight on what can be improved.

Ideally, there would also be a questionnaire to be answered by students who have participated in the physical visits of the laboratory, in order to create a parallel between the two experiences. This would allow us to obtain a more effective feedback on the comparison between the two models and draw better conclusions about their differentiation. However, at the time of writing this article, this is not possible considering the constraints of the COVID-19 pandemic.

6   Conclusions and Future Work

As previously mentioned, field trips with educational purposes are valuable learning tools. When faced with the limitations posed by physical trips, we identified an alternative based on technology, thus giving us the idea of creating a virtual tour of the INL.

With the aforementioned limitations of a physical field trip in mind, we were able to identify the main advantages of a digital version of an educational visit. The fact that, in this way, there are no constraints about scheduling dates or the issue of traveling, and related costs to the place of the visit, is one of the most visible advantages. This will also allow for the exclusive access to spaces that are not available to the public of a physical visit, due to a number of reasons such as the cleanroom's tight air quality control. The interactive videos, podcast and gallery of scientists will also allow room for explanations about the areas by the very scientists that work on them. In essence, a virtual field trip will be accessible any time, any place.

In the future, there must be work done in the matter of accessibility to people with disabilities, such as text to sound features and aid to blind people.

Acknowledgments. This work was carried out within the scope of the "PortLinguE" project (PTDC/LLT-LIG/31113/2017) financed by FEDER under Portugal 2020 and by national funds through Fundação para a Ciência e a Tecnologia, I.P. (FCT, I.P.).

The PortLinguE (More information at http://ceh.ilch.uminho.pt/portlingue/) project is an initiative of the Digital Humanities Group of the Center for Humanistic Studies of the University of Minho. It draws on open access texts, such as those found in scientific repositories, doing justice to the large sums invested in Open Science and in the promotion of Portuguese as a language of scientific communication, in line with European policies on multilingualism. In addition to texts, PortLinguE explores multimodal content, aiming to foster a taste for science in the most diverse audiences, especially the youngest, and also to build bridges between traditionally distant disciplinary areas by blending different angles on science.

We would also like to thank the research group SIIS (More information at www.siis.pt) (Social Innovation and Interactive Systems) for motivating us by integrating us on their research team.

References

1. Shakil, F., Faizi, N., Hafeez, S.: The need and importance of field trips at higher level in Karachi, Pakistan. Int. J. Acad. Res. Bus. Soc. Sci. **2**, 1–16 (2011)
2. Behrendt, M., Franklin, T.: A review of research on school field trips and their value in education. Int. J. Environ. Sci. Educ. **9**(3), 235–245 (2014)
3. Nadelson, L., Jordan, J.: Student attitudes toward and recall of outside day: an environmental science field trip. J. Educ. Res. **105**(3), 220–231 (2012)
4. Carrapatoso, E., Restivo, M.T., Marques, J., Ferreira, A., Cardoso, R., Ferreira Gomes, J.: Motivar os jovens para as áreas da Ciência e Tecnologia Reflexões na Universidade do Porto. In: Global Congress on Engineering and Technology Education, Brazil, pp. 384–387 (2005)
5. Burns, W., O'Connor, J., Stocklmayer, M.: Science communication: a contemporary definition. Publ. Underst. Sci. **12**(2), 183–202 (2003)
6. Ruão, T., Neves, C., Magalhães, R.: Science and strategic communication: how can universities attract high school students? In: Melo, A., Somerville, I., Gonçalves, G. (eds.) Organizational and Strategic Communication Research: European Perspectives II, pp. 111–128. CECS - Centro de Estudos de Comunicação e Sociedade, Universidade do Minho (2015)
7. INL Organisation. https://inl.int/organisation/. Accessed 14 Mar 2021
8. Deterding, S., Dixon, D., Khaled, R., Nacke, L.: From game design elements to gamefulness: defining gamification. In: Proceedings of the 15th International Academic MindTrek Conference: Envisioning Future Media Environments, Finland, pp. 9–15 (2011)
9. Kapp, K.: The Gamification of Learning and Instruction: Game-based Methods and Strategies for Training and Education, 1st edn. Pffeifer, USA (2012)
10. PortLinguE NanoCast. http://ceh.ilch.uminho.pt/portlingue/?page_id=2990. Accessed 15 Mar 2021

Experimental Result Applied to a WISP Network in the Cumbaratza Parish of the Zamora Chinchipe Province

Luis Miguel Amaya Fariño[1]([✉]) [ID], Mónica Karina Jaramillo Infante[1] [ID], Washington Torres[1] [ID], Esther Elizabeth Gonzabay De la A[1] [ID], and Elsy del Roció Villamar Garcés[2] [ID]

[1] State University Santa Elena Peninsula (UPSE), Santa Elena, Ecuador
{mjaramillo,wtorres,egonzabay}@upse.edu.ec
[2] Polytechnic University of Madrid, Madrid, Spain
e.villamar@alumnos.upm.es

Abstract. This report describes the feasibility study that exists in the population of the parish of Cumbaratza, looking for the appropriate methodology to obtain information on the primary data needed on the internet service that is currently provided. This data will be used as a basis, to subsequently propose the solution to the problem, as the design of a wireless service provider, that can be implemented in the future with the best technology and wireless infrastructure, that provides a quality Internet service with an affordable cost, in order to demonstrate the feasibility of the project.

Keywords: Technological advances · Antennas · Radio links · Fresnel zone · Optimal coverage · Line of sight · Wireless services

1 Introduction

Communications have been of great importance since the very beginning of man, since they help to perform many tasks and functions that are necessary in our daily lives. One type of communications is telecommunications, which are remote communications, and within these, radio communications that use the radioelectric space as a physical medium to propagate, carrying the communication information [1].

Radiocommunications have their advantages and disadvantages when making a connection, either because of the area where it is going to be designed and all the factors that intervene in a wireless communication, therefore, the lack of coverage in some parts of the parish of Cumbaratza disappoints to the users, because there are no suppliers interested in these sectors and their needs. Users may be dissatisfied with the service due to delays, poor performance, quality, and in some cases, costs offered by providers [2].

The implementation of the wireless network with services for an optimal quality of coverage and links that are more resistant to the type of climate in each area of Ecuador, requires technological factors, capable of preparing a design in real conditions for a correct implementation both physical and topological. Using a WISP network is preferred

© Springer Nature Switzerland AG 2021
T. Guarda et al. (Eds.): ARTIIS 2021, CCIS 1485, pp. 169–183, 2021.
https://doi.org/10.1007/978-3-030-90241-4_14

since uneven geographic conditions require more power. This type of network is charac-terized by low costs in the installation infrastructure, since it does not require wiring in urbanization areas, trails, historic centers, etc. In addition to the low maintenance cost after network installation [3].

The study to determine the viability of a wireless service provider in Cumbaratza Parish, is very important for the entire population, but especially for the users who are going to use the service. However, it depends a lot on the technology and equipment that they will use in the network infrastructure, above all, the quality of service, the standards to be used, that will result in satisfied customers [4].

2 Materials and Methods

2.1 Software Atoll

Atoll is a comprehensive and intuitive Windows wireless planning environment that supports wireless network operators throughout the entire network lifecycle, from ini-tial design to density and optimization. Atoll is not an engineering tool, but an open, scalable, and flexible technical information system, that can be easily integrated with other IT systems to increase productivity and reduce production times. Atoll supports a wide variety of deployment scenarios, from standalone configurations to enterprise-scale server-based configurations with parallel and distributed processing [5].

2.2 Software Global Mapper

It is a GIS (Geographic Information System) data processing software that contains all kinds of cartography and cartographic information. A powerful and cost-effective GIS application that combines all kinds of spatial data processing tools with access to multiple data formats. Developed for cartographers and GIS professionals, this versatile software is also suitable as a standalone GIS data management tool or as an addition to infrastructure. The Global Mapper contains practically everything needed for a GIS. Complete interoperability with unmatched data support. Easy installation and configu-ration. The perfect balance between the scope of big data processing and ease of use. Unlimited, free, and very affordable technical support [6].

Therefore, according to the SENPLADES projection, by 2020, it has been determined that in Cumbaratza (Fig. 1), a Rural Parish belonging to the Zamora Canton of the Zamora Chinchipe Province, there are 5,310 inhabitants, who due to the current situation have needed having quality internet. However, there is no good Internet Service provider that can provide users with easy access to services and similarly have a broader scope to cover sectors that have never been considered [7].

The parish is located between mountains that reach up to two thousand meters in height and considering that this sector is in the Amazon region, it has extremely abrupt climate changes that can affect communication. These factors can last up to a month, they can even be more extensive, therefore, it must be considered what type of antenna can be used so that these factors do not affect communication and thus, there are no connection lost [8].

The implementation of the wireless network in an urban environment requires factors that can facilitate or influence the normal operation of the network. Using a WISP network is preferred since uneven geographic conditions require more power. This type of network is characterized by low costs in the installation infrastructure, since it does not require wiring in urbanization areas, trails, historic centers, etc. In addition to the low maintenance cost after network installation.

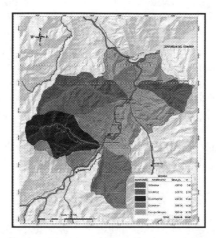

Fig. 1. Geographical location of Cumbaratza (Source [8])

This project has a viable, legal and above all economic technique, the technology that uses a WISP network, since being an irregular geographic location, it needs more powerful power. This type of network is characterized by having a lower cost in the installation infrastructure, since it does not require the need to wire urbanization areas, promenade, historic center, etc. In addition to the low maintenance cost once the network is installed, the infrastructure is adequate to achieve quality of service.

The main advantage of the system that has been chosen, lies in the increase in the number of addresses available. In the same way, it has other additional benefits that make it more innovative. As well as the new packaging system you have an improvement in the addressing, that allows people to create much more efficient networks. It also allows the auto configuration of addresses, thanks to the messages between routers and can even perform the multicast very efficiently, allowing the sender to deliver a flow data to multiple recipients at the same time only once.

It must be emphasized, that telecommunications help social and economic development in any part of the world, since its technological advance opens the doors to systems that have new and interesting voice, video, data services; in which the internet has become in the most effective, cheap, and reliable means for communication, giving itself an essential part for life.

An analysis of a radio link system is necessary for effective signal reception. For this, the use, and specifications of the most important elements of the radio link have to be explained and thus achieve the objectives of the project, A wireless link in the Cumbaratza Parish.

3   Network Topologies and Radio Link

Network topology refers to various communication structures that allows to organize a network that transfers data between devices. For automated components like sensors, actuators, programmable controllers, and robots, they need to exchange information and be physically linked according to a particular structure [9].

It is any interconnection between the different telecommunications terminals used by electromagnetic waves. These radio links are duplex type communications, since they are used to transmit two modulated carrier waves, one is for Transmission and the other for Reception. The frequencies used for each wave are called the radio channel [10].

This type of radio communication system will be located on the earth's surface, and provide the quality, capacity, and availability of information. Radio links usually work between frequencies of 800 MHz and 42 GHz. For the construction of these links, they must be located between points that are visible, that is, they must be at the highest points of the topography [18]. The most important thing in a wireless communication is the transmitting and receiving antenna, but each part that makes the transmission feasible must also be considered.

3.1   Antennas

It is a device that was designed to transmit or receive electromagnetic waves from or to free space. Transmitting antennas cause currents to transform into electromagnetic waves, and receiving antennas do the opposite [11].

The transmitting antenna sends an electromagnetic wave that will be received by the electrical conductor, which is the receiving antenna. This will work as a transducer, since the induction of the OEM in the antenna makes the antenna convert this wave into electrical, and thus the users can interpret it as audio, video, or data (Fig. 2).

Fig. 2. View of a wireless internet antenna (source [12]).

3.2 Cables y Connectors

Many types of cables are used, although they all serve the same purpose, which is to carry information. For radio links it is used to carry data from the switch to the antenna, the most used type of cable is coaxial. These cables are composed of two conductors insulated by a dielectric. There is the core, the wire conductor (copper or aluminum) through which the electrical signal is going to be transmitted. Then, the dielectric, this isolates the two conductors, so that there are no short circuits. They are surrounded by a metallic mesh that protects the signals from noise and distortions. And finally, it is covered on the outside by rubber or plastic, this helps protect from humidity or external electromagnetic interference [17].

This type of cable was designed to carry high-frequency and high-speed signals over long distances, without affecting interference from any external signal. And for this design the RG8 will be used.

Perhaps it can be observed that the use of connectors is very simple, however, this is complicated since there is no regulation that says or specifies how the connectors should be. So, given the situation, there are many different models of connectors.

The type N male connector is the most used in 2.4 GHz and 5 GHz antennas. This type of connector works perfectly with frequencies up to 10 GHz. It is screw type, it is a suitable size, and there is sometimes confusion with UHF connectors. The difference between these two is that UHF cannot be used for 2.4 GHz frequencies. For the connectors used in the cables that are going to be used, there is the RJ49, these have a physical interface that is normally used that are used for this type of cable, it has a meta coating, which is used to ground the equipment of transmission that are in the high part of the tower [19].

3.3 Mast y Equipment Protection

When the antennas are installed, there is the big problem of not having the right place for it, for which a support is required. This bracket allows to hold the antenna and keep it in the given direction. It is not part of the communication, but it is of great importance to improve the range, since it allows to modify the height of the antenna, and thus avoid obstacles.

Components that are part of the wireless link often operate in extremely high ambient temperatures, so protecting the equipment is critical. Since the transmitting and receiving equipment is located at the top of the infrastructure and the electrical control equipment is located at the bottom, two types of cabinets or boxes are required to protect it. The most suitable solution is to use closed cabinets for wireless transmission equipment and metal cabinets for electrical components. This provides the required security for the device and brings convenience to the operational user [20].

3.4 Direct Line of Sight

The term line of sight is often abbreviated as LOS (an acronym for Line of Sight), but if point B can be seen from point A, where it can be seen directly, visible light can be easily understood. Its width is explained by the concept of Fresnel zone.

Therefore, the path is long and there is a phase transition between the direct and indirect rays. If the phase shift is of all wavelengths, constructive interference is achieved, and the signal is optimally synthesized. Following this approach and doing the calculations there is an annular region around the line from A to B that contributes to the destination of the B signal [14].

Note that there are many Fresnel regions, but zone 1 is not dominant. When blocked by obstacles such as trees and buildings, the signal to distant destinations will weaken. Therefore, when planning a wireless connection, it's needed to make sure that there are no obstacles in this area. In fact, in wireless networks, you are happy that the first Fresnel zone is not at least 60% (Fig. 3).

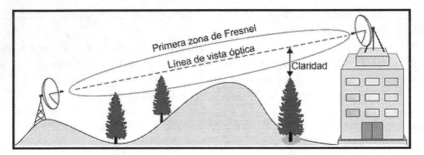

Fig. 3. Fresnel zone

For the design of the project, we used an Antenna PE51YA1005 for transmission. The HyperLink PE51YA1005 (Fig. 4) closed radome yagi antenna features high gain and 30° beamwidth. It is ideal for IEEE 802.11a/n directional and multipoint wireless LAN and WiFi applications and other systems operating in the 5.8 GHz ISM band (Table 1).

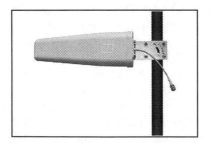

Fig. 4. Antenna PE51YA1005

Table 1. Specifications per antenna band

Description	Band	Units
Rank	5725–5825	MHz
Gain	16.5	dBi
Horizontal beam width	30	Grades
Vertical beam width	25	Grades
Maximum input power	100	Watts

Three locations have been considered for the antennas. The Base Station (Fig. 5) with the location: Longitude: 78°50′57,84″W; Latitude: 3°58′53,24″S.

Fig. 5. Cumbaratza downtown

The following antenna, which is in the La Quebrada de Cumbaratza neighborhood (Fig. 6): Longitude: 78°52′27,48″W; Latitude: 4°0′36,13″S.

Fig. 6. La Quebrada

And finally, for the antenna located in the Barrio Chamico (Fig. 7): Longitude: 78°49′21,04″W; Latitude: 3°55′49,95″S.

Fig. 7. Chamico

Once the corresponding values for each antenna have been placed.

Signal Level Coverage of Transmitting Antennas
The received signal strength indicator (RSSI) is a reference scale (called 1 mW) that measures the power level of a signal received from a device on a wireless network (usually WIFI or a mobile phone). The coverage provided by a satellite, commonly called the satellite footprint, corresponds to the land area covered by the transponder, and determines the diameter necessary for the satellite antenna to efficiently receive satellite signals. Different transponders (or groups of transponders) can have different maps because they can be oriented to cover different parts of the world.

Given the different parameters to analyze the coverage of an antenna, as shown in Fig. 8 the area that the antennas reach in the proposed design.

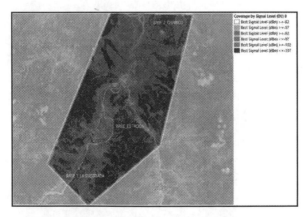

Fig. 8. Signal level coverage of transmitting antennas

Antenna Performance
The efficiency of the transmitting antenna is the ratio between the radiated power and the total power applied to the antenna, which considers the lost power in addition to the radiated power (Fig. 9).

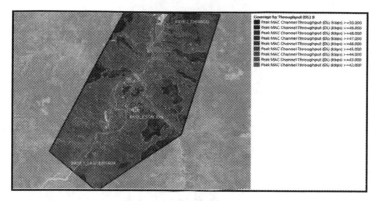

Fig. 9. Antennas performance.

Users per Antennas

Once everything related to the Transmitter Antennas have been designed, repeaters have not been used, since the antenna has a power that reaches what is required.

After it has been defined the users who will acquire the wireless service, Atoll shows a simulation where it can be observed for each antenna the speed and all the parameters that each user has.

The data obtained after starting the simulation is shown at Table 2, Table 3, and Table 4.

Table 2. Users of La Quebrada base

Id	X	Y	Height (m)	Name	User Profile	Terminal	Service	Azimut h (°)	Downti lt (°)	Received Preamble Power (DL) (dBm)	Received Traffic Power (DL) (dBm)	Traffic Total Noise (I+N) (DL) (dBm)	Traffic C/(I+N) (DL) (dB)	Peak MAC Channel Throughput (DL) (kbps)	Received Power (UL) (dBm)	Total Noise (I+N) (UL) (dBm)	C/(I+N) (UL) (dB)	Permutation Zone (UL)
1	78°52'	4°0'52,4	20	Busin	Rooft	FTP D	1,72	-3,41	-66,33	-69,33	-93,17	23,04	38.568,6	-90,27	-103,19	12,92	10 (A
2	78°52'	4°0'29,8	20	Busin	Rooft	FTP D	352,59	-2,82	-66,12	-69,12	-93,17	24,05	38.568,6	-90,06	-102,22	12,16	10 (A
3	78°52'	4°0'29,0	20	Busin	Rooft	FTP D	111,3	-23,55	-67,06	-70,06	-99,19	29,13	9.330,3	-90,19	-103,19	13	10 (A
4	78°52'	3°59'56,	20	Busin	Rooft	FTP D	19,01	-10,3	-63,21	-66,21	-93,17	26,96	38.568,6	-87,15	-99,21	12,06	10 (A
5	78°52'	3°59'57,	20	Busin	Rooft	FTP D	177,76	-9,42	-70,77	-73,77	-99,19	25,42	9.330,3	-90,79	-103,19	12,4	10 (A
6	78°52'	4°0'15,8	20	Busin	Rooft	FTP D	16,63	-5,89	-68,26	-71,26	-93,17	21,91	38.568,6	-92,2	-104,44	12,24	10 (A
7	78°52'	4°0'11,6	20	Busin	Rooft	FTP D	27,44	-5,62	-67,18	-70,18	-93,17	22,99	38.568,6	-91,12	-103,19	12,07	10 (A
8	78°52'	4°0'18,9	20	Busin	Rooft	FTP D	23,33	-5,22	-68,11	-71,11	-93,17	22,05	38.568,6	-92,05	-104,44	12,38	10 (A

Table 3. Users of the station base

Id	X	Y	Height (m)	Name	User Profile	Terminal	Service	Azimut h (°)	Downti lt (°)	Received Preamble Power (DL) (dBm)	Received Traffic Power (DL) (dBm)	Traffic Total Noise (I+N) (DL) (dBm)	Traffic C/(I+N) (DL) (dB)	BLER (DL)	Peak MAC Channel Throughput (DL) (kbps)	Received Power (UL) (dBm)	Total Noise (I+N) (UL) (dBm)	C/(I+N) (UL) (dB)
1	78°52'6,	3°59'18,	5	Bus	Rooft	FTP D	196,05	-3,37	-76,15	-79,15	-99,19	20,04		0	9.330,3	-96,17	-108,24	12,07
2	78°51'59	3°59'36,	5	Bus	Rooft	FTP D	205,88	-5,93	-77,72	-80,72	-99,19	18,47	0	9.330,3	-97,74	-110,46	12,72
3	78°51'55	3°59'15,	5	Bus	Rooft	FTP D	88,99	-9,8	-81,33	-84,33	-99,19	14,86	0,02803	8.293,6	-104,27	-115,23	10,96
4	78°51'56	3°59'33,	5	Bus	Rooft	FTP D	207,22	-5,68	-77,96	-80,96	-99,19	18,23	0,00059	9.330,3	-97,98	-110,46	12,48
5	78°51'49	3°59'18,	5	Bus	Rooft	FTP D	206,77	-5,05	-80,64	-83,64	-99,19	15,55	0,00352	8.293,6	-102,23	-115,23	13
6	78°51'50	3°58'57,	5	Bus	Rooft	FTP D	103,49	-10,16	-81,18	-84,18	-99,19	15,01	0,01868	8.293,6	-104,12	-115,23	11,31
7	78°51'58	3°59'1,9	5	Bus	Rooft	FTP D	98,93	-9,03	-80,08	-83,08	-99,19	16,11	0,08291	9.330,3	-103,02	-115,23	12,21
8	78°51'55	3°59'9,3	5	Bus	Rooft	FTP D	93,64	-9,67	-81,17	-84,17	-99,19	15,02	0,01845	8.293,6	-104,11	-115,23	11,12
9	78°50'27	3°58'30,	5	Bus	Rooft	FTP D	194,76	-12,56	-84,2	-87,2	-99,19	11,98	0,0015	6.220,2	-107,93	-115,23	7,3
10	78°50'57	3°57'36,	5	Bus	Rooft	FTP D	171,08	-7,69	-82,7	-85,7	-99,19	13,49	0	6.220,2	-105,64	-112,22	6,58
11	78°50'59	3°57'31,	5	Bus	Rooft	FTP D	170,17	-7,32	-83,35	-86,35	-99,19	12,64	0	6.220,2	-107,93	-115,23	7,3
12	78°50'49	3°57'44,	5	Bus	Rooft	FTP D	31,93	-4,75	-88,81	-91,81	-99,19	7,38	0,00141	4.146,8	-108,83	-115,23	6,4
13	78°50'51	3°57'41,	5	Bus	Rooft	FTP D	33,32	-4,86	-88,85	-91,85	-99,19	7,34	0,00158	4.146,8	-108,87	-115,23	6,36
14	78°50'55	3°57'32,	5	Bus	Rooft	FTP D	172,16	-7,41	-83,22	-86,22	-99,19	12,97	0	6.220,2	-107,93	-115,23	7,3
15	78°50'44	3°57'53,	5	Bus	Rooft	FTP D	177,9	-9,1	-80,56	-83,56	-99,19	15,63	0,00264	8.293,6	-104,03	-115,23	11,2

Table 4. Users of the Chamico base

Id	X	Y	Height (m)	Name	User Profile	Terminal	Service	Azimuth (°)	Downtilt (°)	Best Server	Received Preamble Power (DL) (dBm)	Received Traffic Power (DL) (dBm)	Traffic Total Noise (I+N) (DL) (dBm)	Traffic C/(I+N) (DL) (dB)	BLER (DL)	Peak MAC Channel Throughput (DL) (kbps)	Received Power (UL) (dBm)	Total Noise (I+N) (UL) (dBm)
1	78°50'31	3°56'42	5	Busin	Rooft	FTP D	43,23	-8,33	Trans	-84,36	-87,36	-99,19	11,83	0,00211	6.220,2	-104,35	-115,23
2	78°50'34	3°56'42	5	Busin	Rooft	FTP D	45,12	-8,13	Trans	-84,6	-87,6	-99,19	11,59	0,00493	6.220,2	-104,62	-115,23
3	78°50'31	3°56'46	5	Busin	Mobil	FTP D	41,65	-7,93	Trans	-85,39	-88,39	-99,31	8,92	0,34034	1.843,5	-115,41	-120
4	78°50'35	3°56'43	5	Busin	Rooft	FTP D	45,03	-7,95	Trans	-84,97	-87,97	-99,19	11,22	0,01862	6.220,2	-104,99	-115,23
5	78°50'30	3°56'39	5	Busin	Rooft	FTP D	44,37	-8,6	Trans	-83,72	-86,72	-99,19	12,47	0	6.220,2	-104,03	-115,23
6	78°50'30	3°55'21	5	Busin	Rooft	FTP D	106,72	-11,76	Trans	-98,24	-101,24	-99,31	-1,93	0	0	-120	-120

Comparison with Radio Mobile Software Simulation

Then, to corroborate the data previously shown, it was proceeded to carry out the simulation in the Radio Mobile software, with the same locations of the antennas and the users. Achieving a clean line of sight with good coverage between each user and antenna, where one of the decisive parameters is the Rx level, that is, the received power level expressed in decibels, since the lower it is, the better the quality of the link (Fig. 10).

Fig. 10. Design in radio mobile

Now, a link is distributed by each sector to cover the entire parish of Cumbaratza (Fig. 11 and Fig. 12).

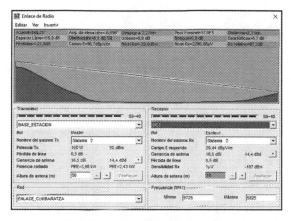

Fig. 11. Link station base to UC1

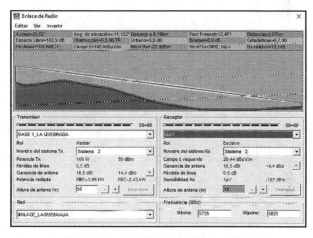

Fig. 12. La Quebrada base link to UQ1

As can be seen, the design could be corroborated by presenting the Atoll software, as Radio Mobile is a very old tool; it only helps to analyze the different designs that may be presented. As conclusion to Atoll, it is that more updated, and allows to be more precise in the characteristics for radio links [2].

4 Results

At Tables 5, 6 and 7 is presented for each station that was in the Cumbaratza parish with the most important data of each radio link obtained through the Radio Mobile software.

---

180   L. M. A. Fariño et al.

Table 5. Station base user measurements

Users	Worst Fresnel	RX Level
UC1	15.4 F1	−39.1 dBm
UC2	9.2 F1	−51.8 dBm
UC3	14.6 F1	−35.8 dBm
UC4	14.9 F1	−36.3 dBm
UC5	12.9 F1	−32.1 dBm
UC6	14.4 F1	−35.2 dBm
UC7	**16.2 F1**	−36.1 dBm
UC8	13.4 F1	*−55.7 dBm*
UC9	15.2 F1	−31.3 dBm
UC10	*7.6 F1*	−39.1 dBm
UC11	9.4 F1	−41.0 dBm
UC12	15.3 F1	−39.6 dBm
UC13	*7.6 F1*	−39.9 dBm
UC14	7.8 F1	−39.5 dBm
UC15	12.2 F1	**−28.7 dBm**

It can be highlighted that among the 15 users, the user registered with the name UC7 will have better coverage compared to the other users, because, at that point, there is a good line of sight, as well as a good coverage evidenced through the level RX. Having its worst Fresnel at 16.2 F1 and RX level at −36.1 dBm.

Table 6. La Quebrada base user measurements

Users	Worst Fresnel	RX level
UQ1	*10.4 F1*	**−26.8 dBm**
UQ2	11.4 F1	−27.0 dBm
UQ3	**19.7 F1**	−27.0 dBm
UQ4	11.3 F1	*−33.1 dBm*
UQ5	12.5 F1	−32.9 dBm
UQ6	15.2 F1	−27.5 dBm
UQ7	13.6 F1	−30.7 dBm
UQ8	18.6 F1	−27.4 dBm

It can be highlighted that, among the 8 users, the user registered with the name UQ3 will have better coverage compared to the other users, because, at that point, there is a good line of sight, as well as a good coverage evidenced through the level RX. Having its worst Fresnel at 19.7 F1 and RX level at −27.0 dBm.

Table 7. Chamico base user measurements.

Users	Worst Fresnel	RX level
UCH1	7.5 F1	−43.6 dBm
UCH2	9.3 F1	−40.5 dBm
UCH3	8.3 F1	−35.7 dBm
UCH4	10.2 F1	−38.5 dBm
UCH5	6.5 F1	−60.6 dBm
UCH6	13.1 F1	−35.9 dBm

It can be highlighted that, among the 6 users, the user registered with the name UCH6 will have better coverage compared to the other users, because, at that point, there is a good line of sight, as well as a good coverage evidenced through the level RX. Having its worst Fresnel at 13.1 F1 and RX level at −35.9 dBm.

Regarding the users who receive coverage from the antennas of each station, it can be mentioned that a good signal reaches all of them, because there is an optimal line of sight between the Base and each user, and it can be done that, evidenced through the worst Fresnel, as well as by the Rx Level, since in the case of the worst Fresnel its values must be higher than 0.6 F1 to be free of obstruction and the Rx Level the closer it is to 0, the better. Fulfilling in each case taken as an example through the Radio Mobile software.

5   Discussion and Conclusions

In this project a WISP network design is carried out in the Cumbaratza parish belonging to the Province of Zamora Chinchipe, considering the main objectives of improving the quality of wireless connection.

Once the analysis and the different studies had been done, difficulties were found to achieve a better quality of connection. This caused the project to have some negative results. Although a suitable choice of antennas was made, and places to locate the transmitting antennas, the radio link was not very acceptable. But good results were also obtained with respect to other users.

Atoll is a tool with great potential in the field of wireless communication technologies, since having a very complex interface has many functionalities that allows to choose the different modules, and thus improve the modeling and simulation process of the design.

In the simulation with the Atoll software, when looking at the spectrum of the signal level radiated by the antennas, an excellent level was observed, but when trying to reach the different users, the opposite was noted.

By not having much information about WISP radio links in the mentioned software, the problems presented could not be solved, however, with the help of another software called Radio Mobile, it allowed to meet the established objectives, and have an acceptable radio communication and thus get better wireless connectivity.

References

1. Huidobro, J.M.: Telecomunicaciones. Ra-Ma, Paracuellos de Jarama (2014). ISBN 9788499642741
2. Ramos Pascual, F., E-Libro, Corp: Radiocomunicaciones. Marcombo, Barcelona (2007). ISBN 1-4492-0960-2
3. Camacho, M.R.M., Jiménez, G.P.Í., Giraldo, H.B.: Red local inalámbrica en la comunidad indígena de Otavalo. Ecuador, 2018. Revista cubana de informática médica **10**(2) (2019)
4. Caisaguano Pérez, P.G.: Diseño y simulación de un WISP Wireless Internet Service Provider para la ciudad de Pedernales en Manabí Ecuador. Bachelor's thesis (2018)
5. Kusmaryanto, S., Sari, S.N., Haromain, I.: Long Term Evolution (LTE) Network Planning at 700 MHz Frequency in Cipali Toll Road Using Atoll Radio Planning Software. In: 2018 Electrical Power, Electronics, Communications, Controls and Informatics Seminar (EECCIS), pp. 218–223. IEEE (2018). https://doi.org/10.1109/EECCIS.2018.8692850, ISBN 153865251X
6. Popovich, V., Schrenk, M., Thill, J., Claramunt, C., Wang, T.: Information Fusion and Intelligent Geographic Information Systems (IF&IGIS'17). Springer, Cham (2017). https://doi.org/10.1007/978-3-319-59539-9, ISBN 9783319595382
7. Tandazo, C.V.G., Galarza, F.Y.P., Benavides, A.V.V.: Digital strategic communication in Ecuador's public organisations Current state and future projection. Revista latina de comunicación social, English ed. **71**(71), 211–231 (2016). https://doi.org/10.4185/RLCS-2016-1092en, ISSN 1138-5820
8. G. p. d. cumbaratza: Microcuencas de la parroquia cumbaratza, Plan De Desarrollo Y Ordenamiento Territorial De La Parroquia Cumbaratza, p. 60, 2015–2019
9. Rocha O'Kelard, G., Toledo, M.: Topologia de Red Segura (2005)
10. Alonso, S., Jesús, J., Mendo Tomás, L.: Simulación del enlace descendente LTE orientada a planificación radio. E.T.S.I. Telecomunicación (UPM), S.l. (2015)
11. Esteban Gómez, J., González Posadas, V., Universidad Politécnica de Madrid Departamento de Teoría de la Señal y Comunicaciones: Diseño y fabricación de antenas de banda ancha para telefonía móvil. J. Esteban Gómez, Madrid (2017)
12. https://wisp.com.mx/uncategorized/internet-inalambrico-a-traves-de-antenas/
13. Vásquez, M.T., Uc, D.A.P.: Analysis and design of communication point for data linking. Pistas Educativas **39**(126) (2017)
14. Quimis Choez, B.J.: Design of a technological infrastructure of category 6 high speed structured cabling under the IEEE 802.3 standard for the telecommunications laboratory of the computer and networks engineering career. Bachelor's thesis, Jipijapa. Unesum (2021)
15. Gómez Martín, J.: Estudio de viabilidad estructural de un soporte para equipos de Telecomunicaciones (2020)
16. Anguera, J., Andújar, A.: Antenas: Elementos Indispensables de las Telecomunicaciones (2018)

17. Sanmartín Núñez, S.: Proyecto de Infraestructuras Comunes de Telecomunicaciones (ICT) para un Edificio de 15 Viviendas en el municipio de Pobla de Vallbona (Valencia). Universitat Politècnica de València, S.l. (2020)
18. Valencia Ramírez, J.R.: Departamento de eléctrica y electrónica y telecomunicaciones
19. Guerra Soto, M.: Interconexión de redes privadas y redes públicas. Ra-Ma Editorial, Madrid (2016). ISBN 9788499646602
20. Martín, P., Fernández, I., Parnás, V.E.: Estudio comparativo de normas para el análisis dinámico de una torre autosoportada bajo carga de viento. Informes de la construcción **70**(552), 274–e274 (2019). https://doi.org/10.3989/ic.15.021, ISSN 0020-0883
21. Sánchez León, M.A., Vargas Cofre, C.E.: Desarrollo de guías para prácticas de laboratorio de la asignatura de comunicaciones inalámbricas. Bachelor's thesis, Quito (2021)
22. Atoll Radio Planning Software Overview (RF Planning and Optimisation) | Forsk. Forsk.com (2021). https://www.forsk.com/atoll-overview

ADDiagnosis: Support Tool for Psychologists in the Diagnosis of Attention Deficit Disorder in Children

Daniel Arias⬭, Camila Calvopiña⬭, and Graciela Guerrero⁽⊠⁾ ⬭

Departamento de Ciencias de La Computación, Universidad de Las Fuerzas Armadas ESPE,
Sangolqui, Ecuador
{daarias10,cmcalvopina,rgguerrero}@espe.edu.ec

Abstract. Currently, Attention Deficit Disorder (ADD) is one of the most common conditions in children, however, there is no technological support tool that facilitates the diagnosis for psychologists. Also, the tools used do not create an interest and entertainment for the patients during their appointment. This article presents the design, development and evaluation of a web application based on a thoughtful game that works as a support tool for psychologists for the diagnosis of children with ADD. The game uses a scoring system based on the decisions that the child makes during its development and their performance in the minigames that are in the game. The psychologist will have the possibility of registering all their patients' scores with a database where the specialist can write down any observations that they have about their patients. The results show that the application has an adequate construction and usability level and that it handles activities according to the stage of development of the patients. Finally, the long-term goal of the application is to expand and support other types of disorders.

Keywords: Attention Deficit Disorder · Psychology · Children · Video game · ADDiagnosis

1 Introduction

Attention Deficit Disorder (ADD) is a disorder of neurobiological origin that starts in childhood and whose symptoms can last into adulthood [1], studies carried out in cultures such as Germany and Puerto Rico have shown that around 5% of the child population, that is 1 in 20 children, is affected by this disorder. ADD has a male predominance of 3 to 1 with respect to women [2]. For this reason, attention problems are more frequently diagnosed during the first year of school. In epidemiological studies with a normal population, teachers reported that almost half of the boys in an average class were distracted and just over a quarter of the girls were distracted as well. In a clinical setting, attention problems prevail over other disorders between 3% and 5% [3]. Many children suffer from such inattention to some extent, but for children with ADD this condition appears to be more serious [4]. The most common symptoms are easy distraction, low understanding of orders and difficulty in organizing. Therefore, inattention suggests that

© Springer Nature Switzerland AG 2021
T. Guarda et al. (Eds.): ARTIIS 2021, CCIS 1485, pp. 184–193, 2021.
https://doi.org/10.1007/978-3-030-90241-4_15

a child may deviate from any type of task showing difficulty with a sustained focus and persistence. However, severity of symptoms tends to decrease with age according to Reddy and Alperin [4].

To make the diagnosis of ADD in children, psychologists usually use a technical sheet that takes around 5 to 10 min [5]. The document is a questionnaire where psychologists evaluate the child according to their decision. This method could be an unattractive activity from the perspective of the patients, making them feel bored and even more distracted, tired or stressed. For this reason, the development of a web application for diagnosing children with ADD that generates attraction is relevant. The creation of this application will be supported by an interactive game with which the child's decisions can be measured to define whether or not he suffers or not of this disorder.

The objective of this article proposes to develop a web application based on video games as a working tool for psychologists in the diagnosis of ADD in children between 8 and 13 years of age. To obtain a correct functioning of this application, working with professionals in the area of psychology is important. Psychologists, who through their support, will establish both symptoms and qualities to take into account in the diagnosis of children with ADD.

The article is structured as follows: Sect. 2, the related works for the diagnosis of ADD symptoms in children through the use in applications are established; Sect. 3 methodology for the implementation of the application; Sect. 4 Research evaluation and design; Sect. 5 Results and Future Work.

2 Related Works

Four relevant databases were consulted for the related works section: IEEE, ACM, PubMed and Scopus. The search was made up of: (Attention Deficit Disorder OR ADD) AND Psychology AND (Children OR Kids) AND (videogames OR games) including a filter of the last 5 years. When executing the search, different numbers of articles were obtained from each one of them, making a total of 6879. However, for the present research work, only 13 articles were considered for their title, abstract and keywords.

Gomes et al. [1] say that attention deficit hyperactivity disorder has been one of the most studied issues in school-age children, where gamification is a strategy used as a treatment for children suffering from this deficit. Thus, this work aims to present software guidelines for the design of gamified educational technologies to patients with this deficit.

To ensure the importance of the use of games for the diagnosis of ADHD, Bahana et al. [6] states that the gaming industry has become one of the fastest growing industries in the world. In recent years, several studies have been carried out that have used games, especially computer-based games, to improve the executive function of children with ADHD. Especially in the improvement of working memory, in terms of evaluation Peñuelas-Calvo et al. [7] states that gamification and cognitive training could be the main mechanisms underlying the usefulness and efficacy as tools. Sanchez-Morales et al. [8] argue that the use of serious games and interactive interfaces for the detection and therapy of problems related to learning has helped to obtain better results.

On the other hand, Colombo et al. [9] describe the planning of another serious game (SG) for the improvement of attention skills in children with ADHD to promote learning and autonomous management of impulsive behaviors and inhibit irrelevant thoughts. Antonyms consists of three mini- games in a single frame and is designed for educational and rehabilitation settings. To avoid a monotonous and uncomfortable environment for children in a hospital Chen et al. [10] propose a system, called COSA, to support the auxiliary diagnosis of ADHD, which is based on the Diagnostic and Statistical Manual of Mental Disorders (DSM-V). COSA assesses ADHD symptoms using three serious game-based contexts. At the same time, multidimensional data is acquired during the tests, including physiological data, motion data and task-related data. The effectiveness and acceptability of COSA are verified through questionnaires for doctors, parents and children. Additionally, Delgado-Gómez et al. [11] proposes a video game called "running raccoon" to assess the severity of inattention in patients diagnosed with ADHD. The proposed tool is an authentic video game in which the patient must make a raccoon avatar jump to avoid falling into different holes. The results obtained, together with the characteristics of the video game, make it an excellent support tool for clinicians in the treatment of ADHD. Another of the serious games that was proposed by Wrońska et al. [12] is a software system with new interaction mechanisms with the aim of improving memory and attention in children with ADHD. The system is based on a set of collaborative games whose interaction with the system is very intuitive and simple, since children interact directly with physical objects instead of using input devices. By using this method, children can play while moving around the room and interact with the games that are projected on the wall.

De la Guía et al. [3] in a social context, using economic games examined the role of individual differences in decision-making related to reward, specifically, the roles of sensitivity to reward and prosocial skills. The results suggest that instead of not understanding the perspective of others, children and adolescents with ADHD were less motivated by justice than controls in simple social situations. The results encourage the use of inexpensive games in ADHD research.

Finally, Hocine Nadia [13] mentions that serious games can provide children the appropriate guidance to develop their self-regulation skills while improving their cognitive functions, such as attention.

3 Design and Implementation

This section describes the design of the proposed architecture for the development of the proposed video game, which is hereinafter called ADDiagnosis, which consists of the development of a serious game. Describes the proposed implementation to meet the objective, which is to provide a support tool for psychologists and through this to diagnose a child between 8 to 13 years of age whether he or she suffers from ADD (attention deficit disorder).

3.1 Architecture Design

As shown in Fig. 1, communication with the application depends on the type of user that is manipulating it, i) the psychologist will be able to access the login/register of the platform. Once inside, the psychologist will have access to the results of each and every one of the patients diagnosed, ii) the patient will have access solely and exclusively to the video game, guided by the psychologist.

Figure 1 shows that the application in question is made in HTML5, as it offers many tools to create clean and optimized code. In addition to the multiple compatibility between browsers and HTML5. It provides a friendly and intuitive navigation to the user. The JS and CSS languages will be used within the HTML; in the realization of the video game for the application, the RPG MAKER MV video game engine was chosen, this tool, in addition to having a relatively low learning curve, allows to implement rpg-type games on the web platform with a wide variety of tools and events, making it easier for the developer to program the video game; For the connection with the application database, the PHP language was used due to the simplicity of both its syntax and architecture, and its easy access and integration with the database service. Finally, the DBMS considered is MySQL because it has a multiplatform system that does not require a very specialized maintenance for the administration of its databases.

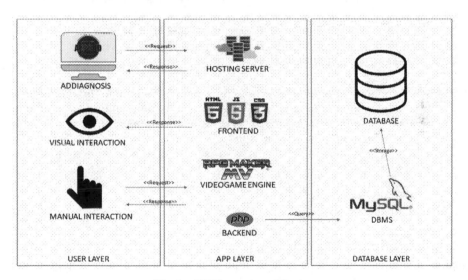

Fig. 1. ADDiagnosis architecture

3.2 Implementation

The implementation of the video game is based on the analysis of research work carried out previously and is divided into four phases: analysis, design and development.

Analysis. The analysis is an important phase in the development of a game. By carrying out a detailed analysis, this will ensure a good planning of resources and time. This analysis must provide brief and clear information (Table 1), which details the requirements and the place where the game will be implemented.

Table 1. Requirements ADDiagnosis application

Requirements	Description
Functional	Software (RPG Maker MV, Html5, CSS, JavaScript, Php, MySql) Hardware (Laptop, Desktop)
Non-functional	Interface (Colors according to color psychology) Character and map design
Environment	Clinical Environment
User	Graphic interface

Design. The relevant aspects provided by this tool to meet the specified objective. Aspects such as: the color of the interface was chosen based on the psychology of colors [14], where blue represents the clinical family and cleanliness; The game design type is 2D Role-Playing Game (RPG) as it is a very familiar interface with children to get their attention and centralize their focus.

Developing. For the development, the database was designed in Power Designer where the Script to create was extracted. For the preliminary tests of the application, the Apache web server was used within the Xamp tool with which it was possible to have access to a local host (localhost) and connection to MySQL. The PhpMyAdmin database manager was used.

The development of the interface was worked with HTML, CSS and JS; With PHP, on the other hand, session management was used to provide security to the application, and it was used as a direct connector with the MySQL database. The data obtained from both the pertinent psychologist and the patients were registered for the video game, RPGMAKERMV was the preferred tool, since, as mentioned above, it provides countless facilities to the programmer, from its learning curve to its multi-platform deployment. The main interface of the application where the record of each one of the patients diagnosed with the serious game is shown in Fig. 2. The psychologist will be able to enter said interface through a logging and registration system.

Fig. 2. Serious 2D RPG game design. Own source

First, both scenarios and characters were created to be related and ordered regarding the development of the story. Once it has been done, validations, events and establishment of diagnostic scores will be generated for the patients. For the resolution of the video game, the patient must consider the indications that are given along, such as following the correct path, pressing the indicated keys, among others.

4   Evaluation and Results

This section will focus on the evaluation design with the different scenarios that were proposed and on certain corrections that were made for a better functioning of the application, all regarding feedback based on questionnaires and suggestions.

4.1   Evaluation Design

The scenarios will be evaluated as follows; the interface of the application, that is, the web environment will be evaluated by professionals within the area of psychology and by experts in HCI. This way, the functionality and usability will be evaluated; this must be measured by means of a SUS questionnaire [15]. On the other hand, the video game design will be the main evaluation tool for children between 8 and 13 years of age, which can be used to diagnose ADD deficit or not, with the implementation of a score based on minigames and decision-making.

Scenarios. The study of scenarios will be carried out to verify the functionality and usability of the web application, for which the scenarios defined below will be taken (Table 2): i) Professionals in psychology: Professionals will diagnose and evaluate the patients according to the game and the score. The specialist will determine a good functioning; ii) HCI experts: It consists of two HCI experts evaluating the interface that is displayed to professionals; and iii) Children between 8 and 13 years old: It consists of children already diagnosed using the video game incorporated into the web application to verify its veracity.

Table 2. Description of proposed scenarios

No. Scenario	Task	Activity	Description	Objective
Activities Professionals in psychology	1	Login/Register at applicative	The psychologist must log in or register in the application	Ensure the correct weighting of scores for patients who are evaluated by the videogame
	2	Registration/Update patient	The psychologist must register a new patient or update the data of an existing one	
	3	Video game test	The psychologist must test the video game to verify that the weightings are applied correctly	
Activities Experts in HCI	1	Login/Register at applicative	The expert must log in or register in the applicative	Check the Right functioning, validation and usability of web application
	2	Registration/Update patient	The expert must register a new patient or update the data from an existing one	
Activities for children between 8 and 13 years old	1	Video game test	The child must play and complete the video game to be able to evaluate it	Evaluate the possibility of disease or not of the disorder attention deficit (TDA)

4.2 Results

The results of the different scenarios were obtained, where each of them is detailed below.

In the Scenario 1 A SUS type usability questionnaire was carried out to professionals in the field of psychology, the game scores and the notes of each patient were reviewed in detail with the help of the clinical psychologist (Table 3).

According to the survey that was carried out, it can be concluded that 86.67% of the respondents liked the application, and 93.33% agree that it is easy to use.

Table 3. .

Question	Professional 1	Professional 2	Professional 3
I think I would like to use this frequently applicative	5 (100%)	4 (80%)	4 (80%)
I found the application unnecessarily complex	2 (40%)	4 (80%)	2 (40%)
I thought it was easy to use the application	3 (60%)	5 (100%)	5 (100%)
I think I would need the support of an expert to go through the application	2 (40%)	4 (60%)	1 (20%)
I found the various possibilities of application quite well integrated	5 (100%)	4 (80%)	4 (80%)
I thought there was too much inconsistency in the application	3 (60%)	2 (40%)	2 (40%)
I imagine that most people would learn very quickly to use the applicative	4 (80%)	5 (100%)	5 (100%)
I found the application very large when walk it	2 (40%)	4 (80%)	2 (40%)
I felt very confident in handling the applicative	5 (100%)	3 (60%)	2 (40%)
I need to learn many things before being handled in the application	3 (60%)	1 (20%)	1 (20%)

On the other hand, in scenario 2 the same SUS type usability questionnaire was carried out to the HCI experts (Table 4), where guidelines and corrections were established regarding the design and usability of the application in question, especially in the intuitive part of it. The results obtained were the following.

Finally, rcfcrring to scenario 3, the percentages that represent the evaluation of 20 children with an age range of 8 to 13 years can be seen where the application diagnosed 14 children with a negative and 6 with a possible case of ADD, from these results and with the help of the clinical psychologist. It was determined that one of the children (1%) has a mild feature of attention deficit hyperactivity disorder ADHD, the other 5 (25%) children have a cognitive problem, and the remaining 14 (70%) children do not present behaviors out of step with their developmental stage.

Table 4. SUS HCI expert survey.

Question	Expert 1	Expert 2
I think I would like to use this frequently applicative	5 (100%)	4 (80%)
I found the application unnecessarily complex	2 (40%)	3 (60%)
I thought it was easy to use the application	4 (80%)	3 (60%)
I think I would need the support of an expert to go through the application	5 (100%)	4 (80%)
I found the various possibilities of application quite well integrated	5 (100%)	4 (80%)
I thought there was too much inconsistency in the applicative	2 (40%)	3 (60%)
I imagine that most people would learn very quickly to use the applicative	2 (40%)	4 (80%)
I found the application very large when I went through it	5 (100%)	3 (60%)
I felt very confident in handling the applicative	5 (100%)	4 (80%)
I need to learn many things before being handled in the application	5 (100%)	3 (60%)

5   Conclusions and Future Work

In this research, a web application was designed, developed and evaluated whose purpose is to be a support tool for psychologists in the diagnosis of children with Attention Deficit Disorder ADD, where the possibility or not of suffering from said disorder will be displayed by means of the score obtained in a serious game, based on the results and decisions of the children.

In the related works, it is observed that most of the applications made for this type of disorders are serious games with an educational approach. However, for project reasons, a clinical approach has been decided, without departing from the objective that is to facilitate the task of the psychologist to diagnose your patients.

At the end of the evaluation of the application, the results corresponding to the SUS questionnaire were obtained, which when processed and speaking in general terms, both those carried out by psychologists and those carried out by HCI experts, presented positive results, indicating that users feel comfortable and find it easy to use the application.

The results of the video game, evaluated in children between the ages of 8 and 13 years of age, indicate positive results regarding the possible condition. However, there are elements at the scoring level that improved because in certain minigames the subtracted score was not adequate either because it was not in accordance with the stage of development of the children or because it did not consider a balance between attention and hyperactivity. However, these considerations were verified and corrected in a timely manner.

ADDiagnosis was initially developed to determine the possibility of suffering from Attention Deficit Disorder ADD through the development of a children's story in a video game. However, the possibility of support for psychologists in other types of conditions has been raised thanks to the existence of an open ending in said story, giving the opportunity to create new adventures with the same protagonist whose scores reveal the probable existence of another disorder.

References

1. Gomes, T., dos Santos, W., Marques, L., da Silva Brito, P.H., Bittencourt, I.: Software requirements for the design of gamified applications for time management and tasks for children and adolescents with ADHD. In: Proceedings of the XV Brazilian Symposium on Information Systems, Brasil (2019)
2. Fernández, A.A.: Niños con déficit de atención e hiperquinesis (TDA/H). Revista Latinoamericana de Psicología **36**(1), 47–58 (2004)
3. De la Guía, E., Lozano, M., Penichet, V.: Educational games based on distributed and tangible user interfaces to stimulate cognitive abilities in children with ADHD. Br. J. Educ. Technol. **46**(3), 664–678 (2015)
4. Reddy, L., Alperin, A.: Children with attention-deficit/hyperactivity disorder. In: Handbook of Child and Adolescent Group Therapy, pp. 344–356 (2016)
5. Ferré, A., Narbona, J.: Escalas para la evaluación del trastorno por déficit de atención con hiperactividad, no. 3. Publicaciones de Psicología Aplicada (2000)
6. Bahana, R., et al.: Performance test for prototype game for children with ADHD. In: Journal of Physics: Conference Series, vol. 978, no. 1, p. 012004 (2018)
7. Peñuelas-Calvo, I., et al.: Video games for the assessment and treatment of attention-deficit/hyperactivity disorder: a systematic review. Eur. Child Adolesc. Psychiatry, 1–16 (2020).https://doi.org/10.1007/s00787-020-01557-w
8. Sánchez-Morales, A., Martínez-González, C., Cibrian, F., Tentori, M.: Interactive interface design for the evaluation of attention deficiencies in preschool children. In: Proceedings of the 7th Mexican Conference on Human-Computer Interaction, Mexico (2018)
9. Colombo, V., Baldassini, D., Mottura, S., Sacco, M., Crepaldi, M., Antonietti, A.: A serious game for enhancing inhibition mechanisms in children with Attention Deficit/Hyperactivity Disorder (ADHD). In: International Conference on Virtual Rehabilitation (ICVR) (2017)
10. Chen, Y., Zhang, Y., Jiang, X., Zeng, X., Sun, R., Yu, H.: Cosa: contextualized and objective system to support ADHD diagnosis. In: International Conference on Bioinformatics and Biomedicine (BIBM) (2018)
11. Delgado-Gómez, D., et al.: Objective Assessment of Attention-Deficit Hyperactivity Disorder (ADHD) using an infinite runner-based computer game: a pilot study. Brain Sci. **10**(10), 716 (2020)
12. Wrońska, N., Garcia-Zapirain, B., Mendez-Zorrilla, A.: An iPad-based tool for improving the skills of children with attention deficit disorder. Int. J. Environ. Res. Public Health **12**(6), 6261–6280 (2015)
13. Hocine, N.: Personalized serious games for self-regulated attention training. In: Adjunct Publication of the 27th Conference on User Modeling, Adaptation and Personalization (2019)
14. Martins, A.I., Rosa, A.F., Queirós, A., Silva, A., Rocha, N.: European Portuguese validation of the system usability scale (SUS). Procedia Comput. Sci. **67**, 293–300 (2015)

Data Intelligence

Innovation Process in Universities – A Bibliometric Analysis

Zornitsa Yordanova(✉) (iD)

University of National and World Economy, 8mi dekemvri, Sofia, Bulgaria
`zornitsayordanova@unwe.bg`

Abstract. Universities are often a dominant stakeholder in the innovation projects of industries, society and government and an active participant in research for innovative development of technologies, economic and political models and education. Furthermore, there is much evidence that universities per se are a key player in the innovation process. Regardless of this active, basic or no role of the university in innovation development, the university must follow a structural and systematic process for the development and management of innovation. This study analyzes innovation processes in universities, using bibliometric analysis to reveal the evolution of the concept and the research sub-streams related to this broad and complex topic, such the innovation process is. The results show interesting insights on the by-words and by-phrases research along with the university innovation process which enclose the sub-streams and co-activities of universities in their innovation management. These sub-streams deserve considerable attention, related to the innovation process in universities such as innovation networks, innovation methods such as design thinking, regional innovation, university-industry cooperation, ecosystem innovation, and innovation systems. The results from the study contribute to the university management and innovation management science fields by mapping the existing research done and discussing the major trends and directions of its evolution. This study contributes to building a comprehensive and structured innovation process in universities to support project management of innovations.

Keywords: Innovation development · Innovation management · Innovation process · Science management · University management

1 Introduction

Ongoing research focuses on the development of innovation in academia, as universities are one of the three components of the Innovation and Knowledge Triangle and a key player in technology transfer [1]. However, the development of innovation in universities is often insufficiently managed due to the specialization of research project managers on the fundamental science on which the project is focused and no professional research managers are used [2]. This current research is motivated by the growing number of failed science projects for innovation development [3, 4], that reach the phase of commercialization as well as the widening gap between science and market needs

© Springer Nature Switzerland AG 2021
T. Guarda et al. (Eds.): ARTIIS 2021, CCIS 1485, pp. 197–208, 2021.
https://doi.org/10.1007/978-3-030-90241-4_16

[5]. Previous researches have already revealed insufficient project management skills in science organizations [6], weak knowledge amongst academics about management of innovation development [7], absence of practical approach for developing innovations which solve real problems [8] and lack of knowledge for developing innovations ready for the market [9].

Most of the research considers academia and university as a team member or a stakeholder in society and business innovation processes [10] and do not focus much on the cycle of the innovation process in universities which some authors acknowledge as critical for the innovation results [11]. However, to determine the scope of the innovation process in universities with all its diversity, we ask these research questions (RQ) to shed light for the research streams for the application of this process in this specific environment, such as universities: (1) Is there a clear and systematic innovation process implemented in universities? (2) What are the research streams dealing with innovation process and university? (3) How innovation process is positioned within university's processes and innovation?

We performed bibliometric analyses to report the status of the study of innovation processes in universities. The chosen research method aimed at handling the large volumes of scientific data on the topic, producing high research impact as well as uncovering emerging trends as Donthu et al. suggested [12]. We conducted a citation analysis and identified influential references, authors, and top-tier journals. The literature is mapped through co-word analysis. In addition, a co-citation network analysis is used to describe the evolution of innovation process research in universities, and a cluster analysis of the main research streams is conducted. Limitation in this research is the common understanding of universities without going deeper and categorize the outcomes of the innovation process according to the specific science or ranking of the university. The contribution of this study is reckoned to be the base for further development of a comprehensive and structural innovation process in universities, embracing the flexible project management methodologies, the best practices in the modern innovation development and the use of technologies.

2 Theoretical Background

In this section, we clarify the concept of innovation process in general and its manifestation in Academia and universities as well as the link between industrial innovation process and universities since it has been the focal research point so far [13].

2.1 Innovation Process and Universities

Innovation process has widely been seen as a predefined sequence of phases. Rogers [14] defined the innovation development as a process consisting all decisions, activities, relationships and considerations of the environment as well as their impacts on an object that materialize from recognition of a need or problem, through research, development, and commercialization of an innovation through diffusion and adoption of the innovation by users, to its consequences. Robert et al. [15] argued that the most successful innovation processes, especially in new product development projects, employ formal processes with well-defined decision-making criteria. The phases and structure of the innovation process generally depend on the field of the project for innovation development, the science and environmental obstacles, the level of uncertainty (Salerno). It may also depend on the actors and contributors involved. Thus, university collaboration as part of the innovation process in industrial firms typically contributes to the early stages of the process whereas the main focus of customer involvement lies in the final stages [16]. Traditionally, an innovation process consists of a preliminary investigation (idea generation), detailed investigation (selection of ideas), Innovation development, Testing and validation, Commercialization, Post implementation [17].

As Salerno et al. [18] suggested, an innovation process may follow a number of different paths and it is not necessarily to traditionally goes through the linear steps from-idea-to-launch. Thus, innovation process is diverse in its nature and may be proceeded according to the purpose, the innovation nature, the science field as well as the object it takes place in (for instance a university). As being a process, the innovation process involves and engages many participants. Academia and universities specifically are often used by business organizations and whole industries in the process' steps of research and development [19]. Research has provided proves that firms increasingly had absorbed and exploited the results of academic research through collaborative university-industry relationships [20].

2.2 Innovation Process in Universities

Innovation development in science organizations and universities covers wide scope and meets a variety of challenges. The literature has already provided some conclusions that universities face fundamental challenges in dealing with the increasing complexity of innovation processes [10].

The most recent research from 2019 and 2020 on innovation process in universities discuss the evolution of innovation capabilities [21], science and education as reliable segments for the diffusion of innovations and the scope and scale of technology parks as one of the most effective organizational and economic form of integration of science and production among all other innovative structures in the world [22]. University–industrial relations as a main factor in the education and innovation development is also in focus [23], as well as the role of scientific and industrial cooperation in assessing the innovative potential of an industrial enterprise and the approach to assessment through joint patent and licensing activities [24]. Knowledge management practices are embedded in the innovation process and thus, have a strong impact on the success of research projects according to Numprasertchai and Igel [25].

Research and Development (R&D) is considered as main function of universities along with education. A review of the latest literature reveals some case studies as those of the University of Oulu, Finland which purpose was to examine knowledge-creating interaction in developing an innovation in a multidisciplinary research community with hermeneutic phenomenology, to understand how previous experiences and future prospects shape the process and to examine the circumstances; which support or limit knowledge creation [26]. Most of the R&D research is discussing concrete science activities outside of the management. However, there are few science articles in the literature analyzing the management side of these processes and they are generally related to project management.

3 Research Design

The research design of the study employs traditional bibliometric analyses to address the research questions. Inclusion criteria for framing the scope of the research and RQ are wide since bibliometric analyses aim at checking the status and evolution of research activity. We performed a Boolean search in the Scopus database with the following formula:

TITLE-ABS-KEY ("innovation process" AND "university") AND (LIMIT-TO (LANGUAGE, "English")).

Scopus database was selected as this source provides the most relevant data for Technology and Innovation Management [27]. The applied inclusion criteria resulted in 697 publications from 475 authors in the years between 1973 to 2021 (the extraction was done in May 2021). We applied exclusion criteria in order to approximate the research close to our re-search questions. Thus, we excluded short surveys and conference reviews as well as editorials, notes and erratum since they are not relevant for our bibliometric analyses and do not represent primary research. As a result, we set the scope of the study on innovation process in universities based on publications with details provided in Table 1.

Table 1. Innovation process in universities research scope

Criteria	Details
Timespan	1973:2021
Sources (Journals, Books, etc.)	468
Documents	680
Average years from publication	8.8
Average citations per documents	19.94
Document types	
Article	412
Book	25
Book chapter	47
Conference paper	172
Review	24
Authors	
Authors	1653
Author Appearances	1804
Authors of single-authored documents	145
Authors of multi-authored documents	1508
Single-authored documents158	

On these 680 publications by 1653 authors, we conducted several bibliometric analyses, such as:

- Author analyses
- Co-word analysis
- Source analysis
- Cross analysis (country, affiliation, research stream)

We applied a bibliometric approach proposed by Cobo et al. [28]. This bibliometric methodological approach combines both performance analysis tools and science mapping tools to analyze a research field on focus, to detect and visualize its conceptual subdomains (particular topics/themes or general thematic areas) and its thematic evolution. The results might be of interest to university administration and management as well as to all researchers in the fields of innovation management and university management.

4   Results and Discussion

The results of the conducted bibliometric analyses provide much insight but here we present only those outcomes relevant to the research questions of this study. First of all, the growth in the research meeting the inclusion criteria of mentioning simultaneously "innovation process" and "university" is ambiguous and it is another reason to focus on these issues, that still remain unanswered. Figure 1 shows the increase in the number of publications on the matter in the recent years.

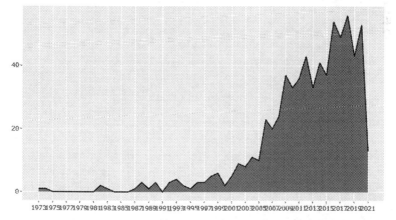

Fig. 1. Number of publications meeting the inclusion criteria

While the number of publications is exploding, the authors involved in the topic are not constant. The reason for this observation is that every university is interested in research about the barriers and stimulation factors that might increase the innovation and often universities are much involve if not in their internal innovation development, then at least as stakeholders and members of others' innovation projects. For many universities, innovation is amongst the priorities and part of the mission. Main contributors from our scoped 680 publications in the last 50 years are Maccari, E.A., Philippi, D.A. who both have five publications on the matter, Brustureany, B., Chian, L.M, Fei, G.C., Heng, L.H., Kowang, T.O., Ogrezeanu. A. with four publications during the years. The next figure (Fig. 2) demonstrates the growth of the publications on the topic in the sources which contain most of the research regarding innovation process in universities. The most relevant sources are: Industry and Corporate Change (11), Industry and Higher Education (10), Technovation (10), Research Policy (9), ASEE Annual Conference and Exposition, Conference Proceedings (9), Journal of Agricultural Education and Extension (9), European Planning Studies (8). Most of these sources and journals from Q1 SJR category in the field of management.

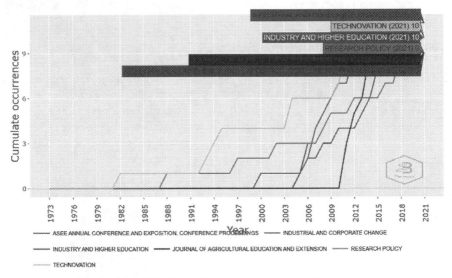

Fig. 2. Growth in the publications in the most relevant sources

No matter the timespan of the research on the innovation process in universities starts in the early 70s, its expansion has started after 2010. The next conducted analysis represents the sources that are cited the most. Usually, it is assumed that the number of citations is taken to represent the relative scientific significance or 'quality' of papers" [29]. Thus, pioneers in this citation race are Research Policy, Technovation, Strategic Management Journal, Management Science, R&D Management and Research Policy which all are SJR Q1 journals. The data from this analysis is provided in Fig. 3.

The following performed analysis aims at revealing countries much involved in these studies and key-words around the major corner stones of the research, i.e. "innovation process" and "university". Figure 4 shows that scientists from the USA, Germany, UK, Netherlands, Spain, Italy, Brazil, Sweden, China and Finland are those. Main key-words (the figure represents author key-words and journal key-words for refined coverage) are: innovation, open innovation, technology transfer, collaboration, innovation management, research and students. This analysis indirectly provides evidence about the

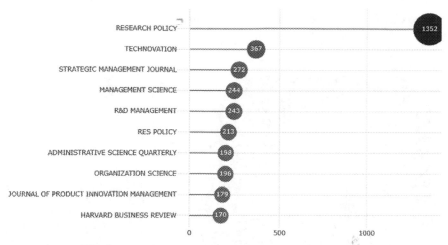

Fig. 3. Most cited sources for university innovation process

co-words of interest and close topics when researching on innovation process in universities. Students, educational processes, research and innovation management in general are among those affected. That would mean that analyzing them separately, innovation process would also be in focus and that it is part of the core university processes.

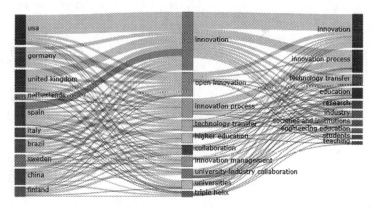

Fig. 4. Countries and top key-words

The keyword and co-word analysis is important for bibliometric analysis because of its powerful vigor to reveal patterns and trends and by measuring the association strengths of terms representative of relevant publications [29]. In the next figure, co-words analyses are performed, revealing with bigram and trigram methods what are the most commonly used words (phrases) in the publications from the scope. Figure 5 discloses phrases used in the context of innovation process in universities by the trigrams method. The results show: university-industry collaboration, factor-driven economy, regional innovation systems, the triangle of university-industry-government, university technology transfer and accelerated radical innovation. All these terms are sub-topics of research in the field of innovation process in universities.

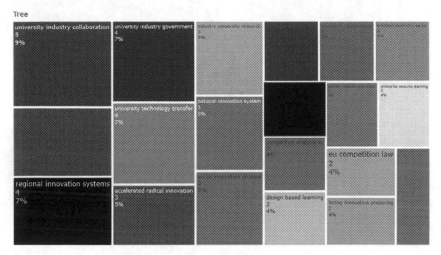

Fig. 5. Trigrams word analysis (title's word)

The following Fig. 6 presents the evolution and growth in the recent years of research on the topic with focus on co-word using bigrams method. The results show that innovation process/es is the main core of this research stream. However, insights come from the revealed co-used concepts such as triple helix, design thinking, innovation networks and regional systems. All these concepts are forming the general sub-streams of research in the field.

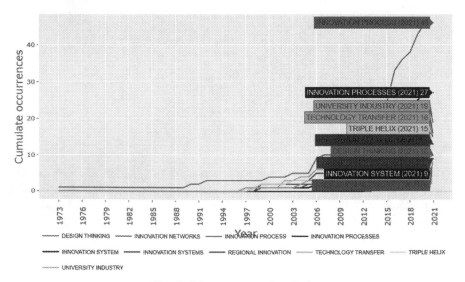

Fig. 6. Bigrams co-word analysis

Figure 7 exposes the evolution of the most research terms and concepts related to university innovation process by using the bigrams method. In the figure it is well visible the importance of these sub-streams, their longitude and centrality. In the last 10 years, major focus has been put on innovation ecosystem, design thinking, innovation system, social innovation, industry collaboration, regional and national innovation, innovation networks and innovation performance. An interesting observation came from this visualization is the beginning of the research development with its core concepts on which basement the whole concept of the innovation process in university is set – technological innovation, product development and intellectual property. These three sub-streams were central from the end of 20th century until 2013/4. Technology transfer from another point of view, has been in the epicenter of research interest for the longest period in the scoped timespan.

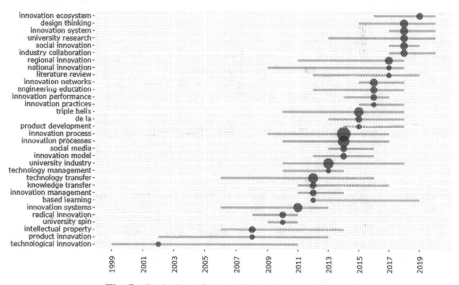

Fig. 7. Evolution of research sub-streams (bigrams)

The thematic evolution is also analyzed by a wave analysis on Fig. 8. It is well perceivable the streams and their inflowing into evolutionary research streams. Significant results from this analysis is sub-stream of innovation systems which has been flowed into innovation models. University industry (usually discussed as relationship or collaboration in the literature) has flowed to triple helix and innovation networks. Innovation performance in the context of university innovation process is rather linked to innovation system in the evolution of the research. The topic of technology transfer from another hand has been inflexed to innovation process and practice based innovation development which additionally prove the significance of the research core-concept: the university innovation process.

As Preez and Louw[30] suggested, a successful innovation requires an integrated design process, i.e. integration in the design of the organizational structure, the design of the product/service, as well as the design and implementation of new technologies.

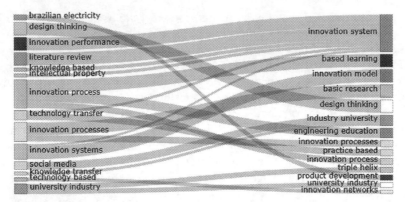

Fig. 8. Evolution of research-sub-streams (inflow method)

This is a close concept to the innovation process required to be implemented in modern higher educational institutions for meeting the current challenges.

Addressing the research questions, we formulated a brief conclusion of each of them and do call for further and deeper research on the sub-streams forming the university innovation processes.

RQ1: No clear and systemic innovation process has been identified in the analysis. Moreover, the university innovation process has been analyzed mostly from the prism of macro perspective for innovation development in general rather than as a process for internal innovation creation.

RQ2: Major research sub-streams are: innovation networks, methods for innovation development as design thinking, regional innovation, university-industry collaboration, innovation ecosystem and innovation systems.

RQ3: Mostly, university innovation process is linked to technology transfer, innovation ecosystem and it has not been researched as an ingredient of the university management.

5 Conclusion

As the results show, most of the literature meeting the inclusion criteria of this bibliometric research, do not focus on innovation process in universities per se. The conducted bibliometric analysis is necessary for such a complex activity as the innovation process in university is as well as its application is. In this respect, we shed light on its core areas, relationships through co-word analyses of the titles, keywords, and abstracts of the relevant literature using visualization and bibliometric mapping tools in order to (1) gain a one-stop overview, (2) identify knowledge gaps, (3) derive novel ideas for investigation, and (4) position their intended contributions to the field as Donthlu et al. suggested [12].

As the results show, one of the barriers to innovation in universities is the lack of a clear, systematized and digitized innovation process to which scientists can adapt and follow to perform methodologically from a management point of view. Some other barriers are provided by Avila et al. [31] with the recommendation for closer cooperation between the university administration, which defines and manages the formal processes and the researchers who implement them. This is why, with this study we call for further research and agenda on creating a framework for Innovation Development and R&D Project Management in Science Organizations and Universities [32].

Acknowledgments. The paper is supported by UNWE NI-NID 09/2021 and BG NSF Grant No KP-06 OPR01/3-2018.

References

1. Gulbrandsen, M., Slipersæter, S.: The third mission and the entrepreneurial university model. In: Bonaccorsi, A., Daraio, C. (eds.) Universities and Strategic Knowledge Creation: Specialization and Performance in Europe, Edward Elgar, Cheltenham, pp. 112–143 (2007)
2. Schuetzenmeister, F.: University Research Management: An Exploratory Literature Review. Institute of European Studies, UC Berkeley (2010). https://escholarship.org/uc/item/77p3j2hr
3. Etzkowitz, H., Zhou, C.: The Triple Helix: University–Industry–Government Innovation and Entrepreneurship, 2nd edn. (2017). ISBN 9781315620183
4. Leahey, E.: From sole investigator to team scientist: trends in the practice and study of research collaboration. Ann. Rev. Sociol. **42**(1), 81–100 (2016)
5. Turel, O., Kapoor, B.: A business analytics maturity perspective on the gap between business schools and presumed industry needs. Commun. Assoc. Inf. Syst. **39**, 6 (2016). http://aisel.aisnet.org/cais/vol39/iss1/6
6. Pinto, J., Winch, G.: The unsettling of "settled science:" the past and future of the management of projects. Int. J. Project Manage. **34**(2), 237–245 (2016)
7. Hauge, S., Pinheiro, M., Zyzak, B.: Knowledge bases and regional development: collaborations between higher education and cultural creative industries. Int. J. Cult. Policy **24**(4), 485–503 (2018). https://doi.org/10.1080/10286632.2016.1218858
8. Pearce, J.: Teaching science by encouraging innovation in appropriate technologies for sustainable development (2019)
9. Stock, G., Greis, N., Fischer, L.: Organisational slack and new product time to market performance. Int. J. Innov. Manage. **22**(04), 1850034 (2018)
10. Kaloudis, A., et al.: How Universities Contribute to Innovation: A Literature Review-based Analysis. NTNU (2019). ISBN 978-82-691902-1-2 (E-bok)
11. Rubenstein, A.H., Chakrabarti, A.K., O'Keefe, R.D., Souder, W.E., Young, H.C.: Factors influencing innovation success at the project level. Res. Manage. **19**(3), 15–20 (1976). https://doi.org/10.1080/00345334.1976.11756350
12. Donthu, N., Kumar, S., Mukherjee, D., Pandey, N., Lim, W.M.: How to conduct a bibliometric analysis: an overview and guidelines. J. Bus. Res. **133**, 285–296 (2021). https://doi.org/10.1016/j.jbusres.2021.04.070, ISSN 0148-2963
13. Perkmann, M., et al.: Academic engagement and commercialisation: a review of the literature on university–industry relations. Res. Policy **42**(2), 423–442 (2013), https://doi.org/10.1016/j.respol.2012.09.007. ISSN 0048-7333
14. Rogers, E.: Diffusion of Innovations, 5th edn. Free Press, New York (2003)
15. Cooper, R.G., Edgett, S.J., Kleinschmidt, E.J.: Optimizing the stage-gate process: what best-practice companies do—II. Res. Technol. Manage. **45**(6), 43–49 (2002). https://doi.org/10.1080/08956308.2002.11671532
16. Kunttu, L., Neuvo, Y.: The role of academics, users, and customers in industrial product development, technology innovation. Manage. Rev. **10**(3), 59–68 (2020)

17. Cooper, R., Kleinschmidt, E.J.: New Products - The Key Factors in Success, 1st edn. South-Western Educational Pub, Mason (1990)
18. Salerno, M.S., de Vasconcelos Gomes, L.A., da Silva, D.O., Bagno, R.B., Freitas, S.L.T.U.: Innovation processes: which process for which project? Technovation **35**, 59–70 (2015). https://doi.org/10.1016/j.technovation.2014.07.012. ISSN 0166-4972
19. Kunttu, L., Neuvo, Y.: Balancing learning and knowledge protection in university-industry collaborations. Learn. Organ. **26**, 190–204 (2018). https://doi.org/10.1108/TLO-06-2018-0103
20. Ankrah, S.N., Al-Tabbaa, O.: Universities-industry collaboration: a systematic review. Scand. J. Manage. (2015). https://doi.org/10.2139/ssrn.2596018, https://ssrn.com/abstract=2596018
21. Efindi, T.H.A.: The development of innovation capabilities. A review paper about the challenges and future research trend in the UAE high education. Test Eng. Manage. **83**, 7299–7307 (2020)
22. Andrusiv, U., et al.: Experience and prospects of innovation development venture capital financing. Manage. Sci. Lett. **10**(4), 781–788 (2020)
23. Zmyzgova, T., Polyakova, E., Prokofyev, K., Chelovechkova, A., Dmitrieva, O.: University relations: university–industrial relations as the main factor in the development of polytechnic education. In: Solovev, D.B., Savaley, V.V., Bekker, A.T., Petukhov, V.I. (eds.) Proceeding of the International Science and Technology Conference "FarEastCon 2019." SIST, vol. 172, pp. 569–579. Springer, Singapore (2020). https://doi.org/10.1007/978-981-15-2244-4_54
24. Kirillova, E.: The role of scientific and industrial cooperation in assessing the innovative potential of an industrial enterprise and the approach to evaluation through joint patent and licensing activities. In: Solovev, D.B., Savaley, V.V., Bekker, A.T., Petukhov, V.I. (eds.) Proceeding of the International Science and Technology Conference "FarEastCon 2019." SIST, vol. 172, pp. 507–516. Springer, Singapore (2020). https://doi.org/10.1007/978-981-15-2244-4_49
25. Numprasertchai, S., Igel, B.: Managing knowledge in new product and service development: a new management approach for innovative research organisations. Int. J. Technol. Manage. **28**(7–8) (2004). https://doi.org/10.1504/IJTM.2004.005776
26. Suorsa, A.R., Svento, R., Lindfors, A.V., Huotari, M.-L.: Knowledge creation and interaction in an R&D project: the case of the energy weather forecast. J. Documentation **76**(1), 145–172 (2019)
27. Chadegani, A., et al.: A comparison between two main academic literature collections: web of science and scopus databases. Asian Soc. Sci. **9**(5), 18–26 (2013). https://ssrn.com/abstract=2257540
28. Cobo, M.J., López-Herrera, A.G., Herrera-Viedma, E., Herrera, F.: An approach for detecting, quantifying, and visualizing the evolution of a research field: a practical application to the fuzzy sets theory field. J. Inf. **5**(1), 146–166 (2011)
29. Cole, J.R., Cole, S.: Social Stratification in Science. The University of Chicago Press, Chicago (1973)
30. du Preez, N.D., Louw, L.: A framework for managing the innovation process. In: PICMET 2008 - 2008 Portland International Conference on Management of Engineering & Technology, pp. 546–558 (2008). https://doi.org/10.1109/PICMET.2008.4599663
31. Ávila, L.V., et al.: Barriers to innovation and sustainability at universities around the world. J. Clean. Prod. **164**, 1268–1278 (2017). https://doi.org/10.1016/j.jclepro.2017.07.025, ISSN 0959-6526,
32. Yordanova, Z.: Innovation development and R&D project management in science organizations and universities - data-driven model and analysis. In: Suhaili, W.S.H., Siau, N.Z., Omar, S., Phon-Amuaisuk, S. (eds.) CIIS 2021. AISC, vol. 1321, pp. 3–12. Springer, Cham (2021). https://doi.org/10.1007/978-3-030-68133-3_1

Contactless Human-Computer Interaction Using a Deep Neural Network Pipeline for Real-Time Video Interpretation and Classification

Regina Sousa⑩, Tiago Jesus⑩, Victor Alves⑩, and José Machado$^{(\boxtimes)}$⑩

ALGORITMI Research Center, School of Engineering, University of Minho,
Gualtar Campus, 4710 057 Braga, Portugal
{regina.sousa,tiago.jesus}@algoritmi.uminho.pt,
{valves,jmac}@di.uminho.pt

Abstract. Nowadays, all applications are developed with the user's comfort in mind. Regardless of the application's objective, it should be as simple as possible so that it is easily accepted by its users. With the evolution of technology, simplicity has evolved and has become intrinsically related to the automation of tasks. Therefore, many researchers have focused their investigations on the interaction between humans and computing devices. However, this interaction is usually still carried out via a keyboard and/or a mouse. We present an essemble of deep neural networks for the detection and interpretation of gestural movement, in various environments. Its purpose is to introduce a new form of interaction between the human and computing devices in order to evolve this paradigm. The use case focused on detecting the movement of the user's hands in real time and automatically interpreting the movement.

Keywords: Human-computer interaction · Hand gesture recognition · Computer vision · Deep neural networks · Desktop task simulator

1 Introduction

1.1 Motivation and Contextualization

Regardless of the objective of an application, it should be as simple as possible so that it is easily accepted and by the users. As technology progressed, the concept of simplicity evolved and became intrinsically connected with the automation of tasks. While "a click away" was considered as simple a few years ago, nowadays "a gesture away" would be simpler, making it possible to do more with less effort and without the need for physical interaction with a machine. With this in mind, this paper presents an environment with a new strategy that has the potential to change the way some operations are performed in computing devices, be it via

This research has been supported by FCT - Fundação para a Ciência e Tecnologia whithin the R&D Units Project Scope: UIDB/00319/2020.

© Springer Nature Switzerland AG 2021
T. Guarda et al. (Eds.): ARTIIS 2021, CCIS 1485, pp. 209–220, 2021.
https://doi.org/10.1007/978-3-030-90241-4_17

hotkeys, the mouse or some other external device. All of the before mentioned can be replaced by gesture interactions.

The usefulness of the provided virtual environment depends entirely on the use case. For instance, when cooking, if the user is following a recipe on the laptop, having dirty hands requires extra work (cleaning/drying hands). By using gestures, it would allow the user to perform some actions on the laptop without getting it dirty. Other use case where gestures can be very usefull is in surgery as surgeons might need to use some kind of computing device and can't use their hands. At last, another important use case would be to use gestures while driving to use computers whithout losing focus on the road.

The user may be using external monitors and the computer may be far away.

If the user doesn't have an external device like a mouse to help them with the tasks shown here and they didn't know how to do them otherwise.

Therefore, the presented prototype was only modeled to perform some operations such as Zoom in, Minimize, and Swiping left.

1.2 Objectives

Taking into account the contextualization stated in the previous section, the work presented here was based on several objectives related to the need for a tool capable of capturing the movement of a user (through the camera of the respective device) and interpret that same movement in real-time, in order to perform a certain operation on the computer. Thus, the detection of movement is foreseen regardless of the environment the user is in, as well as the globalization of this software to any operating system. As such, our first goal would be to develop a general setup capable of capturing and processing movements in real-time. The remaining objectives were stated according to research questions so that in this way the resolution process would have a logical thread from the beginning to the final goal.

2 Related Work

The process of recognizing manual gestures depends on several steps, as illustrated in Fig. 1:

The first step is called "Image Frame Acquisition" and involves the capture of the hand gesture, performed by the computer [9]. This step is very basic and does not require any gadget or special technique. Only a web or depth camera is used to find the user's hand. The second stage, according to the review by [12] on vision-based hand gestures recognition, is called "Hand tracking" which, as the name implies, boils down to the ability that a computer has to track the hand and isolate it from any surrounding environment. As for the characteristics, the extraction phase is the most volatile because the features under consideration can be several: Finger position, thumb state, skin color, alignment, palm position, among others. Thus, it is thought that manual gestures have the potential to be used for interaction with the computer. The work of

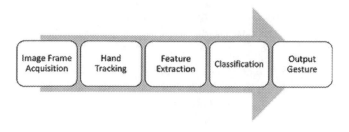

Fig. 1. Hand gesture recognition process.

Weiguo et al. (2017), Chenyang, Yingli & Matt (2016), Rasel et al. (2017), Shaun et al. (2017), Deepali & Milind (2016), Nabeel, Rosa & Chan (2017); and Anshal, Heidy and Emmanuel (2017) proposed the use of manual gesture recognition for American Sign Language (ASL) for people with hearing disabilities, while in Shaun et al. (2017) did not evaluate dynamic letters (such as j and z) [5,8,15,17]. In Nabeel, Rosa and Chan (2017), 36 gestures were studied, including 26 ASL alphabets and 10 ASL numbers [15]. In Anshal, Heidy and Emmanuel (2017), two different translation paradigms were proposed, English characters (alphabet) and complete words or phrases [8].

3   Materials and Methods

Gesture Detection and Recognition. The detection of movements is achieved through a pipeline of neural networks. The developed pipeline has some similarities with personal assistants such as Alexa or Siri [6], in which the detection of a specific word occurs initially. For example, "Hey Siri" triggers the Siri assistant, and only then the following text is processed. Likewise, the developed environment is triggered when it detects a hand with a certain confidence and then processes the given movement, which may or may not be a known gesture to be executed by the operating system.

Trigger Hand. At an early stage in this work, two proposals were taken into account. The first was based on the creation of an in-house dataset and the second on the search for a dataset appropriate to the task at hand. Taking into account the cost and time to gather a reasonable amount of data needed for the deep learning algorithms, it was decided to use a pubicly available dataset. The approach that was taken for this work did not ease the search for a dataset since the trigger hand is not a binary ranking problem, but a bounding box problem. This means that the algorithm does not only detect whether the hand is present, but it also detects its position. It should be made clear that, although the approach adopted increases the complexity of the problem, it is advantageous in that it is intended to continue this research by adding several operations where it is possible to interact with the operating system through a gesture. For example, to scroll continuously, to click on a certain operation on a web page, to open a certain program, among many other actions. All of the above, require spatial coordinates, which can be provided by the proposed method.

Dataset. The chosen dataset had to be the most similar to the environment in which this system is intended to operate, in this case, users who are in front of a computer or computing device and where the quality of the camera, brightness, and adjacent noise can vary innumerably. The first experiment was carried out with a set of data provided by Oxford, the Hands Dataset [2]. Since, the result was not what was desired, an alternative dataset was searched. Given the scarcity of research and availability carried out so far in this area, movement recognition for computing devices (without the use of sensors), a dataset not very appropriate to the terms described above as we can see in Fig. 2, but where the results obtained are satisfactory, was used to show the efficiency of this prototype, Egohands Dataset [3].

Fig. 2. Egohands dataset.

Model. For building the model a transfer learning process was used. The first step to understand this process is to know that this concept is not new specific to deep learning. There is a stark difference between the traditional approach of building and training machine learning models and using a methodology following transfer learning principles [1]. Traditional learning is isolated and occurs purely based on specific tasks, datasets, and training separate isolated models on them. No knowledge is retained which can be transferred from one model to another. In transfer learning, you can leverage knowledge (e.g. features, weights) from previously trained models for training newer models and even tackle problems like having less data for the newer task. This means that we can use an existing model, which has already been trained in a similar area or situation (in this case image detection), and modify the last layers to our benefit. Since neural networks can contain millions of parameters and the training process can take days, weeks, or even months, Transfer Learning proves to be a very interesting solution to help reduce this time. In addition, the choice of the model must take into account the performance of the environment in question. In other words, going back to Siri's example, being this a good analogy, the model is always waiting for the trigger word, "Hey Siri", and it is processing what it receives at all times. The solution we propose uses the same concept, all captured frames are analyzed for potential triggers. In our search for a model already trained in this area we verified that TensorFlow has some models already available, from which was decided to use the _mobilenet_v1coco model as a starting point since it is one of the fastest current models for this sort of task [10].

Training Environment. Model training can be done locally, on local GPUs that would take some time, or in the cloud. For the sake of time optimization, it was chosen to use the cloud. By reference only, the model training on a MacBook Air (Intel i5 2.6 GHZ, 8 GB RAM), ran at a maximum speed of 8 s with CPU and 3 s with GPU. It would take about 17 days to run approximately 200,000 epochs on the Mac, mentioned above, compared to 3 to 4 h on the cloud. Therefore, GoogleColab was used as a platform. It's not the best choice but it was chosen because it's free service and varies the GPU in use so you cannot identify which GPU is used. As this model and API is provided by TensorFlow, Tensorboard was used in the visualization of the models training graphs, being the most significant parameter the accuracy of the same in the validation dataset. Due to the use of the TensorFlow Object Detection Platform API for image recognition, the training graphs were not provided, which will only highlight the loss of the model in the test set. The model was run in 200,000 epochs and the result can be seen in Fig. 3 with a smoothing of 0.5.

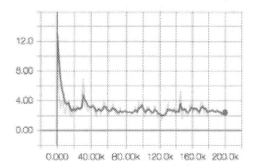

Fig. 3. Model training loss evolution.

After the model was completely trained, it was adapted to capture frames in real-time.

214   R. Sousa et al.

Movement Detection. A vital part of the whole project is the recognition of the operation to be demonstrated and performed by a user in real-time. This is the way this work differs from the others reffered to above that only detect whether or not the hand is in the camera frame, without performing any action after that. The recognition of the operation to be performed was made by another trained neural network, incorporated into the system.

Each excerpt was composed on average of 36 frames, the result of processing the original video from which 12 frames per second were extracted. This implies that any gesture has a 3s time window to be executed, although most frames are transitive movements for the beginning or end of the gesture, the gesture itself has a relatively small presence. The gestures to be recognized are found in the 20BN-JESTER dataset [11] (Fig. 4). For this reason, this dataset was chosen as a basis for movement detection. From the whole dataset, the clips corresponding to four different classes were used: swiping left, swiping down, zooming in with full hand, and doing other things, this last class is applied when none of the gestures are recognized. To complete the dataset some videos of our own were created similar to the existing ones. These videos were processed in the same way, regarding the number of frames (12 per second), however, a feature was added that allowed to increase exponentially the size of the data set: each gesture executed in the video would have 4s of transition actions between them, which allows for the same instance of the same gesture, it can be presented somewhere at the beginning, middle or end of the 3s established by 20BN-JESTER. A sliding window style script has been developed which, having marked the first and last exact frame corresponding, respectively, to the beginning and end of the gesture, makes a sequential sampling that puts this exact frame in the possible positions throughout the 3-second video time. This has become quite useful because, besides increasing the number of data samples, in this case being a process of data augmentation [14], a gesture can theoretically be detected correctly if placed in any position of the clip.

3.1   Data Processing

Given the enormous size of the dataset, resulting from joining the 20BN-JESTER and the self created dataset, which as a whole occupied about 20 GB, Out-of-core Training was used [13,16]. Out-of-core Training is a method used when it is practically impossible to train the models in the entire dataset, since there is not enough memory available, among other cases, and this form, allows the data to be fetched in a sequential way at each step [16]. As such, a customized generator was created, with the Keras API in order to send a predefined amount of gestures to memory.

As previously mentioned, 20BN-JESTER contains gestures that can be lower or higher than 36 frames, so it was decided to set the maximum frame limit to 36, corresponding to 3s, and if any gesture contained less than that, a masking was performed, if it was higher it was cut to 36 frames. Furthermore, all frames are reduced to (100, 250) pixels.

Fig. 4. Frame samples of 20BN-JESTER.

Model Used. In the process of creation and design of the architecture to use for the convolutional network, the possibility of using pre-trained models was considered, but an original model was chosen so that it could contain specific characteristics of the original data. The designed architecture was inspired by an existing C3D [7], which uses several 3D convolutional layers, pooling and dense to remove spatial and temporal attributes from each image. The original architecture presents considerable complexity, which led to the decision to use a relatively simpler approach to the problem in question. The architecture of the model can be seen in Fig. 5.

It has always been a priority to use architectures with as few parameters as possible since it was intended to be used in real-time. The simplification from the original model was based primarily on the reduction of units in each layer, maintaining proportionality between the new numbers. It is important to note that the model presented was not the original, the reduction of units was gradual. What was sought was a decrease in the complexity of the model without compromising the precision values pointed out by the model, values that remained constant until the order of eight hundred thousand parameters.

Platform Used and Model Training. The settings of the workstation used to train this model were Ubuntu 16 as the operating system, an Intel Xeon 12 cores processor (with 64 GB RAM) and a NVIDIA QUADRO P6000 GPU (with 24 GB of GDDR5X dedicated memory), which allowed the tuning, in a few days, of what would be the final model. After passing the dataset to the respective server, in a few hours, it was possible to obtain results and analyze them in order to make potential changes to the model. For the training of the

```
Layer (type)                    Output Shape            Param #
=================================================================
conv1 (Conv3D)                  (None, 18, 38, 50, 16)  1312
_____
pool1 (MaxPooling3D)            (None, 18, 19, 25, 16)  0
_____
batch_normalization_13 (Batc    (None, 18, 19, 25, 16)  64
_____
dropout_13 (Dropout)            (None, 18, 19, 25, 16)  0
_____
conv2 (Conv3D)                  (None, 18, 19, 25, 32)  13856
_____
pool2 (MaxPooling3D)            (None, 9, 9, 12, 32)     0
_____
batch_normalization_14 (Batc    (None, 9, 9, 12, 32)     128
_____
dropout_14 (Dropout)            (None, 9, 9, 12, 32)     0
_____
conv3a (Conv3D)                 (None, 9, 9, 12, 64)     55360
_____
conv3b (Conv3D)                 (None, 9, 9, 12, 64)     110656
_____
pool3 (MaxPooling3D)            (None, 4, 4, 6, 64)      0
_____
batch_normalization_15 (Batc    (None, 4, 4, 6, 64)      256
_____
dropout_15 (Dropout)            (None, 4, 4, 6, 64)      0
_____
conv4a (Conv3D)                 (None, 4, 4, 6, 128)     221312
_____
conv4b (Conv3D)                 (None, 4, 4, 6, 128)     442496
_____
pool4 (MaxPooling3D)            (None, 2, 2, 3, 128)     0
_____
batch_normalization_16 (Batc    (None, 2, 2, 3, 128)     512
_____
dropout_16 (Dropout)            (None, 2, 2, 3, 128)     0
_____
zeropad5 (ZeroPadding3D)        (None, 2, 3, 4, 128)     0
_____
pool5 (MaxPooling3D)            (None, 1, 1, 2, 128)     0
_____
flatten_4 (Flatten)             (None, 256)              0
_____
fc8 (Dense)                     (None, 4)                1028
=================================================================
Total params: 846,980
Trainable params: 846,500
Non-trainable params: 480
_____
```

Fig. 5. Model architecture.

model, the Keras platform was used, characterized by its high-level APIs that allow the production of models at a high pace. The described architecture has been trained with the optimizer SGD with momentum and with a learning rate decay. It trained for 50 epochs, in which callbacks would be used to save only the best models in terms of validation set accuracy.

When observing the learning curves, presented in Fig. 6, it is clear that quickly (in relation to the total number of epochs), satisfactory accuracy values are achieved within the first dozen iterations to the dataset. The callback used to store only the best models last recorded the model of epoch number 13, which indicates that from the second dozen epochs the continuation of the training is no longer necessary, and the final model reaches an accuracy in the validation set of 96% and 98% in the training set for gesture detection.

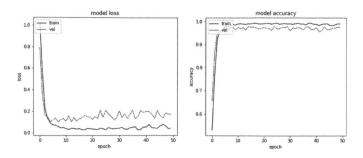

Fig. 6. Accuracy and model loss.

3.2 Real Time Movement Capture

In order to identify the gesture made by users, it is necessary to capture them in real-time. This capture is made thanks to the OpenCV library [4], which allows access to any camera connected to the computer. Using OpenCV means taking the maximum number of frames that a given computer can take per second, also known as fps. In order to counter this act predefined by the library, because we only want 12 frames per second in order to maintain consistency with the dataset used, the following architecture was structured:

Each square represented in Fig. 7 represents 1 s and as can be seen, the first square represents the past, the next represents the present, and, finally, the last represents the future, in this way you get a time array with the user's real-time frames.

Fig. 7. Frame allocation

In this case, the first square contains the past n frames, the second one contains the n current frames, and the third square the n frames that are still to come in the next second, where n denotes the number of frames being used and is dependent on the number of fps of the computer where processing takes place. The advantage of this type of architecture is that the number of frames desired can be changed at any time, in this case only 12 of those to which the computer you can pull out in a second. For this, we use dynamic strides in the choice of successive frames.

Furthermore, the trigger word model fits perfectly in the following architecture, because when the hand is detected, automatically the user is in the second square, the previous 12 frames are already present and the user only has 1 s to perform the gesture, which after several tests was considered sufficient. For all intents and purposes these frames can also be modified, that is, it is possible to have more time to perform the gesture, however, it increases the inconsistency before the dataset used here.

4   Execution of the Operations

With the network trained and ready to detect hands and classify the gestures, the last step is to execute the operation that the gesture represents (minimize, zoom in, or swipe left). For this, hotkeys where simulated.

The simulation is done using packages in Python that allow you to simulate the pressing of keyboard keys. After finding out which hotkeys to carry out the processes related to the gestures in the different operating systems they were implemented e.g. in Windows 10 to switch to the right desktop (swipe left) the key combination is used: WIN + CTRL + right arrow. It's important to mention that other hotkeys can be added easily, changing the source code.

5   Conclusions and Optimizations

Decisions on building a prototype were made throughout this work. These decisions had a practical and effective demonstration of the goal in mind, that is, understanding and remotely executing commands issued by a human entity without the help of equipment.

The use of an existing dataset as a conceptual basis for the definition of the gesture enables a better degree of normalization in relation to a personalized dataset since this is better structured in terms of quantity and quality of the samples. However, this measure is inherently a limitation because it limits the training process to the reality imposed by the data that was not defined by the authors.

As mentioned above, a set of data has been added to the existing dataset. The aim is to create a completely original data set with the desired features such as the speed of the gesture and the frame window in which the gesture is carried out (start, middle, or end). Note that the 20BN-JESTER should be used for this purpose with some manipulation of the existing frames through data sampling strategies that have been designed and already idealized.

The implementation of the pipeline itself, which was developed from scratch, has extremely adaptable properties for various machine types in terms of performance and frames per second, which have a major influence on the designed system. The pipeline was built on the basis of dynamic arrays that complement each other and support the creation of a necessary background for the model created.

There is a lot of room for improvement in terms of threading, efficiency, and flexibility. These aspects of improvement focus primarily on capturing and handling images that are different for each machine. It is necessary to put together the various aspects that contribute to the portability and viability of what could be a commonly used application.

Python's choice for implementation was based on the ease of use and simplicity of the language, mainly in the area of Machine Learning. The simplification as well as the compatibility with various required platforms (such as TensorFlow, Keras, OpenCV) made Python the obvious choice for a first creation. However, the simultaneous use in relation to this language is not the most accurate as it is an interpreter. With this in mind, we intend to use optimized compilers like Numba or a transition to C++.

The implementation of only a small set of gestures is a very important feature as it allows for more efficient maintenance and optimization/debugging to find flaws in the pipeline. However, when developing and improving it is essential to expand the vocabulary associated with the commands that can be interpreted by the model. This is a measure that needs to be developed along with the personalized data to allow better immersion in what would be a motion-driven desktop.

Using a more appropriate dataset for hand recognition or its construction is an important step in improving the environment because the dataset used does not have all the features of real cases, making system performance impractical in certain cases.

Regarding the execution of the process regarding the performed gesture, one possible optimization is to switch from using the simulation (simulate the event of pressing the buttons) to the use of direct calls to the operating system, i.e., instead of using key simulations directly execute the desired process. This optimization would be achieved with the programming language C++ and would be what connects the application with the operating system.

References

1. Aqra, I., Abdul Ghani, N., Maple, C., Machado, J., Sohrabi Safa, N.: Incremental algorithm for association rule mining under dynamic threshold. Appl. Sci. **9**(24), 5398 (2019)
2. Arpit Mittal, A.Z., Torr, P.: Hand detection using multiple proposals. In: Proceedings of the British Machine Vision Conference, pp, 75.1-75.11. BMVA Press (2011). http://www.robots.ox.ac.uk/vgg/data/hands, https://doi.org/10.5244/C.25.75
3. Bambach, S., Lee, S., Crandall, D.J., Yu, C.: Lending a hand: detecting hands and recognizing activities in complex egocentric interactions. In: The IEEE International Conference on Computer Vision (ICCV), December 2015. http://vision.soic.indiana.edu/projects/egohands
4. Bradski, G.: The OpenCV library. Dr. Dobb's J. Softw. Tools **25**, 120–123 (2000)
5. Canavan, S., Keyes, W., Mccormick, R., Kunnumpurath, J., Hoelzel, T., Yin, L.: Hand gesture recognition using a skeleton-based feature representation with a random regression forest. In: 2017 IEEE International Conference on Image Processing (ICIP), pp. 2364–2368. IEEE (2017)
6. Hoy, M.B.: Alexa, Siri, Cortana, and more: an introduction to voice assistants. Med. Ref. Serv. Q. **37**(1), 81–88 (2018). https://doi.org/10.1080/02763869.2018.1404391. pMID: 29327988
7. Jin, K.H., McCann, M.T., Froustey, E., Unser, M.: Deep convolutional neural network for inverse problems in imaging. IEEE Trans. Image Process. **26**(9), 4509–4522 (2017)

8. Joshi, A., Sierra, H., Arzuaga, E.: American sign language translation using edge detection and cross correlation. In: 2017 IEEE Colombian Conference on Communications and Computing (COLCOM), pp. 1–6. IEEE (2017)
9. Liu, G., Zhu, W., Saunders, C., Gao, F., Yu, Y.: Real-time complex event processing and analytics for smart grid. Procedia Compu. Sci. **61**, 113–119 (2015)
10. Liu, W., et al.: SSD: single shot MultiBox detector. In: Leibe, B., Matas, J., Sebe, N., Welling, M. (eds.) ECCV 2016, Part I. LNCS, vol. 9905, pp. 21–37. Springer, Cham (2016). https://doi.org/10.1007/978-3-319-46448-0_2
11. Materzynska, J., Berger, G., Bax, I., Memisevic, R.: The jester dataset: a large-scale video dataset of human gestures. In: 2019 IEEE/CVF International Conference on Computer Vision Workshop (ICCVW), pp. 2874–2882 (2019). https://doi.org/10.1109/ICCVW.2019.00349
12. Murthy, G., Jadon, R.: A review of vision based hand gestures recognition. Int. J. Inf. Technol. Knowl. Manage. **2**(2), 405–410 (2009)
13. Sampaio, L., et al.: A deep-big data approach to health care in the AI age. Mob. Netw. Appl. **23**(4), 1123–1128 (2018). https://doi.org/10.1007/s11036-018-1071-6
14. Perez, L., Wang, J.: The effectiveness of data augmentation in image classification using deep learning. arXiv preprint arXiv:1712.04621 (2017)
15. Siddiqui, N., Chan, R.H.: A wearable hand gesture recognition device based on acoustic measurements at wrist. In: 2017 39th Annual International Conference of the IEEE Engineering in Medicine and Biology Society (EMBC), pp. 4443–4446. IEEE (2017)
16. Sjardin, B., Massaron, L., Boschetti, A.: Large Scale Machine Learning with Python. Packt Publishing Ltd., Birmingham (2016)
17. Zhou, W., Lyu, C., Jiang, X., Li, P., Chen, H., Liu, Y.H.: Real-time implementation of vision-based unmarked static hand gesture recognition with neural networks based on FPGAs. In: 2017 IEEE International Conference on Robotics and Biomimetics (ROBIO), pp. 1026–1031. IEEE (2017)

An Exploratory Analysis of COVID-19 in Latin America Using Functional Principal Component Analysis

Diana Chaglla$^{(\boxtimes)}$![ORCID], Isidro R. Amaro ![ORCID], and Saba Infante ![ORCID]

Yachay Tech University, Urcuquí, Ecuador
{diana.chaglla,iamaro,sinfante}@yachaytech.edu.ec

Abstract. Even though there already exists a wide variety of epidemiological models, it's worthwhile to apply Functional Data Analysis (FDA) techniques to study the shapes of the COVID-19 pandemic in Latin America. In the present work we use Functional Principal Component Analysis (FPCA) to make an exploratory study on a dataset formed by the total cases per million, new cases, new tests, and stringency index of 6 Latin American countries, namely: Mexico, Ecuador, Chile, Peru, Cuba, and Colombia; obtained from the first confirmed case reported to January 2021, measured daily. We identify an increasing pattern in all of the variables and the interesting case of Cuba concerning the management of the pandemic, as well as the influence of stringency index over the growth curve of positive cases, and the mean perturbations with functional principal components (FPC) of the variables. Finally, we suggest more FDA techniques to carry out further studies to get a broad perspective of COVID-19 in Latin America.

Keywords: Functional data analysis · Functional principal component analysis · COVID-19 · Latin America

1 Introduction

On January 30, 2020, the Director-General of the World Health Organization (WHO) declared the outbreak of COVID-19 to be a public health emergency of international concern and issued a set of temporary recommendations [11]. Almost one month later the Brazilian Minister of Health confirmed the first case in his country becoming the first person to be tested positive in the Latin American territory, was a Brazilian man, of 61 years old, who traveled in February, to Lombardy, northern Italy, where a significant outbreak was ongoing [17]. Get to know the implications of the first confirmed case for the rest of the Latin American countries was a matter of time, especially being aware of the already fragile health care system and the lack of appropriate political responses in the

© Springer Nature Switzerland AG 2021
T. Guarda et al. (Eds.): ARTIIS 2021, CCIS 1485, pp. 221–233, 2021.
https://doi.org/10.1007/978-3-030-90241-4_18

majority of them. By the time the WHO declares COVID-19 as a worldwide pandemic countries like Mexico, Ecuador, and Dominican Republic already had confirmed cases.

Over the years various studies regarding functional principal component analysis (FPCA) have been carried out, beginning from [3], where a technique for principal components analysis of data consisting of functions observed at a determined number of argument values is described, and [15] that showed how the theory of L-splines can support generalizations of linear modeling and principal components analysis to samples drawn from random functions. More recent researches include: [6] a study of Sleep Heart Health Study (SHHS) using multilevel functional principal component analysis (MFPCA), [13] an exploratory analysis employing FPCA, functional clustering and principal component analysis on fertility, infant mortality, life expectancy, Multidimensional Poverty Index (MPI), Human Development Index (HDI) and Gross Domestic Product (GDP) growth indexes data sets from twenty Latin American countries during time frames around 1960–2018, [1] an evaluation of Spatial functional data analysis (sFDA) as a tool to regionalize seasonality and intensity precipitation patterns in Ecuador, [5] an analysis to verify the potential utility, as well as the theoretical and practical consistency of the results of functional data analysis applied to the financial risk of credit unions, subject to the control of the Superintendency of Banks of Ecuador. In particular, concerning COVID-19 in [20] an exploration of the modes of variation of the data through a FPCA was done, and a study of the canonical correlation between confirmed and death cases, together with cluster analysis and forecasting based on the dynamic FPCA.

In addition to the FDA techniques, other statistical and computational methods have been used to analyze aspects of the pandemic. In this sense we can mention, for example: [14] where two data visualization techniques are used, specifically Cluster Analysis and Principal Component Analysis Biplot, over a dataset focused on South America, [18] where Cluster Analysis and Canonical Biplot are applied in variables related to the pandemic in the provinces of Ecuador, in the study [8] where a particular type of recurrent neural networks (LSTM) is used to predict the percentage of positive COVID-19 patients in Pakistan.

Besides all existing literature about epidemiological models that have been successfully applied over the years, in the most recent studies FDA has been used due to it offers very powerful approaches to analyze data sets composed of curves or surfaces, can effectively complement traditional epidemiological analyses and provide useful insights [4]. Moreover, offers significant advantages for a better understanding data trends over the time [19]. For this reason, the contribution in this research is the implementation of FPCA a technique from the field of FDA, to make a brief exploration of the growth curve of some COVID-19 data such as new cases, total cases per million, new tests and stringency index of Mexico, Ecuador, Cuba, Chile, Peru, and Colombia.

By the exploratory data approach nature of this study, we have the following remaining sections. In Sect. 2, we make an explanation of the methodology to be applied, together with the description of the data collection. In Sect. 3, we state the main results, with an interpretation and discussion thereof. Finally, in Sect. 4 we give the conclusions and the guideline to continue with this study to get a broad knowledge about the COVID-19 pandemic in Latin America.

2   Material and Method

2.1   Data Collection

The data was collected from Our World in Data (OWID) [12], which is a scientific online publication. Due to the amount of data available on the website is needed to capture and understand the most relevant information. For this reason, the chosen dataset is composed of 324 samples of Total Cases per million (TCPM), New Cases (NC), New Tests (NT), and Stringency Index (SI) from six Latin American countries: Mexico, Peru, Ecuador, Colombia, Chile, and Cuba. Each one has been taken from the first confirmed case reported in the respective country to January 2021. It is important to remark that the data might be attached to limitations, and this can cause a bias in the results.

2.2   Methodology

FDA has recently received a lot of attention in the statistics literature, because in many applied problems of the different branches of science, the observations are modeled by a continuous stochastic process in time or space, where the observations represent a sample of random variables functions i.i.d, $X_1(t), X_2(t), \ldots, X_n(t) \in L^2[0,1]$. Since the measurements are independent, and the functions $X_i(t)$ have smooth trajectories through time t, the FPCA technique can be used to decompose the patterns of temporal or spatial variation.

The functional data $X_i(t)$ can represent a variable characteristic implementation of a stochastic process $\{X(t), t \in \mathbb{T}\}$ for an individual i, $1 \le i \le n$ at time t. Functional measures can be completely observed without noise in an arbitrary point network and the observations $Y_{it} = X_i(t)$ are considered to be available for all $t \in \mathbb{T}$, $i = 1, \ldots, n$, this is an unrealistic but mathematically convenient model. Observations with errors can also be obtained which is the most realistic case:

$$Y_i(t_{ij}) = X_i(t_{ij}) + \epsilon_{ij}, \quad \epsilon_{ij} \sim N(0, \sigma_\epsilon^2) \tag{1}$$

where t_{ij} are the registration times in a regular network, $t_{i1}, \ldots, t_{in_i}$.

The Karhunen-Loève (KL) expansion [10], provides a basic tool for describing the distribution of random functions X_i and can be considered as the theoretical foundation of FPCA. FPCA plays a much more important role in the functional data analysis than the multivariate analysis techniques, due to the distributions in function spaces are complex objects, and the KL expansion seems to be the only reasonable way to access this structure; another reason is that in multivariate analysis, an interpretation of the principal components might be difficult and has to be based on assumptions about the correlation of the principal components with the original variables, this problem does not exist in FPCA, because the eigenfunctions $\gamma_1, \gamma_2(t), \ldots$ represent the main forms of the stochastic process variation $X_i(t)$ in time t.

By definition it follows that if $\gamma_1, \gamma_2 \in L^2[0, 1]$, are basis of functions that satisfy the inner product:

$$\langle \gamma_1(t), \gamma_2(t) \rangle = \int_0^1 \gamma_1(t)\gamma_2(t)dt \tag{2}$$

and let $\|.\| = \langle ., . \rangle^{\frac{1}{2}}$, denotes the usual norm in L^2. FPCA produces a KL expansion in terms of two-dimensional functions $\gamma_j(t) = \{\gamma_{1j}(t), \gamma_{2j}(t)\}$, and coefficients β_{ij}, such that the observations can be expanded as:

$$X_i(t) = \mu(t) + \sum_{r=1}^{\infty} \beta_{ri}\gamma_r, \quad i = 1, \ldots, n \tag{3}$$

where $\mu(t) = \mathbb{E}\left(X_i(t)\right)$ is the mean function, and the $\beta_{ri} = <X_i(t) - \mu(t), \gamma_r>$, are uncorrelated random variables with $\mathbb{E}\left(\beta_{ri}\right) = 0$ and variance $\mathbb{E}\left(\beta_{ri}^2\right) = \lambda_i$, which satisfy: $\lambda_1 \geq \lambda_2 \geq \ldots$ and $\gamma_1, \gamma_2, \ldots$ denoting the eigenvalues and the corresponding orthonormal eigenfunctions of the covariance operator $k(t, s)$ of the functional observations $X_i(t)$, for more details see [2].

Then the random functions dynamics can be evaluated analyzing the functional principal components (FPC) γ_r as well as the distribution of the coefficients β_{ri}. The unknown characteristics λ_r and γ_r are estimated by the eigenvalues and eigenfunctions of the empirical covariance operator, which are estimated as follows: for $r-$ th pair of eigenvalues and eigenfunctions (λ_r, γ_r), is calculated:

$$\int_0^T k(t, s)\gamma_r(s)ds = \lambda_r \gamma_r(t) \tag{4}$$

where:

$$\int_0^T \gamma_r(t)dt = 1, \quad \int_0^T \gamma_r(t)\gamma_m(t)dt = 0, \quad r \neq m \tag{5}$$

replacing smoothed estimations in functional data $X_1(t), X_2(t), \ldots, X_n(t)$, the covariance operator is estimated:

$$k(t, s) = \sum_{r=1}^{\infty} \lambda_r \gamma_r(t)\gamma_r(s) \tag{6}$$

In practice, what is done is to truncate the expansion in M terms, and a certain percentage of the process variance is still retained; this is,

$$k(t, s) = \sum_{r=1}^{M} \lambda_r \gamma_r(t)\gamma_r(s) \tag{7}$$

then, the approximation would be:

$$X_i(t) = \mu(t) + \sum_{r=1}^{M} \beta_{ri} \gamma_r, \quad i = 1, \ldots, n \tag{8}$$

The truncation point M can be chosen as the smallest value that satisfies:

$$\frac{\sum_{r=1}^{M} \hat{\lambda}_r}{\sum_{l \geq 1} \hat{\lambda}_l} \geq M, \qquad 0 \leq M \leq 1 \tag{9}$$

so that a fraction M of the variance is explained, see [7]. To obtain a more detailed theoretical reviewed about FPCA and related techniques, see [16,21], [2] and its references. In the application, the functions of interest are not directly observed, but rather they are regression curves that have to be reconstructed from discrete data measured with errors.

In this context, the standard approach is to first estimate the individual functions in a non parametrical way (for instance, using $B-$splines), and then determine the principal components of the estimated empirical covariance operator. To understand the principal component weight functions $\gamma_r(t)$, a graph can be done $\bar{X}(t) \pm k\gamma_r(t)$, for some suitable multiple k. In this case the perturbed functions $\bar{X}(t) \pm k\gamma_r(t)$ are two-dimensional, and the trajectory is plotted in the space XY as t varies.

3 Results and Discussion

Being aware of the characteristics of the real-world data and the context where it was obtained we make a box-plot exploratory analysis in the raw dataset to know if it contains sparse information and missing values. From now on, the colors: green, pink, light blue, red, black and blue will represent Chile, Colombia, Cuba, Ecuador, Mexico, and Peru respectively, as is presented in Fig. 1 and Fig. 2.

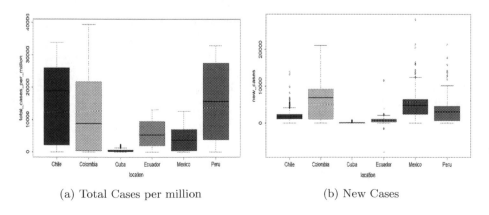

(a) Total Cases per million   (b) New Cases

Fig. 1. Boxplots of raw dataset. Part 1.

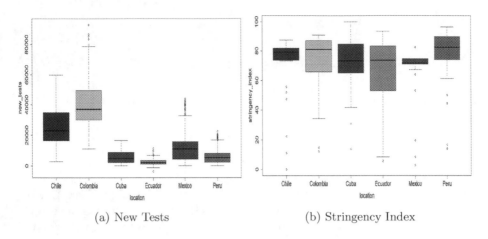

(a) New Tests   (b) Stringency Index

Fig. 2. Boxplots of raw dataset. Part 2.

Regarding Fig. 1a, we can see a wide variance in Chile, Colombia, and Peru comparing to Ecuador and Mexico that have a similar pattern, and Cuba where the TCPM on the time on evaluation remains low compared to the other countries. Moreover, Mexico and Peru have a symmetric distribution, and the rest of them asymmetric distribution.

In Fig. 1b, the negative outliers in Ecuador might be caused by errors in the recollection of the data. Contrary to TCPM boxplots the variance in NC are narrower with the three of them having a symmetric distribution and the others a negative asymmetry, also the presence of atypical values is seen clearly. It is pertinent to highlight the difference among the countries in the amount of NT, leading to the significant contrast in the mean.

Finally, it is understandable that for the steep changing in the political responses of each country the SI, which is a number from 1 to 100 that reflects the containment policies taken by the government, has the behavior shown in Fig. 2b. Even though the SI in all countries is high, the only country to reach the maximum value of political policies contingency is Cuba in a certain period.

Once the exploratory analysis of the raw data is done, to the treatment of missing values the data is interpolated and subsequently the methodology stated in Sect. 2.2 is applied using the R package `fda` [9]. In this case due to the characteristics of the data we choose B-Spline method to get the functional approximations as is shown in Fig. 3.

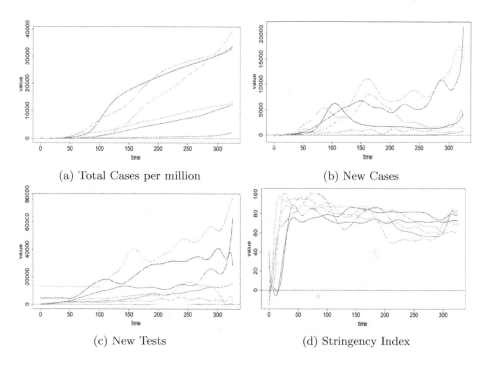

(a) Total Cases per million   (b) New Cases

(c) New Tests   (d) Stringency Index

Fig. 3. B-spline approximations.

Concerning B-Spline plots shown in Fig. 3 we can see an accurate approximation for TCPM, NC, and NT variables, while in SI there might be inaccuracies
at the beginning of the interval. It's interesting to observe the difference among
growth curve of Cuba with respect to the others, and how while the other ones
increase exponentially, the curves of TCPM and NC over time in Cuba remain
flat. Furthermore, respecting SI curve Fig. 3d we can see growth until the day 50
in the majority of the countries except for Cuba that keeps increasing approximately until the day 100; while the days go by SI decrease and TCPM increase
this is presented in all countries, but the most evident one is Ecuador. This may
show us the influence between SI and the growth curve of positive cases.

Now we present the FPCs plotted as perturbations of the mean function
after carrying out the FPCA technique in each one of the variables employing
the same R package, in particular, `pca.fd` function, with parameter `nharm = 4`
that corresponds to the number of FPCs to be computed. In Fig. 4, we notice
that the first two plots obtain almost 99% of the variance and that the last two
plots are not needed since are almost the same as the mean plot, in Fig. 4a the
observations have greater variance, which means that keeps increasing throughout the interval. On the other hand, in Fig. 4b there is a flip near the 250th day
from the first confirmed case, this happens due to the behavior of the TCPM
curve in these countries.

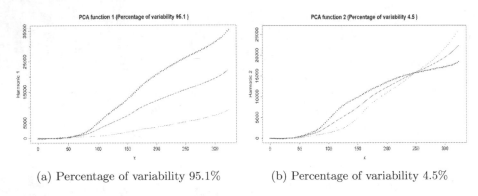

(a) Percentage of variability 95.1%   (b) Percentage of variability 4.5%

Fig. 4. Mean perturbations plot with FPC of total cases per million.

With respect to the NC dataset Fig. 5 we see that the first two plots get approximately 95% of the variance and the last one the remaining 5%, the last two plots have differences with the mean plot this is a result of the volatile and sinusoidal type of the NC dataset. Moreover, this also causes the flips on the 220th day in Fig. 5b, and the others in Fig. 5c and d. In this variable the variance also increase over the interval.

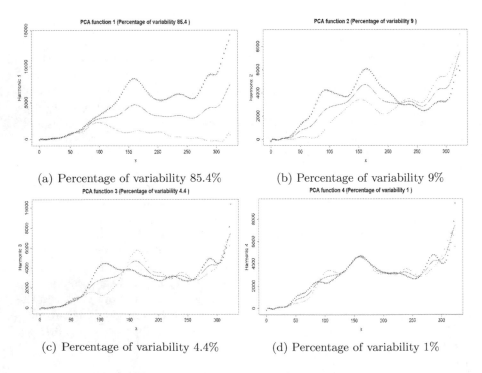

(a) Percentage of variability 85.4%   (b) Percentage of variability 9%

(c) Percentage of variability 4.4%   (d) Percentage of variability 1%

Fig. 5. Mean perturbations plot with FPC of new cases.

The mean perturbation plot of NT are showed in Fig. 6. We see that the first two plots get the majority of the variance with almost 98% of it, all plots are rising over time but at the end present small perturbations that could be interesting to be analyzed in a future study taking into account the variables that influenced in this particular period. Similarly, to the Fig. 5 the last 3 plots present flips because of the behavior of the growth curve of NT in the 324 days when the data was obtained.

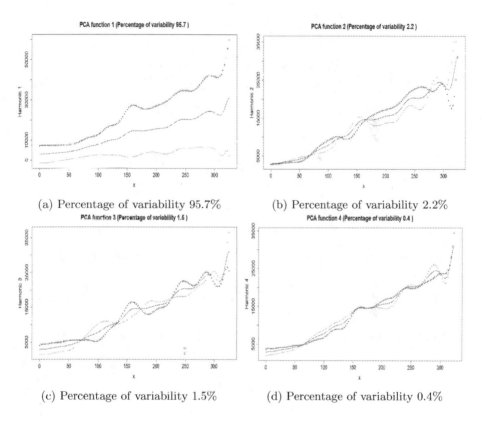

(a) Percentage of variability 95.7%   (b) Percentage of variability 2.2%

(c) Percentage of variability 1.5%   (d) Percentage of variability 0.4%

Fig. 6. Mean perturbation plot with FPC of new tests.

The perturbations of SI is located at the beginning of the interval, this might be caused by the inaccuracy of the B-spline approximation when we transform to functional data or the abrupt change in the policies responses as a result of the COVID-19 breakout. Moreover, the variance of the Fig. 7a and b is less than the mean perturbations plots of the other variables with only 83.6% and produce flips in all plots of the percentages of variability.

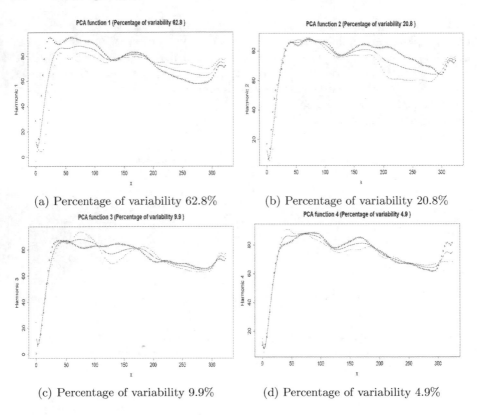

(a) Percentage of variability 62.8%   (b) Percentage of variability 20.8%

(c) Percentage of variability 9.9%   (d) Percentage of variability 4.9%

Fig. 7. Mean perturbations plot with FPC of stringency index.

To summarize the percentage of variability of the four variables we present Table 1.

Table 1. Summary of percentage of variability.

Variable	FPC1	FPC2	FPC3	FPC4	Total
TCPM	95.1%	4.5%	0.4%	0%	100%
NC	85.4%	9%	4.4%	1%	99.8%
NT	95.7%	2.2%	1.5%	0.4%	99.8%
SI	62.8%	20.8%	9.9%	4.9%	98.4%

Finally, we make a score plot to FPC1 and FPC2 to look at their relationship.

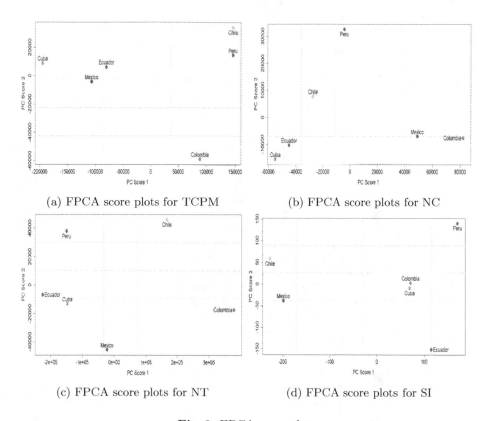

(a) FPCA score plots for TCPM

(b) FPCA score plots for NC

(c) FPCA score plots for NT

(d) FPCA score plots for SI

Fig. 8. FPCA score plots

Since our data set was only acquired in 6 countries of Latin America it's difficult to see if there exists an accumulation for any of the variables according to their behavior. However, in Fig. 8a we can group Ecuador and Mexico, and Cuba and Peru, in Fig. 8b Ecuador and Cuba are closer than the other countries, in Fig. 8c all countries are scattered and in Fig. 8d Cuba and Colombia are together while the others stay separate.

4   Conclusions and Further Studies

The presented work used one method of Functional Data Analysis to make a brief study of the COVID-19 pandemic in a few Latin American countries. In the initial boxplot analysis, we were able to observe the type of distribution, the variance, and the difference among the variables of the 6 countries to be studied. Moreover, by the B-splines approximations plot, we took notice of the variables behavior along the time of observation, seeing an increasing pattern in all of them and the influence of stringency index over the growth curve of positive cases. Regarding the score plot, we have to remark the case of Cuba with respect to the New Cases per day variable that is the lowest and will be worthwhile to analyze in the future the factors that contributed to this result.

In the future researches will be valuable to perform a forecast study of confirmed cases and the influence of political responses in the growth curve of new cases per day using other FDA techniques that allow us to get a broad analysis of the COVID-19 pandemic in more Latin America countries. Therefore, we encourage to continue this study employing more FDA procedures, for instance, those mentioned in [13].

References

1. Ballari, D., Giraldo, R., Campozano, L., Samaniego, E.: Spatial functional data analysis for regionalizing precipitation seasonality and intensity in a sparsely monitored region: unveiling the spatio-temporal dependencies of precipitation in Ecuador. Int. J. Climatol. **38**(8), 3337–3354 (2018)
2. Benko, M., Härdle, W., Kneip, A., et al.: Common functional principal components. Ann. Stat. **37**(1), 1–34 (2009)
3. Besse, P., Ramsay, J.O.: Principal components analysis of sampled functions. Psychometrika **51**(2), 285–311 (1986). https://doi.org/10.1007/BF02293986
4. Boschi, T., Di Iorio, J., Testa, L., Cremona, M.A., Chiaromonte, F.: The shapes of an epidemic: using functional data analysis to characterize COVID-19 in Italy. arXiv preprint arXiv:2008.04700 (2020)
5. Castillo-Páez, S., Flores, M., Herrera Enríquez, G.: Análisis de datos funcionales aplicado al riesgo financiero: un caso de estudio en cooperativas de ahorro y crédito ecuatorianas. Latin Am. J. Comput **4**(1), 9 (2017)
6. Di, C.Z., Crainiceanu, C.M., Caffo, B.S., Punjabi, N.M.: Multilevel functional principal component analysis. Ann. Appl. Stat. **3**(1), 458 (2009)
7. Han, K., et al.: Functional principal component analysis for identifying multivariate patterns and archetypes of growth, and their association with long-term cognitive development. PloS one **13**(11), e0207073 (2018)
8. Iqbal, M., et al.: Covid-19 patient count prediction using LSTM. IEEE Trans. Comput. Soc. Syst. (2021)
9. Ramsay, J.O.: Spencer Graves, G.H.: Package 'fda' for R (2020)
10. Loéve, M.: Elementary Probability Theory. In: Probability Theory I. Graduate Texts in Mathematics, vol. 45, pp. 1–52. Springer, New York (1977). https://doi.org/10.1007/978-1-4684-9464-8_1
11. World Health Organization: A joint statement on tourism and COVID-19 - UNWTO and WHO call for responsibility and coordination. www.who.int/news/item/27-02-2020-a-joint-statement-on-tourism-and-covid-19--unwto-and-who-call-for-responsibility-and-coordination. Accessed 07 Feb 2021
12. OWID: Our world in data. https://ourworldindata.org/ (2020). Accessed 07 Feb 2021
13. Padilla-Segarra, A., González-Villacorte, M., Amaro, I.R., Infante, S.: Brief review of functional data analysis: a case study on regional demographic and economic data. In: Rodriguez Morales, G., Fonseca, C.E.R., Salgado, J.P., Pérez-Gosende, P., Orellana Cordero, M., Berrezueta, S. (eds.) TICEC 2020. CCIS, vol. 1307, pp. 163–176. Springer, Cham (2020). https://doi.org/10.1007/978-3-030-62833-8_14

14. Pozo, S., Carrillo, G., Amaro, I.R.: An exploratory analysis of COVID-19 in South America. In: Iano, Y., Saotome, O., Kemper, G., Mendes de Seixas, A.C., Gomes de Oliveira, G. (eds.) BTSym 2020. SIST, vol. 233, pp. 266–280. Springer, Cham (2021). https://doi.org/10.1007/978-3-030-75680-2_31

15. Ramsay, J.O., Dalzell, C.: Some tools for functional data analysis. J. Royal Stat. Soc. Ser. B (Methodol.) **53**(3), 539–561 (1991)

16. Ramsay, J., Silverman, B.: Functional Data Analysis. Springer, New York (2005). https://doi.org/10.1007/b98888

17. RodrRodriguez-Morales, A.J., et al.: COVID-19 in Latin America: The implications of the first confirmed case in Brazil. Travel medicine and infectious disease (2020)

18. Sabando, M.C., Tallana-Chimarro, D., Amaro, I.R.: Health impact analysis of COVID-19 in Ecuadorian provinces. In: Iano, Y., Saotome, O., Kemper, G., Mendes de Seixas, A.C., Gomes de Oliveira, G. (eds.) BTSym 2020. SIST, vol. 233, pp. 281–292. Springer, Cham (2021). https://doi.org/10.1007/978-3-030-75680-2_32

19. Sánchez-Sánchez, M.L., et al.: Functional principal component analysis as a new methodology for the analysis of the impact of two rehabilitation protocols in functional recovery after stroke. J. Neuroeng. Rehabil. **11**(1), 1–9 (2014). https://doi.org/10.1186/1743-0003-11-134

20. Tang, C., Wang, T., Zhang, P.: Functional data analysis: An application to COVID-19 data in the united states. arXiv preprint arXiv:2009.08363 (2020)

21. Wang, J.L., Chiou, J.M., Müller, H.G.: Review of functional data analysis. arXiv preprint arXiv:1507.05135 (2015)

Multivariate Technical Analysis of Data on the Multidimensional Effects of Pandemics in Chile (1850–1923)

Alexis Matheu[1]([⊠]) [ID], Paola Juica[1] [ID], Francisco Ocaranza[1] [ID],
Juliana Hadjitchoneva[2], Marcelo Ruiz[1] [ID], and Claudio Ruff[1] [ID]

[1] Universidad Bernardo O´Higgins, Centro de Investigación Institucional, Santiago de Chile,
Av. Viel 1497, Santiago, Chile
alexis.matheu@ubo.cl
[2] New Bulgarian University, 21 Montevideo Street, NUB, 1618 Sofia, Bulgaria

Abstract. Introduction: The current crisis situation leads us to reflect on the effects that Chile has had throughout the various pandemics that have hit the world in the last 200 years and on the level of impact that they have had on its social development. **Objective:** To analyze, from a socio-historical perspective, the main elements that characterized the pandemics that occurred between the years 1850–1923 in Chile. **Methods:** Main component techniques were used to analyze multivariate data, in terms of new noncorrelated variables, and multivariate sample techniques in a space of reduced dimension (Biplot). **Results:** The research showed the relative and direct effects of pandemics in Chile on the economic life of the country, and their influence on mortality and birth rates. **Conclusion:** This study confirmed that the consequences of these health crises were multidimensional and that they significantly affected the development of the nation.

Keywords: Pandemics · Sociohistorical analysis · Multivariate data analysis

1 Introduction

Throughout its history, humanity has suffered from devastating consequences of diseases that have hit the world. They have become milestones that have had a disastrous impact on the life and development of society. Chile has not been exempted from suffering as a consequence of these pandemics. Some examples of pandemics are the exanthematic typhus during 1864 and 1866, which originated in the Choapa Valley and attacked mainly low-income, alcoholic, and malnourished populations [1]. Afterward, between 1886 and 1888, the sixth cholera world pandemic [2] arrived in Chile from Argentina through the mountain passes [3]. In Argentina, the virus appeared in the neighborhood La Boca in Buenos Aires [4]. The first cities that informed about the presence of cholera were Valparaíso and its surroundings [5]. In fact, the village Santa María is identified as the starting point of the pandemic, and then it is spread into Putaendo, San Felipe, Los Andes, Limache, Llay-Llay, and Quilpué [6].

© Springer Nature Switzerland AG 2021
T. Guarda et al. (Eds.): ARTIIS 2021, CCIS 1485, pp. 234–246, 2021.
https://doi.org/10.1007/978-3-030-90241-4_19

Later in 1918, it can be found that the "Spanish" epidemic originated in the United States and was spread by its soldiers in Europe. As a consequence of the pandemic, between 45 and 100 million deaths had been counted worldwide. The number has been estimated in 50 million deaths by other researchers [7].

The crisis is manifested in four waves between 1918 and 1921. The first occurred between October 1918 and February 1919, and it constituted the peak period of contagious and deaths. Then between the last quarter of 1920 and the summer of 1921, a new outbreak –although milder than the previous ones– occurred in the provinces of Tarapacá, O'Higgins, Arauco, and Valdivia. Finally, the last episode hit Santiago intensively, between June and December of 1921[8].

Regarding these sociohistorical contexts, it is possible to determine and characterize the constitutive elements of a health crisis process, considering the components of the development of a nation. Thus, it can be evaluated how these events have impacted the growth processes and social progress, according to the predominant cultural and political models of each era.

Without a doubt, Chile has experience in the ways of dealing with adversity, which is based on its geography and political history. That is why it is genuinely significant to examine carefully and exhaustively the historical, political, cultural, and economic processes linked to pandemics that this nation has overcome.

This paper aimed to analyze, from a sociohistorical perspective, the main elements that characterized the pandemics that occurred between the years 1850–1923 in Chile.

2 Methods

The analysis of this research used the Principal Component Analysis (PCA), which was applied to study the multivariate data, non-correlated with Biplot techniques.

Regarding these techniques, the economic impact of pandemics in the development in Chile is analyzed. Thus, statistical studies were considered based on economic variables related to exportations, importations, and Gross Domestic Product (GDP), in contrast to the variables connected to health indicators such as mortality and birth rates.

2.1 Analysis of the Statistical Techniques Used

The historical moments of the pandemics related to economic variables (GDP, exportations, and importations) and health variables (number of deaths per 100,000 inhabitants, and birth rate) were analyzed through different statistical techniques. The analysis sought to establish the consequences and impacts of pandemics in Chile, considering the eras studied.

The statistical methods used were:

- *Scatter diagrams*: They were used to describe the joint behaviors of two variables, in which each case is represented as a point in the plane defined by the variables, in order to detect any relation or correlation between the two variables. In the first analysis, correlations from the graph patterns were found. The patterns could be positive (both values increase in the same direction), negative (one value increases and the other one decreases), null (no correlation), linear, exponential, quadratic, among others. The strength of correlation was determined by the proximity of the points to the pattern graph.

- *Principal Component Analysis (PCA)*: It was a statistical technique of synthesis and reduction of information (number of variables), in which the loss of information is as minimal as possible. The new components were a linear combination of original variables that were also independent between them, which eliminated the problem of collinearity among the possibly correlated variables.

In a PCA, it is vital to give evidence of the variance explained by each of the principal components because it shows how much data is lost considering each component's projections. The summation of all these variances is equal to 1 (100%); consequently, depending on the precision of each study, it could be accepted a variance between values of 60% to 100%.

- *Biplot Methods (HJ-Biplot)*: Multivariate generalization of a scatter diagram from PCA, the multivariate analysis through graphical representations was proposed by Gabriel (1971) [9]. The rows of the matrices generated are represented by points, while vectors represent the columns. In the research, the data were contained in a matrix, in which the rows were the years analyzed, and the columns were the economic and health indicators studied.

Biplot allows to plot the row i of data matrix through the markers pi, and column j through the vectors lj, so when the point pi is projected into the vector lj, this projection overlaps with the value that the indicator has had, i.e., it is a geometric representation of the scalar product.

The representations have a great practical interest because each point of the rows can be projected into all the column variables, thus allowing the localization of the position of these in each indicator variable.

Concerning the multiple ways to represent a Biplot, in this research, the HJ-Biplot was used, which was suggested by Galindo (1986) [10], because this representation made possible that both markers (rows and columns) could be represented with maximum quality in the same reference. In regard to final conclusions, it must be considered the following rules, which are specific to HJ-Biplot visualizations:

1. The length of the vectors approximates the standard deviation of the indicators studied.
2. The cosines of the angles between the vectors approximate the correlations between the indicators. Likewise, the cosines between the vectors and the axis approximate the correlations between both of them.
3. The order of the orthogonal projections of the rows estimates the order of the elements in that vector.
4. The distance of the row markers expresses similarities of the individuals studied.

3 Results

An initial analysis using scatter diagrams provided the first elements of the three pandemic periods studied. Regarding the variations of real GDP, it was slightly affected in the two first pandemics: the typhus during 1864–1866 and cholera in 1886–1888. Nevertheless, in the second part of the Spanish flu pandemic (1920–1921), the GDP reduction was more significant. Figure 1 shows a positive linear correlation between both variables with variations in the three pandemic periods, and during the years when other historical events took place, such as the Pacific War (1879–1883) and the First World War (1914–1918), in which occurred negative correlation changes. The correlation matrix supports the above exposed with a high significance and a strong correlation, close to 1 (0,964).

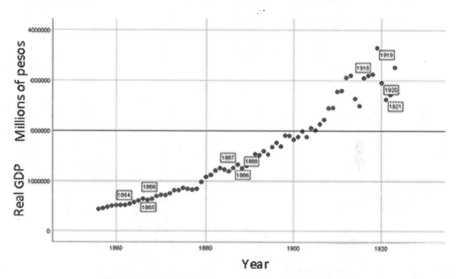

Fig. 1. Scatter between pandemic periods and GDP.

The second economic variable analyzed (exportations) maintained similar trends to the first one, although the reductions (negative correlations) during the three periods of the pandemics were more significant. Likewise, a positive linear correlation was observed until the year 1906 approximately, but it tended to a slight exponential change from that

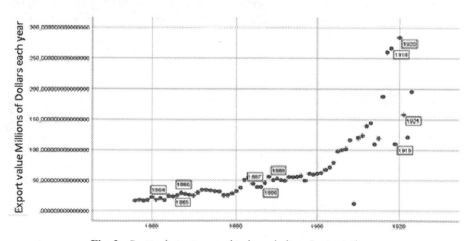

Fig. 2. Scatter between pandemic periods and exportations.

point. The correlation matrix of this variable demonstrated the analysis but not with the strength of the GDP variable (0,787). Furthermore, there was a strong correlation between the behavior of GDP and exportations (0,842) (Fig. 2).

The last economic variable analyzed, importations, changed its trend during the Spanish Flu, in which the value of importations was not affected in the period of the pandemic itself. Nonetheless, it was affected in 1992, a year after the pandemic (Fig. 3).

It is important to highlight that, as in the first two variables, the periods of the two wars had a significant impact than the pandemics. The correlations between the three economic variables showed the strength of the positive relation and a great significance in the analysis conducted[1].

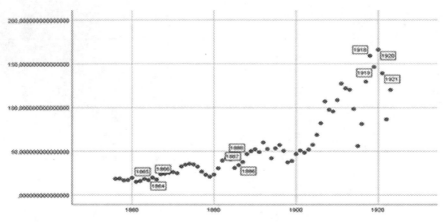

Fig. 3. Scatter between pandemic periods and importations.

Regarding health indicators, the first of them, the number of deaths per 100,000 inhabitants, shows weak correlations in the period, as shown in Fig. 4. However, it impacts the indicator considering the three pandemics, with increases in the number of deaths in the three periods of pandemics. There is a low correlation with the three economic variables described.

The other health variable, birth rate, maintained the trend of linearity as the economic variables, hence their strong correlations with these variables and the low correlation with the other health variable. It is worth noting that in the case of the two first pandemics, the impact on the birth rate was marked with a negative correlation, unlike with the third pandemic, in which the impact of the pandemic was almost null in correlations (Fig. 5).

---

[1] Correlation importations (I) –Year 0,865, I- GDP 0,920, I- Exportations 0,884.

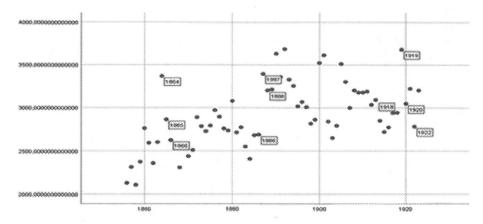

Fig. 4. Scatter between periods of pandemics and number of deaths per 100,000 habitants

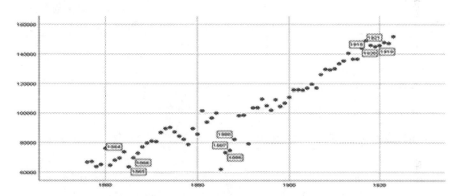

Fig. 5. Scatter between periods of pandemic and importations and birth rates.

Biplot analysis showed in one representation all the elements analyzed. First, considering the periods of pandemics –using PCA–, they were represented with 87% of the explained variance, assuring the feasibility of the analyses conducted. All the variables, except the number of deaths per 100,000 inhabitants, were related to each other. Furthermore, in several years of the pandemics, the individuals of analysis (years) are at the top of Fig. 6. This confirms the effect on the variable deaths per 100,000 inhabitants in the representation. It is important to highlight the evolution (from left to right in the graph) of the economic variables and birth rate in a linear proportion of deviations. Only at certain times of the pandemic, the individuals (years) were in some points to the left of the preceding years, which indicates the slight setbacks in those variables regarding pandemic aspects.

In the first pandemic (1864–1865–1866), the leftward trend of the points as the years increase was an example of the negative impact in the correlation between pandemics and economic variables. The same situation is observed in the years 1920 and 1921.

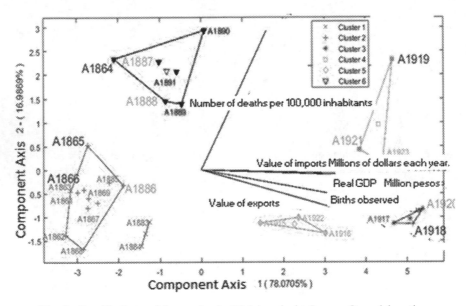

Fig. 6. Specific times of the pandemic, Biplot analysis. Source: Own elaboration.

Following the analysis order, considering the typhoid fever, it was observed that it affected, mainly, low-income people, who worked in farms, aged between 15 and 45 years old, in other words, the pandemic affected the primary productive force on which the Chilean economy depended. The contagion rates were so high that they reached alarming levels in 1865 when a third of the hospitalization was due to this disease.

In Fig. 7, the years in which the pandemic was suffered were analyzed, and they were compared with the three previous years and three subsequent years to this event. In this context, it is significant to note that the year of the beginning of the pandemic, 1864, was when the highest number of deaths was recorded, confirming that the significant impact of pandemics occurs during the first year of their emergence. This number fell in 1865 in correlation to the numbers in the previous year. On the other hand, the value of exportations rose to 40%, encouraged by the governmental policies of the time.

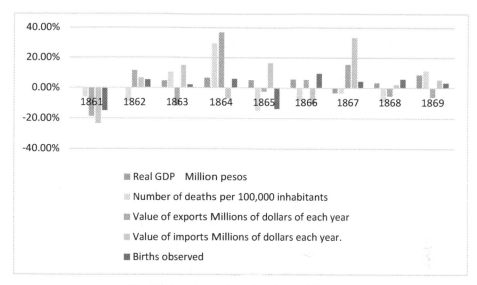

Fig. 7. Exanthematic typhus from 1864–1866.

After this sanitary crisis, there was a strong tendency to reactivate the economy, achieving an increase of over 30% in the value of imports. At the same time, the data showed that, during the pandemic period, Chile's economy was not so heavily damaged. The Real[2] GDP during these years and the value of exports rebounded between 1866 and 1867. However, imports were affected at the end of the pandemic, strengthening significantly due to government policies in the following year.

Figure 8 shows the background analysis for the three years before and after the onset of the cholera epidemic. It is significant to note that the greatest number of deaths from this disease did not occur, as is common in this type of pandemic, in the first year of its appearance, but rather, the greatest number of deaths occurred in the second year. From the point of view of the economy, it was observable how much care was taken to protect it compared to the precautions taken with respect to public health protection measures. However, in any case, the GDP was affected in 1888, showing a decline, but it recovered in 1890, a year before the economy was brutally destroyed in 1891 with the civil war.

Figure 9 shows the statistical data for this pandemic period, which was longer than the previous ones and was divided into two stages. The first shows that in both stages the Spanish flu did have an effect on the economy, evidencing declines in all economic figures. In 1920, however, there was an extraordinary rise in the export index, in the midst of the Spanish crisis, due to a historical fact, the creation of synthetic nitrate by the Europeans, which in 1920 forced Chile to export its natural nitrate stocks.

---

[2] Total and sectorial real GDP, 2003 base, figures extracted from the book *Chile 1810–2010, la República en Cifras* (2016). All research figures are extracted from this text.

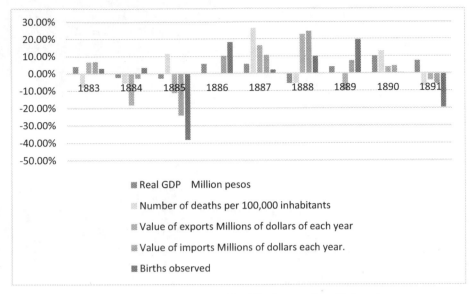

Fig. 8. Cholera between 1886–1888. Source: Own Elaboration

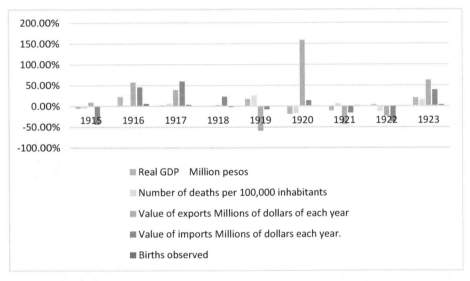

Fig. 9. Spanish flu in 1918 and 1921. Source: Own Elaboration.

The results of this research concluded that the measures taken by the different governments in power at the time of the pandemic had a direct influence on the indexes that show the impact of these crises, both on the economy and on the policies aimed at ensuring public health, with evidence of the government's decision to prioritize one or the other aspect. Under this perspective, it was recorded how the public policies of the past were clearly insufficient to ensure, in the broad sense of the term, the health, economic and social needs of the country.

4 Discussion

The economic and demographic relationships obtained in the results are influenced by the following political and historical elements of the time. According to the data obtained in this study, it is possible to point out some aspects that characterized the Chilean economy during the pandemic times analyzed. Thus, it is pointed out that between 1880 and 1930, Chile lived under a liberal and mono-producer economic system. Coincidentally, at both ends of this period, as already mentioned, the country was hit by two pandemics: cholera (1886–1889) and the Spanish flu (1918).

Since colonial times, the Chilean economy has been closely linked to the production of metals. In the 16th and 17th centuries, it was gold and silver, and in the 18th and 19th centuries, copper. Although Chile had been producing saltpeter since the 1860s, after its victory in the War of the Pacific (1879–1883), its production intensified, thanks, firstly, to the abundance of saltpeter in the northern regions, and then, necessarily, to the associated investment, in this case, from foreign capital, mostly British. In fact, by 1895, 60% of production was in the hands of British capital, which was reversed by 1918, when the same figure corresponded to Chilean participation [11].

To understand the impact of the nitrate industry during the period in question, it should be noted that between 1880 and 1920, its production averaged a growth of 6.1% per year. It should also be noted that, during the 1890s, its exports constituted 50% of the country's total, a figure that rose to 70% between the beginning of the 20th century and World War I [12]. The value of exports amounted to US$ 6.3 million in 1880, increasing to US$ 70 million in 1928, reaching its highest value just at the beginning of World War I (US$ 96 million) [13].

The good performance of nitrate exports meant that it occupied a predominant place in Chile's economic matrix. In fact, between 1900 and 1920, it accounted for an average of 30% of GDP [13]. As a consequence, it contributed 50% of total national taxes between 1895 and 1920 (US$ 1 million in 1880, rising to US$ 20 million at the beginning of the 20th century) [12].

As a result of the increase in tax collection, the State gained a greater share of the national economy (GGP), from 5% to 6% in 1880, to 12% to 14% between 1910 and 1920 [13]. It also resulted in an expansion of the state bureaucracy, from 3000 positions in 1880 to slightly more than 27,000 in 1919; of educational coverage, where if in 1860 there were 18,000 young people participating in primary education and 2,200 in secondary education, by 1900, the figures had increased to 157,000 and 12,600, and in 1920 to 346,000 and 49,000 respectively; and in transportation infrastructure, from 1106 km of railroads in 1890 to 4,579 km in 1920 [13].

The increase in tax collection made it possible to eliminate old taxes such as the alcabala, the contribution of inheritances and donations, the payment of patents for agricultural and industrial machinery, the tobacco stamp tax, and to reduce others, such as the agricultural tax, the tax on movable assets, and the income tax. This dependence on a single tax item generated an "unstable tax situation" [12]. This situation ended up taking its toll as a result of the production of synthetic European saltpeter during World War I, worsening the situation around 1929, when its value dropped to levels close to those of 1880 [14]. For this reason, around 1918–1920, the government had to increase the collection of direct taxes, especially on luxury goods, by at least 50%. In spite of the above, the governmental collection was not sufficient, even after having obtained a loan of 60 million dollars [11].

After the end of the Pacific War, there was a boom in sheep farming in the extreme south. There was also a slight industrial growth phenomenon associated with agricultural production. Milk producers developed their by-products, fruit producers marmalade, tobacco producers cigarettes, grain producers beer, noodles and cookies, and leather producers shoes, thanks to the possibility of installing these goods in the cities and the saltpeter works [11].

Between 1910 and 1920, wheat production slowed down its growth rate due to the impact on sales caused by competition with Australia, Argentina, Canada, the USA, and Russia in the market, in addition to the plagues and climatic instability that affected the central area of the country [11].

The industrializing eagerness led to the creation in 1883 of the Sociedad de Fomento Fabril (SOFOFA), which promoted the technical training of future workers, the presence of Chile in international economic forums, and advocated an increase in taxes on the importation of foreign manufactured goods, in order to encourage local production. In 1897, a Customs Ordinance was issued in this sense, but with the precaution of reducing taxes on industrial machinery and raw materials [11]. The tax base of 25% was maintained, except for 57 products, which were increased to 60%, while industrial supplies were taxed at a rate of 5% [14].

By 1915 there were a total of 7800 industrial plants, primarily small-scale. They employed about 80,000 people, satisfying 80% of the domestic demand. The following year taxes on imports were increased again, from 50% to 80%, which increased the development of local industry [12]. The main industrial centers were located in Santiago, Valparaíso, and Concepción [14].

Between 1908 and 1916, the so-called large copper mining industry gained strength as a result of the investments made by North American capital in the northern and central areas of Chile. In 1915 the Guggenheim family transferred the Chuquicamata and El Teniente deposits to the Kennecott Copper Company, and in 1916 the Anaconda Copper Company opened the Potrerillos ore. Thus, Chile's world participation in copper production increased from 4.3% to 10% [11].

According to an important part of the historiography, the saltpeter cycle is remembered as a "lost opportunity". Of the large amount of resources generated as a consequence of its production, what was reinvested in the country corresponds to a reduced amount, while most of it was taken to developed countries by foreign investors. As Meller says: "This vision corresponds to the 'enclave hypothesis': the export sector, dominated by foreign investment, is more connected to developed countries than to the domestic economy, requires very few national supplies and the profits are sent abroad; consequently, the hosting economy does not benefit at all" [12].

5 Concluding Remarks

From the evidence of all the data collected and their analysis, we can conclude that during the first typhus pandemic, since the authorities were unaware of it, the measures taken were almost null, so the impact on the economy was reduced, but not the number of deaths per 100,000 inhabitants, which increased in the year 1864, growing by almost 700 deaths per 100,000 inhabitants.

In the second pandemic, the case of cholera, although measures were taken such as closing the borders, there was no positive impact on the number of deaths, which grew at the same rate as in the first pandemic. As for the economic consequences, the impact was greater, especially on imports and exports. In this pandemic, the drop in the number of births in the country stands out.

The Spanish flu pandemic had a substantial impact on both the number of deaths in Chile and GDP, but not on imports and exports.

The slight impact on the economic development of the nation and the high impact on the health of the population lead us to conclude that the economy was better protected than health in the three moments of the pandemic.

The historical perspective provides routes to understand the globalizing interest of a study of diseases and their influences on the development of different societies since ancient times, especially for the value that may have been given to health in the history of Chile in pandemic phenomena. The study shows that governmental and political responses were insufficient from the point of view of health protection, not only because of the measures implemented, but also because they were not able to convince the civilian population of the importance of complying with appropriate norms and rules of behavior in the face of these events. Today, in times of a pandemic, with the new COVID-19, society and its leaders are once again facing the same questions, and although it is not yet possible to measure all the impacts and consequences of this new pandemic, it seems that history is repeating itself.

This paper sought to analyze the social and economic effects of pandemics in Chile between the late 19th and early 20th centuries, from a perspective that used multivariate statistics based on historical data. In conclusion, its future research projections are defined by its application to other historical periods as well as to other countries in the region.

References

1. Barros Arana, D.: Estudios Geográficos sobre Chile. Imprenta Nacional, Santiago (1875)
2. Westfall, C., Cáceres, I.: Vidas mínimas y muertes anónimas. Arqueología de la salud pública de Chile. La epidemia de cólera en Santiago, siglo diecinueve. Canto Rodado **201**(6), 167–92 (2011)
3. Salinas, R.: Salud, ideología y desarrollo social en Chile 1830–1950. Cuadernos Historia **3**, 99–126 (1983)
4. Laval, E.: Chile 1918: Las dos epidemias. Rev. Chilena Infectol. **20**, 133–135 (2003)
5. Laval, E.: El cólera en Chile (1886–1888). Rev. Chilena Infectol. **20**, 86–88 (2003)
6. Illanes, M.: En el nombre del pueblo, del Estado y de la ciencia. Historia social de la salud pública. Chile 1880–1973. Colectivo de Atención Primaria, Santiago (1993)

7. López, M., Beltrán, M.: Chile entre pandemias: la influenza de 1918, globalización y la nueva medicina. Rev. Chilena Infectol. **30**(2), 206–215 (2003)
8. Chowell, G., Simonsen, L., Flores, J., Miller, M., Viboud, C.: Death patterns during the 1918 influenza pandemic in chile. Emerg. Infect. Dis. **20**(11), 1803–1811 (2014)
9. Gabriel, K.: The biplot graphic display of matrices with application to principal component analysis. Biometrika **58**(3), 453–467 (1971)
10. Galindo, M., Cuadras, C.: Una extensión del método Biplot y su relación con otras técnicas. Publicaciones Bioestadística Biomatemática **17**, 17–51 (1986)
11. Collier, S., Sater, W.: Historia de Chile 1808–1994. Cambridge University Press, Madrid (1999)
12. Meller, P.: Un siglo de economía política chilena (1880–1990). Uqbar, Santiago (2016)
13. Briones, I., Islas, G.: Comercio exterior de Chile en perspectiva histórica, 1810–2010. Tomo III: Problemas económicos. Fondo de Cultura Económica, Santiago (2018)
14. Correa, S., Figueroa, C., Jocelyn-Holt, A., Rolle, C., Vicuña, M.: Historia del siglo XX chileno. Balance paradojal. Editorial Sudamericana, Santiago (2001)

An Analytical Overview of the Projects Approved by the Portugal 2020 Programme

Helena Adams[1] and Filipe Portela[1,2(✉)] (iD)

[1] Algoritmi Research Centre, University of Minho, Braga, Portugal
a85624@alunos.uminho.pt, cfp@dsi.uminho.pt
[2] IOTECH—Innovation on Technology, Trofa, Portugal

Abstract. The Portugal 2020 programme (PT2020) arose from a partnership agreement between Portugal and the European Commission. This commission brings together the activities of the five European Structural and Investment Funds, where the programming principles of action apply the policy of economic, social, and territorial development are defined to promote, in Portugal, between 2014 and 2020. Thus, Portugal received about 25 billion euros until 2020 to invest in operations related to the thematic objectives defined by the country to stimulate growth and job creation, the necessary interventions to achieve them, and the expected results with this funding. Therefore, the main objective of this article is to characterise the panorama of the PT2020 programme investments in Portugal. It was possible to determine that the North region of Portugal holds almost 40% of all operations approved by PT2020 and most of the financial support made available by the European Commission. It was also found that the financial support implemented per year was always lower than what was initially planned to be used. The number of operations associated with the investment type "Liquidity Support" corresponds to about 45% of the total number of approved operations, an investment planned in about 305 654 193€.

Keywords: Data analytics · Data warehouse · Key Performance Indicators (KPI's) · Business intelligence · Portugal 2020

1 Introduction

Nowadays, programmes such as Portugal 2020 have a significant impact on a country's economy, massive help for economic growth and development and sustainability, better allocation of resources, investment in human capital, and international recognition. Portugal established a partnership with the European Commission to improve between 2014 and 2020 regarding the topics described above. That said, this document seeks to answer a simple question: which thematic areas, operational programmes, national regions, and nature of investment have obtained higher financial support and a higher number of approved operations.

© Springer Nature Switzerland AG 2021
T. Guarda et al. (Eds.): ARTIIS 2021, CCIS 1485, pp. 247–262, 2021.
https://doi.org/10.1007/978-3-030-90241-4_20

It is essential to understand the effectiveness of the PT2020 project from several points: the point of view of citizens [6], the policy applied by PT2020 in the promotion of sustainable territorial development [5], the effects of European Union funds in the central region of Portugal [12, 13], the economic impacts in the North [7] and the financial impact of PT2020, based on the specific case of a company [1]. Although PT2020 funds have been the target of several studies mentioned above, the overview of the applicability and distribution of these funds is still missing. In order to obtain this analytical vision of the applicability and distribution of the financial funds of the PT2020 programme and to better characterise the panorama of the investments made, it was necessary to carry out a practical component, which corresponds to the development of a project inserted in the area of Business Intelligence. In order to explain the process made, this article follows the Kimball Methodology.

For this purpose, in Sect. 2, a description and understanding of the base of the Portugal 2020 programme is made. In Sect. 3, the methodologies, and tools used are described, followed by the analysis of the datasets provided by the project manager and using Data Analytics techniques to determine the quality of the data, detecting anomalies and presenting strategies for their correction and transformation demonstrated in Sect. 4. Subsequently, in Sect. 4, a multidimensional model is proposed to store the most relevant data and implement the Data Warehouse, creating an Extraction, Transformation and Loading process (ETL). Finally, in Sect. 5, four dashboards and a word cloud are demonstrated, developed from the data obtained from the process described in Sect. 4. A discussion of the project results is made to understand better what kind of operations were accepted in the Portugal 2020 programme.

2   Background

This section sets out the business context in question and clarifies the terms used throughout the article referring to it. Portugal 2020 corresponds to a partnership between Portugal and the European Commission, through which the principles that are aligned with smart, sustainable and inclusive growth were defined, based on the Europe 2020 strategy and that apply the economic, social and territorial development policy to promote Portugal between 2014 and 2020 [8].

In this topic, the terms referring to the PT2020 programme are described below. It allows to clarify what each one means in the context of the programme:

- **Operational Programmes**: These are programmes built under Portugal 2020 to align national and European strategic guidelines, mobilising in different domains. This article addresses only the thematic operational programmes, the mainland's regional operational programmes, and the autonomous regions [8].
- **European Union Funds:** There are five European Structural and Investment Funds, aiming to promote investment in the economy, a sustainable and healthy environment and job creation. In this article, only the European Regional Development Fund (ERDF), the European Social Fund (ESF) and finally, the Cohesion Fund (CF) are referred to [2].

- **Nature of Investment:** The nature of investment in operations is divided into six main categories: Infrastructure, Equipment/Material, Intangible Actions/Studies, Technical Assistance, Financing Support and Productive [8].
- **State of the Operation:** Determines the current state in which a given operation is at the time of its application to the PT2020 programme, i.e., at which stage the work of the operation is currently, there being different states: Approved, Accepted by the Entities/Contracted, In Execution and Closed/Completed [8].
- **Thematic Domain:** The thematic domain represents a thematic area in general, in which PT2020 projects are inserted, being divided into four categories: Competitiveness and Internationalisation, Social Inclusion and Employment, Human Capital, Sustainability and Efficiency in the Use of Resources [8].
- **Beneficiaries:** Are entities, such as companies, organisations, that will have access to funding from the European Structural and Investment Funds. They are identified by their tax identification number (TIN) and company/organisation name [8].
- **Location of the Operation:** Parish, Municipality, District and NUTS (Nomenclature of Territorial Units II and III). For investments of a tangible nature, the location of the operation shall be the one where the investment will take place. For non-material investments, the location is the location of the head office or the establishment in charge of the operation [8].
- **Estimated Completion Date of the Operation:** These are expected dates of a possible completion date of the operation, which usually corresponds to the financial term of the investment in a given operation [8].
- **Characteristics of the Operation:** Three attributes characterise the operations: the designation of the operation, which corresponds to a generic name to be given to the project to be developed, the summary of the operation, which represents a short description of what the project consists of [8].

3 Methodologies and Tools

This section describes the tools and methodologies used to develop the practical project and the technical architecture by which it was guided.

3.1 Kimball Methodology

The methodology used for this project's basis and guide was the Kimball Data Warehouse/Business Intelligence Lifecycle Methodology. It was devised in the 1980s by members of the Kimball group and other colleagues at Metaphor Computer Systems. Since then, this methodology has been used as a guiding model, which determines the sequence of high-level tasks for successful Data Warehouse and Business Intelligence projects to support business decision-making [3] (Fig. 1).

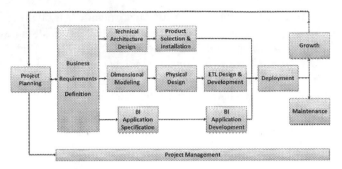

Fig. 1. Kimball data warehouse/business intelligence lifecycle methodology

3.2 Technical Architecture Design

As this is a Data Warehouse and Business Intelligence project, the objective is to process data, storing them in a repository, allowing the Business Intelligence process to be carried out in the future. For this, it is necessary to have a process that represents all the necessary steps so that the data used in Business Intelligence has the appropriate quality. Thus, the ETL process is used:

- It begins by choosing the data sources and then extracts the data from the source (extract) to the tool where the ETL process will occur.
- After that, the data transformation phase begins (clean + conform). It is based on data cleaning and conformity. In this phase, the data is corrected, standardised and treated according to the defined rules.
- Finally, the loading phase (deliver) occurs, where the physical loading of the data to the data warehouse occurs.

3.3 Tool Selection and Installation

According to the defined technical architecture, tools were selected to execute the different phases of the Extraction, Transformation and Loading (ETL) process.

It was necessary to explore which open-source tools exist to perform the entire process of extracting, cleaning, transforming and loading data. Having this said, the tools to be used for the execution of this project are Talend Open Studio for Data Quality, Talend Open Studio for Data Integration, MySQL Workbench and Tableau. These tools were chosen because they are very practical and easy to use, are free, have a lot of documentation explaining how to use them, and are also familiar to the research team.

A short description of each one is given below:

- **Talend Open Studio for Data Quality:** Is an open-source tool that allows performing an analysis of the quality and integrity of a given set of data, that is, if they are following their description, if they have spelling errors, if they have the correct format, among others [10].
- **Talend Open Studio for Data Integration:** Is a free and open-source tool for Data Integration and Big Data. It guarantees all the necessary functionalities for developing

an ETL process, i.e. it houses the entire process of extracting, cleaning, processing and loading data into a Data Warehouse [9].
- **MySQL Workbench:** Is a unified visual tool that provides data modelling, SQL development and comprehensive administration tools for server configuration, user administration, backup, among others [4].
- **Tableau:** Is an analytical platform used in the Business Intelligence industry, which allows data visualisation through the creation of analytical graphs, tables, geographic maps, spreadsheets, dashboards, among others, generated from data coming from relational databases, OLAP's, excel files, among other data sources [11].

4   Case Study

After carrying out the project and obtaining the Gantt diagram, the analysis of the quality of the data started, followed by the treatment/cleaning of the same data, as well as the establishment of Key Performance Indicators, that is, defining metrics that are capable of assessing whether specific attributes are under the expectations.

4.1   Data Quality Analysis

In this phase, an analysis was carried out of the project data sources representing all the information collected from the start of 2014 to 31 December 2020 obtained from four datasets in CSV format.

These datasets contain all the information about the operations approved by the PT2020 program, such as the name of the operations, which operational program they belong to, in which thematic areas they are inserted, which financial support was granted to them, among other characteristics.

All dataset columns were used, except in the dataset "lista-operacoes-pt2020–31122020.csv", as it contained some columns without any records. The name of the operations and the beneficiaries were not used for the sake of security and data protection.

It was decided not to use the dataset "indicadores-trimestrais-pt2020–31122020.csv", as it does not add much value to the business and presents information of little use without much connection to the other datasets. This data is available online, in an open format, on the Portugal 2020 website [8]. It is also noteworthy that the model used for this solution is scalable and updates the results whenever there are new records (Table 1).

Table 1. Description of the datasets used

File name	File size	Number of records
Dotacao-fundo-po-pt2020–31122020.csv	2 KB	22
Lista-operacoes-pt2020–31122020.csv	46419 KB	88355
Operacoes-regionalizadas-pt2020-vrsrevista-31122020.csv	16071 KB	117340

4.2 Definition of the Key Performance Indicators (KPI's)

In order to achieve a successful or valuable result for the project, from the business point of view, it was necessary to define metrics that can assess whether specific attributes are in line with the expectations generated in Table 2.

Table 2. KPI's

KPI	Analytical issues	Target
Check if the incidence of operations in the northern region is higher than 35%	Which region of Portugal holds about 35% of operations?	A target of 35% was set in order to prove that the North region is the region with the highest number of operations approved at a national level
Verify if the FC fund is the one that holds around 15% of the operations belonging to the Operational Programme "Competitiveness and Internationalisation"	What percentage of operations are associated with the Operational Programme "Competitiveness and Internationalisation" and the "CF" fund?	As the "PO Competitiveness and Internationalisation" may be one of the programmes with the most operations associated, given that it is an area on which companies tend to focus, it was intended to verify whether the "CF" fund allocates funds to a considerable percentage of operations of this operational programme, thus choosing the value of 15%
Understand if "Immaterial Actions/Studies" is the main nature of investment in PT2020 project operations, representing 30% of the total	What is the leading investment nature of PT2020 project operations?	The target of 30% was established to prove the predominance of the "Immaterial Actions/Studies" in the nature of the investment. This value would be sufficient given that there are eight types of investment nature
Verify if the Metropolitan Areas of Porto and Lisbon are the cities that have, individually, a percentage of operations above 10% and a rate of approved support above the same value	Which cities host the highest number of PT2020 project operations?	Metropolitan Areas of Porto and Lisbon have expected to receive a higher percentage of support, with 10% for each being the minimum expected

(*continued*)

Table 2. (*continued*)

KPI	Analytical issues	Target
Obtain a difference of less than 50% concerning the amount of approved support and the amount of support implemented in the thematic area "Human Capital"	What is the difference between executed and approved support values for the thematic area "Human Capital"?	The aim was to prove that the financial support's executed value would have already exceeded 50% of the approved value, and the PT2020 project will be close to its end
Ascertain whether 2020 presents the highest percentage of operations under execution	Since the beginning of the PT2020 project, which year presents the highest percentage of operations in execution?	The aim is to prove that 2020 is the year with the most operations in execution
Understand if the Operational Programme "Regional North" presents a percentage of funds allocated in the order of 10% of the total	What percentage of funds are allocated to the "Northern Regional" Operational Programme?	The objective was to prove that the Operational Programme "Regional North" presented a reasonable percentage of the allocation of funds. The North zone, being more industrialised, would tend to be more likely to obtain greater support
Assess if the year 2019 presents 15% of its operations are inserted in the thematic area "Social Inclusion and Employment" in execution	What percentage of operations in 2019 under the thematic area "Social Inclusion and Employment" are under implementation?	As 2019 was a very positive year for Portugal concerning employment growth, it was chosen to assess this thematic area about the number of operations in execution, considering that the 15% figure was sufficient to demonstrate the performance of the operations
Verify if the Operational Programme "Sustainability and Resource Efficiency" presents the lowest rate of approved support in the Central region of Portugal	Which operational programme has the lowest rate of approved support in the Central region?	Of all the regions where this operational programme may be present, the aim is to understand if the Central region of Portugal is the region with the lower approved support rate. This region may give more importance to other types of programmes

4.3 Multidimensional Model Design

This topic shows the physical design of the multidimensional model of the business process in question. It comprises nine dimensions (date, location, state of the operation, nature of investment, operational programme, operations fund, beneficiary operation, thematic domain and operation features) and a fact table (operations management). Each dimension is composed of a single primary key and the attributes that characterise it, with the primary purpose of analysing the data provided.

In turn, the table of facts is composed by foreign keys, coming from the dimensions connected to it, and by a set of numeric attributes, called facts, where the objective is to register data. For practical reasons, the multidimensional model presented in Fig. 2 was developed in English so that the presentation is more accessible, and even when implementing it, there are no typing errors.

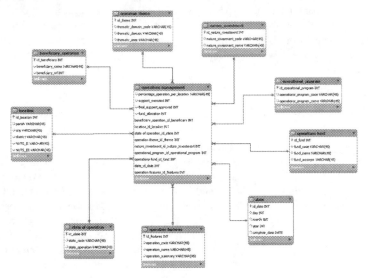

Fig. 2. Multidimensional model

4.4 Extraction, Transformation and Loading System

The entire ETL process was developed in this phase, i.e., extraction, transformation/cleaning, and data loading into the data warehouse. Thus, text capitalisation, empty spaces correction, null values and special characters correction was performed in all dimensions. In the "operational programme" dimension, as it extracted data from three different datasets, it was necessary to transform the different ways of naming the same operational programmes into only one name per operational programme.

5 Results

Once the ETL process was completed, it was possible to move on to the next phase, the Business Intelligence system, which combines data collection, data storage, and knowledge management to extract useful information to support decision-making.

Through these dashboards, it is possible to make an analytical view of the applicability and distribution of the financial funds of PT2020 and discover which type of operations were mostly accepted. Thus, four dashboards and a word cloud were created using the Tableau tool to represent all the resulting information interactively through graphs, tables and filters.

The dashboard presented in Fig. 3 was made to provide an overview of the percentage of operations by the Operational Programme and European Investment Fund. The stacked bar chart presents it just below the filters, where it can be seen that:

- Only five operational programmes do not receive funds from the three investment funds;
- Thirty-two thousand three hundred twenty-one operations belong to the Operational Programme "Competitiveness and Internationalisation", with an investment type "Liquidity Support";
- "Liquidity Support" is the predominant investment with 44.98% of the total;
- "Competitiveness and Internationalisation OP" holds 20.47% of the total funds allocated to the operational programmes.

Through the filters "Nature of Investment" and "Operational Programme", present at the top left of the dashboard, it is possible to select only the desired options, which will affect what kind of information is presented in each of the graphs.

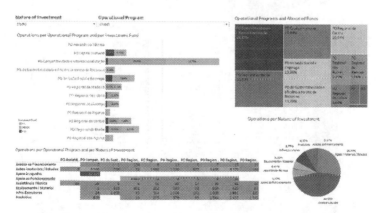

Fig. 3. Dashboard nature of investment/operational programme

Next, a word cloud was developed, represented in Fig. 4, which presents the most frequent words related to the description made by the beneficiaries when filling out the application to the PT2020 project. It is thus possible to verify that the five most used words, which are the most prominent, are "training", "development", "conditions", "creation", and "market". One can also highlight words such as "Covid-19" and "pandemic", which should be among the main reasons for applying several operations throughout 2020. Thus, all these words refer to the description that each beneficiary made of a given operation and the reasons that led him to apply the same.

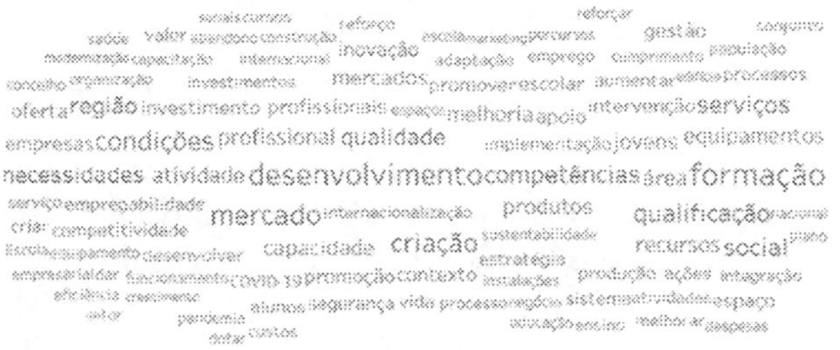

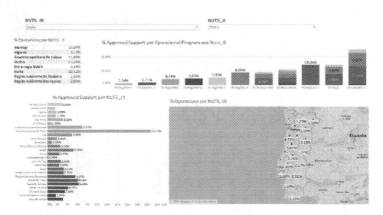

Fig. 4. Wordcloud

Figure 5 shows the percentage of approved support by NUTS_III. It can be seen that the place with the highest support is Porto with 20.73% of the total support, by Operational Programme. The "Sustainability and Resource Efficiency OP" is the operational programme available in more regions. The table below shows the percentage of operations by NUTS_II Region with a dominance in the North, with 38.15% of operations. The NUTS_III Region analysis represented in the map shows that Porto has the highest number of operations, i.e. 16.65% of all operations.

In this dashboard, there are also associated filters, through which one may choose to visualise the information of a particular region, either NUTS_II or NUTS_III.

Fig. 5. Dashboard regions

Figure 6 presents the dashboard that gathers information about, for example, the comparison between the amounts of support approved and implemented over the years. It is possible to verify that the financial support implemented was always lower than the financial support planned. The analysis by the percentage of operations per thematic area and state of the operation is also available. The highest values of approved and executed support per thematic area were "Competitiveness and Internationalisation". Finally, the evolution of the number of operations over the years, taking into account their status, as shown in the graph at the bottom right, denoting a peak of 35.63% of the total number of accepted operations in 2021 represented by the orange line. Some filters allow the choice of years between 2014 and 2023, and another allows the choice of thematic domains.

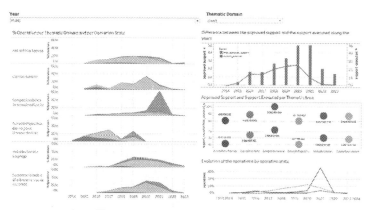

Fig. 6. Dashboard year/thematic area

Lastly, a dashboard, represented in Fig. 7, which gathers information presenting, for example, the comparison of the financial support implemented and the number of operations approved for each operational programme, is presented in the vertical bar chart. There is a considerable discrepancy between these two values regarding the "Human Capital OP", where the percentage of financial support implemented is considerably higher than the percentage of operations. Information is also presented on the financial support implemented by each of the existing thematic areas in the pie chart in the bottom left-hand corner, where "Competitiveness and Internationalisation" dominates. The comparison between financial support approved and implemented by a type of investment, represented in the graph with a marker, in the dashboard's bottom right-hand corner shows that the type of investment is Infrastructure with the highest financial support and Funding Support with the lowest values.

The evolution of the number of operations and the financial support per European Investment Fund can be observed in the area chart below the filters. It can be seen that in the year 2021, there is a peak of 38643 operations funded by the ERDF in light blue. Some filters allow filtering the operational programmes or choose the desired European investment funds.

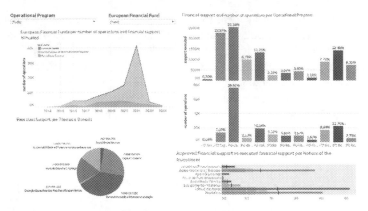

Fig. 7. General dashboard

6 Discussion

Considering all the Key Performance Indicators discussed in Sect. 4, in this section, a brief discussion and analysis of the results obtained will be carried out, verifying whether the KPIs were achieved or not. All the KPIs will be analysed according to Table 2, where they are listed from 1 to 8.

1. **Check if the incidence of operations in the northern area is higher than 35%.** - The purpose of this indicator is to prove that the North Region of Portugal holds about 35% of the total operations approved by the PT2020 project. In the table represented in Fig. 5, all NUTS_II regions and the percentage of operations associated with each one are presented. It is possible to ascertain that the zone with a higher percentage of operations is the North, with about 38.51% of total operations, thus proving that the KPI was achieved since the observed value is above 35%. It should be noted that the regions of Central Portugal, with 27.29%, the Metropolitan Area of Lisbon, with 11.68% and the Alentejo, with 10.86%, stand out, despite having slightly lower percentages than the North region. The higher incidence of operations in these regions may happen due to the existence of more industrialised areas with more population.

2. **Verify if the "FC" fund is the one that holds around 15% of the operations belonging to the Operational Programme "Competitiveness and Internationalisation".** - This indicator aims to prove that the European Investment Fund "CF" holds 15% of the total operations of the Operational Programme "Competitiveness and Internationalisation". Therefore, a chart was developed in order to respond to this KPI. The horizontal stacked bar chart in Fig. 3 shows the percentage of operations by the Operational Programme and European Investment Fund. A careful analysis of the chart in question allows us to conclude that 18.79% of the total operations belong to the "Competitiveness and Internationalisation" operational programme and the "CF" fund, which means that the indicator was achieved. It can also be highlighted that this European investment fund finances all the operational programmes analysed in this article, being the only one of the three different funds to do so.

3. **Understanding whether "Immaterial Actions / Studies" is the main nature of investment in PT2020 project operations, representing 30% of total approved operations.** - The purpose of this KPI is to determine whether the "Immaterial Actions/Studies" is the main nature of investment in the PT2020 project operations, having 30% of the total of the same. It is possible to reach this conclusion through the pie chart in Fig. 3, which shows the percentage of the number of operations by nature of the investment. Thus, it is possible to ascertain that the nature of investment with a higher percentage of the total number of operations is "Liquidity Support" with 44.98%. In comparison, "Immaterial Actions/Studies" holds only 26.20% of operations. Therefore, it was concluded that neither the target of 30% nor the fact that "Immaterial Stocks/Studies" is the primary type of investment nature was achieved.

4. **Verify if the Metropolitan Areas of Porto and Lisbon are the cities that individually have a percentage of operations above 10% as well as a rate of approved support above the same figure.** - A map was drawn up showing the percentage of distribution of operations by the different regions to ascertain this KPI. A horizontal bar graph shows the approved support percentages for each region, shown in Fig. 5. This way, it is plausible to verify through the visualisation of the map that the Metropolitan Area of Porto represents 16.65% of the total number of operations. In comparison, the Metropolitan Area of Lisbon holds 11.68%, thus reaching the first part of the indicator. Regarding the percentage of support approved by each area under analysis, it can be seen that the Metropolitan Area of Porto holds 20.73% of the support and the Metropolitan Area of Lisbon with 7.07%. In this case, the indicator was not achieved in the Lisbon Metropolitan Area, as the percentage of total support approved for this area was less than 10%. What may justify this considerable difference between the percentage of support for Lisbon and Porto is that the operations approved in the Porto region must be larger, thus requiring higher support.

5. **Obtain a difference of less than 50% in relation to the amount of support implemented and the amount of support approved for the thematic area "Human Capital".** - This indicator aims to verify if there is a 5% difference between the amount of support executed and the amount of support approved for the thematic area "Human Capital". The scatter plot in Fig. 6, which shows the amount of support approved and the amount of support implemented by the thematic area, shows that the amount of support approved for the "Human Capital" thematic area was €4,521,293,605 and the support implemented was €2,884,935,921. The variation between these values was calculated, giving a value of 36.19%. So, it can be concluded that this indicator was achieved since the difference between the support approved and the support implemented for this specific thematic area was below the stipulated value of 50%.

6. **Find out if 2020 has the highest percentage of operations being executed** - The objective of this KPI is to ascertain whether 2020 was the year with the highest percentage concerning the number of operations in execution. That said, the line graph, which shows the evolution of the percentage of operations taking into account their status, in Fig. 6 shows that in fact, it was in 2020 that a peak in the number of operations in execution was reached, representing approximately 12% of the total number of operations. Thus, it is concluded that the indicator has been achieved. This graph shows that in 2021 a large part of the operations is currently accepted

by the entities/contractor. There is no information on operations already completed since these ended in the previous year.

7. **Understand if the Operational Programme "Regional North" has a percentage of funds allocated in the order of 10% of the total.** - This indicator aims to understand whether the Operational Programme "Regional North" presents a percentage of allocated funds in the order of 10% of the total, which can be ascertained through the treemap, which shows the percentage of funds allocated by the operational programme presented in Fig. 3. Thus, it was possible to note that the Operational Programme "Regional North" holds 15.78% of the allocation of funds by operational programmes. Since the target was 10%, we conclude that the indicator was achieved. It should also be noted that, apart from the "Regional Operational Programme of the North", the operational programmes that raised most funds were the OP "Competitiveness and Internationalisation" with 20.47% and the OP "Human Capital" with 14.94% of the allocation of funds.

8. **Assess if the year 2019 presents at least 15% of its operations inserted in the thematic area "Social Inclusion and Employment" in execution.** - The purpose of this indicator is to assess whether 2019 has at least 15% of its operations within the thematic area "Social Inclusion and Employment" under execution. Thus, the area chart showing the evolution of the number of operations by thematic area and operation status over the years, presented in Fig. 6, was prepared to respond to this Key Performance Indicator. The analysis of the graph in question allows us to ascertain that the percentage of operations being executed in 2019, relating to the thematic area "Social Inclusion and Employment", is 18.16%. Thus, given that the target of this KPI was 15%, we conclude that it was successfully achieved.

9. **Verify if the Operational Programme "Sustainability and Resource Efficiency" presents the lowest rate of approved support in the Central region of Portugal.** - In order to verify if the Operational Programme "Sustainability and Efficiency in the Use of Resources" is the Operational Programme with a lower rate of approved support in the Central region of Portugal, the stacked bar chart was elaborated, which exposes the percentage of approved support per Operational Programme and NUTS_II region, shown in Fig. 5. Therefore, after evaluating and analysing the mentioned chart, it was found that 2.81% of the approved support in the Central region of Portugal belongs to the Operational Programme in focus, being the lowest value verified. Next, there is the Operational Programme "Social Inclusion and Employment" with 3.15%, the Operational Programme "Human Capital" with 4.80% and the Operational Programme "Competitiveness and Internationalisation" with 9.10% of the total approved support. Thus, it can be concluded that the indicator was achieved. It can also be highlighted that the Operational Programme "Social Inclusion and Employment" is the Operational Programme that is inserted in more zones of Portugal, being present in seven of the main NUTS_II regions.

7 Conclusions

The results achieved from the dashboards allow the understanding of which operational programmes and thematic areas, investment funds, regions, and nature of the investment held a predominance, which is the objective of this article. This analysis considered the number of approved operations and the higher financial funds allocated. It should be noted that seven of the nine stipulated goals were successfully achieved:

- It was possible to verify that the North region holds about 40% of the total approved operations;
- 19% of the operations of the "Competitiveness and Internationalisation OP" were financed by the "CF" fund;
- 36.19% was the difference between the approved and the executed support for the thematic area "Human Capital";
- 2020 was the year where there was a greater number of operations in execution, equivalent to 12% of the total;
- "Northern Regional OP" holds 15.78% of the allocation of funds, that the percentage of operations in execution in 2019;
- "Social Inclusion and Employment" is the most supported thematic area with 18.16%;
- 2.81% of the support approved in Central Portugal belongs to the operational programme in question, being the lowest value verified.

It can be seen that most of the main objectives stipulated were achieved by the comparison made in Sect. 6, while others were not, but by a small margin. Lisbon holding 7.07% of the financial support defined, instead of the 10% stipulated, and that the "Immaterial Actions/Studies" hold only 26.20%, being below the 30% defined and also because it is not the predominant type of investment in the approved operations.

This study addresses a current topic due to the growing concern with sustainability, employment generation and economic development and can help society understanding the PT2020 programme. It strengthens the component of characterisation of the financial support granted and may help analyse funds transparency.

Some analysis will be explored in the future. Text mining to find patterns in operations and data mining to discover which operations are more likely to be approved in a project like this in the future.

Acknowledgements. This work has been supported by FCT – Fundação para a Ciência e Tecnologia within the R&D Units Project Scope: UIDB/00319/2020 and supervised by IOTECH.

References

1. Alberto, V.: Financial impact of Portugal 2020: Case study of a company. In: Estudogeral.uc.pt. (2018). https://estudogeral.uc.pt/handle/10316/84552. Accessed 14 May 2021
2. European Commission. In: Official Site of the European Union (1958). https://ec.europa.eu/info/index_pt. Accessed 19 May 2021
3. Kimball, R., Ross, M., Thornthwaite, W., Mundy, J., Becker, B.: The Data Warehouse Lifecycle Toolkit, 2nd Edition. Wiley, Hoboken (2008)
4. Medeiros, E.: Portugal 2020: an effective policy platform to promote sustainable territorial development? Sustainability **12**, 1126 (2020)
5. MySQL. In: MySQL Workbench (1995). https://www.mysql.com/products/workbench/. Accessed 5 Apr 2021

6. Nishimura, A., Moreira, A., Au-Yong-Oliveira, M., Sousa, M.: Effectiveness of the portugal 2020 programme: a study from the citizens' perspective. Sustainability **13**, 5799 (2021)
7. Oliveira, F., Leitão, A.: Economic impacts of North 2020: an input-output analysis. In: Repositorio.ucp.pt (2021). Accessed 14 May 2021
8. Portugal 2020. In: Approved Projects (2014). https://www.portugal2020.pt/. Accessed 24 Mar 2021
9. Talend. In: How to Get Started with Talend Open Studio for Data Integration (2006). https://www.talend.com/resources/get-started-talend-open-studio-data-integration/. Accessed 5 Apr 2021
10. Talend. In: Introduction to Talend Open Studio for Data Quality (2006). https://www.talend.com/resources/introduction-talend-open-studio-data-quality/. Accessed 5 Apr 2021
11. Tableau. In: Realise the potential of your data with Tableau (2003). https://www.tableau.com/. Accessed 12 May 2021
12. Ribeiro, D., Jesus-Silva, N., Ribeiro, J.: The impact of European Union funding in the "Centro" region of Portugal between 2014–2020. In: Repositorio.uportu.pt (2021)
13. Ribeiro, D., Jesus-Silva, N., Ribeiro, J.: The multiplier effect of european union funds in the alentejo region, portugal, between 2014–2020. Eur. J. Econ. Bus. Stud. **7**, 2411–4073 (2021)

Hybrid Algorithm of Convolutional Neural Networks and Vector Support Machines in Classification

Marcos Yamir Gómez Ramos$^{(\boxtimes)}$ (iD), José Sergio Ruíz Castilla (iD), and Farid García Lamont (iD)

Universidad Autónoma del Estado de México (UAEMEX), Jardín Zumpango s/n, Fraccionamiento El Tejocote, Texcoco, Estado de México, Mexico
{fgarcial,jsruizc}@uaemex.mx, mgomezr008@alumno.uaemex.mx
https://www.uaemex.mx

Abstract. Looking for the improvement of the classification, we propose a hybrid algorithm to identify the corn plant and the weed. With the aim of improving the fertilization and herbicide application processes. An efficient process can avoid wasted fertilizers and decrease subsoil contamination. The purpose is to identify the corn plant to specify the fertilizer application in an automated and precise way. Whereas, the identification of the weed allows to apply herbicides directly. In this work we propose a hybrid method with Convolutional Neural Networks (CNN) to extract characteristics from images and Vector Support Machines (SVM) for classification. We obtained effectiveness results, a percentage of 98%, being higher than those compared to the state of the art.

Keywords: Classification · Convolutional neural network · Support vector machine · Hybrid algorithm

1 Introduction

According to the national agricultural survey in Mexico (NAS, 2019), corn is the second crop in the country in terms of annual production, surpassed only by sugar cane, but above crops such as wheat, sorghum, tomato, Chile and beans [1]. Of the 64 breeds reported in Mexico, 59 can be considered native. Mexico is the cradle of corn. Also, it is the origin of an enormous diversity of varieties. The corn has been the sustenance of their peoples. The population uses corn in countless ways. Finally, corn is the source of cultural and social wealth for Mexicans [2].

Chemical fertilizers unquestionably have effects on the environment. Fertilizers generate a high risk of environmental damage. Fertilizers can contaminate subsoil groundwater in the area of application. A fertilizer is a substance that is used to provide nutrients to the soil. The objective of fertilizers is to increase the concentration of nutrients to favor and promote plant growth [3].

T. Guarda et al. (Eds.): ARTIIS 2021, CCIS 1485, pp. 263–274, 2021.
https://doi.org/10.1007/978-3-030-90241-4_21

We must currently rely on new technologies, for example: sensors, big data or deep learning. We must move towards smart agriculture. Smart farming technology can help increase crop yields. On the other hand, it could also support the control of weeds with high precision in different stages of growth [4].

Weeds are considered one of the main threats in agricultural production. Weeds can cause a significant loss of yield at harvest. Weeds compete for nutrients, sunlight, space, and water. Weeds also cause loss of product quality. Finally, weeds harbor insects or diseases [5].

Therefore, the recognition of weeds automatically with great precision is urgent. A weed identification can help in the application of herbicides and fertilizers in specific spaces.

Deep learning is a sub-area of machine learning. Deep learning is a new way of learning representations from data, images, sounds, or videos. Deep learning uses a series of successive layers of increasingly meaningful representations. The number of layers that contribute to a model of the data is called the depth of the model. Layered representations are almost always learned using models called neural networks. The architecture consists of structured in layers literally stacked one on top of the other. Deep learning often requires tens or even hundreds of successive layers of representations. The model learns automatically from the training data [6].

By definition, a deep architecture is a multi-stage hierarchical structure. Each stage is made up of a neural network with at least three layers. The neural network is trained through the Backpropagation algorithm. Neural network training with multiple layers in between fosters the emergence of several clustered algorithms in an area of study known as deep learning. The algorithms use two or more layers. Algorithms have the main objective of learning, not only to distinguish between classes based on artificial descriptors, but also to be able to learn their own descriptors based on raw data. For images, learning is based on pixel values [7].

Convolutional Neural Networks (CNN) are architectures inspired by biological neurons. CNNs are capable of being trained and learning representations. CNNs can learn without variation in terms of scale, translation, rotation, and similar transformations [8]. CNNs are used with two-dimensional data, which makes them a good choice for the image recognition process [9].

Support Vector Machines (SVM) are used to classify and recognize patterns in various types of data. The SVM are also used in a wide range of applications, such as facial recognition, clinical diagnostics, industrial process monitoring, and image processing and analysis [10].

Image recognition (IR) remains an open research issue. Image recognition requires the exploration of new techniques and methodologies. The IR requires further improvement in: performance in terms of recognition accuracy, execution time, and computational complexity. Therefore, in this work we propose a hybrid CNN-SVM method for the recognition of images of corn and weeds. The objective of this work is to extract the characteristics of the images of corn and weeds using a CNN, then the SVM classifier is applied to the learned characteristics for their classification.

We propose a method that classifies images of corn and weeds automatically. We obtained an excellent percentage of precision compared to those found in the state of the art. In the literature, hybrid methods are being proposed to solve problems involving feature extraction and image classification. Some research works that are mentioned present percentages of precision in the identification of images with a percentage greater than 90% of precision.

2   State of the Art

A number of studies that include the use of deep learning have reported state-of-the-art achievements in a considerable number of tasks. Some achievements are: image classification, natural language processing, speech recognition, symbol and text classification, as well as the classification of plants, weeds and diseases in various crops.

Silva et al. [11] present a tool for the recognition of cattle brands using CNN and SVM. In the experiments, the authors used 12 cattle brands and a set of 540 images and the precision obtained in the experiment reached 93.28%. The same author [12] Silva et al. in another work he carried out two experiments reaching indices of 93.11% and 95.34%, respectively, in the recognition of cattle brands.

Niu et al. [13], present an algorithm that uses a CNN and SVM to solve the problem of text recognition, achieving a recognition rate of 94.40%. Abien et al. [14] proposes a hybrid model capable of recognizing symbols from the MNIST database with an accuracy of 91.86%.

Hend et al. [15] present excellent precisions like the one proposed for recognition of human activity using a pre-trained CNN with 1.2 million high resolution images of the ILSVRC2015 classification training subset of the ImageNet dataset. The results generated were 99.92% Accuracy. In this case, it is necessary to mention that they used a pre-trained network with more than 14 million images. The number of images may be the reason that your tests have returned the excellent percentage.

The use of deep learning is also described in the research carried out by Constante et al. [16], who used a three-layer neural network with input through backpropagation; used this method to classify strawberries and obtained recognition results of 92.5%.

Garcia et al. [17] classified 20 kinds of common fruits in Mexico. The best classified fruits in the experiments were: pineapple and lemon with an effectiveness percentage of 97.68%.

Cervantes [18] mentions that current identification methods involve advanced algorithms to measure the morphological and texture characteristics of the objects contained in the image. These features provide a lot of information for classification.

Yang [19] addresses the problem of distinguishing corn plants from weeds, using an artificial neural network (ANN) using the Backpropagation algorithm. The results obtained were a detection percentage in corn of 100% and in weeds of 80%, that is, 90% on average.

Barufaldi [20] exposes the problem of weed recognition on a cultivated field. He applied Deep Learning techniques. The proposed vision system is based on a CNN and uses an SVM. The results for weed identification was 91%.

Haug et al. [21] proposed an artificial vision approach to discriminate crops and weeds in carrot crops, achieving a precision value of 93.8%. His Hnin et al. [22] developed a method to discriminate between crops and weeds with a classification percentage of 66.7%.

García-Amaro et al. [23] used traditional image processing techniques to detect diseases and pests in the tomato plant. They used the SVM algorithm achieving the best result of 93.86% accuracy.

Lanlan Wu [24] proposed a tool for classifying and identifying weeds in maize fields at the early stage of growth, using an SVM. The results showed that the SVM classifiers were able to successfully identify weeds with 100% accuracy.

In some cases, identification of crops and weeds was made possible by the SVM technique. The objective was to identify three categories: crops, soils and weeds. The identification of crops and weeds undoubtedly allows for various future applications. The proposal reached 94.3% accuracy in identifying the three categories. The solution could be used in vehicles, autonomous tractors [25] and robots.

In the literature we find that there are methods similar to ours, such as that of Campos et al. [25] that classifies crops, soil and weeds with a precision percentage of 94.3%; [26]. Jiang et al. classified corn and weeds with an effectiveness of 96.51%. [27] Yang Li et al. classified corn, apples and grapes with a precision of 94%.

Computer vision is the key technology to correctly identify corn plants and can differentiate them from weeds. The above could improve the fertilization and fumigation processes in an automated and precise way [3].

3   Methodology

LeCun et al. [28] developed the CNN, which is a hierarchical neural network and has an enormous capacity for representation that learns the significant characteristics at each layer of the visual hierarchy. Features are automatically extracted from the input image. Feature extraction has the advantage of being invariant to displacement and shape distortions of the input textural images. Recently, some deep learning architectures are switching from the engineering feature extraction phase to machine processing. With the new method, deep neural networks go directly into the raw data without human intervention to extract deep features [14].

Obtaining the Images: An image dataset of corn and weed plants was not found on the Internet. The image dataset needs specific characteristics according to the experiment of each investigation. In this work, we have used a high resolution image dataset obtained by ourselves. The images were obtained from a corn crop in the municipality of Francisco I. Madero in the state of Hidalgo, Mexico.

Dataset Organization: The problem of classification in unbalanced data sets currently represents a significant challenge for the artificial intelligence, data mining and machine learning scientific communities. There are several factors that make a problem of this type complicated, for example, imbalance between classes, imbalance within classes and anomalous instances [34]. External methods perform pre-processing on unbalanced data sets to meet one or more of the following objectives: balance the data set, remove instances considered noise, remove overlap between classes, or search for prototypes that represent the set of data in a way that is easy to process by classification or grouping methods.

This is the reason why the Dataset used is our own and the images were collected to maintain a balance of data that allows to obtain better results in the classification.

The images used in this investigation were 1000, of which 500 are of corn and 500 of weeds. We create two groups of images. The first group contains 80% for training. Whereas, the second group contains 20% for validation. The set of images were used without prior pre-processing such as normalization or dimensionality reduction, see Table 1.

Table 1. Dataset image features

Class	Quantity	Width	Height	Format
Corn	500	768	1024	JPG
Weed	500	768	1024	JPG

Method: The proposed method includes: the storage of the image dataset, the processing of the algorithm and the visualization of the results. We use a MacBook Pro personal computer with a 2.6 GHz Intel Core i5 processor with 8 GB of RAM. The code was written in Python version 3.5.

The dataset was used, without prior pre-processing such as normalization or dimensionality reduction. There are 1000 high resolution images, where 80% were for training and 20% for validation.

CNNs have the advantage of reducing the number of parameters and connections used in the artificial neural model to facilitate their training phase. The adopted method is a neural network with three convolutional layers.

In this section, we present the architecture of our method based on CNN and SVM. CNN is considered a deep learning algorithm on which the Dropout technique has been applied during training. Our proposed method was adapted by modifying the CNN trainable classifier by a linear SVM classifier. Our goal was to blend the respective capabilities of CNN and SVM. Our algorithms allowed us to obtain a new image recognition process for corn and weeds. We seek successful results inspired by the combination of the two powerful algorithms.

The initial CNN layers extract global features from the original images. However, the last fully connected layers draw out more distinctive features. These layers can extract features, which are increasingly stable to local transformations of the input image. For the training procedure, the SVM takes the results of the units as a vector of characteristics. The training phase continues until a good training is achieved. For the test process, the SVM classifier performs the classification on the test suite using these characteristics automatically. In summary, in the hybrid model that we propose, the CNN functions as a feature extractor and the SVM as a binary classifier.

The architecture of the proposed CNN-SVM hybrid model is described in the Fig. 1:

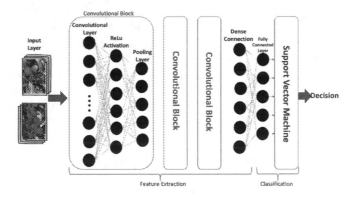

Fig. 1. CNN + SVM hybrid model architecture

The model consists of a 3-layer CNN architecture and an SVM classifier. In the CNN input layer, resize the original image and take a 150×150 matrix of corn or weeds, that is, an image of 150 pixels by 150 pixels of our Data set. In the convolutional layers, a 3×3 convolutional filtering and a stride of size 1 were used. The CNN was trained after executing 50 epochs and until the training process converged. The last layer of the CNN was replaced by an SVM linear classifier. The characteristics of the input image obtained in the third layer were treated as input to the SVM classifier. The SVM classifier is initially trained with these new features automatically generated from the training images. Finally, the SVM classifier is used to recognize the corn or weed images used for the test.

In Fig. 2 we can see the general architecture of a CNN, this to get an idea of the difference between the characteristics that a normal CNN has and the CNN combined with the SVM shown in Fig. 1 and which is our proposed method.

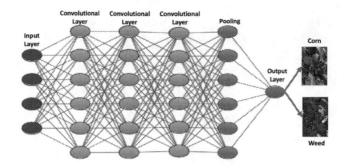

Fig. 2. CNN general architecture.

Common practice in most recent CNN developments focuses on implementing larger and deeper models to achieve better performance. The disadvantage arises when as the model gets bigger and deeper, the parameters of the network increase dramatically; as a result, the model becomes more complex to train and more computationally expensive. Therefore, it is very important to design an architecture that provides better performance using a reasonably fewer number of parameters in the network [35], such as the one proposed in Fig. 1.

Algorithms: The deep learning-based model is considered as one of the best rankings in pattern recognition tasks to improve analytical results [29].

On the other hand, SVMs are considered one of the most robust algorithms in machine learning created by Vapnik [30]. SVMs have become a well-known and exploited approach in many areas such as pattern recognition, classification, and image processing. The SVM was developed for binary classification and its objective is to find the optimal hyperplane.

The difference between a CNN and a multilayer perceptron network is the use of convolutional layers, clustering, and non-linearities like tanh, sigmoid, and ReLU. That is, the multilayer perceptron is an artificial neural network formed by several layers, in such a way that it has the ability to solve problems that are not linearly separable, which is the main limitation of the simple perceptron. The multilayer perceptron can be locally or fully connected. Whereas, CNN is a type of supervised learning neural network that processes its layers to identify different characteristics in the inputs that make it able to identify objects. Specialized hidden layers with a hierarchy can detect lines and curves in the first layers and are specialized until they reach deeper layers that recognize complex shapes such as a face or the silhouette of a plant.

Convolutional neural networks are used to extract features due to their strong ability to extract features [31]. The original images were uploaded to CNN, then the convolution operation of each layer was performed to acquire the characteristics of the image. The lower layer contains more spatial details, while the upper layer has more semantic information [31]. In order to obtain robust features from CNN, the output of the final grouping layer is used as a feature map

of the image. The characteristic map goes directly to the SVM classifier to make
the decision and thus know if an image corresponds to a corn plant or weed.

4   Results and Discussion

The results obtained during the tests performed are shown using the following
abbreviations in Table 2: Acc = Accuracy; S = Sensitivity; E = Specificity;
P = Precision; F-m = F-measure and MCC = Mattew's Correlation Coefficient,
which are the performance measures generated in the results.

Table 2. CNN and SVM results

Algorithm	S	E	P	F-m	MCC
CNN + SVM	**98**	94	**98**	96.96	94

In Table 3 you can see the results compared with the results obtained with
different methods found in the state of the art. The mentioned percentage corresponds to the Accuracy metric.

Table 3. Comparison of results obtained versus state of the art

Name	Images	CNN	SVM	CNN + SVM
Silva et al. 2019	Cattle brands	–	–	93.28
Silva et al. 2020	Cattle brands	–	–	95.34
Niu et al. 2011	Texts	–	–	94.4
Abien et al. 2019	MNIST symbols	–	–	91.86
Campos et al. 2017	Crop, soil and weeds	–	–	94.3
Jiang H. et al. 2020	Corn and weeds	–	–	97.51
Yeshwanth Sai et al. 2020	Dogs	–	–	93.57
Miao Ma et al. 2016	Hand gestures	–	–	96.1
Yang Li et al. 2020	Corn, apple and grape	–	–	94
Zhicheng Wang et al. 2017	Fire detection	95.79	–	–
Dechant et al. 2017	Blight on the corn husk	96.7	–	–
Sibiya 2019	Corn diseases	87 – **99**	–	–
Xihai Shang et al. 2017	Corn diseases	**98.8** y **98.9**	–	–
Sumita Mishra et al. 2020	Corn diseases	88.46	–	–
Zhanquan Sun et al. 2017	Fake images on the web	95.2	89.45	97.2
Proposed method	**Corn and weeds**	–	–	**98**

The proposed method yielded results with an excellent precision percentage,
since it has been proven and it can be seen in the previous table that only two

methods out of the 15 reviewed in the state of the art exceed it. A method very similar to the one proposed is the one used by CNN to detect corn diseases. Sibiya [32] detects corn leaf blight disease with 99% accuracy, but detections of the other diseases do not exceed 87%. In the same way, Zhang [33] detects diseases in the corn leaf with an accuracy percentage of 98.9% with the support of advanced models of pre-trained networks such as GoogleNet and data sets with thousands of images such as CIFAR-10 that helped to obtain 98.8% respectively. Therefore, we can mention that the percentage obtained by our method is highly effective with a precision of 98%.

In the Fig. 3, we can see the ROC curve and in the Fig. 4, the area under the curve (AUC) and its values obtained.

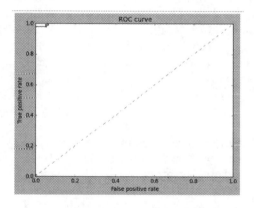

Fig. 3. Graph of the ROC curve.

AUC = 0.9988995598239296

Fig. 4. Value of the area under the curve.

5   Conclusions

The results obtained in the experiments were better than those obtained with the application of the traditional methods reviewed. Therefore, we conclude that a combination of CNN + SVM generates relevant results for the field of image classification by means of convolutional neural networks. The precision obtained by the hybrid algorithm was significant, since the experiment reached 98% precision in the recognition of corn and weeds. The results confirm the performance and reliability of the classifications made by the proposed method. We have demonstrated the efficiency of the system for the recognition of corn and weeds applied to the dataset used.

The method proposed in this research showed better results in terms of precision for the corn and weed image recognition task when compared to what was found in the literature. Overall, we deduce that the CNN model combined with SVM is, in fact, a very promising classification method in the field of corn and weed image recognition. However, it is necessary to extend our Dataset and enrich it to be able to deal with more test images and improve the accuracy rate in validation.

Therefore, the superiority of the proposed method is clearly demonstrated in comparison with the other models of the state of the art. After analyzing the results presented in Table 3, the precision of the CNN + SVM hybrid classifier for the recognition of images of corn and weeds is 98%. The percentage is greater than the image recognition precision shown in said table, thus exceeding 86% of the results shown there.

We conclude that our method obtained the third best performance in the classification of the two classes using its own Dataset. Regarding the two best classification percentages in the table, we can mention in our favor that Sibiya [32] detects the blight disease in the corn leaf with an accuracy of 99%, but the detections of the other diseases do not exceed 87%. In the same way, Zhang [33] detects diseases in the corn leaf with an accuracy percentage of 98.9% with the support of advanced models of pre-trained networks such as GoogleNet and data sets with thousands of images such as CIFAR-10 that helped to obtain 98.8% respectively.

Finally, the collection of images will be promoted to feed the private data set that is available, in order to expand the size and variety of the Dataset. We hope to put the dataset on hand for other researchers for modeling and learning in the future, ultimately wanting to further aid the study in the field. In addition to that, this proposed method can also be used for the classification of images of all kinds, not only for classification of images in the agricultural area.

References

1. INEGI: Gobierno de México. Encuesta Nacional Agropecuaria 2019. "Superficie cultivada y producción de cultivos anuales y perennes por cultivo seleccionado" (2019)
2. Barkin, D.: El maíz: la persistencia de una cultura en México. Cahiers des Amériques latines **40**, 19–32 (2002)
3. Gómez, et al.: Clasificación de plantas de maíz y maleza: hacía la mejora de la fertilización en México. Res. Comput. Sci. **149**(8), 683–697 (2020)
4. Sa, I., et al.: weedNet: dense semantic weed classification using multispectral images and MAV for smart farming. IEEE Robot. Automat. Lett. **3**, 588–595 (2018)
5. Olsen, A., et al.: Deepweeds: a multiclass weed species image dataset for deep learning. Sci. Rep. **9**, 2058 (2019)
6. Chollet, F.: Deep Learning with Python: Fundamentals of Machine Learning. Manning Publications Co., Shelter Island, NY (2018). ISBN 9781617294433
7. Juraszek, G.: Reconhecimento de Produtos por Imagem Utilizando Palavras Visuais e Redes Neurais Convolucionais. UDESC, Joinville (2014)
8. LeCun, Y., Kavukcuoglu, K., Farabet, C.: Convolutional networks and applications in vision. In: Proceedings of 2010 IEEE International Symposium on Circuits and Systems (ISCAS), pp. 253–256. IEEE (2010). https://doi.org/10.1109/ISCAS.2010.5537907

9. Arel, I., Rose, D., Karnowski, T.: Deep machine learning - a new frontier in artificial intelligence research [research frontier]. IEEE Comput. Intell. Mag. **5**(4), 13–18 (2010). https://doi.org/10.1109/MCI.2010.938364
10. Tchangani, A.: Support vector machines: a tool for pattern recognition and classification. Stud. Inf. Control J. **14**(2), 99–109 (2005)
11. Silva, C., Welfer, D., Gioda, F.P., Dornelles, C.: Cattle brand recognition using convolutional neural network and support vector machines. IEEE Latin Am. Trans. **15**(2), 310–316 (2017). https://doi.org/10.1109/TLA.2017.7854627
12. Silva, C., Welfer, D.: A novel hybrid SVM-CNN method for extracting characteristics and classifying cattle branding. Latin Am. J. Comput. LAJC **VI**(1), 9–15 (2019)
13. Niu, X.X., Suen, C.Y.: A novel hybrid CNN-SVM classifier for recognizing handwritten digits. Pattern Recognit. **45**, 1318–1325 (2011). https://doi.org/10.1016/j.patcog.2011.09.021
14. Agarap, A.F.M.: An Architecture Combining Convolutional Neural Network (CNN) and Support Vector Machine (SVM) for Image Classification (2017)
15. Basly, H., Ouarda, W., Sayadi, F.E., Ouni, B., Alimi, A.M.: CNN-SVM learning approach based human activity recognition. In: El Moataz, A., Mammass, D., Mansouri, A., Nouboud, F. (eds.) ICISP 2020. LNCS, vol. 12119, pp. 271–281. Springer, Cham (2020). https://doi.org/10.1007/978-3-030-51935-3_29
16. Constante, P., Gordon, A., Chang, O., Pruna, E., Acuna, F., Escobar, I.: Artificial vision techniques for strawberry's industrial classification. IEEE Latin Am. Trans. **14**(6), 2576–2581 (2016). https://doi.org/10.1109/TLA.2016.7555221
17. Garcia, F., Cervantes, J., Lopez, A., Alvarado, M.: Fruit classification by extracting color chromaticity, shape and texture features: towards an application for supermarkets. IEEE Latin Am. Trans. **14**(7), 3434–3443 (2016). https://doi.org/10.1109/tla.2016.7587652
18. Cervantes, J., Garcia Lamont, F., Rodriguez Mazahua, L., Zarco Hidalgo, A., Ruiz Castilla, J.S.: Complex identification of plants from leaves. In: Huang, D.-S., Gromiha, M.M., Han, K., Hussain, A. (eds.) ICIC 2018, Part III. LNCS (LNAI), vol. 10956, pp. 376–387. Springer, Cham (2018). https://doi.org/10.1007/978-3-319-95957-3_41
19. Yang, C.C., Prasher, S.O., Landry, J.A., Ramaswamy, H.S., et al.: Application of artificial neural networks in image recognition and classification of crop and weeds, 147–152 (2000)
20. Barufaldi, J.M.: Redes neuronales adversarias para el reconocimiento de malezas. Tesis. Facultad de Ciencias Exactas, Ingeniera y Agrimensura. Universidad Nacional de Rosario, Argentina, pp. 47–61 (2016)
21. Haug, S., Andreas, M., Biber, P., Ostermann, J.: Plant classification system for crop/weed discrimination without segmentation. In IEEE Winter Conference on Applications of Computer Vision, pp. 1142–1149 (2014)
22. Hlaing, S.H., Khaing, A.S.: Weed and crop segmentation and classification using area thresholding. IJRET **3**, 375–382 (2014)
23. Amaro, E.G., Canales, J.C., Cabrera, J.E., Castilla, J.S.R., Lamont, F.G.: Identification of diseases and pests in tomato plants through artificial vision. In: Huang, D.-S., Premaratne, P. (eds.) ICIC 2020, Part III. LNCS (LNAI), vol. 12465, pp. 98–109. Springer, Cham (2020). https://doi.org/10.1007/978-3-030-60796-8_9
24. Lanlan, W., Youxian, W.: Weed corn seedling recognition by support vector machine using texture features. African J. Agricu. Res. **4**(9), 840–846 (2009)

25. Campos, Y., Sossa, H., Pajares, G.: Comparative analysis of texture descriptors in maize fields with plants, soil and object discrimination. Precision Agric. **18**(5), 717–735 (2016). https://doi.org/10.1007/s11119-016-9483-4
26. Jiang, H., Zhang, C., Qiao, Y., Zhang, Z., Zhang, W., Song, C.: CNN feature based graph convolutional network for weed and crop recognition in smart farming. Comput. Electron. Agricu. **174**, 105450 (2020). https://doi.org/10.1016/j.compag.2020.105450. ISSN 0168-1699
27. Li, Y., Nie, J., Chao, X.: Do we really need deep CNN for plant diseases identification? Comput. Electron. Agric. **178**, 105803 ((2020). https://doi.org/10.1016/j.compag.2020.105803. ISSN 0168-1699
28. LeCun, Y., Bottou, L., Bengio, Y., Haffner, P.: Gradient-based learning applied to document recognition. Proc. IEEE **86**(11), 2278–2324 (1998)
29. Ahila Priyadharshini, R., Arivazhagan, S., Arun, M., Mirnalini, A.: Maize leaf disease classification using deep convolutional neural networks. Neural Comput. Appl. **31**(12), 8887–8895 (2019). https://doi.org/10.1007/s00521-019-04228-3
30. Cortes, C., Vapnik, V.: Support-vector networks. Mach. Learn. **20**(3), 273–297 (1995). https://doi.org/10.1007/BF00994018
31. Qiao, Y., Cappelle, C., Ruichek, Y., Yang, T.: ConvNet and LSH-based visual localization using localized sequence matching. Sensors **19**(11), 2439 (2019). https://doi.org/10.3390/s19112439
32. Sibiya, M., Sumbwanyambe, M.: A computational procedure for the recognition and classification of maize leaf diseases out of healthy leaves using convolutional neural networks. AgriEngineering **2019**(1), 119–131 (2019). https://doi.org/10.3390/agriengineering1010009
33. Zhang, X., Qiao, Y., Meng, F., Fan, C., Zhang, M.: Identification of maize leaf diseases using improved deep convolutional neural networks. IEEE Access **6**, 30370–30377 (2018). https://doi.org/10.1109/ACCESS.2018.2844405
34. Puente-Maury, L., et al.: Método rápido de preprocesamiento para clasificación en conjuntos de datos no balanceados. Res. Comput. Sci. **73**, 129–142 (2014)
35. Alom, M.Z., Hasan, M., Yakopcic, C., Taha, T.M., Asari, V.K.: Improved inception-residual convolutional neural network for object recognition. Neural Comput. Appl. **32**(1), 279–293 (2018). https://doi.org/10.1007/s00521-018-3627-6

Implementation of an Object Recognizer Through Image Processing and Backpropagation Learning Algorithm

Fabricio Toapanta[1]([✉]), Teresa Guarda[1,2,3] [iD], and Xavier Villamil[1]

[1] Universidad de Las Fuerzas Armadas, Quito, Ecuador
[2] Universidad Estatal Península de Santa Elena, La Libertad, Ecuador
[3] CIST – Centro de Investigación en Sistemas y Telecomunicaciones, Universidad Estatal Península de Santa Elena, La Libertad, Ecuador

Abstract. Artificial neural networks in an effort to emulate the operation of the human brain from the point of view of learning and adaptation, have evolved in such a way that different statistical and mathematical models have inspired biological models, example you have to nerve cells or better known as neurons; the same ones that are composed of dendrites which are responsible for capturing the nerve impulses emitted by other neurons. The present study aims to analyze the Backpropagation model and the multilayer topology using an object recognizer through digital image processing such as object segmentation by detection and edge determination.

Keywords: Backpropagation · Neural network · Synapse · RNA · Digital imaging · Pixel · Machine vision · Perceptron · Optics

1 Introduction

Technological advancement has evolved and incorporated into different modern devices and into people's daily lives. As is the case of capturing better photography's, or the increasingly use of digital assistants on a day-to-day basis. Consequently, people do not skimp on expenses when it comes to using all the technology that exists in them.

Artificial Intelligence (AI) has become a trend, due to its applicability in a large number of devices for daily use.

Artificial Neural Networks emulate the functioning of the human brain, formed by a group of nodes also known as artificial neurons that connect and transmit signals to each other. The signals transmitted from the input to producing the output and whose primary objective of said model will be to learn with the continuous and automatic modification in itself, in such a way that it can perform complex tasks that not be achieved by means of classical programming that it is based on rules. With this it be possible to automate functions that previously could only be performed by human beings [1].

The Artificial Vision or Computer Aided Vision has also been developing alongside, consisting of the automatic deduction of the structure and properties of a three-dimensional, possibly dynamic world, from one or several two-dimensional images of

© Springer Nature Switzerland AG 2021
T. Guarda et al. (Eds.): ARTIIS 2021, CCIS 1485, pp. 275–287, 2021.
https://doi.org/10.1007/978-3-030-90241-4_22

this world. In this area of knowledge, there are concepts of color physics, optics, electronics, geometry, algorithms, and computer systems [2]. Computer Vision (CV) has also been developing alongside AI and Neural Networks, through the analysis of images by computers. CV has been implemented in the field of industry on two fundamental fronts: obtaining the greatest interaction between machines and their environment; and achieve total quality control in the products that are manufactured [2].

The development of new algorithms and the invention of new digital cameras has been the beginning in which the spectrum of applications has expanded in recent years. As is the case of new digital cameras and photographic applications, which can be detected by means of facial recognition the face of the person in the image.

This type of technological advance has opened up new fields of application in industry such as, security, automatic and autonomous driving of vehicles, new ways of interacting with controllers through gestures with the hand the movement of eyes and the growing boom Internet of Things (IoT) [3].

Artificial vision consists of the automatic deduction of the structure and properties of a three-dimensional world, possibly dynamic, from one or more two-dimensional images of that world. In this area of knowledge, concepts of color physics, optics, electronics, geometry, algorithmic, and computer systems are combined [4].

2 Images

An image is a two-dimensional representation of a three-dimensional world scene. The image is the result of the acquisition of a signal provided by a sensor, which converts the information from the electromagnetic spectrum into numerical encodings [5]. Based on this, the transformation in the chosen image representation format is part of a discrete information not only in the used values but also in the parameters that define it.

Without this representation, in a generic way, a digital image can be defined as a matrix of $N \times M$ dimensions, where each element of this matrix contains a discrete value that quantifies the information level of the corresponding element, represented with a finite number of bits (q). Thus, the concept or image criterion can be expressed as a discrete two-dimensional function in the following way:

$$I(x, y) / 0 \ <= x <= N - 1, \ 0 \ <= y <= M - 1 \tag{1}$$

Where N and M can be any numerical value within the natural numbers and the values of each element must be multiples of 2:

$$0 \ <= I(x, y) \ <= p - 1 / p = 2! \tag{2}$$

The values contained in each of the elements of the image i represented from dark levels of luminosity to the lightest values. The darkest level corresponds to the lowest value of the interval represented by the color black, and the lightest level represented by the color white and corresponds to the highest value.

The image is a two-dimensional function that provides certain electromagnetic information for each of its values. Each of these discrete elements is a point or pixel and generally contains the lighting level, or the color of a point in the scene. The set of points or pixels form the image or photograph of the scene. The image comes from the spectral representation received by a sensor. Being the color generated by the superposition of three spectral components [5].

2.1 Lighting

During the design of artificial vision systems, uncontrolled lighting of the environment is usually not acceptable since images with low contrast, specular reflections, being shadows and flares obtained. A well-designed lighting system provides light to the scene in such a way that the image obtained favor the subsequent process on it, maintaining and even improving the information necessary for the detection and extraction of objects and characteristics of interest [6].

Two types of lighting can be consider, those that can affect image processing (natural light such as the sun, moon, and stars) and artificial lights. Artificial are the most commonly used in artificial vision, since these can be adjusted depending on the physical environment that surrounds it; the same one that produces the transformation of electrical energy into photons and produces the different types of lighting with the most common and their own characteristics. That define a type of lighting, which is based on the range of wavelengths emitted by the light, the durability at the time of the wavelength and the variations produced over time and the temperature that can be reach in that instant [6].

2.2 Lighting Techniques

The proper functioning of a vision application is fundamentally dependent on lighting. If adequate lighting is not used, problems in contrasts, brightness and shadows can occur, which make the inspection algorithm difficult, and if this is the case, there may be instances where the algorithm cannot find a solution.

If the intention is to improve the vision system, it is necessary to use an adequate lighting technique, which will be a determining factor in obtaining a correct image to be processed. An example is an image in which the pixels that represent the objects of interest in it, have certain characteristics of similar luminosity, and are very different from the pixels that do not represent other objects of interest. Appropriate lighting is critical for correct image, which do not appear saturated areas or shadows that hide information within the image. Shadows cause false edge detections resulting in measures of either incorrectly [7].

In this context, weak lighting can result in a low signal/noise ratio, which can lead to a quality image with noisy pixels.

To choose a good lighting will be necessary to determine the actions of each component of the vision system at the time of image capture. Each of the components influences the amount of light that reaches the sensor, and therefore this will depend on the quality of the captured image. The aperture of the optics diaphragm directly affects the amount of light reaching the sensor. If the diaphragm is closed, the amount of light coming from the scene must be increase, or the exposure time must be increase, if the aim is to achieve an image with the same brightness values. A small area reflects less light than a large area and as consequence its necessary take into account the point of view of lighting. In this sense, the advantages and disadvantages of lighting techniques should be consider (Table 1) [8].

Table 1. Advantages and disadvantages of the different lighting techniques.

Technique	Description	Disadvantages	Advantages
Directional (Fig. 1)	It is directed to the object	Low price	Brightness
Diffuse	It is directed at the entire work area	Low brightness	Not useful in tight places
Backlighting	It is directed at the shadow of the image	Image edges are sharp	Image details are not visible to the naked eye
Oblique	It is directed only at the object obliquely	The shadow of the image will be skewed by the light	It only focuses on a single object
Dark-Ground (Fig. 1)	It is directed with transparent materials	Useful for highlighting cracks and bubbles within an object	The contrast at the edges is decreased
Coaxial	It is directed with illumination through a mirror	The edges are well defined	The surface is not well defined
Structured	It is addressed both in visible and non-visible space	Has a visibility of the entire object	Loss of color distinction

Figure 1 shows an example of images to which the different lighting techniques applied, fin this case direct lighting and dark-ground lighting.

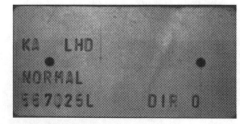 

Fig. 1. Image capture applying Direct lighting (Left) and Dark-Ground lighting (Right). Source: [2]

3   Image Processing

Image processing is a set of techniques that facilitates the search for information from an image or object, through information extraction techniques such as optical methods or by digital means such as the computer, applying different mathematical models, algorithms, among others.

This type of processing uses the Pixel, which is the physical unit of color that is part of the digital image; the images are formed by the succession of pixels, which presents a coherence in the information that is displayed, constituting an information matrix.

Digital image processing is performed by dividing the image into a matrix of values or pixels; it is here where a numerical value is assigned to the average brightness of each pixel and the coordinates of its position, resulting in an image definition complete.

There are several mathematical models that allow the representation of colors in numerical form, using chromatic values: RGB (Red, Green, Blue) and CMYK (Cyan, Magenta, Yellow, Key), which associates a numeric vector in a space color.

3.1   Binarization

Binarization is the process to move to simpler colors, which in this case is black and white. This technique allows reference different regions of the image, which have a similar intensity distribution, making the gray scale histogram show which areas belong to what regions. Threshold binarization is a technique that allows obtaining as much information as possible, since it identifies a threshold as an intensity value from a certain group of pixels, these will be considered within another subgroup and classified as white, while the other subgroup will be classified black.

For the detection of the threshold, the histogram of the image is essential, since it defines the intensity levels by means of their relative frequency.

Assuming that the objects have intensity values greater than those of the environment (Fig. 2), binarization is performed by whether a pixel (x, y) meets the current value of that pixel in the image f, is greater than the threshold, $f(x, y) > T$, then that pixel will be considered as the object, otherwise, this point will be considered from the environment [8].

Explicitly, the threshold value T is obtain by operation of the form:

$$T = T[x, y, p(x, y), f(x, y)] \tag{3}$$

Where, x and y are the coordinates of the pixel in the image f, $f(x, y)$ represents the intensity of the pixel in these coordinates, $p(x, y)$ is a property of the point to discriminate. This threshold obtained by the result of the equation, you can define a binary image $g(x, y)$,

$$g(x, y) = \left\{ \frac{0 \ sif(x, y) > T}{1 \ sif(x, y) \le T} \right\}$$

Examining $g(x, y)$ it is possible to observe that the pixels assigned a value of 0 are objects, while those with a value of 1 are the environment. In Fig. 2, there is an example, with a grayscale image, and its respective image segmented with different thresholds.

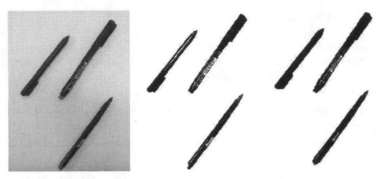

Fig. 2. Original image in grayscale, binarized image with threshold $T = 0.3$ and with threshold $T = 0.6$. Source: [5]

3.2 Edge Extraction

The edges of a digital image are transitions between gray levels in two different regions. Which provide information on the edges or borders of objects, being use for image segmentation, and object recognition, among others.

The edges of each region are different from the background, allowing their detection based on sudden changes in the intensity level.

Edge detection techniques usually employ operators based on discrete approximations of the first and second derivatives of the gray levels of the image. The second Derivative Gradient method, also known as the Laplacian Mask, is the strongest regarding the detection of lines, therefore it is the most used [9].

The Laplacian filter allows the enhancement of linear features in environments, to highlight the elements of greater variability is to subtract from the original image the one obtained by a Laplacian filter (Fig. 3) [6].

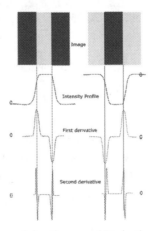

Fig. 3. Laplacian Edge Detector applying the second Derivative (■Laplacian: measures changes in the gradient; ▨Gradient difference). Source: [6]

3.3   Object Recognition Using Hough Transforms

The Hough transform allows you to detect curves in an image. This technique is good against noise and gaps at the edge of the object. For its application, the image it's first binarized to obtain the edge of the object.

The Hough transform aims to find the aligned points in the image, to have the equation of the line, for the values of ρ *and* θ. The equation of the line transformed to polar is $p = x * \cos\theta + y * sen\theta$. Then it is necessary to discretize the parameter space in accumulation cells.

Where ρ is the perpendicular distance from the origin to the line, and θ is the angle formed between the perpendicular to the line and the horizontal axis, which will be measured counterclockwise.

Therefore, each straight line can be associated with the parameters (ρ, θ) and this parameter plane (ρ, θ) is the Hough space [10].

Then the equation of the line is evaluating for each point in the image (x_k, y_k), it is evaluated if the equation is satisfied and the value of the cell is increased by one. If the values are high, this indicates that the point belongs to the line [11].

4   Artificial Neural Networks

Artificial Neural Networks (ANN) are computer systems that try to emulate the functioning of the human brain, from the point of view of learning and adaptation. ANN also called Distributed Processing Systems is a parallel process that is massively distributed and that stores experimental knowledge [12].

The ANNs have as main charactcristics the learning that is through examples or samples, and the interconnection weights "Synapse" that are adjust while learning (Fig. 4).

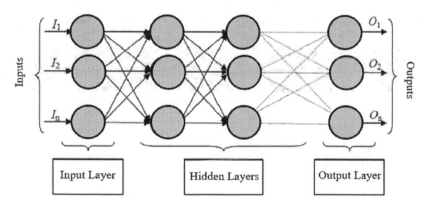

Fig. 4. Connected artificial neural networks. Source: [12]

4.1 Artificial Neuron

The neuron is a fundamental information process unit in an ANN. It is a device that allows calculating from an input vector with values from outside, or from other neurons that provide a response or output, in Fig. 5, the image of a biological neuron and an artificial neuron is observed [13].

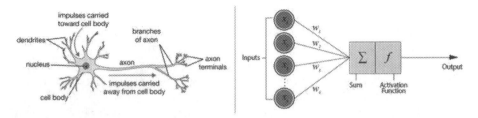

Fig. 5. Biological neuron and an artificial neuron. Source: [13]

In the artificial neuron model we have:

— Link Connection (parameters of synaptic weights W_{jn}
     if $W_{jn} > 0$ the connection is excitatory
     if $W_{jn} < 0$ the connection is inhibitory;
— Sum Point (it is the weighted sum between the inputs and their synaptic weights);
— Activation Function (non-linear transformation function, where the sum value is transformed into a digital signal);
— And Polarization or Network Function (also known as threshold, it allows to shift the value of the inputs).

4.2 Backpropagation Algorithm

Depending on the ANN, there are several connection topologies and learning algorithms, depending on their use. In this case, the model to be review is the Backpropagation Model, [14].

Backpropagation model tries to combine several perceptron's in a type of multilayer network, and carry out the learning using a backward propagation algorithm, backward from the error. The term refers to the calculation method on an error environment of a network, forward.

Backpropagation is a supervised learning algorithm, which expects to know the expected output, and is associated with each input, updating the weights and gains, through the rule of descending steps. To supervise the control of the error made, the error function is redefine, leaving a new error function and is the following:

$$E\left(\vec{w}\right) \equiv \frac{1}{2} \sum_{d \in D} \sum_{k \in outputs} (t_{kd} - o_{kd}) \tag{5}$$

Where each parameter represents: $\left(\overrightarrow{w} \right)$ Weights vector; D Set of training weights; d Concrete training; *Outputs* Neurons vector output; k Output neuron; t_{kd} Correct output that the output neuron k should give when applying the training example to the network d; O_{kd} Output calculated by the output neuron k when applying the training example to the network d [15].

4.3 Learning Process

For the learning process, the weights should be adjust through an interaction between neurons and the environment. A neural network modifies its weights in response to input information. The changes that occur during it are reduce to the destruction, modification and creation of connections between neurons [16]. In this context, in biological systems there is a continuous destruction and creation of connections between neurons.

The RNA models for the creation of a new connection, its weight happens to have a value other than zero. A connection is destroy when the weight equals zero. The Backpropagation algorithm supports error propagation, providing an efficient method to calculate error derivatives $\frac{\delta E}{\delta y}$, which converts the discrepancies between the derivative output and the network output.

5 Implementation of the Object Recognition System

The Object Recognition System (ORS) was develop in the C # programming language and with several Open Sources type libraries. Which allow obtaining the image through a camera and process the images, making it a little easier to implement edge detection algorithms, image segmentation as well as neuron training, so that according to the captured image it has the ability to identify them through a system's own database.

For the processing of the images, the AForge.dll, AForge.Imaging.dll, AForge.Math.dll library was used, which specializes in binary source code specialized in Artificial Intelligence and Computer Vision, developed by Andrew Kirillov for the .NET framework.

The NeuronDotNet.Core.dll library takes care of neuron training, which uses multilayer input and 2 layers output. Vijeth Dinesha develop this library as an Artificial Intelligence project.

At the moment of execute the project, a screen will appear (Fig. 6) where the different options can be shown with which the program will start to carry out the processing of the image using the binarization and detection of edges.

Once the image treatment has done, then network process is perform, with which the neuron is train using the Hough Moments, and the affine matrix which values are obtain to perform the RGB Histogram (Fig. 7).

To perform the training the Error Correction Learning algorithm is applied, with which the weight adjustments are made, differentiating the types of leaves, and the Hough moments; and as input parameters the number of iterations and the percentage (%) of error tolerance.

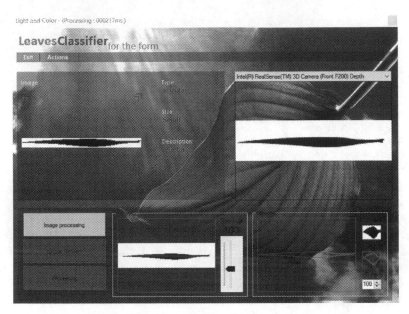

Fig. 6. ORS Image obtain and processing screen.

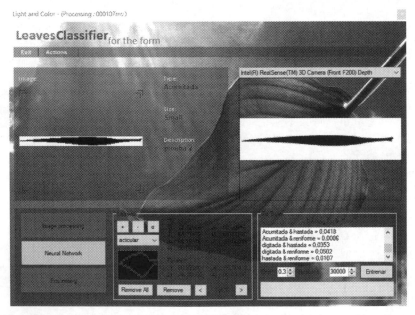

Fig. 7. ORS neuron training and obtaining the weights and related values and hough moments screen.

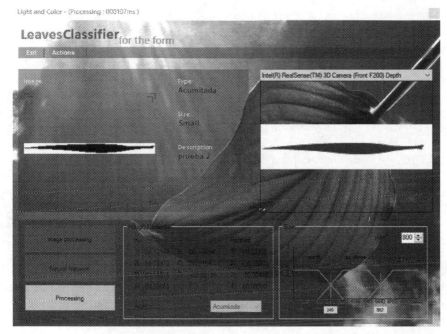

Fig. 8. ORS processing screen, where the weights, hough values, and others are identified, in addition to the Histogram.

Once the neuron is trained, the last step (Processing) is carried out, and the values of the weights, Hough Moments, and the Affine are observed, with which the Histogram of the image can be performed (Fig. 8).

Once the entire Neuron Training Process is perform, these data are save in a file, with the values obtained. This file will help so that when a new process executed and the values are similar, it will automatically identify the same image, appearing it on the screen.

The result of the implementation of the Backpropagation Algorithm is the integration of the different processes of Processing Images and Learning by Correction of Errors, which allows obtaining small output values, according to its structure and training weights.

Backpropagation is a learning algorithm used in Multi Layers of Perceptron, being use to solve complex problems in an efficient way, turning out to be more efficient than traditional programs. Witch can be used in industry as part of Process Control, which allows you to identify whether a manufactured product has a defect in its structure, with the quality of the improved product allowing for the improvement of raw material.

6 Conclusions

There are several models and algorithms of Artificial Neural Networks, even more efficient than the one implemented in this work, like the case of the Kohonen algorithm that is used in many applications of transit, global positioning, among others.

Currently there are tools that perform facial recognition, which use their own knowledge base making it more efficient, they also use more advanced algorithms such as Hopfield, Kohonen.

Amazon has its recognition tool called Amazon Rekognition that is used for facial recognition through mobile devices.

What makes artificial intelligence a tool used to improve times and processes in the industry, since it can be monitored in real time, applying the necessary corrections, so that it is not affected by any errors in production. The aim is to motivate the research and implementation of this type of technology, not only for industry, but also in everyday life, such as in intelligent buildings, thus giving a differential to this type of device.

The purpose of this work is to study the Backpropagation algorithm as a start towards neural networks and their possible utilities, knowing that there are many learning algorithms that are being used in other programming languages such as Python.

What is intended is that it can be applied in other programming languages and for other uses.

We recommend that this type of research work, be use to motivate the development and improvement of new projects, involving new methodologies of Artificial Intelligence and Image Processing, since nowadays they are on the rise, thanks to their low cost, and their easy learning. Thus, innovative projects with social benefit can be perform, such as facial recognition, which would help public security to recognize people who have committed illicit acts, improving the quality of our society.

References

1. Asanza, W.R., Olivo, B.M.: Redes neuronales artificiales aplicadas al reconocimiento de patrones, 2016th ed. Editorial UTMACH, Machala
2. Martinsanz, G.P.: Conceptos y métodos en Visión por Computador. Grupo de Visión del Comité de Automática (CEA), España (2016)
3. Péref, F., Félix, A., Guerra, J.L.: Internet de las Cosas. Perspectiv@s, vol. 10, pp. 45–46 (2017)
4. Gonzalez Galvis, J.L., Parra Abril, J.A.: Diseño E Implementación De Un Sistema De Reconocimiento De Naranjas Para El Robot Gio 1 Usando Visión Asistida Por Computador (2015)
5. Gonzalez, R.C., Woods, R.E.: Digital Image Precessing. Pearson, Chicago (2008)
6. Documentary Educational Resources. Machine Vision: Theory, Algorithms, Practicalities. Academic Press, Oxford (2015)
7. van der Walt, S., Schönberger, J., Nunez-Iglesias, J., Boulogne, F.: Scikit-image: image processing in Python. Peerj (2014)
8. Ruiz, C.A., Basualdo, M.S.: Redes Neuronales: Conceptos Básicos y Aplicaciones. PubliEditorial, Rosario (2001)
9. Wasserman, P.D.: Neural Computing: Theory and Practice. Van Nostrand Reinhold, Netherlands (1989)
10. Montavon, O.M.: Neural Networks: Tricks of the Trade. Springer, Chicago (2012). https://doi.org/10.1007/978-3-642-35289-8
11. Simon, H.: Neural Netwoks and Learning Machines. Prentice Hall, Chicago (2018)
12. Rouhiainen, L.P.: Inteligencia Artificial. Editorial Planeta S.A, Barcelona (2018)
13. Flores, L.R., Fernández, F.J.M.: Las Redes Neuronales Artificiales: Fundamentos Teóricos y Aplicaciones prácticas. NetBiblo, S.L, La Coruña (2015)

14. Bishop, C.M.: Neural Networks for Pattern Recognition. Oxford University Press, Oxford (2006)
15. Guinot, P.M., Ortí, M.: Introduccion A Las Redes Neuronales Aplicadas Al Control Industrial. Pearson, Valencia (2013)
16. González, B., Valdeza, F., Melina, P., Prado-Arechiga, G.: Fuzzy logic in the gravitational search algorithm for the optimization of modular neural networks in pattern recognition. ScienceDirect, pp. 5839–5847 (2015)

Generation of 3D Terrain Surfaces from Satellite Images

Yalmar Ponce Atencio[1](✉) [iD], Francisco Espinoza Montes[2] [iD], Iraida Ortiz Guizado[1],
Mary Luz Huamán Carrion[1] [iD], and Noemi Porras Diaz[1]

[1] Universidad Nacional José María Arguedas, Andahuaylas, Apurímac, Peru
{yalmar,mhuaman}@unajma.edu.pe
[2] Universidad Nacional del Centro del Perú, Huancayo, Junín, Peru

Abstract. The reconstruction of three-dimensional (3D) models of terrain is
important in many applications mainly for photorealistic visualizations of virtual
natural environments, ranging from the representation of a landscape, to doing
analysis and monitoring of coverage, or land use. In addition, could also is used
for the management and planning of the territory. The 3D modeling of territories
or land is very important since many applications requires of this element and
getting a three-dimensional digital model of the surface of some land, which is
could be reliable and accurate, and that allows to be viewed interactively certainly
help many users. In this context, to date, there are few tools that facilitate this
task, among them the most used are ArcGIS, Google® Maps and Google® Earth,
however, for this purpose, these tools are available online and works entirely on
its environment. The main objective of this work is to get digital terrain models to carry out simulations, visualization for monitoring and also the possibility
of a photorealistic representation, thus, we could even think of representing the
entire world in a virtual navigation environment, supporting simulations with representation of objects of different types, from small rocks, plants, bushes, streams,
ponds, rivers, lakes, mountains and other attributes that we can find in real terrain.
As preliminary results, this research work shows some techniques and tools that
can be used for the reconstruction of land that are often necessary to use them in
our own applications and combine them with other elements to achieve the main
objective.

Keywords: 3D terrain surfaces · Satellite images · 3D terrain reconstruction
techniques

1 Introduction

Currently, acquire of Digital Surface Models (DSM) is quite demanded in different
applications. Usually, this is done by using aerial images obtained by drone or from
high-resolution satellite images, where images with high resolution are preferred, but, in
many cases, could not be available and only is possible to use images from some online
applications like google maps.

© Springer Nature Switzerland AG 2021
T. Guarda et al. (Eds.): ARTIIS 2021, CCIS 1485, pp. 288–301, 2021.
https://doi.org/10.1007/978-3-030-90241-4_23

Thus, terrain modeling, Is very important for a large set of applications like the generation of topographic, terrain navigation, simulations for natural phenomena, virtual environments, games, among others. However, in case of use satellite images, correction procedures are also required to provide elevation data, for example, elevation by orthorectification process, using a set of ground control points; therefore, the resulting precision in mapping meets the mapping requirements. There are currently a wide variety of computer programs that allow digital image processing in photogrammetry, based on algorithmic approaches, which seek to solve the problem of the numerical representation of relief. The DSM is a fundamental information layer and various parameters can be extracted from this. This paper presents some existing simplified ways to generate an DSM that reconstructs a 3D surface model by using existing resources like google maps. The process allows to quickly generate 3D surfaces since Google® Maps is used as a tool to provide satellite images. The study involves the use some software like Blender for the generation of an 3D surface model (mesh).

The rest of the document is organized as follows: the related works are presented in the second section, in the third section the details of the process of obtaining the 3D surface model are presented, in the fourth section the results and a discussion about in-process used in comparison with other processes, finally, in the fifth section the conclusions and future works are presented.

2   Related Works

2.1   Traditional Techniques

Traditional terrain creation techniques commonly involve taking data from some source, modifying it using a terrain modeling tool, then adding modeled elements and optimizing it for use in a final application. However, even to achieve a static result, without the possibility of interaction, it takes a considerable effort and time of work and quite a lot of time and then it is only the representation of a small part or a localized part of some territory, which is not satisfactory for many purposes [1].

2.2   Modern Techniques

Given the nature of a geospatial application, it generally uses and displays geospatial data, this could be as 2D maps, as a 3D visualization of the environment, or even to add interaction. Its usefulness can be reflected in a wide range of applications such as: incorporation of objects, for example, vehicles, simulation of logistics systems, communications or other systems, or enabling semi-automated behaviors.

Most simulations are based on local copies of terrain data. As the areas of interest for each sub-application expand and high-fidelity geospatial data becomes more readily available, the needs to store this data have grown exponentially. Although the capacity of the disk drive has also increased, becoming more and more capacity and less expensive, however, the process of copying and re-copying data is still time consuming and prone to errors and/or loss information [2].

Considering the points described above, the best solution is to store a single set of reference data, so that each application accesses this data when necessary. The Open

Geospatial Consortium (OGC) has published a series of web mapping specifications to enable transmission of geospatial data across a network environment that can be leveraged to support this approach. There are defined standards for manipulation of terrain information (according to the OGC), and these are used to provide the basis for delivering images, elevations, feature data and 3D models to be supported in applications that are expected to be executed in real time, both for visualization and simulation. The geospatial data can be provided on demand, avoiding the need to copy large terrain databases to each PC, workstation or imager, and can be controlled in a central location to help manage potential terrain modification and update it automatically on users [3–8].

Applications such as Google® Earth, Google® Maps and many other mapping applications are commonly used, both in standalone environments and in web environments; to view locations, calculate driving directions, or discover other information about a particular location. By using these applications, which are somewhat standard available, we can use the same approaches to achieve real-time simulations of an entire region (a particular territory area). However, the generation of terrain information of an entire region in an agile way requires the support of some specific concepts [9–11], which not often found in traditional terrain navigation systems.

3   Terrain Surface Reconstruction

Until now, some quite used tools are the ArcGIS products, however, their function is somewhat different from the reconstruction of surfaces and more oriented to the field of Geographic Information Systems or GIS and its applications. Fuentes, in his work [12], presents a description of how a Digital Surface Model (DSM) can be obtained from optical satellite images with high spatial resolution and its use for the generation of topographic information. This process should be considered as a practical and affordable methodological alternative for modeling land surfaces. For this purpose, satellite images of the different satellites that exist can be used, however in order to generate an DSM, it is necessary to have more than one image, taken from another angle, of the area that you want to reconstruct the surface. Satellite stereoscopy is essential in the images to be able to obtain the elevation over the desired terrain. The images have the stereoscopic effect because two different fields of view are taken that can be along or across the path of the satellite. The images are obtained from two close but slightly different orbits; one image is taken from an angle between 60° and 75° and the other is taken at an angle oblique to the satellite's path between 60° and 90°. This indicates that the satellite has the ability to rotate in relation to its orbit (see Figs. 1 and 2). Satellite sensors with this capacity can be characterized as stereoscopic image systems by being able to originate data from which three-dimensional coordinates can be calculated and information on the height of the terrain can be obtained.

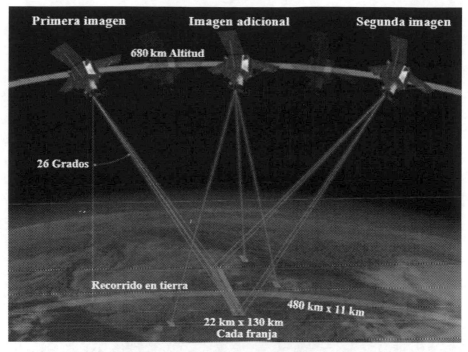

Fig. 1. Illustration of how satellites taking images of the same area.

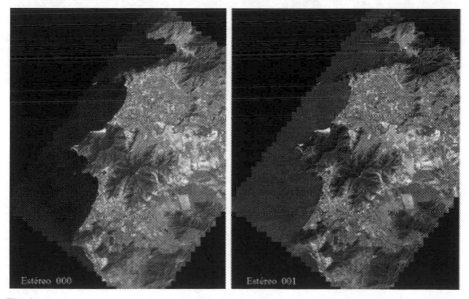

Fig. 2. Stereoscopic images (it consists of take two images of the same place but from different angles).

DSMs are the representation of surface elevation variations present at the time of imaging, either using photogrammetric instruments, Lidar (Light Detection and Ranging) or radar. These can have a regular or irregular data representation structure. The main difference of the Digital Terrain Model (DTM) with the DSM is that the former represents only the elevation values of the lowest points of a surface (terrain), as opposed to the latter which represent the elevation of the surface layer of objects on the ground. DTMs can be a product originated from some DSM process. The term Digital Elevation Model (DEM) corresponds to an elevation attribute in a digital model with a specific projection and a regular data representation structure (see Fig. 3). These terms are often confusing as many uses DEM and DTM synonymously [12].

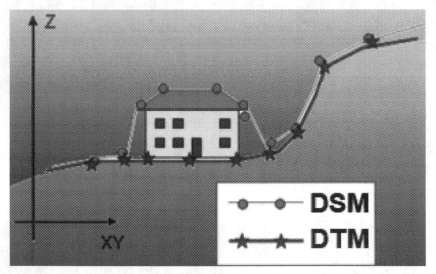

Fig. 3. Differences between a Digital Surface Model (DSM) and a Digital Terrain Model (DTM).

3.1 Reconstruction Process

For this purpose, the Blender software and the AddOn BlenderGIS have been used (https://github.com/domlysz/BlenderGIS). In the Fig. 4 is shown the installation of this AddOn[1].

---

[1] Alternatively, there are similar interesting projects on the GitHub repository (github.com).

Next, by selecting the GIS, Web geodata and Basemap options, we will have the possibility of use Google® Maps in the display mode with satellite images (see Figs. 5 and 6).

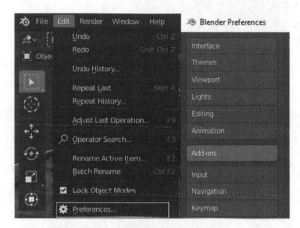

Fig. 4. Installing the BlenderGIS AddOn.

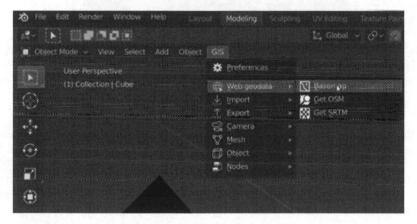

Fig. 5. Choose the basemap option.

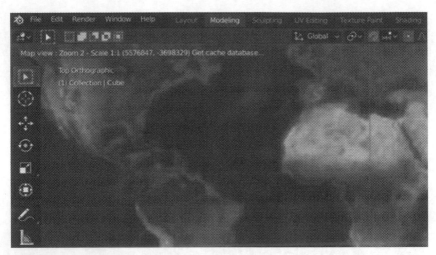

Fig. 6. The basemap option allows navigate on google maps within Blender and mark a region of interest.

Then, we can navigate on Google® Maps, within Blender, and choose the area that we want to rebuild its 3D surface (see Fig. 7).

Next, in order to get the selected area, is recommendable use a zoom value of 15 (see Fig. 8).

In the image you can see quite clearly the details of the terrain, such as roads, rocks, lagoons, small houses and vegetation.

Once we have the area where we want to reconstruct the surface, we simply press the 'e' key in the computer keyboard.

The selected region has been delimited, so we must choose the option "GetSRTM".

The Digital Surface Model is automatically generated, as shown in the Figs. 9 and 10.

Later, in order to obtain a surface model (mesh) with better details, it must be subdivided several times until an adequate level of detail will be obtained (see Fig. 11).

The subdivision generates flat surfaces, and must be corrected with interpolation or smoothing techniques (see Fig. 12). In addition, to achieve the characteristics of surfaces such as vegetation, it is necessary to use some effects like "bumpmapping" (see Fig. 13).

The process is quite simple using the Blender GIS plugin for Blender, however, the main difficulty lies in the equipment to be used to perform all the processing, since all these options used in each step of the reconstruction consume a lot of memory, and capacity of prosecution.

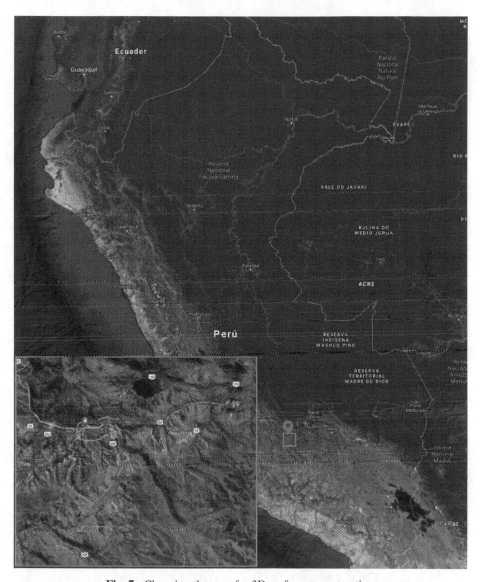

Fig. 7. Choosing the area for 3D surface reconstruction.

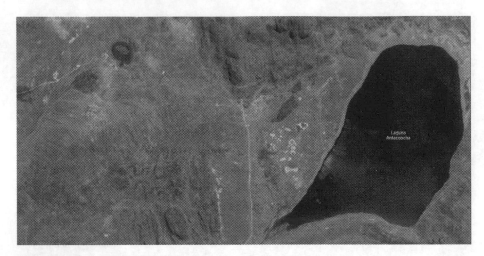

Fig. 8. Zoom value is set to 15.

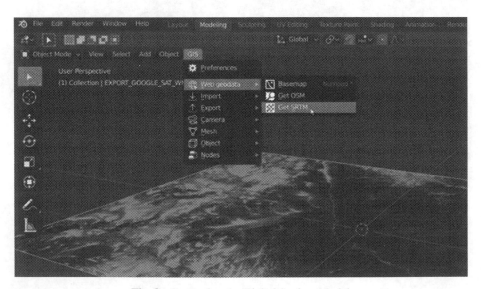

Fig. 9. Generating the Digital Surface Model.

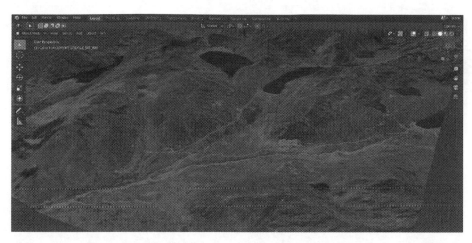

Fig. 10. The generated Digital Surface Model.

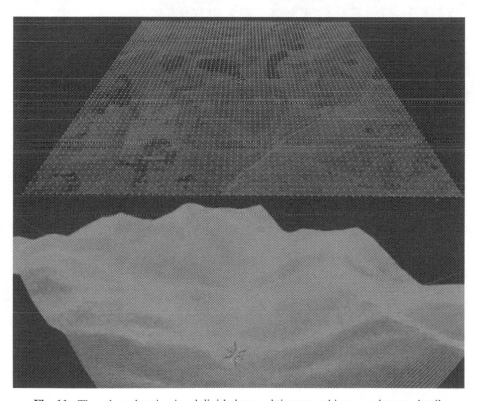

Fig. 11. The selected region is subdivided several times to achieve an adequate detail.

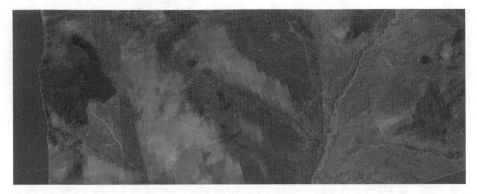

Fig. 12. Subdivision generates flat parts.

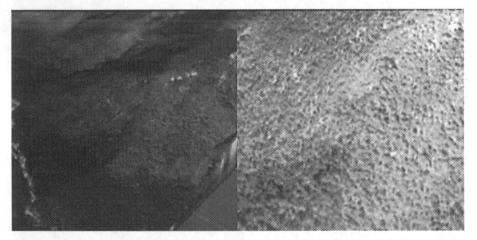

Fig. 13. The generated 3D surface does not consider the ground level; however, better results can be achieved using "bummapping".

3.2 Reconstruction Process

After making several attempts to reconstruct land surfaces corresponding to images obtained from Google® Maps, it has been noted that Google® Maps images are considerably heavy, and once the reconstruction area is selected, Blender consumes a good amount of memory, between 2 GB and 4 GB.

Thus, a computer equipped with an Intel i7 5820K processor (6cores/12threads), 16 GB DDR4 memory, and a NVidia TITAN Xp GPU has been used.

Despite being a fairly well-equipped computer, the 16 GB of memory is insufficient to perform the processing. In several attempts, the computer stopped working, since the subdivision process only remained at level 6, managing to consume around 12 GB of RAM.

In this sense, it is very likely that to perform terrain reconstructions of larger areas or surface dimensions, and with greater detail, it will be necessary at least 32 GB or better 64 GB, or 128 GB of RAM.

Once the reconstruction of the selected area has been generated, it must be saved in a file so that the digital model of the terrain surface can be used later. This process also took several minutes, and the generated file occupied around 1 GB, considering a territory area of approximately 15 Km^2.

4   Results

It was possible to reconstruct the area of the micro-basins of the Chumbao river, belonging to the Andahuaylas province, in the department of Apurímac in Peru. The terrain surface was obtained with satisfactory levels of detail, however, there is a great difficulty in the processing time, achieving few results in a few hours of attempts. The Fig. 14 shows the 3D terrain surface of the micro-basins, and with enough realism to the place.

Fig. 14. 3D surface of the Chumbao river micro-basins area.

In a second experiment, the saved file was recovered, since memory consumption is very high for a program that allows handling 3D model files, delaying loading for several minutes (see Fig. 15).

Nombre	Estado	14% CPU	89% Memoria
> 🔹 Blender (2)		13.1%	11,683.3 ...
> 🌐 Microsoft Edge (31)		0.1%	353.3 MB

Fig. 15. Memory consumption when reading the generated terrain surface file.

The generated model file has 4208975 vertices and 4200448 quadrilaterals, so it occupies around 10 GB in memory when the model is loaded. Notice that this model was not re-meshed or cleaned on its generated elements.

The saved model file was successfully displayed. The Fig. 16 shows the generated mesh, which can be used in other applications and for different purposes. Notice that the retrieved model still has the original dimensions so it must be processed and treated at a predefined scale.

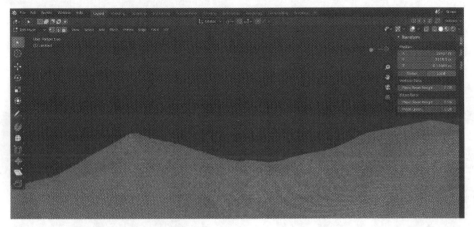

Fig. 16. Model of the terrain surface retrieved from a .ply file, the same one that was previously saved with Blender.

5   Conclusions and Future Work

In the experiments carried out, the processing of satellite images requires a computer with good enough capacities, in memory, on disk, as well as in processing.

The manual processing performed, using the Blender software, has some disadvantages, since we must wait for the reconstruction of a selected area to finish the processing, so reconstructing larger regions would be quite tedious to be able to process with acceptable levels of detail.

As future work, it has been considered to do the reconstruction processing in our own software without depending on Blender. An alternative is to use the BlenderGIS AddOn separately, since it is developed in Python, and it is possible to reuse the algorithms and data structures, on other hand, there are many other tools for terrain surface reconstruction, similar to BlenderGIS, and it is possible to customize and get better results by processing large areas of terrain.

Additionally, we consider to clean the surface of the terrain surface in order to get only the Digital Terrain Model (DTM), and later incorporate different kind of objects like vegetation, buildings, and others.

Acknowledgements. We wish to thank the CONCYTEC - FONDECYT, Perú and UNAJMA. This project has received funding from FONDECYT and UNAJMA and was supported under grant agreement N° 098-2018-FONDECYT-BM-IADT-AV., under the call E041-2018-01-BM.

References

1. Toutin, T.: Elevation modeling from satellite data (2006)
2. Eltner, A., Kaiser, A., Castillo, C., Rock, G., Neugirg, F., Abellan, A.: Image-based surface reconstruction in geomorphometry - merits, limits and developments. Earth Surf. Dyn. **4**, 359–389 (2016)
3. Forghani, A., Nadimpalli, K., Cechet, R.: Extracting terrain categories from multi-source satellite imagery. Int. J. Geoinform. **14**, 25–34 (2018)
4. Xiao, Z., Yang, B., Zhang, H.: Positioning accuracy analysis and application for worldview-1 stereo imagery. ISPRS – Int. Arch. Photogramm. Remote Sens. Spat. Inf. Sci. **XL**(4), 311 (2014)
5. Poon, J., Fraser, C., Zhang, C.: High-resolution satellite imaging for digital surface models (2020)
6. Poon, J., Dousse, T., Santosuosso, D.: Digital terrain model generation from worldview-1 stereo imagery (2020)
7. Qin, R.: Automated 3D recovery from very high-resolution multi-view satellite images (2017)
8. Rathore, M.M., Ahmad, A., Paul, A.: Real-time continuous feature extraction in large size satellite images. J. Syst. Architect. **64**, 122–132 (2016)
9. Nemade, N., Wagh, S.: Feature extraction in large size satellite images using GIS concept for remote sensing technique, pp. 1–6 (2017)
10. Dinkov, D., Vatseva, R.: 3D modelling and visualization for landscape simulation (2016)
11. Perko, R., Raggam, H., Gutjahr, K., Schardt, M.: Advanced DTM generation from very high-resolution satellite stereo images. ISPRS Ann. Photogramm. Remote Sens. Spat. Inf. Sci. **II**(3/W4), 165–172 (2015)
12. Fuentes Delgado, J.E.: Modelo digital de superficie a partir de imágenes de satélite ikonos para el análisis de Áreas de inundación en santa marta Colombia. Investig. Mar. **41**, 251–266 (2012)

Digital Influencers and Tourist Destinations: Cristiano Ronaldo and Madeira Island, from Promotion to Impact

Pedro Vaz Serra[1]([✉]) [iD] and Cláudia Seabra[1,2,3] [iD]

[1] Faculty of Arts and Humanities, University of Coimbra, Coimbra, Portugal
cseabra@uc.pt
[2] CEGOT - Centre of Studies in Geography and Spatial Planning, Coimbra, Portugal
[3] CISeD - Research Center in Digital Services, Viseu, Portugal

Abstract. With the advent of the internet and the consequent emergence of social networks, a new era in the way of communicating and interacting began. Its influence on tourism and on the destination's image also emerged. When the most followed person worldwide on social networks, Cristiano Ronaldo, regularly promotes the image of Madeira, where he was born, it is pertinent to assess the impact of this combination on the significant number of awards obtained by the Island over the past few years, within the scope of the World Travel Awards. The present work will answer two research questions: i) Do Cristiano Ronaldo influence, in a positive and significant way, the perception of the image of Madeira Island? ii) Do the island's natural attributes overlap, in a positive and significant way, over the others, in the perception of the image of Madeira Island? The results, under a descriptive research plan—obtained from mix method approach with secondary data and a questionnaire with 477 participants—support the association of phenomena between the awards obtained by Madeira and the publications made by Cristiano Ronaldo on social networks. It is recognized by the respondents the influence that the football player has in the promotion of the Island, as well as the prevalence of natural factors compared to the others in the perceived image. The results give a relevant contribution to the various local stakeholders, from public entities to private operators, opening space for future investigations with the intervention of new participants in the study and other variables in the research.

Keywords: Digital influencers · Tourist destinations · Cristiano Ronaldo · Madeira Island · Destination image · Digital technologies

1 Introduction

With de internet advent and, especially, social media, the *WoM* - Word-of-Mounth term has gained a new amplitude, in the online context, and was renamed *e-WoM* - electronic-Worth-of-Mounth, emerging its influence on tourist activity, in general, and on the destinations image, in particular [1].

Madeira Island has several conditions to a good tourism offer: the friendliness and hospitality of its inhabitants, good infrastructures and services and high-quality hotels.

© Springer Nature Switzerland AG 2021
T. Guarda et al. (Eds.): ARTIIS 2021, CCIS 1485, pp. 302–317, 2021.
https://doi.org/10.1007/978-3-030-90241-4_24

In addition, a setting mapped by dense and green landscapes, between the blue of the Atlantic and the brightness of the sun, we are facing a magnificent scenery. When this horizon, which is also a destination, is a depository of paths that add and experiences that tell, lived in a safe and peaceful environment, then the conditions for a positive differentiation are met.

Cristiano Ronaldo is considered one of the best football players of the present time, and he is a well-known Madeira born, so his image is closely linked to that of the Atlantic island. This athlete carries with him the most valuable brand among the world's footballers, with levels of media potential, notoriety, popularity and reputation never before achieved [2]. When the resulting records are supported, furthermore, by a professional management of communication and image, with a scale effect that induces planetary recognition [3], then we are faced with a case worthy of study.

In the context of the *World Travel Awards* (WTA) [4], Madeira Island was elected, between 2013 and 2020, as *Europe's Best Island Destination* seven times – 2013, 2014, 2016, 2017, 2018, 2019 and 2020 – and, between 2015 and 2020, consecutively, as *World's Best Island Destination* [4].

Simultaneously, between 2013 and 2020, Cristiano Ronaldo has walked a gradual and consistent path—he was distinguished by FIFA - Fédération Internationale de Football Association, in 2008, 2013, 2014, 2016 and 2017, as *Best Player in the World*; and by UEFA - Union of European Football Associations, in the 2013–14, 2015–16, 2016–17 seasons, as *Best Player in Europe*, in addition to dozens of other individual and collective awards [5]—that enshrines him as one of the most followed people on the main social networks [6] and at the date of October 2020, it is even the most-followed in the world, by registering 451 million followers [7].

That is, on the various platforms, Cristiano Ronaldo has a relevant exposure, being the footballer with the highest visibility worldwide, with the resulting status of *digital influencer* [2].

Besides the previous studies on the impact of social networks on tourist destination image, a greater empirical analysis evidencing its real impact on the tourist experience and the image of the destination is needed [8]. The main goal of this paper is to close this gap, specifically by establishing a connection between the topic of digital influencers and the promotion of tourist destinations.

By using the case study of Cristiano Ronaldo influence on Madeira destination image, the main aim is to analyse how individuals perceive the image of the Island. The present work will answer to two research questions: i) Do Cristiano Ronaldo influence, in a positive and significant way, the perception of the image of Madeira Island? ii) Do the island's natural attributes overlap, in a positive and significant way, over the others, in the perception of the image of Madeira Island?

2   Literature Review

The importance of the tourist destination image is emphasized by most authors [9, 10] and, given the influence it exerts on the choices, expectations, behaviour and evaluations of tourists [11, 12] this must be coherent with the reality of the destination and consequently due to the highlight of its differentiating factors [10].

Destinations compete, fundamentally, for the perception of their image in the target segments in direct comparison with the perceived images of their competitors' destinations [13]. It is noticeable, particularly in the last decade, an increased competition between tourist destinations. This is mainly due to the effects of globalization, which allow mobility – real and virtual – to be more accelerated and expressive, supported by an increasingly effective communication in the media and more efficient in the content [14].

Models and paradigms changed, with the consequent change in terms of marketing—also in tourist destinations and digital influencers themselves—which, outlined in a strategic perspective, reaches the target segments by its operational impact [15].

In fact, it is not only predictable but also essential, the connection of marketing and technology, in general, and to the internet and social media, in particular [6], areas where synergies and scope for action are increasingly expressive, assuming these as a critical success factor in attracting, engaging and monitoring tourist flows [16].

In this way, we see a whole new reality in the way tourists interact—before (through the analysis), during (through the narrative), and after (through the experience) with a tourism destination [17, 18]. They interact in a more dynamic and flexible environment, increasingly accessible and therefore more popularized [17].

Through long-range platforms and mobile equipment that, combining functionality with technology, enshrine the moment, new forms of content emerge, supported by an overlap of emotion (positive or negative) and mediation in information channels [18]. Aware of this reality, tourism destinations offer increasingly personalized products and enhancers of intensely unique experiences [19, 20].

Thus, the importance of social networks and digital content becomes evident. An investigation [21] concluded that 55% of respondents changed their travel plans after using social networks and 52% stated that their friends' posts on Facebook inspired them in choosing a holiday destination. There are strong evidences that social media constitute an essential instrument and form of interaction for those promoting tourist destination [21, 22].

An *influencer* is someone likely to impact the behaviour or ideas of others, based on the dissemination of a message [23, 24], alternatively is considered as the individual able to change other people's attitudes, by their communication or by their example [25], referring to a *digital influencer* whenever this occurs in a digital environment and carrying, as a rule, a very significant number of followers in the social networks, the context in which they place their publications [26–29].

Identifying digital influencers is, due to its potential, a relevant action for marketing, also in the promotion of tourist destinations and the most influential followers can also contribute to a marketing campaign can go viral [30]. In the identification process, criteria such as the number of followers, interactions—views, likes, comments, shares—are used in order to determine which are the most suitable digital influencers for pursuing a strategy and achieving the underlying goals [31].

In summary, the importance of digital influencers and their potential in promoting tourist destinations is revealing. However, quantity does not overlap with quality, which implies a planned, developed and executed strategy with criteria and professionalism [32], where one of the fundamental elements is its image [33].

The strategic and operational marketing process linked with tourist destinations is therefore particularly important, although there is no consensus on how the image is defined [34] and it should be noted that it results from a mental construct consisting of factors—external and internal—to the individual [35], i.e., impressions and ideas [36]; a representation built over time [37]; an elaborate image about the destination [38]—that is, the image comprises impressions, perceptions and beliefs [39].

Although it is not a unanimous approach, authors [40, 41] tend to consider that this mental construct incorporates two components: one cognitive and the other affective. Anyway, although the recognition of the existence of these two components prevails in the literature, it is important [42] study both and not only emphasize one of them, since tourist destinations are formed both by physical characteristics, at the level of attributes, and by intangible characteristics, at the level of feelings.

In summary [43], the cognitive component corresponds to knowledge, memory and the way tourists perceive the attributes and characteristics of the destination, which includes its landscape, attractions and built environment, using different scales, such as Likert type, or the combination of this with the semantic differential, or with open questions, adapted according to the purposes of the investigation [44].

In its turn, the affective component corresponds to a special feeling about the destination [43], that stems from the different emotions granted by the tourist and their affective associations - which can be positive, neutral, or negative. However, the measurement of these components must be produced with support for semantic differential scales, as they increase the perception of the environment [36, 45].

3   Methodology

The research will be supported by the literature review, after which statistical data is collected, using multiple sources of evidence, synonymous with a more robust analysis in case studies [46], because it gives space to the convergence of lines of investigation as a data triangulation process.

In this context, the relevance of the approach through a case study [46] stems from the relevance of investigating complex social phenomena: the definition of a case study corresponds to an empirical investigation that studies a contemporary phenomenon in its context, inserted in real life, especially when the boundary between the phenomenon and the context is very tenuous [46].

The research plan will be descriptive—distinguished by making the connection between the comprehensive methods of reality and the explanatory ones—structured in the collection of data that allow describing the reality inherent to the theme.

To answer the research questions, we used a mix methodology approach (see Table 1) with secondary data.

Regarding the Cristiano Ronaldo's publications analysis, we focused on the period of seven years, between 2013 and 2019, in order to coincide with the Madeira awards' schedule time—although Madeira was elected, also in 2020, *Europe's Best Island Destination* and *World's Best Island Destination*, we chose not to include that year in the analysis given the pandemic situation and the consequent difficulty in obtaining comparable data—and the promotion made by Cristiano Ronaldo.

Table 1. Selected variables

Designation	Description (2013–2019)
Cristiano Ronaldo's publications promoting Madeira	• Views/Likes (No.) • Comments (No.) • Shares (No.)
Awards won by Madeira in the WTA	No
Madeira Tourism's official website (www.vis itmadeira.pt)	• Site views (No.) • Facebook, Instagram, Twitter (Followers; No.)
Tourists in Madeira	• Arrivals (No.)
Worldwide visibility of Madeira	Records (No., Social networks; Google)
Tourists and worldwide visibility in Madeira's 6 competing destinations in the WTA	• Europe: Balearic Islands, Canary Islands, Azores (No., Social networks; Google) • World: Bali, Maldives, Seychelles (No., Social networks; Google)
Madeira Island image as a tourist destination and Cristiano Ronaldo's influence on it	Questionnaire to assess participants' perception of: • The image of Madeira • Cristiano Ronaldo's influence on the Island's image

Source: [4, 47–60]

The worldwide visibility indicator was obtained from the *web* dimension and considering the records on the main social networks, a method [2] which assesses reputation, popularity and notoriety based on 6 dimensions—revenue, media, *web*, history, social and impact.

To complement also we collected empirical data with a questionnaire to assess the participants' perception regarding the Madeira Island's image as a tourist destination and the Cristiano Ronaldo's influence on it.

The questionnaire was carried out online, the period between 16 and 30 November 2020 for data collection was defined, and has two sections: the first, dedicated to the formulation of questions inherent to the image of the tourist destination, using scales from the literature to measure the participants' perception of the concepts related to cognitive image [61, 62] and regarding the affective image factors [45]; the second, focused on the socio-demographic characterization of the participants.

The *Top-of-Mind* approach was also used, in order to assess spontaneous recall, one of the most important elements in the strategy of affirming a destination and an important enhancer of its appreciation [63].

Finally, an open question was asked with an appeal to Cristiano Ronaldo, in order to assess the opinion of respondents regarding his influence on the image of the Madeira destination.

With a snowball sampling approach, it was possible to collect 477 answers. The sample (see Table 2) is mainly composed of females (71,9%), 33,5% of the participants are between 46 and 55 years old, 45,3% with graduation and 52,0% are middle/senior officers.

Table 2. Sample profile

		N	%
Participants		477	100,0
Gender	Female	343	71,9
	Male	134	28,1
Age group	≤25	62	13,0
	26–35	81	17,0
	36–45	88	18,4
	46–55	160	33,5
	56–65	73	15,3
	>65	13	2,7
Education level	Up to 12 years	100	21,0
	Graduation	216	45,3
	Master's degree	119	24,9
	Doctorate	42	8,8
Professional occupation	Unemployed	20	4,2
	Domestic	5	1,0
	Sole proprietor	42	8,9
	Student	53	11,1
	Commercial/administrative	83	17,4
	Factory worker	4	0,8
	Pensioner/retired	22	4,6
	Middle/senior officer	248	52,0

Source: The authors

4 Results

4.1 Madeira Island and Cristiano Ronaldo's Publications Impact

The election of Madeira, simultaneously, as the *Europe's Best Island Destination* and the *World's Best Island Destination*—in 2016, 2017, 2018 and 2019—coincides with the increase in Cristiano Ronaldo's publications interactions on the part of his followers who, in the same period, went from 238 to 401 million on social networks.

Also, the number on Madeira's official website interactions and the followers on its official social network increased since Cristiano Ronaldo promotes the Island (see Table 3).

Table 3. Madeira's awards; Cristiano Ronaldo's publications; *Madeira Tourism*'s official website (2013–2019)

		2013	2014	2015	2016	2017	2018	2019
Madeira's awards at the WTA	*Europe's best island destination*	x	x		x	x	x	x
	World's best island destination			x	x	x	x	x
Cristiano Ronaldo's publications promoting Madeira	Followers (No.; millions)	114	152	197	238	297	345	401
	Views/likes (No.; millions)	0	0,463	1,388	17,109	10,139	12,724	37,617
	Comments (No.)	0	4.394	16.500	74.407	46.164	24.152	178.991
	Shares (No.)	0	0	14.700	12.107	5.594	7.988	15.194
Madeira Tourism's official website	Followers (No.; millions)	0,046	0,068	0,094	0,159	0,206	0,280	0,390
	Views (No.; millions)	1,151	1,482	2,728	3,675	3,917	3,740	3,672

Source: [4, 47–52]

The number of tourists/years (see Table 4) in Madeira is lower, with the exception of the Azores and Seychelles, than in other competing destinations here considered.

In the case of the Balearic and Canary Islands, they receive much more tourists in a month than Madeira receives over the course of a year.

Table 4. Number of tourists (2013–2019; millions)

	2013	2014	2015	2016	2017	2018	2019	Total
Madeira	1,083	1,140	1,029	1,163	1,396	1,395	1,383	**8,590**
Balearic Islands	13,050	13,525	13,995	15,370	16,341	16,596	16,453	**105,330**
Canary Islands	12,188	12,924	13,301	14,981	15,976	15,560	15,111	**100,040**
Azores	0,373	0,397	0,506	0,626	0,768	0,841	0,972	**4,480**
Bali	3,279	3,767	4,002	4,928	5,698	6,071	6,275	**34,020**
Maldives	1,125	1,205	1,234	1,286	1,390	1,484	1,700	**9,420**
Seychelles	0,230	0,233	0,276	0,303	0,350	0,362	0,384	**2,140**

Source: [47, 53–58]

With the exception of the Azores, all other competing destinations here considered have a much larger number of records with worldwide visibility, especially on Google, when compared to Madeira (see Table 5).

Table 5. Worldwide visibility - number of followers/records (October 2020; millions)

	Madeira	Balearic Islands	Canary Islands	Azores	Bali	Maldives	Seychelles
Instagram	0,221	0,117	0,146	0,079	0,457	0,261	0,084
Facebook	0,201	0,047	0,445	0,096	0,359	0,681	0,078
Twitter	0,013	0,035	0,071	0,007	0,003	0,049	0,014
Google	92,700	146,600	193,635	62,900	437,000	306,000	297,000
Total	**93,135**	**146,799**	**194,297**	**63,082**	**437,819**	**306,991**	**297,176**
		European awards' competing destinations			World awards' competing destinations		

Source: [49, 51, 59, 60]

In other words, based on the empirical data presented, we can conclude that Madeira, despite having fewer tourists than most of its competitors, and also having fewer worldwide visibility indicators, repeatedly obtains awards in direct dispute.

This finding suggests the existence of an external factor able to significantly influencing Madeira's voting.

4.2   Madeira Island Destination Image

About the answers (see Fig. 1) to the first question of the questionnaire, designed to assess cognitive image participants' perception—*Taking into account Madeira Island image that you retain, indicate, for each of the attributes listed, which option you identify with, considering the scale from 1 to 5 (1 = strongly disagree; 5 = strongly agree)*— the highest averages were recorded in the variables *The landscape is magnificent*, *The climate is pleasant* and *The mountains are inspiring*.

The worst averages correspond to the variables *There are many interesting monuments, The bars are cozy* and *The accommodations are good value for money.*

Thus, with regard to the cognitive image, the Madeira Island's natural attributes outweigh the others, namely the built heritage and the provided services.

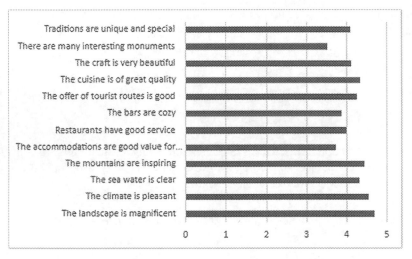

Fig. 1. Cognitive image participants' perception Source: The authors.

In the second question (see Fig. 2)—*Tick, considering a scale from 1 to 7, how do you rate the Madeira Island destination*—we intend to measure the affective image participants' perception and the highest average was obtained by *Pleasant*, followed by *Relaxing, Exciting* and *Breath-taking*.

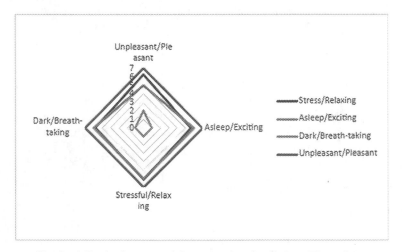

Fig. 2. Affective image participants' perception Source: The authors.

The spontaneous evocation, *Top-of-Mind*, corresponding to the third question—*Indicate 3 words that come to mind when you think about Madeira Island*—the *Sea*, *Nature* and *Beauty* words are the most remembered (see Table 6).

Table 6. Spontaneous evocation, *Top-of-Mind*

		N	%
Words	*Sea*	91	19,0
	Nature	85	18,0
	Beauty	45	9,0
Total (partial)		221	46,0
Grand total		477	100,0

Source: The authors

The answers to the open question—*In your opinion, do Cristiano Ronaldo positively or negatively influence the Madeira Island's image as a tourist destination? Please justify your answer*—they were analysed, taking into account the sample considerable size, through a *Word Cloud* [64], where the terms (see Fig. 3)—*positive, island*, Cristiano, *image, yes,* world, *player, influence, Madeira, born, tourism* and *destiny*—clearly prevail.

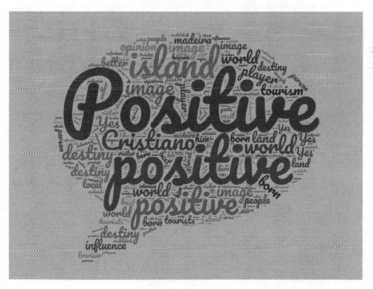

Fig. 3. Cristiano Ronaldo's influence on the image of Madeira Island Source: [64].

Thus, there is a dominant convergence among the participants regarding the Cristiano Ronaldo's positive influence on Madeira Island's image: in this context, his global dimension was highlighted, also evoking the fact that he was born on the Island.

312   P. Vaz Serra and C. Seabra

5 Conclusions, Implications and Limitations

Technological advances in this area, the instruments of interaction and the affirmation of personalities, especially with a global impact also in the area of Tourism, with the status of *influencers*, are relatively recent and the implication between these realities has been ascertained [16, 22].

In view of the above and for this reason, the approach to the theme is of an increased relevance, not only by the architecture of the present, but also by the design of the future.

The present work was based in two research questions. The first: Do Cristiano Ronaldo influence, in a positive and significant way, the perception of the image of Madeira Island? The second: Do the island's natural attributes overlap, in a positive and significant way, over the others, in the perception of the image of Madeira Island?

Regarding the first question and taking into account the questionnaire's open question data, we can conclude that *yes*. In its unequivocal majority, the participants believe that Cristiano Ronaldo positively influences the Madeira's image, having justified this position by its worldwide high notoriety, his capacity to influence and also the fact that he was born in the Island.

As for the second question, the obtained data, both of cognitive image and spontaneous evocation, clearly indicate that *yes*, the Madeira Island's natural attributes prevail over any others, constituting positive differentiation factors.

It is clear that, nowadays, there is a relationship with a virtuous potential between digital influencers and tourist destinations, as their capacity to influence attitudes, reactions and behaviours with touristic impact [9–12].

However, with the speed at which information flows, monitoring must be permanent and communication strategies, of the influencer and the destination, must converge, highlighting the various authors that a digital influencer is of little use when there is no coherent purpose of the tourist destination, at the levels of communication and image, which, in some way, complements, supports and gives consistency to a plan based on strategic objectives.

Cristiano Ronaldo's status as a digital influencer is unanimous. Even for those who do not appreciate the person, or who do not value his career, it is unavoidable to consider—it is not subjective, it is factual—that, from all the indicators considered to assess the reach of a digital influencer and the impact of its influence degree, Cristiano Ronaldo obtains the full in all the approaches carried out, at world level and whatever the comparison terms, on this date.

It is also unquestionable that the awards that, since 2013, Madeira Island has consecutively been able to obtain within the WTA's scope are far beyond what Madeira represents in terms of tourist destination, so it is legitimate to question whether or not there is an external factor that, in some way, influences the Island's image, in general, and induces its expressive votation, in particular.

The empirical data and the comparative analysis carried out support the association of phenomena between Cristiano Ronaldo and the Madeira's awards' temporal chronology.

However, the Madeira destination's cognitive image suggests the need to work on some aspects, such as the price-quality ratio in accommodation or the attractiveness of entertainment spaces such as bars, as well as an additional effort in promoting monuments: all these aspects are less valued by the participants, although the natural surroundings, with stunning landscapes, are much appreciated, as is the quality of its cuisine.

Also in the affective image, the Island is perceived as a less vibrant destination, with few solutions that provide exciting moments, being identified as an essentially relaxing and pleasant destination, indicating that there is a way to go, namely in attracting younger segments, more identified with events and activities.

This work confirms the importance that digital influencers can have on the image of a destination, highlighting the relevance of social networks as a support vehicle for multi-scale and impact marketing campaigns and actions—which promotes new working tools and new communication channels, with an undeniable importance for senders and receivers, as previous works had already concluded [20, 23].

This approach also highlighted the potential of the relationship between digital influencers and the promotion of tourist destinations, as well as the need to obtain greater knowledge as to what tourists most evoke in the perception of image in a market that, being global, it will increasingly need to appeal to creative and innovative forms of affirmation and attraction.

As stated, this is a recent and understudied area. The present work deepened the scientific knowledge, as the approach to the subject, which is not yet frequent, proves to be timely and pertinent.

Considering the need for destinations to structure competitive and sustainable offers, in an increasingly demanding and competitive market, the resulting attractiveness is built on the destination image constructed by the interaction between territorial specificities and the way in which they are perceived.

In this regard, it is worth reiterating the little expression that Madeira has in worldwide visibility indicators, when compared to some of its competing destinations, which translates into greater vulnerability in the affirmation and communication of its designs, becoming more dependent on other factors to obtain results.

Hence, the importance of this research for stakeholders—from public institutions to private operators—who, based on the results obtained, will have relevant information for the destination management, the strategies' definition, the actions' implementation, which, based on if in current and up-to-date facts and perspectives, allow for more faster, effective and efficient measures, based on the resources optimization and the value chain as a whole involvement.

We are aware, however, that because it is an ideal case in view of the proposed approach, considering the Cristiano Ronaldo's superlative configuration as a digital influencer, we are facing a very particular context, because exceptional, with the consequent difficulty of generalization from the conclusions that we can draw from it. That is, the distinctive factor conditions the way we can frame this case study, because being transferable, it is not generalizable, considering its uniqueness and its contexts, which constitutes a limitation of its representativeness.

From the above, there is an opportunity for, in the future, this to be a subject susceptible of revisiting, incorporating new angles of analysis to the study, involving new interlocutors and variables to the investigation, configuring an adding value approach to the relationship between digital influencers and tourist destinations.

Acknowledgments. This research received support from the Centre of Studies in Geography and Spatial Planning (CEGOT), funded by national funds through the Foundation for Science and Technology (FCT) under the reference UIDB/04084/2020.

References

1. Bronner, F., De Hoog, R.: Consumer-generated versus marketer-generated websites in consumer decision making. Int. J. Mark. Res. **52**(2), 231–248 (2010)
2. IPAM - The Marketing School: Avaliação da marca Cristiano Ronaldo. Gabinete de Estudos de Marketing para Desporto (2017)
3. YouGov: World's most admired 2020 (2020)
4. WTA - World Travel Awards: Madeira Tourism Board nominee profile (2020). https://www.worldtravelawards.com/profile-32572-madeira-tourism-board
5. Cristiano Ronaldo (2020). https://www.cristianoronaldo.com
6. Cosenza, V.: World Map of Social Networks. Vincos - il blog di Vincenzo Cosenza (2021)
7. Globo: Top 20, as contas mais seguidas nas redes sociais (2020)
8. Gretzel, U., Sigala, M., Xiang, Z., Koo, C.: Smart tourism: foundations and developments. Electron. Mark. **25**(3), 179–188 (2015). https://doi.org/10.1007/s12525-015-0196-8
9. Gallarza, M.G., Saura, I.G., García, H.C.: Destination image: towards a conceptual framework. Ann. Tour. Res. **29**(1), 56–78 (2002)
10. Loureiro, S.M.C., Stylos, N., Bellou, V.: Destination atmospheric cues as key influencers of tourists' word-of-mouth communication: tourist visitation at two Mediterranean capital cities. Tour. Recreat. Res. **46**(1), 85–108 (2021)
11. Martín Santana, J.D., Reinares-Lara, P., Reinares-Lara, E.: Spot length and unaided recall in television: Optimizing media planning variables in advertising breaks. J. Advert. Res. **56**(3), 274–288 (2016)
12. Pop, R.-A., Săplăcan, Z., Dabija, D.-C., Alt, M.-A.: The impact of social media influencers on travel decisions: the role of trust in consumer decision journey. Curr. Issues Tour. 1–21 (2021)
13. Beerli, A., Martín, J.: Tourist's characteristics and the perceived image of tourist destinations: a quantitative analysis – a case study of Lanzarote, Spain. Tour. Manag. **25**, 623–636 (2004)
14. Baloglu, S., Mangaloglu, M.: Tourism destination images of Turkey, Egypt, Greece and Italy as perceived by US-based tour operators and travel agents. Tour. Manage. **22**(1), 1–9 (2001)
15. Song, H., Li, G., Cao, Z.: Tourism and economic globalization: an emerging research Agenda. J. Travel Res. **57**(8), 999–1011 (2017)
16. Buhalis, D., Foerste, M.: SoCoMo marketing for travel and tourism: empowering co-creation of value. J. Destin. Mark. Manag. **4**(3), 151–161 (2015)
17. Kráľová, A., Pavlíčeka, A.: Development of social media strategies in tourism destination. In: 3rd International Conference on Strategic Innovative Marketing. Elsevier Ltd., Madrid (2015)
18. Pirolli, B.: Travel information online: navigating correspondents, consensus, and conversation. Curr. Issue Tour. **21**(12), 1337–1343 (2016)

19. Serrano-Puche, J.: Digital technologies: mapping the field of research in media studies. London School of Economics and Political Science Working Paper Series, 33 (2015)
20. Sigalat-Signes, E., Calvo-Palomares, R., Roig, B., García-Adán, I.: Transition towards a tourist innovation model: the smart tourism destination: reality or territorial marketing? J. Innov. Knowl. **5**(2), 96–104 (2020)
21. Bennett, S.: The impact of social media on travel and tourism (2012)
22. Hua, L., Ramayah, T., Ping, T., Jacky, C.: Social media as a tool to help select tourism destinations: the case of Malaysia. Inf. Syst. Manag. **34**(3), 265–279 (2017)
23. Song, S., Yoo, M.: The role of social media during the pre-purchasing stage. J. Hosp. Tour. Technol. **7**(1), 84–99 (2016)
24. Francalanci, C., Hussain, A.: A visual analysis of social influencers and influence in the tourism domain. In: Tussyadiah, I., Inversini, A. (eds.) Information and Communication Technologies in Tourism 2015. Springer, Cham (2015). https://doi.org/10.1007/978-3-319-14343-9_2
25. Coelho, R., Almeida, M., Gomes, A., Filho, A.: O impacto dos influenciadores espontâneos nas métricas de engajamento de uma rede social virtual. 11° Congresso Latino-Americano de Varejo: Engaging and Interactive Shopper Experience (2017)
26. Suciati, P., Maulidiyanti, M., Lusia, A.: Cultivation effect of tourism TV program and influencer's Instagram account on the intention to travel. In: The 1st International Conference on Social Sciences, Indonesia (2017)
27. Mariano, A., Anjos, F., Silva, V., Santos, M.: Tornando-se um Digital Influencer: Um estudo dos fatores que influem a sua concepção. In: XXVI Congreso Internacional AEDEM, v. XXVI, Italy (2017)
28. Francalanci, C., Hussain, A.: Discovering social influencers with network visualization: evidence from the tourism domain. Inf. Technol. Tour. **16**(1), 103–125 (2015). https://doi.org/10.1007/s40558-015-0030-3
29. Santos, S., Silva, P., Santos, J.: Gabriela Pugliesi: uma análise sobre o marketing de influência na rede social Instagram. In: XVIII Congresso de Ciências da Comunicação na Região Nordeste, Brasil (2016)
30. Watts, D., Dodds, P.: Influentials, networks, and public opinion formation. J. Consum. Res. **34**, 441–458 (2007)
31. Li, Y.-M., Lee, Y.-L., Lien, N.-J.: Online social advertising via influential endorsers. Int. J. Electron. Commer. **16**(3), 119–153 (2014)
32. Patel, N., Lopez, C., Partalas, I., Avouac, P., Segond, F.: Detecting influential users in social network conversations: a linguistic approach. viseo technologies (2017)
33. Freberg, K., Grahamb, K., McGaughey, K., Freberg, L.: Who are the social media influencers? A study of public perceptions of personality. Public Relat. Rev. **37**(1), 90–92 (2011)
34. Hunter, W.: The social construction of tourism online destination image: a comparative semiotic analysis of the visual representation of Seoul. Tour. Manag. **54**, 221–229 (2016)
35. Servidio, R.: Images, affective evaluation and personality traits in tourist behaviour: an exploratory study with Italian postcards. Tour. Manag. Perspect. **16**, 237–246 (2015)
36. Hallmann, K., Zehrer, A., Müller, S.: Perceived destination image: an image model for a winter sports destination and its effect on intention to revisit. J. Travel Res. **54**, 94–106 (2015)
37. Añaña, E., Anjos, F., Pereira, M.: Imagem de destinos turísticos: avaliação à luz da teoria da experiência na economia baseada em serviços. Revista Brasileira de Pesquisa Em Turismo **10**, 309 (2016)
38. Onder, I., Marchiori, E.: A comparison of pre-visit beliefs and projected visual images of destinations. Tour. Manag. Perspect. **21**, 42–53 (2017)
39. Lai, K., Li, X.: Tourism destination image: conceptual problems and definitional solutions. J. Travel Res. **55**(8), 1065–1080 (2016)

40. Beerli, A., Martín, J.D.: Tourists' characteristics and the perceived image of tourist destinations: a quantitative analysis—a case study of Lanzarote, Spain. Tour. Manag. **25**(5), 623–636 (2004)
41. Stylidis, D., Shani, A., Belhassen, Y.: Testing an integrated destination image model across residents and tourists. Tour. Manag. **58**, 184–195 (2016)
42. Hosany, S., Ekinci, Y., Uysal, M.: Destination image and destination personality. Int. J. Cult. Tour. Hosp. Res. **1**, 62–81 (2007)
43. Moraga, E.T., Artigas, E.A.M., Irigoyen, C.C.: Desarrollo y propuesta de una escala para medir la Imagen de los Destinos Turísticos (IMATUR). Revista Brasileira de Gestão de Negócios **14**(45), 400–418 (2012)
44. Stylidis, D., Belhassen, Y., Shani, A.: Destination image, on-site experience and behavioural intentions: path analytic validation of a marketing model on domestic tourists. Curr. Issue Tour. **20**, 1–18 (2015)
45. Yacout, O.M., Hefny, L.I.: Use of Hofstede's cultural dimensions, demographics, and information sources as antecedents to cognitive and affective destination image for Egypt. J. Vacat. Mark. **21**(1), 37–52 (2015)
46. Yin, R.: Estudo de Caso Planejamento e Métodos. Bookman, Porto Alegre (2005)
47. Direção Regional de Estatística da Madeira: Estatísticas do Turismo (2020). https://estatistica.madeira.gov.pt/dre-3/pesquisa.html?q=estat%C3%ADsticas+de+turismo
48. Facebook: Cristiano Ronaldo's official page. Publications, followers, shares and comments, 2013–2019 (2020). https://www.facebook.com/Cristiano
49. Facebook: Madeira Island's official page; Balearic Islands' official page; Canary Islands' official page; Azores's official page; Bali official page; Maldives's official page; Seychelles' official page: Followers, 2013–2019 (2020). https://www.facebook.com/search/top?
50. Instagram: Cristiano Ronaldo's official page. Publications, followers, shares and comments, 2013–2019 (2020). https://www.instagram.com/cristiano/
51. Instagram: Madeira's official page; Balearic Islands' official page; Canary Islands' official page; Azores's official page; Bali's official page; Maldives's official; Seychelles' official page page. Followers and publications, 2013–2019 (2020). https://www.instagram.com/
52. Turismo da Madeira: Registos no sítio oficial do Turismo da Madeira. [Informação reservada, não acessível ao público] (2020). www.visitmadeira.pt
53. Gobierno de Canarias: Estadísticas de Turismo 2013–2019 (2020). https://www.gobiernodecanarias.org/buscador/search?query=Estadisticas+Turismo+&fqtr=&fbt=false&ambitos=gobcan
54. Govern Illes Balears: Estadísticas del Turismo, anuários de turismo 2013–2019 (2020). https://www.caib.es/sites/estadistiquesdelturisme/es/anuarios_de_turismo-22816/
55. Government of Seychelles: National Bureau of Statistics – Tourism (2020). https://www.nbs.gov.sc/statistics/tourism
56. Serviço Regional de Estatística dos Açores: Estatísticas anuais do Turismo 2013–2019 (2020). https://srea.azores.gov.pt/Conteudos/Relatorios/lista_relatorios.aspx?idc=392&idsc=6454&lang_id=1
57. The World Bank: Number of arrivals – Maldives 2013–2019 (2020). https://data.worldbank.org/indicator/ST.INT.ARVL?locations=MV
58. Tourism Statistics of Bali Province: Statistik Bali 2013–2019 (2020). https://bali.bps.go.id/searchengine/result.html
59. Google: Madeira Island's records; Balearic Island's records; Canary Islands' records; Azores's records; Bali's records; Maldives's records; Seychelles' records (2020). https://www.google.com/search?
60. Twitter: Canary Islands' official page; Azores's official page; Bali's official page; Maldives's official page; Seychelles' official page Followers, 2013–2019 (2020). https://twitter.com/

61. Santana, L., Gosling, M.: Imagem de destino turístico: Ilhéus/BA na perspectiva de visitantes e moradores. Caderno Virtual de Turismo – Rio de Janeiro **18**(2), 58–79 (2018)
62. Seabra, C., Paiva, O., Abrantes, J., Pereira, A., Reis, M.: Imagem do Centro de Portugal: Uma abordagem geracional. In: Correia, A., Homem, P.B. (Coord), Turismo no Centro de Portugal – Potencialidades e Tendências, pp. 81–104. Actual, Coimbra (2018)
63. Wang, Y., Hsiao, S.-H., Yang, Z., Hajli, N.: The impact of sellers' social influence on the co-creation of innovation with customers and brand awareness in online communities. Ind. Mark. Manag. **54**, 56–70 (2016)
64. Word Cloud (2020): https://www.wordclouds.com/

Analysis of Chaos and Predicting the Price of Crude Oil in Ecuador Using Deep Learning Models

Naomi Cedeño$^{(\boxtimes)}$ (ID), Génesis Carillo (ID), María J. Ayala (ID), Sebastián Lalvay (ID), and Saba Infante (ID)

Universidad Yachay Tech, Urcuquí, Imbabura, Ecuador
{helen.cedeno,genesis.carrillo,maria.ayalab,sebastian.lalvay,
sinfante}@yachaytech.edu.ec

Abstract. This paper studied deterministic chaotic behaviour and prediction of WTI crude oil daily price time series from 2015 to 2020 in Ecuador. To understand the price of crude oil, the dynamics and time delay of the system were reconstructed through the Average Mutual Information and False Nearest Neighbours methods, the chaotic characteristics was determined using the Lyapunov exponent, and finally a BDS test was applied to determine the nonlinearity of the series. Then, three neural networks are used to predict oil prices, which were validated by estimating four goodness-of-fit measures. The results show that the neural network models produce a good prediction rate, confirmed by a maximum error of 0.0058927% from the Radial Basis Function, which indicates a significant similarity between the prediction and the real data. Predictions made with monthly values perform better than those made with daily values, possibly due to the level of noise in the daily time series. Among the three models, NARX performs best, with a percentage error of $2.6213 \cdot 10^{-13}$%.

Keywords: Chaotic time series · Neural networks · Time series prediction · Crude oil

1 Introduction

Determining the behavior of phenomena that are modeled by a deterministic dynamical system is a complex task due to its irregular nature, nonlinear structure, high sensitivity to changes in initial conditions, and restriction of the dynamics in the immersion space [22,31].

Suppose that the data x_t is generated by a non-linear auto-regressive model that satisfies:

$$x_t = f(x_{t-m}, x_{t-m+1}, \ldots, x_{t-1}), \quad 1 \leq t \leq n \tag{1}$$

where $m \in \mathbb{Z}$ is the immersion dimension, and f is an unknown nonlinear function. System (1) does not converge to a fixed point or to a cycle limit, but exhibits a random behavior known as chaos.

© Springer Nature Switzerland AG 2021
T. Guarda et al. (Eds.): ARTIIS 2021, CCIS 1485, pp. 318–332, 2021.
https://doi.org/10.1007/978-3-030-90241-4_25

Traditionally, chaos was studied in deterministic dynamical systems and has been developed in mathematics, biology and physics, but its applications have extended to fields such as meteorology, ecology, epidemiology, economic systems and stock markets [8, 11, 19, 28]. In particular, literature shows that chaotic behaviour is related with oil price markets [2, 10, 18, 30]. On the other hand, the analysis of econometric series that results from crude oil prices is relevant because it is one of the most highly valued primary resources in the world, playing an important role in the development of world economies. Previous articles studied the chaotic characteristics and prediction of monthly prices of WTI crude oil using prediction models as ANN and Chaos type models [16, 34], including architectures as evolutionary and multi-recurrent networks [9, 26]. On the other hand, Boullé [5] used deep neural networks to classify univariate time series based on its chaotic behavior and obtained that convolutional neural networks without batch normalization layers outperforms the latest generation classifiers.

In this work, we aim to use statistical techniques to analyze real systems where data have non-linear dynamics and a lot of variability. The proposed objective is to determine chaos and not linearity using criteria such as Mutual Information, False Nearest Neighbors, Lyapunov Exponent and the BDS test. Also, we propose deep learning models testing various hidden layer structures to predict oil prices in Ecuador over short periods.

The main contributions of the article are based on the combination of two mathematical modeling techniques: the reconstruction of the dynamics and the computation of the time delay of system by means of the Average Mutual Information and False Nearest Neighbours methods. In addition, the chaotic characteristics and the nonlinearity of the time series are determined through the estimation of the Lyapunov Exponent and the BDS Test, respectively. Then, based on this information, three structures of neural network models are used to predict the oil prices in Ecuador: Nonlinear Auto-Regressive model with Exogenous Input, Multilayer Perceptrons, and Radial Basis Function. Finally, four performance measures are calculated: RSME, MAE, Percentage error, $1 - R^2$ to validate the estimation quality of the models.

The article is presented as follows: in Sect. 2 the techniques that determine chaos and non-linearity of time series are described. Furthermore, deep learning models and its characteristics are defined. In Sect. 3, the performance measures that will be used to calibrate the prediction quality of the proposed models are introduced. In Sect. 4, a detailed description of the dataset is given and the results obtained are analyzed. Finally, in Sect. 5, the discussion is presented and the conclusions are established.

2   Methodology

Deterministic dynamical systems describes the time evolution of a system in some phase space $\Gamma \subset \mathbb{R}^n$. They can be expressed, for example, by ordinary differential equations: $\dot{x}(t) = f(x_t)$ where $f : \Gamma \subset \mathbb{R}^n \to \mathbb{R}^n$ and Γ is an open subset. Here, $x_t \in \mathbb{R}^n$ denotes the variables to be studied at a time $t \in \mathbb{R}$, the space $\mathbb{R}^n$ is called phase (or state) space, while $\mathbb{R}^n \times \mathbb{R}$ is known as the space of motions. In discrete-time $t = n\Delta t$, the solution is charted by maps that have the form $x_{t+1} = f(x_t)$. If we know the true state of x_t and $f(.)$, then we can accurately forecast the values of x_{t+1}. The system generated by $f(.)$ is usually defined on an attractor A, which has dimension $m < n$.

2.1   Time Delay

This method consists of choosing a time delay and construct a series of $m-$ dimensional vectors as follows: $y_i = (x_1, x_{i-\tau}, x_{i-2\tau}, \ldots, x_{i-m\tau})$ for an index $i \in \{1, \ldots, n\}$. Here, the number m is the dimension of y_i called embedding dimension, τ is the delay time, and y_i is the reconstructed phase space vector. If n scalar measurements are available, the number of embedding vectors is $n - m\tau$.

Average Mutual Information. One strategy of choosing τ is by using the average mutual information delay time suggested by [12]. Taking the measurements $x(t) \in X$ and $x(t + \tau) \in Y$, if x_t in a time t is connected $x_{t+\tau}$ in a time $t + \tau$, the Average Mutual Information (AMI) between these two measurements can be defined as:

$$I(\tau) = \sum_{x_t} \sum_{x_{t+\tau}} p(x_t, x_{t+\tau}) \log \left[\frac{p(x_t, x_{t+\tau})}{p(x_t)p(x_{t+\tau})} \right]$$

where $I(\tau)$ is greater or equal to zero.

When τ gets very large, the chaotic behavior of the signal makes the measurements x_t and $x_{t+\tau}$ independent in a practical sense, causing $I(\tau)$ to approach zero. The selection criterion for the delay value was established by [12] and consists of selecting some τ such that the first minimum of $I(\tau)$ occurs. This selection ensures that the measurements are somewhat independent, but not statistically independent. When there is no clear minimum of mutual average information, this criterion can be substituted by choosing τ as the time for which the average mutual information reaches four-fifths of its initial value. According to [27], $\frac{I(\tau)}{I(0)} \approx \frac{4}{5}$.

False Nearest Neighbors. This method is based on iterating through the immersion dimension from an $m-$dimensional space to an $m + 1-$dimensional space to determine the immersion dimension m [20]. Considering that all points of the attractor that are close in $\mathbb{R}^m$ must be close in $\mathbb{R}^{m+1}$, the False Nearest Neighbor is the point where is located the nearest neighbor in the $m-$dimensional space, but it is not in $m + 1$. When the number of points classified as nearest false neighbors arising through the projection is zero in d_E, the attractor has been displayed in that dimension [7]. Each point $y_t = (x_{t+\tau}, x_{t+2\tau}, \ldots, x_{t+m\tau})$ has a close neighbor $y_t^{NN} = (x_{t'+\tau}, x_{t'+2\tau}, \ldots, x_{t'+m\tau})$. For a pair of neighbors y_t and y_t^{NN} in $\mathbb{R}^m$ the dimension is increased by one unit, so $\hat{y}_t = (x_{t+\tau}, \ldots, x_{t+m\tau}, x_{t+(m-1)\tau})$ and

$\hat{y}_t^{NN} = (x_{t'+\tau}, \ldots, x_{t'+m\tau}, x_{t'+(m-1)\tau})$ may or may not be close. Increasing the distance between the last components:

$$\|\hat{y}_t - \hat{y}_t^{NN}\|^2 - \|y_t - y_t^{NN}\|^2 = \left(x_{t+(m-1)\tau} - x_{t'+(m-1)\tau}\right)^2$$

Replacing the immersion dimension from m to $m+1$ in the delay time creates a new coordinate $x(t+\tau)$ in each of the delayed vectors $y(t)$. The normalized increment to the distance between the false neighbors is computed as:

$$\frac{|x_{t+(m-1)\tau} - x_{t'+(m-1)\tau}|}{\|y_t - y_t^{NN}\|} > R_{tol} \tag{2}$$

where R_{tol} is some threshold that depends on the spatial distribution of the embedded data y_t, with $10 \leq R_{tol} \leq 30$ as the tolerance criterion for the identification of false closest neighbors [7]. The immersion dimension will be the one in which the percentage of false closest neighbors tends to zero when the dimension of the components of the lagged vectors is increased from m to $m+1$.

2.2   Lyapunov Exponent

This method describe the behavior of non-linear dynamical systems by measuring the exponential (infinitesimal) speed at which nearby trajectories separate. For some initial condition x_0, consider another initial condition y_0 close to x_0, at $z_0 = y_0 - x_0$. Assuming that y_t is close to x_t, we have that:

$$z_{t+1} = f(y_t) - f(x_t) \approx Jf(x_t) z_t \tag{3}$$

Equation (3) determines the evolution of the small displacement of the path concerning the undisturbed path $\{x_t\}$, where J is the Jacobian matrix of the map f, z_t is the tangent vector, $\frac{z_t}{\|z_t\|}$ determines the direction of the shift after t steps, $\|.\|$ is the Euclidean norm, and $\frac{\|z_t\|}{\|z_0\|}$ is the factor that determines the growth of the tangent vector after t steps. Then, we have that $z_{t+1} = Jf_{t+1}(x_0) z_0$, where $Jf_{t+1}(x_0) = Jf(x_t).Jf(x_{t-1})\ldots Jf(x_0)$. The Lyapunov Exponent for x_0 and an initial direction $u_0 = \frac{z_0}{|z_0|}$ is given as:

$$\lambda(x_0, u_0) = \lim_{t \to \infty} \frac{1}{t} \ln\left(\frac{|z_t|}{|z_0|}\right) = \lim_{t \to \infty} \frac{1}{t} \ln(Jf_t(x_0) u_0)$$

where f_i is the vector field of the components of f. When the largest Lyapunov Exponent is positive, the difference between two initially close trajectories will grow exponentially and the system will preserve the sensitive dependence of its initial condition:

$$\frac{\|z_t\|}{\|z_0\|} \approx \exp(\lambda_{max} t) \tag{4}$$

The largest Lyapunov Exponent describes the mean divergence between neighboring trajectories in phase space by $d(t) = D \exp(\lambda_1 t)$, where D is the initial separation between neighboring points and λ_1 is the largest Lyapunov exponent. If we assume that the $j-$th closest neighbors diverge at a rate given by:

$$d_j(i) \approx D_j \exp\left(\lambda_1(i\Delta t)\right) \tag{5}$$

where D_j is the initial distance between the j pairs of points, and $d_j(i)$ is the distance between nearest neighbors after $i\Delta t$ seconds. Rewriting (5), we get:

$$\ln\left(d_j(i)\right) \approx \ln\left(D_j\right) + \lambda_1(i\Delta t), \quad j = 1, 2, \ldots, M \tag{6}$$

Equation (6) represents a set of approximately parallel lines, where each one has a slope approximately proportional to λ_1. Finally, the largest Lyapunov Exponent is calculated using a linear regression:

$$y(i) = \frac{1}{\Delta t}\langle\ln\left(d_j(i)\right)\rangle \tag{7}$$

where $\langle ., . \rangle$ denotes the average over all the values of j.

2.3   BDS Test

In general, the BDS test verifies time-based dependence in a series. It can be used for testing against a variety of possible deviations from independence, including chaos. It is applied to a series of estimated residuals to prove if the residuals are i.i.d. Taking a distance ϵ such that $0 < \varepsilon < \max(x) - \min(x)$, then consider two points. If the series observations are i.i.d., then for any pair of points the probability that the distance between those points is less than or equal to ϵ will be constant, and it will be known as $c_1(\epsilon)$. For a embedding dimension m, sets of multiple pairs of points can also be considered, so given observations s and t from a series X, a set of pairs can be constructed by:

$$\{\{x_s, x_t\}, \{x_{s+1}, x_{t+1}\}, \ldots, \{x_{s+m-1}, x_{t+m-1}\}\} \tag{8}$$

Let $c_m(\epsilon)$ be the joint probability of each pair of points in the set that satisfies the epsilon condition. If the time series is i.i.d., $c_m(\epsilon)$ can be rewritten as the product of the individual probabilities of each pair, i.e. $c_m(\epsilon) = c_1^m(\epsilon)$. To estimate the probability for a particular dimension, the correlation integral $c_{m,n}(\varepsilon)$ in a finite space is used [14]. It is given as:

$$c_{m,n}(\epsilon) = \frac{2}{(n-m+1)(n-m)}\sum_{s=1}^{n-m+1}\sum_{t=s+1}^{n-m+1}\prod_{j=0}^{m-1} H_\epsilon\left(X_{s+j}, X_{t+j}\right) \tag{9}$$

where H_ϵ is the Heavyside function. On the other hand, we have that:

$$w_{m,n}(\epsilon) = \sqrt{n}\frac{c_{m,n}(\epsilon) - c_{1,n}^m(\epsilon)}{\sigma_{m,n}(\epsilon)} \tag{10}$$

converges in distribution to $N(0, 1)$ [13] and,

$$\sigma_{m,n}^2(\epsilon) = 4 \left[k^m + 2 \sum_{j=1}^{m-1} k^{m-j} c^{2j} + (m-1)^2 c^{2m} - m^2 k c^{2m-2} \right] \tag{11}$$

where c is estimated by $c_{1,n}(\epsilon)$ and k can be estimated by:

$$k_n(\varepsilon) \equiv \frac{2}{n(n-1)(n-2)} \sum_{t=1}^{n} \sum_{s=i+1}^{n} \sum_{r=s+1}^{n} \Big\{ H_\varepsilon(x_i, x_s) H_\varepsilon(x_s, x_r)$$

$$+ H_\varepsilon(x_t, x_r) H_\varepsilon(x_r, x_s) + H_\varepsilon(x_s, x_i) H_\varepsilon(x_i, x_r) \Big\} \tag{12}$$

This test consists of assuming as a null hypothesis H_0 that the series are i.i.d. against an unspecified alternative hypothesis H_a [6]. The rejection of the null hypothesis can be interpreted as a test of non-linearity for the series and could imply that there exists some type of dependence on prices because the stochastic process that models the data is not stationary, is non-linear, or is a deterministic system that appears to be random. The test procedure consists of choosing the values of ϵ and of the embedded dimension m.

2.4   Prediction Based on Artificial Neural Networks

The non-linear nature of artificial neural networks makes them an appropriate instrument to solve multi-step prediction problems in chaotic systems [3]; in addition to its ability to recognize non-visible or unknown functional relationships within given data. In the context of this work, neural networks will be grouped into static and dynamic. In static networks, each output is related only to the immediately previous point; while in dynamic networks, each past input and output is closely related to the predicted output [33]. One dynamic and two static neural networks will be tested to predict a sequence states of WTI Ecuadorian oil daily price.

Nonlinear Auto-regressive Model with Exogenous Inputs (NARX). Is a dynamic neural network that model nonlinear dynamical systems [17], characterized through one main and one secondary and external time-series input. Features, such as its computational power similar to the Turing machine [21], its strong nonlinear mapping ability [33], and its auto-regressive structure that predicts values based on past behavior make it an useful tool when current values of the time series correlate with the ones that precede and succeed them. The architecture of the NARX neural network is given by an input layer, hidden layer, output layer, and two time delays one for inputs and one for outputs. In mathematical terms, NARX is a non-linear discrete system given by:

$$y(n+1) = f\left[y(n), \ldots, y(n-d_y); u(n), \ldots, u(n-d_u)\right], \tag{13}$$

where $f(\cdot)$ is unknown, $u(n) \in \mathbb{R}$ represents the input of the model at time n, $y(n) \in \mathbb{R}$ is the corresponding output, and $d_y, d_u \geq 1$ ($d_u \leq d_y$) are the input and output delays, respectively [24]. In this work, we will use a network with two vector inputs and one vector output.

Multilayer Perceptrons (MLP). Is a static neural network that was widely used for function approximation, and, adding time delays, for time series prediction. This network presents good results in noisy or incomplete data set. Also, if it has an additional bias and a sigmoid function applied in its hidden layers it can approximate every function with finite discontinuity points [21], and using a hidden layer every any continuous function can be approximated [15]. This network charts a mapping $f : R^m \to R^n$, where m and n are the number of inputs and outputs, respectively. These values define the total of input and output layers, where in the first unit, the network holds the input, while in the second the overall mapping of the network is shown, producing outputs that are composed by the organization in series of mutually exclusive sets of neurons or layers [29]. This architecture is given as the following equation:

$$Y = \sum_1 v_1 F' \left[\sum_j w'_{jl} F \left(\sum_i w_{ij} x_i + b_{1j} \right) + b_{2k} \right] + b_{31}, \qquad (14)$$

where Y is the output, w_{ij} and w'_{jl} are, respectively, the weights from input to hidden layers and from hidden to output layers, v_l was analogously stated, b_{ij} are the biases, F is the function applied to the hidden layer, and F' is the function applied to the output layer [21].

Radial Basis Function (RBF). Is a static neural network that consists of computing the output of a distance function at a central point. It provides a powerful alternative when it comes to approximate or classify a pattern system. The output layer is expressed as follows:

$$y_k(\mathbf{x}) = \sum_{j=1}^{M} w_{kj} \phi_j \left(\| \mathbf{x} - \mathbf{u}_j \| \right)$$

where i is the dimension of the input vector $\mathbf{x}$, $\mathbf{u}_j$ is the vector that determines the center of the basis function, w_{kj} is the connection weight of the output layer and ϕ_j is called a radial basis function. In this case, we denote ϕ_j as a Gaussian function with a width value β:

$$\phi_j \left(\| \mathbf{x} - \mathbf{u}_j \| \right) = \exp \left(\frac{- \| \mathbf{x} - \mathbf{u}_j \|}{\beta^2} \right)$$

A three-layer feed-forward network with one hidden layer was proposed, where each neuron is activated in a determined region of the input patterns [25]. The input layer has i neurons, which determines the size of $\mathbf{x}$. From there, $\mathbf{x}$ goes to the hidden, while the calculations are done in the occupied layer and go to the output layer, where the network evaluate the results through linear combinations.

3   Performance Metrics for Prediction Models

Literature shows a large number of metrics that are based on the difference between true and predicted values to measure the accuracy of a model. Measures based on squared differences place more emphasis on outliers, predictions that are far from the true values are penalized more strongly than closer predictions.

3.1   Root Mean Squared Error (RMSE)

The RMSE is the square root of the mean square error, known also as quadratic loss or L_2 loss. Let the original prices and the predicted prices be $x(n)$ and $x_p(n)$ respectively. Also, define the error $E(n) = x(n) - x_p(n)$ and N_p as the number of predicted samples. It follows that:

$$RMSE = \sqrt{\frac{\sum_{n=1}^{N_p} E^2(n)}{N_p}}$$

3.2   Mean Absolute Error (MAE), Percentage Error (Perr), and R^2

MAE measures the average of the sum of the absolute differences between observation and predicted values, while Perr is an adjusted measuring of the percentual error. Using the notation given above, there are respectively defined as:

$$MAE = \frac{1}{N_p} \sum_{n=1}^{N_p} |E(n)|, \quad \text{and} \quad Perr = \frac{\sum_{n=1}^{N_p} E(n)^2}{\sum_{n=1}^{N_p} x^2(n)} m$$

On the other hand: $1 - \mathbf{R}^2 = 1 - \dfrac{\sum_{n=1}^{N_p} E(n)^2}{\sum_{n=1}^{N_p} [x(n) - \bar{x}_p]^2}$ where $\bar{x}_p$ is the arithmetic mean of the observed points. We use $1 - \mathbf{R}^2$ as a performance metric so that smaller values are better, which makes this measure comparable to the other metrics considered here.

4   Results

4.1   Data Description

In this work, 2076 data points corresponding to daily oil prices from January 2015 to September 2020, along with 69 data points belonging to its corresponding monthly means were obtained from the Ecuadorian Central Bank [4]. Monthly and daily data sets present frequent fluctuations, and a significant drop in April 2020 were observed, giving this series non-regular features.

4.2   BDS Test

In this section, the results obtained by the estimation of the BDS Test are presented for the embedding dimensions $m = 2, 3, 4, 5$ and for values of $\epsilon = 0.25, 0.5, 1, 1.5$, the analysis was carried out using the R statistical package tseries [32]. In Table 1 shows the results for the series analyzed. The critical values to compare the BDS Test are obtained from the normal distribution and, the null hypothesis is accepted or rejected considering the following theoretical values 1.64 (10%), 1.95 (5%), y 2.57 (1%). It can be seen that the values of the BDS statistic confirm that the series is not independent. It means that they have an underlying non-linear character structure. Given that the $p - value < 0.05$ for each of the embedding dimensions with different values of ϵ. All of the above shows statistically significant results to reject H_0.

Table 1. BDS test with m and ϵ in terms of the standard deviation.

m	ϵ_1	ϵ_2	ϵ_3	ϵ_4
2	20.3851	13.8300	12.2293	11.2718
3	28.0740	15.1628	12.0150	10.8111
4	36.8693	16.9121	11.7807	10.1958
5	49.7833	18.5811	11.7477	9.7730

4.3   Deterministic Chaos

In this section, the chaotic behavior of the time series corresponding to the monthly oil prices in Ecuador is identified by computing the largest Lyapunov Exponent of the reconstructed phase space.

Phase Space Reconstruction. Time delay is estimated by using the Average Mutual Information (AMI) method. The first minimum value of the AMI is chosen as the time delay value. The result is displayed in Fig. 1(a), where the firts minimum of the AMI is for a lag equal to 8. On the other hand, the embedding dimension is obtained by False Nearest Neighbors method as the point with the smallest percentage of False Nearest Neighbors. Figure 1(b) shows that $m = 3$ is the first embedding dimension that gives a small percentage of false nearest neighbours in the observed time series.

Maximum Lyapunov Exponent(MLE). In chaos recognition theory, the sign of the MLE allow us to classify the dynamic behavior of the prices time series. If the MLE is positive, the evolution of oil prices differs significantly from the original prices. Moreover, there is an increase in the observation errors. Figure 2 shows the evolution of the logarithm of the mean distance between the reference points and their closest neighbors in the reconstructed trajectory, the

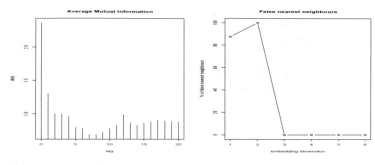

(a) Average Mutual Information.   (b) False Nearest Neighbours.

Fig. 1. Phase space reconstruction.

slope of the linear fit is an estimate of the maximum Lyapunov exponent. The estimate of the Maximum Lyapunov Exponent is $\lambda = 0.30$, which is greater than 0. Thus the time series of WTI crude oil prices is chaotic.

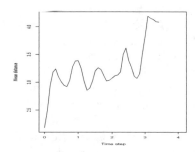

Fig. 2. Evolution of the logarithm of the mean distance between closest points.

4.4   Artificial Neural Networks:

Nonlinear Auto-regressive Model with Exogenous Input (NARX). The NARX neural network considers the data corresponding to the monthly means as the main series, while the second series is composed by the monthly means of the WTI prices of Petro-ecuador EP, the largest oil company in Ecuador. This network was trained with MATLAB's Neural Net Time Series Toolbox [23], with a Levenberg-Marquardt optimization function, MSE loss function and equal input and output time delays within the compact interval [1, 2].

Figure 3 shows the actual values contrasted with the estimated values by fitting a NARX model, showing a graphical overlap between the estimated and observed values, which implies a low error rate. The proposed model proves to be effective in determining the dynamics of WTI crude oil prices.

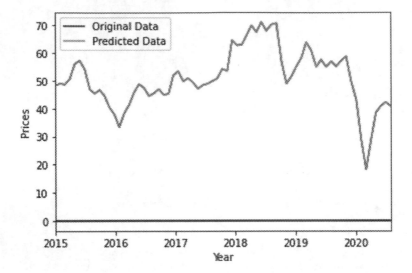

Fig. 3. Real vs. Predicted values in NARX network.

Multilayer Perceptrons (MLP). Two tests in the Multilayer Perceptrons network were performed. In the first graphic, the entire dataset was used while in the second only the monthly means were used, both datasets were divided into progressive sequences of cardinality three. This network was compiled with Python's Tensorflow [1], using the ReLu activation function, MSE loss function, and the Adam automatic parameter optimizer. To simplify the network model, biases and time lags were omitted.

Figure 4(a) shows a graphical representation of the observed daily sales prices and the prices estimated using the MLP model, where similarity between both curves can be observed. The prices predicted by this model have slight differences with respect to the observed ones. Figure 4(b) shows the same dynamics but with monthly sales prices, showing a similar pattern.

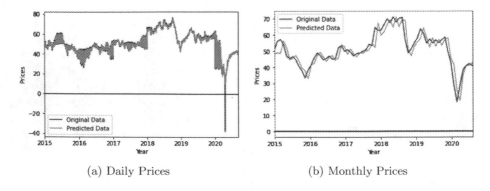

(a) Daily Prices   (b) Monthly Prices

Fig. 4. Real vs. Predicted values in multilayer perceptrons network.

Radial Basis Function (RBF). In the RBF network, the entire dataset and monthly averages of the time series were used. Python's Tensorflow library was required to develop the code. On the other hand, $\frac{1}{\beta}$, the amplitude of the Gaussian function, was modified as follows: $\frac{1}{\beta_1} = \frac{1}{25}$, $\frac{1}{\beta_2} = \frac{1}{50}$, and $\frac{1}{\beta_3} = \frac{1}{75}$, improving the rate of prediction on each step. It implies that the larger β is, the predicted outputs are more precise.

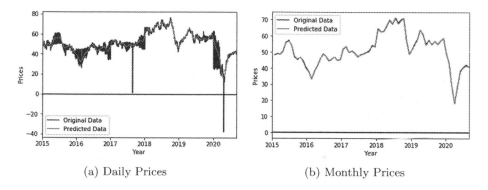

(a) Daily Prices   (b) Monthly Prices

Fig. 5. Real vs. Predicted values in radial basis function network.

Figure 5(a) shows a graphical representation of the actual behavior of sales prices and the estimated prices using the RBF model, observing a relatively similar pattern between both curves. Figure 5(b) replicates the time series shown in Fig. 5(a), but using the average monthly sales prices, where the similarity between both series is high, overlapping one over the other. The results prove that the proposed model can be an effective alternative for oil price prediction, especially with monthly data, and can become an useful tool to determine short-term prices in real time. Table 2 shows four performance metrics estimated for daily sales prices using the MLP and RBF models, showing low variability and small errors. Similarly, Table 3 presents four metrics estimated for monthly sales prices using the NARX, MLP and RBF models, showing generally decreasing estimation errors, approaching zero in some of the architectures.

Table 2. Performance measures for daily values.

Neural network	RMSE	MAE	Perr	$1 - R^2$
MLP	3.37352675	1.59527893	0.00418776	0.09372298
RBF	1.5597379	2.4327824	0.0058927	0.1464123

Table 3. Performance measures for monthly values.

Neural Network	RMSE	MAE	Perr	$1 - R^2$
NARX	2.6981e-05	2.2224e-05	2.6213e-13	6.6940e-12
MLP	4.57582611	3.56268875	0.00774235	0.19061066
RBF	0.481955409	0.232281029	4.301172e-05	0.001032302

5   Discussion and Conclusions

Considering the current weakening of the global financial structures, it is essential to study the behavior of primary values, including oil prices, so that policymakers and economists restructure investment models in order to reactivate the economy. However, the application of methodologies that allows modelling the behaviour of crude oil prices shows difficulties due to its volatile nature. In this work, a study was carried out on a dynamic system with chaotic characteristics. A time series generated by measurements of oil prices in Ecuador, which represents the dynamics of the system, was analyzed.

The delay time τ and the embedding dimension m were determined using techniques such as false nearest neighbors and mutual information criterion. The estimation of both parameters allows the reconstruction of the series attractor in the corresponding phase space. Taking the dimension of the phase space as the smallest integer such that it is greater than the correlation dimension, the Lyapunov Exponent was computed. The presence of a positive Lyapunov Exponent was found, which indicates that the nearby trajectories diverge. It implies greater variability in the representation of the map, which shows the presence of chaos in the series. The BDS test was also estimated to verify the non-linearity hypothesis of the system. The values of the BDS statistic confirm that the analyzed series are not i.i.d., which means that the series has an underlying structure of a non-linear nature. Also, the p-value confirms the rejection of H_0.

Since the price system reveals chaotic characteristics, short-term predictions through deep learning model architectures were proposed. The neural network models training produced a good prediction rate, confirmed by a maximum error of 0.0058927% from the Radial Basis Function, indicating a significant similarity between the prediction and the actual data. Predictions made with monthly values have better results than those made with daily values, possibly due to the level of noise presented by the daily time series. Among the three models, NARX performs better, with a $2.6213 \cdot 10^{-13}\%$ percentage error. The empirical study shows that dynamic neural networks have a better response than static networks. Finally, the results obtained may lead to future research, in which a new neural network model can be developed in order to improve accuracy.

References

1. Abadi, M., et al.: TensorFlow: large-scale machine learning on heterogeneous systems (2015). http://tensorflow.org/
2. Alvarez-Ramirez, J., Cisneros, M., Ibarra Valdez, C., Soriano, A.: Multifractal hurst analysis of crude oil prices. Phys. A Stat. Mech. Appl. **313**, 651–670 (2002)
3. Ardalani-Farsa, M., Zolfaghari, S.: Chaotic time series prediction with residual analysis method using hybrid elman-narx neural networks. Neurocomputing **73**, 2540–2553 (2010)
4. BCE: Sector Petrolero (2020). https://contenido.bce.fin.ec/documentos/ Administracion/bi_menuPetroleos.html#
5. Boullé, N., Dallas, V., Nakatsukasa, Y., Samaddar, D.: Classification of chaotic time series with deep learning. Phys. D Nonlinear Phenom. **403**, 132261 (2019)
6. Broock, W., Scheinkman, J., Dechert, W., Lebaron, B.: A test for independence based on the correlation dimension. Econometric Rev. **15**, 197–235 (1996)
7. Bruijn, S., Meijer, O., Beek, P., Van Dieen, J.: Assessing the stability of human locomotion: a review of current measures. J. R. Soc. Interface **10**, 20120999 (2013)
8. Chirivella, X., Ortega-Becea, J., Infante, S.: Análisis no lineal de la frecuencia cardíaca fetal. Revista de obstetricia y ginecología de Venezuela **71**(3), 174–182 (2011)
9. Chiroma, H., Abdulkareem, S., Herawan, T.: Evolutionary neural network model for west texas intermediate crude oil price prediction. Appl. Energ. **142**, 266–273 (2015)
10. Drachal, K.: Forecasting spot oil price in a dynamic model averaging framework: have the determinants changed over time? Energ. Econ. **60**, 35–46 (2016)
11. Farmer, J., Sidorowich, J.: Exploiting chaos to predict the future and reduce noise. In: Evolution, Learning and Cognition, January 1988
12. Fraser, A., Swinney, H.: Independent coordinates for strange attractors from mutual information. Phys. Rev. A **33**, 1134–1140 (1986)
13. Garcia, M., Ruiz, J., Sanz, B.: El test BDS: Posibles limitaciones. Rect@ Actas **9** (2001)
14. Grassberger, P., Procaccia, I.: Measuring strangeness strange attractors. Phys. D Nonlinear Phenom. **9**, 189–208 (1983)
15. Greenwood, P., Nikulin, M.: A Guide to Chi-squared Testing, vol. 39. Wiley-Interscience, Hoboken (1996)
16. Gupta, N., Nigam, S.: Crude oil price prediction using artificial neural network. Procedia Comput. Sci. **170**, 642–647 (2020)
17. Hagan, M., Demuth, H., Beale, M.: Neural Network Design, vol. 2 pp. 2–14. Pws Pub, Boston (1996)
18. He, L.Y., Chen, S.P.: Are crude oil markets multifractal? evidence from MF-DFA and MF-SSA perspectives. Phys. A Stat. Mech. Appl. Phys. A **389**, 3218–3229 (2010)
19. Infante, S., Ortega, J., Cedeño, F.: Estimación de datos faltantes en estaciones meteorológicas de venezuela vía un modelo de redes neuronales. Rev. Climatol. **8**, 51–70 (2008)
20. Kennel, M., Brown, R., Abarbanel, H.: Determining embedding dimension for phase-space reconstruction using a geometrical construction. Phys. Rev. A **45**, 3403 (1992)
21. Kuchaki Rafsanjani, M., Samareh, M.: Chaotic time series prediction by artificial neural networks. J. Comput. Methods Sci. Eng. **16**, 1–17 (2016)

22. Kugiumtzis, D., Bjørn, L., Christophersen, N.: Chaotic time series part i: estimation of invariant properies in state space. Model. Identificat. Control **15** (1994)
23. MATLAB: Neural net time series toolbox (2010). https://la.mathworks.com/help/deeplearning/ref/neuralnettimeseries-app.html
24. Menezes, J.M., Jr., Barreto, G.: Long-term time series prediction with the narx network: an empirical evaluation. Neurocomputing **71**, 3335–3343 (2008)
25. Moody, J., Darken, C.: Fast learning in networks of locally-tuned processing units. Neural Comput. **1**, 281–294 (1989)
26. Orojo, O., Tepper, J., Mcginnity, T., Mahmud, M.: A multi-recurrent network for crude oil price prediction (2020)
27. Piorek, M.: Analysis of Chaotic Behavior in Non-linear Dynamical Systems Models and Algorithms for Quaternions. Springer International Publishing, Cham (2019). https://doi.org/10.1007/978-3-319-94887-4
28. Schuster, H.: Deterministic Chaos: An Introduction. Wiley-VCH Verlag, Weinheim (1984)
29. Shiblee, M., Kalra, P., Chandra, B.: Time series prediction with multilayer perceptron (mlp): a new generalized error based approach. In: Advances in Neuro-Information Processing: 15th International Conference, pp. 37–44, November 2008
30. Singh, V., Kumar, P., Nishant, S.: Feedback spillover dynamics of crude oil and global assets indicators: a system-wide network perspective. Energ. Econ. **80**, 321–335 (2019)
31. Smith, R.: Estimating dimensions in noisy chaotic time series. J. R. Stat. Soc. Ser. B (Methodol.) **54**, 329–351 (1992)
32. Trapletti, A., Hornik, K.: Tseries: time series analysis and computational finance (2020). https://CRAN.R-project.org/package=tseries
33. Xiu, Y., Zhang, W.: Multivariate chaotic time series prediction based on narx neural networks. In: Proceedings of the 2nd International Conference on Electrical, Automation and Mechanical Engineering, pp. 164–167 (2017)
34. Yin, T., Wang, Y.: Predicting the price of WTI crude oil using ANN and chaos. Sustainability **11**, 5980 (2019)

Analytical Dashboards of Civil Protection Occurrences in Portugal

Francisco Barros[1] and Filipe Portela[1,2]($\boxtimes$) (iD)

[1] Algoritmi Research Centre, University of Minho, Braga, Portugal
a85918@alunos.uminho.pt, cfp@dsi.uminho.pt
[2] IOTECH—Innovation on Technology, Trofa, Portugal

Abstract. This study is focused on analysing Civil Protection occurrences for a better understanding of this type of events. This study collected all data on Civil Protection occurrences (Portugal Population) in the time interval from 2016 to 2019. The data comes from a public repository of Civil Protection. The results revealed that the most common type of occurrence is regarding Health Care (±47%). Assistance and Prevention of human activities, Accidents and Rural Fires appear in a second line of the most common types. Data were used to perform a more detailed analysis (compared to type), and trauma is the most frequent value with nearly 41% of the occurrences. Its evolution over the years of study deserves attention. It was possible to see that Lisbon and Porto dominate the number of occurrences by district and together have nearly one third (33%) of the occurrences. Summer (30.6%) is the most "favourable" time for this type of event, and in the opposite is winter (18.9%).

Keyword: Data analysis · Occurrences · Analytical vision · Data transformation

1 Introduction

Understanding the occurrences of Civil Protection is very important for a better knowledge of Portugal and helps identify trends and needs with which it must be debated and concerned. So, a study was accomplished to identify the areas and words of the occurrences, creating a descriptive analysis. Every summer, there is much information about fires and how Civil Protection has mobilised its resources for these events. Still, it is essential to know that Civil Protection is in charge of many more activities, and one of the biggest motivations for this study is to understand what they are and demystify some myths. After finishing this step, it was possible to characterise, at various levels, the most common groups of occurrences. First, it was analysed the quality of the dataset. This dataset gathers all occurrences from 2016 to 2019. After the data quality analysis has been completed and all data problems and errors have been detected, the ETL (Extract, Transform and Load) tasks were realised. They were performed all corrections/modifications necessary to change the original data and later loaded it into the database, depending on the created Multi-Dimensional Model. Finally, dashboards were

© Springer Nature Switzerland AG 2021
T. Guarda et al. (Eds.): ARTIIS 2021, CCIS 1485, pp. 333–345, 2021.
https://doi.org/10.1007/978-3-030-90241-4_26

created for complete data analysis. There have always been growths in terms of the number of occurrences by year at the national level, making the study focus on identifying the areas of the country where these increases in occurrences occur, the reasons, the time intervals among Civil Protection, being this the main research topics and questions.

This article has six sections. After the introduction, "Background" contextualises the topics. The "Materials and Methods" section presents much of the support used for the project, emphasising technologies. The "Case Study" shows some of the essential points and topics necessary to complete the project. The "Results" chapter presents the global results of the analysis and compares 2016 to 2017 and 2018 to 2019. The "Discussion" section gives the answers to the analytical questions that were made in the project.

2 Background

This section will explain some of the context and mains topics necessary to understand the findings from the research study.

2.1 What is Civil Protection?

Civil Protection [1] is an activity in charge of the State of Portugal to prevent collective risks inherent in situations of accidents or catastrophes, mitigate its effects, and protect and rescue people and goods in danger when those situations occur. Civil Protection is developed throughout the national territory.

The civil protection policy's conduct is the Government's responsibility, and the Prime Minister is responsible for directing civil protection policy. It is the responsibility of the member of Government responsible for the area of civil Protection, at the district level, to trigger, in the imminence or occurrence of a severe accident or catastrophe, the civil protection actions of prevention, relief, assistance and rehabilitation appropriate to each case, with the aid of the District Operational Commander and the collaboration of the competent civil protection agents, under the legal terms. In the exercise of the functions of municipal responsible for the civil protection policy, the mayor's responsibility is to trigger, in the imminence or occurrence of a severe accident or catastrophe, the civil protection actions of prevention, relief, assistance and adequate recovery in each case.

There are many civil protection agents: Fire brigades, Security forces, Armed forces, National Maritime Authorities, the National Civil Aviation Authority, INEM and other health care providers and Forest sappers. In the autonomous regions, civil protection policies and actions are the responsibility of the Regional Governments. Within the framework of international commitments and applicable rules of international law, the activity of civil Protection can be carried out outside the national territory in cooperation with foreign States or international organisations to which Portugal is a party.

2.2 What Are Occurrences?

Occurrences are the type of situations referred at Sect. 2.1 as civil protection activities, which is the article's main topic. The data about the occurrences refer from 2016 to 2019 [2]. This occurrence has associated the location (district, county, parish, locality, latitude and longitude), start and end date, state of occurrence, kind, number of land and air resources, and number of land and air operations.

3   Materials and Methods

The Kimball methodology [3] was used for the construction of the Data Warehouse. Data Warehouse is a data repository oriented to a specific area (company, organisation, etc.) and helps make decisions in the entity in which it is used. This approach allows for the creation of adequate planning and organisation by phase. In Fig. 1, it is possible to see how this methodology is divided. It is focused on the essential steps. Project planning, where it was planned the costs and deadlines between others. Definition of business requirements that are the basis of the project, giving it a direction. As outputs of this last phase, the analytical questions that were important for data analysis were determined. Then the multi-dimensional model with the eight dimensions and the fact table was transported to a physical model. This last phase served as the basis for the ETL, where the necessary changes were made and later uploaded to the database. The only difference observed between what was stipulated by this approach and what happened was creating dashboards and reports. These phases were only performed in the end. Python [4] and, more specifically, the pandas' library [5] were used for the Data Quality phase and the ETL [10, 11]. MySQL Workbench [6, 9] was used to store data after its transformations. The dashboard's analytical and building part was rendered using the Tableau Desktop [7, 8].

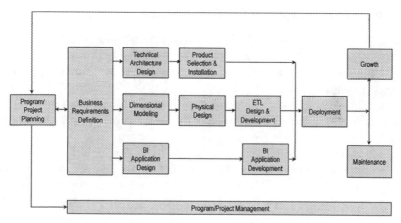

Fig. 1. Kimball Methodology Structure [1], adapted from The Data Warehouse Lifecycle Toolkit, 2nd Edition (Wiley, 2008)

4   Case Study

The analysis dataset represents the occurrences of Civil Protection from 2016 until 2019, being the aim of this study understanding, through Data Analysis and Data Visualization, trends and familiar words to a better knowledge of this type of activities and their details (ex: location, date, kind, status, number of air and overland means and the number of air and overland operatives). The dataset has 818396 rows and comes from a repository of Civil Protection.

A plan was defined for each of the stipulated phases, and in total, it was estimated that it would take about 50 days to complete the project. According to what was planned, the phases that lasted the most hours were ETL, the development of analytical dashboards and data quality, which was verified.

The project's database and dashboards were stored "locally" by the authors.

4.1 Analytical Questions

The following analytical questions were identified for a better direction of the project and to determine the fundamental points of analysis:

- Which areas of the country have more occurrences?
- How has the number of occurrences evolved over the years?
- What are the months to take more "serious"?
- Where do the occurrences selected as the most frequent occur at the kind level?
- When do the occurrences selected as the most frequent occur at the kind level?
- What days of the week have the highest number of occurrences?
  How are the average values of terrestrial means by area?

4.2 Multi-dimensional Modelling and ETL Design

After analysing the quality of the data, the Multi-Dimensional Model was built. This model (star schema), which can be seen in Fig. 2, has eight dimensions (date, time, place, coordinates, kind, status, air_means and air_operatives) and 1 table of facts (occurrence_management).

For the ETL phase, the tables identified in the multi-dimensional modelling were previously created in the database. Before loading the data into the tables, many changes were made.

To get an idea of what kind of changes were made, for example, Substitution of null values and values that were registered incorrectly (ex: in the column "EstadoOcorrência" there were lines with the value: "2") by "Unknown", splitting a column in several for easier reading, converting types, removing duplicate combinations and more.

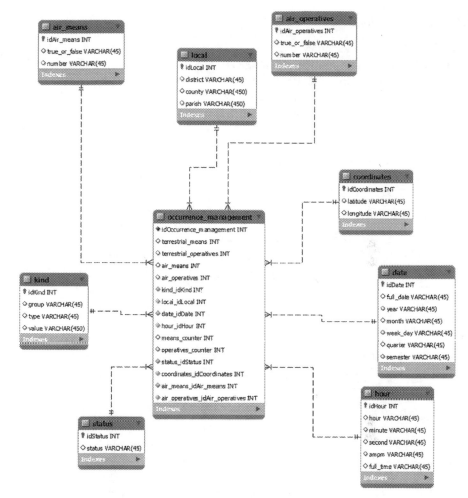

Fig. 2. Multi-dimensional model

5 Results

In this chapter, the results of the project are presented. Analysing achieved results made it easier to understand the occurrences' where, when, how, and why. Thus, there will be conditions to respond to these events more effectively. First, the focus will be on the overall results over the four years under analysis. Then there will be a comparison of the results from 2016 to 2017 and 2018 to 2019. This comparison will help to understand differences in 2 years with a completely different number of occurrences (2016 and 2017) and two years with a very similar number of occurrences (2018 and 2019).

5.1 Global Results

Once analysed, it was identified that the most significant number of records appeared in Lisbon (16.7%) and Porto (15.9%). Braga (7.6%), Setubal (7.4%) and Aveiro (7.1%) are the districts that appear next. On the other hand, Beja (2.1%), Portalegre (1.9%) and Évora (1.8%) are the less common districts. In this study, the project approach was divided the kind column into three columns: group, type and value, because kind was a column with much information and could have multiple levels of detail. The analysis says that Health Care was the most common value with nearly 47% of the records. Assistance and Prevention of Human Activities, accidents and rural fires are in a second line of the most common types. In Fig. 3, it is possible to see all the values.

Type	
Health Care	46,55%
Assistance and Prevention of human activities	
Accidents	10,16%
Rural Fires	8,55%
Total or partial commitment to security, services or structures	4,19%
Urban Fires or in Building Areas	2,86%
Fires in Debris	1,71%
Fires in Equipment and Products	1,47%
Transport Fires	0,92%
Industrial and technological accidents	0,38%
Operations	0,28%
Natural Phenomena	0,02%
Intervention in legal conflicts	0,01%

Fig. 3. Percentage of type records during the study

The "value" that can also be considered as the origin of the problem in itself has as primary records: "Trauma", "Prevention of leisure activities", and "Intoxication" with nearly 41%, 7% and 6%, respectively.

This parameter has 108 different values, so in Fig. 4, it is possible to see only the ten most common values because there are many irrelevant values for this study.

Value	
Trauma	41,03%
Prevention of leisure activities	5,69%
Intoxication	5,03%
Patrol, Recognition and Surveillance	5,00%
Bush	4,71%
Road collision	4,42%
Road Crash	4,21%
Road Cleaning and Hazard Signaling	3,50%
Cutting or Removal of Fall Hazard Elements	3,29%
Housing	2,05%

Fig. 4. Percentage of value records during the study

According to Fig. 5, of the total occurrences analysed, the month that most frequently appeared was August (11.1%). On the other side, January was the month with lower numbers (5.9%). Analysed by the year's season, the 3rd quarter was the most common with 250685 records (30.6%). The 4th and second quarters occupied the second and third positions with 219705 (26.9%) and 193089 occurrences (23.6%).

Finally, the 1st quarter has registered only 154910 (18.9%) occurrences. Something that can be said is that during the four years of analysis, all quarters had an increase in records concerning the homologous quarter from the past year.

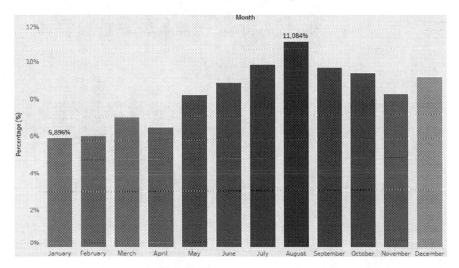

Fig. 5. Occurrence by month

The analysis says that the weekend days have more records, with Saturday and Sunday having 18.4% and 17.2% of the records, respectively. From Monday (10.4%) to Friday (14.9%), the records increase every day. The state of the occurrences closed (74%) was a very typical state. Next, the most frequent values were 1st Alert Dispatch (10%) and Ongoing (5%). In Fig. 6, it is possible to see an overview dashboard of some of the most important results of the analysis.

5.2 Analysis of the years: 2016 vs 2017

It is necessary to understand that there was an increase of about 80% in the number of occurrences from 2016 to 2017. So, it is expected that all or almost all of the values increased in many of the analyses.

All districts increased the number of occurrences at the geographic level, emphasising Vila Real and Viana do Castelo, which more than doubled the records, corresponding to a rise of 106.83% (+3549) 101.54% (+3034), respectively.

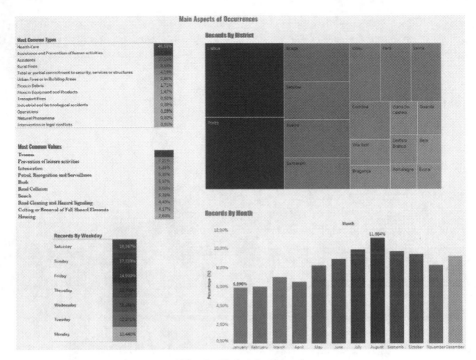

Fig. 6. Global dashboard

Districts such as Évora, Viseu and Beja also registered very positive growth, around 92%. Santarém, Portalegre and Setubal were the districts where growth was lowest, being 66.87% (+5138), 71.09% (+1692) and 71.92% (+6540), respectively. It is possible to see the top 10 of the most significant evolutions in Fig. 7.

The analysis says (Fig. 8) that, from 2016 to 2017, the 1st quarter had an evident growth of 26309.83% (+45516). The reason for this increase is that there were only 173 records in 2016. In 2017, were analysed 45689 records.

The low number of records in the 1st quarter of 2016 is carried over to the 2nd quarter of that year. It means that there are only 24270 records, allowing an increase of 111.37% for 2017, setting the value 51300. The evolution of the 3rd and 4th quarters was "normal", being 18.32% (+9704) and 32.72% (+14318), respectively.

District		Year	
		2016	2017
Vila Real	Number of Occurences	3 322	6 871
	Diference (%)		106,83%
Viana Do Castelo	Number of Occurences	2 988	6 022
	Diference (%)		101,54%
Évora	Number of Occurences	2 111	4 068
	Diference (%)		92,70%
Viseu	Number of Occurences	6 377	12 284
	Diference (%)		92,63%
Beja	Number of Occurences	2 367	4 551
	Diference (%)		92,27%
Guarda	Number of Occurences	3 127	5 894
	Diference (%)		88,49%
Bragança	Number of Occurences	3 271	6 156
	Diference (%)		88,20%
Castelo Branco	Number of Occurences	2 721	5 068
	Diference (%)		86,26%
Lisboa	Number of Occurences	19 981	35 839
	Diference (%)		79,37%
Faro	Number of Occurences	6 254	11 191
	Diference (%)		78,94%

Fig. 7. 2016 vs 2017: district

Quarter		Year	
		2016	2017
1	Diference (%)		26 316,18%
	Number of Occurences	173	45 700
2	Diference (%)		111,62%
	Number of Occurences	24 270	51 359
3	Diference (%)		18,46%
	Number of Occurences	52 976	62 758
4	Diference (%)		32,87%
	Number of Occurences	43 760	58 144

Fig. 8. 2016 vs 2017: quarter

"Natural Phenomena", "Total or partial impairment of security, services or structures" and "Urban Fires or in Building Areas" suffered the most considerable increases, with 346.15% (+45), 148.05% (+4283) and 141.21% (+3735), respectively. Operations appear at the other extreme, having a growth of only 10.04% (+47).

Once analysed the records of the attribute: "value", the focus was on the evolution of the most common records and only these, because in 108 possible values for this attribute, there will be many that are not relevant to study.

For this, a minimum of 1000 records each year was considered. The analysis says also that "Tree Falls", "Housing" and "Forestry" suffered the biggest evolutions with +245.44% (+2501), +153.47% (+2767) and +135.57% (+2546). "Search, and Rescue of Land, Animals" and "Water Supply to Private Entities" also registered increases, but the "shiest" with both around 40%. Once analysed the aerial means, there was a huge growth of 442.62% (+3417) compared to the number of occurrences involving this type of means in 2016.

5.3 Analysis of the years: 2018 vs 2019

At the geographic level, the districts with the most significant growth were Bragança, Braga and Évora, with this evolution being 12.80% (+704), 10.15% (+1694) and 9.62% (+381), respectively. The only districts with negative growth were Vila Real and Beja, with a decrease of 189 and 19 records. It is equivalent to −2.68% and −0.39, respectively. It is possible to see the top 10 of the most significant evolutions in Fig. 9.

District		Year 2018	2019
Bragança	Number of Occurences	5 719	6 416
	Diference (%)		12,19%
Braga	Number of Occurences	17 273	18 973
	Diference (%)		9,84%
Évora	Number of Occurences	4 095	4 489
	Diference (%)		9,62%
Castelo Branco	Number of Occurences	5 167	5 627
	Diference (%)		8,90%
Viseu	Number of Occurences	11 917	12 919
	Diference (%)		8,41%
Setúbal	Number of Occurences	17 288	18 281
	Diference (%)		5,74%
Porto	Number of Occurences	37 022	39 104
	Diference (%)		5,62%
Aveiro	Number of Occurences	16 535	17 443
	Diference (%)		5,49%
Santarém	Number of Occurences	14 051	14 775
	Diference (%)		5,15%
Faro	Number of Occurences	12 354	12 880
	Diference (%)		4,26%

Fig. 9. 2018 vs 2019: district

Analysed the kind, the types: "Total or partial commitment to safety, services or structures", "Assistance and Prevention to human activities" and "Accidents", had positive evolutions of 23.97% (+2596), 8.36% (+4370) and 5.70% (+1387), while "Natural Phenomena", "Operations" and "Intervention in Legal Conflicts" registered decreases corresponding to −45.95% (−34), −42.31% (−341) and −26.83% (−11).

About the records of the attribute: "value", only values that have at least 1000 records each year were considered, due to the above reasons. The results say that "Tree Falling", "Water Supply to the Population", and "Search and Rescue of Land, Animals" got the biggest evolutions with +38.13% (+1814), +35.72% (+654) and +25.55% (+753). There was a negative evolution in some values, but only a minority. Despite this, the note remains for: "Forest Settlement" and "Bush", as they had the most significant decreases, being in the order of −18% and −11%, respectively.

About the time (Fig. 10), it can be concluded that the 4th quarter suffered the most significant evolution, growing 14.19% (+7806). The remaining quarters remained practically unchanged, suffering variations between +0.04% and +1.88%. In terms of

Quarter		Year 2018	2019
1	Number of Occurences	54 075	54 875
	Diference (%)		1,48%
2	Number of Occurences	58 626	58 703
	Diference (%)		0,13%
3	Number of Occurences	66 764	68 030
	Diference (%)		1,90%
4	Number of Occurences	54 938	62 737
	Diference (%)		14,20%

Fig. 10. 2016 vs 2017: quarter

aerial means, there was a decrease of 64.45% (−4301) compared with the number of occurrences involved in 2018.

6 Discussion

Considering all the Analytical Questions presented in Sect. 4, a discussion and analysis of the results obtained will be performed, trying to answer the questions. The questions will be analysed in the order in which they appear in Sect. 4.

1. Which areas of the country have more occurrences?
Lisbon (16.7%) and Porto (15.9%) lead the number of occurrences, starting with the areas of occurrences. Districts like Braga, Aveiro, Setubal and Santarém also register a considerable number of events. The Interior of the country has low records.

2. What are the months to take more "serious"?
The evolution of the number of occurrences over the years is important. The first analysis is that the number of occurrences of 2016 compared to the years that followed is low. It is due to the 1st semester of that year. To explain this situation, the numbers are almost non-existent in January and February, with 4 (0.003%) and 1 (0.0008%) occurrences, respectively. March and April also registered low values: 168 (0.14%) and 321 (0.26%), respectively. The situation starting to normalise in May/June and remained so until the end of 2019. Because of this, the evolution from 2016 to 2017 is enormous. From 2017 to 2018 and 2018 to 2019, it already registers moderate growth.

3. How has the number of occurrences evolved over the years?
Some months are more important than others because of the difference in the occurrences. The summer months and the closer ones, which typically have more mobilisation, have the most records. August and July, respectively, are the ones that "lead". At the other end, January and February, respectively, are the ones with lower records.

4. Where do the occurrences selected as the most frequent occur at the kind level?
Psychological trauma is a problem that deserves attention due to its growth. The district of Lisbon has almost 47% (64024) of its occurrences, being the maximum of all districts. This last data helps explain the high number of trauma records because Lisbon has the most occurrences. When analysing the remaining districts, it was noticed that this

percentage is higher in Littoral districts, where there may be more conditions to combat this problem. At the same time, they are typically more modern and "open" districts. Bragança has the lowest percentage, not even reaching 30% (6385). Road accidents are more likely in large cities and with large populations and are now confirmed in numbers. Lisbon, Porto, Braga, Setubal, Aveiro and Leiria have the highest percentages of this type of accident, being around 11% or 10%. Bragança is the city with the lowest rate, not reaching 7%. Then, there is a big difference in some districts regarding patrolling - Portalegre has around 16.6% (maximum) of the occurrences are of this type, and Beja has only about 1.8% (minimum).

5. When do the occurrences selected as the most frequent occur at the kind level?

Rural fires are widely spoken in Portugal during each summer, so it is crucial to understand how this time of the year influences the rise of these occurrences due to high temperatures. Something that leads us to agree with this idea is that January has 2183 (3.05%) records, while August, which is the "worst" month, has 12948 (18.08%). High temperatures may not be the only reason because July is also a typically hot month and "only" had 7871 (10.99%) records (clearly less than August). To have a better idea, September and October, which are months when it is customary to have lower temperatures than July, have more records of rural fires. Viana do Castelo has the highest percentage of rural fires, with around 16.3% (3496). It is almost triple (in terms of percentage!) of Setubal, which presents about 5.6% (3383). There is a tendency for these percentages to be higher in Northern and/or Interior districts. A good climate generates a lot of mobilisation of people, which may be one reason for the patrolling actions to occur precisely in July, August, and September. These last few months represent around 63% of patrolling occurrences, one of the most frequent data source values.

6. What days of the week have the highest number of occurrences?

The weekdays have the highest records: the weekend days have more records, with Saturday and Sunday having 18.4% and 17.2% of the records, respectively. It probably happens due to the greater mobility typical of these days. From Monday (10.4%) to Friday (14.9%), the records increase every day.

7. How are the average values of terrestrial means by area?

The number of terrestrial means used by the district was analysed to understand if low numbers, in any case, gave the feeling that the geographical condition could lead or not to the lack of this type of means. The average is quite similar in all districts, being the minimum reached in Porto, with around 1.41 and the maximum in Castelo Branco, with 1.71. The Littoral districts have lower numbers than in the Interior, although they are always similar. As many of these districts are among the most developed in the country, it leads to believe that it is the very type of occurrences in the Interior that require terrestrial means in more situations than in the Littoral.

7   Conclusions

This section helps to understand the leading indicators that were studied. Kind (later transformed to group, type and value) is one of the most exciting attributes of the data source, leading the project to notice several aspects of the occurrences and some of the most important words, which was one of the main goals of this project. Psychological traumas, road accidents, fires, and patrolling are examples of the most common values seen further. Trauma deserves much attention because it has nearly 41% of records, doubling the value in the interval time of this study. Because of the last data, Health Care (46.5%) is the most common type with almost half of the records. These values were related to place, time, between others for a more complete analysis. The district variable was analysed to understand the most common areas and, in most cases, Lisbon and Porto dominant. Lisbon (16.7%) and Porto (15.9%) together have about one-third of all occurrences to understand this idea better. In the temporal aspect, the occurrences evolved favourably over the years, and it was possible to observe the times of the year in which this type of event is most frequent. The high temperatures and great human mobilisation typical of the summer months lead (probably) to this time of year that registers the most events. August (11.1%), July (9.9%) and September (9.7%) are the months with more records, respectively. The number of terrestrial means per district is quite balanced, with the average of this number varying between 1.41 (Porto) and 1.71 (Castelo Branco).

For the future, an important analysis is about the pandemic and how it affects the occurrences. A reduction in values is expected, but more important is to analyse where they will occur, at what times of the year and which types are most affected. Observing the trends through a real-time monitoring mechanism is also essential to obtain more complete results and take the project to another level.

Acknowledgements. This work has been supported by FCT – Fundação para a Ciência e Tecnologia within the R&D Units Project Scope: UIDB/00319/2020 and supervised by IOTECH.

References

1. Prociv.pt. http://www.prociv.pt/pt-pt/Paginas/default.aspx. Accessed 29 Mar 2021
2. Antunes, J. https://github.com/centraldedados/protecao_civil. Accessed 20 Mar 2021
3. Ralph Kimball, M.R., Thornthwaite, W., Mundy, J., Becker, B., Wiley (eds.): The Data Warehouse Lifecycle Toolkit, 2nd edn. (2008)
4. Python Software Foundation. Python Language Reference, version 2.7. http://www.python.org
5. McKinney, W.: pandas: a python data analysis library. http://pandas.sourceforge.net
6. M. AB, M. Press (ed.): MySQL Language Reference: The Official Guide to the MySQL Language and APIs (2004)
7. Albert Nogués, J.V. (ed.): Business Intelligence Tools for Small Companies. Apress (2017)
8. Murray, D.G. (ed.): Tableau Your Data!: Fast and Easy Visual Analysis with Tableau Software. Wiley (2016)
9. MySQL: MySQL WorkBench (1995)
10. Sonia Bergamaschi, F.G., Orsini, M., Sartori, C., Vincini, M.: A semantic approach to ETL technologies (2011)
11. Ziawasch Abedjan, L.G., Naumann, F.: Profiling Relational Data – A Survey (2015)

Hindcasting with Cluster-Based Analogues

Carlos Balsa[1]([✉]) [ID], Carlos V. Rodrigues[2] [ID], Leonardo Araújo[3],
and José Rufino[1] [ID]

[1] Research Centre in Digitalization and Intelligent Robotics (CeDRI), Instituto
Politécnico de Bragança, Campus de Santa Apolónia, 5300-253 Bragança, Portugal
{balsa,rufino}@ipb.pt
[2] Vestas Wind Systems A/S, Design Centre Porto, Porto, Portugal
calvr@vestas.com
[3] Universidade Tecnológica Federal do Paraná, Campus de Ponta Grossa,
Ponta Grossa 84017-220, Brazil
leonardoa.2016@alunos.utfpr.edu.br

Abstract. The reconstruction of meteorological observations or deterministic predictions for a certain variable and station may be performed
with data from other variables at that station, or from other nearby stations. This is a hindcasting problem, known from some time to be solvable
using the Analogues Ensemble (AnEn) method. However, depending on
the dimension and granularity of the datasets used for the reconstruction,
this method may be computationally very demanding, even if parallelization is used. In this paper, the AnEn method is combined with K-means
clustering, allowing for a considerable acceleration of the reconstruction
task, while keeping the accuracy of the results.

Keywords: Hindcasting · Analogues ensemble · K-means · Time series

1 Introduction

Short-range weather prediction by correlation with similar past states (analogues) was initially hypothesized by Lorenz [14], who conjectured that if two
atmospheric states are very close initially, they will remain somewhat close for
some time in the future. This was introduced as an alternative to classical
weather forecast, based on systems of equations underlying deterministic Numerical Weather Prediction (NWP) models. However, for many years, Lorenz's proposal was discarded, due to limited historical data available on past weather
conditions (specially over wide geographical areas), and insufficient computing
processing capabilities to undertake his approach. Two decades later, van den
Dool [9] revisited analogue-based short-range weather forecasting and found it
feasible and effective when applied to limited geographical areas.

Afterwards, Monache [16] showed the applicability of an analogue scheme
(named AN) to postprocess numerical weather predictions, in order to reduce

© Springer Nature Switzerland AG 2021
T. Guarda et al. (Eds.): ARTIIS 2021, CCIS 1485, pp. 346–360, 2021.
https://doi.org/10.1007/978-3-030-90241-4_27

systematic and random errors. The rationale is that if past forecasts (analogues) exist, similar to the current NWP forecast (predictor), it is possible to produce an AN forecast by averaging the observations corresponding to those past forecasts; then, the analogue forecast is compared with the NWP forecast to infer the prediction error and thus improve the NWP forecast.

Later, Monache refined the use of analogues, to estimate the probability distribution of the future state of the atmosphere [15]. Instead of focusing on improving a single deterministic NWP prediction, the goal was to derive a Probability Density Function (PDF) of the range of possible future states (forecasts), a more realistic approach due to imperfect initial conditions and model limitations that generate prediction errors. In the same work, the term *analogue ensemble* (AnEn) was coined, naming both the observations corresponding to the past analogue forecasts, and the method used to the select those observations.

Since its inception, the AnEn method gained traction in other contexts, like renewable energy management, namely for wind power and solar power forecasting [2,3]. It was also combined with other approaches, like artificial neural networks, e.g. to predict the power generated by photovoltaic power plants [6].

Another use of the AnEn method, particularly relevant in the scope of this paper, is *hindcasting*. Classical weather hindcasting is the recreation of past weather conditions by applying a forecast model on a past starting point (reanalysis); this is done to validate the forecast model, if comparable past observations are available; it may also be used to derive absent past data (non-recorded past observations) from the forecast model (reconstruction). Hindcasting with the AnEn method allows to reconstruct data of a meteorological variable i) based on data of other variable(s) at the same location, or ii) based on data of the same or other variable(s), from one or several nearby locations.

The last approach (hindcasting with multistations) was exploited in [5] where, in addition to the classical Monache similarity metric, others were used to select the analogues, namely cosine similarity, normalization, and K-means clustering; the results showed the potential of the AnEn method coupled with K-means (especially with two predictor stations), but also pointed to the need of comparing K-means with alternative clustering methods, and to study the influence of variations on several important parameters. Part of this parametric study was already presented in [4], for the reconstruction of a single meteorological variable, using the classical Monache, K-means clustering and C-means clustering methods for the selection of analogues; the study revealed K-means to ensure the best accuracy, and identified heuristics to define the number of clusters, number of analogues and the analogue time span, that minimize prediction errors.

This paper focus on the coupling of the AnEn method with K-means clustering for hindcasting with multistations. The mathematical formulation of the resulting approach is introduced in order to highlight the parameters that directly influence its numerical accuracy. A parametric study is carried out, in which the preliminary research presented in [4] is expanded to hindcast other three meteorological variables in addition to the gust speed (GST), namely: the pressure (PRES), the air temperature (ATMP) and the wind speed (WSPD). Additionally, the computational efficiency of the proposed clustering-based approach is compared with the classical Monache method.

In what follows, Sect. 2 revises the classical AnEn method and introduces a clustering variant; Sect. 3 presents the results obtained in a hindcasting problem with real meteorological datasets, using both the classical and the new cluster-based AnEn variant; finally, Sect. 4 concludes and lays out future work.

2   Combining the AnEn Method with Clustering

The original AnEn method can be adapted to reconstruct meteorological data of a predicted weather station, based on meteorological data from nearby predictor stations. The methodology is illustrated in Fig. 1 for the case of a single predictor station. In the figure, the *historical dataset* corresponds to a full record of past observations at the predictor station, and the *observation dataset* is an incomplete record of past observations at the predicted station (this record is complete for a training period, but incomplete or absent for a prediction period).

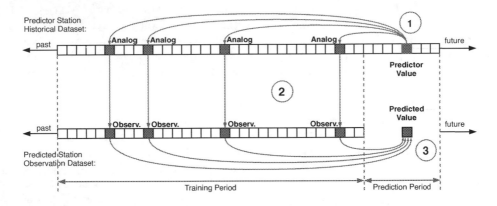

Fig. 1. Hindcasting with the Analogues Ensemble method.

The hindcasting of a missing value (predicted value) of the predicted station, concerning a certain instant in time t', goes through three different stages.

Firstly (step 1), a certain number of analogues are selected in the historical dataset, due to being the past observations most similar to a predictor at instant t'. Both the predictor and each analogue are in fact vectors of $2k + 1$ elements, where each element is the value of a meteorological variable at successive $2k + 1$ instants of the same time window, and k is a positive integer that represents the width of each half-window (into the past, and into the future) around the central instant of the time window. Comparing vectors, and not single values, takes into account the evolutionary trend of the meteorological variable around the central instant of the time window, allowing for the selection of analogues to take into account weather patterns instead of single isolated values.

Secondly (step 2), the analogues map onto observations in the training period of the predicted station. This mapping is done only for the central instant of the analogue time window, meaning that for each analogue vector a single observational value is selected in the observation dataset. Thirdly (step 3), the observations selected are used to estimate (hindcast) the missing predicted value. If this value is indeed available as real observational data (as assumed in this paper), it then becomes possible to assess the prediction/reconstruction error.

Before moving on to the formalization of the approach discussed in this paper, some notation is introduced: H represents the historical timeseries, from where analogues are defined; O represents the measurements/observations timeseries for the station/feature to be predicted, and P is the outcome prediction. Whilst O and P can be viewed solely as function of time, t, when using multistations the history H will be an aggregate of timeseries at multiple meteorological stations, in which case it will be a function also of the station s, that is, $H = H(s, t)$.

2.1 Error-Based Score Metrics

In this section the techniques used to find analogues are presented. The techniques are based on the score obtained through given metrics. The choice of these metrics will depend on whether or not predictor stations are considered independent or dependent. In the independent case, the choice of analogues for a predictor station is independent of the choice made for other stations. In the dependent case, the analogues of the different stations must coincide in time.

Independent Analogues. Following [16], a univariate metric can be defined as:

$$\epsilon(t, \tau) = \sqrt{\sum_{j=-k}^{k} [H(t + j\,\Delta t) - H(\tau + j\,\Delta t)]^2}, \tag{1}$$

where H is the historic timeseries from where analogues are identified, t is the prediction time, τ is the time defining an analogue, and Δt is the timeseries period. Both t and τ are the central instants of vectors with $2k + 1$ consecutive records (Δt apart in time), with k past (future) records that immediately precede (succeeded) them. The resulting metric, ϵ, is an Euclidian Distance between a possible analogue and the predictor, such that the best analogues are those that yield the lowest ϵ. The $\epsilon(t, \tau)$ metric can be directly expanded to multiple measurement stations at different locations, identified through an index s, as

$$\epsilon_i(s, t, \tau) = \sqrt{\sum_{j=-k}^{k} [H(s, t + j\,\Delta t) - H(s, \tau + j\,\Delta t)]^2}, \tag{2}$$

where $s = 1, \ldots, N_s$ and N_s is the total number of predictor stations. The metric ϵ_i allows to identify the best analogues for each station s, independently of those found for other stations, hence ϵ_i is designated as an *independent* score.

These analogues are used to define the best predictor periods from which to derive the prediction. This is equivalent to find, for each predictor station s, the N_a analogues with the lowest scores for each specific prediction time t, i.e.,

$$a_{s,n} = \operatorname*{argmin}_{\tau} \left[\epsilon_i(s, t, \tau), \text{ if } \tau \notin \{t, a_{s,1}, \ldots, a_{s,n-1}\} \right]$$

$$\text{for } n = 1, \ldots, N_a \text{ and } s = 1, \ldots, N_s, \tag{3}$$

Then, the prediction follows from the mean of the observations corresponding to the analogues selected:

$$P(t) = \frac{1}{N_s N_a} \sum_{s=1}^{N_s} \sum_{n=1}^{N_a} O(a_{s,n}). \tag{4}$$

Dependent Analogues. A time dependency between the analogues from different predictor stations may be forced so that the score metric for time τ considers all stations. This may be designated as *dependent* score and is given by

$$\epsilon_d(t, \tau) = \sqrt{\sum_{s=1}^{N_s} \epsilon_i(s, t, \tau)^2}. \tag{5}$$

The equivalent expression to Eq. (3) for the best analogues now becomes

$$a_n = \operatorname*{argmin}_{\tau} \left[\epsilon_d(t, \tau), \text{ if } \tau \notin \{t, a_1, \ldots, a_{n-1}\} \right] \quad \text{for } n = 1, \ldots, N_a \tag{6}$$

leading to predictions performed by

$$P(t) = \frac{1}{N_a} \sum_{n=1}^{N_a} O(a_n), \tag{7}$$

2.2 Cluster-Based Analogues

The classical search for analogues in the training period of the historic timeseries H may take a considerable amount of time, due to the need to go through every instant in the training period and compare the record centered in that instant, with the predictor vector, in order to compute the metrics given by Eq. (2) or (5). A faster alternative way to define and select the best analogues is through the use of *clustering*. Next, a formal description of this approach is provided.

The historic timeseries H of a station s may be broken into smaller overlapping subsets (vectors of size $2k+1$), such that each subset is given by

$$\mathbf{x}_{s \cdot j} = \{H(s, (j-k)\Delta t), \ldots, H(s, (j+k)\Delta t)\}$$

$$\text{for } s = 1, \ldots, N_s \text{ and } j = k+1, \ldots, N_t - k, \tag{8}$$

and the set of all $\mathbf{x}_i$ subsets is

$$\mathbf{X} = \{\mathbf{x}_1, \ldots, \mathbf{x}_{(N_t - k)\, N_s}\}, \tag{9}$$

where N_t is the dimension of the timeseries included in the training period.

The clustering method can be described as a function f mapping the set $\mathbf{X}$ into a set of clusters c_i, for a maximum number of clusters N_c, i.e.,

$$f : \mathbf{X} \to \{c_1, \ldots, c_{N_c}\} \tag{10}$$

where each cluster c_i will include a certain number of $\mathbf{x}_i$ subsets that share some aggregation criteria, for example, minimizing the variance of the subsets within each cluster. The aggregation of the $\mathbf{x}_i$ subsets into a cluster will depend on the clustering algorithm employed and respective efficiency metric employed. N_c may be specified or estimated from $\mathbf{X}$, depending on the technique employed.

After the application of the clustering algorithm, each cluster will have a centroid $\bar{\mathbf{c}}_i$ equal to the mean of the respective subsets, given by

$$\bar{\mathbf{c}}_i = \frac{\sum_{\mathbf{X} \in c_i} \mathbf{X}}{\sum_{\mathbf{X} \in c_i} 1} \quad \text{for } i = 1, \ldots, N_c, \quad \text{where } \bar{\mathbf{c}}_i \equiv \bar{\mathbf{c}}_i(\tau), \quad \tau \in [-k\,\Delta t,\, k\,\Delta t], \tag{11}$$

Each vector $\bar{\mathbf{c}}_i$ acts as an individual analogue, that may be compared against the historic value $H(s, t)$ for prediction time t. Then, a metric similar to Eq. (5) may be used to determine which are the best $\bar{\mathbf{c}}_i$ analogues:

$$\epsilon_c(s, t, i) = \sqrt{\sum_{j=-k}^{k} [H(s, t + j\,\Delta t) - \bar{\mathbf{c}}_i(j\,\Delta t)]^2}, \tag{12}$$

As each $\mathbf{x}_i$ subset has a time correspondence to the observation timeseries O that can be mapped into a matching subset,

$$o_{s \cdot j} = O(j\,\Delta t), \quad \text{for } s = 1, \ldots, N_s \text{ and } j = k + 1, \ldots, N_t - k, \tag{13}$$

each centroid $\bar{\mathbf{c}}_i$ will have an associated observation value $\bar{o}_i$, that is the average of all the observations o_i that match the vectors $\mathbf{x}_i \in c_i$. Solving a problem similar to Eq. (6) for time t, in order to determine the analog clusters, one may compute a prediction as:

$$P(t) = \frac{1}{N_a} \sum_{i=1}^{N_a} \bar{o}_i. \tag{14}$$

As in this work we only use a single analog cluster (the one with the best score ϵ_c), the prediction is simply $P(t) = \bar{o}_i$.

In the case of dependent stations, the dependent metric ϵ_d will be given by

$$\epsilon_d(t,\, i) = \sqrt{\sum_{s=1}^{N_s} \epsilon(s,\, t,\, i)^2} \tag{15}$$

and the prediction follows from (7).

Compared to other metrics, the big advantage of clustering is that it is done only once, before making predictions. Then, for each prediction time, it is only necessary to compute the score metric, given by Eq. (12), with the centroids $\overline{c}_i$, with $i = 1, \ldots, N_c$, which are usually much less than the total number of subsets, given by $(N_t - k)N_s$. This advantage translates into a great reduction in the computational effort required.

In this variant of the AnEn method, clustering is achieved using the K-means algorithm, whereby $m = (N_t - k)N_s$ historical data subsets $x_i \in \mathbb{R}^{2k+1}$ are to be classified in N_c clusters (with N_c predetermined). The data is organized as lines in a matrix $X \in \mathbb{R}^{m \times (2k+1)}$. To describe the K-means method as proposed in [10], a partition of the subsets vectors $\mathbf{x}_1, \ldots, \mathbf{x}_m$ in N_c clusters is denoted as $\prod = \{\mathbf{c}_1, \ldots, \mathbf{c}_k\}$, where

$$\mathbf{c}_j = \{\ell : \mathbf{x}_\ell \in \text{cluster } j\} \tag{16}$$

defines the set of vectors in cluster j. The centroid, or the arithmetic mean, of the cluster j is then

$$\overline{\mathbf{c}}_j = \frac{1}{n_j} \sum_{\ell \in \mathbf{c}_j} \mathbf{x}_\ell \tag{17}$$

where n_j is the number of elements in cluster j. The sum of the squared distance, between the data points and the j cluster centroid, known as *coherence*, is

$$\mathbf{q}_j = \sum_{\ell \in \mathbf{c}_j} \epsilon_c(s,\, \ell,\, j)^2 \tag{18}$$

The closer the vectors are to the centroid, the smaller the value of $\mathbf{q}_j$. The quality of a clustering process can be measured as the *overall coherence*:

$$\mathbf{Q}\left(\prod\right) = \sum_{j=1}^{N_c} \mathbf{q}_j \tag{19}$$

K-means is considered an optimization method once it seeks a partition process that minimizes $\mathbf{Q}(\prod)$ and, consequently, finds an optimal coherence. The problem of minimizing *overall coherence* is NP-hard [11] and, therefore, very difficult to solve. The basic algorithm for K-means clustering is a two step heuristic procedure. First, each vector is assigned to its closest group. Then, new centroids are computed using the assigned vectors. In the K-means version presented in Algorithm 1, adapted from [10], these steps are alternated until the changes in the *overall coherence* are lower than a certain tolerance previously defined.

Algorithm 1. K-means
1. Start with an initial partitioning $\prod^{(0)}$ and compute the corresponding centroid vectors $\bar{\mathbf{c}}_j^{(0)}$ for $j = 1, \ldots, N_c$. Compute $Q(\prod^{(0)})$. Set $z = 1$.
2. For each vector $\mathbf{x}_i$ find the closest centroid. If the closest centroid is $\bar{\mathbf{c}}_p^{z-1}$ assign i to $\mathbf{c}_p^{(z)}$.
3. Compute the centroids $\bar{\mathbf{c}}_j^{(t)}$ for $j = 1, \ldots, N_c$ of the new partitioning $\prod^{(z)}$.
4. If $\left\| \mathbf{Q}(\prod^{(z)}) - \mathbf{Q}(\prod^{(z-1)}) \right\| < \text{tol}$, stop; Else $z = z + 1$ and return to step 2.

This work uses the K-means implementation available in the R software package through the built-in function `kmeans` [17].

3   Cluster-Based Analogues on Meteorological Datasets

In this section the cluster-based AnEn method presented in the previous section is applied to a hindcasting problem with real-world meteorological data.

3.1   Meteorological Stations Datasets

The datasets used in this paper originate from the United States National Data Buoy Center [1], concerning specifically to three weather stations on the east coast of the state of Virginia, in the United States – see Table 1. These stations were selected because its records were previously found to be correlated [5,8].

Table 1. Meteorological stations.

Station	Code	Location	Role
s_1	*ykt*	37° 13' 36" N 76° 28' 43" W	Predicted
s_2	*ykr*	37° 15' 5" N 76° 20' 33" W	Predictor
s_3	*dom*	36° 57' 44" N 76° 25' 27" W	Predictor

The stations collect several meteorological variables, such as pressure (PRES), air temperature (ATMP), wind speed (WSPD) and gust speed (GST), which are studied in this work. Records are made mostly every 6 min ($\Delta t = 6$ min), but data is not always complete (there are periods with missing data).

A period of 9 years was considered, spanning from 2011 to 2019. The data was separated into two groups: i) data for a training period, from the beginning of 2011 to the end of 2017; ii) data for a prediction period, from the beginning of 2018 to the end of 2019. Data from station s_1 in the prediction period are predicted from data available at stations s_2 and s_3, that act as predictor stations.

Having data for a period of 9 years, with $\Delta t = 6\,\text{min}$, implies a large number of record vectors, originating a considerable computational burden when applying either the classical AnEn method or even the K-means based approach exploited in this paper. For that reason, the historic dataset was filtered: only records between 10 a.m. and noon were used, which translated into $N_t = 43238$.

As real data is available for the predicted period, it is possible to compare the predictions with the observed values, and thus assess the accuracy of the methods through different types of error metrics. In agreement with the recommendations by Chai and Draxler [7], several metrics are used, namely: Bias (a basic indicator of the *systematic error* in a prediction), RMSE (Root Mean-Squared Error), SDE (Standard Deviation of the Error, an indicator of the *random error*) and MAE (Mean Absolute Error); for the respective formulae and explanation see [7].

3.2 Number of Clusters

The number of clusters is a fundamental parameter of the proposed method. The fewer clusters formed, the greater the number of subsets in each. As all subsets x_i $(i = 1, \ldots, m)$ included in the selected cluster are considered analogues, then the prediction must take into account a number of observations in equal number.

This section presents the values of the errors in the prediction of the meteorological variables PRES, ATMP, WSPD and GST, when varying the number of clusters (N_c). This concerns only the independent stations scenario, such that a cluster is selected in each predictor station to make the forecast. The results, shown in Fig. 2, were obtained with $k = 5$ (hence, each subset x_i has 11 values, corresponding to a 66 min time window, for a total of 86466 subsets).

Observing the Fig. 2, it is possible to notice a similarity in the behaviour of the errors, with the variation of N_c, for the variables ATMP, GST and WSPD: the errors initially decrease a lot with the increasing of N_c, but then stabilize for values of $N_c > 300$. For the variable PRES, a distinct behaviour is observed: errors continue to progressively decrease as the number of clusters increases; this is possibly due to the fact that the PRES variable does not have large fluctuations over a short period of time and as such the smaller clusters, with lesser variance (coherence), are the ones that best describe its behaviour.

3.3 Temporal Window Size

The impact of changing the analogues size was verified by changing the k parameter defined in Sect. 2.1. Note that changing k to $k + 1$ is equivalent to increase the analogue size by $2\,\Delta t = 12\,\text{min}$. In the tests performed, k varied between 1 and 10 (with unit increments), corresponding to time periods varying between 18 min and 2 h. In agreement with the results of the previous section, the value of the number of clusters was fixed at $N_c = 350$ for all variables.

The results of varying the temporal window size by varying k are shown in the sub-tables of Table 2. As may be observed, the lowest error values (in bold) are obtained with k between 5 and 7. However, their differences are minimal.

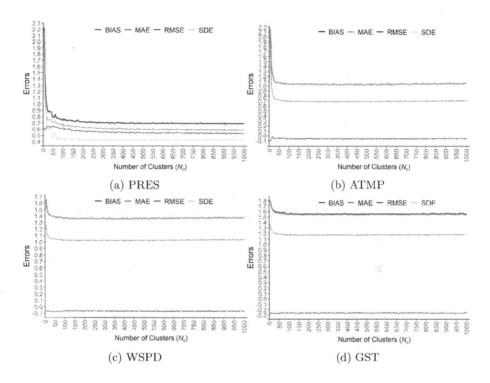

Fig. 2. Impact of the number of clusters (N_c) on the prediction errors.

3.4 Dependent Stations Method

This section compares the results obtained using datasets from the two predictor stations s_2 and s_3 in a independent and dependent way (see Sect. 2.1). In the first approach the clustering of subsets $\mathbf{x}_i$ was made for each station independently through the metric of Eq. (12), and a cluster of analogues is selected at each of these two stations. In a dependent approach only one cluster is determined through Eq. (7). In both approaches, $N_c = 350$ and $k = 5$ were set.

The results (see Table 3), show that the use of the dependent method translates into a reduction in the errors obtained, although this reduction is modest.

3.5 Prediction with Variables Different from the Predicted

So far, in all predictions made, the data from the predictor stations corresponded to data from the variable that was being predicted. For instance, if the variable in focus was ATMP, only data from this same variable was used to carry out the analogue selection. But in a scenario where the stations that are used as predictors do not have historical records of the variable that is to be predicted, making predictions with a different variable is the only alternative and the impact of this approach will vary, depending on the correlation between the variables at stake.

356   C. Balsa et al.

Table 2. Effect of the temporal window half-size (k) on the prediction errors.

k	Bias	RMSE	MAE	SDE	k	Bias	RMSE	MAE	SDE
1	−0.574	0.717	0.628	0.430	1	−0.067	1.043	0.690	1.041
2	−0.571	0.712	0.622	0.425	2	−0.060	1.038	0.690	1.036
3	−0.557	0.704	0.612	0.430	3	−0.059	1.046	0.697	1.044
4	−0.570	0.713	0.623	0.428	4	−0.058	1.049	0.699	1.047
5	−0.550	0.703	0.607	0.438	5	**−0.053**	**1.031**	**0.685**	**1.029**
6	−0.554	0.708	0.610	0.441	6	−0.049	1.039	0.693	1.038
7	**−0.548**	**0.701**	**0.605**	**0.437**	7	−0.047	1.048	0.699	1.047
8	−0.549	0.705	0.608	0.442	8	−0.043	1.045	0.700	1.044
9	−0.554	0.708	0.612	0.441	9	−0.034	1.044	0.705	1.043
10	−0.557	0.713	0.618	0.445	10	−0.040	1.042	0.699	1.041

(a) PRES   (b) ATMP

k	Bias	RMSE	MAE	SDE	k	Bias	RMSE	MAE	SDE
1	−0.063	1.364	1.028	1.362	1	−0.258	1.556	1.172	1.535
2	−0.060	1.366	1.029	1.365	2	−0.258	1.558	1.169	1.537
3	−0.060	1.359	1.026	1.357	3	−0.257	1.557	1.172	1.536
4	−0.062	1.365	1.029	1.364	4	−0.256	1.558	1.176	1.537
5	−0.055	1.361	1.027	1.359	5	**−0.261**	**1.556**	**1.171**	**1.534**
6	**−0.064**	**1.357**	**1.025**	**1.356**	6	−0.258	1.557	1.171	1.536
7	−0.061	1.357	1.027	1.355	7	−0.266	1.566	1.180	1.543
8	−0.066	1.368	1.032	1.367	8	−0.258	1.568	1.186	1.546
9	−0.062	1.364	1.030	1.363	9	−0.251	1.562	1.180	1.542
10	−0.071	1.379	1.038	1.377	10	−0.257	1.561	1.176	1.539

(c) WSPD   (d) GST

Table 3. Prediction errors obtained with dependent and independent stations.

Dependency	Variable	Bias	RMSE	MAE	SDE
Yes	PRES	**0.561**	**0.712**	**0.618**	**0.439**
No	PRES	0.653	0.732	0.685	0.332
Yes	ATMP	**−0.037**	**1.040**	**0.695**	**1.039**
No	ATMP	−0.051	1.047	0.685	1.045
Yes	WSPD	**−0.059**	**1.355**	**1.024**	**1.354**
No	WSPD	−0.086	1.558	1.193	1.555
Yes	GST	**−0.263**	**1.559**	**1.172**	**1.537**
No	GST	−0.278	1.681	1.290	1.658

Table 4 exhibits the prediction errors for each meteorological variable when using any of the variables as predictor. The predictor stations were used in a dependent way and, as before, the parameters $N_c = 350$ and $k = 5$ were adopted.

Table 4. Prediction errors for different variables used as predictors.

Predictor	Predicted	Bias	RMSE	MAE	SDE
PRES	PRES	0.564	**0.713**	**0.619**	**0.435**
ATMP	PRES	−0.642	6.651	5.216	6.620
WSPD	PRES	−0.210	6.518	5.085	6.515
GST	PRES	−0.162	6.590	5.169	6.588
PRES	ATMP	0.343	7.998	6.621	7.991
ATMP	ATMP	−0.050	**1.038**	**0.693**	**1.037**
WSPD	ATMP	−0.558	8.771	7.670	8.754
GST	ATMP	−0.519	8.916	7.802	8.901
PRES	WSPD	0.222	2.587	2.067	2.577
ATMP	WSPD	−0.015	2.443	1.901	2.443
WSPD	WSPD	−0.059	**1.359**	**1.024**	**1.358**
GST	WSPD	−0.070	**1.327**	**1.005**	**1.325**
PRES	GST	0.012	3.196	2.549	3.196
ATMP	GST	−0.198	3.073	2.402	3.067
WSPD	GST	−0.261	**1.609**	**1.203**	**1.588**
GST	GST	−0.257	**1.554**	**1.171**	**1.533**

As can be seen in Table 4, for the variables PRES and ATMP the results are worse when using a predictor variable other than the one being predicted. However, for the WSPD and GST variables, the results obtained when one of them is used to predict the other are very similar to those obtained with self prediction, indicating that these two variables are strongly correlated. From these results, it is expected that the best analogues should be obtained when using predictors which are well correlated with the variable being predicted.

3.6   Computational Efficiency

The classic AnEn method compares the predictor value with all the historical values of the training period (step 1 of Fig. 1) through the metrics of Eqs. (2) or (5). This requires a considerable computational effort, specially if performed in a pure sequential manner. Although it is possible to parallelize the analogues search [13], this effort will be greater the longer the prediction period.

A significant advantage of determining analogues via clusterization with the K-means algorithm is the reduction in total computational time. This reduction originates from the fact that cluster formation (which, done only once, still is the most time-consuming phase in this approach) followed by the comparison of each cluster centroid with the predictor, is much faster than going through all possible analogues of the historical dataset and compare them with the predictor.

The K-means based AnEn variant used in this work was implemented in R [17], taking advantage of the parallel implementation in R of many operations with large-scale matrices and vectors. All tests for this paper where performed in a Linux machine with a 16-core AMD EPYC 7351 CPU and 64 GB of RAM.

Table 5 presents a comparison between the best results obtained with the classic AnEn method and with the K-means clustering version. The errors shown are the Bias and the SDE, that represent the systematic and the random errors, respectively. The parameters used in the classical version are $N_a = 150$ and $k = 2$ and in the K-means version are $N_c = 350$ and $k = 5$. The prediction times of each version, for a different numbers of CPU cores used, are also included.

Table 5. Comparison between Classical and K-means based AnEn

Variable	AnEn variant	Errors		Prediction time (seconds)			
		Bias	SDE	1 core	2 cores	4 cores	8 cores
PRES	Classic	0.278	0.412	206	107	73	41
PRES	K-means	0.561	0.431	9	6	5	4
ATMP	Classic	0.000	1.070	205	111	52	39
ATMP	K-means	−0.037	1.027	9	6	5	4
WSPD	Classic	−0.206	2.064	186	98	50	27
WSPD	K-means	−0.059	1.353	12	10	7	7
GST	Classic	−0.530	2.132	200	98	53	27
GST	K-means	−0.257	1.535	13	11	8	7

In general, the K-means variant leads to more accurate predictions. Only in the case of variable PRES does this not occur and even there the differences in errors are small. This is linked with the discussion in Sect. 3.2, namely that due to its lack of variance for short time scales, variable PRES requires an higher number of clusters such that each cluster characterizes a smaller sample.

It may also be seen that, for the same AnEn variant, the prediction time does not vary much between variables. However, between the two AnEn variants, the prediction times are quite different, separated up to two orders of magnitude, with the K-means variant being much faster than the classic one. On the other hand, the classic version benefits greatly from the increase in the number of CPU cores used, since the computation of the similarity metric, in step 1 of Fig. 1, for each analogue candidate, is independent of any other candidate and, as such, is done in parallel. In turn, the K-means version does not benefit as much from the increased number of CPU cores because only the centroids similarity to the predictor can be calculated in parallel and their number is much smaller than the number of analogue candidates in the classical variant.

4   Conclusion

The clustering-based AnEn variant introduced in this paper, built on the K-means algorithm, proved to be an alternative to the classical AnEn method, exhibiting the same or better accuracy, and much better computational efficiency.

The prediction accuracy of this new AnEn variant depends on some of its most important parameters, specially the number of clusters (N_c) and the temporal window dimension around the time to be predicted. The results show that, for most of the meteorological variables considered, N_c had to be greater than 300, though needn't be too high. However, for variables whose values are more regular, such as atmospheric pressure, the number of clusters must be high in order to capture its well-defined profile. Concerning the temporal window size, it seems that $k = 5$ is a good all-round choice for all the variables.

The determination of the clusters of analogues was achieved through the K-means algorithm. This algorithm aggregated similar (or coherent) time periods in the same cluster, where the coherence of the cluster was based on the squared 2-norm of the difference between the vectors representing the time periods. It is known that this measure does not capture certain similarities between the data that well. It would be interesting to implement K-means with other metrics that would allow to better capture the similarity between the various time periods that will be compared. A comparison with the results of machine-learning based techniques in this field [12] is also another direction for future work.

References

1. National Data Buoy Center. https://www.nature.com/nature/. Accessed 20 Oct 2020
2. Alessandrini, S., Monache, L.D., Sperati, S., Cervone, G.: An analog ensemble for short-term probabilistic solar power forecast. Appl. Energy **157**, 95–110 (2015). https://doi.org/10.1016/j.apenergy.2015.08.011
3. Alessandrini, S., Monache, L.D., Sperati, S., Nissen, J.N.: A novel application of an analog ensemble for short-term wind power forecasting. Renew. Energy **76**, 768–781 (2015). https://doi.org/10.1016/j.renene.2014.11.061
4. Araújo, L., Balsa, C., Rodrigues, C.V., Rufino, J.: Parametric study of the analog ensembles algorithm with clustering methods for hindcasting with multistations. In: Rocha, Á., Adeli, H., Dzemyda, G., Moreira, F., Ramalho Correia, A.M. (eds.) WorldCIST 2021. AISC, vol. 1366, pp. 544–559. Springer, Cham (2021). https://doi.org/10.1007/978-3-030-72651-5_52
5. Balsa, C., Rodrigues, C.V., Lopes, I., Rufino, J.: Using analog ensembles with alternative metrics for hindcasting with multistations. ParadigmPlus 1(2), 1–17 (2020). https://journals.itiud.org/index.php/paradigmplus/article/view/11
6. Cervone, G., Clemente-Harding, L., Alessandrini, S., Delle Monache, L.: Short-term photovoltaic power forecasting using artificial neural networks and an analog ensemble. Renew. Energy **108**, 274–286 (2017)
7. Chai, T., Draxler, R.R.: Root mean square error (RMSE) or mean absolute error (MAE)? - Arguments against avoiding RMSE in the literature. Geosci. Model Dev. **7**(3), 1247–1250 (2014). https://doi.org/10.5194/gmd-7-1247-2014
8. Chesneau, A., Balsa, C., Rodrigues, C.V., Lopes, I.M.: Hindcasting with multi-stations using analog ensembles. In: CEUR Workshop Proceedings, vol. 2486, pp. 215–229. CEUR-WS (2019)
9. Dool, H.M.V.D.: A new look at weather forecasting through analogues. Mon. Weather Rev. **117**(10), 2230–2247 (1989). https://doi.org/10.1175/1520-0493a(1989)117⟨2230:ANLAWF⟩2.0.CO;2

10. Eldén, L.: Matrix Methods in Data Mining and Pattern Recognition. SIAM, Philadelphia (2007)
11. Garey, M.R., Johnson, D.S.: Computers and Intractability: A Guide to the Theory of NP-Completeness. W. H. Freeman & Co., New York (1990)
12. Hu, W., Cervone, G., Young, G., Monache, L.D.: Weather analogs with a machine learning similarity metric for renewable resource forecasting. ArXiv abs/2103.04530 (2021)
13. Hu, W., Vento, D., Su, S.: Parallel analog ensemble - the power of weather analogs. In: Proceedings of the 2020 Improving Scientific Software Conference. pp. 1–14. NCAR, May 2020. https://doi.org/10.5065/P2JJ-9878
14. Lorenz, E.N.: Atmospheric predictability as revealed by naturally occurring analogues. J. Atmos. Sci. **26**(4), 636–646 (1969). https://doi.org/10.1175/1520-0469(1969)26⟨636:aparbn⟩2.0.co;2
15. Monache, L.D., Eckel, F.A., Rife, D.L., Nagarajan, B., Searight, K.: Probabilistic weather prediction with an analog ensemble. Mon. Weather Rev. **141**(10), 3498–3516 (2013). https://doi.org/10.1175/mwr-d-12-00281.1
16. Monache, L.D., Nipen, T., Liu, Y., Roux, G., Stull, R.: Kalman filter and analog schemes to postprocess numerical weather predictions. Mon. Weather Rev. **139**(11), 3554–3570 (2011). https://doi.org/10.1175/2011mwr3653.1
17. R Core Team: R: A Language and Environment for Statistical Computing. R Foundation for Statistical Computing, Vienna, Austria (2017). http://www.R-project.org/

Big Data as an Orientation Tool for Networking Marketing

Bogart Yail Márquez[✉], Luis Alberto Partida-Ramírez, and Maribel Guerrero-Luis

Tecnológico Nacional de México Campus Tijuana, Av Castillo de Chapultepec 562,
Tomas Aquino, 22414 Tijuana, B.C, Mexico
{bogart,m21210016,maribel.guerrero}@tectijuana.edu.mx

Abstract. This research work pursues to present information relevant to advertising on social networks presented in other research works, this in order to provide a project to guide small businesses to advertise in the most optimal way on different social networks, considering the gender and age of the clients to be reached. The project will implement the use of big data with multiple databases to determine the best social network to advertise according to the parameters offered by the user. This will help small and even medium-sized companies have a better overview that helps them make the decision on which social network to invest advertising resources in according to the market they are looking.

Keywords: Big data applications · Marketing management · Metadata ·
Classification models · Data analysis · Machine learning

1 Introduction

Marketing has evolved a lot in recent years thanks to digitization, taking the form of web pages instead of advertising magazines, ads on recognized pages instead of newspaper ads, even the advertising we consume when we watch television now interrupts us the videos that we want to see on social networks offering us products that we might like. However, this reality has also been overcome, now most users do not surf the internet, just like that, if not limited to browsing social networks, such as Facebook, Instagram, Twitter, among others. So marketing is no longer the same as years ago, now we must adapt to advertise efficiently on different social networks, although we cannot ignore that different social networks have their own network of users that vary in ages and genders. Depending on the social network you want to work with. And this can become complicated for a small company or a personal business if they have a not very high budget, in these cases it is best to have a good marketing plan to invest in the most intelligent way, for this we will develop a project that uses big data to offer support for decision making in advertising [1].

This project will be based on three main databases: "Which Social Media Millennials Care About Most" by A. Halper, "Social Influence on Shopping" by A. Halper and "data of usage of social media by students between age 17–22" By M. Maheep. With these three databases, the big data algorithms will be implemented for the analysis and development

© Springer Nature Switzerland AG 2021
T. Guarda et al. (Eds.): ARTIIS 2021, CCIS 1485, pp. 361–371, 2021.
https://doi.org/10.1007/978-3-030-90241-4_28

of the data statistics and thus provide a better orientation of which social network is more suitable to advertise in them according to the market that the user seeks to reach with their products [2, 3].

2   The Problem of the Project

For small companies and independent businesses, it is usually a problem to decide about which medium to use to advertise, in addition to the fact that in many cases they do not have good management of social networks and it is difficult to decide which social network would be the best to advertise and invest in having a better reach on one platform. In addition, financial problems are present in the same way, requiring a payment to advertise on a large scale and not always all the social networks used can be covered. It is critical to advertise the company or business on social networks because of their great reach, but which of them is better for the company or business?

3   State of the Art

Advertising has always been a useful tool for companies looking to sell their products by offering them to a certain sector of the market. However, the techniques of how to advertise has been evolving by leaps and bounds, going from advertising only by recommendations that go from people to people, newspapers and until now social networks which can be quite a difficult change for many to digest, for This seeks the best way to adapt and advise the advertiser in this new form of marketing [4].

Historical Evolution of Knowledge and Current Situation. As is well known, social networks have revolutionized the world and the way people interact with each other and with each other, changing the way information is handled. Likewise, traditional advertising media such as the newspaper, magazines, radio and a little more recent television are already becoming obsolete not because they are not effective but because their scope is already very limited compared to the number of people and information that is handled today. So, what resources could be used to this intention?

Social networks are used by many people worldwide and these in turn have been evolving and constantly changing information management [5].

Social media is said to have evolved by Giant steps, as have many other technologies. Before, you were only provided with an application that was only capable of sending and receiving messages, now with the passage of time these characteristics have been improved, in order to offer a list of new possibilities so that the user is satisfied. On the other hand, the number of users continues and continues to increase over time, which requires measurements by trained engineers for the analysis and storage of huge amounts of data provided by users.

Today it is well known that on social networks we are exposed to a lot of publicity, both in videos, images and in the middle of the news page. But how viable is it to advertise here on social media? Everything will depend on the target market, the different social networks such as Facebook, Twitter, Instagram among others, handle a user base mostly of a certain age range and this is where it can be used as an advertising medium targeting a specific sector [6, 7].

Big Data emerges as a new era in the exploration and use of data. From the business perspective Big Data does not represent only large volumes of data, the patterns extracted from the data and that can generate innovation processes must be considered [8, 9].

In the enterprise world and the business world, during the last decade of the last century and the first years of this, we started talking of Business Intelligence (BI) to refer to the set of strategies and tools that a company had at its disposal to be able to analyze your organization's data. With BI, forecasts and analysis were made [10].

3.1 Theoretical-Conceptual Framework

Before entering the analysis of data from social networks we need to understand how market is handled within social networks as Veeramani handles it, in his paper Impact of Social Media Networks Big Data Analysis for High-Level Business, there are different elements such as such as: the market maker which is a company that seeks to work online by associating with distributors, merchants and the consumers themselves, sellers in social networks would have the role of being independent people who in turn act as a sales center, the merchants who are companies with large quantities of products that remotely sell their products and the buyers who are all potential customers who buy the products [11].

In this case, we are interested in approaching the management of social networks as a merchant, since the generalization of the data to recommend the way to advertise allows us to better target the market and in this way to better manage the advertising resources. Although being an independent seller this could also be of interest, although in general the public is much wider, and it is not necessary to focus so much in this case [11].

The best way to apply a classification method is to know its functionality and the data that are needed to make it work, it is from this knowledge that different strategies for data collection and identification of useful data for the algorithm begin to be developed. When the data that will be used for the implementation of the algorithm is known, it is cleaned, distributed and applied in the algorithm, commonly they are divided into training data and test data to build the algorithm. In the area of social networks and advertising, the most important data are likes, clicks, comments and feelings within these comments and responses, it is from these that work begins [12].

The following data normalization formulas, as Abu-Salih says in his paper Time-aware domain-based social influence prediction, are applied to an environment based on likes, comments, replies (responses), and feelings that exist in them. They represent the way to analyze and manipulate the data obtained from the different social networks analyzed. Mention is also made of different supervised classification methods and machine learning and the metrics used to evaluate the performance of the applied methods [12].

Big Data is also related to what has been known as data mining, a field of Computer Science that tries to discover patterns in large volumes of data. Data mining (part of BI), like Big Data, uses the methods of Artificial Intelligence (AI) and Statistics to analyze the patterns in the databases with which it works [13].

Domain-based relativeness factor. This formula is used to calculate Ru based on the score obtained from u for each domain d.

$$R'_{u,d} = \frac{R_{u,d}}{max(R_{*d})} \qquad (1)$$

Where:

$R'_{u,d}$: Represents the normalized value of R.

$R_{u,d}$: Represents the frequency of retweets for each content in a user's domain d.

$max(R_{*d})$: Represents the maximum number of retweets obtained by users in domain d.

Normalization of Lu, d. In this formula L represents the number of likes those users make in a given domain, so this formula represents the normalization of this data, that is, the likes.

$$L'_{u,d} = \frac{L_{u,d}}{max(L_{*d})} \qquad (2)$$

Where:

$L'_{u,d}$: Represents the normalized value of L.

$L_{u,d}$: Represents the percentage of likes for each content in a user's domain d.

$max(L_{*d})$: Represents the maximum percentage of likes obtained by users in domain d.

Pu normalization, d. In this formula P represents the number of replies that users make in each domain, so this formula represents the normalization of this data, that is, the responses.

$$P'_{u,d} = \frac{P_{u,d}}{max(P_{*d})} \qquad (3)$$

Where:

$P'_{u,d}$: Represents the normalized value of P.

$P_{u,d}$: Represents the number of responses (replies) for each content in the domain d of a user.

$max(P_{*d})$: Represents the maximum percentage of responses obtained by users in domain d.

Normalization of Su, d. In this formula, the normalization of this variable represents the difference between positive or negative feelings in all the responses of user u in domain d.

$$S'_{u,d} = \frac{S_{u,d} - (S_{*d})}{(S_{*d}) - (S_{*d})}, \; where \; S_{u,d} = SP_{u,d} - |SN_{u,d}| \, for \, each \, domain \, of \, d \qquad (4)$$

Where:

$S'_{u,d}$: Represents the normalized value of S.

$S_{u,d}$: Represents the difference between the positive or negative feelings of the responses of the users in a domain d of a user.

$max(S_{*d})$: The maximum represents the difference between the positive or negative feelings of the responses of the users in a domain d of a user.

(S_{*d}): Represents the minimum difference between the positive or negative feelings of the responses of the users in a domain d of a user.

$SP_{u,d}$: Represents the sum of the positive score of the responses of user u in domain d.

$SN_{u,d}$: Represents the sum of the negative score of the responses of user u in domain d.

Relationship of the user's followers and friends (User followers-friends relation). In this formula the last dimension in the list of key attributes of the user is the ratio between the number of followers and friends of each user.

$$FF\_R_u\{\frac{FOL_u - FRD_u}{Age_u}, \; si\, FOL_u - FRD_u \neq 0 \frac{1}{Age_u}, \; si\, FOL_u - FRD_u - 0 \quad (5)$$

Where:

FF_R_u: It refers to the difference between the number of followers and friends that the user obtains according to the age of the user's profile.

FOL_u: It is the number of followers of user u.

FRD_u: It is the number of friends of user u.

Age_u: It is the age of the user profile u in years.

FF_Ru normalization.

To perform the normalization of the data obtained with the formula FF_Ru, the following formula is used:

$$FF\_R'_u = \frac{FF\_R_u - (FF\_R)}{(FF\_R) - (FF\_R)} \quad (6)$$

Where:

$FF\_R'_u$: It is the value resulting from the normalization.

(FF_R): Represents the highest friend-follower ratio of all users on the data network.

(FF_R): Represents the minimum ratio of friends-followers of all users on the data network.

Once the data to be worked on is known, it is required to know the different methods to use, for this case two methods are particularly identified to work with this information, which are NBC (Naive Bayes Classifier), LC (Logistic Classifier) and GBTC (Gradient Boosted Tree Classifier). The usefulness of these classification methods lies in the fact that some use probability formulas to obtain results, others use linear sums of characteristics and other methods of applying trees to make predictions.

3.2 Naive Bayes Classifier

It is a classification method with high bias and low variance, capable of building an acceptable model even with a small dataset. Easy to develop due to its low computational cost even with huge amounts of data to use.

The following formula explains the probability function on which this classification method works:

$$P(X) = P(x_1|c) \times P(x_2|c) \times \ldots \times P(x_{12}|c) \times P(c) \quad (7)$$

Where:

$P(X)$: Indicates the probability of the user being in a particular domain c.

$P(x_i|c)$: Indicates the probability of the user of having the characteristic x_i when the user is in domain c.

$P(c)$: It is the probability that the user is in c.

3.3 Logistic Classifier

This method is frequently used for dual classification tasks, in this method the probability of predicting the social influence of a user is determined by the logistic function consisting of the linear sum of all its characteristics. This function is the following:

$$f^{LR}(\underline{x}) = P(\underline{x}) = \frac{1}{1 + exp\left(-\left(b_0 + \sum_{i=1}^{12} .b_i \cdot x_i\right)\right)} \tag{8}$$

Where:

$f^{LR}(\underline{x})$: Represents the social influence of a user.

$b_0, b_1, \ldots, b_{12}$: They are the logistic coefficients which are determined by maximizing the probability.

When and is large, there is a high probability that the user is in the domain, whereas when y is 1, the user is in the domain-based social influence category.

Gradient Boosted Tree Classifier.

The approach is like Random Forest, except that the normalized weights are multiplied by the decision tree models instead of averaging all the models equally. Try to give great weight to the model that can achieve accurate predictions.

$$f^{GB}(\underline{x}) = \sum_i .w_i \cdot f_i^{DT}(\underline{x}) \tag{9}$$

$f^{GB}(\underline{x})$: It is the weighted sum of the multiple decision trees.

$f_i^{DT}(\underline{x})$: Represents multiple decision trees.

$\sum_i .w_i$: All the w_i are determined based on the gradient-based method that tries to minimize the discrepancies between the predictions and the actual samples [12].

"Maintaining a presence on platforms like Facebook and Twitter is important because it allows people to act with the company on a seemingly personal level that helps companies on multiple fronts. It is also vital for the typical client" [14].

It is very important that emphasis be placed on the great impact that social networks have today when a company decides to advertise, since it will allow interaction with the client, give an image that can provide trust and recommendations from others users about the advertised company.

Big data refers to the set of data that grows in an excessive way, surpassing the possibility of being managed and analyzed using common and traditional data processing techniques, this being a modern problem since most of the information that we seek to analyze on a daily basis. today it is simply huge. Big data is made up of unstructured and multi-structured data often coming from interactions between people and machines, Web applications, social networks and sensors [15].

To analyze the massive data that social networks offer us regarding user activity, we need to use different tools that facilitate their management and analysis. These tools can be known as machine learning techniques and methods that are very important when analyzing big data, which are previously developed algorithms that are highly efficient to handle exorbitant amounts of data [11].

Social media marketing refers to how advertising, sales and purchases of products and services are handled today. Since the way of offering products on social networks is very different and taking advantage of this change, a tool can be implemented that helps us focus on how we advertise on social networks according to statistics based on big data [14].

As we see, Big Data analysis potentially constitutes an option for the design of public policies with the technical possibility of taking into account the totality of the data generated and not just a sample, this has the potential to generalize a statistic with greater precision or to make a prediction with greater accuracy [16, 17].

4   Research Methodology

The methodology for conducting the diagnosis seeks to see what indicators exist among network users and the networks themselves. Once the problem that is how social networks influence advertising given to the information provided to the networks by users has been generated and defined, the points or approaches to be applied are determined. Once the points are determined, an action plan for the in-depth investigation of the project is generated, context is given, the results are applied and interpreted in order to reach a relevant conclusion.

The methodological approach used is mainly social and economic since we focus on the trends of people within social networks and how these trends influence the economic field of advertising and companies. In this social approach we can see trends such as the "level of education" or "types" of users, as well as appealing to certain figures of social networks, or trends that are generated in them. In the case of the economic approach, we can see what types of products users are more likely to observe on the networks.

The sample used for the research is based on a specific range of ages, those considered millennials (approximately born between 1981 to 1999). The data collected from this sample was regarding which platform has most influenced this sector of the population in terms of online shopping, in a total of 2,676 people of different ages and different universities throughout the United States.

The methods for obtaining information in this case were surveys that were conducted among different groups within the United States population with a total of 2,676 people, while the data used in this research was collected from the "Social Influence on Shopping" uploaded by Adam Halper and provided by the data. World page.

To perform the analysis of the data within our database, different techniques and machine learning methods are used for the processing and classification of information within the respective Big Data methods. Some of these classification methods are usually:

- Linear Regression
- Logistic Regression

- Decision trees
- Support Vector Machines (SVM)
- K methods, such as K-NN (K-nearest neighbors), K-means, among other K methods.
- Another tool for data analysis and transport to implement these different methods is with libraries such as
- Scikit Learn with its focus on applications developed in python
- Apache Spark whose main focus is Scala, but also has support for Python, R, Java.

It is through these libraries that applications for massive data analysis can be made, using the methods mentioned above, providing the developer with tools for easy implementation and readability in the code.

5 Results and Analysis

Experimentation/Testing. Data analysis tests were carried out using tools in python and pyplot to obtain the necessary graphs to give a statistical reference that provides a better understanding and improves the decisions about social media marketing that the client wants to obtain in order to have a more effective campaign and with better results. The previous analysis of the data resulted in the following graphs that were obtained from Adam Halper's "Social Influence on Shopping" database for a more effective analysis (Fig. 1).

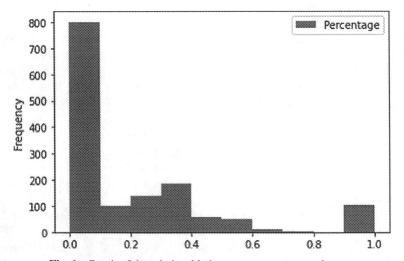

Fig. 1. Graph of the relationship between percentage and count.

As can be seen, there is a higher percentage in values that are between 0.0 and 0.1, this is where the relationship that exists between the platform that has the most influence when making online purchases can be analyzed (Fig. 2).

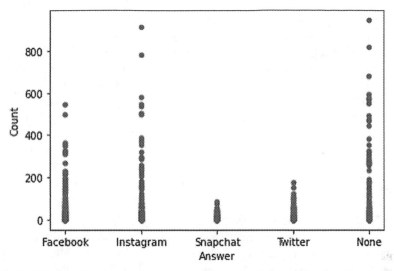

Fig. 2. Relationship between the number of responses in each of the social networks.

As can be seen, Snapchat and Twitter are the social networks with the least influence in terms of online transactions (Fig. 3).

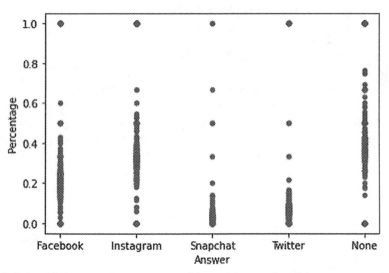

Fig. 3. Relationship between the percentage of the social network and the percentage of positive responses.

As you can see, there are certain peaks in the percentage, but the majority is between 0.2 and 0.5% of selection between the social networks of Facebook and Instagram and in "None" as observed.

It can be seen in this descriptive analysis, the number of people who buy through online services using the most popular social networks today. In this case, 3 variables were taken for the organization and structuring of the data, which are: Answer, Count and Percentage. The operation of these variables ranges from selecting the type of social network that was used by the user, showing the number of votes that a specific response had and the amount in percentage that people vote in a social network. It can be specified that most of the population is inclined to make online purchases through some social networks, due to their degree of popularity or influence in the market, such as Facebook and Instagram.

6 Conclusions

By using social networks as a means of marketing for SMEs, you have the advantage of being low cost, easy to implement and making use of different big data methods for recommendations, predictions and data analysis, will help to improve the results obtained in the performance of these businesses, thus obtaining an increase in the scope that the company has over its potential clients.

This project is formed to show us how big data can be linked to the large amounts of data that are generated through social networks and with this provide a service to users. This service can be as much as simply seeing the general data of the behavior of users in social networks, as well as its use for advertising purposes in them.

This project will provide a lot of help to all those businesses that do not have a high budget to do marketing studies but that want to have effective advertising, which is why the reason to use social networks as an advertising medium and offer a guide with this project, for those little ones. companies and independent businesses, in the world of digital marketing in social networks.

The project that is being carried out aims to specify information about big data and also to provide viable information to those users interested in establishing advertising between different social networks, for example, among which age ranges it would be more important to establish specific advertising or more necessary for the user in question.

7 Future Work

Some possible paths to follow by this project in the medium-term future that could be developed as a result of this research to take what is embodied in this research to the practical field are the following.

- Investigate, experiment, and apply new algorithms or big data methods to obtain better results in recommendations made by the system for the user's target market.
- Collect a greater amount of data for a more specific and accurate data analysis when recommending the social network for digital marketing.
- Develop a platform in a virtual environment that allows obtaining a recommended statistic to advertise that the user searches according to the market of his business. Also, this platform would be hosted on a web server for easy access.

- Develop a mobile application that allows you to monitor the business and the change in its market according to its objective. This application will be able to make recommendations for the social media platform that best suits the market to be reached.
- Start a company that offers consulting services in digital marketing using data analysis tools as a basis to provide the best option according to the client's needs.

References

1. Chalawadi, A.M.: Impact of social media on big data and green computing and solution 5(3), 102–106 (2019)
2. Mahat, M.: Data of usage of social media by students between age 17–22 (2018). https://data.world/maheepmahat/data-of-usage-of-social-media-by-students-between-age-17-22
3. Esfahani, H., et al.: Big data and social media: A scientometrics analysis 3(3), 145–164 (2019)
4. Tidd, J., Bessant, J.R.: Managing Innovation: Integrating Technological, Market and Organizational Change. Wiley (2020)
5. Cross, R.L., Cross, R.L., Parker, A.: The Hidden Power of Social Networks: Understanding How Work Really Gets Done in Organizations. Harvard Business Press (2004)
6. Turban, E., et al., Electronic commerce 2018: a managerial and social networks perspective. 2017: Springer.
7. Gentina, E., Chen, R., Yang, Z.: Development of theory of mind on online social networks: evidence from Facebook, Twitter, Instagram, and Snapchat. J. Bus. Res. 124, 652–666 (2021)
8. Hernández-Leal, E.J., Duque-Méndez, N.D., Moreno-Cadavid, J.J.T.: Big Data: una exploración de investigaciones, tecnologías y casos de aplicación 20(39), 17–24 (2017)
9. Fathi, M., et al.: Big data analytics in weather forecasting: a systematic review, pp. 1–29 (2021)
10. Rasmussen, N.H., Goldy, P.S., Solli, P.O.: Financial Business Intelligence: Trends, Technology, Software Selection, and Implementation. Wiley (2002)
11. Veeramani, T., et al.: Impact of social media networks big data analysis for high-level business. Int. J. Recent Technol. Eng. (IJRTE) 7(552), 87–92 (2019)
12. Abu-Salih, B., et al.: Time-aware domain-based social influence prediction 7(1), 1–37 (2020)
13. Tascón, M.: Introducción: Big Data. Pasado, presente y futuro, pp. 47–50. Cuadernos de comunicación e innovación, Telos (2013)
14. Sahatiya, P.: Big data analytics on social media data: a literature review 5(2), 189–192 (2018)
15. Yamagata, Y., Seya, H.: Spatial Analysis Using Big Data: Methods and Urban Applications. Academic Press (2019)
16. Myers, J.L., Well, A.D., Lorch Jr., R.F.: Research Design and Statistical Analysis. Routledge (2013)
17. Baesens, B.: Analytics in a Big Data World: The Essential Guide to Data Science and Its Applications. Wiley (2014)

Multivariant and Geo-Statistical Analysis of the Effects of the COVID 19 Pandemic of the Microenterprise Business Segment in Ecuador (Province of Santa Elena Case)

Fausto Calderón Pineda(✉) ⓘ, Juan Carlos Olives ⓘ, Divar Castro Loor ⓘ, and Alonso Pirela Añez ⓘ

Península de Santa Elena State University, La Libertad, Ecuador
{fcalderon,jolives,dcastro,apirela}@upse.edu.ec

Abstract. The COVID-19 pandemic has had a very strong negative impact on the world's economies and small and medium-sized companies have not been the exception. To mitigate the impact, it is necessary for small and medium enterprises (SMEs) to develop contingency plans, based on their reality. This research, by its design is of a causal descriptive type and its objective is to determine, based on the appreciation that those responsible for SMEs in sectors related to agriculture, commerce, industry, services, information, and communication technologies (ICTs) and other technological services, which is their situation in the face of the COVID-19 crisis and measure its affectations degree. In the methodological analysis, a sample of 376 SME's was used, from a population of 11,670 companies officially registered in the Santa Elena province. Statistical processes of correlational hypothesis tests such as Pearson and Chi-square were applied for a probabilistic trend analysis between explanatory variables logit models and for geospatial references, a multicriteria analysis of raster and vectors throughout the province. The main results are that SME's have been severely affected by the pandemic in two out of every three companies, with high losses in their income, decreased sales and production capacity, limitations in supply chains, lack of accessibility to tools of telecommuting. In addition, 8 out of 10 companies project that the negative effects of Covid-19 will continue to impact their business in the next 12 to 16 months. And that financial and non-financial supports at the state level have been insufficient or non-existent in some cases.

Keywords: Causality · Economic impact · Development · Small and medium scale enterprises

1 Introduction

The Coronavirus outbreak crisis (Covid-19) that originated in Wuhan, China in December 2019 has spread globally to more than 200 countries, including Asia, Europe, America, and Australia.

© Springer Nature Switzerland AG 2021
T. Guarda et al. (Eds.): ARTIIS 2021, CCIS 1485, pp. 372–384, 2021.
https://doi.org/10.1007/978-3-030-90241-4_29

This outbreak has been classified as a pandemic by the World Health Organization (WHO 2019) a growing human infection (Qiu et al. 2017) which caused more than 200,000 deaths within three months of the start of the outbreak (OMS 2020). In fact, Covid-19 recalled high infection rates and deaths compared to other outbreaks of coronaviruses such as MERS-CoV, SARS-CoV and Influenza (Liu et al. 2020; Peeri et al. 2020).

The effects of Covid-19 are altering the world's economies. The pandemic has disrupted tourism, global value chains and labour supply, affecting trade, investment and total production in countries leading to widespread damage to economic growth (Alonso 2020).

Undoubtedly, the main victims of the COVID-19 outbreak are micro, small and medium-sized enterprises (SMEs) because SMEs, compared to large enterprises, are more complex in that SMEs do not have adequate and sufficient resources, especially financial and management, and are therefore not prepared to address this problem beyond what is expected (Bartik et al. 2020; Prasad et al. 2015) In Latin America, SMEs account for 99.5% of enterprises in the region, employ 60% of the economically active population and account for 25% of regional GDP (IADB 2020).

Small and medium-sized enterprises (SMES) are the backbone of the economies. In Ecuador, SMEs have been identified as the drivers of the economy to their ability to stimulate productivity, provide employment opportunities and improve people's wellbeing (Abosede and Onakoya 2013; Ariyo 2005).

Most small and medium-sized enterprises can be considered dependent on their daily business operations and a limited number of recurring customers (Williams and Schaefer 2013).

For Ecuador, a country of just 17.5 million inhabitants, with a business fabric of more than 900 thousand companies in all sizes, which hosts about 3,150,000 workers with formal employment (INEC 2019), the situation becomes extremely critical, the forecasts made by chambers of commerce, production, economic analysts and international bodies, they estimate an unemployment rate of 21% at the end of 2020, this would mean a projected loss of more than 510,000 jobs by the end of 2020, as the risk rises more and more for employees and employers, by reducing their productive equipment, which at the moment still has about 65% of semi-paralized business units, in a bleak picture. Unfortunately the layoffs do not stop, sales are almost nothing, without allowing to achieve the balance points for the sustainability of organizations and businesses. From what has been researched so far, it is felt and observed that the Ecuadorian businessman is already in the intensive care room, with a reserved prognosis (Ponce et al. 2020).

The Santa Elena province, one of the 24 provinces of Ecuador, has a vulnerable situation, with a population of 308,000 thousand inhabitants, 11,662 registered companies, with a multidimensional poverty rate of 38% and poverty per income of 25% and the unemployment rate is 6% (INEC 2019). The Santa Elena province before the pandemic, as of December 2019, despite being a tourist destination par excellence, it reported a share of business structure (productive enterprises) of just 1% nationally, 0.7% in the share of global sales, 1% in the employment generation registered with the Institute of Social Security and the last place in the number of companies per ten thousand inhabitants (INEC 2019).

In this context, some studies offer some addresses for understanding and sizing the crisis from the micro-business approach. According to (Katz et al. 2020) they consider that the Covid-19 pandemic has brought challenges to the global socio-economic system and emphasize the role of digital technologies used to counteract isolation, disseminate prophylactic measures and facilitate the operation of the economic system in isolation, distancing and definitive exit.

The Zwanka and Buff (2020) study predicts that the impact of the pandemic will bring changes in consumer behavior and point out that online shopping will be a recurring practice during and after this public health problem.

In order to determine how Covid-19's confinement measures impact the economic activities of small and medium-sized enterprises in Santa Elena province, it isproposed to develop a study of the impact of the Covid-19 pandemic on small and medium-sized enterprises, in order to determine on the basis of the appreciation of SMEs in the agro-related sectors, trade, industry, services, ICT and other technological services, what is their situation in the face of the COVID-19 crisis and to size their degree of impact.

To fulfil this purpose and to check the proposed assumptions explaining the effects of the pandemic versus a system of indicators related to telework conditions, capacity of the company's response, adaptability, industrial relations, and motivation and working climate in SMEs, four phases were developed. The first, a descriptive analysis of the application of the survey technique; the second item refers to an econometric analysis of the pandemic variable. The third phase presents the correlational hypothesis test analyzes; and finally, the geostatistical model was carried out.

2 Methodology

This research has a methodology consisting of three phases:

1. 1: Descriptive analysis of the application of the survey technique: At this stage, a univariate and bivariate analysis of the results is applied, where response trends are verified, and which factors have the greatest weight can be identified in a possible system of variables that explain the behavior of the ventures through Covid-19.
2. 2: Econometric analysis of the Pandemic variable: Once the univariate trends of responses have been analyzed, it is important to identify in a single system which variables (independent) turn out to be significant at 95% confidence and that they can explain to the dependent variable (Pandemic Covid-19). A model is established with variables that identify the effects dependent on entrepreneurship under the effects of Covid-19.
3. 3: Correlational hypothesis test analysis: At this stage, it is intended to verify the independent correlational effect of established socio-economic parameter indicators, such as: Telework; Responsiveness; Adaptability; Industrial relations; and Job motivation. This section includes variables that in a multiple linear regression system were both significant and non-significant.
4. 4: Geostatistical model: Finally, the georeferencing process of micro-undertakings together with a covid-19 contagion model will show the areas with the highest degree of affectation in terms of the processes of: Transmission, Contagion, based on socioeconomic variables.

The data were collected cross-cuttingly in October 2020. It was applied to entrepreneurs, micro-entrepreneurs, managers and delegates of ventures and medium-sized industries located in Santa Elena province. Through the survey technique, a total of 376 primary data were collected.

3 Development and Results

Phase 1: Descriptive analysis of the application of the survey technique.

- Within the sample raised, there were 62.77% of companies whose economic activity focuses on commerce, 26.86% dedicated to services, and minimum values related to the sectors: industrial, agricultural, technological, among others.
- The economic sectors most affected by the Covid-19 pandemic in Santa Elena proved to be commercial, services, agriculture, aquaculture, and the industrial.
- The economic sectors that, despite the crisis caused by the Covid-19 pandemic, were not significantly affected were food and technology. This result is to be expected, since with the isolation of the families, it was necessary to adequately supply food, which was a casual demand for these products accelerated to the point of feeling a shortage effect, so the food industry had to increase its production, this achieves this effect. On the other hand, for the same reason of isolation, technological resources such as computers, laptops, cameras, and the internet increased exponentially, managing to keep this economic sector active.
- According to the results between variables such as the effects of the Covid-19 pandemic and the time of the ventures, it is evident that the closure and drop in sales caused by confinement affects a young business in the same way as one that has been in the market for some time. Basically, in Santa Elena, no establishment anticipated this condition, so the experience turned out to be indifferent under these circumstances.
- As for the normal functioning of the ventures, more than half continue to advance despite the pandemic but under slowed effects, with almost zero sales.
- More than half of the ventures, although they have computer media, were not prepared to be used in telework or telecommunication. Currently, despite low sales, some invested in adequate technology to ensure that they did not disappear into competition and be viewed through digital media. The same response trend is evident in the use of specialized computing applications for these two virtual modalities.
- The administration and planning of the ventures did not incorporate risk events related to biological aspects, so from the beginning of the confinement coupled with the new modalities involved training in new uses and modalities of work and trade.
- These new work modalities did not have the expected effects, both the entrepreneurship and the execution of work from home was slowed down by external factors, from the company by new technological adaptations and at home by environmental distractions such as: family, friends, emergency situations, purchase planning under conditions of vehicular restriction and traffic lights, among others.
- It was clear that both businesses and households did not have the technological infrastructure of Wifi networks to adequately cope with all their planning under this new normal. The effect turned out to be more significant in homes, as they went from basic

to premium internet service packages to better cope with all the activities carried out from home such as: tele-education, telework, entertainment and so on.
- Despite all these pandemic effects, what is expected in each of the undertakings is a slight improvement as the months go by, if the biosecurity measures referred to by the main national health security agencies exist and are followed.
- An expected time, according to the ventures to stay under these growth parameters, is at least six more months.
- Among the main parameters of management decisions to better cope with the evolution of ventures are: Family support, support among entrepreneurship partners, and partner with other entrepreneurs. These elections have managed to keep the undertakings running, waiting for their recovery through a possible economic revival.
- Support from the authorities on duty has been scarce, slow, and insufficient. So, the internal decisions between entrepreneurs have been the union, training and a momentary forgiveness of credits and interest in arrears.
- Among the main conditions and strategies suggested by entrepreneurs to stay active under pandemic conditions are: Expert training, subsidies to finance wages, seed capital contributions, deferment of tax obligations, and in case of dismissal or completion of activity agile access to public unemployment insurance.
- One of the fundamental pillars of economic revival suggests entrepreneurs, which restrict foreign consumption to increase the domestic market, energizing the economic sectors through the projection of aggregate demand.

Phase 2: Econometric analysis of the pandemic variable.
Econometric analysis is a mathematical modeling that guarantees, under concepts and applications of statistics and linear algebra, the significant identification of variables that explain each other under conditions of elasticity, determining a dependent variable and several independent ones. The method applied for this phase will be to estimate models under ordinary least squares (OLS) criteria.

The regression model established as a dependent variable "Impacts of Covid-19 on ventures" versus a system of indicators related to telework conditions, company response capacity, adaptation capacity, labor relations, and motivation and work environment (Tables 1 and 2).

Table 1. The regression model

Model summary				
Model	R	R square	Corrected R square	Standard error
1	,475[a]	0,226	0,191	0,665

a. Predictor variables: (Constant), Labour regulatory facilities (employers' contributions, remote work regulation), Households do not have a quality and capacity internet connection, how do you think your entrepreneurial activity will evolve in the coming month?, Based on your projections and speculations, how long can you keep your entrepreneurship active?, What impacts is the Covid-19 crisis having on your entrepreneurial activity?, we have tools (computers) to work remotely, strengthen and facilitate access to unemployment insurance.

Table 2. Coefficients[a]

Model	Non-standardized coefficients		Typed coefficients	t	Sig.
	B	SD	Beta		
(Constant)	3,333	0,418		7,974	0
What effects are the Covid-19 crisis having on your entrepreneurial activity?	−0,251	0,081	−0,237	−3,1	0,002
Do we have tools (computers) to work remotely?	0,282	0,116	0,19	2,428	0,016
Households do not have a quality and capacity internet connection	0,319	0,116	0,214	2,741	0,007
How do you think your entrepreneurial activity will evolve in the coming month?	−0,1	0,046	−0,165	−2,162	0,032
Based on your projections and speculations, how long can you keep your entrepreneurship active?	−0,088	0,041	−0,155	−2,136	0,034
Strengthen and facilitate access to unemployment insurance	−0,135	0,071	−0,232	−1,904	0,049
Labour regulatory facilities (employers' contributions, remote work regulation)	−0,162	0,073	−0,269	−2,221	0,028

a. Dependent variable: What extent is the current Covid-19 crisis negatively impacting the mood and motivation of the entrepreneurial team?

Depending on the econometric conditions of the model, they establish a square r close to 50%, in other words, the generated model maintains a relevant significance condition between the dependent variable and the explanatory variables that were significant.

Applying a methodology from the general to the particular in terms of eliminating variables that turned out to be statistically insignificant (significance less than 5%), seven variables prevail that meet adequate conditions to remain in the system estimated under OLS. Here is his explanation:

The negative sign of the variable "Effects of the pandemic" establishes that as adverse conditions to the normality that we were used to present arise, these effects negatively condition the enterprise and its operation.

The positive sign of the variable "Tools to work (computers)" highlights the importance of having the electronic means necessary for the free exercise of an enterprise, to the point that if these are overcrowded, the impacts of the pandemic in micro-enterprises.

The positive sign of the variable "Internet at home" establishes the basic and efficient condition of connectivity, as houses are affected by connection, this increases the possibilities of overloading the impact of the pandemic on businesses.

The negative sign of the variable "Evolution of entrepreneurial activity" inversely conditions the negative effects of the pandemic, since if there are favorable contexts of economic reactivation, the impacts of the pandemic on businesses are significantly reduced.

The negative sign of the variable "Estimated time of activity of the enterprise" refers to the fact that as stability policies and economic reactivation of the enterprise are maintained, the impacts on them due to the pandemic will be less and less.

The negative sign of the variable "Access to unemployment insurance" inversely conditions the negative effects of the pandemic on businesses, because as there are guarantees of access to unemployment insurance, companies and / or businesses can be activated by temporarily reducing personnel, until an ideal state is achieved, to rehire the dismissed personnel, meanwhile it is guaranteed that the worker receives a proportional monthly income.

The negative sign of the variable "Labor regulations" also establishes an inverse condition against the impacts of the pandemic, because by knowing adequately the interpretations of regulations and laws under health emergency conditions, the enterprise may be subject to benefits that help to form a field of economic reactivation from the state.

Phase 3: Correlational hypothesis test analysis.
The variables to be contrasted are qualitative cross-sectional, or at least a quantitative-qualitative combination, therefore the technique to verify the existence of a relationship between them turns out to be Pearson's Chi-Square.

The Chi-Square technique involves the formulation of two types of hypothesis, the null and the alternative. To test hypotheses and define which is accepted and rejected, specialized statistical software (SPSS) will be applied.

According to the statistical process, if the value of significance (bilateral) turns out to be greater than 0.05 (95% confidence), the null hypothesis is accepted, confirming the non-existence of some type of relationship; but if it turns out to be lower, the null hypothesis is rejected in favor of the alternative, that is, if there is a relationship between the study variables. Here are the results:

Ho: There is no relationship between the variables "Covid-19 impacts on SMEs" and "Business time".

Ha: There is a relationship between the variables "Impacts of Covid-19 on SMEs" and "Business Time" (Table 3).

According to the test data and significance, the null hypothesis is rejected in favor of the alternative, that is, "there is a relationship between these variables", which implies, according to the data, that despite the existence of years of experience and learning economies of entrepreneurship, this if it can be affected by the pandemic.

Table 3. Chi-square test A

	Value	gl	Asymptotic Sig. (bilateral)
Pearson's Chi-square	23,674[a]	12	0,023
Likelihood ratio	27,049	12	0,008
Linear-to-linear association	0,717	1	0,397
N of valid cases	376		

a. 5 squares (25.0%) have an expected frequency of less than 5. The minimum expected frequency is .43.

Ho: There is no relationship between the variables "Impacts of Covid-19 on SMEs" and "Telework".

Ha: There is a relationship between the variables "Covid-19 impacts on SMEs" and "Telework" (Table 4).

Table 4. Chi-square test B

	Value	gl	Asymptotic Sig. (bilateral)
Pearson's Chi square	21,463[a]	12	0,003
Likelihood ratio	22,365	12	0,007
Linear-to-linear association	0,423	1	0,321
N of valid cases	376		

a. 5 squares (25.0%) have an expected frequency of less than 5. The minimum expected frequency is .43.

According to the test data and significance, the null hypothesis is rejected in favor of the alternative, that is, there is a relationship between these variables, which implies, according to the data, that the telework conditions that are generated within the enterprise do affect positive or negative, so an adequate teleworking and communication environment from home must be guaranteed.

Ho: There is no relationship between the variables "Covid-19 impacts on SMEs" and "Adaptability".

Ha: There is a relationship between the variables "Impacts of Covid-19 on SMEs" and "Adaptability" (Table 5).

According to the test data and significance, the null hypothesis is rejected in favor of the alternative, that is, there is a relationship between these variables, which implies, according to the data, that if the appropriate adaptation conditions are met within the enterprise, this will cause a contraction of the negative conditions of the pandemic, improving the good administrative and commercial performance of the enterprise, as long as spaces are created for adaptation and institutional survival.

Ho: There is no relationship between the variables "Impacts of Covid-19 on SMEs "and "Motivation and Working Climate".

Table 5. Chi-square test C

Chi-square tests		
Value	gl	Asymptotic Sig. (bilateral)
58,056[a]	18	0,0000
56,676	18	0,0000
29,277	1	0,0000
376		

a. 15 squares (53.6%) have an expected frequency of less than 5. The minimum expected frequency is,06.

Ha: There is a relationship between the variables "Impacts of Covid-19 on SMEs" and "Motivation and Working Climate" (Table 6).

Table 6. Chi-square test D

Chi-square tests			
	Value	gl	Asymptotic Sig. (bilateral)
Pearson's Chi-square	28,648[a]	12	0,004
Likelihood ratio	30,758	12	0,002
Linear-to-linear association	0,503	1	0,478
N of valid cases	376		

a. 5 squares (25.0%) have an expected frequency of less than 5. The minimum expected frequency is .45.

According to the test data and significance, the null hypothesis is rejected in favor of the alternative, that is, there is a relationship between these variables, which implies, according to the data, that if the conditions of economic reactivation are guaranteed under parameters of motivation and stimulus of the work environment within the enterprise, it will be possible to reduce the impact related to the pandemic.

Phase 4: Geostatistical analysis.
For Covid-19 geostatistical contagion analysis, socioeconomic variables are established that are significant to explain the state of contagion or not in the population, especially SMEs.

To do this, a logistical probability model (logit) is first established that shows what variables explain a population's contagion trends in each territory.

The econometric model to be tested is as follows:

$$P(y = 1|x) = \lambda(+++\ldots\ldots+\beta_0\beta_1 x_1 \beta_2 x_2 \beta_k x_k) \tag{1}$$

Where:

$P(y = 1) = \lambda$ Probability that a person will be infected.

$P(y = 0) = (1 - \lambda)$ Probability that a person is not infected.

Being the variables:

$\beta_1 = Overcrowding$; Significance: 0.02.

$\beta_2 = Does\ not\ have\ public\ insurance$; Significance: 0.043.

$\beta_3 = Can\ not\ read\ or\ write$; Significance: 0.08.

$\beta_4 = Population\ over\ 65\ years$; Significance: 0.001.

$\beta_5 = Work\ outside\ the\ locality$; Significance: 0.098.

$\beta_6 = Informal\ work$; Significance: 0.03.

The database that was applied is the one determined under the projections of the INEC (2019) for the cross-sectional provincial territory. Following the methodology from the general to the particular, variables that did not turn out to be significant to explain the socioeconomic conditions of contagion were eliminated. Therefore, the variables that must remain in the model are (significance less than 0.05): Overcrowding, not having public insurance, population over 65 and informal work.

This resulting model only determines which variables explain the contagion condition or not of a population, a dichotomous stage, therefore, to calculate the level of probability, based on the variables present in the territory where the micro-enterprises are located, it is applied the following transform reference:

$$\lambda(z) = \frac{\exp(p)}{1+\exp(p)} \tag{2}$$

The value of (p) is the result of replacing variables that turned out to be significant in the main logit model, present in the territorial context of census micro-undertakings. By replacing them in expressions (2), values between 0 and 1 are obtained, which reflect the probability of being infected under the parameters set in each territorial context.

By possessing, for each data raised from the undertaking, its probability of contagion based on the territory, is elaborated by means of a frequency table to establish more detailed ranges of probabilistic contagion scenarios, below the reference values (Table 7):

Table 7. Probabilistic contagion scenarios

Range (%)	Probability status
81–100	Very high probability
61–80	High probability
41–60	Median probability
21–40	Low probability
0–20	Very low probability

The values, for a better territorial understanding, through the application of vector layers, and multi-criteria over position methodology, are generated by means of a GIS software heat maps references under the territorial context of the ventures, the result below (Fig. 1):

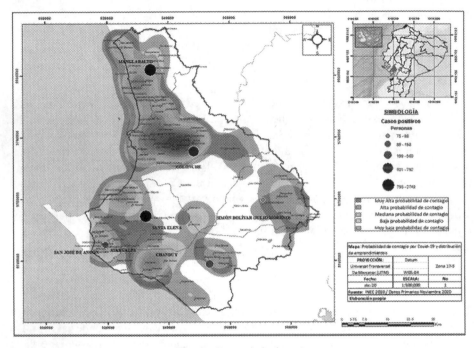

Fig. 1. Geostatistical map.

Values with a larger scale of reds have a higher tendency to contagion by Covid-19, while a larger scale of greens results in lower risk.

According to the locations of the SMEs translated into heat map colors, those that have, according to their geographical location, a greater tendency to contagion and therefore impact on their business development, marketing and sales of their products turn out to be the ones located in the centers of the cantonal and parochial capitals; those close to tourist places such as the beach; located in shopping centers; and concentrations of informal trade demonstrations.

All the SMEs close to these territorial conditions are those that have, under the multicriteria model and heat maps, the greatest probability of being affected in terms of their administrative, commercial, and human talent development. So yes, at the beginning of 2021, management policies that address continuous improvement and biosafety measures are not incorporated under the parameters of the variables that turned out to be significant in the logit model, the enterprise will have fewer and fewer opportunities for its activation. and economic recovery over time.

4   Conclusions

The study determined that there is a relationship between COVID-19 and the variables (hypotheses) determined in phase 2, namely:

a) Time of permanence of the SMEs in the market, which involved that despite the experience generated over time since its creation and knowledge of the business acquired, it can be directly affected by the pandemic.
b) Telework, in other words, although the teleworking conditions and environments were modeled based on a positive or negative impact of COVID-19, an adequate teleworking and communication environment from home must be guaranteed.
c) Adaptability. Today SMEs should aspire to implement new management models that promote resilience, accept failures, value differences, and encourage the expression of what is new and critical analysis of what is current as the only formula not to succumb to the dramatic changes they face today. accelerated by COVID-19, such as digital transformation, automation, and new skills
d) Motivation and the working climate. Motivation is dynamic, it is in constant flux, it is a state of perpetual growth and decline. The crisis caused by the pandemic further accentuated this aspect. Motivation also implies a qualitative change, along with a pleasant and proactive environment where its members feel fulfilled and assume the values of the brand, for all this, motivation in times of crisis, and at any other time, is a good investment for SMEs.

The geostatistical analysis carried out in phase 4 allowed the identification of geographic areas with greater or lesser exposure to contagion by Covid 19, in the population, especially SMEs. This will allow the generation of public policies for a better handling of the crisis. Since if social distancing is required to be maintained for a considerable period, then a profound transformation of the business cycle dependent scheme is required towards an intertemporally sustainable and crisis-proof economy; that is, the construction of a resilient economy. (Lange and Santarius 2020).

References

Alonso, J.: The economic pandemic of Southeast Asia. Universidad Nacional del Rosario. Argentin (2020).https://bit.ly/31cG7v5
Abosede, A.J., Onakoya, A.B.: Intellectual entrepreneurship: theories, purpose and challenges. Int. Daily Bus. Adm. **4**(5), 30–37 (2013)
Bartik, A.W., Bertrand, M., Cullen, Z.B., Glaeser, E.L., Luca, M., Stanton, C.T.: How are small businesses adjusting to COVID-19? Early evidence from a survey. In: Harvard Business School Working Paper, vol. 20 (102), pp. 1–37 (2020)
Katz, R., Jung, J., Callorda, F.: The state of Latin America's digitization in the face of the COVID-19 pandemic. CAF (2020). https://bit.ly/3k31O9F
IADB: Financing instruments for micro and medium-sized enterprises (2020). https://publicati ons.iadb.org/publications/spanish/document/Instrumentos-definanciamiento-para-las-micro-pequenas-y-medianas-empresas-en-America-Latinay-el-Caribe-durante-el-Covid-19.pdf
ILO: COVID-19 and the world of work: Impact and policy responses. ILO Monitor, 1st ed., International Labour Organization (2020)

Lange, S, Santarius, T.: Less work, less consumption,time online (2020). https://www.zeit.de/wir tschaft/2020-04/corona-volkswirtschaft-resilienz-beschaeftigunggrundeinkommen

Liu, Y., Gayle, A.A., Smith, A.W., Rocklov, J.: The reproductive number of Covid-19 is higher compared to SARS coronavirus. J. Travel Med. **27**(2), **taaa021** (2020)

Prasad, S.H., Altay, N., Tata, J.: Building disaster-resilient micro enterprises in the developing world. Disasters **39**(3), 447–466 (2015)

Qiu, W., Rutherford, S., Mao, A., Chu, C.: The pandemic and its impact. Health Cult. Soc. **9**(10) (2017). https://doi.org/10.5195/hcs.2017.221

Steiner, A., Gurrí, A.: How to avert the worst development crisis of this century. United Nations Development Program (2020). https://www.undp.org/content/undp/en/home/blog/2020/how-to-avert-the-worst-development-crisis-of-this-century.html. Accessed 15 Nov 2020

Williams, A.: Schaefer small and medium-sized enterprises and sustainability: managers' values and engagement with environmental and climate change issues. Bus. Strateg. Environ. **22**(3), 173–186 (2013)

World Health Organisation: Coronavirus disease (Covid-2019) situation reports (2020). https://www.who.int/emergencies/diseases/novel-coronavirus-2019/situation-reports/

Peeri, N.C., et al.: The SARS, MERS and novel coronavirus (COVID-19) epidemics, the newest and biggest global health threats: what lessons have we learned? Int J Epidemiol. **49**(3), 717–726 (2020). https://doi.org/10.1093/ije/dyaa033.PMID:32086938;PMCID:PMC7197734

Ponce, J., Palacios, D., Palma, A., Salazar, G.: Pre- and post-pandemic economic crisis: its impact on the mortality of MSMEs in Ecuador. Observatory J. Latin Am. Econ. (2020). ISSN: 1696-8352. https://www.eumed.net/rev/oel/2020/09/crisis-ecuador.html

INEC: Business Directory 2019 (2019). https://www.ecuadorencifras.gob.ec/

Zwanka, R.J., Buff, C.: COVID-19 generation: a conceptual framework of the consumer behavioral shifts to be caused by the COVID-19 pandemic. J. Int. Consum. Market. **0**(0), 1–10 (2020). https://bit.ly/33gbx6v

Identification of Breast Cancer Through Digital Processing of Mammograms

Enrique V. Carrera[1]([⊠])(iD), Bernarda Sandoval[2](iD), and Christian Carrasco[1]

[1] Departamento de Eléctrica, Electrónica y Telecomunicaciones,
Universidad de las Fuerzas Armadas – ESPE, Sangolquí 171103, Ecuador
evcarrera@espe.edu.ec
[2] Facultad de Ingeniería y Ciencias Aplicadas, Ingeniería de Software,
Universidad de las Américas – UDLA, Quito 171204, Ecuador
bernarda.sandoval@udla.edu.ec

Abstract. Breast cancer is one of the main types of cancerous diseases in terms of its mortality rate, although it can normally be cured if the disease is detected early enough. For this reason, it is very important to have computer-assisted diagnosis systems that allow the early detection of breast cancer, especially in underdeveloped countries where women do not have the opportunity to access specialist physicians. Thus, this work proposes a system for the identification of breast cancer on mammograms, whose main objective is to keep the implementation of the system simple, efficient and effective, reducing the need for complex operations or expensive hardware. For this, the current proposal uses digital image processing techniques for the enhancement and segmentation of the regions of interest. Machine learning algorithms (*e.g.*, naive Bayes, artificial neural networks, decision trees, and nearest neighbors) are subsequently used to classify a reduced set of features extracted from the processed mammograms, according to labels that have been validated by specialist clinicians. The evaluation results show that the current proposal is straightforward and, at the same time, precise enough to identify breast cancer on mammograms with accuracy and sensitivity values greater than 99%.

Keywords: Breast cancer · Digital image processing · Machine learning algorithms · Mammograms

1 Introduction

Breast cancer is the most common malignant tumor among women in the world [3,7]. However, the early detection of this disease takes an important role in reducing the death rate of breast cancer. Therefore, the most standard screening technique for detecting this type of cancer is mammography, which is basically an X-ray image of a woman's breast [12]. However, mammograms have some limitations due to the need for a specialist physician to interpret those gray-scale images that generally have high levels of noise [19].

© Springer Nature Switzerland AG 2021
T. Guarda et al. (Eds.): ARTIIS 2021, CCIS 1485, pp. 385–396, 2021.
https://doi.org/10.1007/978-3-030-90241-4_30

Due to the difficulties in interpreting mammograms, many computer-assisted diagnosis (CAD) systems have been proposed in recent years to detect breast cancer [6]. The advances in digital image processing techniques and the computational power of today's digital computers open the possibility of having accurate systems for breast cancer detection [8,18]. Furthermore, the progress in machine learning and deep learning algorithms has increased the possibility of generating cheap and effective CAD systems [2,17]. However, it should be noted that these breast cancer detection systems do not replace specialist physicians, but could be used in underdeveloped countries as an aid to improve the early detection of this deadly disease [11,15].

It is also important to mention that although deep learning has been outperforming traditional machine learning lately, the complexity and computational cost of deep learning make this technique too expensive for systems without sufficient computing power [2]. In addition, deep learning requires a lot of examples for training, while medical applications have trouble accessing enough positives and negative examples of a certain disease [19]. Because of that, we are particularly interested in a simple implementation that can be deployed even in an embedded system.

Based on the above, this work proposes a CAD system to identify breast cancer on mammograms using simple but effective digital image processing techniques [1,9], and some well-known machine learning algorithms [5]. The main objective of this proposal is to keep the system simple, efficient and effective, reducing the need of complex operations or expensive hardware. The fulfillment of this objective will allow us to build cheap and accurate breast cancer detection systems that could be distributed in small hospitals and healthcare centers.

The digital image processing techniques used in this work permit the enhancement and segmentation of the regions of interest [10,21], while the machine learning algorithms are used to classify a small set of features extracted from the processed mammograms, according to the labels that have been verified by specialist clinicians [11]. Among the various machine learning algorithms described in the literature, this work specifically assesses: naive Bayes, artificial neural networks, decision trees, and nearest neighbors [5], because of their fast recall processing.

The results obtained in the corresponding evaluation of this system show that the current proposal is quite straightforward, but precise enough to identify breast cancer on mammograms, presenting accuracy and sensitivity values greater than 99%. It is expected that these results will allow us to implement low-cost processing systems that can be employed in remote locations where there are no specialist physicians, for a successful identification of women with breast cancer.

The rest of this document is organized as follows. Section 2 reports the materials and methods that have been used throughout this work. The proposal for the computer-assisted diagnosis system is presented in Sect. 3. Section 4 shows and analyzes the main results generated by the proposed system. Finally, Sect. 5 concludes this paper.

2   Materials and Methods

2.1   Breast Cancer and Mammograms

Breast cancer is a particular type of cancer that attacks breast cells in both men and women. After skin cancer, which also has a high fatality rate, breast cancer is the most common type of cancer diagnosed in women around the world [3]. The strong support given for breast cancer awareness and research funding has helped to advance in the diagnosis and treatment of this disease, which has decreased the number of deaths associated with this serious disease [7]. However, the cure for breast cancer depends heavily on its early detection.

Therefore, mammograms are the most traditional technique for detecting breast cancer to this day [12]. A mammogram is an X-ray image of the breast, where physicians look for early signs of cancer [12]. Today, mammograms are the best and most widespread tests that physicians have to detect this mortal disease.

2.2   Digital Image Processing

Digital image processing is basically the use of digital computers to process digital images through various useful algorithms [9]. In fact, digital image processing enables a much wider range of algorithms that analog image processing does, avoiding problems such as increased noise or distortion during the corresponding digital processing [18].

In addition to the basic digital image transformations, the digital processing of images allows to filter the information in both time and frequency domains [9]. These techniques have lately been applied to medical imaging for the processing of X-ray images, computer tomography scans, among many other medical applications [14].

2.3   Machine Learning

Machine learning basically teaches computers to do what is already natural for humans and animals: learn from experience [5]. Therefore, these algorithms use computational methods to 'learn' directly from the data without relying on a predetermined equation or model. Currently, there are many machine learning algorithms that adaptively improve their performance based on the examples available for learning. However, this work is fundamentally based on supervised learning, with the evaluation of four main algorithms: naive Bayes, artificial neural networks, decision trees, and nearest neighbors [4].

In order to evaluate the models built through machine learning, the system was trained with a subset of the examples and verify the behavior of the model in the remaining samples. However, when the number of training examples is limited, techniques such as k-fold cross-validation are typically used [4]. Cross-validation randomly divides the set of N examples into k subsets, then trains the model with $k-1$ subsets, and verifies its behavior in the remaining subset.

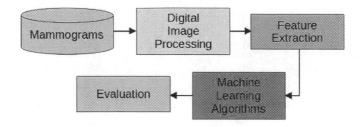

Fig. 1. Block diagram of the CAD system for identification of breast cancer.

This procedure is repeated k times with each of the subsets utilized as testing examples.

Finally, the most common metrics used in machine learning for the evaluation and comparison of the different algorithms/models are accuracy, sensitivity, specificity and precision. These metrics are defined in function of the number of negative examples classified as true negatives (TN), the number of positive examples classified as true positives (TP), the number of positive examples classified as false negatives (FN), and the number of negative examples classified as false positives (FP) [5]. The TP, TN, FP and FN values are generally obtained from the so-called confusion matrix. Moreover, another way of analyzing the results in machine learning is the ROC (Receiver Operating Characteristic) curve, as this plot illustrates the diagnostic capacity of the classifier based on a discrimination threshold. In particular, the area under the curve (AUC) is a quite important metric that is also known as the predictive capability of the model [4].

3   A Computer-Assisted Diagnosis System

The CAD system proposed in this work is summarized in the block diagram of the Fig. 1. Basically, the images from the mammogram database are first processed using digital techniques, before to extract a minimum set of features. Those features are then presented to the machine learning algorithms and their results are evaluated. As was already mentioned, the main idea of this work is to keep the system as simple as possible in order to implement an efficient, fast, and effective breast cancer detection system. Thus, this proposal uses a very small number of features to classify employing simple machine learning algorithms.

3.1   The Mamogram Database

The database used in this work is the Digital Database for Screening Mammography (DDSM) from the University of South Florida [13,16]. This database is publicly available and has 236 mammograms in standard JPG format between 330×185 pixels and 370×257 pixels. From the 236 mammograms, 141 of them correspond to images of patients with breast cancer, while the remaining 95

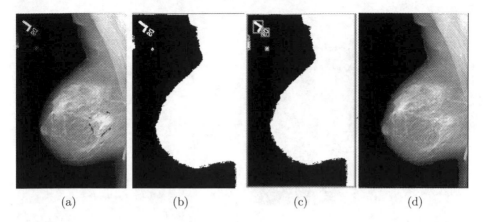

(a)   (b)   (c)   (d)

Fig. 2. Tag removal from the original mammogram: *(a)* original image, *(b)* binary image, *(c)* identified continuous regions, and *(d)* image without tags.

images correspond to healthy women. Although this is an unbalance database, it is a validated and very used dataset for comparing the performance of systems for automatic breast-cancer detection. An example of the mammograms provided by the DDSM is shown in Fig. 2(a), where it can be seen that all the images are in gray-scale despite of using the JPG format.

3.2 Digital Image Processing

Since the JPG format uses three color channels for each image, the first digital transformation is to convert each mammogram into a gray-scale image (*i.e.*, a single matrix of integers) with 256 levels of gray (*i.e.*, 8 bits per pixel) according to the equation

$$W = 0.299R + 0.587G + 0.144B$$

where the gray-scale value W of each pixel depends only on the values of the original R, G and B channel values for that pixel.

The next processing step corresponds to the removal of tags inside the image; for that, the process starts with the binarization of the original image [10]. As it is shown in Fig. 2(b), the binary image describes only the main elements associated to the original image. Using this basic information, the system is able to find the continuous regions according to a default connectivity of 8-connected white pixels [9] (see Fig. 2(c)). Next, all the small continuous regions are removed, and a binary mask is created to apply it to the original image. After applying the mask to the original image, the new mammogram image contains only the breast region without tags or labels, as is shown in Fig. 2(d).

The following processing step is required for increasing the contrast of abnormal masses through an image intensity inversion. This simple transformation for image enhancing is shown in Fig. 3 and basically applies the equation

$$W = 256 - W$$

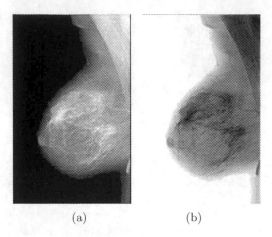

(a)   (b)

Fig. 3. Image intensity inversion: *(a)* image without tags, and *(b)* intensity inversion applied to previous image.

where W is the gray-scale value of each pixel. After that, the image is ready to segment the areas of interest in the mammogram.

As already mentioned, the segmentation is oriented to isolate the areas of interest removing the less relevant regions. This is the most important operation of the digital image processing applied in this work, since allows us to identify the area where some abnormality could be present. For that, using the gray-scale image with intensity inversion, the algorithm tries to segment the image pixels according to the discontinuities and similarities found among the pixels [18]. However, medical images as the mammograms present non-uniform noise layers, making difficult to use fixed threshold values for detecting discontinuities. Because of that, multi-layer segmentation algorithms are preferred, as they increase the quality of this operation.

Therefore, the Otsu's method is used to segment several layers according to adaptive thresholds that highlight some possible areas of interest, as seen in Fig. 4(a). Although this operation is very sensitive to the luminosity of the image, the image intensity inversion helps us to stabilize the result of the operation [10]. In order to effectively segment the breast area, a following flood-fill operation on the background pixels of the image is required, as shown in Fig. 4(b). After that, the convex envelope of the breast region is determined fixing a predefined number of pixels as the thickness of that envelope. This convex envelope correspond to the white region defined in Fig. 4(c). Using this binary mask of the internal region of that convex envelope, the mammogram is segmented to include only the internal breast region, as seen in Fig. 4(d).

The final stage of the digital image processing is the application of some morphological operations that allow us to isolate the possible abnormal masses. Basically, a dilatation operation is applied to the segmented breast to increase

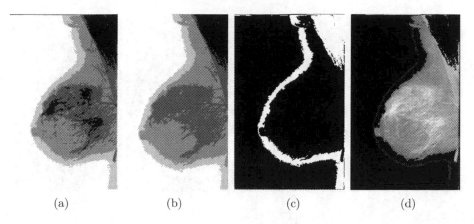

(a)   (b)   (c)   (d)

Fig. 4. Breast segmentation in a mammogram: *(a)* Otsu segmentation, *(b)* filling operation, *(c)* convex envelope, and *(d)* segmented breast.

its contrast (see Fig. 5(a)). Next, the processing suppresses the structures in the image that are darker than their surroundings and connected to the image border, as shown in Fig. 5(b). This operation tends to reduce the overall intensity level of the image, in addition to suppress border structures. Finally, a erosion operation is applied, followed by a new segmentation by thresholding, as shown in Fig. 5(c, d). Figure 5(d) is the input to the feature extraction stage, since this last image shows the possible abnormal masses in the mammogram.

3.3 Feature Extraction

In this work were tested various combinations of possible features that can be obtained from the last image in which the breast abnormalities are isolated. However, since the main objective of this work is to simplify the computer-assisted diagnosis system, only three features that produce excellent results have been chosen. In summary, the selected features are:

- The number of pixels contained in the segmented areas.
- The average intensity of the pixels contained in that segmented areas.
- The variance of the intensity of the pixels contained in the segmented areas.

These three features are normalized in order to be presented to the machine learning algorithms, keeping simple and efficient the proposed classifier. In general, a positive diagnosis of breast cancer is associated to a small number of pixels in the segmented areas, with a high average of the pixel values (*i.e.*, mainly white pixels), and a small variance of them (*i.e.*, uniform color).

3.4 Machine Learning Algorithms

In order to validate which machine learning algorithm is more effective classifying the mammograms, four of the most fast algorithms have been tested in this work, namely:

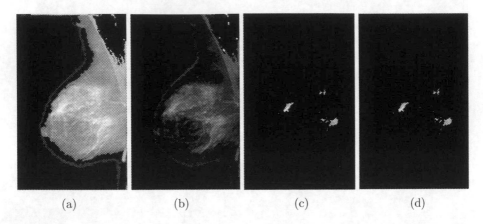

(a)   (b)   (c)   (d)

Fig. 5. Morphological operations in a mammogram: *(a)* dilatation operation, *(b)* removal of image surroundings, *(c)* erosion operation, and *(d)* final segmented image.

- Naive Bayes (Bayes).
- Artificial neural networks (ANN).
- Decision trees (DT).
- k-nearest neighbors (kNN).

The evaluation of all these algorithms is done through a 10-fold cross validation approach [5]. In this way, because there is a small number of examples for training (*i.e.*, 236), the statistical significance of the results is guaranteed using the average value of 10 random training processes [20].

It is also important to consider that in function of the results of the 10-fold cross validation, the parameters of the considered machine learning algorithms were optimized to improve their performance. In particular, the ANN implements a single hidden layer with 10 neurons, the DT is a binary decision-tree without pruning, and the kNN algorithm uses $k = 3$ and Euclidean distance.

4   Results and Discussion

The CAD system described in the previous section was implemented in Matlab, as this platform offers important functions for digital image processing and machine learning. Currently, the Matlab implementation includes 3 free parameters related to the segmentation process:

- The number of quantization levels used by the Otsu segmentation (OQL).
- The convex envelope definition value (*Solidity*).
- The erosion threshold (*Threshold*).

All these 3 parameters have been varied throughout the different machine learning techniques to find the best combination in each case. In particular, the number of quantization levels was varied between 1 and 10, the convex envelope

Table 1. Best combination of parameters that produces the maximum accuracy and lowest training time for the different machine learning algorithms.

Algorithm	OQL	Solidity	Threshold	Accuracy	Training time
Bayes	2	0.3	0.3	98.3%	0.20 s
ANN	1	0.7	0.5	98.7%	6.12 s
DT	1	0.1	0.2	99.2%	0.65 s
kNN	1	0.1	0.3	99.2%	0.36 s

Table 2. Confusion matrices for the four machine learning algorithms with $N = 236$ samples.

Bayes	$N = 236$	Predicted: healthy	Predicted: cancer
	Actual: healthy	$TN = 93$	$FP = 2$
	Actual: cancer	$FN = 2$	$TP = 139$
ANN	$N = 236$	Predicted: healthy	Predicted: cancer
	Actual: healthy	$TN = 94$	$FP = 1$
	Actual: cancer	$FN = 2$	$TP = 139$
DT	$N = 236$	Predicted: healthy	Predicted: cancer
	Actual: healthy	$TN = 95$	$FP = 0$
	Actual: cancer	$FN = 2$	$TP = 139$
kNN	$N = 236$	Predicted: healthy	Predicted: cancer
	Actual: healthy	$TN = 94$	$FP = 1$
	Actual: cancer	$FN = 1$	$TP = 140$

definition value was modified between 0.1 and 0.9, and the erosion threshold was also varied between 0.1 and 0.9.

Although there are several combinations of parameters that give us high accuracy rates, the combination of parameters that minimize the training time was selected. The values selected for these parameters and the accuracy obtained as a function of the machine learning algorithm are presented in the Table 1. As it can be seen, DT and kNN are the best algorithms, since they present an accuracy of 99.2% with a quite reduced training time. Note also that ANN have the longest training time without necessarily improving its classification accuracy.

On the other hand, Table 2 presents the complete confusion matrices for all the four machine learning models. It can be seen that the number of incorrect classifications, in all the cases, varies between 2 and 4 in the 236 analyzed examples. However, as established in any other medical diagnosis applications, the number of FN has a significant relevance in this application. In this particular case, the number of FN varies in the range of 1 to 2. Although the number of FP also matters, automatic medical diagnosis normally is a previous step for more sophisticated medical exams.

Table 3. Sensitivity, specificity and precision for the four machine learning algorithms evaluated in this work.

Algorithm	Sensitivity	Specificity	Precision
Bayes	98.6%	97.9%	98.6%
ANN	98.6%	98.9%	99.3%
DT	98.6%	100%	100%
kNN	99.3%	98.9%	99.3%

Based on the confusion matrices in Table 2, Table 3 presents the values of sensitivity, specificity and precision for the four machine learning models. As mentioned, the value of sensitivity depends on the value of FN and represents an important metric for medical diagnosis applications. It can be seen that in addition to have an accuracy of 99.2%, kNN also shows a sensitivity of 99.3%. The other models reach a sensitivity of 98.6%.

Finally, Fig. 6 shows the receiver operating characteristic curve of the kNN model. It is important to mentions that the other 3 ROC curves are quite similar, since the values of accuracy, sensitivity and specificity are very close. The area under the curve or predictive capability of the model for this case is approximately 99%.

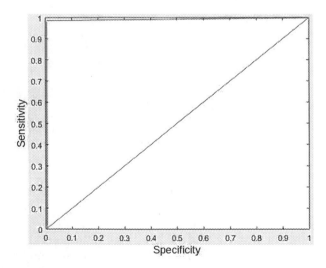

Fig. 6. The ROC curve for the kNN model.

5   Conclusions

This paper has proposed a simple but efficient computer-assisted diagnosis system for detecting breast cancer. This system uses digital signal processing and machine learning algorithm for the automatic screening of cancer in mammograms. This proposal could be used in underdeveloped countries to detect breast cancer with high accuracy and sensitivity, while requiring a minimal processing capacity.

Basically, this work has evaluated four machine learning algorithms, showing that the digital image processing techniques are robust enough to achieve similar classification performances using the four studied algorithms. In summary, the accuracy and sensitivity metrics for the proposed CAD system are above 99%, ensuring an effective mammogram screening.

We look forward to work with more mammogram databases in the near future, increasing the number of training samples and the resolution of such mammograms. We also plan to compare these simple machine learning algorithms with more sophisticated classification techniques based on deep learning.

References

1. Andrade, F., Carrera, E.V.: Supervised evaluation of seed-based interactive image segmentation algorithms. In: 2015 20th Symposium on Signal Processing, Images and Computer Vision (STSIVA), pp. 1–7. IEEE (2015)
2. Arora, R., Rai, P.K., Raman, B.: Deep feature-based automatic classification of mammograms. Med. Biol. Eng. Comput. **58**(6), 1199–1211 (2020)
3. Azamjah, N., Soltan-Zadeh, Y., Zayeri, F.: Global trend of breast cancer mortality rate: a 25-year study. Asian Pac. J. Cancer Prev. (APJCP) **20**(7), 2015 (2019)
4. Bishop, C.M.: Pattern Recognition and Machine Learning. Springer, New York (2006)
5. Bonaccorso, G.: Machine Learning Algorithms. Packt Publishing Ltd., Birmingham (2017)
6. Bouarara, H.A.: A computer-assisted diagnostic (CAD) of screening mammography to detect breast cancer without a surgical biopsy. Int. J. Softw. Sci. Comput. Intell. (IJSSCI) **11**(4), 31–49 (2019)
7. Carioli, G., Malvezzi, M., Rodriguez, T., Bertuccio, P., Negri, E., La Vecchia, C.: Trends and predictions to 2020 in breast cancer mortality in Europe. Breast **36**, 89–95 (2017)
8. Carrera, E.V., Ron-Domínguez, D.: A computer aided diagnosis system for skin cancer detection. In: Botto-Tobar, M., Pizarro, G., Zúñiga-Prieto, M., D'Armas, M., Zúñiga Sánchez, M. (eds.) CITT 2018. CCIS, vol. 895, pp. 553–563. Springer, Cham (2019). https://doi.org/10.1007/978-3-030-05532-5_42
9. Dougherty, E.R.: Digital Image Processing Methods. CRC Press, Boca Raton (2020)
10. Escobar, J.A.M.: Clasificación de mamografías usando la función de base radial de rango tipo M. Master's thesis, Instituto Politécnico Nacional, Mexico, March 2007
11. Fatima, M., Pasha, M., et al.: Survey of machine learning algorithms for disease diagnostic. J. Intell. Learn. Syst. Appl. **9**(01), 1 (2017)

12. Gardezi, S.J.S., Elazab, A., Lei, B., Wang, T.: Breast cancer detection and diagnosis using mammographic data: systematic review. J. Med. Internet Res. **21**(7), e14464 (2019)

13. Heath, M., et al.: Current status of the digital database for screening mammography. In: Karssemeijer, N., Thijssen, M., Hendrik, J., van Erning, L. (eds.) Digital Mammography. Computational Imaging and Vision, vol. 13, pp. 457–460. Springer, Dordrecht (1998). https://doi.org/10.1007/978-94-011-5318-8_75

14. Li, Y., Chen, H., Cao, L., Ma, J.: A survey of computer-aided detection of breast cancer with mammography. J. Health Med. Inf. **4**(7), 1–6 (2016)

15. Rodríguez-Ruiz, A., et al.: Detection of breast cancer with mammography: effect of an artificial intelligence support system. Radiology **290**(2), 305–314 (2019)

16. Rose, C., Turi, D., Williams, A., Wolstencroft, K., Taylor, C.: Web services for the DDSM and digital mammography research. In: Astley, S.M., Brady, M., Rose, C., Zwiggelaar, R. (eds.) IWDM 2006. LNCS, vol. 4046, pp. 376–383. Springer, Heidelberg (2006). https://doi.org/10.1007/11783237_51

17. Sadoughi, F., Kazemy, Z., Hamedan, F., Owji, L., Rahmanikatigari, M., Azadboni, T.T.: Artificial intelligence methods for the diagnosis of breast cancer by image processing: a review. Breast Cancer Targets Therapy **10**, 219 (2018)

18. Tyagi, V.: Understanding Digital Image Processing. CRC Press, Boca Raton (2018)

19. Wang, X., Liang, G., Zhang, Y., Blanton, H., Bessinger, Z., Jacobs, N.: Inconsistent performance of deep learning models on mammogram classification. J. Am. Coll. Radiol. **17**(6), 796–803 (2020)

20. Wong, T.T., Yang, N.Y.: Dependency analysis of accuracy estimates in k-fold cross validation. IEEE Trans. Knowl. Data Eng. **29**(11), 2417–2427 (2017)

21. Zebari, D.A., Haron, H., Zeebaree, S.R., Zeebaree, D.Q.: Enhance the mammogram images for both segmentation and feature extraction using wavelet transform. In: 2019 International Conference on Advanced Science and Engineering (ICOASE), pp. 100–105. IEEE (2019)

Ethics, Security, and Privacy

The Impact of Cloud Computing and Virtualization on Business

Teresa Guarda[1,2,3,6(✉)] ⓘ, Maria Fernanda Augusto[1,2,4] ⓘ, Ismael Costa[6] ⓘ,
Pedro Oliveira[5] ⓘ, Datzania Villao[1] ⓘ, and Marcelo Leon[7] ⓘ

[1] Universidad Estatal Península de Santa Elena, La Libertad, Ecuador
[2] CIST – Centro de Investigación y Innovación en Sistemas y Telecomunicaciones,
Universidad Estatal Península de Santa Elena, La Libertad, Ecuador
[3] Algoritmi Centre, Minho University, Guimarães, Portugal
[4] BiTrum Research Group, Leon, Spain
[5] Polytechnic Institute of Bragança, Bragança, Portugal
pedrooli@ipb.pt
[6] ISLA Santarém, Santarém, Portugal
[7] Universidad Tecnológica Empresarial de Guayaquil, Guayaquil, Ecuador

Abstract. In the begin cloud computing was seen as a thing of "startup" and visionary users, but nowadays it is a reality in organizations of any sector, type and size. Investments in data centers are replaced by the consumption of IT resources from a cloud provider. There are several types of virtualization, and that essentially means the abstraction of computational resources for different purposes; one of the ways, widely used, is to create virtual machines, which simulate a complete environment with software and hardware resources for the user. Despite being a technique that has existed for a long time, the growth of cloud computing has made this concept to be widely discussed. Significant innovations in virtualization, distributed computing, high-speed communications, and IoT, have aroused more and more interest in Cloud Computing. In this sense, we will analyze and evaluate the impact of cloud computing and virtualization on organizations.

Keywords: Cloud computing · Virtualization · Business impact · Security issues

1 Introduction

Cloud computing is currently a major challenge in the management of organizations, being a technology that allows you to distribute your computing services and access them online without the need to install programs. As it does not require the installation of programs or data storage.

The emergence of Cloud Computing services has changed the economics of IT organizations. The Cloud has come to standardize and automate resources in many of the tasks performed manually, being currently a commercial success, making it clear that in the coming years it will have an indisputable role in the IT areas.

© Springer Nature Switzerland AG 2021
T. Guarda et al. (Eds.): ARTIIS 2021, CCIS 1485, pp. 399–412, 2021.
https://doi.org/10.1007/978-3-030-90241-4_31

Despite the obstacles and limitations presented by some managers, the evolution of the Cloud Computing market has been happening at an accelerated pace. Services can be accessed remotely, from anywhere and anytime. The distribution of services is done through a platform of cloud services via the Internet with a price definition according to use.

Improving resource utilization through virtualization of IT infrastructures is a priority for many companies. A successful deployment requires prior preparation to determine the appropriate component infrastructure as well as the architecture, which is also suitable.

Virtualization refers to technologies created to provide an abstraction layer between computer hardware systems and the software that runs on those systems. It is a way to hide the physical characteristics of a computational platform from users.

There are several reasons for organizations to move from traditional IT infrastructures to Cloud Computing. One of the most impactful benefits is its economy.

This change will have a profound impact on the structure cost of organizations, and therefore can have a significant effect on the creation of new businesses, and probably on the economic performance of a country.

In this paper we will analyze and evaluate the impact of cloud computing and virtualization on organizations. The document has organized in six sections. The second section present cloud computing and virtualization concepts, and security issues. The third section, analyses the relation between virtualization and cloud computing. In turn, the fourth section assesses the impact of cloud computing and virtualization on the business, identifying the advantages and disadvantages. In the last section, the conclusions has presented.

2 Background

2.1 Cloud Computing

Cloud computing is the provision of computer services (servers, storage, network, software, analysis) over the Internet to make flexible resources and scaling savings faster.

The concept of Cloud arises from the physical arrangement of the elements involved in the model. The servers that host data and applications are located in data centers of companies anywhere in the world, which led to the need for a term that abstracted this location. The term Cloud, has adopted with the meaning of a tangle of servers available via the Internet.

2.1.1 Cloud Computing Models

There are different models of cloud, and not all are suitable for all companies. These models, types, and corresponding services have evolved a lot in the last few years. Facilitating access to appropriate solutions for the different needs of companies [1].

For each organization, must be determined the type of cloud computing architecture in which the cloud services will be implemented.

In its typology, cloud computing can be classified based on the deployment model, or based on the service model offered by the provider [2] (see Fig. 1).

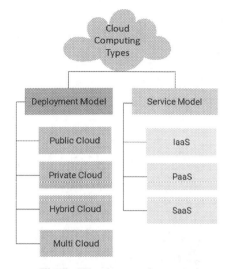

Fig. 1. Cloud computing types.

We present in Fig. 2 the deployment models. In the case of public clouds, organizations can use the cloud functionality of others that offer services to users outside the organization, which they can exploit their own purposes. In this sense, companies can outsource their services, reducing the infrastructure costs [1, 3].

Generally, private clouds propriety of the respective organization, that is, their use are dedicate to a single organization [3]. In a typical private cloud implementation, companies are committed to consolidating distributed resources and virtualizing those resources in data centers. This allows to provide a more profitable management and provide faster services [2].

Public clouds allowing companies to outsource parts of its infrastructure for cloud computing users, and that may causes the loss of control over resources, and data management, which is not a viable option for companies [3]. It is in this context that hybrid clouds appear, which, are a mix of private and public cloud infrastructures, allowing reduce costs through outsourcing, maintaining the control over sensitive data applying private cloud policies [1].

With the evolution of cloud services, and the needs of customers, Multi cloud appears. Multi cloud characterized mainly by the mixed use of various cloud services.

The multi cloud initially allowed circumventing the problems that resulted in data loss and downtime. There are some tendency to compare hybrid cloud & multi cloud systems, due to some confusion. Multi cloud refers to the administration of cloud services from multiple partners without the requirement of interconnection between the functions of the systems the hybrid cloud requires this interdependence, since the hybrid cloud structure works as a combination of private and public cloud services, so that both are integrated and interconnected, so that the service can work correctly [2].

Cloud vendors typically have a specific type of provisioning, although there is no potential restriction on not being able to offer different types at the same time [1].

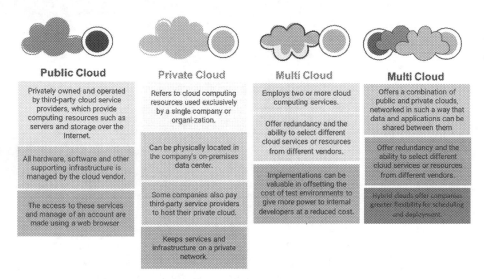

Fig. 2. Cloud computing implementation models.

Cloud Computing is the present, people are spending money on a good computer for their homes and businesses, they will hire services in the cloud to meet their needs and leave all the boring part of taking care of computer in the hands of big companies like Google, Microsoft and Amazon.

A cloud is a set of virtualized computing resources, which support a variety of different workloads, allowing them be scaled quickly through rapid provisioning of virtual machines or physical machines; provide redundant support, programming models, and self-recovery; and monitor the use of resources in real time, in order to allow the rebalancing of the assignments whenever necessary.

In the case of the service model, we have three types of services: Infrastructure as a Service (IaaS); Platform as a service (PaaS); and Software as a service (SaaS). The Infrastructure as a Service (IaaS) model is very successful in organizations. Instead of having its own server in its facilities, the organizations hires this type of service, for example, using Amazon AWS, for which you can have data or processing servers at super affordable prices.

It is important to note that the prices of infrastructure use may seem cheap; depending on the usage profile, it can be quite expensive and lead companies to seek new alternatives.

Platform (PaaS), offers a platform for development, testing, making applications available on the web for developers. It allows integration with web services, database and includes middleware as a service, message as a service, integration as a service, information as a service, and connectivity as a service. Such a layer makes it possible to meet the needs of users by providing infrastructure based on demand. For this type of service, we have Google App Engine.

Software-as-a-service (SaaS), offers implementations for specific business functions and for business specific processes, which are provide by specific cloud capabilities, that is, provide applications / services using an infrastructure (IaaS) or platform (PaaS). The same software can be used by multiple users, whether people or organizations. This type of service is performed and made available by servers in data centers that are the responsibility of a supplier company, that is, the software is developed by a company that instead of using it for exclusive benefit, makes it available at a certain cost for multiple organizations or users. In this model, users instead paying licenses for the complete software, which often has several features that we will never use, they pay for how much they use it. A classic example is Google Drive or SalesForce.

Infrastructure as a Service (IaaS), offers a platform for development, testing, making applications available on the web for developers. It allows integration with web services, database and includes middleware as a service, message as a service, integration as a service, information as a service, and connectivity as a service. This layer allows meet the needs of users by providing infrastructure based on demand.

2.1.2 Security Issues for Cloud Computing

There are several security concerns in a cloud computing technology, more specifically data security, data privacy and data safety [4].

Due to the nature of cloud computing architecture most clients are able to connect to the cloud computing via web browser or web service, which in turn means the cloud computing is vulnerable to web service attacks. Exchanging resources in a cloud-based network is done by Simple Object Access Protocol (SOAP) messages. The SOAP relies in XML signatures to secure the communication. It is then possible to attack the cloud system utilizing an XML wrapping attack. This attack consists on inserting the body of the SOAP message therefore creating a new body with the operation that the attack desires to do [5].

Browser security is another point of vulnerability for the cloud computing technology. Generally, web browser does the access to a remote cloud computing system. The user needs authorization and authentication to request services from the cloud, however web browser possess a security issue in which they can't provide XML Signature or encryption to WS-Security for authentication of an user and protect the data from users that are not authorized [6]. Another characteristic of cloud computing is the allocation of resources based on use, creating a dynamic adaption of hardware requirements to the actual workload occurring. In a security perspective, this concept can lead to several vulnerabilities. One of these is the ease of being attacked by a flooding attack or a Denial of Service attack. To perform this attack, the intruder floods the cloud computing system with non-sense requests for a service causing an increased workload for the server [5]. The cloud computing system has several more vulnerabilities than those mentioned above, which stem from the unique characteristics of the system. It is vital for the organization to be aware of the shortcomings and weak points of the cloud computing technology and prepare counter measures to mitigate the risk of utilizing this technology.

There are several data security risks in the cloud; we will are mention some of them: the APIs and unsafe protocols; Data interception; the leakage of data; public cloud storage; and virtualization [5].

Insecure APIs and security protocols can authorize access to data in the cloud. A basic cloud architecture depends on interfaces for management, orchestration and monitoring. APIs are an integral part of the security and availability of services in the cloud and specify how certain software components should interact with each other [7].

Data interception is a risk that occurs in the cloud due to the flow of data that circulates from side to side. The data in transit can be targeted by attackers, who can for example change the data. Encryption methods must be applied in order to ensure the integrity of the data that circulates between the user and the cloud [4].

Data leakage is one of the data security risks resulting from multi-use. Sharing the same computing resources by multiple users can result in accidental leakage of private data to other users. On the other hand, a system failure can allow other users or attackers to have access to the rest of the data. A security measure to counter this risk is the authentication of users before accessing data [8].

Public cloud storage is also a risk to data security, due to the sharing of computational resources between several users. One way to ensure data security is to use a private cloud for extremely sensitive data. Another way is to use a community cloud mode that adds the privacy protection module based on the Hadoop MapReduce concept. In this way, computing in the cloud will be performed based on the retention of privacy [6]. This community cloud mode consists of separating tasks; sensitive private data is disposed in the private cloud and non-sensitive data in the public cloud. The user must assign the sensitive data, otherwise the mode (community cloud based on privacy) will not do anything to the sensitive data.

Other data security risks result from virtualization, such as: compromising the functioning of the hypervisor, which can result in data exposure to other VMs. Resource allocation and deallocation also poses a risk to data security in the cloud. The careful use of resources, and the proper authentication of data before the resources are depleted are factors to be taken into account.

2.2 Virtualization

Virtualization allows to create a virtual computing environment (also known as a virtual machine), instead of running each environment on its own unique hardware. With sufficient resources (CPU, RAM, Storage) a single system can host countless guests, thus saving companies money and helping them to become more agile [9].

There are several types of virtualization, and that means the abstraction of computational resources for different purposes [10].

One of the ways, widely used, is to create virtual machines, which simulate a complete environment with software and hardware resources for the user [11]. However, the technique is quite broad and used for other purposes, such as application, desktop and server virtualization, for example.

Despite being a technique that has existed for a long time, the growth of cloud computing has made this concept to be widely discussed.

2.2.1   Types of Virtual Machines

They are virtual replicas of the entire logical component of a real computer, and it is not noticeable to the user whether a virtual machine or a physical computer is used. Regarding the kernel of a virtual machine, its system is purely logical, consisting of a series of files that store the configuration, the memory status, disk space, system logs and snapshots (small restores points) [12].

The creation and management has done by software installed on a physical machine called Hypervisor. There are two types of Hypervisors: type 1 and type 2. Hypervisors type 1 or bare metal are installed on the physical machine and consist of an operating system kernel for hypervisor functions in which it uses only the resources established for virtual machines. A good example of usage for these types of hypervisors are the servers and datacenters [13].

Hypervisors type 2 or hosted works as an application in an operating system and that allows applications to be run om the physical machine that are hosted on the virtual machines. The best example in the creation of a website, the installation of the web server is done on a virtual machine and running or testing the website on the physical machine (host) [14].

System containers, they function as an instance of the real system, called "lightvisors" because they share the same kernel as the real machine. In fact, this is one of their limitations, if we update or change libraries and frameworks the kernel remains the same [15]. There are two types of containers, system containers and application containers. Applications containers. They work creating a dedicated container for each application, being isolated form the operating system and other applications. The application requires various modules, and each module would be place in a container [16].

One of the most well known containers platforms are Dockers and Kubernetes. One great advantage of application containers is that permit the developer teams and the operations teams working at same time (devops). Docker platform nowadays supports containers of Linux systems, Windows and Mac in which with virtual machines for each System ensures that containers from different operating systems can be run on the same host operating system, containing tools that allow to integrate and interconnect the various containers to work as one. Docker's containers can run in the real System, in a virtual machine or inside the container itself [17].

The Kubernetes Platform that, in the execution of an application, creates and destroys containers according to your needs, automating the necessary configurations for the execution of the applications [18].

2.2.2   Virtualization Security

In recent years, virtualization has enjoyed considerable acceptance in companies and, more than a trend, it has become a standard in the security industry. The adoption of this technology includes benefits mainly related to the storage and processing capacities in an increasingly reduced infrastructure.

In the process of adopting and migrating to these types of solutions, several issues must be consider to keep services reliable and available. For this reason, security becomes a necessary element to mitigate digital threats, in order to prevent the functioning of virtualized systems from being impact by an eventual incident.

Digital threats can affect systems that operate in physical or virtual environments. However, for protection there are specific conditions for each environment, as well as the implementation of security measures [19]. Especially if we consider that the management of virtualized systems works from a hypervisor.

The hypervisor is the software that allows imitating the hardware on which the virtual machines are running, in such a way that it can work directly on the hardware of the physical equipment or on an operating system. Regardless of how it works, the risks can be hidden. It is possible to identify threats that escape the virtual environment, as in the case of Venom, a vulnerability that allowed a cybercriminal or a malicious program to leave the environment of a virtual machine and affect the host computer or other virtual machines, running on the equipment [20].

The vulnerability was present in the hypervisor's source code, considering that the flaw could affect the main operating systems found in virtual environments. The vulnerability corresponded to an overflow of data, after sending data from specially modified parameters to the hypervisor controller, which would allow the execution of arbitrary code and gain access to the system.

In addition, if the hypervisor is running on an operating system, there may be greater exposure to threats that can affect not only virtualized systems, but also those that seek to affect the host operating system. In other words, you need to deal with threats that are properly focused on operating systems that have been virtualized and targeted to host systems.

Is essential to know how to deal with potentially sensitive data and code, they can affect systems. It is important to ensure, before moving to the Cloud, that the security management processes are properly defined, and that the chosen provider is able to implement them.

3   Virtualization Versus Cloud

It is easy to confuse virtualization with the cloud, mainly because both involve creating usable environments from abstract resources. However, virtualization is a technology that allows you to create multiple simulated environments or dedicated resources from a single physical hardware system, while clouds are IT environments that abstract, group and share scalable resources across a network. In short: virtualization is a technology and the cloud is an environment.

Typically, they are created to enable cloud computing, which is the execution of workloads within that system.

The cloud infrastructure can consist of a variety of elements, including bare metal, virtualization or container software, used to abstract, group and share scalable resources across a network and create the cloud [9]. At the base of cloud computing, there is a stable operating system, such as Linux. This layer gives users independence to operate in public, private and hybrid environments.

If we have access to the Intranet, the Internet or both, virtualization can be use to create clouds, although this is not the only option.

In virtualization, a software called hypervisor resides in physical hardware to abstract the machine's resources, which, in turn, made available in virtual environments, called virtual machines. These resources may include raw processing capacity, storage, or cloud-based applications containing all the resources and execution environment code required for deployment. Up to this point, it is a virtualization process, not a cloud process [15].

We could say that a cloud has created, if we have configured an IT system, and can be accessed by other computers, through a network; that contains a repository of IT resources; and that can be provisioned and scaled quickly.

Clouds provide the additional benefits of self-service access, automated infrastructure scaling and dynamic resource pools, which is the main distinction between cloud and traditional virtualization.

Virtualization has its own benefits, such as server consolidation and hardware optimization, which reduces the need to increase data center power, space and cooling. In addition, virtual machines are isolated environments and are therefore a good option for testing new applications or setting up a production environment.

Virtualization has three characteristics that make it ideal for cloud computing, which are [21] (see Fig. 3).

Partitioning	Isolation	Encapsulation
Run multiple operating systems, and many applications on one physical machine	Each virtual machine is isolated from its physical host system and other virtualized machines	A virtual machine can be represented as a single file, so that it can be easily identified based on the service it provide
Full use of server services	Isolate faults and security at the virtual machine level	Encapsulate the entire state of the virtual machine in hardware-independent files
The available resources being divided according to the needs of each one	Dynamically control CPU, disk and network resources per virtual machine	The encapsulated process could be a business service
Support high availability by clustering virtual machines	Data is not shared between one virtual container and another	Save the virtual machine state as a snapshot in time
	Guarantee service levels	Reuse or transfer whole virtual machines with a simple file copy

Fig. 3. Virtualization has three characteristics.

The more virtualized the environment, the better the results will be in the cloud deployment process. The main benefits will be the improvement of the management of the IT environment, information security and the considerable cost reduction. Because they have broad and interconnected concepts, it is necessary to analyze each of the technologies so that there is no confusion and to understand what the needs and objectives of each company have.

With virtualization, a single resource is able to behave like many. With cloud computing, different departments or companies have access to the same pool of automatically provisioned resources, through a private or public cloud, respectively.

Virtualization projects have been the focus of many IT professionals, especially those trying to consolidate servers or data centers.

Virtualizing IT resources can be toughed for organizations to increase processing power, memory, and bandwidth and storage capacity for the fewest hardware platforms possible and then allocate those resources to operating systems and applications on a time-sharing basis.

Thus, organizations will be able to reduce a significant number of physical servers; and can simply instead having multiple physical servers running, having on a single machine with multiple virtual servers. This allows IT departments to have the possibility of have more than one operating system, applications and services running on a single machine, controlled by a virtualization management console.

In this sense, infrastructure costs are fixed and constant, and not aligned with the mission of reducing complexity and problems. Reducing the number of physical devices reduces costs, energy consumption, and more free space.

Virtualization contributes to higher levels of business continuity in several ways. With the decoupling of applications, operating systems and hardware platforms, less physical device redundancy is required to serve primary machines [22]. To achieve high availability in traditional configurations, a 1:1 ratio of primary device to backup device is often required, in addition to a 1:1 ratio of software to hardware. In the virtualized environment, however, multiple servers can fail over to a set of backup servers.

This then allows for a many-to-one configuration ratio, which increases the availability of the service.

At the configuration level, virtualization sometimes comes down to simple clicks, and in server and network virtualization, companies can define their own policies, such as priority applications, request for competing resources, among others. Therefore, with fewer servers and consequent less maintenance, virtualization allows support a higher-level management, security and monitoring, allowing a better cost and efficiency ratio.

These features make virtualization and cloud computing very compatible. These two technologies are at the top of the priorities for IT professionals.

4   Impact on Business

The organization's motivation to implement and use a system in the cloud computing, it is dependent on the benefits that it may achieve.

Cloud computing providers insistently promote the change of workloads to a Cloud environment, as a fundamental factor for cost reduction that they justify with the elimination of the expenses of buying hardware and software.

Cloud computing represents a paradigm shift in the way information technology services are invented, developed, deployed, scaled, updated, maintained, and paid for [23].

To develop more efficient and sustainable processes and operations, the focus of business organizations will be directed to their core business. In this way, organizations will be able to achieve excellence business success [24]. Cloud Computing has become a fact of existence essentially originated by 3 factors, the rapid technological evolution, changing concepts at the management executive level and the accessibility of abundance figuring limits to giants like Google or Amazon [25]. The ease of adaptation and use, sharing and cooperation, protection and security, reliability, and minimization of costs, are characteristics of high relevance at the time of decision by business organizations for solutions based on cloud computing [26, 27].

The reduced cost, unlimited scalability, flexibility, better mobility, improved communication, reliability, increased storage, easier updates, disaster recovery, security, can be identified as the main benefits of cloud computing. These benefits are at the basis of the motivation of business organizations to migrate their local infrastructure to a cloud computing solution. Instead of building their own infrastructure, organizations prefer to take advantage of the services offered by cloud computing. This solution is an important help to achieve business goals, allowing increasing revenue and having a positive impact on business organizations. However, there are also challenges to be faced, some of which are interoperability, security and privacy in the cloud, sensitive data, and portability, imprisonment of suppliers, organizational aspects, and regulatory and legal restrictions. Using encryption techniques, alternate backups, hiring qualified and experienced professionals, subcontracting security services, investing in education, adequate selection of cloud providers, auditing the services present in the cloud and selective migration of business applications, will be some of the solutions to follow by business organizations to overcome the challenges of migration to cloud computing [28].

In OECD countries (Organization for Economic Cooperation and Development), small and medium-sized business organizations (SMEs) account for approximately 2 thirds of total employability (60–70%). These organizations (SMEs) represent 95% of all business organizations. For these organizations, cost reduction or the economic factor will not be the most relevant factors to consider when migrating to a cloud solution. On the other hand, the factors "Ease of use and convenience" and "security and privacy" are the most important facts for this migration. Cloud computing is having a real impact on SMEs, slowly infiltrating the business strategy in the present and in the near future [29].

According to a Gartner study published in 2020, cloud technology will continue its growth as organizations continues to move to distributed, hyper scale, and hybrid solutions in cloud. The crisis of COVID-19 and the consequent technological needs, have led to greater investments in IT by business organizations, thus accelerating the migration to the cloud. These investments represented 9.1% already in 2020 and, according to the consultant's projection; they will represent 14.2% of the total investments of the organizations in 2024. In 2025, transformational business models will be adopted in more than 50% of organizations. These models will be implemented through solutions based on distributed cloud, located anywhere of choice. Compared to less than 1% in 2020, the consultant also predicts that by the end of the year 2023, hyperscale cloud providers will manage 20% of installed edge computing platforms [30].

Boosting greater efficiency in the use of data and system resources, the virtualization layer must adapt its state over time according to the resources available, thus overlapping some activities and decisions specific to the management of organizations. The requests made by the customer are translated into actions sent to the virtualization system, which implies a close and strong coordination between this system and the organizations' own management system. These two systems are difficult to separate, and their effective functioning is dependent on their joint treatment. A virtualization layer should be one of the components of the organization's management system, with its own assessment, advice, and action resources [31]. Solving several complex problems and providing a superior computing experience, this type of technological solution will have a high impact on SMEs, considering that it allows a reduction in hardware, administration, and system maintenance costs. Virtualization should therefore be considered as an important component of the organization's management, enhancing its success and sustainability. According to the Mordor Intelligence consultant report published in January 2021, the desktop virtualization market represented a volume of $ 6.712,8 million in 2020. The same consultant predicts that a volume of US $ 12.290,22 million will be reached in 2026, with a CAGR growth of 10.6% over the forecast period (2021–2026) [32].

5 Conclusions

With Cloud Computing, it will also be possible to have equipment operating more efficiently and, therefore, less expensive than in traditional organizations' environments.

However, the benefits of Cloud Computing are not that obvious. The savings provided by the Computing Cloud, as well as the increase in efficiency, would depend on many factors: the intensity of the workload, the frequency with which the application will be use in the coming years, the necessary storage capacity, among others. It also depends on the approach and the previous study done by the organizations in order to meet what they really want and thus facilitate a smooth migration.

In general, companies are moving to the Cloud at a good pace, starting a giant tide that multiplies the number of new implementations. Hiring paid cloud computing services according to the user's needs becomes a good solution. The systems adapt to the requirements of the business. Among the main suppliers, Google, Microsoft and Amazon can be highlight, offering a wide range of solutions for organizations.

Migrating to the Cloud Computing is a complex evolution for many companies, and it is essential that IT companies and executives are align with the initiatives. It is necessary to carry out a preliminary study of the real organization's needs, and how it is going to do, so it is therefore important to prepare IT professionals for such a change. Only then and being properly prepared, an organization can remove the due performance from the Cloud Computing.

Moving a company's workloads to the Cloud Computing is see as a factor in reducing costs. At a minimum, it eliminates the capital expenditures necessary to purchase equipment and software. The savings provided in the Cloud Computing will depend on many factors: the intensity of the workload, the frequency with which the application will be used in the coming years, the storage capacity required and the software licensing costs.

References

1. Frantsvog, D., Seymour, T., John, F.: Cloud computing. Int. J. Manag. Inf. Syst. (IJMIS) **16**(4), 317–324 (2012)

2. Senyo, P.K., Addae, E., Boateng, R.: Cloud computing research: a review of research themes, frameworks, methods and future research directions. Int. J. Inf. Manage. **38**(1), 128–139 (2018)
3. Varghese, B., Buyya, R.: Next generation cloud computing: new trends and research directions. Futur. Gener. Comput. Syst. **79**, 849–861 (2018)
4. Gupta, A., Thakur, S.: Cloud computing: its characteristics, security issues and challenges. Rev. Comput. Eng. Stud. **4**(2), 76–81 (2017)
5. Zissis, D., Lekkas, D.: Addressing cloud computing security issues. Future Gener. Comput. Syst. **28**(3), 583–592 (2012)
6. Venkatesh, A., Eastaff, M.S.: A study of data storage security issues in cloud computing. Int. J. Sci. Res. Comput. Sci. Eng. Inf. Technol. **3**(1), 1741–1745 (2018)
7. Walia, M.K., Halgamuge, M.N., Hettikankanamage, N.D., Bellamy, C.: Cloud computing security issues of sensitive data. In: Research Anthology on Architectures, Frameworks, and Integration Strategies for Distributed and Cloud Computing. IGI Global, pp. 1642–1667 (2021)
8. Fu, X., Gao, Y., Luo, B., Du, X., Guizani, M.: Security threats to Hadoop: data leakage attacks and investigation. IEEE Network **31**(2), 67–71 (2017)
9. Shukur, H., Zeebaree, S., Zebari, R.Z.D., Ahmed, O., Salih, A.: Cloud computing virtualization of resources allocation for distributed systems. J. Appl. Sci. Technol. Trends **1**(3), 98–105 (2020)
10. Khalid, M.F., Ismail, B.I., Mydin, M.N.M.: Performance comparison of image and workload management of edge computing using different virtualization technologies. Adv. Sci. Lett. **23**(6), 5064–5068 (2017)
11. Feoktistov, A., et al.: Multi-agent approach for dynamic elasticity of virtual machines provisioning in heterogeneous distributed computing environment. In: International Conference on High Performance Computing & Simulation (HPCS) (2018)
12. Alqahtani, A.S., Daghestani, L.F., Ibrahim, L.F.: Environments and system types of virtual reality technology in STEM: a survey. Int. J. Adv. Comput. Sci. Appl. (IJACSA) **8**(6), 77–89 (2017)
13. Vojnak, D.T., Đorđević, B.S., Timčenko, V.V., Štrbac, S.M.: Performance comparison of the type-2 hypervisor VirtualBox and VMWare workstation. In: 7th Telecommunications Forum (TELFOR) (2019)
14. Norine, C., Shaffer, A., Singh, G.: Artifact mitigation in high-fidelity hypervisors. In: Proceedings of the 54th Hawaii International Conference on System Sciences (2021)
15. Karmel, A., Chandramouli, R., Iorga, M.: Nist definition of microservices, application containers and system virtual machines. National Institute of Standards and Technology (2016)
16. Sharma, P., Chaufournier, L., Shenoy, P., Tay, Y.C.: Containers and virtual machines at scale: a comparative study. In: 17th International Middleware Conference (2016)
17. Modak, A., Chaudhary, S.D., Paygude, P.S., Ldate, S.R.: Techniques to secure data on cloud: Docker swarm or Kubernetes? In: Second International Conference on Inventive Communication and Computational Technologies (ICICCT) (2018)
18. Shah, J., Dubaria, D.: Building modern clouds: using Docker, Kubernetes & Google cloud platform. In: IEEE 9th Annual Computing and Communication Workshop and Conference (CCWC) (2019)
19. Hashizume, K., Rosado, D.G., Fernández-Medina, E., Fernandez, E.B.: An analysis of security issues for cloud computing. J. Internet Serv. Appl. **4**(1), 1–13 (2013)
20. Abdoul-Kader, C., Chang, S.H.: A novel VENOM attack identification mechanism in cloud virtualization environment. Commun. CCISA **24**(1), 61–72 (2018)
21. Ahmed, I.: A brief review: security issues in cloud computing and their solutions. Telkomnika **17**(6), 2812–2817 (2019)

22. Sehnem, S., Campos, L.M., Julkovski, D.J., Cazella, C.F.: Circular business models: level of maturity. Manag. Decis. **57**(4), 1043–1066 (2019)
23. Srivastava, P., Khan, R.: A review paper on cloud computing. Int. J. Adv. Res. Comput. Sci. Softw. Eng. **8**(6), 17–20 (2018)
24. Khan, S.: Cloud computing paradigm: a realistic option for the business organizations -a study. J. Multi Disc. Eng. Technol. **12**(2), 85–97 (2018)
25. Rajaraman, V.: Cloud computing. Resonance **19**(3), 242–258 (2014)
26. Devasena, C.L.: Impact study of cloud computing on business development. Oper. Res. Appl. Int. J. **1**, 1–7 (2014)
27. Viswanathan, S.: A study on influence of cloud computing on business developments. Int. J. Pure Appl. Math. **118**(18), 3637–3643 (2018)
28. Dar, A.: Cloud computing-positive impacts and challenges in business perspective. Int. J. Comput. Sci. Eng. **7**(1), 786–789 (2019)
29. Gupta, P., Seetharaman, A., Raj, J.R.: The usage and adoption of cloud computing by small and medium businesses. Int. J. Inf. Manage. **33**(5), 861–874 (2013)
30. Gartner: Gartner Forecasts Worldwide Public Cloud End-User Spending to Grow 18% in 2021, 17 September 2020. https://www.gartner.com/en/newsroom/press-releases/2020-11-17-gartner-forecasts-worldwide-public-cloud-end-user-spending-to-grow-18-percent-in-2021. Accessed 28 Mar 2021
31. Sven, G., Ralf, K., Vijay, M., Jim, P., Sahai, A., Aad van, M.: Impact of virtualization on management systems. Hewlett-Packard Laboratories, 1501 Page Mill Road, Palo Alto, CA 94304, USA (2003)
32. Mordor Intelligence, Desktop Virtualization Market - Growth, Trends, Covid-19 Impact, DND Forecasts (2021–2026) (2021). https://www.mordorintelligence.com/industry-reports/desktop-virtualization-market-industry. Accessed 28 Mar 2021

Use of Social Networks and Other Digital Platforms as Tools for Education. Systematic Literature Review

Tatyana K. Saltos-Echeverría[1](✉), Silvia Arciniega[1], Daisy Imbaquingo[1,2], and José Jácome[1]

[1] Universidad Técnica del Norte, Avenida 17 de julio y Gral., José María Córdova 100150, Imbabura, Ecuador
{tksaltos,deimbaquingo}@utn.edu.ec

[2] Universidad Nacional de La Plata, La Plata Calle 1 y 50, 1900 Buenos Aires, Argentina

Abstract. Social networks are increasingly used in education due to their great potential to support the teaching-learning process. Student participation in face-to-face environments, in some cases, is diminished by a lack of confidence and self-esteem, that is why using social networks is an effective way to decrease frustration, isolation, and loneliness of the students. The objective of this research is to carry out a systematic descriptive and literature study. This study focuses on the investigation of the main benefits and identification of the use of social networks and digital platforms, such as Virtual Learning Environments (VLE), at university education. 52 scientific and review articles from the last 15 years are studied and analyzed from 5 bibliographic databases: Scopus, EBSCO, ScienceDirect, ERIC, and Dialnet, which answer three research questions. The results obtained present the benefits of social networks in universities as the most-used social network and technological platforms in this field.

Keywords: Social networks · education · Digital platforms · Learning

1 Introduction

Currently, knowledge and technology advance quickly and efficiently, generating a new interaction between human beings using fast, global, and mobile media [1]. In this context, this research shows the benefits of using social networks and digital platforms in education.

The Internet has become a considerable communication tool, which appeared at the beginning of the 21st century [2]. WEB 2.0, a term promoted by Tim O´Really, has generated two main aspects in the evolutionary process: the ability to make the most of collective intelligence and the creation of content produced in a collaborative sense by users [3]. Thus, WEB 2.0 allows the exchange of information between users, as can be seen in the most relevant emerging social networks today, such as Facebook (2004) and Twitter (2006) [4]. Social networks and other WEB 2.0 technologies use in the educational field, and it constitutes an essential part of students' lives, from ages 12 and

© Springer Nature Switzerland AG 2021
T. Guarda et al. (Eds.): ARTIIS 2021, CCIS 1485, pp. 413–429, 2021.
https://doi.org/10.1007/978-3-030-90241-4_32

up [5]. In the same way [6, 7] point out that they have a significant influence in modern society, becoming progressively part of the lives of individuals on a daily.

WEB 2.0 presents more and more possibilities to increase virtual education regardless of whether it is developed in an e-learning or b-learning modality, incorporating various technological tools, social networks, and digital platforms, mainly used for educational purposes. There are cases of students who become discouraged and abandon their studies because they have a feeling of isolation and loneliness due to the technological restrictions they present in their learning [8].

Social Networking Sites (SNS) have improved the learning process because students have increased their well-being, social interactivity, and skills [9]. In the same way, according to [10], SNS allows the creation and exchange of user-generated content, aggregation of knowledge and information, as well as its subsequent revision [11]. Likewise [12] considers social networks as "constructivist tools" that support the interaction between students and teachers. Social networks that are transforming academic practices in higher education are gradually being adopted, including general-purpose social networking sites such as Facebook, Twitter, and Instagram, or video-sharing media like YouTube and content creation services as blogs or wikis or those research-oriented social networks like Research Gate [13].

Facebook and Twitter are the most used social networks in universities [2]. Students have a positive perception regarding using Facebook as a learning support tool. Facebook is the most popular and used social network with more than 1.49 billion users worldwide. Twitter is used in university classrooms, and its benefits are allowing students to search for and share content, fostering relationships with their peers, improving social presence and interaction between students [14]. The use of YouTube to support teaching practice is increasing, as is the case of the study carried out by [15], in the use of YouTube in anatomy education, which has a positive impact improving the instruction of the subject, as well as, represents an opportunity in the teaching of the new generations.

The purpose of this work is to carry out a Systematic Review of Literature (SLR), contemplating the personalization phase with search Google Scholar, of articles selected by the research team for a better approach to identify the main benefits of using social networks as tools for higher education and other digital platforms. The methodology used in this study for the preparation of the SLR is detailed below.

2 Materials and Methods

This research is quantitative, qualitative, and descriptive, focused on the analysis of the main benefits and identifying the use of social networks and digital platforms as Virtual Learning Environments (EVA) in university education. The search for articles is carried out in 5 bibliographic databases: Scopus, ScienceDirect, Eric, Ebsco, and Dialnet. Scientific and Review articles are selected and analyzed from the main quartiles: Q1, Q2, Q3, Q4, equally indexed and non-indexed articles but relevant to the study are collected considering the last 15 years. An article search in Google Scholar was added, which the research team determined necessary to cover more articles to improve the quality of research in the universe proposed for this study.

The methodology applied for the study focuses on the search for information related to the use of social networks for educational purposes and their benefits and which social network and digital platform are the most used in this field. The study includes a Systematic Literature Review [16], who quotes [17–19] and search on Google Scholar added that the research team considers necessary to cover more articles to improve the quality of research the universe proposed for this study. The review process is presented in Fig. 1, composed of four phases: (I) Research Questions, (II) search for documents, (III) selection of articles, (IV) extraction of relevant data. Each of the phases is explained below: The methodology used in this study for the preparation of the SLR is detailed below.

2.1 Research Questions

For the development of this study, three research questions (PI) are established, Table 1, which constitute the guidelines for the review process on the study topic. In Table 1 describes the SLR research questions.

Table 1. Research questions (RQ)

N°	Research questions	Motivation
PI1	¿What are the benefits of using social networks in the university educational environment?	Identify the benefits of using social networks in education
PI2	¿What social networks are used in the educational field?	Identify the social networks used in education
PI3	¿What digital platforms are used in education?	Know the digital platforms that are used in education

2.2 Research Questions

Text strings used to search for documents such as Social networking sites ("SNS" "OR Education") AND ("SNS and Learning") OR (SNS and Education and students) OR (Virtual platforms and SNS) OR (Facebook and Higher education) AND (SNS and Higher

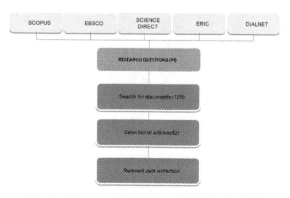

Fig. 1. Diagram of the protocol used in the SLR

Table 2. Search strings used in scientific databases

Criterion	Scopus	EBSCO	Science direct	ERIC	DIALNET
Search strings	(("SNS" OR "Education") AND ("SNS and Learning"))	(SNS) and (Students behaviour) (Higher Education and (SNS) (Facebook and Higher Education)	(SNS and Education and students) SNS and Facebook and higher education	(SNS and Education) And (SNS and Platforms) (SNS and Higher Education) And (Facebook and Higher Education)	(Virtual platforms and SNS) and (Facebook and Higher education)
Total	51	21	11	12	14

Education). Auxiliary words like SNS, digital platforms, Facebook, and Education are selected to obtain more documents in different bibliographic databases, as seen in Fig. 1.

Table 2 presents the search strings in each database and the combinations used, considering that the databases have different search criteria and capabilities. A total of 109 documents were obtained, found in the databases, 51 belong to Scopus, 21 to EBSCO, 11 to ScienceDirect, 12 to ERIC, and 14 to Dialnet. Table 2 shows the search string of articles investigated for the writing of the SLR.

The search strings consulted for each database are sectioned. In the SCOPUS database, information regarding the use of Social Networking Sites. While at EBSCO the search chain focuses on the behavior of students regarding the use of SNS for educational purposes, the use of Facebook, and Universities. In ScienceDirect, the search accentuates the usage of SNS in education and students and the use of Facebook and universities. Finally, Dialnet highlights the search for Virtual Platforms and SNS, as well as Facebook and universities. In consensus with the research team, the bibliographic databases to be consulted are agreed upon.

2.3 Selection of Articles

For the selection of articles, we consider three stages. In the first phase, take into consideration the criteria of inclusion and exclusion. The inclusion criteria considered by the authors are (i) Scientific articles, (ii) literature reviews, and other indexed and non-indexed articles but relevant to the study. All the works are related to the field of study of computer science and engineering (Computer Science e Engineering), and education, published during the last 15 years (2005–2020) in English and Spanish languages. The exclusion criteria considered by the authors are (i) duplicate works, (ii) chapters of books, (iii) thesis, (iv) studies published in other areas of knowledge.

Regarding the second phase, criteria related to search strings are considered to give greater importance to the Systematic Literature Review (SLR) and respond to the three research questions posed. The documents researched are ordered by year of publication, the title, abstract, and keywords are initially analyzed. Finally, in a third phase, the sections of the publications corresponding to the Introduction and Conclusions are reviewed to verify if the information contained contributes and is related to the proposed RQs. The total number of documents recovered after applying the three phases are presented in Table 3.

Table 3. Selection of articles for the SLR.

Database	Phase I	Phase II	Phase III
Scopus	51	23	21
EBSCO	21	9	8
Science Direct	11	5	5
Eric	12	6	4
Dialnet	14	14	14
Total	109	57	52

2.4 Extraction of Relevant Data

Table 4 shows the 52 articles finally selected, which were reviewed again by the four members of the research team, who verified the filtration and selection of the articles. If the papers answered more than one of the RQs, they grouped into a single collection for a better study and interpretation of the results and discussion. The data extracted from the articles obtained considering the PI. Firstly, researchers identified the benefits and advantages of social networks in education, then distinguished the most used social networks in education, and finally, recognized the platforms used in this field. Table 4 shows the detail of the 52 finally selected scientific articles:

Table 4. Selected articles for SLR

Code	Title	Bibliographic data base	Year
A1	Social networking sites and cognitive abilities: ¿Do they make you smarter?	Eric	2013
A2	Teaching and learning 24/7 using Twitter in a university classroom: Experiences from a developing country	Dialnet	2016
A3	A theoretical model of intentional social action in online social networks	ScienceDirect	2010
A4	Social networks, communication styles, and learning performance in a CSCL community	Ebsco	2007
A5	Social networks as motivation for appendix: the opinion of teenagers	Dialnet	2016
A6	Exploring the views of students on the use of Facebook in university teaching and learning	Eric	2014
A7	Understanding students' perceptions of the benefits of online social networking use for teaching and learning	Scopus	2015
A8	The social exchange that produces lanes in Venezuelan education	Scopus	2018
A9	Social networking sites and learning in international relations: The impact of platforms	Ebsco	2019
A10	Social Networks as a New University Venue	Scopus	2019
A11	Predicting Student Performance Based on Online Study Habits: A Study of Blended Courses	Scopus	2019
A12	Training of professors for the European Higher Education Department	Dialnet	2012

(continued)

Table 4. (*continued*)

Code	Title	Bibliographic data base	Year
A13	The social networks applied to the formation	Scopus	2015
A14	Gender differences in using social networks	Eric	2011
A15	Social Networks and Information Technology and Communication in Education: collaborative approximation, gender differences, age and preferences	Scopus	2016
A16	Use of social networks as well as adoption strategies. Educ Educational transformation?	Ebsco	2011
A17	Facebook as virtual classroom – Social networking in learning and teaching among Serbian students	Ebsco	2015
A18	An education in Facebook	Eric	2012
A19	A multi-stakeholder view of social media as a supporting tool in higher education: An educator–student	Scopus	2019
A20	Social networks as an associate professor: analysis of the use of facebook in university docencia	Ebsco	2012
A21	Using Twitter for Education: Beneficial or Simply a Waste of Time?	ScienceDirect	2017
A22	Social networks to promote motivation and learning in higher education from the students' perspective	Scopus	2019
A23	An Analytical Study of the Use of Social Networks for Collaborative Learning in Higher Education	Scopus	2017
A24	The application of physics e-handout assisted by PBL model use Edmodo to improve critical thinking skills and ICT literacy of high school student	Scopus	2020
A25	Edmodo as Web-Based Learning to Improve Student's Cognitive and Motivation in Learning Thermal Physics	Scopus	2018
A26	The effect of Edmodo social learning network on Iranian EFL learners writing skill	Scopus	2018
A27	A content analysis in the studies of YouTube in selected journals	ScienceDirect	2013

(*continued*)

Table 4. (*continued*)

Code	Title	Bibliographic data base	Year
A28	University students explore social media and education as a means of adoption	Scopus	2020
A29	Blogs like virtual engagement and upgrading in Higher Education	Dialnet	2015
A30	The social networks as an educational environment in the formation of the professional university	Scopus	2019
A31	Implementation of an educational platform in an institution of higher middle level as well as in their docent activities	Dialnet	2015
A32	The technological platforms in the contemporary university	Ebsco	2016
A33	Comparative Analysis of Virtual Educational Platforms Moodle and Docs	Dialnet	2013
A34	Methodology for instructional design in b-learning mode from educational Communication	Dialnet	2017
A35	Virtual upgrade platforms, an offer for online educational investigation	Dialnet	2015
A36	Evaluation of induction by means of online line-up platforms by UNED students	Dialnet	2015
A37	Use of educational platforms and their impact on practical pedagogy in Institutions of Higher Education in San Luis Potosí	Dialnet	2017
A38	Experimenting learning platforms	Dialnet	2016
A39	The use of DOKEOS e-learning platform in a Moroccan Business School	Scopus	2014
A40	Importance of the Dokeos platform for teaching histology	Scopus	2015
A41	A fundamentals of financial accounting course multimedia teaching system based on dokeos and Bigbluebutton	Scopus	2018
A42	Interactive e-learning through second life with blackboard technology	Science Direct	2015
A43	Adaptive learning in Moodle: three practical cases	Dialnet	2015
A44	Evaluating the Usability and accessibility of LMS "Blackboard" at King Saud University	Scopus	2016

(*continued*)

Table 4. (*continued*)

Code	Title	Bibliographic data base	Year
A45	Indicators for evaluating the level of satisfaction with the use of blackboard	Ebsco	2016
A46	A blackboard system for generating poetry	Ebsco	2016
A47	Didactic possibilities of Moodle tools to produce courses and educational materials	Scopus	2015
A48	The effects of a flipped classroom approach on class engagement and skill performance in a blackboard course	Scopus	2017
A49	Interacción comunicativa con Blackboard Collaborate y el rendimiento académico en estudiantes de educación a distancia	Dialnet	2016
A50	A Study about Using E-learning Platform (Moodle) in University Teaching Process	Science Direct	2015
A51	Use of Moodle in business management teaching-learning processes: new student profile in the EEES	Scopus	2015
A52	Analysis of the Blackboard platform in the implementation of the semi-face-to-face course (b-learning) at the UAEH	Dialnet	2015

3   Results

The results obtained in each of the three research questions proposed for analysis are indicated below.

P1: ¿What are the benefits of using social media in the university educational environment?

Collaborative Work and Learning. [20] state that the use of a social network has a tangible impact on individual learning performance, and on directed self-learning as indicated (Hamid, Waycott, Kurnia, & Chang, 2015), because social networks allow interaction between the student and knowledge, who alone or with their peers discover new knowledge through collaborative work. Similarly, social networks enhance active and collaborative learning, which contributes to the acquisition of high-level cognitive skills and strategies because students must employ information localization skills, analysis, synthesis, discrimination, evaluation, construction of the message, and meta-evaluation, therefore we would be talking about metacognitive strategies [21].

Social networks provide a knowledge integration platform that contributes significantly to collaborative learning, for instance, with a collaborative writing activity on wikis to produce a "social text" that facilitates sharing action the content created by users globally [11]. Similarly, social networks link to new active and participatory method-ologies and in a particular way with collaborative work, understood as the exchange and development of knowledge by small groups of equals, aimed at achieving the same academic goals [22]. Learning at their own pace is another advantage of using social networks due to Students have at their disposal the range of materials and services made available by teachers [23]. Furthermore, Social networks in education encourage mean-ingful learning that develops critical thinking, empowers autonomous, cooperative, and collaborative work, inserting new forms of guidance and tutoring [24].

Communication and Interaction. [2] point out the usage of social networks at universi-ties facilitates communication between students and teachers, becoming didactic com-munication, consisting of the "transmission of knowledge, understanding, and dialogue in the teaching-learning" where students feel more confident and independent. In the same way [21] indicate that social networks promote, in addition to communication, the interaction between participants, which contributes to the collective construction of knowledge, and also increase connectivity [25]. On the other hand, It promotes dialogue and the creation of research communities, which allows academic development through the production of new knowledge (Ollarves et al. 2018).

In the study carried out by [26], students perceive that interaction with their peers and teachers is better with the social networks, which contributes to improving their mastery of the classes and the development of skills in the course. Critical thinking, therefore, using social networks, they can comment on the work of their colleagues, and in the same way, they await their comments. In fact, the students' fascination with social networks makes it a highly communicative didactic possibility [2]. Similarly [27] states that social networks allow the development of specific cognitive skills in students, including the interaction with peers and instructors, improvement of critical thinking, and self-control for learning. Furthermore, as indicated [28], it contributes to student identification of learning styles, providing them with new ways of participating and developing verbal skills.

P2: ¿What social networks are used in the educational field?
Several social networks found on the Internet are used currently in universities due to collaborative work open between students, contributions of experiences and knowledge, communication between peers anywhere in the world without geographical barriers [2].
Here are some of the social networks used in education:

Facebook: [11] indicate that the most used social networks are Facebook and Twitter in the educational field. For [29], Facebook is a literacy 2.0, who comes to instruct all people without distinction in the use of tools and applications of the social Web, as well as establish contacts and spontaneous social relations [30]. More than 90% of students in the US use this network as a learning aid [31]. According to [32] the main reasons universities adopt Facebook for academic purposes are collaboration, the exchange of resources, the perception of enjoyment, and social influence because it meets the needs of students in the interaction between their peers and teachers, thence affirm [33, 34].

Similarly, Facebook is used in face-to-face teaching at universities because the resources have a proactive dimension and contribute to improving student-teacher relationships since teaching is cyclical and is not limited to a schedule settled down [35].

Likewise, [27] point out that the use of Facebook for more than one year in young people between 12 and 18 years of age is a factor that enhances the development of memory, verbal ability, and spelling for a large amount of information that presented to you, you must process and manipulate it or judge it as a guide in future action.

For its part, [31] expose that Facebook uses as a virtual classroom aimed at university students, is a support tool in the execution of tasks, improving the quality of the educational process and expanding of knowledge. Similarly, the content shared on Facebook acquires a pro-activity dimension by bringing the class material closer to the student, and they do not feel the obligation to "I am going to study o I am going to visit a teaching space" on the contrary, they enter a space staff that is part of their daily activities [36].

Twitter: [1] point out that the social network Twitter was created in 2006, and it is possible to use it for educational purposes in specific activities such as homework assignments, a reminder of important dates, discussions between students, or as a system of quick questions to the teacher. In the same way [37] state that Twitters are used by teachers as a formative assessment platform to collect feedback and instant reactions from students towards teaching and learning. [38] state that the use of Twitter produces greater motivation in the student and encourages informal learning with student participation. Furthermore, Twitter is a tool that allows students to contextualize the learning results concerning the course objectives and their comprehensive knowledge in which they support each other individually or collectively [39].

YouTube uses in education for interventions with teachers and students sharing topics of interest to the audience [1]. YouTube, makes its appearance in 2005, as a leading online video-sharing destination, with great potential for the development of knowledge and mental models of technological functions in planning lessons with technology [40]. On the other hand, YouTube can improve student participation and commitment to the course and the subject of the class, as evidenced by [35] in their study during the program of marketing communication where some videos ads referring presented the topic of communication on this subject, making students feel more comfortable with participating in the field of study and the contribution to the co-creation of knowledge.

PI3: ¿What digital platforms are used in education?
Digital platforms are technological devices that help in university education, integrating various functions, which facilitates academic activity, both for teachers and students. Digital platforms are classified as free software that is free to the public; commercials have all privileges; and self-developed [41]. Below are some of the most important digital platforms:

Blackboard: Platform used in more than 60 countries since 2005 [41]. For [42], it is a software company used to manage online learning and electronic commerce; In addition, it is of great acceptance and easy use [43]. To [44], Blackboard integrates collaboration, communication, publishing and knowledge production benefits. Allows interaction in the teaching-learning process from collaborative environments based on the constructivist model [45]. Likewise, for [46], Blackboard has updated and diverse content, practical relevance of the course, in addition to the technical performance and stability of the platform. It Lets add the assumptions of Baar's Theory, which simulates the creativity platform [47]; as well as virtual classes as if they were real to attract students [48]. Inverted teaching in a Blackboard course allows students to control their self-learning, promoting better performance and using technology. In the same way [49, 50] deduce that teachers already have these valuable e-learning software for their virtual classes.

Moodle: Open source platform in the commercial system, created by MartinDougiamas, has spread since 1987 in more than 46,000 sites worldwide [51]. Provides teachers with technological tools that promote learning [52] it is a useful platform for educational uses [53]. [43] considers Moodle as software that supports teachers to create online courses, very easy to install, flexible, and personalized. For [54], Moodle has facilitated the contact of teachers with the students, generating a positive attitude in the academic development of the institutions, since a set of scenarios for the teacher and it is the software open to different training itineraries. Similarly [55, 56] point out that Moodle can encompass passive resources, assets, and asynchronous and synchronous communication tools. Moodle supports the teacher's performance in a better organization of time and content, which enables centralizing information and communication with students [57]. It is a system based on constructivist pedagogy, where knowledge can be assessed and learning facilitated [58].

Dokeos: For [52], Dokeos is a platform that allows the management, administration, and evaluation of online teaching-learning activities and is an excellent option to develop online courses. [59] states that the use of DOKEOS regarding the pedagogical content, students have a positive evaluation since they have access to study materials, such as exams and solved exercises, and the use of platforms has helped reinforce your skills and knowledge. Concerning the technical part, they have not had any difficulty accessing this platform. [60] point out that Dokeos enables communication and learning assessment in educational settings, is easy to use and is highly intuitive. In addition, it uses to monitor classroom, blended, or distance teaching. In the same way [61] states that it is an open-source network course teaching and management system it allows teachers to manage and create course websites in Explorer, Opera, and other browsers that support the world's 34 principal language interfaces.

Further, [57] describe other Anglo-Saxon digital platforms such as Coursera, EdX, UdacytyMiriadaX in the Ibero-American sphere. In this sense, [62] refer to learning platforms such as LMS (LearningManagementSystems), such as Blackboard, Moodle, and others like Canvas, Brightspace known as D2L (UniversityofWisconsinSystem, 2016), Sakaiy Schoology.

4   Discussion

As evidenced in the results of this research, universities use social networking sites as support for the teaching practice to which they have transformed it [13]. Social networks improve the students' well-being [9] because their confidence is better to comment on their points of view on the tasks developed by their classmates and expect their feedback. They also show that the interaction between teachers and their peers increases using social networks [26].

One of the most used social networks in university education is Facebook, as students have a positive perception of its use as a support tool in the academic field [2]. Universities adopt Facebook in their educational process because it has a range of possibilities for collaboration, the exchange of resources, support in the execution of tasks, improving the quality of the educational process, and expanding knowledge. [29, 31, 32] consider Facebook as a literacy 2.0 that comes to instruct all people without distinction in the use of tools and applications of the social Web, as well as establish contacts and spontaneous social relationships.

Another of the networks that incorporate as support tools in academic work is Twitter. It presents tangible benefits when students manage to establish relationships with their peers, share content, and strengthen their social presence [14], fact as point out [38], t is a social network that encourages informal learning and produces greater motivation in the student for learning. YouTube is a social network uses to support teaching practice because from any point of view is to replace a master class with a video, its contribution in the educational field is broad and can be used to strengthen the knowledge of various subjects, such as the case of the anatomy study, the results of which contribute to better subject instruction [15].

On the other hand, regarding digital platforms [44, 45], indicates that Blackboard integrates benefits of collaboration, communication, publication, and production of knowledge. As well [46], states that this platform allows interaction in the teaching-learning process from collaborative environments based on the constructivist model. According to [47], Blackboard has updated and diverse content, the practical relevance of the course, moreover to the technical performance and stability of the platform. Furthermore, it allows adding the assumptions of the Baar Theory, which stimulates creativity.

Moodle is a helpful platform in education. [63], states that it is software to support the teacher's achievement and enables them to create online courses. Similarly [54] consider that it is a medium that facilitates contact between teachers and students, which allows good academic development within higher-level educational institutions; In addition, it contains a series of passive, active, and effective asynchronous and synchronous communication resources [56].

5 Conclusions

During this research, 52 articles, published since 2010. First, the great interest of the scientific community in the use of social networks in higher education is prominent. Second, the tendency to use networks is increasingly growing both in online classes and in person. From the analysis of the research, we obtained motivating results regarding the widespread use of social networks in the teaching-learning process due to their great potential for the development of cognitive skills, including verbal, memory, critical thinking, and self-learning. Additionally, its positive contribution to significant student learning was determined, as it is an effective tool that facilitates communication and inter-action between students and teachers, according to the security and independence that is generated in the students to raise their concerns and contributions in the construction of knowledge, through social networks.

This research showed that Facebook is the most used network in the university environment. In the first place, it is a support tool in university education due to the presentation of proactive resources that contribute to the execution of students' tasks and improve the quality of the educational process. Second, it allows interaction between students and teachers who consider the enjoyment and social influence, without limited to a set schedule. Some research revealed that Twitter is an effective tool that makes it easier for students to search and share documents, fosters relationships with their peers, and improves social presence and interaction between students. Researchers consider in the same way that YouTube is a social network to support university academic activities, to strengthen the content presented by teachers through videos. On the other hand, digital platforms have a positive impact on educational action because facilitating academic activity with the support of content and courses. The results of this research show that the most widely used platform worldwide is Moodle because of its ease, flexibility, and customization.

For future research, it is proposed to study the safe use of social networks and digital platforms in education as their impact on students' academic performance.

References

1. Ollarves, M., Hernández, M., Pirela, D.: El cambio social que producen las redes en la educación venezolana. Quórum Académico **15**, 119–131 (2018)
2. Rivera-Rogel, D., Yaguache Quichimbo, J., Velásquez Benavides, A.V., Paladines Galarza, F.: Social networks as a new university venue. In: Túñez-López, M., Martínez-Fernández, V.-A., López-García, X., Rúas-Araújo, X., Campos-Freire, F. (eds.) Communication: Innovation & Quality. SSDC, vol. 154, pp. 495–513. Springer, Cham (2019). https://doi.org/10.1007/978-3-319-91860-0_30
3. O'Reilly, T.: Web 2.0 Compact Definition: Trying Again - O'Reilly Radar. http://radar.ore illy.com/2006/12/web-20-compact-definition-tryi.html. Accessed 2 Mar 2020
4. Ahmad, S., Mustafa, M., Ullah, A.: Association of demographics, motives and intensity of using Social Networking Sites with the formation of bonding and bridging social capital in Pakistan. Comput. Human Behav. **57**, 107–114 (2016). https://doi.org/10.1016/j.chb.2015.12.027
5. Greenhow, C., Askari, E.: Learning and teaching with social network sites: a decade of research in K-12 related education. Educ. Inf. Technol. **22**(2), 623–645 (2015). https://doi.org/10.1007/s10639-015-9446-9
6. Alkhathlan, A., Al-Daraiseh, A.: An analytical study of the use of social networks for collaborative learning in higher education. Int. J. Mod. Educ. Comput. Sci. 9, 1–13 (2017). https://doi.org/10.5815/ijmecs.2017.02.01.
7. Raghavendra, P., Hutchinson, C., Grace, E., Wood, D., Newman, L.: "I like talking to people on the computer": Outcomes of a home-based intervention to develop social media skills in youth with disabilities living in rural communities. Res. Dev. Disabil. **76**, 110–123 (2018). https://doi.org/10.1016/j.ridd.2018.02.012

8. Regan, K., et al.: Experiences of instructors in online learning environments: identifying and regulating emotions. Internet High. Educ. **15**, 204–212 (2012). https://doi.org/10.1016/j.iheduc.2011.12.001

9. Yu, A.Y., Tian, S.W., Vogel, D., Chi-Wai Kwok, R.: Can learning be virtually boosted? An investigation of online social networking impacts. Comput. Educ. **55**, 1494–1503 (2010). https://doi.org/10.1016/j.compedu.2010.06.015

10. Kaplan, A.M., Haenlein, M.: Users of the world, unite! The challenges and opportunities of Social Media. Bus. Horiz. **53**, 59–68 (2010). https://doi.org/10.1016/j.bushor.2009.09.003

11. Cabero, J., Barroso, J., Llorente, M.C., Yanes, C.: Redes sociales y Tecnologías de la Información y la Comunicación en Educación: aprendizaje colaborativo, diferencias de género, edad y preferencias. Rev. Educ. Distancia. 1–23 (2016) https://doi.org/10.6018/red/51/1

12. Hernández, S.: El modelo constructivista con las nuevas tecnologías : aplicado en el proceso de aprendizaje (2008). http://rusc.uoc.edu

13. Manca, S., Ranieri, M.: Yes for sharing, no for teaching! Social Media in academic practices. Internet High. Educ. **29**, 63–74 (2016). https://doi.org/10.1016/j.iheduc.2015.12.004

14. Junco, R.: Comparing actual and self-reported measures of Facebook use. Comput. Human Behav. **29**, 626–631 (2013). https://doi.org/10.1016/j.chb.2012.11.007

15. Jaffar, A.A.: YouTube: an emerging tool in anatomy education. Anat. Sci. Educ. **5**, 158–164 (2012). https://doi.org/10.1002/ase.1268

16. Pusdá-chulde, M., Salazar, F., Sandoval, L., Herrera, E., García-santillán, I., Giusti, A.: Análisis de imágenes basado en arquitecturas heterogéneas para agricultura de precisión : una revisión sistemática de literatura (2019)

17. Fernandez, A., Insfran, E., Abrahão, S.: Usability evaluation methods for the web: a systematic mapping study. Inf. Softw. Technol. **53**, 789–817 (2011)

18. Kitchenham, B., Charters, S.: Guidelines for performing systematic literature reviews in software engineering. Presented at the (2007).https://doi.org/10.1145/1134285.1134500

19. Género, M., José, C.-L., Piattini, M.: Métodos de Investigación en Ingeniería del Software. Madrid-España (2014)

20. Cho, H., Gay, G., Davidson, B., Ingraffea, A.: Social networks, communication styles, and learning performance in a CSCL community. Comput. Educ. **49**, 309–329 (2007). https://doi.org/10.1016/j.compedu.2005.07.003

21. Vázquez-Martínez, A.I., Cabero-Almenara, J.: Las redes sociales aplicadas a la formación. Rev. Complut. Educ. **26**, 253–272 (2015). https://doi.org/10.5209/rev_RCED.2015.v26.47078

22. Vázquez, A., Alducin-Ochoa, J., Marín Díaz, V., Cabero Almenara, J.: Formación del profesorado para el Espacio Europeo de Educación Superior. Aula abierta **40**, 25–38 (2012)

23. Sheshadri, A., Gitinabard, N., Lynch, C.F., Barnes, T., Heckman, S.: Predicting student performance based on online study habits: a study of blended courses. In: Proceedings of 11th International Conference on Educational Data Mining, EDM 2018 (2019)

24. Álvarez de Sotomayor, I., Muñoz Carril, P.C.: Las redes sociales como motivación para el aprendizaje: opinión de los adolescentes. Innoeduca. Int. J. Technol. Educ. Innov. **2**, 20 (2016). https://doi.org/10.20548/innoeduca.2016.v2i1.1041

25. Cheung, C.M.K., Lee, M.K.O.: A theoretical model of intentional social action in online social networks. Decis. Support Syst. **49**, 24–30 (2010). https://doi.org/10.1016/j.dss.2009.12.006

26. Hamid, S., Waycott, J., Kurnia, S., Chang, S.: Understanding students' perceptions of the benefits of online social networking use for teaching and learning. Internet High. Educ. **26**, 1–9 (2015). https://doi.org/10.1016/j.iheduc.2015.02.004

27. Alloway, T.P., Horton, J., Alloway, R.G.: Social networking sites and cognitive abilities: do they make you smarter? Comput. Educ. **63**, 10–16 (2013). https://doi.org/10.1016/j.compedu.2012.10.030

28. Pallas, J., Eidenfalk, J., Engel, S.: Social networking sites and learning in international relations: the impact of platforms. Australas. J. Educ. Technol. **35**, 16–27 (2019). https://doi.org/10.14742/ajet.3637
29. Islas Torres, C., Carranza Alcántar, M.: Uso de las redes sociales como estrategias de aprendizaje. Transformación educativa? Apert. Rev. Innovación Educ. **3**, 6–15 (2011). https://doi.org/10.18381/198
30. Mazman, S.G., Usluel, Y.K.: Gender differences in using social networks. Turkish Online J. Educ. Technol. **10**, 133–139 (2011)
31. Milošević, I., Živković, D., Arsić, S., Manasijević, D.: Facebook as virtual classroom - Social networking in learning and teaching among Serbian students. Telemat. Inform. **32**, 576–585 (2015). https://doi.org/10.1016/j.tele.2015.02.003
32. Sharma, S.K., Joshi, A., Sharma, H.: A multi-analytical approach to predict the Facebook usage in higher education. Comput. Human Behav. **55**, 340–353 (2016). https://doi.org/10.1016/j.chb.2015.09.020
33. Donlan, L.: Exploring the views of students on the use of Facebook in university teaching and learning. J. Furth. High. Educ. **38**, 572–588 (2014). https://doi.org/10.1080/0309877X.2012.726973
34. Allen, M.: An education in Facebook (2012)
35. Stathopoulou, A., Siamagka, N.T., Christodoulides, G.: A multi-stakeholder view of social media as a supporting tool in higher education: an educator–student perspective. Eur. Manag. J. **37**, 421–431 (2019). https://doi.org/10.1016/j.emj.2019.01.008
36. Túñez López, M., Sixto García, J.: Las Redes Sociales Como Entorno Docente: Análisis del Uso de Facebook en la Docencia Universitaria. Soc. Netw. Learn. Environ. Anal. Facebook Use Univ. Teach. **41**, 77–92 (2012)
37. Tang, Y., Hew, K.F.: Using Twitter for education: Beneficial or simply a waste of time? Comput. Educ. **106**, 97–118 (2017). https://doi.org/10.1016/j.compedu.2016.12.004
38. Hortigüela-Alcalá, D., Sánchez-Santamaría, J., Pérez-Pueyo, Á., Abella-García, V.: Social networks to promote motivation and learning in higher education from the students' perspective. Innov. Educ. Teach. Int. **56**, 412–422 (2019). https://doi.org/10.1080/14703297.2019.1579665
39. Chawinga, W.D.: Teaching and learning 24/7 using Twitter in a university classroom: experiences from a developing country. E-Learning Digit. Media. **13**, 45–61 (2016). https://doi.org/10.1177/2042753016672381
40. Alias, N., Razak, S.H.A., elHadad, G., Kunjambu, N.R.M.N.K., Muniandy, P.: A content analysis in the studies of YouTube in selected journals. Procedia Soc. Behav. Sci. **103**, 10–18 (2013). https://doi.org/10.1016/j.sbspro.2013.10.301
41. Arias, A., Gracia, R., Talamantes, C., Valenzuela, F.: Implementación de una plataforma educativa en una institución de nivel medio superior como apoyo en las actividades docentes, pp. 1–19 (2015)
42. González Hernando, C., Valdivieso-León, L., Velasco González, V.: Estudiantes universitarios descubren redes sociales y edublog como medio de aprendizaje. RIED. Rev. Iberoam. Educ. a Distancia **23**, (2020). https://doi.org/10.5944/ried.23.1.24213
43. Mora, F., Valero, C.: Evaluación de la inducción al uso de las plataformas de aprendizaje en línea a estudiantes de la UNED, pp. 77–88 (2015)
44. Torres, M., Hernández, S.: Análisis de la plataforma blackboard en la implementación del curso semi-presencial (b-learning) en la UAEH. Etic@net. **2**, 196–206 (2015)
45. Montenegro Díaz, D.J.: Interacción comunicativa con Blackboard Collaborate y el rendimiento académico en estudiantes de educación a distancia. Hamut'Ay **3**, 68 (2016). https://doi.org/10.21503/hamu.v3i2.1322
46. Guel González, S., Pintor Chávez, M., Gómez Zermeño, M.: Indicadores para la evaluación del nivel de satisfacción del uso de Blackboard. Campus Virtuales. **5**, 36–47 (2016)

47. Misztal-Radecka, J., Indurkhya, B.: A Blackboard system for generating poetry. Comput. Sci. **17**, 265 (2016). https://doi.org/10.7494/csci.2016.17.2.265
48. Alenezi, A.M., Shahi, K.K.: Interactive e-learning through second life with blackboard technology. Procedia Soc. Behav. Sci. **176**, 891–897 (2015). https://doi.org/10.1016/j.sbspro.2015.01.555
49. Elmaadaway, M.A.N.: The effects of a flipped classroom approach on class engagement and skill performance in a Blackboard course. Br. J. Educ. Technol. **49**, 479–491 (2018). https://doi.org/10.1111/bjet.12553
50. Alturki, U.T., Aldraiweesh, A., Kinshuck, D.: Evaluating the usability and accessibility of LMS "Blackboard" at King Saud University. Contemp. Issues Educ. Res. **9**, 33–44 (2016). https://doi.org/10.19030/cier.v9i1.9548
51. Campos, R.: Las plataformas tecnológicas en la universidad contemporánea1, vol. 1, pp. 46 57 (2016)
52. Estrada Lizárraga, R., Colado Zaldívar, A., Peraza Garzón, J.F.: Análisis Comparativo de las Plataformas Educativas Virtuales Moodle y Dokeos Análisis Comparativo de las Plataformas Educativas Virtuales Moodle y Dokeos. Rev. Iberoam. para la Investig. y el Desarro. Educ. **10**, 1–14 (2013)
53. González Morales, L.: Metodología para el diseño instruccional en la modalidad b-learning desde la Comunicación Educativa. Razón y palabra. **21**, 4–50 (2017)
54. Ramirez Valdez, W., Barajas Villarruel, J.I.: Uso de las plataformas educativas y su impacto en la práctica pedagógica en instituciones de educación superior de san luis potosí. Edutec. Rev. Electrónica Tecnol. Educ. **60**, 1–13 (2017). https://doi.org/10.21556/edutec.2017.60.798
55. Romero Díaz, J.J., Martínez, T.S., Trujillo, J.M.: Posibilidades didácticas de las herramientas Moodle para producción de cursos y materiales educativos. Digit. Educ. Rev. 59–76 (2015). https://doi.org/10.1344/der.2015.28.59-76
56. López, D., Muniesa, F., Gimeno, Á.: Aprendizaje adaptativo en Moodle: tres casos prácticos. Educ. Knowl. Soc. **16**, 138 (2015). https://doi.org/10.14201/eks201516138157
57. Padilla-Meléndez, A., del Águila-Obra, A.R., Garrido-Moreno, A.: Empleo de moodle en los procesos de enseñanza-aprendizaje de dirección de empresas: Nuevo perfil del estudiante en el eees. Educ. XX1 **18**, 125–146 (2015). https://doi.org/10.5944/educXX1.18.1.12314.
58. Oproiu, G.C.: A study about using E-learning platform (Moodle) in University teaching process. Procedia Soc. Behav. Sci. **180**, 426–432 (2015). https://doi.org/10.1016/j.sbspro.2015.02.140
59. El Khalkhali, I.: The use of DOKEOS e-learning platform in a Moroccan Business School. Int. Conf. Multimed. Comput. Syst. Proc. 633–638 (2014). https://doi.org/10.1109/ICMCS.2014.6911146
60. Vilaça, F.A., Brito, A. de S., Schimiguel, J., do Val, M.L., dos Santos, M.E.K.L.: Importância da plataforma Dokeos para o ensino de histologia. Espacios, vol. 36 (2015)
61. Han, W.: A fundamentals of financial accounting course multimedia teaching system based on dokeos and Bigbluebutton. Int. J. Emerg. Technol. Learn. **13**, 141–152 (2018). https://doi.org/10.3991/ijet.v13i05.8433
62. Juárez, A., Aguilar, A., de León, L., Alanís, J., Guerrero, S.: Experimentación de Plataformas de Aprendizaje. In: Instituto Tecnológico de Monterrey (2016)
63. Linarez, G.: Las plataformas virtuales de aprendizaje, una propuesta para la investigación educativa en línea, vol. 2 (2015)

Eliciting Preferences to Find Your Perfect Laptop: A Usability Study

Jhoan Almeida[(✉)] and Ixent Galpin

Facultad de Ciencias Naturales e Ingeniería,
Universidad de Bogotá Jorge Tadeo Lozano, Bogotá, Colombia
{jhoans.almeidac,ixent}@utadeo.edu.co

Abstract. Effective search tools are of paramount importance for users of an e-commerce site to feel confident that they are buying the right product. Most e-commerce websites that sell technological items provide a simplified Query-by-Example preference elicitation approach to enable users to search for the product that they desire by specifying constraints over criteria and filtering results. Such an interface may be adequate when the technical specification is known to the buyer. In this work, the usability of an alternative preference elicitation approach, Pairwise Comparisons, that enable users to specify trade-offs between various potentially conflicting criteria, is compared and contrasted to the traditional Query-by-Example approach.

The two approaches are evaluated by implementing two search tools that implement each preference elicitation approach to collect data about user behaviour. An experiment is carried out to evaluate performance and usability to search for laptops over a web scraped data set for varied tasks. It is found that while Query-by-Example tends to be preferred for cases where the technical specification criteria are precisely specified, the result sets generated for the Pairwise Comparisons approach are preferred when it is less clear what the criteria values should be. As such, the Pairwise Comparisons preference elicitation is deemed to be a worthwhile complementary approach for such e-commerce websites.

Keywords: Usability · Preference elicitation approaches · Pairwise comparisons · Query-by-Example

1 Introduction

Choosing which laptop to buy can be a daunting prospect. For many people, the acronyms and technical specifications may be hard to parse. Even experienced computer users are likely to find that technology has moved on since they purchased their last device, and that getting up to date with the latest developments is a cumbersome chore. To aid with this difficulty, there are numerous sites on the Web (e.g., http://www.which.co.uk or http://www.techradar.com) that purport to advise consumers about the best computers to buy, and in order to contend with the high number of products available may provide a ranking

© Springer Nature Switzerland AG 2021
T. Guarda et al. (Eds.): ARTIIS 2021, CCIS 1485, pp. 430–446, 2021.
https://doi.org/10.1007/978-3-030-90241-4_33

of models for different prices. This is often coupled with tips to take into consideration when selecting a laptop. In most cases, the purchase of a laptop has significant implications on a household budget, and it is therefore important to make the right decision.

Most e-commerce sites such as Amazon or Ebuyer incorporate search tools that assume that the purchaser knows the technical specifications of the laptop that they wish to buy (even if they do not understand them). Typically, they are presented with an interface that enables them to filter in terms of attributes that denote laptop characteristics. For example, a user may specify requirements in terms of the minimum RAM available, or screen size required, usually dictated by the anticipation of tasks that they wish to perform. As such, a user may filter for laptops whose RAM is greater than 16 GB if the laptop is required for certain memory intensive tasks. This approach, which essentially comprises a subset of the widely used *Query-by-Example* (QBE) graphical query language proposed by [16], has a demonstrated track record of being an intuitive way for users to find the information that they require [15].

However, using a filtering approach such as QBE may be less effective if a buyer is unsure about the specific threshold values that are required for certain criteria (e.g., RAM). Furthermore, trade-offs may present themselves among the various criteria associated with a laptop, and a buyer may understand the relative importance between criteria even if he/she is not able to assign threshold values for these criteria. For example, the lighter a laptop is, the fewer computing resources (in terms of memory or CPU) it is likely to have. Such nuances cannot be captured using a preference elicitation approach such as QBE. Other elicitation approaches such as Pairwise Comparisons (PCs) have been proposed [9] that enable the relative importance of pairs of criteria to be specified by a user, rather than constraints in terms of specific thresholds.

In the paper, we carry out an exploration of the effectiveness of QBE and PCs as elicitation techniques and measure factors including performance and usability. By *performance* we mean how fit-for-purpose the results obtained by the search tool are considering the requirements of the buyer. On the other hand, *usability* refers to the subjective user experience when using the search tools. For the experimentation, we consider two categories of laptop buying tasks:

- Those in which the criteria threshold values to consider are *explicit*, and thus arguably lend themselves better to the QBE approach; and
- Those in which the criteria threshold values are *implicit* (even if the relative importance between them is not), and which may therefore lend themselves better to PC elicitation.

The contributions of this paper are threefold:

1. The implementation of two web-based laptop buying search tools, one for QBE and the other one for PC, to perform data collection about performance and usability;

2. The design of an experiment to measure the performance and usability of both preference elicitation techniques, using the search tools created in (1);
3. The analysis of the data collected from the experiment in (2).

This paper is structured as follows. Section 2 presents related work. In Sect. 3, we present a description of the tools evaluated, and the associated paradigms employed by each tool. The usability experiment is described in Sect. 4. Subsequently, in Sect. 5 we describe results. We present a discussion in Sect. 6. Section 7 concludes.

2   Related Work

The importance of usability in e-commerce websites for commercial success is highlighted in several works, e.g., [7,14]. Muhtaseb *et al.* [8] identify factors such as interactivity, personalisation, privacy and security, learnability, consistency, navigation and memorability as being important characteristics to consider when designing a successful e-commerce website. Furthermore, they emphasise the importance of effective tools to "overcome decision paralysis and facilitate sales" [8].

With regards to pairwise comparisons (PCs) as an elicitation method, the verbal Saaty scale, shown in Table 1, is a widely used scale used to enable users to denote strength of preference between criteria [9]. Although this preference elicitation approach was originally conceived for the Analytic Hierarchy Process (AHP) methodology [10], it has been used as a preference elicitation more widely in diverse computing applications. A number of usability studies have been carried out to show its effectiveness in relation to other techniques. For example, Galpin *et al.* [3] and Abel *et al.* [1] show that it is able to obtain improved performance and usability in the domain of source selection (the problem in data integration whereby a subset of data sources needs to be chosen) when compared to constrained optimisation as an elicitation technique. Leon-Medina *et al.* [5] also demonstrate that they are preferred by users in the domain of data cleaning.

There has also been discussion about the effectiveness of pairwise comparisons as a preference elicitation approach in the field of recommender systems. Kalloori *et al.* [4] consider how pairwise preferences may be elicited in a Recommender System and effectively combined with absolute ratings, and demonstrate that pairwise preferences enable better recommendations to be made to users. They conclude that the most effective preference elicitation approach is inextricably linked to the user's personality. Sepliarskaia *et al.* [13] also uses relative preference questions combined with a latent factor model to improve recommendation quality.

The usability of QBE has been explored since its inception. Thomas *et al.* [15] compare three approaches: the "English-like" IQF and SQL languages, and the graphical QBE language. They find that QBE is effective as users tend to not confuse disjunctive and conjunctive queries, and easily learned by novice users. It is likely for this reason that subsets of QBE are used by search tools on e-commerce websites pervasively.

While usability studies have been carried out about QBE and PC preference elicitation techniques in isolation, the authors are not aware of any usability studies in which these two techniques are directly compared to one another.

Table 1. The verbal Saaty scale [9]

Verbal preference strength	Numerical
Equal importance	1
Weak or slight importance	2
Moderate Importance	3
Moderate plus	4
Strong Importance	5
Strong plus	6
Very strong importance	7
Very very strong	8
Extreme importance	9

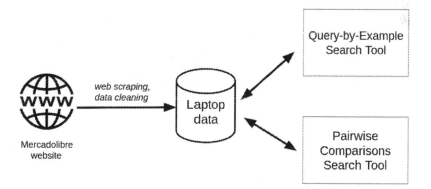

Fig. 1. Overall system architecture

3 System Architecture and Search Tools

Figure 1 shows the overall architecture employed. Data pertaining to 90 laptops was scraped from the Mercadolibre website[1] using the scrapy[2] Python library. Mercadolibre is an e-commerce website similar to e-Bay and is currently the company with the highest market capitalisation in Latin America [6]. Data was scraped from "official" vendors only (as opposed to private individuals) because it was found to be of higher quality. Not only was it significantly more complete, it was also available in a structured format rather than the free-text format from non-official vendors. Data cleaning was carried out using the pandas[3] and NumPy[4] Python libraries. The data set was stored in a PostgreSQL database and made available for querying by the search tools using the Python pg2psyco library[5]. In this section we describe the search tools that we implemented using QBE and PC preference elicitation approaches. The search tools were implemented using Python 3.8 with the PyCharm IDE and Django[6] framework.

3.1 Query-by-Example Search Tool

Figure 2 presents an example of the user interface for the QBE tool. The preference elicitation interface allows a user to enter one or more constraints or filter conditions to specify the technical specification required. The constraints must be given in terms of a criterion, a comparison operator, and a threshold value for the criterion. The criteria available are {brand, price, RAM, screen size, screen type, storage, webcam, weight}. For numerical criteria, there are five different comparison operators to choose from $\{<, \leq, =, \geq, >\}$ however these are presented verbally (e.g., "greater than or equal to") in the drop-down menu to ease of understanding of non-mathematically minded people and for consistency with the Pairwise Comparisons tool (described ahead). The threshold value depends on the criterion selected, e.g., for *Brand* the options available are {Acer, Asus, Compumax, Dell, HP, Huawei, Lanix, Lenovo, Toshiba}. The Add and Remove buttons allow a user to add as many constraints as desired.

When the Evaluate button is clicked, a result set of up to five laptops that meet the constraints given are shown. These are chosen at random from the database. It is possible that less than five results are shown or indeed, none, if the constraints are too restrictive. For the purposes of the experimental evaluation, the user is only given one opportunity to carry out the search, and then is asked to state whether he or she likes the result or not.

In Fig. 2(a), the user seeks a laptop with at least 4 GB RAM and large display size. However, the user has a maximum budget of 6 million Colombian pesos. All the results in Fig. 2(b) meet these constraints.

---

[1] https://www.mercadolibre.com.co/.

[2] https://scrapy.org/.

[3] https://pandas.pydata.org/.

[4] https://numpy.org/.

[5] https://pypi.org/project/psycopg2/.

[6] https://www.djangoproject.com/.

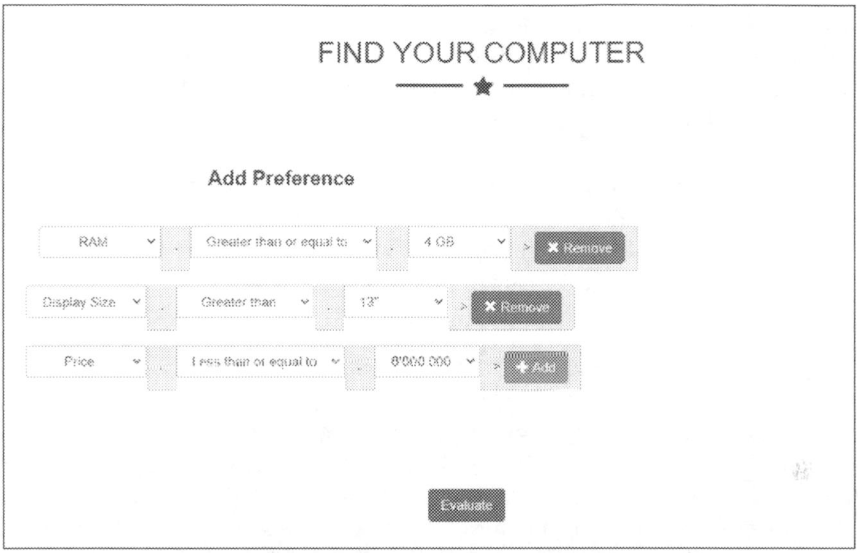

(a) Example preference elicitation

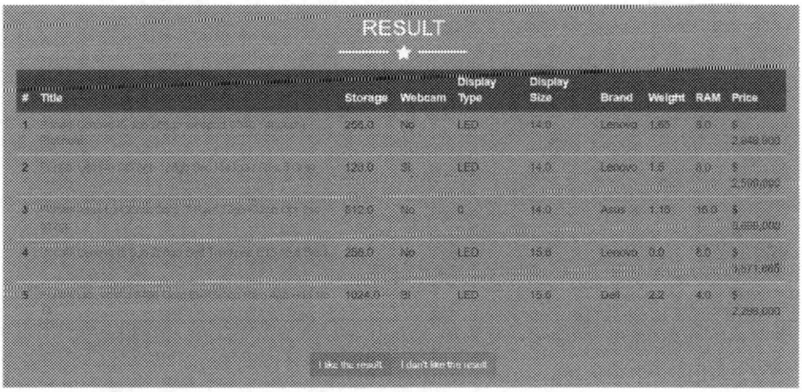

(b) Example results

Fig. 2. The *Query-by-Example* interface

3.2   Pairwise Comparisons Search Tool

Figure 3 presents an example of the user interface for the PC tool. The interface aims to appear visually as similar as possible to the QBE tool in order to ensure fairness of the comparison we carry out in the subsequent experimental evaluation. This is achieved by, as far as possible, using the same type of user interface elements and layout in both cases.

The preference elicitation interface allows a user to enter a series of preferences in terms of two criteria and an operator to express the degree of preference between the left-hand and right-hand side criteria. The set of criteria used are the same as for the QBE tool. However, the preference operator is a subset of the verbal Saaty scale shown in Table 1. Five points in the scale are chosen, so that the number of scale points is the same as with the QBE tool. Unlike the QBE tool, no threshold values are given, as the idea is to specify the relative importance of criteria.

Once the user preferences are elicited, the well-known Analytical Hierarchy Process (AHP) methodology [10] is applied in order to select the laptops which best meet the user preferences. In Fig. 3(a), the user gives a series of preferences, and the result set produced is shown in Fig. 3(b).

4   Experiment Design

We designed an experiment to measure the performance and usability of both preference elicitation techniques. For this, the tasks shown in the Table 2 were defined. This table shows two types of tasks: those that stipulate an explicit value for the thresholds of the criteria, and those that express the user's requirements without specifying specific values for the criteria. It is expected that for tasks whose criteria values are explicitly defined, the requirements can be directly expressed using QBE. In contrast, for task requirements where only specific values are specified, the expectation is that these can be expressed using PC more easily.

The structure of the experiment is defined as follows:

– A short two-minute tutorial is carried out explaining each of the elicitation techniques and the steps to be followed;
– The participant carries out the four tasks in Table 2 using Technique 1. For each task, the user gives the requirements according to their interpretation, and the tool returns the result sets. The user must then indicate whether he is satisfied with the results, indicating whether they are deemed to be useful or not.
– The participant answers four questions about the usability of Technique 1;
– The participant carries out the four tasks in Table 2 using Technique 2;
– The participant answers four questions about the usability of Technique 2;
– The participant answers a question comparing the usability of both elicitation techniques, giving a qualitative answer.

Two groups of participants of equal size are created. For the first group, Technique 1 corresponds to Query-by-Example, and Technique 2 to Pairwise Comparisons. For the second group, the reverse is done. This is to avoid giving an advantage to one of the techniques over the other, taking into account that the second technique will always have an advantage since participants become more familiar with the interface. Two versions of a guide with instructions were created for each group, with the respective links to the tools and the usability questions.

The metrics used for evaluation aim to consider two aspects, user performance and usability. *User Performance* is related to the F-measure of the result set

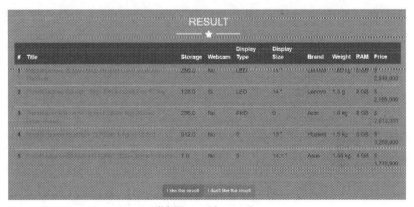

(a) Example preference elicitation

(b) Example results

Fig. 3. Pairwise comparisons

obtained for a given preference elicitation. F-measure is a widely used measure within information retrieval that provides a measure of accuracy combining both precision and recall [12]. It also enables result sets that may be of different sizes to be compared in a succinct manner. The F-measure obtained for a given result set $\mathbf{R}$ for a task T and elicitation e, denoted $F(\mathbf{R}_e^T)$, is calculated thus:

$$F(\mathbf{R}_e^T) = 2 \cdot \frac{\text{Precision}(\mathbf{R}_e^T) \cdot \text{Recall}(\mathbf{R}_e^T)}{\text{Precision}(\mathbf{R}_e^T) + \text{Recall}(\mathbf{R}_e^T)} \tag{1}$$

Table 2. Tasks given to participants of the usability experiment

Task	Description	Criteria values
1	I am a video game designer and I need to select a computer for my work. The price and weight are not important to me	Implicit
2	I manage a team for a large company. Usually I need a computer to use MS Office applications, to send emails, web-browsing and video-conferencing. It is important that it not be too heavy as I travel frequently, and that the price is between the 3 to 5 million Colombian pesos assigned in the budget	Explicit
3	I am a person without much technical knowledge and I need a computer to get in touch with my children, view photos and use social networks. I don't want to spend much money	Implicit
4	I am a web page developer and I need a computer that supports several programs in parallel to give good customer support, possibly with 4 GB of RAM, or higher, and a screen size larger than 13 in. My maximum budget is 6 million Colombian pesos	Explicit

where $\mathbf{R}_e^T$ is result set obtained using elicitation e and

$$\text{Precision}(\mathbf{R}_e^T) = \frac{|TP_e^T|}{|TP_e^T \cup FP_e^T|} \tag{2}$$

and

$$\text{Recall}(\mathbf{R}_e^T) = \frac{|TP_e^T|}{|TP_e^T \cup FN_e^T|} \ . \tag{3}$$

The set of true positives TP_f^T is defined thus:

$$TP_e^T = \{r|r \in \mathbf{R}_e \wedge r \in \mathbf{F}_T\} \tag{4}$$

where $\mathbf{F}_T$ is the set of true positives, i.e., the rows in the results which are deemed to be adequate according to the natural language description for task T. By true positive is meant a record corresponding to a laptop computer which deemed to be suitable for the task described. For example, for Task 2 in Table 2, which specifies a budget of between 3–5 million, an example of a true positive would be a laptop computer in that range. Conversely, a laptop with the price outside that range would be deemed to be a false positive.

Table 3. Subset of SUS questions employed

Question	Type
I found the system unnecessarily complex	Negative
I would imagine that most people would learn to use this system very quickly	Positive
I thought the system was easy to use	Positive
I needed to learn a lot of things before I could get going with this system	Negative

For usability, we consider the two metrics to measure subjective user preference. Firstly, we compute the frequency of *likes* vs. the frequency of *dislikes* of the result sets obtained for each query. Furthermore, we calculate a usability score based on the well-established System Usability Scale (SUS) [11]. We use a variant of the SUS score which only involves four questions, in a similar fashion to Leon-Medina *et al.* [5]. The four questions used are shown in Table 3. We collect the responses using the Likert scale [2], the options strongly disagree, slightly disagree, neither agree nor disagree, slight agree and strongly agree. The usability score is each technique calculated as follows:

- The positive questions take the value assigned by the user minus one.
- The negative questions are 5 minus the value assigned by the user.

The individual scores for the questions are summed. Subsequently, a score in the range of 0 to 100 is computed:

$$U = \sum_{i=1}^{N}(score_i) \times \frac{100}{4N} \tag{5}$$

where N is the number of questions (four in this case), $score_i$ is the score awarded to the ith question, and the constant 4 represents the maximum score for any given question.

5   Results

Twenty volunteer participants were recruited to carry out the usability experiment described. Thirteen participants were Computer Science students at Jorge Tazeo Lozano University in Bogotá, Colombia. The remaining seven participants were friends and family members of the authors. The people who took part had a diverse range of IT skills knowledge, ranging from elementary to advanced.

Frequency of Criteria Employed. Figure 4 shows the frequency of use for the criteria Query-by-Example and Pairwise Comparisons respectively. The price and RAM criteria are most frequently used for both elicitation approaches. The third most frequently used criterion is *Screen Size* and *Weight* for Query-by-Example and Pairwise Comparisons respectively. The least frequently used criteria are *Brand* for Query-by-Example and *Screen Type* for the Pairwise Comparisons elicitation approach. It is broadly observed that the criteria employed reflect the descriptions of the tasks given in Table 2.

Frequency of Comparison Operators Employed. Figure 5(a) shows the frequency of use of the types of comparison operators for the Query-by-Example approach. The *greater than or equal to* or *less than or equal to* comparison operators are the most frequently used, a direct reflection of the tasks in the experiments which tend to mention inclusive ranges when thresholds are given. In contrast, Fig. 5(b) shows that users prefer to provide their preferences in positive terms (i.e., a criterion X being preferred to Y) rather than negative terms (i.e., Y being *less* preferred to X). This observation suggests that the PC interface may be simplified to exclude the negative options, which appear to be less intuitive.

User Performance. Figure 6 presents scatterplots showing precision vs. recall for each of the four tasks. Overall, it is observed that precision and recall tend to be higher for the Query-by-Example elicitation approach rather than Pairwise Comparisons. For Tasks 1 and 3, while it is observed that most users obtain full precision for Query-by-Example, the recall obtained is quite variable. This is most likely due to constraints over the criteria at times leading to less than five results being returned by the tool.

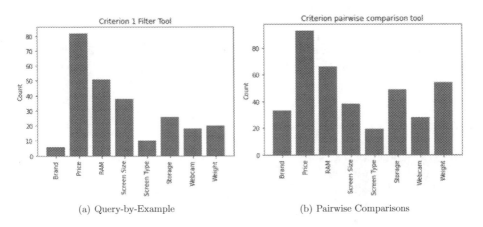

(a) Query-by-Example   (b) Pairwise Comparisons

Fig. 4. Frequency of criteria use

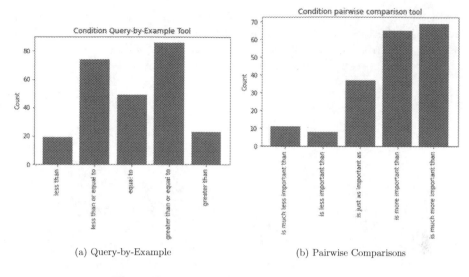

(a) Query-by-Example   (b) Pairwise Comparisons

Fig. 5. Frequency of comparison operator use

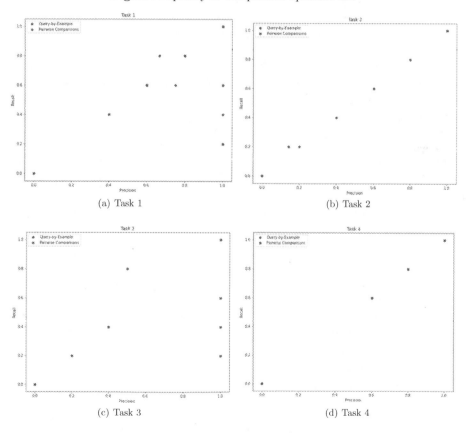

(a) Task 1   (b) Task 2

(c) Task 3   (d) Task 4

Fig. 6. Precision vs. Recall

Usability Score. Figure 7 shows the Usability Scores obtained for each person. On average, the Usability Scores were 75.3 for Query-by-Example, and 72.5 for Pairwise Comparisons. The difference is negligible and a paired t-test shows that the difference between the two distributions is not significant.

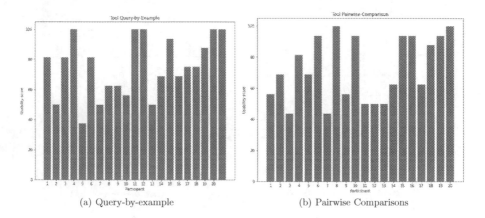

(a) Query-by-example   (b) Pairwise Comparisons

Fig. 7. Usability score (per person)

User Result Set Evaluation. Figures 8 and 9 show user result set evaluation for the Query-by-Example and Pairwise Comparison elicitations approaches respectively. It is observed that for Tasks 1 and 3, with implicit criteria, that participants are happy with the result set given by the Pairwise Comparisons elicitation approach 46.2% and 13.5% resp. more often than the Query-by-Example approach. A paired two-tailed t-test shows that this is very significant in the case of Task 1 ($p = 0.0140$) and less so in the case of Task 3 ($p = 0.336$). On the other hand, for Tasks 2 and 4, which have explicit criteria, participants are happy with the result set given by Query-by-Example approach 4.05% and 6.86% more often that with the Pairwise Comparisons. However, these results are not statistically significant.

Usability Score vs. F-measure. Figure 10 shows the relationship between Usability Score and F-measure obtained. For the case of QBE, a positive, albeit slight, correlation is observed for all four tasks. This suggests that participants who tend to perform well using this elicitation approach also tend to prefer it more. Conversely, there is no correlation (or a very slight negative one) in the case of PCs.

6   Discussion

Due to the space constraints, we present a sample of the most representative comments recorded in the final part of the experiment, in which participants are asked to compare the two elicitation approaches:

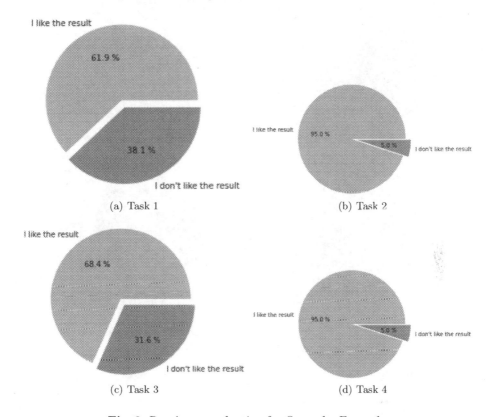

Fig. 8. Result set evaluation for Query-by-Example

C1 *Even though QBE does not always return results, it enables a simpler and more specific search.*

C2 *The PC approach requires greater knowledge about computers than the QBE approach.*

C3 *PC may be a better option for a user who is unsure of the technical specs required.*

C4 *QBE mimics the process of purchasing a computer more realistically.*

C5 *With PC it is hard to understand which criterion is most important.*

C6 *Generally when buying a laptop I do not prioritise certain criteria over others, and I prefer to consider them separately.*

The above comments reflect the usability scores awarded to each elicitation approach. In general, the QBE approach is favoured particularly for the tasks where criteria values are explicit because it is easier to translate a technical specification to a QBE formulation (C4). However, the potential drawback posed by tasks where criteria values are not stated explicitly are that QBE may result in a empty result set is noted (C1). Indeed, all e-commerce sites known to the authors that sell technological items use a QBE-based (rather than PC-based) approach to search for results, so this is probably the most familiar way for the

444   J. Almeida and I. Galpin

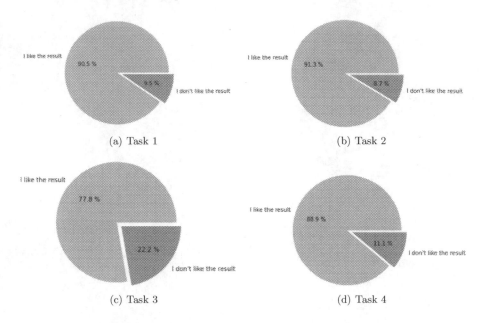

(a) Task 1   (b) Task 2

(c) Task 3   (d) Task 4

Fig. 9. Result set evaluation for Pairwise comparisons

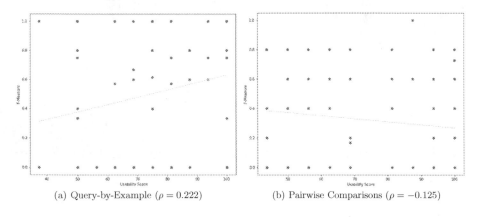

(a) Query-by-Example ($\rho = 0.222$)   (b) Pairwise Comparisons ($\rho = -0.125$)

Fig. 10. Correlation between Usability score and F-measure

participants to select a laptop computer. We note that the QBE approach is often coupled with filters that suggest sensible ranges, to avoid the potential problem of an empty result set being returned.

The comments given about the PC approach are somewhat ambiguous. While one participant considers it may lend itself better to people with less knowledge about the technical specifications ($C3$), others consider that a deeper understanding is required ($C2, C5, C6$), possibly because the trade-offs that present themselves between different criteria (e.g., price vs. weight) may not always be apparent to less technically-minded people. The results in the previous section indicate that in cases where requirements are not precisely stated, i.e., Tasks 1 and 3 where the criteria values are implicit rather than explicit, there is considerably higher satisfaction with the result sets obtained. As such, the PC elicitation approach may prove useful as a complementary elicitation approach to QBE for technology e-commerce websites.

While these results provide important insights, it should be noted that they may not be applicable across diverse domains. For laptop search on an e-commerce website, QBE is the most popular technique and will therefore be familiar to many users. Thus, the results of our study may be differ for other domains.

7   Conclusions

Effective search tools are of paramount importance for users of an e-commerce site to feel confident that they are buying the right product and, consequently, boost sales. In this paper, we compare the performance and usability of QBE and PC as preference elicitation techniques for search tools envisioned to be used on a e-commerce laptop computer sales websites. We find that while users do not directly express a preference for one tool over the other, for tasks where criteria values are not defined explicitly that PCs offers a promising preference elicitation approach. We note that for the domain selected, i.e., laptop search on an e-commerce website, QBE is the habitual form of searching for results. As such, the results may be rather domain dependent, and fruitful future work may involve the exploration of usability of Pairwise Comparisons for other domains.

References

1. Abel, E., Galpin, I., Paton, N.W., Keane, J.A.: Pairwise comparisons or constrained optimization? a usability evaluation of techniques for eliciting decision priorities. Int. Trans. Oper. Res. (2020)
2. Albaum, G.: The likert scale revisited. Mark. Res. Soc. J. **39**(2), 1–21 (1997)
3. Galpin, I., Abel, E., Paton, N.W.: Source selection languages: a usability evaluation. In: Proceedings of the Workshop on Human-In-the-Loop Data Analytics, pp. 1–6 (2018)
4. Kalloori, S., Ricci, F., Gennari, R.: Eliciting pairwise preferences in recommender systems. In: Proceedings of the 12th ACM Conference on Recommender Systems, pp. 329–337 (2018)
5. Leon-Medina, J.C., Galpin, I.: RefDataCleaner: a usable data cleaning tool. In: Florez, H., Leon, M., Diaz-Nafria, J.M., Belli, S. (eds.) ICAI 2019. CCIS, vol. 1051, pp. 102–115. Springer, Cham (2019). https://doi.org/10.1007/978-3-030-32475-9_8
6. Mander, B.: How mercadolibre emerged as an ecommerce titan: Latin America's answer to alibaba valued at $63bn as consumers turn to online shopping. Financial Times, November 2020. https://www.ft.com/content/446558a8-c0b2-449c-97a5-53b3956cd427
7. bt Mohd, N.A., Zaaba, Z.F.: A review of usability and security evaluation model of ecommerce website. Procedia Comput. Sci. **161**, 1199–1205 (2019)

8. Muhtaseb, R., Lakiotaki, K., Matsatsinis, N.: Applying a multicriteria satisfaction analysis approach based on user preferences to rank usability attributes in e-tourism websites. J. Theor. Appl. Electron. Commer. Res. **7**(3), 28–48 (2012)
9. Saaty, T.L.: A scaling method for priorities in hierarchical structures. J. Math. Psychol. **15**(3), 234–281 (1977)
10. Saaty, T.L.: Decision Making for Leaders: The Analytic Hierarchy Process for Decisions in a Complex World. RWS publications (1990)
11. Sauro, J.: Measuring usability with the system usability scale (SUS). https://measuringu.com/sus/. Accessed 10 May 2019
12. Schütze, H., Manning, C.D., Raghavan, P.: Introduction to Information Retrieval, vol. 39. Cambridge University Press, Cambridge (2008)
13. Sepliarskaia, A., Kiseleva, J., Radlinski, F., de Rijke, M.: Preference elicitation as an optimization problem. In: Proceedings of the 12th ACM Conference on Recommender Systems, pp. 172–180 (2018)
14. Singh, T., Malik, S., Sarkar, D.: E-commerce website quality assessment based on usability. In: 2016 International Conference on Computing, Communication and Automation (ICCCA), pp. 101–105. IEEE (2016)
15. Thomas, J.C., Gould, J.D.: A psychological study of query by example. In: Proceedings of the May 19–22, 1975, National Computer Conference and Exposition, pp. 439–445 (1975)
16. Zloof, M.M.: Query by example. In: Proceedings of the May 19–22, 1975, National Computer Conference and Exposition, pp. 431–438 (1975)

Internationalization at Home (IaH) as an Alternative for Academic Cooperation: A Mexico-Colombia Case

Rubén Hernan Leal-López[1] , Rafael Humberto Rojas-Millán[2] ,
Jorge Guadalupe Treviño-Montemayor[1] ,
and Rafael Enrique Casadiego-Cardona[2]([✉])

[1] Universidad Autónoma de Nuevo León, Pedro de Alba S/N, Niños Héroes,
Ciudad Universitaria, San Nicolás de los Garza, N.L., México
[2] Corporación Universidad de La Costa, Cl. 58 ##5566, Barranquilla, Atlántico, Colombia
rcasadie@cuc.edu.co

Abstract. The concept of internationalization at home is broad and, depending on the academic tradition and the place where it takes place, includes different elements. That is why this article has been structured in three fundamental parts: at the beginning, a review of the concept is made and also examines the evolution that internationalization at home (IaH) has achieved in recent years. It explores in a special way the trends followed in Europe, North America, Australia, Mexico and Colombia. It continues with a debate on the definition of internationalization at home, through a journey through the different analytical currents to later explore its manifestations. The article concludes with an analysis of an internationalization project at home carried out between the Autonomous University of Nuevo León in Mexico and the Universidad de la Costa Corporation in Colombia, where a set of recommendations will also be given that give a comprehensive vision of the aspects that a higher education policy should consider to ensure that a broader base of students and teachers can access the opportunities that are configured in a globalized world, and in the so-called knowledge society, through internationalization at home.

Keywords: Internationalization at home (IaH) · Academic cooperation · Higher education mobility · International cooperation

1 Introduction

Academic and student mobility occurs thanks to academic cooperation between countries. Since 1977, with the reestablishment of relations between Mexico and Spain, higher level academic cooperation has increased and regulated through normative instruments that intensify exchanges of both academics and students. Mexico, together with the countries that have signed cooperation mechanisms, are part of collaboration networks that promote academic and student mobility among them. In addition, the acquisition of Highly Qualified Human Resources (RHAC) is essential for these countries

© Springer Nature Switzerland AG 2021
T. Guarda et al. (Eds.): ARTIIS 2021, CCIS 1485, pp. 447–459, 2021.
https://doi.org/10.1007/978-3-030-90241-4_34

to develop technological innovations and scientific advances. In this article we seek to determine whether immigration and academic cooperation policy for RHAC influences talent retention.

International academic cooperation between educational systems occurs in a global context, highly unequal (due to the existence of countries-center and countries-periphery where knowledge is produced), of massification of Higher Education (HE) and in which science is communicates in a common language with a predominance of English [6]. Similarly, new technologies facilitate and promote the internationalization of HE and alliances between university associations on a global, regional and national scale. Therefore, internationalization is one of the guiding principles of the SE. Its importance lies in the fact that through it and the cooperation mechanisms it will be possible to strengthen the universities, as well as a greater dissemination of knowledge [4].

Academic and student mobility stands as a reflection of the international logic of the international circulation of knowledge [20] and the capacity of countries to attract and retain RHAC through migration policies. In fact, due to their importance for developing technological innovations, RHACs experience less restricted mobility due to their quality of human capital, since there are other types of opportunities to enter developed countries thanks to their credentials [1–3] and selective migration policies [9].

Academic exchanges have occurred since the appearance of the first universities and, according to Altbach, the organizational structures of Higher Education Institutions (HEIs) tend to standardize as an effect of globalization [6]. These synergies promote mobility not only for students but also for teachers, researchers and administrative staff. Examples are the cases of the Pacific Alliance Mobility Program and the European Higher Education Area (EHEA). The first is a device for student academic exchange, and involves 4 countries: Mexico, Colombia, Chile and Peru. In the second case, it is an intraregional university project sponsored by the European Union (EU) and its starting point is found in the Green Paper "The European Dimension of Education" (1993), the final result of which has been supranational compatibility between European higher-level systems.

In this environment, universities are fundamental actors, since it is in these institutions where technological innovations occur that must respond to the increase in the demand for Highly Qualified Human Resources (RHAC) required in the scenario of the Knowledge and Information Society [12]. It should still be noted that RHACs weigh the difficulties they encounter in their countries of origin to carry out research, living conditions, educational options for their children, political conditions and the possibilities of obtaining a job related to their training [17]. These contextual antecedents have positioned academic cooperation in the sights of politicians, representatives of educational institutions, researchers, and agencies that financially finance such mobility.

In addition to the above and taking into account the rise of Information and Communication Technologies (ICTs) in the last 20 years as well as the presence and importance that they have acquired in the different areas of human life, Internationalization arises at Home (IaH) as a natural result of these trends and evolution in the education sector.

Internationalization at home comprises all activities that help our students, teachers, researchers, administrators and graduates to develop international understanding and intercultural skills within the institution's campuses. The dimension of this strategy permeates the curriculum, collaboration in research, foreign languages, curricular internationalization, liaison with international multidisciplinary groups and many other academic activities.

It is in this sense that this article will address what internationalization at home (IaH) is, an analysis will be made of countries whose educational systems have been adapting, to a greater or lesser extent, this new alternative of academic cooperation to finally, present the case of an exercise carried out by the Universidad Autónoma de Nuevo León, located in the city of Monterrey, Mexico, and the Universidad de la Costa, located in the city of Barranquilla, Colombia, an exercise that achieved a transversal integration of students and teachers who had the opportunity to live an international experience through the Columbus Hub Academy program of the Columbus Association, this being a case of Internationalization at home (IaH).

2 Origin and Evolution of the Concept of Internationalization at Home (IaH)

[11] Beelen (2012) points out that the term internationalization at home was coined in 1999 by the Swede Bengt Nilsson, when faced with the fact that the newly established University of Malmö did not yet have an international network that could offer its students the traditional study abroad experience. For this reason, the students had to look for the opportunity to live this experience "at home". From that moment on, there was a growing interest in exploring and formally analyzing an idea that led to multiple interpretations.

The concept has been the subject of deep reflection in Europe (Malmö, 2003; Rotterdam, 2005, 2006 onwards, EAIE) and has led to the creation of a Special Interest Group in the European Association for International Education (EAIE). In this sense, the term internationalization at home evolved in the European context from an initial stage in which it was associated with interculturality, diversity and inclusion of immigrant populations, towards a systemic conception that includes the incorporation of international references in all areas of higher education institutions (HEIs).

In the North American case, the concept has assumed the connotation of "Internationalization on Campus" and refers to one of the two currents into which the concept of internationalization has been divided [34]: internationalization abroad (education transnational or cross-border), which includes all forms of education existing across borders: student and teacher mobility, and project, program and provider mobility. The second, internationalization on campus, which consists of a series of activities that help students develop an international understanding of global phenomena and intercultural skills [11]. This approach has also led to the concept of comprehensive internationalization or comprehensive internationalization, which positively converges with the systemic vision that has characterized the European perspective. Thus, internationalization cannot be seen as a list of fragmented activities carried out by the International Relations Offices (ORI) and a small group of motivated internationalists among administrators and students. On the contrary, internationalization must be comprehensive, comprehensive and must become a pillar of the institution [13].

The Australian context, with a significant impact on the international mobility of students, has focused internationalization at home on the incorporation of international references in the training processes, particularly in the internationalization of the curriculum, understood from a perspective of integration of multiple training experiences that they allow the development of professional and interdisciplinary profiles with global competencies.

In Mexico, programs have been promoted for the internationalization of higher education such as the Alban Program, whose purpose is to grant scholarships to high-level Latin American students to carry out postgraduate studies in the European Union and thus contribute to the education and training of global citizens [22]. The European Union also has the Erasmus Worlds program, which works through the promotion of master's programs that grant scholarships to students with the idea of preparing European citizens for a global life [23]. One of its strengths is that it allows the student to move to third countries, thereby increasing cultural baggage and interpersonal relationships [42].

The Fulbright scholarship program contributes to the improvement of cross-border and internationalization practices between Mexico and the United States. Fulbright was developed within the framework of relations between the two countries in 1948, with the purpose of granting scholarships to Mexican students to carry out higher studies in the United States. As a result, in 1990 the United States-Mexico Commission for Educational and Cultural Exchange (COMEXUS) was created, through which the economic resources contributed by these countries are administered [45]. Hence, this program has encouraged the formation of academic networks in the cross-border area between the two countries.

For the Colombian case, internationalization at home is related to the evolution of different institutional aspects. Starting in the 1990s, a legal reorganization was introduced in Colombia that offered greater openness. With the issuance of the National Constitution in 1991, the promulgation of Law 30 of 1992 that grants autonomy to HEIs, and the promulgation of national development plans, universities are protected by a legal framework that allows them to face the challenges of internationalization. In 1996, the Colombian Association of Universities (ASCUN), a private non-governmental entity founded in 1957, supported and coordinated the Colombian Network for International Cooperation for Higher Education (RCI) seeking to complement the efforts made by higher education institutions. This network brings together the ORIs with the fundamental purpose of stimulating, promoting and strengthening the culture of internationalization in Colombian universities [8]. The RCI is undoubtedly the oldest articulation effort in university internationalization in Colombia that is accompanied by the evolution of the entire higher education system and the concept of university that has been promoted by the public and private institutions that are members of ASCUN. Its effect has been seen in a particular way in young universities or those with increasing levels of development that, through networking experiences, have managed to incorporate good practices from national and international universities with a greater tradition.

In October 2003 ASCUN and the RCI presented to the CX Council of Rectors the document entitled "Towards an internationalization of the university with its own meaning" [8], in which an internationalization model and a model are proposed. evaluation of the same, adapted to the Colombian reality. There, the internationalization of the curriculum is pointed out as a training strategy, closely linked to internationalization at home, which allows the inclusion of external references in the study plan, in the domain of foreign languages, in the use of new technologies, in environments libraries and teacher training [8]. In other words, a first approximation is established on the way in which IaH manifests itself in the concert of Colombian universities.

3 Comprehensive Internationalization: The Double Integration Strategy

From the review of the concept of internationalization at home and the analysis of the distinctive features that this concept involves, three fundamental aspects become evident:

1. Internationalization at home is a systemic concept that requires a conducive institutional environment so that its different manifestations can have the desired impact. This implies the inclusion of international references in all its functions and university activities.
2. In the Colombian case, it can be seen that the approach to the concept of internationalization at home has been done in an instrumental way. However, there is no direct or explicit articulation with the strategic and tactical levels from which the orientations of the other academic activities are defined, generating a low impact on the multiple actions.
3. In an effective implementation of internationalization at home, all members of the educational community (teachers, students, administrative staff and graduates) must participate and therefore, it is essential that the international relations office, or the unit that develops its functions, be aware of the role you must play at all organizational levels: awareness and support at the strategic level (policies and planning) and dynamization at the tactical (planning) and operational levels (projects and actions).

These three elements determine that a fundamental step in the effective implementation of the concept of internationalization at home in an HEI is the integration of the international dimension in all institutional policies and programs at the three levels of the educational process: the macro (taking of decisions and design of institutional policies), the environment (curricular structures and policies) and the micro (the teaching and learning process in the classroom and other educational spaces) [46].

4 The Universidad Autonoma de Nuevo León (UANL) and the UANL School of Business

The Universidad Autonoma de Nuevo León (UANL) is a higher education institution with 87 years of history, considered the third largest public university in Mexico and has the largest educational offer in the northeast of the country.

Its main coverage is in Nuevo León (northeast of México) and the surrounding states. Its headquarters include six university campuses: University City, Health Sciences, Mederos, Agricultural Sciences, Sabinas Hidalgo and Linares, which make up a total of 26 faculties, the Institute of Social Research and 29 high schools.

It currently offers 334 educational programs at the upper, upper and postgraduate levels, of which 20 undergraduate and 12 graduate offer double degrees with foreign institutions. And in short, with these programs more than 214 thousand students are served, under the advice of more than 7 thousand teachers.

Its educational model promotes the comprehensive training of students and is based on two structuring axes: education focused on learning and education based on competencies; an operational axis: the flexibility of educational programs and processes; and three transversal axes: academic innovation, internationalization, and social responsibility.

Similarly, within the framework of the mobility and academic exchange program, more than 900 UANL students carry out partial studies a year in other national and foreign institutions and more than 380 are incorporated from other institutions.

The Business School of the Universidad Autonoma de Nuevo León was founded on October 13, 1952. It currently has a student population that exceeds 18,000 students. The UANL School of Business mission is to train professionals in the field of business that contribute to the socio-economic development of the region and the country, through quality educational programs that provide them with critical skills to function in global scenarios, as well as strengthen research oriented to the generation of knowledge in our disciplines, cultivating an innovative, ethical and socially responsible spirit in its community.

The UANL School of Business seeks to be the most influential business school in the region due to the quality of its educational programs, with national and international recognition and accreditation, through research and innovation in areas of knowledge that ensure that our graduates are promoters of the development of the environment in which they work.

Currently the UANL School of Business offers 4 undergraduate or programs: Public Accountant, Bachelor of Administration, Bachelor of Information Technology and Bachelor of International Business, being in this last educational program where the activity of Internationalization at Home (IaH) was developed that is analyzed in this research work.

The mission of the Bachelor of international business is to train professionals with academic excellence in the areas of international business, in administration, operations, finance and international legal framework, who are recognized for their creativity, innovative capacity and competitiveness, in addition to a solid formation of values, ethics with high commitment in economic, social, scientific and cultural development with a global approach.

Regarding postgraduate studies, the Faculty has 8 Master's programs in the areas of accounting, administration, information technology and international business. Similarly, it has 2 doctoral programs: the Doctorate in Accounting and the Doctorate in Philosophy with a specialty in Administration.

5 The Universidad de la Costa CUC and the Specialization in Integral Logistics

With the purpose of contributing to regional educational development at a higher level, the UNIVERSIDAD DE LA COSTA -CUC was created on November 16, 1970, a non-profit organization dedicated to the training of professionals in the area of science, technology, humanities, art and philosophy.

On January 3, 1971, the new center began work on Carrera 42F No. 75B-169 in this city, offering Architecture, Administration, Law and Civil Engineering programs, with an enrollment of 154 students. The transfer to its current headquarters, Calle 58 No. 55–66, took place in January 1974. Its legal status was granted on April 23, 1971, through Resolution No. 352 of the Government of Atlántico.

Subsequently, studies began at the Faculty of Educational Sciences, in the specialties of Psychopedagogy, Mathematics, Modern Languages and Physical Education, as well as in Economics in International Trade.

In 1975, the Department of Socioeconomic Research (DIS) attached to the Faculty of Economics was created, a fact that marked the beginning of the investigative process at the CUC. Postgraduate programs began on March 16, 1987 with a Specialization in Finance and Systems, authorized by Agreement 203 of October 30, 1986, issued by the ICFES Board of Directors.

In the 90's, the ICFES authorized the operation of the programs of Electrical Engineering, Electronic, Industrial, Sanitary and Environmental Engineering, Analysis and Programming of Computers, Information Technology and Telecommunications, then the Psychology program.

Then, it was decided in mid-2000 to create the Consulting and Service Delivery Division attached to the CID , taking into account its environment and the strengths that the institution possesses or generates during the next few years, with the purpose that the institution maintains its role of social, economic and environmental change in the Caribbean Region.

5.1 The Specialization in Integral Logistics

The Integral Logistics Specialization Program seeks to train professionals with technical, managerial and investigative capacities for the management, planning and control of logistics systems with a systemic approach to the supply chain, with the ability to generate efficient solutions aimed at adding value in any link in the logistics chain. The focus of the Comprehensive Logistics Specialization program is aimed at generating skills in all links of the logistics chain: Procurement, Inventory Management, Transportation and Distribution, and Customer Service.

Currently logistics is a key area in the development of the industry in a competitive and sustainable way. As a consequence of this, professionalization in the area of logistics and supply chains continues to gain strength, which is why many educational institutions worldwide offer programs related to logistics issues such as Supply Chain Management, International Physical Distribution, Transportation Logistics among other specific topics in the area.

For all the above, the university aims to train specialists in comprehensive logistics with a systemic approach, qualified to meet the needs in design, planning and control of logistics systems in industrial and service organizations, achieving cost reduction and improving the use of resources., in such a way that an efficient response is given to the market, adding value and aiming for the increase in the competitiveness of the industry in a regional, national and international scope.

By the end of 2013: The program is created through AGREEMENT No. 526 of November 2013 of the Board of Directors, it is offered at the postgraduate academic level, in the face-to-face methodology, with a cut-off duration of two (2) semesters. Already in 2015, the qualified registration is obtained. The offer to the public of the postgraduate program: Specialization in Integral Logistics is made official. Finally, on March 4, 2016 the classes of the first class of the Specialization in Integral Logistics begin. This specialization has a total of 24 credits divided into 8 subjects and a duration of 2 academic semesters.

6 The Columbus Hub Academy Program

Columbus Hub Academy is an online platform that seeks to stimulate the design and implementation of international educational projects through online media, involving institutions from Europe and Latin America in its first phase of collaboration.

Columbus seeks to encourage Internationalization at Home (IaH), which has become an option for the improvement of learning and teaching, by providing students with an international experience without having to leave the country, and by helping them develop an international awareness and intercultural skills, that is, it prepares them to be active in a much more globalized world [18].

It is important to mention that the Columbus Association created the Columbus Hub Academy because despite the fact that student mobility increases, it is a fact that around 90% of students will never experience an opportunity to go study abroad. In addition to economic reasons, there are also cultural reasons, as not all students see opportunities for intercultural and international learning. This situation is similar for academics/teachers. Between 30 and 40% are mobilized in the institutions that best achieve it.

The Columbus Hub Academy program supports the development of International Collaborative Online Learning projects using an innovative approach to teaching and learning, which provides teachers and students with the possibility of collaborating with international peers through the use of online tools (Fig. 1).

The Columbus Hub Academy program seeks to develop competencies in its participants, whether they are students or teachers, which will be tools for their professional practice. These competences are:

- Work in teams located in different countries.
- Manage projects: focus on meeting objectives, organize complex tasks, manage time, lead teams. Communicate interculturally and develop attitudes such as tolerance and recognition of one's own cultures.
- Work with digital tools
- Search and analyze information
- Work on interdisciplinary themes.

It is important to note that the development of these competencies is increasingly relevant for:

- Respond to global societal challenges
- Access an increasingly global job market
- Expanding horizons beyond local-national barriers, critical thinking
- Build tolerance and respect for other cultures, global citizenship.

Inspired by other initiatives such as COIL-SUNY and OIL-Coventry, Columbus Hub Academy offers a value-added opportunity, through:

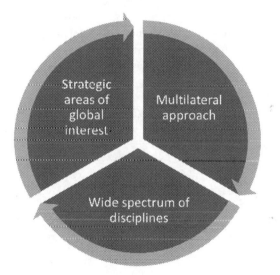

Fig. 1. Columbus Hub Academy model approach. Source: Columbus Association (2019).

7   UANL-CUC Case: An Exercise of Integration of Logistics and International Business Through Internationalization at Home (IaH)

The project carried out in a period of three months during the second semester of 2019, was entitled Analysis of the current situation of the management of international physical distribution between Mexico and Colombia, and in which students of the Bachelor of International Business of the UANL School of Business, within the course "Logistics" by Professor Rubén Hernán Leal López. His teammates were students of the Logistics Specialization at the Universidad de la Costa, with Professor Rafael Humberto Rojas Millán in charge of the course. The project was developed within the framework of the Columbus Hub Academy program of the Columbus Association, through the use of its platform, tools and resources, also highlighting the guidance and accompaniment of the Columbus Association officials, who were key to the success of this activity.

The Mexican students carried out an analysis of the state that keeps the physical distribution for commercial exchange from Mexico to Colombia. For their part, the Colombian students carried out an analysis of the situation of physical distribution for commercial exchange from Colombia to Mexico. Once both analyzes had been carried out, a joint conclusion could be developed regarding the current situation of the management of international physical distribution between Mexico and Colombia. Once the project was completed, it became the first to be successfully concluded by the UANL School of Business and the University of the Coast within the Columbus Hub Academy.

The evaluation carried out by Columbus Hub staff shows that there was a marked enthusiasm on the part of the participants, where 68.5% of the students considered that the project was relevant or very important, and that it added value to their learning processes. Additionally, 88.4% of the students indicated that it was the first internationalization initiative in an academic context in which they participated.

Once the project concluded, the students developed competencies, which will be tools for their professional practice. These competences developed by the students were:

- Work in teams located in different countries.
- Manage projects: focus on meeting objectives, organize complex tasks, manage time, lead teams. Communicate interculturally and develop attitudes such as tolerance and recognition of one's own cultures.
- Work with digital tools
- Search and analyze information
- Work on interdisciplinary themes.

It is necessary to highlight that the aforementioned competencies are the competencies that the Columbus Hub Academy Program establishes as objectives, which is why it can be affirmed that the fulfillment of these objectives was achieved and that this exercise really had the expected impact on the participants.

Finally, all the students who participated in the project recommended their other teachers to include similar activities in their courses, since it allows them to live an international experience without having to leave the country and helps them develop a global vision and strengthens their intercultural skills. In other words, it prepares them to be active in a much more globalized world.

8   Conclusion

The concept of "Internationalization at Home" (IAH) refers to any international or intercultural activity carried out by a higher education institution, with the exception of outgoing exchanges [11]. This modality of understanding the internationalization of higher education was developed for the first time in 1999, by Nilson (1999), who observed that despite the existence of more than 10 years of student mobility programs such as ERASMUS MUNDUS, it is still not known. it achieved the minimum objective that 10% of university students and professors in the European community had completed a period of study at a foreign university.

Internationalization at home comprises all activities that help our students, teachers, researchers, administrators and graduates to develop international understanding and intercultural skills within the institution's campuses.

The dimension of this strategy permeates the curriculum, collaboration in research, foreign languages, curricular internationalization, liaison with international multidisciplinary groups and many other academic activities.

It is important to take advantage of the advantages that Internationalization at Home (IaC) offers to improve learning and teaching, by giving students an international experience without having to leave the country, and by helping them develop international awareness and intercultural skills, that is, it prepares them to be active in a much more globalized world.

Undoubtedly, internationalization at home (IaH) has positioned itself as one of the most effective and accessible options to train professionals who can develop successfully in a knowledge society, in a knowledge economy where the constant is the multiculturalism of its actors. This alternative represents a great opportunity for the educational systems of Latin American countries to internationalize.

References

1. Alarcón, R.: Skilled immigrants and cerebreros: Foreign-born engineers and scientists in the high-technology industry of Silicon Valley. In: Foner, N., Rumbaut, R.G., Gold, S.J. (eds.) Immigration research for a new century: Multidisciplinary perspectives, pp. 301–321. Russell Sage Foundation, New York (2000)
2. Alarcón, R.: Immigrant niches in the U.S. high technology industry. In: Cornelius, W.A., Espenshade, T.J., Salehyan, I. (eds.). The International Migration of the Highly Skilled, pp. 235–263. Center for Comparative Immigration Studies, San Diego (2001)
3. Alarcon, R.: The free circulation of skilled migrants in North America. In: Pécoud, A., de Guchteneire, P. (eds.), Migration Without Borders: Essays on the Free Movement of People, pp. 243–257. Berghahn, New York (2007)
4. Alcántara, A.: Tendencias mundiales en la educación superior: El papel de los organismos multilaterales. En Inter-Ação: Revista da Faculdade de Educação da Universidade Federal de Goiás e do Programa de Pós-Graduação em Educação da FE/UFG 31(1), 11–33 (2006). jan./jun. http://www.revistas.ufg.br/index.php/interacao/article/view/1490/1474
5. Álvarez, S.: La adquisición de la nacionalidad española por estudiantes extranjeros, Diario La Ley, N° 7979, Sección Doctrina, 5 dic. 2012, Editorial LA LEY 18157/2012 (2012). https://www.academia.edu/4774562/La_adquisici%C3%B3n_de_la_nacionalidad_espa%C3%B1ola_por_estudiantes_extranjeros
6. Altbach, P.: Globalisation and the university: myths and realities in an unequal world. Tertiary Educ. Manag. 10, 3–25 (2004). https://link.springer.com/article/10.1023/B:TEAM.0000001 2239.55136.4b
7. Asociación Nacional de Universidades e Instituciones de Educación Superior [ANUIES]. Internacionalización de la educación superior en México: La visión estratégica de la ANUIES (2018). http://www.rimac.mx/internacionalizacion-de-la-educacion-superior-en-mexico-la-vision-estrategica-de-la-anuies/
8. Aponte, C., De Toro, A., Krausova, E., Pinzón, N.: Hacia una Internacionalización de la universidad con sentido propio, Coordinado por Isabel Cristina Jaramillo. ASCUN, CX CONSEJO NACIONAL DE RECTORES, Bogotá (2003). http://secretariageneral.univalle.edu.co/consejo-academico/temasdediscusion/2003/Agenda%20de%20Pol%EDticas.pdf

9. Appleyard, R.: International Migration and Development: An Unresolved Relationship. Tenth IOM Seminar on Migration and Development. IOM, Geneva (1992)
10. Batalova, J. Fix, M., & Creticos, P. (2008). Uneven progress: The employment pathways of skilled immigrants in the United States. Migration Policy Institute. http://www.migrationpol icy.org/pubs/BrainWasteOct08.pdf
11. Beelen, J.: La internacionalización en casa en el mundo. In: Martínez, P., David, L., Helena, P.C. (eds.) La Internacionalización de la Eduación Superior en América Latina y Europa: retos y compromisos. de 1 Pontificia Universidad Javeriana Bogotá (2012)
12. Bell, D.: El advenimiento de la sociedad post-industrial: Un intento de prognosis social. Alianza, Madrid (1976)
13. Brandenburg, U., De Wit, H.: The end of internationalization. En: International Higher Education (62), 15–17 (2011). Consultado en: http://www.bc.edu/research/cihe/ihe/issues/2011. html Mestenhauser, 2007, 70
14. Brewer, E., Leask, B.: Internationalization of the Curriculum. In: Deardorff, D.K., de Wit, H., Heyl, J., Adams, T. (eds.) The Sage Handbook of International Higher Education (Sage) (2012)
15. Castells, M.: La era de la información economía, sociedad y cultura. Alianza, Madrid (1997)
16. Castells, M.: La société en réseaux, L'ère de l'information, tome I. Fayard, Paris (2001)
17. Cheng, L., Yang, P.: Global interaction, global inequality and migration of the highly trained to the United States. Int. Migr. Rev. **32**(3), 626–653 (1998)
18. De Wit, H.: Globalisation and internationalisation of higher education. Int. J. Educ. Technol. High. Educ. **8**(2), 241–248 (2011)
19. Didou, S., Durand, J.P.: Extranjeros en el campo científico mexicano: Primeras aproximaciones. Revista Electrónica de Investigación Educativa **15**(3), 68-84 (2013). http://redie.uabc. mx/vol15no3/contenido-didoudurand.htm
20. Didou, S., Gérard, E.: El Sistema Nacional de Investigadores, veinticinco años después: la comunidad científica entre distinción e internacionalización. Asociación Nacional de Universidades e Instituciones Educativas de Educación Superior, México, D.F. (2010)
21. Didou, S., Renaud, P.: Introducción. In: Didou, S., Renaud, P. (Coords.) Circulación internacional de los conocimientos: miradas cruzadas sobre la dinámica Norte-Sur, 11–23. Ciudad de México: Organización de las Naciones Unidas para la Educación, la Ciencia y la Cultura-Instituto Internacional para la Educación Superior en América Latina y el Caribe (2015)
22. European Commission. Final Evaluation of ALBAN Program, December, Brussels (2010)
23. European Commission. Final Evaluation Erasmus Program, December, Brussels (2010)
24. Gacel-Ávila, J.: Los retos de La Internacionalización del Currículo en América Latina. In: Martínez, P., David, L., Helena, P.C. (eds.) La Internacionalización de la Eduación Superior en América Latina y Europa: retos y compromisos, de 1 Pontificia Universidad Javeriana Bogotá (2012)
25. Gacel-Ávila, J., Ávila, R.: Universidades latinoamericanas frente al reto de la internacionalización. en Casa del Tiempo **1**(9), 2–8 (2008)
26. Gandini, L.: Escapando de la crisis? Un estudio comparativo de trayectorias laborales de migrantes argentinos en la Ciudad de México y Madrid. CRIM-UNAM, Cuernavaca (2015)
27. Gérard, E.: "Fuite de cerveaux" ou mobilité: La migration pour études en question. In: Gérard, E., Balac, R., Kail, B., Lanour, E., Proteau, L. (eds.) Mobilités étudiantes Sud-Nord: Trajectoires scolaires de Marocains en France et insertion professionnelle au Maroc, pp. 13–28. Paris-Publisud (2008)
28. Gérard, E., Grediaga, R.: Entre brèches et héritages. Mobilité académique mexicaine dans la seconde moitié du 20è siècle. Colloque La migration en héritage dans les Amériques, París, 6–8 junio (2012)

29. Gérard, E., Maldonado, E.: De la movilidad académica a la circulación de conocimientos: Pistas de investigación. Casa del Tiempo **24**, 3–6 (2009)
30. Gómez, N.: Conacyt busca revertir la "fuga de cerebros" (2014). https://archivo.eluniversal.com.mx/nacion-mexico/2014/impreso/conacyt-busca-revertir-la-8220fuga-de-cerebros-8221-221576.html
31. E Góngora 2012 Prestigio académico: estructuras, estrategias y concepciones. El caso de los sociólogos de la UAM. Asociación Nacional de Universidades e Instituciones de Educación Superior (ANUIES) México (2012)
32. Góngora, E.: Movilidad, alojamiento y socialización de estudiantes de posgrado en la Casa de México en París. In: Ramírez, R., Hamui, M. (Coords.) Perspectivas sobre la internacionalización en educación superior y ciencia. CINVESTAV-RIMAC: Ciudad de México (2016)
33. Gonzálcz, M.: Estudio sobre la movilidad de talentos. Fundación Carolina, Madrid (2015)
34. Hoyos, J., Velasques, O., Domínguez, O.: Problemas nodales de la Internacionalizacion de la Educacion Superior en Colombia, principios orientadores y lineamientos para la construccion de politica publica. ASCUN, Mesa de Internacionalizacion de la educacion superior (2013)
35. Instituto de los Mexicanos en el Exterior [IME]. Estadísticas de Mexicanos en el Exterior (2018)
36. http://www.ime.gob.mx/gob/estadisticas/2016/mundo/estadistica_poblacion.html
37. Knight, G.: Higher Education in Turmoil; The Changing World of Internationalization. Sense Publishers, Rotterdam (2008)
38. MEN & CCYK: Informe Final Proyecto. Estudio sobre la internacionalización de la educación superior en Colombia y modernización de indicadores de internacionalización del Sistema Nacional de Información de la Educación Superior. Anexo 4. Informe análisis exploratorio de la encuesta. (Anexo), p. 125, Bogotá (2013)
39. Nelson, L.: Obama's immigration plan. Inside Higher Ed. (2013). https://www.insidehighered.com/news/2013/01/30/obamas-immigration-plan-would-expand-stem-visas-fund-science-education-offer-path
40. UNESCO. Global flow of tertiary-level students (2019). http://uis.unesco.org/en/uis-student-flow
41. Sacristan, F.: La irrupción de las nuevas tecnologías de la información en los ámbitos educativos. España (2006)
42. Salmi, J.: The Challenge of Establishing World-Class Universities. Directions in Development. Human Development. The World Bank (2007)
43. Spinelli, G.: Títulos colaborativos. Cátedra Europa. Universidad del Norte, Barranquilla (2010)
44. United States Department of State's Bureau of Educational and Cultural Affairs (ECA). Fulbright Foreign Student Program (2007)
45. Van der Wende, M.: Theoretical and methodological contributions of various disciplines to the study of the international dimension: drawing on sciences of education as a theoretical and practical framework. In: Smith, A., Teichler, U., Van der Wende, M. (eds.) The International Dimension of Higher Education: Setting the Research Agenda. IFK/ACA, Vienna (1994)
46. Vigil, C.: Aprendiendo de la experiencia ALBAN para mejorar la cooperación en materia de educación superior entre la Unión Europea y América Latina. Investigación y Desarrollo, **21**(1) (2013)
47. Xalma, C.: El renovado auge de la Cooperación Sur-Sur: La experiencia iberoamericana. Revista Integración y Comercio (Integration and Trade Journal), Inter-American Development Bank, INTAL **36**(17), 29–42 (2013). https://ideas.repec.org/a/idb/intala/jouintegycomv36y2013i17p29-42.html

Corruption in Public Contracts: Improvement of Control Through Quality Management Tools

Pablo Dávila[2]([⊠]) [iD], Guido Villacis[1] [iD], Rubén León[1] [iD], and Marco González[1] [iD]

[1] Universidad Central del Ecuador, Quito 170129, Ecuador
[2] Polytechnic University of Madrid, Madrid, Spain
pablo.davila.pinto@alumnos.upm.es

Abstract. In this study we developed a novel anti-fraud and anti-corruption control model during the public procurement process considering the following processes: i) compliance, ii) risk management and iii) ISO 37001 anti-bribery. This exploratory research included participation from expert auditors in public procurement was requested, who provided criteria that were quantified. We identified concepts and reporting that made it possible to reveal acts of corruption and fraud. Then, specialized bibliography was reviewed to decipher theories and methodologies that are applied in risk control processes. Audit reports were also studied to identify the causes and consequences of the application of public procurement processes. In contracting, risks were identified in all components of the model, which were made visible to make corrections or store a risk. In practice, this model can aid in decreasing corruption and fraud in the contracting process.

Keywords: Public contracts · Risk management · Rules and regulations · Contracts · Quality control · Quality management

1 Introduction and State of the Art

Corruption has been gaining ground in public management, as the easiest way to win contracts with the State is for a group of officials to agree to favor unscrupulous contractors, who in exchange for a commission, obtain getting contracts is the benefit. When this occurs, the Law becomes permissible and the weakness of the controls is evident. The largest number of contracts in recent years stem from criminal activities such as collusion, extorsion, illicit enrichment and illicit association. Vega, León and Nieves define the internal control "as an element of the management process that most contributes to improving the performance of the system" [29]. In other words, when the internal control fails within contracting activities, management is handling these processes poorly.

Public procurement is permeable when it is handled by certain officials who seek to evade the system and help suppliers for their personal benefit. Castañeda conclude that "if nothing is done in this regard, it is reasonable that corruption gradually becomes a norm or is considered necessary to deal with public administration" [6]. In this paper we delve into public procurement by reverse auction, which has contracts of various kinds and amounts, being as diverse as the institutional framework within the public sector. The objective of this work was to establish a preventive model for anti-fraud

© Springer Nature Switzerland AG 2021
T. Guarda et al. (Eds.): ARTIIS 2021, CCIS 1485, pp. 460–473, 2021.
https://doi.org/10.1007/978-3-030-90241-4_35

and anti-corruption control, executed before, during and after public procurement; thus, preventing crime in all the phases of this process.

This model intends to consolidate itself as a strategy for the formulation of public policies that improve the public procurement process, and that greatly reduce the financial damage for the State. Once these intermediate controls are implemented, it will be possible to considerably reduce fraud and corruption in Ecuador.

1.1 Corruption and Fraud in Public Contracts

Corruption is present in all societies, the elimination of it in a country is a panacea, controlling it involves all civil society actors and the coordinated collaboration of all control bodies, in addition to certain cross-cutting Laws that allow expediting the complaints and proceed diligently with the capture and reparation of damages by the administrators of justice. González and Dávila indicate that "The new ethical profile of the professional is based on the interaction that the individual has between the environment and the system in which he/she develops professionally and personally" [17], that is, these factors influence in some way the individual to consider performing an immoral act.

The concept of corruption has been defined by several authors.

Castañeda points out that:

"There is a wide set of political, socioeconomic and institutional factors that define acts of corruption, but not necessarily thanks to an altruistic or disinterested behavior of bureaucrats and politicians, but through an institutional order that makes their deviations costly in relation to precepts that society deems morally acceptable" [6].

On the other hand, fraud involves deception with certain damages for the State. Gutierrez states that "the objective of fraud is to intentionally deceive a person, company or organization, with the purpose of obtaining an unfair advantage to the detriment of the rights or interests of another person or entity" [19].

According to the Instituto Internacional de Auditores:

"Any illegal act characterized by deception, concealment or breach of trust. These acts do not require the application of threat of violence or physical force. Frauds are perpetrated by individuals and organizations to obtain money, goods or services, to avoid payments or loss of services, or to secure personal or business benefits" [21].

In other words, the illegal act translates into a threat of violence and is carried out by individuals and organizations to obtain money and benefits. Frett states that "Fraud comprises a wide range of irregularities and illegal acts characterized by the intention to deceive or provide false information" [13]. The raising of false information to commit acts of corruption and fraud also implies fraudulent acts, which lead to the evidence of corruption. Fraud is a deception that reveals the crime of breach of trust and when the system allows these intentional acts to develop when a group of officials agree to harm an organization, emphasis is placed on the crime of breach of trust, in such a way that, said act executed in the public administration contravenes a mistaken appreciation of the officials within the financial crimes.

On the other hand, Bakhtigozina et al. point out that "according to auditing standards, actions with the objective of extracting illegal profits, which have led to significant errors in the accounting records, are considered unfair" [23] this appreciation shows that when companies already fulfill their objective, which is to participate in a corruption contract, an important economic benefit is achieved, while for the State that offered such contract, it is an unfair act that harms economic development.

Villalta indicates that "in addition to economic losses and expenses aimed at protecting against crime, companies are also affected by the suspension or cancellation of actions or business decisions, for reasons again related to criminal victimization" [30]. Here an action of kleptocracy is mentioned, this action has become widespread and now it is common to observe that politics has an intrinsic relationship with corruption.

In the current context, economic crimes have an influence on the economy of a country. Fraud and corruption influence people's behavior. Modernity in business takes into account the transactions that are carried out to win a contract within the public action, in this environment the public and private companies participate, some as suppliers and others as demanders of a good or service.

For this research we focused on the causes and effects of public procurement, considering ethics as a fundamental variable.

According to SERCOP [27] the number of processes in contracts in the reverse electronic auction type add up to 2470, representing an allocation of 331.9 millions USD, and is the tool with the highest amount adjudicated representing 41.7% of total contracts of this type adding up to 961.8 million USD, between January and February 2020.

Complex digital transactions are used to carry out these types of contracts through online platforms.

Public companies and the different Ministries and National Secretaries include the purchase of goods and services in their public procurement plans to meet institutional objectives; therefore, each institution has a team of specialists in public procurement. Below, certain ethical aspects are included that, based on experience and from practice, must be considered in order to comply with a public procurement process with a certain level of quality (Table 1):

Table 1. Ethical aspects in public procurement.

Ethical aspects in procurement	Business ethical aspects
• Determining ethical and moral values at the time of procurement	• Ethical and moral values are left out and are not relevant
• Procedures are carried out in planned times, meeting scheduled deadlines	• Speed, simplicity, and fraud prevail in the specifications when preparing the contracting process
• There is a collective interest in the process	• Individual interest in the process prevails
• The results are based on the availability of financing	• The results are overwhelming and at any price without paying attention to the quality
• There is transparency in the negotiation	• There is no transparency in the negotiation

Gallego, Rivero and Martínez, state that "transparency is crucial to curb undesirable outcomes in public procurement, such as malfeasance, breaches of contract, and general inefficiency" [14]. Transparency in business with the State has been seriously questioned by the public media and the State Attorney General's Office. Ethical and moral values are important elements to take into account when negotiating a contract, however these are not considered by computer platforms, which only focus on contractual processes.

Within the procurement procedure there are actions that are considered robbery, in private companies they are called criminal organizations and in public institutions it is called organized crime. Both denominations have an intrinsic relationship because they conclude in the same immoral act.

From the previous idea, public morality can be mentioned as a series of acts that positively or negatively interfere with people's behavior. When the immoral act is already carried out, people continue to do it and it becomes a vicious circle.

For this reason, it is necessary to promote professional awareness, so that criminal acts do not occur in the procurement processes.

It is logical to assume that regulation is linked to the regulatory and control entity that for our country is the State Comptroller General. However, the control system must apply independence in its management, with this, the guarantees for adequate control allow it to have a greater scope because it will evidence fraud and will reach civil, administrative and criminal instances.

1.2   Organizational Culture

If we focus on the integral quality that a public company must have, then the business culture must be considered, this important element that is part of the business organization takes into account the behavior of individuals within any organization.

According to Chiavenato, "the organizational culture represents the informal, unwritten norms that guide the daily behavior of the members of the organization and direct their actions in the realization of the organizational objectives" [9]. In other words, it places a lot of emphasis on what does not appear in its codes of ethics and is based on something intangible that is the behavior of people in an organization.

Baracaldo points out that "the objectives of corporate governance, which is established to be a safeguard for shareholders, is to promote fair treatment, strengthen the transparency of information, increase social responsibility, guarantee sustainability and increase investment in organizations" [4]. However, in reality, when it is intended to ignore these goals, they are left out and it is possible to violate methodologies and add fraudulent actions.

1.3   The Codes of Ethics

This element is recommended as a quality seal in the proper functioning of organizations. Its application depends on the management, and in public organizations, officials must know its principles and objectives, promulgation, implementation and monitoring.

Franklin notes that "principle-based statements, also known as corporate creeds, define the core values that underpin the organizational culture" [22]. Likewise, "the code of ethics is the declaration of the values of an organization in relation to social ethical aspects. It is generally based on two types of statements: principles and policies".

Public institutions are constantly changing, and corruption and fraud can interfere when they are committed by unscrupulous people who, knowing the consequences of such actions, still commit this type of crime.

According to Mantilla, "the so-called disruptive innovation, which is the product of new and emerging technologies" [31], aims to be a phenomenon to which much attention is being paid due to the effects and risks that it entails, by neglecting legal and regulatory frameworks. This includes the control of public procurement, for which there is a technological platform with many limitations.

Pérez, Garzón and Ibarra, point out in [11] that "business ethics guarantees the continuity of credibility and trust, from the external sphere to the inside of the company and vice versa, through a set of rules" [24]. In this way, ethical conduct is reflected in the codes of ethics, and these parameters make it possible to adapt the actions of officials, limiting their actions to ethical positions and moral conduct that do not allow corruption.

Public procurement arises from institutional need and ends in the assessment of the delivery of the good or service. When an act of corruption occurs, it allows risks to arise at the beginning and end of the hiring process.

Large contracts where costs exceed millions of dollars are much more permeable to fraud and corruption. Regarding this, Castro and Otero point out:

"Large works or infrastructure projects, telecommunications or those related to the energy and defense sectors are also considered prone to corrupt practices, as the technological complexity of these sectors offers a greater opportunity to hide diverse and varied corrupt practices" [8].

In fact, the organization Transparency International affirms that "corruption in public procurement is currently recognized as the main factor of waste and inefficiency in the management of resources" [28]. These are transferred to society, but for fraudulent officials and for companies that committed corruption, the loss of reputation and loss of prestige in their work falls on themselves.

Many times the contracting of certain identical projects and in which no measurement has been carried out, are also subject to corruption. As noted by Rodrigues and Zucco, "the choice of the contracting model had no causal relationship with the evaluated results" [26]. These contracts, due to the urgency of the officials, grant several procedures to a certain company, whose choice is fraught with irregularities and comes to light when a special examination is carried out.

This type of crime affects the economy and the few resources that we have become even more insufficient. In this regard Ramírez points out that:

"The explanation of crime has been generated in two aspects: from the perspective of the economic cycle and from the economic development. Each of them specifies a particular mechanism and a group of independent variables to explain the variation in crime: unemployment in the case of the business cycle and growth and wealth indices in the case of economic development" [25].

In this set of ideas, it should be considered that the best cost is crime prevention, and this is where our research focused.

2   Methodology

For this study, the opinion of 10 experts on the subject was considered. This type of sample is frequent in some studies to generate more precise hypotheses or raw material for the design of questionnaires [20]. Based on a set of directed questions, the auditors selected those that are displayed on the radar charts. This exploration was carried out based on the fraud and corruption events in public procurement selected from the confidential reports of public companies. From the set of questions selected by the expert auditors, the preventive anti-fraud and anti-corruption control model was born. This was addressed from a qualitative and quantitative approach as the questions with the highest assessment were validated to define the three processes: i) compliance, ii) risk management and iii) ISO 37001 anti-bribery.

Risk prevention in public procurement allows establishing a set of measures to minimize risk through control in organizations, meeting the strategic objectives of State institutions and safeguarding insufficient resources, as well as considering demands which are unlimited.

Within corporate government the goal is to review structures and responsibilities under strategic-level policies and directives. The goal of this commitment is to fulfill the control models applied, as a best practices code for middle and operational levels. The development of parameters and directives fulfilled by the upper layers of public management is achieved, they say that as the strategic level is fulfilled the middle and operational levels must do so as well. In this sense, compliance with the control standards, established by companies through best practices, code of ethics, anti-bribery practices, risk prevention and data protection, becomes a priority to combat corruption. Within the quality of public procurement processes, the following quality processes must be related and coordinated.

2.1   Compliance

This process is called compliance and must be applied by all levels of an organization, at the strategic, medium and operational levels. Its functions are focused on preventing, detecting and managing, for which a compliance program must be established, and all efforts made within this program make it possible not to violate the activities. It focuses on standardization, that is, the program must be assumed and must be an example to be followed by senior management,

Results are produced after implementing fulfillment correctives.

According to García:

"Compliance management systems (guidelines) provide guidance for implementing, evaluating, maintaining or continuously improving a compliance management system. As mentioned in the previous chapter, compliance must encompass the entire organization and people with a certain responsibility in it must have maximum involvement" [16].

2.2   Risk Management

It is a mechanism to identify damage, either due to an event that may be operational, legal, or of corruption and money laundering and financing of terrorism. The culture of an organization is based on values, attitudes and beliefs, the way in which institutions work in a system where corruption is institutionalized counts on activities related to the contracting process, which become bad practices which generate organizational fraud risks.

Part of the contextual analysis of how they work is related to organizational culture, because the non-adjustment of best practices is present in public contracting, later a follow up and evaluation are done to quantify it, they can minimize corruption and fraud cases in any institution, public or private.

In summary, the main activities in quality risk management taken from the COSO model are the following:

"The new ISO 9001: 2015 standard speaks especially about risk management, which is one of the most prominent developments in professional quality circles. We have commented on one of the mechanisms or methodologies that we can use to carry out this management, referring to COSO I and COSO II. The third version, COSO III, was published in 2013" [21].

2.3   ISO 37001

"This norm was developed by 59 member countries of the International Organization for Standardization (ISO) and published in October 2016, making it the first internationally recognized antibribery norm" [28].

In Ecuador, the creation of an anti-bribery law is pertinent, as it could establish ethical positions and the identification of unfair practices in an organization. In this sense, bribery becomes a powerful weapon to carry out immoral acts, and the results are a decrease in the reputation and trust of the companies that commit such crime. Promoting an ethical and organizational culture stands out, completely eliminating this type of actions, the generation of anti-bribery regulations considerably reduces fraud and leaves aside the traces of its happening again, because it sensitizes personnel to the risks and its measures prevent corruption.

According to SMS Latin-American [28], applying an anti-bribery management system as a result of the application of the ISO 37001 standard, provides the following benefits:

– Communicates the organization's commitment to prevent bribery from occurring.
– Provides clarity on the measures that organizations can reasonably expect to manage bribery risk
– It allows identifying organizations that are serious about the fight against bribery from those that are not.

The elements that allow this ISO to be complied with consider: preventing, discovering and addressing bribery, in such a way that the people who carry out these illegal activities are exposed and are not hired. This process must be tied with the national public procurement system.

In order for these measures to be adopted, it is suggested: i) implement an institutional policy, ii) appoint a compliance officer in contracting, iii) verification and evaluation with training for those responsible, iv) financial and accounting controls, v) promotion of procedures for internal and external complaint, and vi) socialize the policy to all staff.

3 Results

3.1 Model Proposed to Improve Public Procurement with Comprehensive Quality

Three elements of quality within public procurement were reviewed, which promote and encourage ethical values and public principles as a fundamental premise that organizations must incorporate to combat corruption and fraud in the public procurement process. Taking prevention into account, it seems necessary and essential to achieve the coordination, management, systematization and implementation of this model. From the orderly application and its follow-up, a new research process can be highlighted that manages to provide information for continuous improvement (Fig. 1).

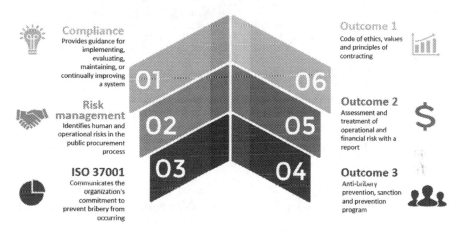

Fig. 1. Model with elements of ISO quality and internal control

The proposed model considers three fundamental processes within the identification, prevention and management of risks in public procurement: the systematization, coordination and continuous evaluation of the model. Its implementation will establish the guidelines for the progressive reduction of fraud and corruption by promoting prevention.

In the analysis carried out, we focused on the causes and effects in the public procurement process, obtaining the following causes and consequences (Table 2):

3.2 Identification of Causes and Consequences in Public Procurement: Reverse Auction Case

Table 2. Causes and consequences

Causes	Consequences
– Unethical practices – Directed contracting for few suppliers – Anti-competitive rating – Values in contracts for retailers – The contracting law protects contractors and not the State – Electronic fraud in the public procurement portal – Connectivity problems in the portal – Failures in the contracting system – Circumvention of processes that evade public procurement – Ignorance of the regulations at all levels – Consulting products are uploaded for very small amounts – Special regime with guidance in contracting – Fair competition for suppliers is not promoted – The platform allows ways to circumvent processes and requirements – Hiring officers direct processes – Avoidance of processes with guidelines – Low quality of services and goods – Deficiency in the quality of materials for works	– Institutionalized corruption – Collusion between officials and bidders – Disinterest of the private sector in sales with the State – Competitors are eliminated applying criteria at discretion – In the electronic bid you communicate with the selected bidder – Failure to verify requirements – Organized mafias of contracting companies – Illegal practices in the process – Large contracts to monopolies – Companies without experience and without certifications are qualified – Only the previously colluded ones sign contracts – Providers and community are both affected – Economic and financial damage to the State

3.3 Application of the Components of the Proposed Anti-fraud Control Model

We conducted an analysis of the proposed model taking as a reference the deficiencies in the contracting processes and placing emphasis on the components of the model. We determined a series of elements for each component, and these were weighed according to the availability of actions that are framed in the public institutions that carry out public contracting And validated under the experience of the auditors. These actions include the empirical observation that currently exists in the contracting process, the provision of the institutional needs emanating from the contracting plans, the design of the terms of reference and the contract specifications, the requirements of the good or service, the award of the contract and its execution.

Next, we present the specific analysis for each of the components with their respective elements:

Compliance. The experts selected this set of specific questions within the recruitment process. In order to observe the variables, an analysis was carried out after the hiring process. We can see that two variables were met, the establishment of a monitoring commission and the variable of training of officials to comply with hiring guidelines.

For the rest of the variables, the experts indicated that contract management was not evaluated, that no internal guidelines were established and, most seriously, that a contract compliance program was not planned. In other words, the contracting was not considered in the annual contracting plan (Fig. 2).

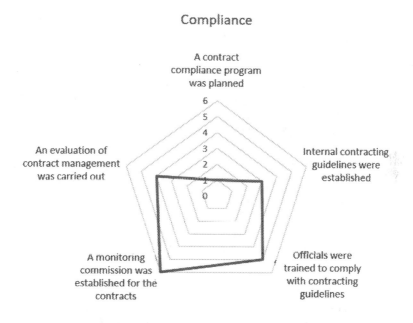

Fig. 2. Compliance component

Risk Management. For this variable, the risk assessment is carried out in the contracting process, considering the products and its fundamental requirements. Here the variable is influenced by three elements: private collusion, targeted verification of requirements, and the experience of providers. The other two elements, supplier certification and contracts with the same companies, are valued moderately. As a whole, the mentioned variables are decisive for accessing a contract with the public sector, and it is clear that collusion and targeted verification of requirements cause corruption and fraud in the public procurement process (Fig. 3).

ISO 37001. According to the experience of the expert auditors, this element is considered a prevention mechanism that allows the level of anti-bribery commitment to be adjusted. Additionally, the company must have a compliance officer to monitor the code of ethics in advance, in order to identify anti-bribery and collusion practices. Finally, corrupt companies and officials are evaluated and sanctioned. Here it is important to highlight the creation of the technical, legal, and financial administrative committees; all of them made up of people with ethical behavior and high values of honesty and integrity (Fig. 4).

Risk management

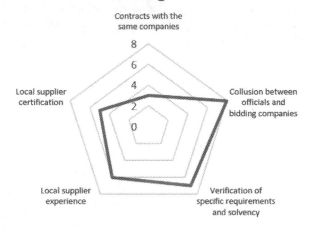

Fig. 3. Risk management component

ISO 37001

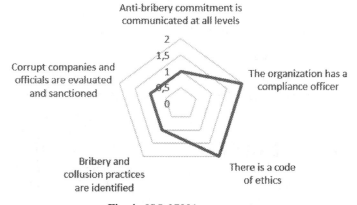

Fig. 4. ISO 37001 component

Figure 2 shows that the organization has a compliance officer who enforces a code of ethics, but only partially tries to identify anti-bribery and collusion practices, not being able to evaluate and sanction corrupt companies and officials. Likewise, and with the same partial assessment, there is no adequate anti-bribery commitment at all levels, which means that the different levels of control are not carried out and therefore bribery may occur in the public procurement process.

We can highlight that contracts with the same companies are a significant risk, as is the identification of local suppliers and the addressing of contracting requirements. On the other hand, in the risk component, private collusion stands out and there is a focus on the requirements and experience of the contractors, these two elements allow fraud and corruption to proliferate. Finally, in the anti-bribery component the main aspect is the work of the compliance officer who verifies that the code of ethics is complied with, but there is only a partial coverage of the identification, evaluation, and communication of corrupt and anti-bribery practices between officials and companies that provide goods and services with the State.

4   Discussion

Establishing a preventive model for the control of public procurement is a challenge for public institutions and for the State. Gutierrez points out that "to promote an integrity regime through the vision of a system that brings together the efforts of multiple institutions and social actors in favor of an honest and effective government regime" [19]. This author argues that preventive efforts should be with all institutions and actors related to contracting; however, this is a limitation of the model because it focuses on the different contracting processes and handles the preventive part, that is, it acts to strengthen the process through its elements: compliance, risk management and the anti-bribery ISO 37001. This is intended to anticipate the corrupt process and eliminate it whenever possible.

The crimes committed in the public sector are evident and increasingly progressive, the terms of fraud and corruption are not unrelated to public contracts, these crimes are to the detriment of society and development policies in every sense. Collusion is not a superfluous act, rather its actions are immeasurable, when officials and contractors make an agreement not even the best internal control can identify it. In relation to this idea, Galvis points out that "collusion is a phenomenon that affects all selection processes indistinctly" [15] the fact of reaching an agreement between officials and contractors is an act of corruption. Arellano [1] points out that "de-normalizing" corruption is then a necessary step and extremely difficult to carry out. Difficult because it implies entering into social relationships, into processes that have made a series of behaviors a routine that may be already rationalized. Corruption for this type of process is considered normal, therefore the culture of corruption and institutionalized impunity in this type of malpractice must be eliminated.

5   Conclusions

This work had the collaboration of 10 expert auditors who have carried out audits for more than 20 years in the public sector. The limitation of the study was that the audit reports made by these experts could not be disclosed due to confidentiality; therefore, the questions were classified based on the perception of the audits carried out. The results obtained were closely related to what the experts answered, within the three components an analysis of the information provided by the regulatory entities regarding fraud and corruption was carried out. The model was developed based on the qualitative analysis of the control body's reports and specialized bibliography. This model allows to identify and clarify the concepts and methodologies that are currently used in financial crimes.

Considering the public procurement portal, we focused on the reverse auction process and the causes and consequences of a type of public procurement were identified, clarifying its elements. In this way, this study is a contribution that allows fighting corruption in public institutions.

The cause and consequences analysis revealed the weaknesses of the contracting system, this also allows people who manage contracting processes to apply this type of filter via alerts, in order to identify how operating risk can generate negative effects leading to fraud and corruption. This study is for identifying these deficiencies; the fundamental process is based on prevention this element is a quality driver within the contracting process, because once functionaries know the procedural deficiencies and the effects that could arise from improperly developing a contract with corruption, they must take responsibility.

Also allows for people interested in managing contracting processes to establish their alertness, taking as a premis their localization. Considering some of them allows for assuming that said causes can generate negative effects on public contracting. This study is for observing such processes, and the fundamental process within this study is based on prevention, with this element becoming a specific quality driver.

An anti-fraud and preventive model were designed to make the surveillance and risk control processes in public procurement transparent. This model must be developed in all its phases and with the committees mentioned as control guidelines.

By applying control processes in public procurement, improvement actions are positioned in an organization, the application of models that have quality premises promote and strengthen the organizational culture and leadership in corporate governance, which becomes a prop that intervenes in the organization so that acts of corruption are alerted, and fraud and economic crimes are reduced. For this reason, the implementation of this model must have institutional policies and commitments. It is necessary to rescue that ethical values such as honesty, loyalty, empathy, and integrity have an intrinsic relationship with the proposed model, because these are verified in all its phases. This means that by implementing the model it is possible to establish conditions to reduce the acts of corruption that do so much harm to the State.

References

1. Arellano, D.: Corrupción como proceso organizacional: comprendiendo la lógica de la desnormalización de la corrupción. Contaduría y Administración **62**(3), 810–826 (2017)
2. Asamblea Nacional del Ecuador. https://tbinternet.ohchr.org/Treaties/CEDAW/Shared%20Documents/ECU/INT_CEDAW_ARL_ECU_18950_S.pdf. Accessed 15 Jan 2021
3. Bakhtigozina, E., Efremova, E., Shevere, E., Shevereva, A., Nalbatova, E.: Fraud in the organization and direction of control in order to prevent it. Espacios **39**(39), 29 (2018)
4. Baracaldo, N.: Diagnóstico de gobierno corporativo como mecanismo en la prevención del fraude en empresas familiares* (Aplicación de método de casos). Cuadernos de Contabilidad **14**(35), 581–615 (2015)
5. Carrera, I.: Hacía una estrategia nacional anticorrupción. Marca publicity, Quito (2007)
6. Castañeda Rodríguez, V.: La moral tributaria en América Latina y la corrupción como uno de sus determinantes. Revista Mexicana de Ciencias Políticas y Sociales **60**(224), 103–132 (2015)
7. Castañeda, V.: Una investigación sobre la corrupción pública y sus determinantes. Revista Mexicana de Ciencias Políticas y Sociales **61**(227), 103–136 (2015)
8. Castro, A., Otero, P.: Prevención y tratamiento punitivo de la corrupción en la contratación pública y privada. Dykinson, Madrid (2016)

9. Chiavenato, I.: Administración de Recursos Humanos: El capital humano en las organizaciones. Mc Graw Hill, México (2009)
10. Cooter, R., Ulen, T.: Law and Economics. Pearson Addison-Wesley, Boston (2011)
11. Donohue, J., Siegelman, P.: Allocating resources among prisons and social programs in the battle against crime. J. Leg. Stud. **27**(1), 1–43 (1998)
12. Franklin, E.: Auditoria administrativa: evaluación y diagnóstico empresarial. Pearson, México (2013)
13. Frett, N.: http://nahunfrett.blogspot.com/2014/09/14-tipos-de-fraudes.html. Accessed 18 Mar 2021
14. Gallego, J., Rivero, G., Martínez, J.: Preventing rather than punishing: an early warning model of malfeasance in public procurement. Int. J. Forecast. **37**(1), 360–377 (2020)
15. Galvis, D.: La colusión como una práctica restrictiva de la competencia que afecta gravemente los procesos de selección de contratistas. Universitas **65**(132), 133–196 (2016)
16. García, A.: https://1library.co/document/y62mm35z-impacto-compliance-tributario-tejido-empresarial-espanol.html
17. Gonzalez, M., Dávila, P.: Definición de criterios éticos para los nuevos profesionales de las carreras de la Universidad Central del Ecuador. Ética e Política **1**(1), 106–110 (2019)
18. Gutierrez, M.: https://360bestpracticesmethodology.wordpress.com/2015/12/12/el-auditor-interno-y-su-responsabilidad-hacia-el-fraude/. Accessed 27 Mar 2021
19. Gutierrez, M.: La auditoría superior de la federación y la conformación del Sistema Nacional Anticorrupción. Cuestiones Constitucionales **37**, 51–83 (2017)
20. Hernández, R., Fernández, C., Bautista, P.: Metodología de Investigación. McGrawHill, México (2007)
21. Instituto Internacional de Auditores: https://www.isotools.org/2015/01/19/iso-90012015-metodologia-coso-iii-gestion-riesgos/. Accessed 25 May 2021
22. Jareño, A.: La corrupción en la contratación pública. Pasajes **42**, 14–21 (2013)
23. Mantilla, S.: Auditoria del Control Interno. Ecoe Ediciones, Bogotá (2018)
24. Pérez, L., Garzón, M., Ibarra, A.: Código de ética empresarial para las Pymes: marco de referencia para la sostenibilidad y responsabilidad social empresarial (RSE). Espacios **36**(2), 11 (2016)
25. Ramírez, L.: Crimen y economía: una revisión crítica de las explicaciones económicas del crimen. Argumentos **27**(74), 261–290 (2014)
26. Rodrigues, B., Zucco, C.: Una comparación directa del desempeño de una CCP como modelo tradicional de contratación pública. Revista de Administração Pública **52**(6), 1237–1257 (2018)
27. SERCOP, S.N.: https://portal.compraspublicas.gob.ec/sercop/wp-content/uploads/downloads/2020/03/BoletIn_Feb_2020_v3_13032020.pdf. Accessed 8 June 2021
28. SMS Latinoamerica: https://smsecuador.ec/iso-37001-anticorrupcion-y-etica-empresarial/. Accessed 15 June 2021
29. Vega, O., León, Y., Nieves, A.: Propuesta de un índice para evaluar la gestión del control interno en entidades hospitalarias. Contaduría y administración **62**(2), 683–698 (2017)
30. Villalta Perdomo, C.J.: When kleptocracy is not enough: crimes against businesses. Economía Sociedad y Territorio **17**(55), 837–866 (2017)
31. Zambrano, N., Jaramillo, M., Pérez, D., Serrano, M.: Fórmulas de selección económica de contratistas en adjudicación de obras de infraestructura vial: estudio de caso Valle del Cauca. Colombia. Entre Ciencia e Ingeniería **12**(24), 60–67 (2018)

Social Engineering: The Art of Attacks

Nelson Duarte[1] , Nuno Coelho[2] , and Teresa Guarda[1,3,4,5(✉)]

[1] ISLA Santarém, Santarém, Portugal
nelson.duarte@islasantarem.pt
[2] ISLA Gaia, Santarém, Portugal
nuno.coelho@islagaia.pt
[3] Universidad Estatal Peninsula de Santa Elena, Santa Elena, Ecuador
[4] CIST – Centro de Investigación en Sistemas y Telecomunicaciones,
Universidad Estatal Península de Santa Elena, La Libertad, Ecuador
[5] Algoritmi Centre, Minho University, Guimarães, Portugal

Abstract. The correct management of information systems security is often over-looked in technological measures and management efforts, and although there are now many tools to address security threats, the human aspect has been neglected. This paper discusses the human factors that could potentially lead to intrusions with social engineering. Social engineering is a method used by hackers to obtain access to systems by manipulating flaws in behavior known as mental preconceptions. Social engineering is a risk to security information and must be considered just as important as in technological areas. In this paper we also approach social engineering, taking an introductory brief in its history, what is psychological manipulation and human weaknesses, what are the social engineering attacks, how they use authority and fear establishment, it is also approached how a social engineering attack is executed, providing value monetizing the scam, and identity exploration.

Keywords: Social engineering attacks · Psychological manipulation · Human weaknesses · Identity exploration

1 Introduction

The internet is the largest means of communication available to us today, it is through the internet that we communicate in most diverse ways, using different means of communication. Social networks have become one of the privileged ways for us to get in touch with other people, whether on a personal or professional level. Organizations increasingly expect their employees to be connected to the company, either by devices that the company provides or by their own devices [1]. Decentralized access to online data and services has brought about a paradigm shift in information sharing and an increase in platforms for doing so. People post all kinds of information on social media without realizing that what they are sharing could be used by someone who might want to compromise the security of systems of the company they work for. Although systems are constantly being updated in terms of security, they end up being not very effective when employees are

© Springer Nature Switzerland AG 2021
T. Guarda et al. (Eds.): ARTIIS 2021, CCIS 1485, pp. 474–483, 2021.
https://doi.org/10.1007/978-3-030-90241-4_36

manipulated through social engineering [2]. The expression "knowledge worker" was introduced by Peter Drucker about 50 years ago and still applies to employees where their main characteristic is knowledge [3].

One of the most powerful tools a hacker has to access privileged information is Social Engineering, where people are manipulated into giving out information they shouldn't. It is a technique superior to most other hacking techniques because it allows them to breach the most secure systems, since users are the most vulnerable part of any system. Social engineering does not require great technical skills and can be performed on a large scale. Social engineering is widely exploited on social networks and sharing platforms, allowing large companies worldwide to fall target to advanced attacks on their computer structures [2].

One can refer to the attack on Google's system in 2011 [4], where it was compromised, the attack on Facebook in 2013 [5], or the attack on the New York Times in the same year where hackers allegedly connected to the Chinese government attacked the computer systems, taking over some passwords [6].

Regarding security and privacy of systems there has been a strengthening of these issues due to the high number of attacks that have been reported in the media, with main focus on attacks by email, which is the main method of communication used for this type of attack by hackers and social engineers, however this awareness in services on the cloud and social networks is still relatively small [7].

The contributions of this paper aim to make an introduction to the history of Social Engineering, what is psychological manipulation and human weaknesses, Social Engineering attacks, how to perform a Social Engineering attack, how to obtain value and how can the attacker benefit from identity exploitation. This article aims to alert companies, employees, public and private entities to the different types of attacks perpetuated through Social Engineering, showing how they are executed, so that the reader can be enlightened and consequently prevent these same attacks that cost companies millions. It is also intended to help other authors in the study and research of this subject.

2 Social Engineering Human Manipulation

Human manipulation in social engineering, in information technology, is the manipulation of the behavior of people to have certain behaviors that could endanger computer systems, whether personal or corporate. Human personality is prone to be manipulated to carry out social engineering attacks [8]. These attacks are mainly aimed at getting an individual to perform certain actions unconsciously, as explained by [9].

2.1 Psychological Manipulation

The goal of psychological manipulation is to get a person to perform a certain action or to reveal confidential information without realizing that they are doing so. People are considered to be the most vulnerable link in an information system, which is why they are also the preferred targets of hackers [10] in computer infrastructures there are firewalls that cost companies a lot of money, information systems have implemented access controls with very tight rules about who has access to what and also have antiviruses that block malicious code from entering servers and other devices on the network, but despite the existence of all these security mechanisms we have the human vulnerability, the people who are inside the network and have access to information. This paradox leads us to Social Engineering, where all these security systems can be compromised by a person in the company who has access to confidential information and advanced permissions [11].

2.2 Human Weaknesses

One of the most exploited human weaknesses in Social Engineering is greed, offering something that the person wants or needs. It is common to use emails offering cash prizes by email as a form of phishing, of course then more information will be requested from the user that will allow other types of attacks. Another weakness is fear, where the attacker scares the user and convincingly threatens him to the point of providing privileged information. Curiosity is another form of weakness, people are curious by nature and this curiosity can lead to problems. Facebook is an example of how click-jacking scam schemes can be realized where a video appears with a text that arouses the user's curiosity and when the user clicks on the video, he loses control over his computer [12].

3 Social Engineering Attacks

Social Engineering is the art of making someone to compromise computer structures and infrastructure. The Social Engineering life cycle, as referenced in Fig. 1, shows us that attackers first identify potential victims by searching for relevant information and selecting the best attacks, then they try to gain the victim's trust through social engineering schemes, using that information to execute attacks and gain control over the systems, and finally they remove the traces of their interaction so that they cannot be incriminated or related to the attack [2].

3.1 Reverse Social Engineering

Hackers target people with privileged access to systems and try to contact potential victims indirectly by posing as a credible entity. The goal is to get victims to make contact and ask the attacker for assistance. This approach is called "reverse social engineering" [13] and consists of damage, assistance, and publicity [14]. The first approach consists of sabotaging the organization's computer system, it can range from disconnecting users from the network to manipulating software installed on the victim's computer. Hackers may later contact the company saying they can fix the problem. When the hacker is asked for help, the hacker will ask for the victim's password to solve the problem or ask the victim to install a certain program [13].

Preparing the ground for the attack:
· Identifying the victim(s).
· Gathering background information.
· Selecting attack method(s).

Closing the interaction,
ideally without arousing suspicion:
· Removing all traces of malware.
· Covering tracks.
· Bringing the charade to a natural end.

Deceiving the victim(s) to gain a foothold:
· Engaging the target.
· Spinning a story.
· Taking control of the interaction.

Obtaining the information over a period of time:
· Expanding foothold.
· Executing the attack.
· Disrupting business or/and siphoning data.

Fig. 1. Social engineering attack lifecycle

3.2 The Technical Approach

The Internet is one of the main means used for cyber-attacks. Granger [13] tells us that the web is very attractive for hackers to get passwords, since people frequently use the same (mostly very simple) passwords for the various systems they have online. Users are unaware that they are giving out critical information. Hackers use search browsers to get private information from potential targets. Some tools are available that allow attackers to collect information from other resources on the web, one such tool is Maltego [15]. Social networks are a valuable source of information for these types of individuals.

3.3 Office Communication

The new online communication platforms have dramatically changed the way teams communicate with each other in companies, making it possible to share information at a great speed. Although these platforms are protected with security devices and software, social engineering attacks are still not properly addressed in security plans. In enterprises face-to-face communication has largely been substituted by email and chat applications, creating a new opportunity for hacker attacks. Social engineering attacks initiated from inside accounts or known emails are easier to succeed with a prospective victim. Parsons et al. [16] performed an experiment with 117 participants where they were tested on their ability to distinguish between phishing emails and authentic emails. They found that people with a high level of awareness were capable to detect substantially more phishing emails has shown in Fig. 2, private information obtained across social engineering had direct effects, such as gaining access to bank accounts or indirect consequences such as identity theft [17].

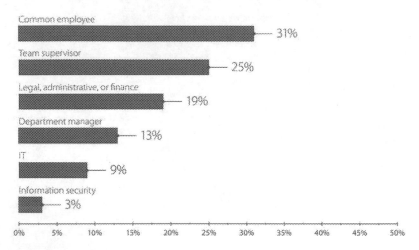

Fig. 2. Phishing attacks on employees by department

3.4 Authority and Fear Establishment

In this kind of attack the hacker uses fear trying to convince the victim that his computer may have a virus, pretending to be a credible entity, like Microsoft, making the victim believe he's being contacted because he's using a Windows operating system and that Microsoft knows what's going on with his computer, establishing authority in this case. As most users have little experience with computers, they become afraid, and that's when the attacker tries to convince the victim that the best solution will be to remotely access his computer to solve the problem. What the hacker really wants is to create authenticity regarding the serious problem that may be on the victim's computer [15]. After gaining control of the victim's computer the blackmailing for value begins.

3.5 Identity Exploration

For identity exploitation there are several tools available on the Internet, some paid and some free, and they are widely used by hackers to obtain information about potential victims. There is a tool called pipl that is a people search engine and allows you to search various sites for data a person has online. It is one of the most powerful tools to find personal and corporate information, emails, phone numbers, files, and posts. In a short time, a hacker can gather enough information to carry out a successful attack [2].

3.6 Personal Contact

In these types of attacks hackers personally contact the victim, interacting with the victim, to get information that will allow them to perform an attack on the victim or the company where the victim works. This type of information may vary depending on what the hacker wants, usually it will be information related to the target. Another way to get information will be to rummage through garbage bins looking for papers that may have been thrown in the trash and may contain relevant information about the company, often employees throw papers away when they should shred them so they cannot be read. These papers may have information about employees, reports about the company and in some cases even information about computer access such as users and passwords. One of the practices of some less informed employees can lead them to write their passwords on papers so that they don't forget them and throw them in the trash absentmindedly. Other types of personal attacks involve stealing or extorting people to get data [13].

3.7 Tailgating

The common characteristic in this type of attack is that the attacker creates a character and invents a false story around the character trying to exploit the victim's basic emotions, sympathy, greed and fear [18]. The technique, basically, consists of following a person with authorized entry into a restricted access location. Less enlightened employees may be easily misled. Employees in less senior positions may fear that they will be denied access by senior managers and the potential (undue) reprisals that will ensue. The social engineer may use a variety of techniques to gain access to the site, such as access, such as using conversation and sympathy to gain the victim's trust in order to provide access, convincing access, convincing them that he has forgotten or lost his card, pretending to be a new colleague at work, using a fake card and excusing himself with a possible malfunction, or pretending to be someone in authority [19].

3.8 Socially Engineered Attacks

One of the most common ways of carrying out social engineering attacks are social approaches. By socially approaching victims, hackers use social-psychological methods to persuade victims. An example of this is the use of authority, or curiosity employed in spear-phishing and baiting attacks. These types of attacks are only successful if the hacker can establish some sort of trust relationship with the victim. Most of these attacks are carried out by phone calls [13].

The majority of attacks in 2018 were aimed at direct financial profit or obtaining sensitive information. However, attacks aimed at data theft often have financial implications: data can be used for stealing money, blackmailing, and can even be sold on the dark web. The graph in Fig. 3 shows us the most common reasons for hackers to carry out attacks.

3.9 Attacks on Social Networks

Although you can get information in traditional ways as mentioned in the previous topic, not all hackers are predisposed to this type of attacks, nowadays; through social networks, you can easily access information about almost everyone. This information can be a starting point to initiate attacks. This kind of information allows you to get phone numbers, emails, places often visited by victims, family members and workplaces [20]. LinkedIn is one such social network, where people post on their profile where they work, in which department and often even the computer equipment the company uses. An employee who posts his or her email address on their profile may be opening the

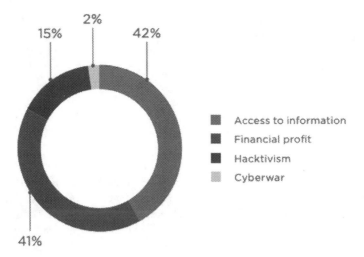

Fig. 3. Most common attacker motives

door to a spam or phishing attack that could compromise the company they work for. Phishing is a widely used attack on the Internet, this type of attack can direct victims to fake websites where hackers can try to collect passwords to access the real sites or bank card information. Many of these phishing attacks are very successful because the hacker pretends to be a friend of the victims, which increases his credibility [21].

3.10   Most Commonly Used Attacks in Enterprises

Data provided by PORDATA (2012), indicates the rate of Internet use by companies with 10 or more employees was 98%. Among the various activities carried out through the internet, email processing (sending and receiving) and information search are the most used activities, and in contact with public bodies and financial institutions the internet is the preferred medium. With the growing importance of the use of this medium, attacks have been aimed at exploiting its vulnerabilities. In the use of various services - email, online contacts with financial institutions and public bodies, chat services, downloads, among others - companies are vulnerable to various types of attack - malware, spying, phishing, interesting software, hoaxing, pop-ups, etc. [22].

For example, when using email services, institutions are vulnerable to attacks, especially malware. A virus infection can result in the installation of backdoors in order to guarantee to malicious third parties' access and control of the infected machines, with potential disclosure of information and also the execution of attacks on other systems from the former. On another note, it is universally recognized that companies, in order to reduce costs with the storage of information, are turning to storage services and file sharing in the cloud. In their use, institutions hand over the management of their information to third parties, losing control over the processes that are running or where data is stored. Before subscribing to these services, customers, in order to reduce the risks associated with their use, should certify that the supplier guarantees the integrity, availability, confidentiality, authenticity and non-repudiation of the information [15].

According to the study developed by ISACA, which included more than 1500 companies from more than 50 countries in Europe, Middle East and Africa, one in five companies that are cloud computing clients do not value the risks of using the technology. Nearly two-thirds were willing to assume a certain level of risk, (12%) of IT managers said they were willing to take the risk to maximize business return.

In the analysis of the services that are used over the phone, it appears that this is the preferred means of contact with partners (98%), with this channel being associated with the possibility of various types of attacks - impersonation/pretexting, smishing, vishing, among others. By including the use of smartphones in the analysis, one should add the attacks associated with the use of the internet, since this type of equipment allows access to the service [22]. The graph in Fig. 4 shows us which sectors have the most business attacks.

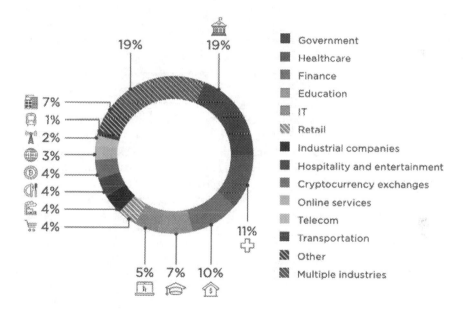

Fig. 4. Organization victims' category

4   State of Future Attacks in Enterprises

According to Kevin Haley, Security Response Specialist at Symantec, the attack risks will tend toward: cyber conflicts; emergence of Ransomware [23]; emergence of malware for mobile devices - madware [24]; scams linked to social networks and attacks on mobile platforms and cloud services.

Regarding cyber-attacks, Kevin states that conflicts between nations, organizations and individuals will tend to be developed in the virtual world. The application of espionage technique, in the virtual world, may be successful.

New malware [25] will emerge, including Ramsomware and Madware. Ramsomware is a type of attack consisting of malicious software that locks the computer and demands a ransom fee to unlock it.

Mobile devices are increasingly used both inside and outside corporate networks, containing sensitive data and information increase the information security risks and arouse interest in the development of attacks. Madware is a type of malware developed for mobile devices, which aims to collect information. This type of threat installs itself on devices through app downloads. This type of attack has increased significantly in the last months. A significant part of these attacks is carried out by social engineering [26].

5   Conclusions

In this paper, we described common attack scenarios for modern social engineering attacks on victims. Policies and distributed collaboration as well as communication over third-party channels offers a variety of new attack vectors for advanced social engineering attacks. We believe that a detailed understanding of the attack vectors is required to develop efficient countermeasures and protect knowledge workers from social engineering attacks. Situations were presented that happen on a daily basis, regarding advanced attacks used in organizations, in communications on online platforms and social networks. Social engineering attacks are attacks that exploit individuals' social and psychological vulnerabilities, attacking weaknesses such as vanity, loneliness, self-centeredness, and others, taking advantage of these weaknesses to target companies through their weakest link, which is the human being. It is extremely important that companies invest in the training and dissemination of this type of attack so that employees can be more alert. We hope this article can contribute to alert organizations and employees to the importance of these attacks, which are increasingly frequent and cost companies millions.

References

1. Ballagas, R., Rohs, M., Sheridan, J.G., Borchers, J.: BYOD: bring your own device. In: Proceedings of the Workshop on Ubiquitous Display Environments (2004)
2. Krombholz, K., Hobel, H., Huber, M., Weippl, E.: Advanced social engineering attacks. J. Inf. Secur. Appl. **22**, 113–122 (2015)
3. Drucker, P.F.: Landmarks of Tomorrow: A Report on the New "Post-Modern" World, 1st edn. Harper, New York (1959)
4. RSA: Anatomia de um ataque. RSA, 17 Julho 2013. http://blogs.rsa.com/anatomy-of-an-att ack/
5. Schwartz, M.J.: Microsoft Hacked: Joins Apple, Facebook, Twitter, InformationWeek, 25 February 2013. https://www.darkreading.com/attacks-and-breaches/microsoft-hacked-joins-apple-facebook-twitter/d/d-id/1108800? Accessed 26 Feb 2021
6. Perlroth, N.: Hackers in China attacked the times for last 4 months. N. Y. Times (2013). https://www.nytimes.com/2013/01/31/technology/chinese-hackers-infiltrate-new-york-times-computers.html. Accessed 26 Feb 2021
7. Huber, M., Mulazzani, M., Leithner, M., Schrittwieser, S., Wondracek, G., Weippl, E.: Social snapshots: digital forensics for online social networks. In: 27th Annual Computer Security Applications Conference (2011)

8. Maurya, R.: Social Engineering: Manipulating the Human, vol. 1. Scorpio Net Security Services (2013)
9. Kamis, A.: Behavior Decision Theory, istheory.byu.edu (2011). http://istheory.byu.edu/wiki/Behavioral_. Accessed 1 Sept 2017
10. Jackson, S.: Research Methods and Statistics: A Critical Thinking Approach. Wadsworth, Cengage Learning, Belmont, CA (2008)
11. Qin, T., Burgoon, J.K.: An investigation of heuristics of human judgment in detecting deception and potential implications in countering social engineering. Intell. Secur. Inf., 152–159 (2007)
12. Peltier, T.: Social engineering: concepts and solutions. Inf. Syst. Secur. 5(15), 13–21 (2006)
13. Granger, S.: Social engineering fundamentals, Part I: hacker tactics. SecurityFocus (2001)
14. Foozy, C.F.M., Ahmad, R., Abdollah, M.F., Yusof, R., Mas'ud, M.Z.: Generic taxonomy of social engineering attack and defence mechanism for handheld computer study. In: Alaysian Technical Universities International Conference on Engineering & Technology, Batu Pahat, Johor (2011)
15. Wagner, A.: Social Engineering Attacks, Techniques & Prevention. Lightning Source, UK (2019)
16. Parsons, K., McCormac, A., Pattinson, M., Butavicius, M., Jerram, C.: Phishing for the truth: a scenario-based experiment of users' behavioural response to emails. In: FIP Advances in Information and Communication Technology (2013)
17. Tam, L., Glassman, M., Vandenwauver, M.: The psychology of password management: a tradeoff between security and convenience. Behav. Inf. Technol., 233–244 (2010)
18. Workman, M.: A Teste of Interventions for Security Threats From Social Engineering. Emerald Group Publishing Limited (2008)
19. Mitnick, K.D., Simon, W.L.: The Art of Intrusion: The Real Stories Behind the Exploits of Hackers, Intruders, & Deceivers. Wiley, Indianapolis (2006)
20. Huber, M., Kowalski, S., Nohlberg, M., Tjoa, S.: Towards automating social engineering using social networking site. In: CSE 2009 International Conference on Computational Science and Engineering, vol. 3, pp. 117–124 (2009)
21. Huber, M., Mulazzani, M., Leithner, M., Schrittwieser, S., Wondracek, G., Weippl, E.: Social snapshots: digital forensics for online social networks. In: Proceedings of the 27th Annual Computer Security Applications Conference (2011)
22. Silva, F.: Classificação Taxonómica dos Ataques de Engenharia Social (2013)
23. Kharraz, A., Robertson, W., Balzarotti, D., Bilge, L., Kirda, E.: Cutting the gordian knot: a look under the hood of ransomware attacks. In: International Conference on Detection of Intrusions and Malware, and Vulnerability Assessment, pp. 3–24, July 2015
24. Feizollah, A., Anuar, N.B., Salleh, R., Wahab, A.W.A.: A review on feature selection in mobile malware detection. Digit. Investig. 13, 22–37 (2015)
25. Sahs, J., Khan, L.: A machine learning approach to android malware detection. In: 2012 European Intelligence and Security Informatics Conference, pp. 141–147, August 2012
26. Haley, K.: Symantec's Cloud Security Threat Report Shines a Light on the Cloud's Real Risks, 24 June 2019. https://symantec-enterprise-blogs.security.com/blogs/feature-stories/symantecs-cloud-security-threat-report-shines-light-clouds-real-risks. Accessed 9 Mar 2021

A Look at Usability, Accessibility and Cybersecurity Standards in Software Development

Miguel Hernández Bejarano[1] (ID), Erika Tatiana Páez Cruz[2](✉) (ID),
and Fredys A. Simanca H.[3] (ID)

[1] Escuela Tecnológica Instituto Técnico Central, Bogotá, Colombia
mhernandezb@itc.edu.co
[2] Fundación Universitaria Los Libertadores, Bogotá, Colombia
etpaezc@libertadores.edu.co
[3] Universidad Libre, Bogotá, Colombia

Abstract. The access and use of the websites regardless of the hardware, software, geographic location or network infrastructures available to the user, are a necessity and topics addressed in the usability and accessibility standards. In this sense, the World Wide Web Consortium (W3C) has provided the set of Web Content Accessibility Guidelines (WCAG), in order to ensure an equivalent user experience for people with disabilities, as well as cybersecurity has gained widespread attention in organizations in the attention of the dependence on ICT, and information management as an asset, managed by technologies and vital for decision making.

Keywords: Software disasters · Usability · Accessibility · Security · Standards

1 Introduction

Web applications are active virtual spaces on the web, made up of a structure of programs implemented on a server, used for user interaction and other purposes. Nowadays organizations independent of sector and size have a presence on the Internet, as well as the development of software applications has now moved from desktop to web applications. The growing popularity of web applications makes them a target for malicious users, therefore, security must be a continuous process to mitigate existing attacks, being security a challenge that organizations must assume in the face of risks coming from various technological or human sources.

1.1 Software Disasters

A failure can be determined as an accidental circumstance that, if it occurs, may cause the application or system component to not function as designed. Furthermore, the software implementation procedure involves the transcription of data from one form to another, that is, from the user's needs to the requirements, construction, design, and character of

© Springer Nature Switzerland AG 2021
T. Guarda et al. (Eds.): ARTIIS 2021, CCIS 1485, pp. 484–496, 2021.
https://doi.org/10.1007/978-3-030-90241-4_37

the application. The above allows this procedure to be carried out by a person, so it is possible that errors are caused during the development phases of the program.

In the area of information technology, several problems in software development have persisted over time. Ongoing activities on software construction aim to integrate existing best practice guidelines, security standards and possible solutions, but often lack a knowledge base or do not involve all requirements, particularly in human influence [1].

Software plays an important role in any complex system of humanity, mainly in areas of critical implementation for security such as the financial sector, astronautics, aeronautics, medicine, transportation industries, development of nuclear energy, among others. When operated in these systems and other industries, software is generally the guarantor of controlling the procedure of electromechanical devices and tracking their interactions, so it must be given big priority in the model and manipulation of such systems [2].

Likewise, software systems are internally complex and have a structure in constant development. They provide quality software during and after development, being an indispensable task for individuals involved in software construction [3].

Among the many notable incidences of software failure that have been recorded and that provide evidence of the need for software quality are some of those shown in Table 1.

Table 1. Software failures.

Name	Description
Radiotherapy equipment	Radiotherapy machine emitting radiation doses of different intensities and the system blocked the mask that was placed on the patient, which was an unfortunate event
Misdirected torpedo	While conducting a test, an engine failed and the torpedo got stuck, the mission was abandoned and when the ship turned 180°, it exploded in the gun tube
Aimless sailor	A rocket, on an in-space investigation, deviated from the flight path which caused the rocket to self-destruct 293 s after liftoff, due to a programming error by skipping a hyphen in the expression
The collapse of the Hartford Coliseum	A stadium structure collapses because the developer calculated that the supports could only support the weight of the roof, not including the weight of the snow
CIA gives gas to the Soviets	CIA agents, introduced in an error in a control software that produced a duress in the gas pipeline, causing one of the largest explosions caused by man, to avoid strategic plan of the Soviets

(continued)

Table 1. (*continued*)

Name	Description
NASA probe	It flew over the planet of Mars at 57 km, instead of the planned 150 km, which caused the Martian atmosphere to be destroyed
Knight Capital	Software of a company starts buying and selling shares without any human control for half an hour
Death of AT&T lines	A communication company stopped working for 9 h due to an erroneous line of code, which caused the network to crash
Patriot Missile	An American missile system failed at the intersection of a missile, due to a rounding error that caused the timing to be incorrectly calculated, destroying a U.S. Navy barracks
Pentium's failure in INTEL's long divisions	Intel's Pentium chip produced rounding errors when dividing a floating point unit with an error of 0.006%. For example, dividing 4195835.0/3145727.0 resulted in 1.33374 instead of 1.33382
Amazon	The error, initially caused by a severe storm, caused one of Amazon's servers to be disabled, which deprived many people of data stored in the cloud

Source: Adapted from [4].

The results reveal how software flaws cause mistrust. Likewise, it can be verified that the denial of service occurs if the existing assumptions of authenticity are violated, and generally these can be violated when there are software failures.

1.2 Software Usability

According to the ISO/IEC 9126 standard (Software Product Evaluation - Quality Characteristics and Guidelines for the User) [5] usability is an attribute of software quality. The term is used to refer to the ability of a product to be used easily. This corresponds to the delineation of use as part of software quality, software quality being defined by the standard as: "A set of software attributes that are supported by the effort required for use and the individual assessment of such use by a set of stated or implied users". This is directly related to the capability of the software product to be understood, taught, used and interesting to the user, used under specific conditions.

In the ISO 9126-1 [6], part of this standard, usability is analyzed in terms of its comprehensibility, learnability, operability, attractiveness, and pleasantness, as described by [7] and restates [8]:

- **Understandability.** Defines the ability of the software product to allow the user to understand whether the software is adequate.
- **Learning.** Refers to the software product's ability to allow users to learn how to use its applications.
- **Operability.** It is the capacity of the software product permit the user to operate and control it. Aspects of conformance, mutability, flexibility, and installation can disturb operability. Also, this attribute resembles to fail tolerance, and diminution to user expectations.
- **Attractiveness.** It is the ability of the software product to be interesting for the user. It refers to the particularities of the software designed to make the application more attractive to the user, such as the color used and the graphic design environment.

Conformance to Standards and Guidelines. Refers to the ability of the software product to conform to standards, conventions, style guides or rules related to use.

In this sense, an Internet user plays an important role in the optimal functioning of any virtual space system, therefore, it is necessary that the interfaces of each navigator meet the demands that customers require. There are many websites and other web-based systems that are useful for customers to interact on the network according to their needs such as communication, fun, business, etc., however, this leads to generating in some cases inconvenient operational. Therefore, it is an obligation that promoters or specialists in these techniques improve cyberspaces and web systems to create trust in users using evaluation tools and methodologies to improve good practice on the Internet [9].

Usage evaluations are a mechanism where direct observations are made of communications with the customer interested in a specific product, this to calculate the proper functioning when using the product. The ease of use of the product, its efficiency and flexibility to admit any errors is known as usability. Therefore, to validate the usability of certain applications and virtual sites, it is carried out under the traditional observation procedure, including the interaction, the disposition of use, the design, and a variety of devices level [9].

ISO (9241-9, 2005) describes "as the ease of effective and satisfactory use of a product, service, environment or instrument by people of differing abilities".

ISO (9241-20), states "The usability of the product, service or environment by people with the widest range of abilities".

There are several proposed methods for the evaluation of usability, which use certain means and techniques that attempt to measure different aspects listed in Table 2.

Table 2. Evaluation techniques.

Methods	Techniques
Inspection. It is a technique that employs the work of experts (usability evaluators or consultants with experience in personal interface design related to Web-related disciplines)	• *Heuristics.* This is the most widely used and well-known technique in the context of usability evaluation, where the interface is checked for conformance to a set of rules (heuristics) previously determined through the inspection of several expert evaluators
	• *Cognitive walkthrough.* Focuses on evaluating the ease of learning through system prototypes, which helps to evaluate the software in the early stages of development
	• *Standards inspection.* Verifies that the user interface under evaluation is in accordance with the standards established in industry standards
Inquiry. Users are observed using the application in real time and are then asked verbally or in writing	• *Field observation.* This is intended to capture all activity related to the task and the context of its performance,
	• *Focus group discussion.* Collection of data from the meeting of six to nine people to discuss aspects related to the system
	• *Interview.* Used to know the opinion of users or potential users of a Website. They are exploratory techniques and in no case can constitute any measurement of usability. The main contribution is that it allows us to know the degree of satisfaction that the user has with the Web site and their evaluations on the contents
	• *Questionnaire.* Exploration of uses and motivations of current or potential users that allow us to know preferences about contents, connection times, familiarity with the Internet and interests
Test. Selected users work on specific tasks using the system and evaluators use the results to see how the user interface supports them with their tasks	• Thinking aloud individual users to express aloud and freely their thoughts, feelings and opinions on any aspect about the system or prototype
	• Card sorting technique used to find out how users visualize the organization of information

Source: Adapted from Source [10].

1.3 Software Accessibility

Web accessibility refers to the ability to access the contents of the pages by all people, regardless of any type of disability they may present or derive the context of the communication process (technological or environmental). When websites are designed with accessibility in mind, all users can have equal access to the contents. The concept was developed in the Web Accessibility Initiative (WAI) by the Word Wide Web Consortium (W3C). The W3C developed a set of standards and design recommendations to facilitate the development of accessible pages, being the WCAG 2.0 one of the most important, as well as the Accessibility Guidelines (WCAG) 3.0, which provides a wide range of recommendations to make web content more affordable for people with disabilities, taking into account the needs of users with low vision, blind and other visual impairments, hearing loss and deafness, limited mobility and dexterity, as well as speech disabilities, sensory and cognitive disabilities, learning difficulties and combinations of these, among others [11, 12].

Access to the web is intended to ensure that the web pages are used by the maximum number of people, regardless of their knowledge, personal skills or the technical parameters of the devices used to access the network [13].

The need for the Network to be worldwide and available for anyone is unavoidable according to [14] Tim Berners-Lee, and it has been in force since the beginning of the Web, since it was a requirement contemplated in its design model made by its creator Tim Berners-Lee: "The power of the Web is in its universality. Access for all regardless of disability it is an aspect".

WCAG 2.0 models are designed for any website: industry, commercial, academia, among others. Models are classified into three levels of compliance: A (basic accessibility compliance), AA (medium level of accessibility compliance), and AAA (highest level of accessibility compliance described in the WCAGs). Level A represents a minimum level of compliance, with AA and AAA above (the higher levels contain all the requirements of each lower level) [15].

In the UNE 139803:2012 standard, the web accessibility requirements are organized into three levels according to the degree of demand for compliance. The most basic and simple level to satisfy is called level A. The requirements of this level together with other more demanding one's form level AA. Finally, level AA, together with some even more complex requirements, constitutes level AAA. In other words, each level encompasses the previous one.

To make web content accessible, WCAG has developed the so-called Web Content Accessibility Guidelines (WCAG), whose main objective is to define the design of web pages, achieving an accessible model, and thus reducing information barriers. The Guidelines also composes a series of validations points that detect possible errors and there are usually two versions of these (WCAG: 1.0 and 2.0) [16].

The rapid increase in technological progress favored the evolution of the web in activities such as economy, communication, education, business, among others. The use of the web today is not only necessary to interact and relate, but web technologies are rapidly progressing globally towards diversity of web genres. However, web technologies highlight the interactions of users within the network, so implementers must also identify the best procedure to meet the needs of users with disabilities or with some type of complexity [17].

1.4 Cybersecurity in Software

Currently, the security of data and virtual information is of great importance in institutions and organizations. For which, organizations have implemented penetration tests (pentesting) that simulate the behavior of an aggressor in a targeted manner in a chosen environment, to identify their weaknesses and thus find a way to validate the security of infrastructures, networks, developed web applications and other assets. In terms of penetration testing, organizations like OWASP offer security for data and records, through testing methods, risk assessment, and penetration testing tools [18].

With the integration of the Internet in organizational information systems and social interactivity, the Internet is transforming the way in which individuals relate and operate, but it also leads to an increasingly marked risk that compromises in the generation of security threats. In this sense, cybersecurity is a set of techniques and models designed to safeguard processors, networks, software and data against unauthorized access, risks, or attacks of damage to systems and loss of information. A security system consists of a network protection method and techniques for computer security, providing firewalls, antivirus software, and intrusion detection procedures (IDS) [19, 20].

Cybersecurity has become a risk for internet users, organizations, and states, since reports of cyberattack, information theft, system lockdown, scam and hate speech generate fear and anxiety about the use of new technologies, and the so-called cybercrimes. To combat this, cybersecurity technologies, policies and measures are implemented [21].

It is necessary not only to protect oneself and be up to date with the recently launched means for frequent risks, but also to establish a constant method of testing and monitoring that facilitates receiving notifications of possible vulnerabilities of the virtual system and at the same time allows catalog the most significant risks through artificial intelligence developed to avoid possible information fraud. In addition, the OWASP Top 10 is the industry baseline that provides the most widely used framework when it comes to monitoring vulnerabilities in web applications [22]. The Open Web Application Security Project (OWASP) typically inspects the top 10 risks of applications used in deployed web spaces. These are: A1 Database Management, A2 Broken Authentication, A3 Reserved Records Display, A4 External XML Entities (XXE), A5 Broken Access Control, A6 Security Misconfiguration, A7 Cross-Site Command Strings (XSS), Insecure deserialization A8, A9 Use of devices with known vulnerabilities, A10 Poor data logging and tracking.

1.5 Standards and Best Practices

This framework is one of the most respected and used standard cybersecurity techniques. Its objective goes beyond implementing the IT security requirements of individual organizations. It was created to serve as a guide in the innovation of the nation's cyber resilience structure and, for that reason, it favors a safe and secure cyber environment.

The National Institute of Standards and Technology (NIST) developed the NIST Cybersecurity Framework or CSF NIST; is a framework that provides a taxonomy of cybersecurity results and a methodology [23] to evaluate and manage those results around five functions (Identify, Protect, Detect, Respond, Recover) and basic activities that intersect with the guidelines, accreditations, and current frameworks. In addition, this framework offering a common language to detail cybersecurity operations, risk environments, trade objectives, and enhancement purposes. It is designed to meet specific business needs, degrees of risk tolerance and generate security tools for public and private organizations [24].

Software standards can help to solve software failures. There are many patterns related to software engineering. Some of those patterns are generic and some are specific to any industry. Also, some of the standards come from procurement agencies and others are developed by certified bodies or are related to certain categories of software [25].

The Common Criteria is a standard based on ISO/IEC 15408:2005 and ISO/IEC 18405:2005.8, developed as a useful guide to facilitate the development of products such as hardware, software or firmware with security functionalities, is so ISO 15408-1: is an introduction and general model that presents the main conceptions of this family, as well as the basis for the unification of criteria in software security evaluation [26].

Also the ISO/IEC 29110 standard Software Engineering oriented to the life cycle profiles for small organizations focuses on the good technical and management practices related to software processes that can be adopted and applied by small development organizations. Software, and defined by and organizations, consisting of less than 25 people [27]. Considering that in software development plans it is very significant to carry out validations of both the process and the result of the application. It is also true in the quality of the ISO/IEC 29110 software process, where it allows small software organizations to achieve a competitive advantage in the market [28].

Likewise, OWASP autonomous, non-profit organization dedicated to finding and fighting the causes of insecure software. It is an entity that has organized itself into chapters and projects around the world. Its documentation, tools and open-source standards are licensed under the gpl, gfdl, and gpl certificates [29]. The OWASP Testing Guide is a comprehensive controller that is freely accessible, open, and constantly updated and used for vulnerability testing [30].

The W3C Consortium is an international body that regulates the development of standards used on the Internet, is carrying out the global standardization of Web technologies [31]. To achieve full accessibility and universal design, regulations and standardization are needed to guide, orient and, in some way, require developers to consider the criteria to be reserved into account in the development of interactive products and web applications.

Therefore, the SWEBOK Guide distinguishes the error, which represents the cause of the bad execution of a software system, and difficulty, which indicates the unwanted or not validated result in a service executed by a software system. The introduction of the Guide records that software without the required parameters and sufficient level of operability is an indicator of failed or deficient software engineering [32].

In this sense, the most significant and authoritative vulnerability repository in the world, and the changes in the information of Common Vulnerability Exposures (CVE) reflect the guidelines of the software weaknesses exhibited already at the end of 2018, the number has reached 16555, which is 2.5 times more than in 2016 [33]. The Fig. 1 presents the number of new vulnerabilities exhibited each year from 2009 to 2018, showing the degree of vulnerability and IT security risks, prevalent worldwide from 2009 to 2019. In the most recent year, 12,174 new IT vulnerabilities Common vulnerabilities were discovered, the first decline since 2016, some common vulnerabilities are present in Fig. 1.

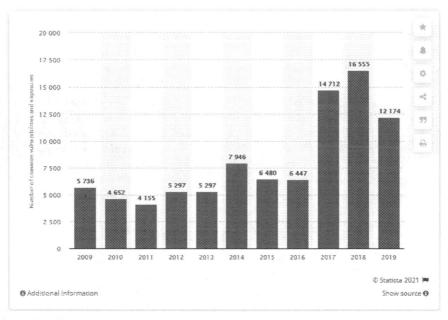

Fig. 1. Number of common IT security vulnerabilities and exposures (CVE) worldwide from 2009 to 2019. Source: Statista (https://bit.ly/3sPIJMo)

Today, web systems are among the most important targets of cyber-attacks. This is due to the growing dynamics (interactivity) of the networks that tolerate, through a composition of approaches, and using programming techniques in favor of the user and the server risks that affect the applications. Penetration testing is therefore a necessary security validation mechanism intended to assess the risks of an organization's network infrastructure and services. Oriented to collect information and take control of a vulnerable system in any environment [34].

Likewise, within best practices, there are various software design and programming techniques with different use today, and one of the most common used is the implementation of agile software with SCRUM [35]. SCRUM since its inception, allows adaptation by adding use and accessibility tasks in the process of values, roles, frameworks, and artifacts, which have been applied in development projects and with the implementation and experience of the IT team, they have observed notable changes both in development and in the results of the product, the same that has been validated and approved by the end users [36].

Access, usability, and inclusion are characteristics closely related to developing a website that works for everyone. Their approaches, goals, and guidelines overlap significantly. So, it is more practical to address them together when developing and designing web sites and applications, therefore the web content access standards (WCAG) will always be the international standard ISO/IEC 40500 as a checklist for complying with these standards, focuses primarily on users with disabilities; these access requirements improve use for all, particularly in constrained circumstances [37]. In this sense, when the website follows the guidelines framed by the W3C or some country-specific guidelines relevant to the WCAG, then the site is universally accessible.

To safeguard applications from cyberattacks, it is essential to take care of the security aspects of the application or system at each stage of the software development life cycle (SDLC) and provide a second layer of protection in the application and after implement the request for this. According to the foregoing, secure coding practices involve appropriate disinfection and coding of user access, verification of input data, parameterization of queries, use of storage techniques, among others [38]. As well as OWASP, helps to create vulnerable web applications to test security mechanisms.

2 Discussions and Conclusions

Advances in technology as well as the growth of web-oriented products in response to the presentation of content in different audio and video formats, as well as access to the web from mobile devices and the appearance of new platforms such as Internet of the things and at the same time the digitization that in these times has become a source of access to information on the status of organizations in the educational and financial sectors, among others, has generated the presentation of a set of accessibility recommendations from the W3C like WCAG, to provide access to people with disabilities, reduced abilities who need to access websites, navigate, and interact with technological devices on the Internet. The access of Internet users to websites is a scenario that offers the possibility of being in equality and equity of conditions of access to information and knowledge.

It should be noted that as technology advances, new solutions appear, new ways of programming, new languages and a host of tools that try to make the developer's job a little easier. However, it is not an easy task, since as observed in the study presented, human errors are the ones that have led to the greatest computer disasters throughout history, so much so that a single coma could cause the death of millions of people.

For this reason, one of the situations that must be considered before starting the built project is to go through a series of testing and pilot phases to achieve a software of very good quality and being sure that there will be no problems or inconveniences in a future.

Usage and accessibility are key components for systems implementation, because, for example, the accessibility of web content plays a significant role for both individuals with disabilities and most users of the web system. Accordingly, the World Wide Web Consortium (W3C) has issued the Web Content Accessibility Guidelines 2.0 (WCAG 2.0), to make web content accessible to all users, including those with disabilities. So, it is necessary that the web content meets the required success criteria. Therefore, web content must meet the criteria for success. In this sense, web usability has the objective of providing users with the guide in instruments in order not to get lost within the platform;

which improves the experience and satisfaction of users in a context of interaction, becoming one of the key factors in the success or failure of a website.

With growing cybersecurity challenges for organizations and individuals as a result, among others, of the increasing number and sophistication of threats, the accessibility and availability of web applications have made them a target for cyber attackers and some of the most well-known risks of the network applications are SQL injection, buffer failure, cross-site scripting, and cross-site request spoofing.

Cybersecurity patterns and guidelines such as ISO/IEC 27001 or NIST SP 800-53 are refined to delineate the target environment and are listed as mandatory, characteristic, or recommended as required by organizations, as well as it is necessary for organizations to develop a culture of cybersecurity, which is a responsibility in senior management roles that range from the generation of a security policy, communication and dissemination of cybersecurity in the organization, to protect one of its most valuable assets, which is information source for decision-making, in order to raise awareness, identify cyber threats and notify them to the security departments of the company, training and awareness allows to reduce security breaches caused by ignorance, or conscious acts of employees that may affect the organization's information systems and therefore l to business continuity.

Furthermore, the quantity of people interconnected to the Internet and web sites with different devices has increased due to its ease of use and accessibility. Likewise, web application security has become an important challenge since insecure applications and software can affect different sectors of society, which makes it necessary for organizations to generate security and training policies as a need urgent to reinforce the security of network applications, making use of standards and good practices that allow mitigating the risks to which applications are exposed on the Web.

Also, current version control systems, such as GitHub, contain bug tracking techniques that developers use to highlight the presence of bugs. This is done through error reports, that is, they detail verbatim and warn of the problem and the causes that led to the failure event [39].

In this sense, as Internet technology and web applications increase, cyberattacks continue to evolve and, as a result, society in general faces a greater security risk in cyberspace, organizations must design and implement policies of cybersecurity, as well as, the allocation of resources for the acquisition, updating of technological infrastructure, training and having updated human resources, to face the challenges of cyberattacks to which organizations are exposed.

References

1. Adi, K., Hamza, L., Pene, L.: Automatic security policy enforcement in computer systems. Comput. Syst. **73**, 1456–171 (2018)
2. Wong, W.E., Li, X., Laplante, P.A.: Be more familiar with our enemies and pave the way forward: a review of the roles bugs played in software failures. J. Syst. Softw. **133**, 68–94 (2017)
3. Özakıncı, R., Tarhan, A.: Early software defect prediction: a systematic map and review. J. Syst. Softw. **144**, 216–239 (2018)
4. Norris, M., Rigby, P.: Ingeniería de Software aplicada. Noriega Editores, México (1994)

5. ISO: ISO 9126: Software product evaluation - Quality characteristics and guidelines for their use. ISO, Ginebra (1991)
6. ISO: ISO/IEC 9126 - p1: Software Engineering – Product quality. Part 1: 2001 – Parts 2 to 4. ISO, Ginebra (2001)
7. Bevan, N., Azuma, M.: Quality in use: incorporating human factors into the software engineering lifecycle. In: Proceedings of the Third IEEE International Software Engineering Standards Symposium and Forum ISESS 1997, pp. 169–179 (1997)
8. Chi, E.: Improving web usability through visualization - predictive web usage visualizations can help analysts uncover traffic patterns and usability problems. IEEE Internet Comput., 64–72 (2002)
9. Kaur, R., Sharma, B.: Comparative study for evaluating the usability of web based applications. In: 2018 4th International Conference on Computing Sciences (ICCS), pp. 94–97. IEEE Xplore (2019)
10. Perurena Cancio, L., Moráguez Bergues, M.: Usability of web sites, methods and evaluation techniques. Revista Cubana de Información en Ciencias de la Salud **24**(2), 176–194 (2013)
11. Jaume, M., Fontanet Nadal, G.: A web accessibility improvement tool. In: 6th Iberian Conference on Information Systems and Technologies (CISTI 2011), pp. 1–5. IEEE Xplore (2011)
12. W3C: W3C Accessibility Guidelines (WCAG) 3.0, 8 June 2021. https://www.w3.org/TR/wcag-3.0/. Accessed 11 June 2021
13. Garrido, A., Firmenich, S., Rossi, G., Grigera, J., Medina-Medina, N., Harari, I.: Personalized web accessibility using client-side refactoring. IEEE Internet Comput. **17**(4), 58–66 (2012)
14. Riaño, J., Ballesteros, J.: Web accessibility. Study web accessibility in public places of the Colombian State. In: 2015 XLI Latin American Computing Conference (CLEI) (2015)
15. Spingola, E., Reid, K.: Accesibilidad de las páginas web "Introducción a la ingeniería. In: 2019 IEEE Frontiers in Education Conference (FIE), pp. 1–7. IEEE Xplore (2019)
16. W3C: Web Content Accessibility Guidelines (WCAG) (2012). https://www.w3.org/WAI/intro/wcag.php
17. Isa, W.: Accessibility evaluation using Web Content Accessibility Guidelines (WCAG) 2.0. In: 2016 4th International Conference on User Science and Engineering (i-USEr), pp. 1–4. IEEE Xplore (2016)
18. Serrão, C., Vieira, T.: Web security in the finance sector. In: 2016 11th International Conference for Internet Technology and Secured Transactions (ICITST), pp. 255–259 (2016)
19. Aftergood, S.: Cybersecurity: the cold war online. Nature **547**, 30–31 (2017)
20. Milenkoski, A., Vieira, M., Kounev, S., Kounev, A., Payne, B.D.: Evaluating computer intrusion detection systems: a survey of common. Evaluating computer intrusion detection systems: a survey of common **48**, 1–41 (2015)
21. Chang, L.Y., Coppel, N.: Building cyber security awareness in a developing country: lessons from Myanmar. Comput. Secur. **97**, 101959 (2020)
22. Loureiro, S.: Security misconfigurations and how to prevent them. Netw. Secur. **2021**, 13–16 (2021)
23. Gupta Gourisetti, S., Mylrea, M., Patangia, H.: Cybersecurity vulnerability mitigation framework through empirical paradigm: enhanced prioritized gap analysis. Future Gener. Comput. Syst. **105**, 410–431 (2020)
24. Benz, M., Chatterjee, D.: Calculated risk? A cybersecurity evaluation tool for SMEs. Bus. Horiz. **63**, 531–540 (2020)
25. Khan, H.H., Malik, M.N.: Software standards and software failures: a review with the perspective of varying situational contexts. IEEE Access **5**, 17501–17513 (2017)
26. ISO: ISO/IEC 15408-1:2009 Information technology—Security techniques—Evaluation criteria for IT. ISO, December 2019. https://www.iso.org/standard/50341.html. Accessed 11 June 2021

27. Buchalcevova, A.: Using ArchiMate to model ISO/IEC 29110 standard for very small entities. Comput. Stand. Interfaces **65**, 103–121 (2019)
28. Castillo-Salinas, L., Sanchez-Gordon, S., Villarroel-Ramos, J., Sánchez-Gordón, M.: Evaluation of the implementation of a subset of ISO/IEC 29110 Software Implementation process in four teams of undergraduate students of Ecuador. An empirical software engineering experiment. Comput. Stand. Interfaces **70**, 103430 (2020)
29. OWASP: OWASP (2021). https://owasp.org/. Accessed 11 June 2021
30. Nanisura, D., Venia, N., Sunaringtyas, S.U.: Secure code recommendation based on code review result using OWASP code review guide. In: 2020 International Workshop on Big Data and Information Security (IWBIS), pp. 153–1258. IEEE Xplore (2020)
31. Ashimura, K., Nakamura, O., Isshiki, M.: TV accesible basada en la arquitectura W3C MMI. In: 2014 IEEE 3rd Global Conference on Consumer Electronics (GCCE), pp. 157–158. IEEE Xplore (2014)
32. Monarch, I.: Understanding software engineering failure as part of the SWEBOK. In: Proceedings 14th Conference on Software Engineering Education and Training. In Search of a Software Engineering Profession, pp. 191–192. IEEE (2001)
33. Wu, X., Zheng, W., Chen, X., Wang, F., Mu, D.: CVE-assisted large-scale security bug report dataset construction method. J. Syst. Softw. **160**, 110456 (2020)
34. Caturano, F., Perrone, G., Romano, S.P.: Discovering reflected cross-site scripting vulnerabilities using a multiobjective reinforcement learning environment. Comput. Secur. **103**, 102204 (2021)
35. Morandini, M., Coleti, T.A., Oliveira, E., Pizzigatti Corrêa, P.L.: Considerations about the efficiency and sufficiency of the utilization of the Scrum methodology: a survey for analyzing results for development teams. Comput. Sci. Rev. **39**, 100314 (2021)
36. Romero, C.: Adaptación de la metodología SCRUM para desarrollar sitios web accesibles. In: 2019 International Conference on Inclusive Technologies and Education (CONTIE), pp. 112–124. IEEE Xplore (2019)
37. W3C: Accessibility, Usability, and Inclusion, 6 May 2016. https://www.w3.org/WAI/fundamentals/accessibility-usability-inclusion/. Accessed 10 June 2021
38. Deepa, G., Santhi Thilagam, P.: Securing web applications from injection and logic vulnerabilities: approaches and challenges. Inf. Softw. Technol. **74**, 160–180 (2016)
39. Catolino, G., Palomba, F., Zaidman, A., Ferrucci, F.: Not all bugs are the same: understanding, characterizing, and classifying bug types. J. Syst. Softw. **152**, 165–181 (2019)

Computational Modeling of the Thermal Effects on Composite Slabs Under Fire Conditions

Carlos Balsa[1]([✉]) [ID], Matheus B. Silveira[2], Valerian Mange[3], and Paulo A. G. Piloto[4] [ID]

[1] Research Centre in Digitalization and Intelligent Robotics (CeDRI),
Instituto Politécnico de Bragança, Bragança, Portugal
`balsa@ipb.pt`
[2] Universidade Tecnológica Federal do Paraná, Campus Pato Branco, Via do Conhecimento,
s/n - KM 01 - Fraron, Pato Branco, PR 85503-390, Brazil
`matheussilveira@alunos.utfpr.edu.br`
[3] ENSEEIHT - IRIT-UFTMiP, Toulouse, France
`valerian.mange@etu.toulouse-inp.fr`
[4] LAETA-INEGI and Instituto Politécnico de Bragança, Bragança, Portugal
`ppiloto@ipb.pt`

Abstract. This paper presents finite element thermal models to evaluate the thermal behavior of composite slabs with steel deck, submitted to standard fire exposure. Composite steel/concrete slabs are a mix of a reinforced concrete layer with a profiled steel deck reinforced by steel bars between its ribs. The resulting transient and non-linear thermal problems are solved numerically with three-dimensional multi-domain finite element models. The models were developed for normal weight concrete and lightweight concrete, and for different steel deck geometries (trapezoidal and re-entrant). The results of the numerical simulations are used to present a new calculation method to determinate the temperatures on the steel deck components and on the rebars and, consequently, to determine the bending resistance of composite slabs under fire conditions.

Keywords: Nonlinear energy equation · Finite element method · Composite slab · Standard fire · Fire rating

1 Introduction

Composite steel/concrete slabs are an alternative construction elements that ensure some advantages to structures, such as the reduction of the self-weight of the structures while speeding up the construction process. The slabs are composed by a profiled steel deck which can be used as permanent formwork, and a reinforced concrete placed on the top (see Fig. 1). The use of composite slabs in buildings has become very popular in North America since 1960. However, due to the fact that there was insufficient information regarding its structural safety, only after 1980 has become popular in Europe. The slab's overall depth usually varies between 100 to 170 mm. The thickness and geometry of the steel deck depends on the producer of the profiles, and usually includes a zinc coating on the exposed surface to resist corrosion [8].

© Springer Nature Switzerland AG 2021
T. Guarda et al. (Eds.): ARTIIS 2021, CCIS 1485, pp. 497–511, 2021.
https://doi.org/10.1007/978-3-030-90241-4_38

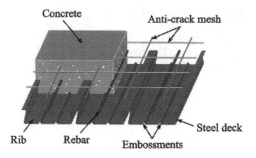

Fig. 1. Composite slab with trapezoidal steel deck (adapted from [14]).

In addition to the corrosion problem, the composite slabs may suffer significant damage when exposed to fire, since the steel elements which are responsible for ensuring the slabs bending resistance capacity are significantly affected under fire conditions. Therefore, it is necessary to perform a thermal analysis previously to the structural analysis, thus guaranteeing that this building element has the fire resistance according to regulations and standards. The fire rating of this type of element is then determined by standard fire tests, accounting for load-bearing (R), Integrity (E), and Thermal Insulation (I). This means that for a composite slab to demonstrate the fire resistance in agreement to the criteria established by the European standard EN 13501-2 [5], it must have the capacity to prevent large deformation or rate of deformation whenever in service, which means the load-bearing, it must also provide thermal insulation, thus limiting the increase in temperature on the unexposed side. Finally, the slabs must keep fire in the exposed side, preventing the passage of flames and hot gases through cracks or holes, which comprises the Integrity criterion.

This work is concerned with the determination of the thermal behavior of composite slabs under a standard ISO-834 fire [9], specially focused on the temperature evolution on the components of steel deck (upper flange, web, lower flange), and the rebars. An accurate and reliable estimation of the temperatures in these components is required, especially to determine the load-bearing criterion, since these temperatures directly influence the steel and concrete strength reduction factors and consequently the bending resistance of the slabs.

Among several ways to determine the fire rating of a composite slab, the development of experimental standard fire tests are the most expensive and time-consuming. Alternatively, the Annex D of the EN 1994-1-2 [4] provides the guidelines for estimating the fire resistance based on the simplified calculation method, but this method is based on studies that have been carried out a long time ago and are currently outdated. The third method consists of simulating the experimental fire tests through finite elements. Computational simulations are of great importance in this field because this can promote a reliable and realistic description of the physical phenomena.

The year of 1983 was very important to the dissemination of composite slabs as an alternative and functional construction process. In this year, the European Convention for Constructional Steelwork ECCS [7], published the design rules for composite concrete slabs with a profiled steel deck, exposed to a standard fire. According to this document, the explicit fire design calculation for composite slabs is not required when the fire requirements are smaller or equal than 30 min and for other fire rating the calculation methods were based on conservative approximations for a safer design procedure. This standard was developed to guarantee structural safety according to the fire resistance classes established by ISO 834-1 [9] without the obligation to carry out experimental tests. This document should only be applied if the composite slab was safely designed for room temperature.

Hamerlinck was a pioneer in proposing mathematical models to estimate the fire resistance of composite slabs. In 1990, he proposed a numerical calculation model that includes thermal and mechanical models for the cross-section analysis and a structural analysis model for composite slabs [8]. Later, in 1991, Hamerlinck [8] describes in detail all the methods conducting numerical and experimental studies regarding the thermal and mechanical behaviour of reinforced composite slabs under fire. Current standards are still based on his work.

In the last years, an extensive range of thermal and structural models have been developed in different finite element software to predict the structural behavior of steel-concrete composite slabs under fire conditions. In 2018, Piloto et al. [18] analyzed the fire resistance of composite concrete slabs with profiled steel deck, in this case also reinforced by a steel mesh at the topside, including reinforcing bars between its ribs. The key objective of this study was to develop two-dimensional numerical models using the Matlab and ANSYS softwares in order to evaluate the fire resistance of different slab configurations according to the insulation criterion. For the development of this research, the fire rating for insulation (I) criterion was evaluated using numerical and simple calculation methods, and then validated against experimental fire tests. The results obtained by the authors allowed the demonstration of the fire resistance (I) increase with concrete thickness for both calculation methods. However, using the numerical method, the simulation predicts a lower fire resistance (I) when compared to fundamental standards, consequently ensuring more structural safety when using this method. Therefore, a new and better approach was proposed, considering a quadratic variation between the fire resistance and the effective thickness of the composite slab. More recently, the same methodology was applied to different slab geometries under the action of different types of standard fires in [14–17].

In 2021 Bolina et al. [1], determined the thermal behavior of composite steel-concrete slabs exposed to a standard fire. The main objective of the work was to develop a comparison of the temperature distribution in the cross-section through several methods: experimental, numerical, and analytical. The authors carried out eight full-scale fire tests which were used to calibrate the numerical models developed using the ABAQUS software. The numerical methods were compared with the analytical method provided by Eurocode 1994-1.2 [4]. The authors noticed a convergence of the analytical method with the numerical and experimental methods only for the steel deck, but not for the concrete, the rebars (positive and negative), and the thermal insulation. Therefore, a new analytical approach was developed to determine the temperature in the rebars and new factors to evaluate the performance of the thermal insulation.

In the present work, aiming to optimize the analytical temperature calculation presented by the simplified calculation method provided in the Annex D of Eurocode

1994 1-2, a parametric study was performed in order to analyze the thermal behavior of composite slabs. The temperature distribution along slabs using normal weight and lightweight concrete (NWC and LWC) was determined for four different types of steel deck geometries, which were chosen to present two different geometric classes, trapezoidal and re-entrant, using different concrete thickness over the steel deck h_1.

Three-dimensional models are presented to simulate the thermal effects of standard fire exposure on composite slabs. The reduce scale models where simulated with three dimensional finite elements using the Matlab Partial Differential Equations Toolbox (PDE Toolbox) [12]. The numerical models comprise different physical domains with different thermal properties, corresponding to the components of the slab such as concrete, steel deck and rebars. In addition, to simulate the debonding effects, air-gap with 0.5 mm of constant thickness is included between the steel deck and concrete.

The heat transfer problem is solved numerically through the Finite Element Method (FEM) with thermal models, already validated with experimental tests by Piloto et al. [13, 18], available in the Matlab PDE Toolbox. The temperature evolution on the steel deck components and on the rebars is evaluated for all the four different composite slabs with different concrete thickness h_1, and subsequently the results are compared with the simplified method provided in the Annex D of Eurocode 1994-1.2. Additionally, a new formula based on the parametric results is proposed to analytically calculate the temperature of slabs components.

2   Heat Transfer Problem

This section presents all the methodology necessary to develop the finite element thermal model, which will be used to solve the nonlinear transient thermal problems. Therefore, the heat transfer problem in this study has to be solved in the multi-domain body corresponding to the composite slab under standard fire conditions. It is worth mentioning that the heat flux applied to the unexposed side depends on the ambient temperature and the heat flux applied to the exposed side depends on the standard fire established by the ISO-834 fire curve.

2.1   Physical Domains

The three-dimensional (3D) transient heat transfer problems will be solved on four different composite slabs with different geometries presented in Fig. 2. First, two composite slabs with trapezoidal geometry were selected: Confraplus 60 and Polydeck 59 s. For this category, the following values were adopted for the h_1 thickness: 50, 70, 90, 110, and 125 mm. However, for other two slabs with re-entrant geometry (Multideck 50 and Bondek) the following thicknesses h_1 where used: 60, 70, 90, 110, and 125 mm.

The 3D models were developed in agreement with a realistic representation of the composite slabs physical model. The geometry of the models consider the exact shape of the surfaces from a representative volume of the slab. The cross-section which was selected has the side edges delimited by the centroid of the upper flange and comprising one rib. The length of the specimens is 250 mm (see Fig. 3).

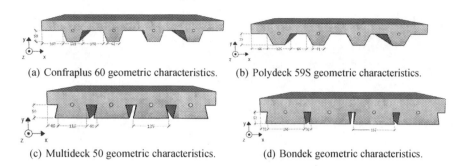

(a) Confraplus 60 geometric characteristics. (b) Polydeck 59S geometric characteristics.

(c) Multideck 50 geometric characteristics. (d) Bondek geometric characteristics.

Fig. 2. Composite slabs geometric characteristics and dimensions [mm].

The multi-domain developed comprises four sub-domains: the steel deck, the air-gap, the concrete, and the rebar. Thus, the materials that compose the physical sub-domains of the slabs are carbon steel (steel deck and rebars), the concrete (concrete topping), and airgap (to simulate the debonding effect between the steel deck and concrete).

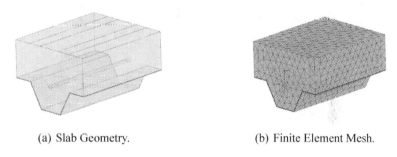

(a) Slab Geometry.   (b) Finite Element Mesh.

Fig. 3. Example of a modelled composite slabs specimen [mm].

Confraplus 60 is a trapezoidal model profile produced by ArcelorMittal. The colab-orating steel deck is produced with S350 steel and the model with 1.25 mm of thick-ness has been selected. The geometric characteristics are presented in the Fig. 2(a). The Polydeck 59S model is the second trapezoidal profile selected. The Polydeck 59S model from ArcelorMittal, presented in Fig. 2(b) is made by a steel deck with S450 steel and 1 mm of thickness. The re-entrant model presented in Fig. 2(c) is the Multideck 50 produced by Kingspan Structural Products. This product has a steel profile with steel grade S450 and 1 mm of thickness. The second type of re-entrant slab studied is Bon-dek, which is developed and produced by the Lysaght company. The deck consists of a steel profile with grade S350 and the 1 mm thickness model was selected (see Fig. 2(d)). These geometries have been selected based on the geometric difference and current use.

The heat transfer inside the models, through the discretization of the domain in a finite element mesh as illustrated in Fig. 3, is exclusively made by conduction. The heat conduction inside the physical domain is mathematically modelled by the energy conservation equation

$$\rho(T)C_p(T)\frac{\partial T}{\partial t} = \nabla \cdot (\lambda(T)\nabla T),\qquad(1)$$

where T represents the temperature ($^\circ$C), $\rho(T)$ is the specific mass (kg/m^3), $Cp(T)$ is the specific heat (J/kgK), $\lambda(T)$ is the thermal conductivity (W/mK), t is the time (s) and $\nabla = (\partial_x, \partial_y, \partial_z)$ is the gradient. Equation (1), is based on the heat flow balance, for the infinitesimal material volume, in each spatial direction.

The thermal properties of the materials that compose the slabs are determined by the Eurocodes [2–4] (steel and concretes) and by [6] (air), and are temperature dependent. Therefore, the specific mass $\rho(T)$, the specific heat $Cp(T)$ and the thermal conductivity $\lambda(T)$ vary with the temperature, introducing the non-linearity of the Eq. (1). Figure 4 describes the thermal properties of the four different types of materials that constitute the studied composite slabs.

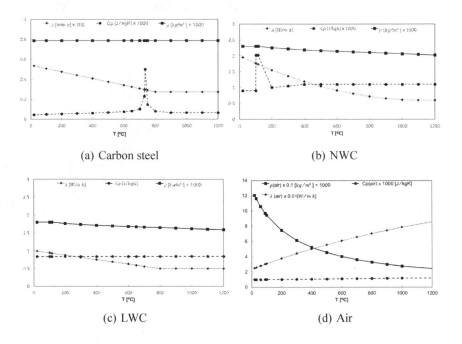

(a) Carbon steel　　　　　　　　(b) NWC

(c) LWC　　　　　　　　(d) Air

Fig. 4. Thermal properties of composite slab components.

Once the heat flux on the fire exposed surface changes with time, the Eq. (1) is time-dependent and holds a transient thermal state for the slab. So, in order to determine the temperature field along the time, the solution of Eq. 1 is required. Furthermore, for the correct solution of the problem, it is necessary to apply the boundary conditions according to the ISO-834 fire curve in the physical domain.

2.2   Boundary Conditions

The boundary conditions are used in numerical simulations to solve the differential equations intrinsic to the model. Therefore it is necessary to master the different natures of heat transfer that act on the slabs, that is, the conduction, convection, and radiation. In thermal analysis, the finite element mesh is generally used to model solids in which conduction is the predominant heat transfer method, and the radiation and convection are imposed through boundary conditions. The composite slabs are subjected to three main boundary conditions comprising the exposed surface, the unexposed surface, and the adiabatic surfaces. All of them follow the guidelines of Eurocode 1991-1.2 [4].

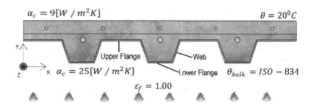

Fig. 5. Boundary conditions.

The boundary conditions in the exposed side of the slab, comprise the heat transfer by convection and radiation and are given by

$$\lambda\left(T\right)\nabla T.\overrightarrow{n} = \alpha_c\left(T_\infty - T\right) + \phi\varepsilon_m\varepsilon_f\sigma\left(T_\infty^4 - T^4\right) \tag{2}$$

where $\overrightarrow{n}$ is the unitary vector normal to the external face, ϕ is the view factor, α_c is the convection coefficient, ε_m is the emissivity of the material, ε_f is the emissivity of fire, σ is the Stefan-Boltzmann constant and T_∞ is the gas temperature of the fire compartment. In Eq. (2), the convection coefficient is $\alpha_c = 25$ W/m^{2}K, the emissivity of steel is $\varepsilon_m = 0.7$ and the fire emissivity is $\varepsilon_f = 1$. This equation represents the amount of energy (or the heat flow) that arrives to the steel deck by radiation and convection based on the gas bulk temperature, which will be transferred though the slab by conduction. The boundary conditions parameters are represented in Fig. 5.

The view factor (ϕ) is a term of great relevance in studying the thermal behavior of structures exposed to fire, that quantifies the geometric relation between the surface emitting radiation and the receiving surface. Thus, it is an adimensional parameter and dependends on the rib surfaces orientations, and the distance between the radiative surfaces. The emissivity for the lower flange is 1 and the values for the web and upper flange are usually smaller than 1.

The view factor has high variability due to complexity in its determination. For this reason, to determine the view factor associated with web and upper flange of steel deck, the Crossed-Strings Method, proposed by Hotell H. C. in 1950 [6], was used in this study. Following this rule, Fig. 6 shows the parameters required for the approximation of the view factor in composite slabs.

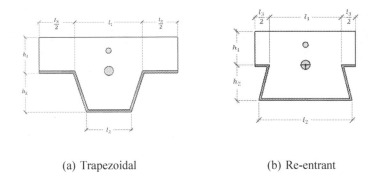

(a) Trapezoidal   (b) Re-entrant

Fig. 6. Geometric parameters used to determine view factors according to each slab profile.

The view factor of the lower flange is $\phi = 1$, and the resulting equations for the upper flange (ϕ_{up}) and web (ϕ_{web}) view factors are presented in Eqs. (3) and (4).

$$\phi_{up} = \frac{\sqrt{h_2^2 + \left(l_3 + \frac{l_1 - l_2}{2}\right)^2} - \sqrt{h_2^2 + \left(\frac{l_1 - l_2}{2}\right)^2}}{l_3} \tag{3}$$

$$\phi_{web} = \frac{\sqrt{h_2^2 + \left(\frac{l_1 - l_2}{2}\right)^2} + (l_3 + l_1 - l_2) - \sqrt{h_2^2 + \left(l_3 + \frac{l_1 - l_2}{2}\right)^2}}{2\sqrt{h_2^2 + \left(\frac{l_1 - l_2}{2}\right)^2}} \tag{4}$$

The Eq. (5) presents the gas temperature of the fire compartment following the standard fire curve ISO-834 ($T_\infty = T_{ISO}$) given by

$$T_{ISO} = 20 + 345 \log_{10}(8t + 1), \tag{5}$$

where T_{ISO} is given in °C and t in minutes [9].

The top part of the composite slab (unexposed side) is also an important side to determine the temperature evolution. After all, it will determine the heat transfer from the slab to the above compartment allowing the calculation of the fire resistance with respect to the insulation criterion. Following the Eurocode recommendations, the heat effect on the unexposed side may be defined by the heat flux by convection, using $\alpha_c = 9$ W/m²K, to include the radiation effect [3]. The boundary condition in the upper surface of the slab is given by Eq. (6),

$$\lambda(T)\nabla T.\overrightarrow{n} = \alpha_c(T - T_\infty) \tag{6}$$

where T_∞ is the room temperature.

The other four surfaces of the slab (front, back, left and right) are considered insulated, i.e., the boundary conditions applied to these faces are given by Eq. (7),

$$\lambda(T)\nabla T.\overrightarrow{n} = 0 \tag{7}$$

Equation (7) which is based on the adiabatic condition, applied to the external lateral surfaces of the slab.

3   Numerical Solution Through Finite Element Method

In order to perform a thermal analysis on composite slabs, the Eq. (1) must be solved through the FEM on 3D domain using Matlab PDE Toolbox. The generated thermal models are composed of sub-domains corresponding to different materials with 3D finite elements resulting from the discretization of the domain (see Fig. 3).

Equation (1) is solved by FEM based on the weak-form Galerkin model and the minimum condition to the weighted residual method, thus leading to the energy matrix formulae

$$C(T)\dot{T} + K(T)T = F \tag{8}$$

where C is the capacitance matrix, $\dot{T}$ is the vector of time derivatives of the temperatures, K is the conductivity matrix and F is the vector of the thermal loads (for details see, for instance, [10]). The vector of the thermal loads F includes the boundary conditions. The solution of the first order non-linear system of ordinary differential equations given by Eq. (8), considering $T(t_0) = T^0$ and the boundary conditions, enables to determine the temperature at each node of the finite element mesh, illustrated in Fig. 3 (b), over the time interval $[t_0, t_f]$.

3.1   Computational Solution with Matlab

The Matlab (R2019a) PDE Toolbox was used to develop and solve the nonlinear transient thermal analysis. The finite element model of the composite slab created with Matlab uses only one type of finite element. The tetrahedral finite elements are defined by four nodes and use linear interpolation functions. The finite element mesh is composed by four different sub-domains: concrete, steel deck, rebar and air-gap. Thus, 3 different materials are used (concrete, steel and air). Additionally, two different types of concrete are considered: NWC and LWC.

Regarding the finite element mesh size on the models, the maximum mesh edge length varies according to each steel deck profile. Figure 3 (b) presents the finite element mesh in one of the studied models, in which the element size was selected by a convergence of results with the mesh refinement, which means the size of mesh elements was adjusted until the relative error in nodal temperature calculations has the maximum value of 10^{-4} in the worst scenario.

In Matlab PDE Toolbox the Eq. (8) is converted in

$$C(T)\dot{T} = \bar{F}(T) \tag{9}$$

where $\bar{F}(T) = F - K(T)$. The solution of Eq. (9) is computed by the built in function ode15s [19]. The algorithm implemented in this function is based on the discretization of the time derivative by numerical differentiation formulas (NDFs) of orders 1 to 5. The order of accuracy of the solution can be explicitly controlled through the absolute or relative tolerance parameters. In this work a value of 10^{-6} is set to the absolute tolerance, and 10^{-3} is set to the relative tolerance. In each time step, the non-linear system of algebraic equation is solved through the Newton-Raphson method whose stopping criterion can be monitored by means of the maximal number of iterations, set to 25, and the residual tolerance, set to 10^{-4} (for more details see [12]).

4   Simplified Calculation Method and Numerical Results

A parametric study is conducted in order to investigate the influence of the concrete thickness h_1 on the temperatures used to determine the fire resistance of composite slabs according to the load-bearing criterion (R). As already mentioned, the load-bearing resistance depends on the temperatures in the steel deck components and rebar. A simplified calculation method is proposed by the standard Eurocode 1994 1.2 [4]. But this model hasn't been updated for a long time and needs to be revised. The proposed methodology is based on solving numerically the thermal problem, presented in the previous section, for different thicknesses of the concrete cover (h_1) and compare the results with the simplified method.

4.1   Simplified Calculation Method

The simplified calculation method used for the load-bearing criterion (R) presented in Eurocode 1994 1.2 [4] can be applied to simply support composite slabs when exposed to an ISO-834 standard fire [9]. In order to calculate the bending moment resistance of the composite slab (sagging moment), the standard defines the temperature for each steel deck component (upper flange, web and, lower flange) according to the formula

$$\theta_a = b_0 + b_1 \frac{1}{l_3} + b_2 \frac{A}{L_r} + b_3 \phi + b_4 \phi^2 \tag{10}$$

and the rebar component θ_s by the formula

$$\theta_s = c_0 + c_1 \frac{u_3}{h_2} + c_2 z + c_3 \frac{A}{L_r} + c_4 \alpha + c_5 \frac{1}{l_3} \tag{11}$$

where the temperatures θ_a and θ_s are given in [°C], the parameter ϕ is adimensional and corresponds to the view factor of the steel deck component (upper flange only), given by Eq. 3, and the terms b_i and c_i refer to the coefficients given by Eurocode 1994 1.2 [4], which depends on the type of concrete used in the composite element and changes according to the standard fire resistance that must be achieved. The component u_3 represents the distance from the rib centroid to the lower flange in [mm], the z-factor represents the position of the rebar concerning the slab rib given in [mm$^{-0.5}$], and the term α corresponds to the angle formed between the web component of the steel deck and the horizontal direction in degrees [°].

4.2   Numerical Results

A total of 40 numerical simulations were carried out, using an air-gap of 0.5 mm. This air-gap value has been obtained through the previous calibration [13]. The computational simulations took into account h_1 values equal to 60, 70, 90, 110, and 125 mm for the two trapezoidal geometries (see Figs. 2 (a) and (b)), and equal to 50, 70, 90, 110, and 125 mm for the two re-entrant geometries (see Figs. 2 (c) and (d)). All simulations were done for NWC and LWC.

Figure 7 and Fig. 8 show the distribution of temperatures inside the slab after 120 min and the evolution of average temperatures, computed numerically (N), in the three parts of the steel deck and in the rebar. For comparison, values calculated using the simplified method (S), given by Eqs. 10 and 11 are also included. Additionally, the T_{ISO} given by Eq. 5 is also depicted in these figures.

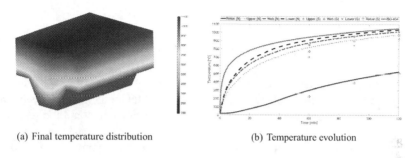

(a) Final temperature distribution   (b) Temperature evolution

Fig. 7. Polydeck 59S with NWC.

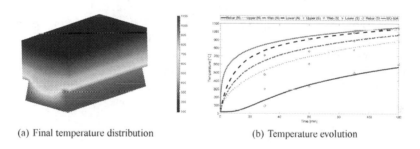

(a) Final temperature distribution   (b) Temperature evolution

Fig. 8. Multideck 50 with LWC.

Figure 7 shows the thermal behavior of the trapezoidal Polydeck 59S slab with $h_1 = 90$ mm using NWC, and Fig. 8 presents the thermal behavior of the re-entrant Multideck 50 slab with $h_1 = 90$ mm using LWC. It is observable that, in general, the temperatures predicted by the simplified model are below the numerical results. This is especially true for the fire ratings of 30 and 60 min, in the case of the Multideck 50, and 60 min, in the case of the Polideck 59S geometry.

4.3 New Calculation Proposal

Based on the simulation results, new coefficients b_i and c_i are proposed for the simplified model. In addition, the original models, given by Eqs. 10 and 11, are modified by including a new term that depends on h_1, in order to take into account the effect on temperatures of the thickness of the concrete topping. The thickness h_1 is explicitly included in the model multiplied by coefficient b_5, in the case of the steel deck temperatures, and by c_6, in the case of the rebar temperature. Thus, the new proposal for the steel deck temperature is

$$\theta_a = b_0 + b_1 \frac{1}{l_3} + b_2 \frac{A}{L_r} + b_3 \phi + b_4 \phi^2 + b_5 h_1 \tag{12}$$

and for the rebar is

$$\theta_s = c_0 + c_1 \frac{u_3}{h_2} + c_2 z + c_3 \frac{A}{L_r} + c_4 \alpha + c_5 \frac{1}{l_3} + c_6 h_1. \tag{13}$$

The coefficients for these new proposal methods have been determined by fitting the mathematical models, represented by Eqs. 12 and 13, to the numerical results obtained with the parametric study with h_1, two different types of concrete and the four different composite slab geometries. The coefficients were determined using the nonlinear least-squares method. This method consists of minimizing the sum of the squared deviations between the temperatures proposed by Eqs. 12 or 13 and those obtained through simulations. This sum was minimized using the Generalized Reduced Gradient (GRG) nonlinear solver [11].

The resulting coefficients for the calculation of temperatures on the steel deck components, through Eqs. 12, are presented in Table 1. For the calculation of the temperatures on the rebar, through Eqs. 13, the proposed coefficients are presented in Table 2. It is worth mentioning that additionally to the standard fire resistance ratings of 60, 90 and 120 min for NWC and 30, 60, 90 and 120 min for LWC, the new proposal also comprises the coefficients for the fire rating of 45 min.

4.4 Comparing Results

In order to verify the differences between the Eurocode 1994-1.2 [4] for the simplified method (S), the numeric results (N), and the new calculation proposal (P), comparison graphs were developed. Figure 9 a) establish this comparison for each steel deck component and the rebars for NWC, while Fig. 9 b) plays the same role for LWC.

Comparing with the Eurocode proposal, the new proposal contributes to improve the temperature estimation according to each fire resistance time. For both types of concrete (NWC and LWC), the new proposal matches very well with the numerical results. It is also possible to verify that the analytical method, proposed by the Eurocode, predicted much lower temperatures than the numerical results, mainly for lowest fire ratings.

Table 1. New b_i coefficients proposal for the steel deck components.

Concrete	Fire resist.	Flange	b_0	b_1	b_2	b_3	b_4	b_5
NWC	45 min	Upper	139.9655	620.7460	7.6958	1421.9882	−1204.0686	−0.0564
		Web	404.1556	−1623.2839	6.7521	1109.9125	−1060.6480	−0.0187
		Lower	860.8523	−2427.8085	1.0349	−40.2277	36.9805	−0.0033
	60 min	Upper	224.5881	−2852.6026	10.8539	1428.8794	−1312.5261	−0.1046
		Web	599.8829	−13427.3660	17.2020	327.3531	−522.0016	−0.0346
		Lower	917.5108	−3173.1570	2.0515	−47.7229	15.2644	−0.0061
	90 min	Upper	578.7070	−18369.1630	22.9583	139.6578	−322.2799	−0.1799
		Web	542.0284	633.9895	4.6194	1398.3091	−1361.2018	−0.0674
		Lower	982.2585	3077.4610	2.3687	3.3250	−52.4300	−0.0166
	120 min	Upper	691.0625	−14595.5356	18.2749	212.0806	−340.0106	−0.2667
		Web	666.1045	−416.2267	4.8378	1158.5088	−1146.7154	−0.1088
		Lower	955.4042	4109.1835	−3.8674	492.9857	−407.7782	−0.0189
LWC	30 min	Upper	302.1644	−5233.6445	10.9946	614.9448	−529.2700	−0.0111
		Web	491.6762	−3193.5831	6.6500	522.4295	−491.2013	−0.0003
		Lower	871.2783	−4956.7858	3.0851	−469.3452	438.6676	0.0006
	45 min	Upper	388.5675	−7171.2080	12.8469	755.4877	−743.7176	−0.0422
		Web	486.1987	1073.6509	3.5221	1137.2531	−1073.2821	−0.0110
		Lower	868.1465	−1328.8180	0.6831	22.4003	−24.4881	−0.0005
	60 min	Upper	389.9821	114.9104	5.8948	1325.8176	−1200.0499	−0.0713
		Web	632.6120	−4880.4634	8.4873	662.5945	−722.1706	−0.0232
		Lower	904.4639	−277.6849	−0.0679	115.2137	−106.1585	−0.0026
	90 min	Upper	578.3817	−425.0477	4.8700	1042.2053	−944.7059	−0.1217
		Web	629.7576	5806.3988	−1.5116	1364.7899	−1243.5193	0.0478
		Lower	986.6232	−834.2380	0.4527	39.8315	−44.2602	−0.0070
	120 min	Upper	686.5569	1931.2433	1.5912	994.6118	−861.4596	0.1382
		Web	820.5056	−1457.3952	4.0784	632.9442	−642.8140	−0.0599
		Lower	1042.9854	−1215.3431	0.8033	−14.9962	2.3697	−0.0108

Table 2. New c_i coefficients proposal for the rebars.

Concrete	Fire resist.	c_0	c_1	c_2	c_3	c_4	c_5	c_6
NWC	45 min	99.8233	100.1983	106.0042	−11.8333	2.0660	−3983.0834	−0.0566
	60 min	−880.0008	923.7717	389.1767	−30.6981	2.9630	−5263.7252	−0.1241
	90 min	117.6928	961.6281	−526.6992	28.0940	0.7423	−5803.2055	−0.3510
	120 min	−151.2236	834.6475	31.9477	−8.0649	2.2052	−7000.3192	−0.6032
LWC	30 min	−496.7732	430.0693	326.4075	−25.8183	2.4637	−3419.6974	−0.0099
	45 min	−2463.4757	2829.0060	49.4180	−9.8686	2.0244	−4509.8827	−0.0558
	60 min	317.3687	53.5299	179.5837	−19.0716	2.4341	−5491.2669	−0.1346
	90 min	528.3687	−181.2998	395.2534	−33.4968	2.9036	−6393.0551	−0.3148
	120 min	−373.7261	−325.9842	1616.5151	−112.2265	6.0518	−7756.3731	−0.4362

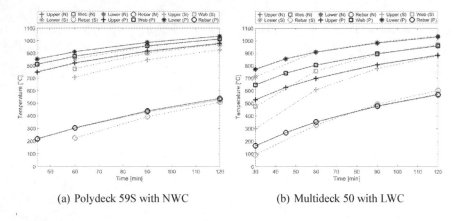

(a) Polydeck 59S with NWC   (b) Multideck 50 with LWC

Fig. 9. Temperature corresponding to different fire rating times.

5   Final Considerations

In this work, new and more realistic computational models were developed to represent the thermal behavior of composite slabs under standard fire conditions. The results of the parametric analysis enable us to determine the temperatures for different slab geometries and compare them with the ones provided by the simplified calculation method of Eurocode 1994-1.2. The new proposed model aimed to comprise some effects that the current Eurocode neglects, such as the debonding effect between the steel deck and concrete and the thickness of the concrete topping.

In order to optimize the analytical calculation proposal, a new calculation proposal for determining the temperature in the steel deck components and the rebars based on the numerical results is presented. The new formulation includes in the actual formula, provided by the Eurocode, an additional term in order to include the effect of the concrete thickness. The new coefficients were determined by fitting the new proposal to the numerical results by non-linear least-squares. The new proposal provide an improvement of the temperature estimation that affects the reduction coefficients in all the slab components and, consequently, an accurate estimation of the load-bearing resistance criteria. The load-bearing resistance criteria will be based on the reduction coefficients applied to yield strength of each component. Future work should include the moisture effect in the thermal behaviour of the concrete and the mechanical effect of the airgap on the load-bearing capacity.

Acknowledgements. This work has been supported by FCT - Fundação para a Ciência e Tecnologia within the Project Scope: UIDB/05757/2020.

References

1. Bolina, F., Tutikian, B., Rodrigues, J.P.C.: Thermal analysis of steel decking concrete slabs in case of fire. Fire Saf. J. **121**, 103295 (2021). https://doi.org/10.1016/j.firesaf.2021.103295

2. CEN: EN 1993-1-2: Design of steel structures. Part 1–2: General rules - structural fire design eurocode (2002)
3. CEN: EN 1992-1-2: Design of concrete structures. Part 1–2: General rules - structural fire design (2004)
4. CEN: EN 1994-1-2: Design of composite steel and concrete structures. Part 1–2: General rules - structural fire design (2005)
5. CEN: EN 13501-2: Fire classification of construction products and building elements. (2016)
6. Cengel, Y.A., Ghajar, A.J.: Heat and Mass Transfer: Fundamentals and Applications. McGraw-Hill Education, Europe (2014)
7. ECCS: Calculation of the fire resistance of composite concrete slabs with profiled steel sheet exposed to the standard fire (1983)
8. Hamerlinck, A.F.: The behaviour of fire-exposed composite steel/concrete slabs. Ph.D. thesis, Eindhoven University of Technology (1991)
9. ISO: International standard ISO 834 - fire-resistance tests: Elements of building construction (1975)
10. Gartling, D.K., Reddy, J.N.: The Finite Element Method in Heat Transfer and Fluid Dynamics, 3 edn. CRC Press, Boca Raton (2010)
11. Lasdon, L.S., Fox, R.L., Ratner, M.W.: Nonlinear optimization using the generalized reduced gradient method. Revue française d'automatique, informatique, recherche opérationnelle. Recherche opérationnelle **8**(V3), 73–103 (1974). https://doi.org/10.1051/ro/197408v300731
12. MathWorks: Partial Differential Equation Toolbox^{TM} User's Guide, Heat Transfer Problem with Temperature-Dependent Properties. The MathWorks, Inc.
13. Piloto, P.A.G., Balsa, C., Ribeiro, F.F., Santos, L.M., Rigobello, R., Kimura, É.: Three-dimensional numerical modelling of fire exposed composite slabs with steel deck. MATTER Int. J. Sci. Technol. **5**(2), 48–67 (2019). https://doi.org/10.20319/mijst.2019.52.4867
14. Piloto, P.A.G., Balsa, C., Ribeiro, F.F., Rigobello, R.: A new calculation method for the temperature of the components of composite slabs under fire. J. Comput. Appl. Mech. (2021). https://doi.org/10.22059/jcamech.2021.316216.584
15. Piloto, P.A.G., Balsa, C., Ribeiro, F.F., Rigobello, R.: Three-dimensional numerical analysis on the fire behaviour of composite slabs with steel deck. In: Piloto, P.A.G., Rodrigues, J.P., Silva, V.P. (eds.) CILASCI 2019. LNCE, vol. 1, pp. 12–30. Springer, Cham (2020). https://doi.org/10.1007/978-3-030-36240-9_2
16. Piloto, P.A.G., Balsa, C., Ribeiro, F., Rigobello, R.: Computational simulation of the thermal effects on composite slabs under fire conditions. Math. Comput. Sci. **15**(1), 155–171 (2020). https://doi.org/10.1007/s11786-020-00466-0
17. Piloto, P.A.G., Balsa, C., Santos, L.M., Kimura, É.F.: Effect of the load level on the resistance of composite slabs with steel decking under fire conditions. J. Fire Sci. **38**(2), 212–231 (2020). https://doi.org/10.1177/0734904119892210
18. Piloto, P.A.G., Prates, L., Balsa, C., Rigobello, R.: Numerical simulation of the fire resistance of composite slabs with steel deck. Int. J. Eng. Technol. **7**(2.23), 83 (2018). https://doi.org/10.14419/ijet.v7i2.23.11889
19. Shampine, L.F., Reichelt, M.W.: The MATLAB ODE suite. SIAM J. Sci. Comput. **18**(1), 1–22 (1997)

Optimal Control of a Passive Particle Advected by a Point Vortex

G. Marques[1], T. Grilo[2], S. Gama[1(✉)], and F. L. Pereira[3]

[1] CMUP - Department of Mathematics, FCUP, University of Porto, Porto, Portugal
smgama@fc.up.pt
[2] CFisUC - Department of Physics, FCTUC, University of Coimbra,
Coimbra, Portugal
[3] SYSTEC - Department of Electrical and Computer Engineering, FEUP,
University of Porto, Porto, Portugal

Abstract. The objective of this work is to develop a mathematical framework for modeling, control and optimization of the movement of a passive particle advected by a point vortex. Dynamic equations are rewritten in polar coordinates, where the control acts only on the radial coordinate. The optimal control found is explicitly time dependent. This framework should provide a sound basis for the design and control of new advanced engineering systems arising in many important classes of applications, some of which encompass underwater gliders and mechanical fishes.

The research effort has been focused in applying necessary conditions of optimality for some class of flow driven dynamic control systems, by using the vortex methods. The control problem of moving a passive particle between two given points driven by this class of flow in a prescribed time and minimizing the energy of the process has been solved by using the maximum principle.

Keywords: Optimal control · Vortex methods · Pontryagin's maximum principle · Ordinary differential equations · Dynamical systems

1 Introduction

In this paper, we present a research work being developed in the framework of optimal control of dynamic systems, whose state evolves through the interaction of ordinary differential equations [1–3], which will provide a sound basis for the design and control of new advanced engineering systems. In Fig. 1, two representative examples of the class of applications are considered: (i) underwater gliders, i.e., winged autonomous underwater vehicles (AUVs), which locomote by modulating their buoyancy and their attitude in its environment; and (ii) robotic fishes. Motion modeling of these two types of systems can be found in [4–8].

A vortex [9, 10] is a point with circulation that generates a rotational flow field. Let us consider a 2D flow specified in the complex plane by N point vortices

© Springer Nature Switzerland AG 2021
T. Guarda et al. (Eds.): ARTIIS 2021, CCIS 1485, pp. 512–523, 2021.
https://doi.org/10.1007/978-3-030-90241-4_39

Fig. 1. Underwater glider (left), robotic fish (right).

each one located in $z_i, i = 1, \ldots, N$ [11–14]. In this context, the motion of any passive particle advected by this flow is given by the following dynamic equation

$$\dot{z}^* (t) = \frac{1}{2\pi i} \sum_{i=1}^{N} \frac{k_i}{z(t) - z_i(t)}. \tag{1}$$

However, in this article, we consider the case for which the dynamic system is driven by one vortex and we solve a control problem that consists in moving a particle between two given points, by applying necessary conditions of optimality in the form of a maximum principle [15, 16].

2   Velocity Field Driven by a Vortex

Consider a flow with a point vortex at the origin $(0,0)$, with vorticity k, and let $z(t) = x(t) + y(t)i$ be the position of the particle placed in this flow, at time t. In the complex form, the dynamic equations of the particle positioned in z subject to the velocity field given by the vortex is

$$\dot{z}^* (t) = \frac{1}{2\pi i} \frac{k}{z(t)}. \tag{2}$$

In polar coordinates, the position of the particle is given by

$$z(t) = \rho(t) e^{i\theta(t)}, \tag{3}$$

and the derivative, with respect to t, is

$$\dot{z}(t) = \dot{\rho}(t) e^{i\theta(t)} + i\rho(t) \dot{\theta}(t) e^{i\theta(t)}. \tag{4}$$

Therefore, the complex conjugate of the derivative is

$$\dot{z}^* (t) = \dot{\rho}(t) e^{-i\theta(t)} - i\rho(t) \dot{\theta}(t) e^{-i\theta(t)}, \tag{5}$$

and, from (2) and (5), we obtain

$$\dot{\rho}(t) - i\,\rho(t)\,\dot{\theta}(t) = -i\,\frac{k}{2\pi}\,\frac{1}{\rho(t)}. \tag{6}$$

By separating the equalities of the real and imaginary parts of both sides of this equation, we have the following dynamic equations of the particle in polar form

$$\begin{cases} \dot{\rho}(t) = 0 \\ \dot{\theta}(t) = \dfrac{k}{2\pi}\,\dfrac{1}{\rho^2(t)} \end{cases} \tag{7}$$

So, the position of the particle, in each time t, is given by

$$z(t) = \rho(0)\,e^{\,i\left(\dfrac{kt}{2\pi\rho^2(0)} + \theta(0)\right)}. \tag{8}$$

In Fig. 2, we have the trajectory of the particle with the initial position in (x_0, y_0), where the circulation of the vortex is $k > 0$. For the case $k < 0$, the trajectory would be the same, but with clockwise motion.

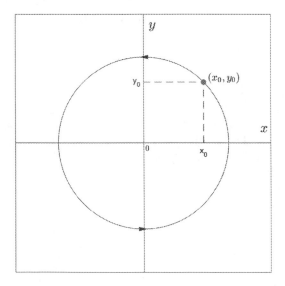

Fig. 2. Trajectory of a free particle, initially located at (x_0, y_0), advected by a point vortex located at the origin ($k > 0$).

3   Control Problem

Consider a flow like the one presented in Sect. 2 and a passive particle placed in
the flow with initial position (x_0, y_0). The objective of this work is to determine
the control function $u(\cdot)$ to be applied to the particle, so that it will move in
the flow from the given initial position to the end point (x_f, y_f), minimizing the
cost function $g(X(T))$, while subject to the flow field. Let $X(t) = (x(t), y(t))$ be
the position of the particle at time t.

The control problem can be then formulated as follows:

$$\begin{cases} \text{Minimize} \quad g(X(T)) \\ \text{subject to} \\ \dot{X}(t) = F(X(t), u(t)) \\ X(0) = (x_0, y_0) \\ X(T) = (x_f, y_f) \\ \dot{X}(T) = 0 \\ \|u(t)\|_\infty \leq 1 \end{cases} \quad , \quad \forall t \in [0, T]. \tag{9}$$

The maximum principle [15], allows us to determine the optimal control $u^*(\cdot)$
by using the maximization of the Pontryagin's function $H(X, P, u)$ (here, P is
the adjoint variable satisfying $-\dot{P} = \nabla_X H(X, P, u)$, being ∇_X the gradient of
H with respect to X) almost everywhere with respect to the Lebesgue measure
(from here onwards, functions are specified in this sense), together with the
satisfaction of the appropriate boundary conditions.

3.1   Minimum Energy Problem

Here, our cost function is the total control power consumption, or energy,

$$E = \int_0^T u^2(t)\, dt.$$

We want to minimize the energy, E, spent to move the particle between the
initial and final points so that, at the final prescribed time T, the particle is at
(ρ_T, θ_T).

To obtain the Mayer's problem [17], we consider a new time dependent variable $w(\cdot)$ that satisfies $\dot{w} = u^2$. Thus, our control problem is formulated as
follows:

$$
\begin{cases}
\text{Minimize} \quad w(T) \\
\text{subject to} \\
\dot{\rho}(t) = u(t) \\
\dot{\theta}(t) = \dfrac{k}{2\pi} \dfrac{1}{\rho^2(t)} \\
\dot{w}(t) = u^2(t) \\
\rho(0) = \rho_0 \\
\rho(T) = \rho_T \\
\dot{\rho}(T) = 0 \\
\theta(0) = \theta_0 \\
\theta(T) = \theta_T \\
w(0) = 0 \\
\|u(t)\|_\infty \leq 1
\end{cases}
\qquad , \qquad \forall t \in [0, T].
\tag{10}
$$

We impose the radial velocity $\dot{\rho}$ to go to zero at $t = T$, so that the control is smooth and differentiable during the arrival at the circular trajectory of radius ρ_T. For simplicity, we will consider only the case where $\rho_T < \rho_0$. The case $\rho_T > \rho_0$ follows analogously.

For this problem, the Pontryagin's function is

$$
H(t, \rho, \theta, w, p_\rho, p_\theta, p_w) = p_\rho u + p_\theta \frac{k}{2\pi\rho^2} + p_w u^2,
\tag{11}
$$

and the dynamic equations for the adjoint variables are

$$
\begin{cases}
-\dot{p}_\rho = -p_\theta \, \dfrac{k}{\pi\rho^3} \\
-\dot{p}_\theta = 0 \\
-\dot{p}_w = 0
\end{cases}
\qquad ,
\tag{12}
$$

and, thus,

$$
\begin{cases}
p_\rho = C_\rho - C_\theta \, \dfrac{k}{\pi} \displaystyle\int_t^T \rho^{-3}(\tau) \, d\tau \\
p_\theta = C_\theta \\
p_w = -1
\end{cases}
.
\tag{13}
$$

where C_ρ and C_θ are integration constants. Furthermore, we know that the optimal solution should maximize the Hamiltonian H. From $\dfrac{dH}{dt} = 0$, it is possible to conclude that the optimal control u^* satisfies

$$
u^*(t) =
\begin{cases}
\min\left\{\dfrac{p_\rho}{2}, 1\right\}, & \text{if} \quad p_\rho \geq 0 \\[2mm]
\max\left\{\dfrac{p_\rho}{2}, -1\right\}, & \text{if} \quad p_\rho < 0
\end{cases}
\qquad ,
\tag{14}
$$

and, thus, it is possible to distinguish between two different behaviors on the radial motion of the passive particle:

1. If $u^*(t) = \pm 1$, we have

$$\dot{\rho} = \pm 1 \Rightarrow \rho(t) = \rho(t_0) \pm (t - t_0). \tag{15}$$

2. If $u^*(t) = \dfrac{p_\rho}{2}$, we have

$$\dot{\rho} = \frac{p_\rho}{2} \quad \Rightarrow \quad \ddot{\rho} = \frac{\dot{p}_\rho}{2} = \frac{C_\theta k}{2\pi \rho^3}. \tag{16}$$

The second order ordinary differential equation (16) can easily be integrated once to obtain ($\dot{\rho}$ is an integrating factor)

$$\dot{\rho}^2 = A^2 - \frac{C_\theta k}{2\pi \rho^2},$$

for some $A^2 \in \mathbb{R}^+$.

Since we impose $\dot{\rho}(\rho = \rho_T) = 0$, we conclude that

$$\dot{\rho}^2 = A^2 \left[1 - \left(\frac{\rho_T}{\rho} \right)^2 \right], \quad A^2 = \frac{C_\theta k}{2\pi \rho_T^2}, \tag{17}$$

and, thus,

$$-\dot{\rho} = |A| \sqrt{1 - \left(\frac{\rho_T}{\rho} \right)^2}, \tag{18}$$

where we take the negative square root, for the reason of $\rho_T < \rho_0$.

The possible radial trajectories of the particle are clearly seen, if we analyze the behavior of $\dot{\rho}$. In Fig. 3, we plot we plot $-\dot{\rho}$ against ρ. The different black lines correspond to different values of $A = \sqrt{\dfrac{C_\theta k}{2\pi \rho_T^2}}$ and, thus, possible trajectories for the passive particle.

The horizontal blue line corresponds to a control $u = -1$, and the movement of the particle has to happen on this line or below it. Therefore, there are two possible types of trajectory for a particle starting at ρ_0.

If $A^2 \left[1 - \left(\frac{\rho_T}{\rho_0} \right)^2 \right] \leq 1$, then the particle is never driven by the control $u = -1$, but by the variable (that is, time-varying) control, describing a curve like the pink one until it reaches ρ_T.

On the other hand, assuming $A^2 \left[1 - \left(\frac{\rho_T}{\rho_0} \right)^2 \right] > 1$, then the particle is driven by the control $u = -1$, for some time, before switching to the variable control law (16) until it reaches ρ_T, as depicted by the red curve in the figure.

We will identify these types of trajectory by type I and type II, respectively. Notice that the trajectory depends solely on the value of A^2, which we have yet to determine.

We now analyze these two different types of trajectory in more detail in order to determine A.

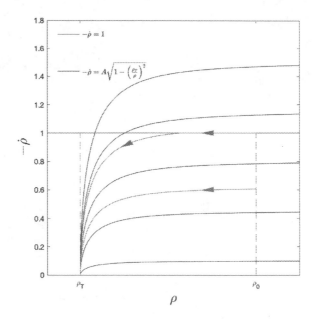

Fig. 3. Illustration of the possible dynamics for the solution of the problem. The different black lines correspond to different values of $A = \sqrt{\frac{C_0 k}{2\pi \rho_T^2}}$. The horizontal blue line corresponds to the control $u = -1$, and so the dynamics can happen above this line. There are two qualitatively different types of trajectories: (i) the particle follows a variable (that is, time-varying) control, until it reaches a trajectory with radius ρ_T (pink curve); (ii) the particle is first pulled by a control $u = -1$, which then switches into a variable control that is active until the particle reaches a trajectory with radius ρ_T (red curve). (Color figure online)

Trajectory of Type I. In a trajectory of type I, the particle starts its motion under the variable control that diminishes its radius until it arrives at ρ_T, at some time t^*. From this point onwards, the particle will describe a circular motion with constant radius around the vortex until it arrives at the prescribed angle θ_T, at time T.

In the time interval $[0, t^*]$, the movement of the particle is given by the solution of the IVP

$$
\begin{cases}
\dot{\rho} = -A\sqrt{1 - \left(\dfrac{\rho_T}{\rho}\right)^2} \\
\dot{\theta} = \dfrac{k}{2\pi}\dfrac{1}{\rho^2} \\
\rho(0) = \rho_0, \quad \theta(0) = \theta_0
\end{cases}
, \tag{19}
$$

which is

$$
\begin{cases}
\rho^2\left(t\right) = \rho_0^2 + A^2 t^2 - 2A\sqrt{\rho_0^2 - \rho_T^2}\, t \\[2mm]
\theta\left(t\right) = \theta_0 + \dfrac{k}{2\pi A \rho_T}\left[\tan^{-1}\left(\sqrt{\left(\dfrac{\rho_0}{\rho_T}\right)^2 - 1}\right) - \right. \\[4mm]
\left. \qquad\qquad - \tan^{-1}\left(\sqrt{\left(\dfrac{\rho_0}{\rho_T}\right)^2 - 1} - \dfrac{At}{\rho_T}\right)\right]
\end{cases}
, \quad t \in [0, t^*]. \quad (20)
$$

The time t^* can be easily calculated from the condition $\rho\left(t^*\right) = \rho_T$, and we get $t^* = \dfrac{1}{A}\sqrt{\rho_0^2 - \rho_T^2}$.

In the time interval $]t^*, T]$, the radius remains constant $\rho\left(t\right) = \rho_T$, while the angular position obeys the equation

$$
\dot{\theta} = \frac{k}{2\pi \rho_T^2},
$$

and, thus, we get

$$
\begin{cases}
\rho\left(t\right) = \rho_T \\[2mm]
\theta\left(t\right) = \theta\left(t^*\right) + \dfrac{k}{2\pi \rho_T^2}\left(t - t^*\right)
\end{cases}
, \quad t \in]t^*, T]. \quad (21)
$$

Notice that we can have $t^* = T$ and, in this scenario, the particle arrives at the final point at the same time, as the variable control goes to zero.

Since we are dealing with a circular motion, one can actually still arrive at the final position with an angle of $\theta_T + 2N\pi$, $N \in \mathbb{N} \cup \{0\}$. Thus, from $\theta(T) = \theta_T + 2N\pi$, we can write

$$
\begin{aligned}
\theta_T + 2N\pi = {}& \theta_0 + \frac{k}{2\pi A \rho_T}\tan^{-1}\left(\sqrt{\left(\frac{\rho_0}{\rho_T}\right)^2 - 1}\right) \\[2mm]
& + \frac{k}{2\pi A \rho_T^2}\left(T - \frac{1}{A}\sqrt{\rho_0^2 - \rho_T^2}\right),
\end{aligned}
\quad (22)
$$

from where we can determine A as

$$
A = \frac{k\,\rho_T\left[\tan^{-1}\left(\sqrt{\left(\frac{\rho_0}{\rho_T}\right)^2 - 1}\right) - \sqrt{\left(\frac{\rho_0}{\rho_T}\right)^2 - 1}\right]}{2\pi \rho_T^2\left(\theta_T - \theta_0 + 2N\pi\right) - k\,T}, \quad (23)
$$

and, thus, the optimal trajectory and optimal control, as long as this value is compatible with $A^2\left[1 - \left(\frac{\rho_T}{\rho_0}\right)^2\right] \leq 1$.

Trajectory of Type II. In a trajectory of type II, the particle starts its motion under the constant control $u = -1$, until some time $\tilde{t}$, reducing the trajectory to one with a radius $\tilde{\rho}$.

At this point, the control switches into the variable control law that further diminishes the trajectory radius to ρ_T, at some time t^*.

In the remainder of the trajectory, the particle will describe a circular motion with constant radius around the vortex, until it arrives at the prescribed angle θ_T, at time T.

In the time interval $[0, \tilde{t}]$, the trajectory of the particle satisfies the IVP

$$
\begin{cases}
\dot{\rho} = -1 \\
\dot{\theta} = \dfrac{k}{2\pi} \dfrac{1}{\rho^2} \\
\rho(0) = \rho_0, \quad \theta(0) = \theta_0
\end{cases}
, \tag{24}
$$

which has the solution

$$
\begin{cases}
\rho(t) = \rho_0 - t \\
\theta(t) = \theta_0 + \dfrac{k}{2\pi A \rho_0} \dfrac{t}{\rho_0 - t}
\end{cases}
, \quad t \in [0, t^*]. \tag{25}
$$

The time $\tilde{t}$ is such that $\rho(\tilde{t}) = \rho_0 - \tilde{t} = \tilde{\rho}$, and $A\sqrt{1 - \left(\frac{\rho_T}{\tilde{\rho}}\right)^2} = 1$. Thus, we arrive at

$$
\begin{cases}
\tilde{\rho}^2 = \dfrac{A^2}{A^2 - 1} \rho_T^2 \\
\tilde{t} = \rho_0 - \sqrt{\dfrac{A^2}{A^2 - 1}} \rho_T
\end{cases}
\tag{26}
$$

Remark: $\theta(\tilde{t}) = \theta_0 + \dfrac{k}{2\pi \rho_T}\left[\sqrt{\dfrac{A^2 - 1}{A^2}} - \dfrac{\rho_T}{\rho_0}\right] = \tilde{\theta}.$

In the time interval $]\tilde{t}, t^*]$, the motion of the particle is ruled by the variable control and it satisfies the same differential equations of the IVP (19), although with initial conditions $\rho(\tilde{t}) = \tilde{\rho}$, and $\theta(\tilde{t}) = \tilde{\theta}$.

The solution is thus

$$
\begin{cases}
\rho^2(t) = \tilde{\rho}^2 + A^2(t - \tilde{t})^2 - 2A\sqrt{\tilde{\rho}^2 - \rho_T^2}(t - \tilde{t}) \\
\theta(t) = \tilde{\theta} + \dfrac{k}{2\pi A \rho_T}\left[\tan^{-1}\left(\sqrt{\left(\dfrac{\tilde{\rho}}{\rho_T}\right)^2 - 1}\right) - \right. \\
\qquad\qquad \left. - \tan^{-1}\left(\sqrt{\left(\dfrac{\tilde{\rho}}{\rho_T}\right)^2 - 1} - \dfrac{A(t - \tilde{t})}{\rho_T}\right)\right]
\end{cases}
, \quad t \in]\tilde{t}, t^*]. \tag{27}
$$

Finally, on the time interval $]t^*, T]$, the movement is the same as in the correspondent time interval of a trajectory of type I: the radius remains constant $\rho(t) = \rho_T$, while the angular position obeys the equation $\dot\theta = \dfrac{k}{2\pi\,\rho_T^2}$. Thus,

$$
\begin{cases}
\rho(t) = \rho_T \\
\theta(t) = \theta(t^*) + \dfrac{k}{2\pi\rho_T^2}(t - t^*)
\end{cases}, \quad t \in]t^*, T].
\tag{28}
$$

Opposite to what happened in a trajectory of type I, it is not possible to write an explicit expression of A.

From $\theta(T) = \theta_T + 2N\pi$, $N \in \mathbb{N} \cup \{0\}$, after some calculation, we can write an implicit equation for A:

$$
\frac{2\pi\rho_T}{k}\left[\theta_T - \theta_0 + 2N\pi\right] + \frac{\rho_T^2 + \rho_0^2}{\rho_T\rho_0} - \frac{T}{\rho_T}
$$
$$
= \frac{1}{A}\left[2\sqrt{A^2 - 1} + \tan^{-1}\left(\frac{1}{\sqrt{A^2 - 1}}\right)\right].
\tag{29}
$$

This equation is consistent with the expression (22), since, in the limit $\tilde{t} \to 0$, we recover that expression. By taking this limit would correspond to the scenario without constraints on the control.

It is also important to notice that the family of curves

$$
\dot\rho^2 = A^2\left[1 - \left(\frac{\rho_T}{\rho}\right)^2\right],
$$

with $A > 0$, constitutes the family of curves with minimal energy, E, for this problem. Thus, if there is any trajectory of type I that is a solution to the problem, it is also the minimal energy solution. In this scenario, any trajectory of type II, that takes the particle from the initial point to the final point, will have higher energy cost.

In Fig. 4, we show the optimal trajectory for the problem of moving a particle originally placed in the initial position $(x_0, y_0) = (2, 2)$ to the final position $(x_f, y_f) = (1, 1)$, in $T = 100$ units of time, in an environment controlled by a point vortex, located at the origin, with circulation $k = 1$. In the red-depicted part of the trajectory, the particle is under the influence of the variable control, while in the black-depicted part, it is only under the influence of the velocity field generated by the vortex. We found $A \approx 0.0460$ and the energy spent in moving the particle was $E \approx 0.9685$.

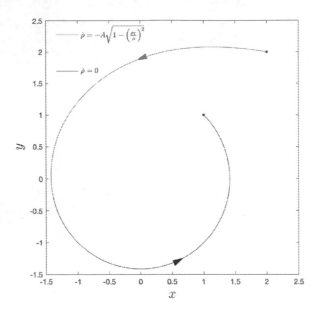

Fig. 4. Optimal trajectory of a particle that moves from $(2, 2)$ to $(1, 1)$, in $T = 100$ units of time, on an environment controlled by a point vortex of circulation $k = 1$, located at the origin. The other parameters are $\rho_0^2 = 8$, $\rho_T^2 = 2$, $\theta_0 = \theta_T = \frac{\pi}{2}$, $N = 1$. The optimal trajectory corresponds to $A \approx 0.0460$, and the energy spent was $E \approx 0.9685$.

4 Conclusions and Future Work

The problem discussed in this work is simple, since the dynamics of the control system are defined by a set of autonomous ODE's. Also, the conditions resulting from the application of the maximum principle can be solved in an explicit way.

In this problem, only the radius is directly affected by the control, since we just need to either pull the particle closer to the vortex or push it farther away in a way that minimizes the cost function and reaches the desired final position at the instant T. We plan to investigate further in this problem, studying and comparing different scenarios by changing the constants in the problem and eventually tackle it in an environment constituted by a viscous vortex or a set of N vortices.

Acknowledgments. This work was partially supported by CMUP (UID/MAT/ 00144/2019), which is funded by FCT with national (MCTES) and European structural funds through the programs FEDER, under the partnership agreement PT2020; by SYSTEC - POCI-01-0145-FEDER-006933/SYSTEC funded by ERDF - COMPETE2020 - FCT/MEC - PT2020; by project MAGIC - POCI-01-0145- FEDER-032485, funded by ERDF NORTE 2020; and by project SNAP - reference NORTE-01-0145-FEDER-000085, co-financed by the European Regional Development Fund (ERDF), through the North Portugal Regional Operational Programme (NORTE2020), under the PORTUGAL 2020 Partnership Agreement.

References

1. Clarke, F., Ledyaev, Y., Stern, R., Wolenski, P.: Nonsmooth Analysis and Control Theory. Springer, New York (1998). https://doi.org/10.1007/b97650
2. Lions, J.: Optimal Control of Systems Governed by Partial Differential Equations. Springer, New York (1971)
3. Protas, B.: Vortex dynamics models in flow control problems. Nonlinearity **21**(9), R203 (2008)
4. Mahmoudian, N., Geisbert, J., Woolsey, C.: Dynamics and control of underwater gliders I: steady motions, Virginia Center for Autonomous Systems, Technical report no. VaCAS-2007-01 (2009)
5. Mahmoudian, N., Woolsey, C.: Dynamics and control of underwater gliders II: motion planning and control, Virginia Center for Autonomous Systems, Technical report no. VaCAS-2010-02 (2010)
6. Liu, J., Hu, H.: Biological inspiration: from carangiform fish to multijoint robotic fish. J. Bionic Eng. **7**, 35–48 (2010)
7. Pereira, F.L., Grilo, T., Gama, S.: Optimal multi-process control of a two vortex driven particle in the plane. IFAC-PapersOnLine **50**(1), 2193–2198 (2017)
8. Pereira, F.L., Grilo, T., Gama, S.: Optimal power consumption motion control of a fish-like vehicle in a vortices vector field. In: OCEANS 2017, Aberdeen, pp. 1–4. IEEE (2017)
9. Aref, H.: Integrable, chaotic, and turbulent vortex motion in two-dimensional flows. Annu. Rev. Fluid Mech. **15**(1), 345–389 (1983)
10. Babiano, A., Boffetta, G., Provenzale, A., Vulpiani, A.: Chaotic advection in point vortex models and two-dimensional turbulence. Phys. Fluids **6**(7), 2465–2474 (1994)
11. Batchelor, G.K.: An Introduction to Fluid Dynamics. Cambridge University Press, New York (1992)
12. Newton, P.K.: The N-Vortex Problem - Analytical Techniques. Springer, New York (2001). https://doi.org/10.1007/978-1-4684-9290-3
13. Chorin, A.J.: Vorticity and Turbulence. Springer, New York (1994). https://doi.org/10.1007/978-1-4419-8728-0
14. Gama, S., Milheiro-Oliveira, P.: Statistical properties of passive tracers in a positive four-point vortex model. Phys. Rev. E **62**(1), 1424 (2000)
15. Pontryagin, L., Boltyanskiy, V., Gamkrelidze, R., Mishchenko, E.: Mathematical theory of optimal processes. Interscience Publish, New York (1962)
16. Arutyunov, A.V., Karamzin, D.Y., Pereira, F.L.: The maximum principle for optimal control problems with state constraints by RV Gamkrelidze: revisited. J. Optim. Theory Appl. **149**(3), 474–493 (2011)
17. Levi, M.: Classical Mechanics with Calculus of Variations and Optimal Control: An Intuitive Introduction, vol. 69. American Mathematical Society, Providence (2014)

Challenges of Online Learning During the COVID-19: What Can We Learn on Twitter?

Wei Quan[(⊠)] [iD]

Sungkyunkwan University, Jongno-Gu, Seoul 03063, Korea
weiquan01@skku.edu

Abstract. The COVID-19 pandemic is an ongoing global pandemic. With schools shut down abruptly in mid-March 2020, education has changed dramatically. With the phenomenal rise of online learning, teaching is undertaken remotely and on digital platforms, making schools, teachers, parents, and students face a steep learning curve. This unplanned and rapid move to online learning with little preparation results in a poor experience for everyone involved. Thus, this study explores how people perceive that online learning during the COVID-19 pandemic is challenging. We focus on tweets in English scraped from March to April 2020 with keywords related to the COVID-19 pandemic and online learning. We applied the latent Dirichlet allocation to discover the abstract topics that occur in the data collection. We analyzed representative tweets from the qualitative perspective to explore and augment quantitative findings. Our findings reveal that most challenges identified align with previous studies. We also shed light on several critical issues, including mental health, the digital divide, and cyberbullying. Future work includes investigating these critical issues to enhance teaching and learning practices in the post-digital era.

Keywords: Online learning · COVID-19 · Social media

1 Introduction

The COVID-19 pandemic is an ongoing global pandemic declared by the World Health Organization on March 11, 2020 [1]. Throughout March and early April, several state and local governments imposed "stay at home" quarantines to stem the spread of the virus (including prohibitions and cancellation of large-scale gatherings and the closure of schools) after a national emergency declared in the US on March 13, 2020 [2, 3].

With schools shut down abruptly in mid-March 2020, it forced teachers to develop online learning materials, whereby teaching is undertaken remotely and on digital platforms. As a result, with the phenomenal rise of online learning, education has changed dramatically. Meanwhile, parents had to figure out how to set up home schools while balancing jobs. It is a massive change affecting 6.2 million K-12 public school students and about 500,000 private school students [4]. Thus, schools, teachers, parents, and students face a steep learning curve as they have switched to online learning in the wake of the COVID-19 pandemic.

© Springer Nature Switzerland AG 2021
T. Guarda et al. (Eds.): ARTIIS 2021, CCIS 1485, pp. 524–535, 2021.
https://doi.org/10.1007/978-3-030-90241-4_40

This unplanned and rapid move to online learning, with no training, little preparation, and insufficient bandwidth, results in a poor experience for everyone involved. Thus, this study explores how people perceive that online learning during the COVID-19 pandemic is challenging. We focused on tweets in English scraped from 03/29/2020 to 04/30/2020 with hashtags related to the COVID-19 pandemic and keywords on online learning. In this study, we used mixed methods. Specifically, we applied the latent Dirichlet allocation (LDA) to discover the abstract topics in the data collection. These abstract topics that emerged from the tweets illustrated what people focused on during the first month after the school closure. We then analyzed representative tweets in each topic from the qualitative perspective to explore and augment LDA findings. Furthermore, we summarized and discussed several critical issues, including mental health, the digital divide, and cyberbullying.

2   Related Work

Although online learning has begun in the mid-1990s with the widespread use of the internet, it is the newest development in education compared to the traditional courses taken in a school [5]. Learner experience is typically asynchronous but may also incorporate synchronous elements [6]. However, no single best practice standard has emerged, given the range of learning and teaching styles, the potential ways technology can be implemented, and how educational technology itself is changing [7]. Various pedagogical approaches or learning theories may be considered in designing and interacting with online learning. As theories of distance education evolve, digital technologies to support learning and pedagogy continue to transform as well [8]. However, the complexity of technology and the poor design of the learning system either cause students to spend significantly more time on learning how to use these technologies or distract students with the innovative features and complexities of the online learning environment than learning [9].

Previous studies identified several challenges faced in online learning. Technological literacy and competency have become necessary for both students and teachers in modern education [9–12]. Since learning materials are being embedded in technologies, gaining access to these materials depends on an individual's technological literacy and competency. Students suffer from inability to effectively use technology for learning, while teachers lack confidence, time and willingness to learn new technology for teaching [10, 11, 13–15]. Students also face challenges in self-regulation, isolation, technological sufficiency and technological complexity [11, 12, 16–20]. Under technological sufficiency, there is the digital divide issue. Some students without reliable internet access and technology struggle to participate in online learning. There is a significant gap between the 15-year-olds from the privileged and the disadvantaged backgrounds in the US. All from the privileged background said they had a computer to work on. In contrast, nearly 25% of those from disadvantaged backgrounds did not [21]. While teachers usually face challenges in the technological operation and negative beliefs regarding using technology for teaching [11, 22]. Educational institutions face challenges mainly on technological provision and teachers training [10, 12].

There has been a significant surge in education technology usage since the COVID-19, including language apps, virtual tutoring, video conferencing tools, and online learning software [21]. However, there have not been many studies yet investigating any specific challenges during the pandemic. Thus, this paper aims to uncover the challenges faced in education during the pandemic by applying mixed methods to analyze social media data.

3   Method

In this study, we used mixed methods. Specifically, we applied the latent Dirichlet allocation (LDA) to discover the abstract topics in the data collection. These abstract topics that emerged from the tweets illustrated what people focus on during the first month after the school closure. We then analyzed representative tweets in each topic from the qualitative perspective to explore and augment LDA findings. Furthermore, we summarized and discussed several critical issues, including mental health, the digital divide, and cyberbullying.

3.1   Data Collection

Shane Smith [23] provides the original dataset. It contains tweets of users who have applied the following hashtags: #coronavirus, #coronavirusoutbreak, #coronavirus-Pandemic, #covid19, #covid 19, #epitwitter, #ihavecorona. This dataset spans from 03/29/2020 to 04/30/2020. Selected dataset columns and details are in Table 1. For this study, we focus on English tweets that contain keywords related to online learning. We use a list of online learning related keywords consisting of "online/remote/distance/e" and "education/learning/teaching" for the extraction. With these filtering criteria, the final dataset contains 19,935 tweets.

Table 1. Dataset columns and details

Column name	Details
user id	The ID of the user account that Tweeted
text	The text of the Tweet
lang	The language of the Tweet
status id	The ID of the actual Tweet
created at	The date and time of the Tweet
source	The type of app used
screen name	The screen name of the account that Tweeted
verified	Whether the account that Tweeted is verified

3.2   Text Pre-processing

First, we removed URL, @mention, hashtags, emojis, and punctuations. Then, we applied lemmatization, the process of determining the lemma of a word based on its intended meaning, to transform words into their base forms [24]. We also removed digits, single strings, and stopwords. In this way, we extracted unigrams from the original textual data. We automatically detected common phrases using the Phrase function from the gensim library [25] on the unigrams we generated. Our final dataset consists of unigrams and phrases, which contain meaningful information for topic modeling.

3.3   LDA

LDA is an unsupervised statistical model that is routinely used for topic modeling task [26]. It groups sets of documents into clusters with a mixture of a small number of topics and that each word's presence is attributable to one of the document's topics. To decide on a suitable number of topics for LDA, we calculated topic coherence scores for topic models with a different number of topics and chose the model that gives the highest topic coherence score [27], see Fig. 1. Figure 1 suggests that fitting a model with seven topics may be the right choice. Thus, we chose the model with seven topics with the highest topic coherence score of 0.392.

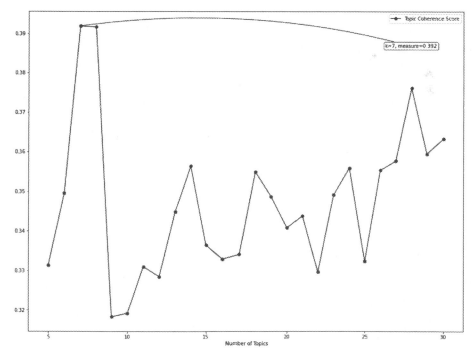

Fig. 1. Topic coherence scores of LDA models with different number of topics

4 Results and Discussions

Table 2 shows the LDA model with seven different topics where each topic is a combination of keywords, and each keyword contributes a certain weight to the topic. We listed the top ten keywords for each topic and each keyword's weight (importance) in Table 2. Instead of inferring a name/label for each topic, which is more art than science, we reported weight * keywords in the table. It describes the tweets clustered in a topic with a certain combination of weighted keywords. For example, topic 1 contains tweets discussing "school", "student", "distance learning", "year", "due", "continue", "plan", "close", "district", and "internet" with the weights 0.151, 0.099, 0.059, 0.033, 0.031, 0.029, 0.018, 0.017, 0.015, and 0.015 respectively.

Table 2. LDA model with seven different topics and corresponding weight*keywords.

Topic #	Weight * Keyword	Weight * Keyword	Weight * Keyword	Weight * Keyword	Weight * Keyword
1	0.151*school	0.099*student	0.059*distance_learning	0.033*year	0.031*due
	0.029*continue	0.018*plan	0.017*close	0.015*district	0.015*internet
2	0.066*free	0.060*resource	0.049*learn	0.043*access	0.025*educator
	0.023*offer	0.022*provide	0.019*platform	0.018*tool	0.017*response
3	0.069*learn	0.063*support	0.038*check	0.034*crisis	0.020*people
	0.016*join	0.016*impact	0.016*health	0.016*closure	0.014*team
4	0.076*student	0.033*teach	0.026*challenge	0.022*world	0.021*give
	0.020*experience	0.019*move	0.019*transition	0.017*face	0.017*university
5	0.073*work	0.072*home	0.047*child	0.044*parent	0.043*kid
	0.040*learn	0.032*family	0.027*tip	0.026*stay	0.019*live
6	0.074*time	0.056*teacher	0.054*make	0.046*day	0.044*class
	0.035*share	0.030*week	0.028*video	0.026*start	0.023*virtual
7	0.029*read	0.026*good	0.021*today	0.020*lesson	0.016*create
	0.015*post	0.015*miss	0.014*love	0.014*week	0.014*grade

Then, we used the pyLDAvis package [28], designed to help interpret the topics in a topic model and visualize the LDA model to examine the produced topics and the associated keywords, see Fig. 2. Each circle represents a topic. The number on the circle corresponds with the topic number in Table 2. The larger the circle, the more prevalent the topic is. A good topic model will have reasonably big, non-overlapping circles scattered throughout the chart instead of clustered in one quadrant. Thus, Fig. 2 shows that the LDA model is good because all the seven topics are non-overlapping and scattering throughout the chart. In Fig. 3, the bar chart shows the corresponding keywords (terms), overall term frequency in blue, and estimated term frequency within the selected topic in red. We can see from Fig. 3 that all the top 30 most relevant terms for Topic 1 have matching overall term frequency and estimated term frequency within Topic 1, except for the terms "student", "today", and "high" which also appear in other topics.

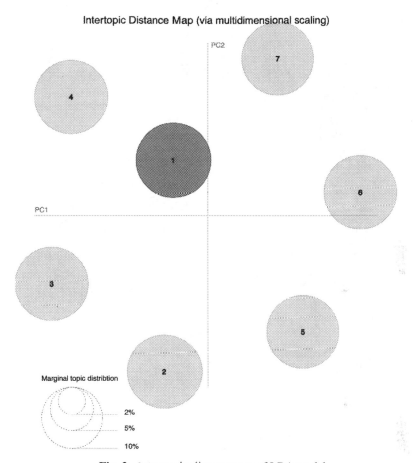

Fig. 2. Inter-topic distance map of LDA model

To understand the volume and distribution of topics to measure how widely it is discussed, we looked at the topic distribution across tweets, see Table 3. We grouped tweets in each topic, counted the number of tweets and calculated the percentage in each topic. We also listed the top ten weighted keywords. Table 3 shows that all the seven topics are relatively evenly distributed, which is in line with the similar-sized circles in Fig. 2.

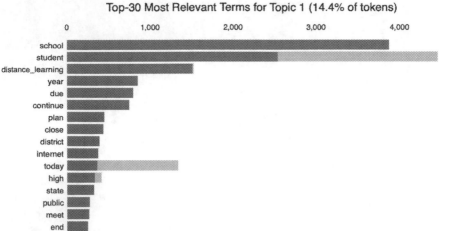

Fig. 3. Top-30 most relevant terms for topic 1

Table 3. Topic volume distribution.

Topic	Keywords	# of tweets	Percentage
1	School, student, distance_learning, year, due, continue, plan, close, district, internet	2654	0.1331
2	Free, resource, learn, access, educator, offer, provide, platform, tool, response	3539	0.1775
3	Learn, support, check, crisis, people, join, impact, health, closure, team	2233	0.112
4	Student, teach, challenge, world, give, experience, move, transition, face, university	3130	0.157

(*continued*)

Table 3. (*continued*)

Topic	Keywords	# of tweets	Percentage
5	Work, home, child, parent, kid, learn, family, tip, stay, live	2503	0.1256
6	Time, teacher, make, day, class, share, week, video, start, virtual	2687	0.1348
7	Read, good, today, lesson, create, post, miss, love, week, grade	3189	0.16

To identify topics with potential challenging issues, we quantitatively analyzed representative tweets. We summarized and discussed our findings below.

We found that most topics in Table 2 align with previous studies [9–12]: students facing challenges to learn independently even though some may need technological literacy skills (Topic 4); parents facing challenges as they figure out how to home school their children while working (Topic 5); facing challenges to launch a comprehensive online learning program which often requires years of careful planning, investment, training, and engagement with the entire school community (Topic 6, 7). Besides, we also found actions in the plan by analyzing the most representative tweets for each topic: stay engaged and productive from home; professional staff/organizations offering online learning materials; news on school closure through the end of the school year; tips on a smooth transition to online learning and ways to encourage learning at home.

Moreover, we shed light on several critical issues discussed in previous studies [21, 29, 30] below, including mental health, the digital divide, and cyberbullying. These issues are not only critical in online learning but also have negative social impacts. Future work will investigate these issues to enhance teaching and learning practices in the post-digital era.

Mental Health includes emotional, psychological, and social well-being. It affects how we think, feel, and act. A nationwide survey assessing the pandemic's effects on the emotional well-being of US adults showed that 90% respondents were experiencing related emotional distress [31]. Younger students not attending school may have protected them from some of the usual factors (schoolwork, bullying), leading to poor mental health. However, graduating students are coping with a shrinking job market and huge changes to their workplaces due to the pandemic. They cannot overlook the pandemic's potential toll on their mental health.

"I'm sick of hearing what other people think schools should do. What do they want from us? Education shouldn't trump mental health. Weeks of kids being at home & staff being on the front line/running online learning. We'll need a break! #edutwitter #COVID19"

"Am I the only teacher that is struggling to make #distancelearning awesome for her kiddos because she is battling her own mental health issues & fears? It was already hard before, now #COVID19 has escalated my issues onto another level. #MentalHealthMatters"

"#Covid 19 and #onlinelearning are destroying my mental health. I can't, I'm stressed and depressed at once."

By analyzing quoted tweets above (related keywords in bold), we should also consider teachers' mental health during this pandemic. We see more teachers tweet about having a panic attack and sobbing breakdown at school. If unaddressed, this challenge will have long-term implications for teachers, students, education, and society.

The Digital Divide is an uneven distribution in the access to information and communications technologies (ICT) between distinct groups. It is another challenge that emerged in our dataset.

"Online learning due to #COVID19 has "widened the digital divide that creates major impediments for lower-income families and those in remote areas." Many students do not have devices, or high-speed internet, or a safe space to work. #onted #cdned"

"Pandemic response lays bare America's digital divide - but we believe together, we can make sure every student has access to the internet. #onlinelearning #COVID19"

"One of the biggest challenges with remote learning in Hawaii is a lack of Internet access and tech devices for many kids. The coronavirus pandemic puts the digital divide into sharper focus #COVID19"

As in the quoted tweet above, lower-income families and those in remote areas who do not have access to the internet and devices face the prospect of starting school without the essentials needed for online learning. To make things worse, schools across the US face shortages in getting the laptops and other equipment needed for online learning, which compounds the inequities [32]. As the digital divide has been studied for quite some time now, we have some basic understanding of investigating the causes, processes, and potential remedies. Future work should focus on what to do during a pandemic or other natural disasters to bridge the digital divide and facilitate people's meaningful participation in the digital society.

Cyberbullying has been studied via conversational social media interactions on Twitter. With the significant increase in online learning amid the COVID-19 pandemic, there has been a 70% increase in cyberbullying in a few months [33].

"Device usage has increased with the change to distance learning. It may cause a rise in cyberbullying. Consider monitoring how & when your students are using their devices. #anonymousalerts #distancelearning #cyberbullying #covid19"

"To help decrease cyberbullying during #distancelearning, educators should set expectations, make standards clear, and explain disciplinary actions for poor online behavior #AnonymousAlerts #Coronavirus #Cyberbullying"

It is important to recognize the struggle the students are going through to prevent the damaging effect. Future research should focus on this topic and discuss what parents and educators can do to lessen the likelihood that it will happen or to minimize the impact if it does occur.

5   Conclusion

This study aims to uncover the challenges people faced in online learning during the COVID-19 pandemic by applying mixed methods to analyze data from Twitter. According to our analyses, people involved in online learning during the COVID-19 pandemic generally had a poor experience due to the unplanned and rapid move to online learning, with no training, little preparation, and insufficient bandwidth. Our findings revealed that most challenges that emerged from the data align with previous studies. We pointed at several critical issues (including mental health, digital divide, and cyberbullying) that have negative social impacts that need to be investigated to enhance teaching and learning practices in the post-digital era. What has been made clear through this pandemic is the importance of disseminating knowledge across all parts of society. Future work will focus on dealing with challenges associated with online learning during the time of pandemic or other natural disasters.

References

1. WHO: Who characterizes covid-19 as a pandemic (2020). https://www.who.int/director-gen eral/speeches/detail/who-director-general-s-opening-remarks-at-the-media-briefing-on-cov id-19. Accessed 11 Mar 2020
2. White House: Proclamation on declaring a national emergency concerning the novel coronavirus disease (covid-19) outbreak (2020). https://trumpwhitehouse.archives.gov/president ial-actions/proclamation-declaring-national-emergency-concerning-novel-coronavirus-dis ease-covid-19-outbreak/
3. All Things Considered: Arkansas governor among the few not to issue stay-at-home order so far (2020). https://www.npr.org/2020/04/06/828303852/arkansas-governor-among-the-few-not-to-issue-stay-at-home-order-so-far
4. Renner, L.: Education vs. covid-19: the shift to online learning (2020). https://capitolweekly. net/education-vs-covid-19-the-shift-to-online-learning/
5. Kaplan, A.M., Haenlein, M.: Higher education and the digital revolution: about MOOCs, SPOCs, social media, and the cookie monster. Bus. Horiz. **59**(4), 441–450 (2016)
6. Cleveland-Innes, M.F., Randy Garrison, D.: An Introduction to Distance Education: Understanding Teaching and Learning in a New Era. Routledge (2010)
7. Meredith, S., Newton, B.: Models of e-learning: technology promise vs learner needs literature review. Int. J. Manage. Educ. **3**(3), 43–56 (2003)
8. Selwyn, N.: Education and Technology: Key Issues and Debates. Bloomsbury Publishing (2016)
9. Prasad, P.W.C., Maag, A., Redestowicz, M., Hoe, L.S.: Unfamiliar technology: reaction of international students to blended learning. Comput. Educ. **122**, 92–103 (2018)
10. Brown, M.G.: Blended instructional practice: a review of the empirical literature on instructors' adoption and use of online tools in face-to-face teaching. Internet High. Educ. **31**, 1–10 (2016)
11. Lightner, C.A., Lightner-Laws, C.A.: A blended model: simultaneously teaching a quantitative course traditionally, online, and remotely. Interact. Learn. Environ. **24**(1), 2 (2016)
12. Rasheed, R.A., Kamsin, A., Abdullah, N.A.: Challenges in the online component of blended learning: a systematic review. Comput. Educ. **144**, 103701 (2020)

13. Zacharis, N.Z.: A multivariate approach to predicting student outcomes in web-enabled blended learning courses. Internet High. Educ. **27**, 44–53 (2015)

14. Cheng, G., Chau, J.: Exploring the relationships between learning styles, online participation, learning achievement and course satisfaction: an empirical study of a blended learning course. Br. J. Edu. Technol. **47**(2), 257–278 (2016)

15. Boelens, R., De Wever, B., Voet, M.: Four key challenges to the design of blended learning: a systematic literature review. Educ. Res. Rev. **22**, 1–18 (2017)

16. Henrie, C.R., Bodily, R., Manwaring, K.C., Graham, C.R.: Exploring intensive longitudinal measures of student engagement in blended learning. Int. Rev. Res. Open Distrib. Learn. **16**(3), 131–155 (2015)

17. Broadbent, J.: Comparing online and blended learner's self-regulated learning strategies and academic performance. Internet High. Educ. **33**, 24–32 (2017)

18. Long, T., Cummins, J., Waugh, M.: Use of the flipped classroom instructional model in higher education: instructors' perspectives. J. Comput. High. Educ. **29**(2), 179–200 (2016). https://doi.org/10.1007/s12528-016-9119-8

19. Gopalan, C., Bracey, G., Klann, M., Schmidt, C.: Embracing the flipped classroom: the planning and execution of a faculty workshop. Adv. Physiol. Educ. **42**(4), 648–654 (2018)

20. Maycock, K.W., Lambert, J., Bane, D.: Flipping learning not just content: a 4-year action research study investigating the appropriate level of flipped learning. J. Comput. Assist. Learn. **34**(6), 661–672 (2018)

21. Li, C., Lalani, F.: The covid-19 pandemic has changed education forever. This is how (2020). https://www.weforum.org/agenda/2020/04/coronavirus-education-global-covid19-online-digital-learning/

22. Bower, M., Dalgarno, B., Kennedy, G.E., Lee, M.J.W., Kenney, J.: Design and implementation factors in blended synchronous learning environments: outcomes from a cross-case analysis. Comput. Educ. **86**, 1–17 (2015)

23. Smith, S.: Coronavirus (covid19) Tweets. Kaggle (2020). https://www.kaggle.com/smid80/coronavirus-covid19-tweets

24. Guerra, J., Quan, W., Li, K., Ahumada, L., Winston, F., Desai, B.: SCOSY: a biomedical collaboration recommendation system. In: 2018 40th Annual International Conference of the IEEE Engineering in Medicine and Biology Society (EMBC), pp. 3987–3990. IEEE (2018)

25. Řehůřek, R., Sojka, P.: Software framework for topic modelling with large corpora. In: Proceedings of the LREC 2010 Workshop on New Challenges for NLP Frameworks, pp. 45–50, May 22 2010

26. Blei, D.M., Ng, A.Y., Jordan, M.I.: Latent Dirichlet allocation. J. Mach. Learn. Res. **3**, 993–1022 (2003)

27. Röder, M., Both, A., Hinneburg, A.: Exploring the space of topic coherence measures. In: Proceedings of the Eighth ACM International Conference on Web Search and Data Mining, pp. 399–408 (2015)

28. Mabey, B.: pyLDAvis: Python library for interactive topic model visualization. Port of the R LDAvis Package (2018)

29. Babvey, P., Capela, F., Cappa, C., Lipizzi, C., Petrowski, N., Ramirez-Marquez, J.: Using social media data for assessing children's exposure to violence during the covid-19 pandemic. Child Abuse Negl. **116**, 104747 (2021)

30. Dhawan, S.: Online learning: a panacea in the time of covid-19 crisis. J. Educ. Technol. Syst. **49**(1), 5–22 (2020)

31. Henderson, E.: Survey reveals significant mental health impact during covid-19 pandemic (2020). https://www.news-medical.net/news/20200702/Survey-reveals-significant-mental-health-impact-during-COVID-19-pandemic.aspx

32. Gecker, J., Liedtke, M.: AP EXCLUSIVE: US faces back-to-school laptop shortage (2020). https://apnews.com/article/virus-outbreak-ap-top-news-ca-state-wire-technology-lifestyle-01e9302796d749b6aadc35ddc8f4c946

33. L1ght. Rising levels of hate speech & online toxicity during this time of crisis (2020). https://l1ght.com/Toxicity_during_coronavirus_Report-L1ght.pdf

Periodontopathies Prevention in Children Through the Digitalization of Play Activities

Patricio Navas-Moya[1]([✉]), Santiago Viteri-Arias[1], Carlos Casa-Guayta[1],
and Camila-Estefanía Navas-Mayorga[2]

[1] Universidad De Las Fuerzas Armadas ESPE Sede Latacunga, Latacunga, Ecuador
{mpnavas,csviteri1,cwcasa}@espe.edu.ec
[2] Universidad Autónoma de los Andes UNIANDES, Ambato, Ecuador
oa.camilaenm21@uniandes.edu.ec

Abstract. Digitization is a strategy for adapting common activities to a virtual environment, in which stimulation and design techniques can be applied to improve the results obtained when performing these activities. Video games allow people to participate in digital activities, starting from going through a stage to perform certain tasks to be satisfied with the activity performed. The development of video games in recent years has made it easier to assimilate knowledge that was previously difficult to acquire, while at the same time increasing the permanence of knowledge in people's memory. The importance of having a mobile device today can be harnessed to transmit through its applications, knowledge and customs that have lost relevance. One of them is dental health correctly practiced, oral pathologies are conditions that develop over time, due to the little importance that has been given to dental health care since childhood has led to many pathologies in adult patients. However, thanks to the application of modern entertainment media such as video games, it has been possible to create a playful environment in which children can play and learn the correct method for the care of their oral health, a fundamental basis for preventing future oral pathologies.

Keywords: Video game · Digitalization · Prevention · Caries · Periodontopathies

1 Introduction

Inadequate oral care can cause serious long and short term diseases such as: dental caries, periodontopathies, canker sores, odontoliths, halitosis, oral manifestations of HIV, trauma and noma (a serious gangrenous disease that begins in the mouth and affects mostly children). For this reason, prevention is essential in the upbringing of children, their initial education during the first years of life, mainly in the second childhood between 3 to 6 years of age, where new activities are interpreted and the personality and motor skills of the infant are developed [1, 2].

It is also important to remember that untreated caries is the most common dental health disorder that leads to tooth loss at an early age. Some 530 million children suffer from it, stressing that treatment is so expensive that it is not covered by universal health

© Springer Nature Switzerland AG 2021
T. Guarda et al. (Eds.): ARTIIS 2021, CCIS 1485, pp. 536–546, 2021.
https://doi.org/10.1007/978-3-030-90241-4_41

coverage (UHC) In high-income countries, dental treatment represents an average of 5% of total health expenditure and 20% of out-of-pocket expenditures, a situation that is aggravated in low-income countries, where the costs of these services are increasing [3].

There are several factors responsible for oral pathologies in the pediatric patient. One of them is the technological evolution. Due to the number and variety of devices, it is easier to entertain a child with content on television or to a greater extent on the Internet or with games that grab their attention, neglecting the oral and personal hygiene of children so that they do not receive adequate education.

Another relevant factor is the amount of time that parents dedicate to the education of infants. In the past, play activities such as games, puppet shows, and storytelling were done with the purpose of helping the infant to develop useful behaviors or skills for the future [4]. Television programs, Internet videos and even video games have become the main sources of education, tools that, if misused, provide incorrect or unhelpful information to children [5].

The objectives of the research are to analyze techniques to influence the behavior of infants in order to motivate patterns of action in favor of learning with respect to oral health, an action that will allow the loyalty of the co-knowledge acquired by the infant [6], the primary stage of learning is the second childhood between 3 to 6 years of age, in this stage it is appropriate to manage oral hygiene in conjunction with parents and treating dentist at the time, at this stage the information is acquired by imitation of actions.

Another objective is to transform playful activities into the pillars of video game design. Playful activities are useful tools that allow emotional and creative development, as well as the acquisition of skills by the child [6]. The aim is to create attractive 2D environments in which images, characters, color patterns, eye-catching scenes and music are presented in order to maximize attention and consequently improve the reception and understanding of the elements presented on the screen [7].

Activities such as brushing teeth, recognizing the correct toothbrush and toothpaste, knowing how to apply toothpaste to the toothbrush will be transformed into entertaining game mechanics to encourage repetition and maximize the amount of knowledge received. The correct influence of video games on children can develop values and improve manual skills [8]. Finally, the integration of the above points in a game for mobile platforms will have statistical analysis within the game, revealing results on the evolution of the child during the time he/she has used the game, to evaluate the effectiveness of the activities performed.

The document is organized in 6 sections which detail each of the steps followed to obtain the results of the proposed research: as the first item we have the introduction where the problem is specified both at the framework and micro level, the possible causes according to experts and other documents on the topic of study, the state of the art where there is information about the tools and works related to the research, in the third point we have the development and implementation of the serious game in which patients made the evaluation to this alternative treatment, and whose results were encouraging and met the objectives of the research, the discussion raises the issue to be addressed on the serious games, tools and alternative treatment as a form of prevention. In the same way, a segment of future works is proposed in which it is suggested to continue with the research as a way to eradicate periodontitis, finally the conclusions obtained from the research.

2 State of the Art

2.1 Video Games as a Learning Tool

Video games as an educational tool (Serious Games) are already considered feasible in different fields of study. They provide attractive environments that stimulate children's learning process and serve as support tools for both teachers and parents [9, 10]. However, not all of them can transmit a message. The large number of elements involved in their development can generate an imbalance in the focus of attention, which is detrimental when seeking to convey knowledge [11].

The graphical presentation is the element that can provide the most knowledge, giving context to a situation, introducing game mechanics and even serving as a hooking or attraction tool [12]. Video games become easy and fun for children when they base their mechanics on images that can be recognized everywhere, geometric figures, animals, objects, expanding the reception of information and its persistence [13], strategy that scales the learning environment from the gaming platform to everyday life. Another visual factor to consider is the image style and how it is presented. Commonly preschool students prefer games that feature colorful shapes and animations [14].

The effort of any form of audiovisual entertainment must lie in attracting the viewer's attention, especially when the information presented seeks to transmit knowledge. The students consolidate the knowledge when they can see the importance of it, without interest there will be no progress [14].

A simple strategy for the creation of mechanics is the memory game, with this type of game the development of the right hemisphere of the child is sought, increasing their ability to learn, implemented through the deployment of simple cards, with an image and short text, easy to read [15].

The use of a video game design framework based on the identification of strategic points in an image has simplified the way in which children recognize different figures, resulting in a simple game that contributes to the development of the imagination [10, 16]. The use of video games as educational tools in infants increases the development of multiple aspects such as relationships, recognition, interpretation, categorization, affective development, aspects that contribute to the social growth of the individual from an early age [17].

For the implementation of all the ideas mentioned above in a mobile device with Android platform, several tools will be used. The first one is Unity, a multiplatform software, partially free, designed for the development of 3D and 2D video games, with an extensive documentation and one of the largest communities in the world of independent game development, also allowing export to various mobile devices [18, 19].

The development of the game behavior will be done using C#, an object-oriented programming language that allows, among other things, the coding of behaviors for each of the objects within a scene, facilitating testing and optimization processes [20]. The code modification will be done in Visual Studio 2019 Community, integrated development software which will play the role of script editor, sequences of instructions oriented to perform an action or solve a problem [21].

3 Implementation

Mobile applications are currently growing, and their technology is what generates the most money worldwide, as they are immersed in all areas of people's daily lives. Applications on mobile devices have become an increasingly popular trend, alternative treatments through mobile devices have become a way to keep patients in constant medical or psychological procedures (Fig. 1).

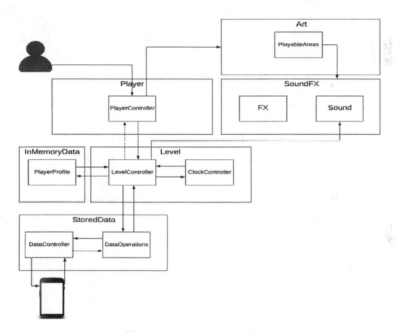

Fig. 1. Logical structure of app

The mobile application for the preventive treatment of periodontopathies in infants through the digitalization of play activities, is based on 6 clearly defined processes within the application, which begins with the interaction of the user (player), The sound consists of soft music so as not to distract the child's attention while playing with the application, since he/she must have the ability to focus on how to destroy cavities and not learn any song that is in the game. After the user interaction interfaces with the equipment and the game, it goes to the level of controls of the devices and software used to solve the problem posed, the storage is being done in the game's own memory that in our case will interact with the equipment in which it is installed, the operations, and the data that the game will show each time it is executed will be used for statistical calculations to measure the performance of patients and their evolution in the proposed activity (Fig. 2).

DEVELOPMENT   IMPLEMENTATION   EXECUTION

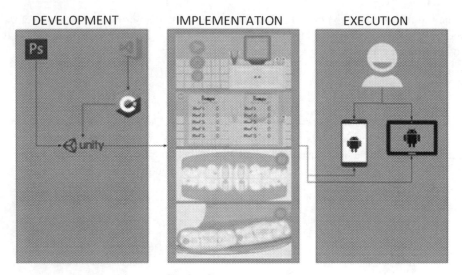

Fig. 2. App design diagram

The design of interfaces and in-game art was done using Photoshop, which is an image editor, which helped in this project for the application of filters and tonalities. It was used to posterize images and add motion blur [22].

The background images were designed using colors that could be found in a bathroom, predominantly light blue, used to create buttons that simulate bubbles. This same technique was used for the implementation of informative and pause windows, to give a childlike aesthetic to the game. This enhances the playful activity within the cognitive capacity of the children [6].

Based on the advice of dental students and according to their knowledge, each of the levels contains a part of the mouth in which the accumulation of biofilm is greater. For the development of the research and according to the contribution of the experts, the modified Bass brushing technique was used [2], which details the proper use of the brush to achieve the expected results, from the design of the buttons were implemented areas in the form of grooves of different colors, which serve the function of brushing space and is where the action of the player will take effect. These areas lose transparency as they are traversed. It should be taken into account that the technique is very complex for children and what they do is to opt for a different brushing technique, which makes it not very effective, the research focuses on proposing a circuit that helps to meet the proposed objective.

The application fulfills the need for children to be accompanied by an adult, as it would act as a tutor, helping both parents and dentists to optimize their time (Fig. 3).

A music system is implemented, which will play a song at a moderate volume, increasing only when the player goes through the brushing area, and this will decrease again if the player raises his hand or leaves the area. To improve the playful part of the game, small germs were created, which play the role of enemies to be followed and that when a correct brushing is performed, they are eliminated little by little, giving the sensation of fulfilling the mission of a correct activity.

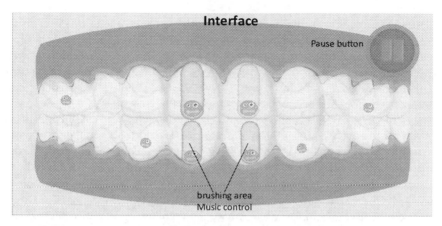

Fig. 3. Structure of the levels based on the Bass Modified brushing technique

The main mechanics consist of allowing the player to touch any part of the screen, however, their action will only take effect when they hold down and move through the brushing areas. In addition, to ensure the movement, the player has been prevented from staying in a single point of the area, otherwise it will not be affected. For the evaluation of the results obtained within the application, the creation of a chronometer is proposed for each level, which is responsible for measuring the time in which the player completes the route of all the brushing areas, contributing to the optimization of time and route in the application. This information measures the capacity of adaptation and practice in the movement to be made. The results of each level will be stored in two lists, the first will contain the time achieved for the first time in each level, the second will be updated as each level is completed again, allowing to measure the evolution of the player (Fig. 4).

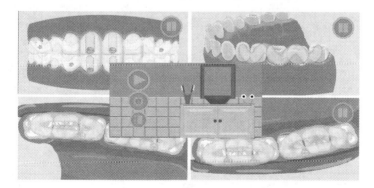

Fig. 4. Videogame structure

Using Unity's particle system, feedback functionalities were created, which consist of displaying small particles that simulate bubbles in the player's position as long as he/she is inside the brushing area. Under this same system, a destruction effect was implemented for the brushing area, alerting the player when he has finished his run.

Choosing a platform for mobile development is not easy, rather it is complicated because you must consider the market to which it should be applied, you should know that a mobile application is of vital importance today for treatment with children as they are considered a complement to certain activities such as treatments. The application by its nature was designed for both cell phones and tablets, trying to take advantage of the potential of patients who come to the appointment with the dentist.

The effectiveness of this application has been measured in terms of the time it takes the player to effectively complete each of the levels. Thanks to the validation of correct movements, the execution time will decrease if the user is performing the brushing correctly.

To complete this time, a simple interface is implemented in which the results (in seconds) obtained in the first time each level was completed are shown together with the time it takes the user to complete each activity in the following attempts, always taking the most recent attempt (Fig. 5).

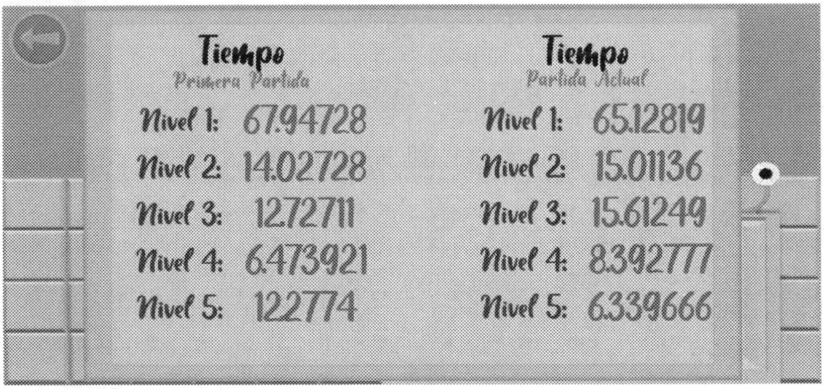

Fig. 5. Time results interface by level

The time in the first game is recorded only once, and the time of each subsequent game is updated as the user repeats each level, always taking the last attempt.

After collecting data obtained from 5 different players who tested the application 3 times, the following results have been obtained:

Table 1. Overall results obtained

	Player 1		Player 2		Player 3		Player 4		Player 5	
	1st set	2nd set	1st set	2nd set	1st set	2nd set	1st set	2nd set	1st set	2nd set
Level 1	67.95	65.13	67.95	75.96	66.04	67.57	64.23	57.07	79.79	79.44
Level 2	14.03	15.01	13.68	12.91	13.31	13.53	24.53	12.94	10.09	11.95
Level 3	12.73	15.61	15.31	13.73	16.76	13.46	16.85	14.34	9.76	11.16
Level 4	6.47	8.39	8.46	6.39	8.69	7.98	6.56	6.61	5.2	7.66
Level 5	12.28	6.34	12.43	7.81	6.42	6.91	6.87	21.87	8.99	5.48

In Table 1, the amount of time in which the player completes each level satisfactorily decreases as a function of the number of repetitions, it can be concluded then that learning the correct movement influences the time that a player takes to perform the cleaning of each of the areas of the mouth proposed by the application, it could be observed that this level became a challenge for the children since they refused to change levels until the time of compliance was lowered as much as possible.

Table 2. Average times per level

Level	Average time (first batch) seconds	Average time (current item) seconds
Level 1	69.19	69.03
Level 2	15.13	13.27
Level 3	14.28	13.66
Level 4	7.08	7.40
Level 5	9.40	9.68

Table 2 shows how the average time required to complete each level decreases, even considering those cases in which the time in which each level was completed for the third time increased. This average does not exceed one second of difference.

It can also be concluded that the previous knowledge of the movement to be performed in each zone of the mouth directly influences the amount of time required to complete each one of them. Thus, causing that the more times each level is repeated, the more the player will remember how the movement should be performed correctly for subsequent attempts, developing a muscle memory that allows him to put into practice these movement patterns, decreasing the time required to complete each one. The application proves to be intuitive and easy to handle, which helps children feel identified with this activity and does not cause boredom in the tests performed in the office.

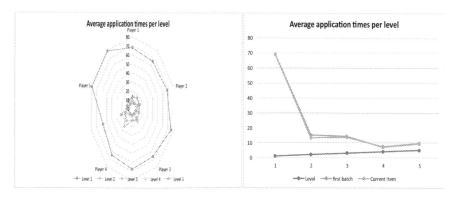

Fig. 6. Graphical representation of application results.

As can be seen in Fig. 6, the distribution of the results is very uniform, since the children to whom the game was applied generated a rapid adaptation and knowledge to the operation of the devices. Children of this generation are very identified with video games and any treatment that requires technological interaction is successfully overcome and each time optimizing time and resources.

In the market of applications there are other similar programs, but in this case, there is an additional value that is the results both the last and the previous one so that you can measure their improvements, this makes children always seek to improve and therefore apply this knowledge in their daily lives for personal hygiene. Likewise, it does not have advertising as it is an application developed for a group of patients.

4 Discussion

The application of video games for educational purposes is a strategy that involves the perception of the elements presented on the screen in favor of a better assimilation of knowledge, improving the player's ability to remember behaviors and patterns.

The application, with its 5 levels, was successful in presenting the correct movements for toothbrushing, using graphic resources that encourage the player to repeat each of the patterns several times and consequently cause him to memorize each one of them. These techniques, when applied from an early age, contribute to the prevention of periodontopathies such as caries, gingivitis, periodontitis, among others.

Thanks to the combination of visual and sound elements, this application has allowed players to learn about habits to preserve their dental health. In addition, the execution platform used, mobile devices, allows portability and convenience of use being complemented by a minimalist aesthetic style focused on attracting the attention of children.

5 Future Works

For future work, we plan to expand the range of knowledge about dental health provided by the application by implementing levels in which the player must recognize which foods are harmful to teeth, classify different toothpastes according to their use, and puzzles that help the player understand which areas accumulate the most plaque. In addition, we plan to refine the technique to measure the evolution of the player to obtain more accurate results.

6 Conclusions

Through the results obtained from the players, it was possible to determine the correct assimilation of the movements necessary to perform a satisfactory dental cleaning.

The implementation of eye-catching visual resources, reinforced with a simple and colorful interface, made the application aesthetically appealing.

The application has also made it possible to control the learning process through the implementation of a statistical interface, which allows people to easily control their progress during the use of the application.

In relation to the above, it can be concluded that the development of video games for educational purposes can be widely explored, generating strategies to transmit and reinforce knowledge.

Additionally, it can be concluded that interactive applications represent an advantage in the current era, due to the great presence of mobile devices in everyday life not only for adults and young people, but also for infants, since currently all the benefits of technology and the Internet are being exploited for a better quality and more controlled development of infants in their learning stage of skills and habits.

References

1. Peres, M.A., et al.: Oral diseases: a global public health challenge. Lancet **394**(10194), 249–260 (2019). https://doi.org/10.1016/S0140-6736(19)31146-8
2. Millissen, S.: Eficacia de las técnicas Bass y Bass nodificada en pacientes atendidos en el CAo con un índice de O'leary inicial a partir del 10%. Universidad De Las Américas (2020)
3. Hosseinpoor, A.R., Itani, L., Petersen, P.E.: Socio-economic inequality in oral healthcare coverage: results from the world health survey. J. Dent. Res. **91**(3), 275–281 (2012). https://doi.org/10.1177/0022034511432341
4. Perez, B., Vera, F.H., Gonzalez, D., V-Nino, E.D.: Designing educational video games to improve spatial learning. In: Proceedings of the 2016 42nd Latin American Computing Conference CLEI 2016 (2017). https://doi.org/10.1109/CLEI.2016.7833386
5. Lecuyer, A., Lotte, F., Reilly, R.B., Leeb, R., Hirose, M., Slater, M.: Brain-computer interfaces, virtual reality, and videogames. Comput. (Long. Beach. Calif.) **41**(10), 66–72 (2008). https://doi.org/10.1109/MC.2008.410
6. Cando, Y.M.: Actividades Lúdicas Para Fomentar Hábitos En Los Infantes Desde la Práctica Docente En El Marco Del Buen Vivir. Universidad Técnica de Machala (2015)
7. Hu, F., Wang, H., Chen, J., Gong, J.: Research on the characteristics of acrophobia in virtual altitude environment. In: 2018 International Conference on Intelligence and Safety for Robotics, ISR 2018, pp. 238–243 (2018). https://doi.org/10.1109/IISR.2018.8535774
8. Verástegui, C.A.: Influencia de los videojuegos en los infantes. Universidad nacional de Tumbes (2018)
9. Ramic-Brkic, B.: Enhancing progressive education through the use of serious games. In: 2018 10th International Conference on Virtual Worlds Games Serious Appl. VS-Games 2018, Proceedings, pp. 1–4 (2018) https://doi.org/10.1109/VS-Games.2018.8493422
10. Lorenzini, C., Carrozzino, M., Evangelista, C., Tecchia, F., Bergamasco, M., Angeletaki, A.: A virtual laboratory: an immersive VR experience to spread ancient libraries heritage. In: 2015 Digital Heritage International Congress (DigitalHERITAGE 2015), pp. 639–642 (2015). https://doi.org/10.1109/DigitalHeritage.2015.7419587
11. Ismai, M., Azman, F.Z.R., Zuhairi, S.F., Nazi, M.N.M.: Which game tells a story to children? In: IC3e 2014 - 2014 IEEE Conference on e-Learning, e-Management e-Services, pp. 156–159 (2015). https://doi.org/10.1109/IC3e.2014.7081259
12. Abubakar, J.A., Bahrin, A.S., Ahmad, M.K., Zulkifli, A.N.: Conceptual model of game aesthetics for perceived learning in narrative games. Int. J. Adv. Sci. Eng. Inf. Technol. **7**(3), 993–999 (2017). https://doi.org/10.18517/ijaseit.7.3.2201
13. Fan, L., Pang, M., Cheng, R.: A general framework for designing and implementing unicursal games for children. In: Proceedings of the 2015 International Symposium on Educational Technology. ISET 2015, pp. 15–19 (2016). https://doi.org/10.1109/ISET.2015.12

14. Eridani, D., Santosa, P.I.: The development of 3D educational game to maximize children's memory. In: 2014 1st International Conference on Information Technology, Computer, and Electrical Engineering. Green Technology and Its. Applications for a Better Future, ICITACEE 2014, Proceedings, pp. 188–192 (2015). https://doi.org/10.1109/ICITACEE.2014.7065739

15. Hui, L.T., Hoe, L.S., Ismail, H., Foon, N.H., Michael, G.K.O.: Evaluate children learning experience of multitouch flash memory game. In: 2014 4th World Congress on Information and Communication Technologies. WICT 2014, pp. 97–101 (2014). https://doi.org/10.1109/WICT.2014.7077309

16. Christopoulos, D., Mavridis, P., Andreadis, A., Karigiannis, J.N.: Using virtual environments to tell the story: 'the battle of thermopylae. In: Proceedings of the - 2011 3rd International Conference on Games and Virtual Worlds for Serious Applications. VS-Games 2011, pp. 84–91 (2011). https://doi.org/10.1109/VS-GAMES.2011.18

17. Beltran, J.E.P., Castro, Y.P.C., Mantilla, M.I.: Pedagogical training and research with video game for strengthening in knowledge processes. In: Proceedings of the 2017 European Conference on Electrical Engineering and Computer Science. EECS 2017, pp. 332–334 (2018). https://doi.org/10.1109/EECS.2017.68

18. Tyers, B.: Platform Game. Pract. GameMaker Proj., pp. 155–172, December 2018 https://doi.org/10.1007/978-1-4842-3745-8_7

19. Gadre, S., Rawalgaonkar, V., Warde, M., Balasubramanian, D., Gore, G., Joshi, J.: Implementation and design issues for augmented reality applications on mobile platforms. In: 2018 International Conference on Advances in Computing, Communications and Informatics. ICACCI 2018, pp. 1341–1344 (2018). https://doi.org/10.1109/ICACCI.2018.8554456

20. Taylor, A.G.: Develop Microsoft HoloLens Apps Now, pp. 91–100 (2016). https://doi.org/10.1007/978-1-4842-2202-7

21. Yin, Q., Yang, W., Ding, K., Huang, M.: The software design of energy efficiency data acquisition and management of operational ships. In: Proceedings of the 2017 4th International Conference on Transportation Information and Safety. ICTIS 2017, pp. 722–726 (2017). https://doi.org/10.1109/ICTIS.2017.8047847

22. Dayan, E.: ARGAMAN: rapid deployment virtual reality system for PTSD rehabilitation. In: Proceedings of the 4th International Conference on Information Technology: Research and Education, ITRE 2006, pp. 34–38 (2006). https://doi.org/10.1109/ITRE.2006.381528

Comparison of Test D2 with Electroencephalographic Signals to Measure Attention and Concentration in University Students

David Asael Gutiérrez-Hernández[1]([✉]) [iD], Miguel S. Gómez Díaz[1] [iD],
Mario Iram García-Quezada[1], Daniel A. Olivares-Vera[1] [iD],
and Mario Díaz-Rodríguez[2]

[1] Universidad De La Salle Bajío, León, Guanajuato, Mexico
david.gutierrez@leon.tecnm.mx
[2] Tecnológico Nacional de México, Instituto Tecnológico de León, León, Guanajuato, Mexico

Abstract. The objective of the experiment is to register the electroencephalographic signals (EEG) during the application of a selective attention test to measure the level of attention and concentration that university students have. The test that has been selected for this work is the called D2 attention test. The D2 is a time-limited test that assesses selective attention through a cancellation task. It measures the processing speed, the following of instructions and the goodness of the execution in a discrimination task of similar visual stimuli. For this experiment the data is coming from 10 undergraduate participants. A commercial headband called "Muse headband" was used, which allows us to acquire EEG signals in real time while applying the d2 attention test. When evaluating the test, a relationship can be observed between the EEG signals taken during the application of the test, this indicates that it is possible to obtain a favorable result to measure the level of attention through this type of signals without the need of the D2 test application, this is thinking in future measurements can be done for future works. As a result, in comparison of the application of the D2 test and the EEG signals, a correlation was found between the scores of the hand-made test and the increase or decrease of brain activity. Frequently denoting the cerebral electrical activity remained according to the current state of the participants in their different stages of concentration and results calculated in the D2 test of attention.

Keywords: EEG · Selective attention · Concentration · Test d2

1 Introduction

Attention is a process in the activation and functioning of selective processes and maintenance of psychological activity [1]. In other words, it is the ability to select, direct and maintain an appropriate level of activation to carry out relevant information processes. It is a complex process that consists of several subprocesses that allow the establishment of classifications associated with different neural circuits [2].

© Springer Nature Switzerland AG 2021
T. Guarda et al. (Eds.): ARTIIS 2021, CCIS 1485, pp. 547–558, 2021.
https://doi.org/10.1007/978-3-030-90241-4_42

Selective attention allows processing of relevant stimuli and suppressing irrelevant stimuli that appear in the visual field, usually the observer ignores irrelevant stimuli [3]. It is responsible for controlling the processes and mechanisms by which the body processes only a small part of all the information, and responds only to those environmental demands that are important to the individual. Many researchers now propose that attention is a basic neuropsychological function that allows cognitive activities to be carried out, as a system capable of processing and monitoring information from various sources of stimuli [4]. The main functions of attention are based on the ability to maintain a state of alertness towards a certain objective [5].

Sustained attention is the activity carried out by the processes by which the body is able to maintain the focus of attention and keep alert in the presence of certain stimuli for relatively long periods of time [6].

Selective attention and sustained attention are regulated by cortical and subcortical structures. Among the cortical structures is the prefrontal cortex and sensory cortices, and in the case of subcortical structures, the optic thalamus, the striatum, the septal and Meynert nuclei and the cerebellum, as it is shown in Fig. 1.

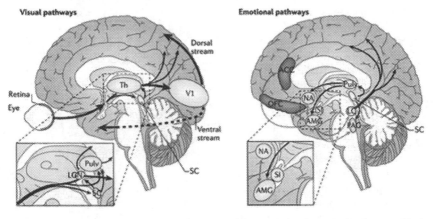

Fig. 1. Cortical and subcortical pathways for vision and emotion. (Color figure online)

Figure 1 shows the cortical and subcortical pathways for vision and emotion. The primary visual pathway (shown by thick arrows) originates from the retina and projects to the primary V1 in the occipital lobe via an intermediate station in LGN of Th. From V1, visual information reaches the extrastriate cortex along the ventral (occipitotemporal) and the dorsal (occipitoparietal) stream. However, a minority of fibres originating from the retina take a secondary route (shown by thin arrows) and reach both SC and Pulv. These two subcortical sites are connected and also send direct projections to the extrastriate visual cortex, bypassing V1. Another V1-independent visual pathway consists of the direct projections between the superior colliculus and LGN that, in turn, send efferents to extrastriate cortices in the dorsal stream. The 'emotion system' includes several cortical and subcortical areas. Among the subcortical structures are AMG and SI (shown in green), which are buried deeply in the temporal lobe and in the basal forebrain, respectively, NA in the basal ganglia (shown in green) and brainstem nuclei (shown in yellow), such as PAG and LC. Among cortical areas (shown in red) are OFC and ACC. The visual and emotional systems are extensively interconnected, especially at the subcortical level, where the superior colliculus is connected to the amygdala via the pulvinar. Direct connections also exist between subcortical and cortical emotion regions (for example, between the amygdala and OFC or ACC), between subcortical structures for emotions and cortical visual areas (for example, between the amygdala and temporal cortex) (not shown) and between brainstem nuclei and the cortex via diffuse projections (shown only from the LC). Grey arrows indicate connections within the emotion system. ACC = anterior cingulate cortex; AMG = amygdala; LC = Locus coeruleus; LGN = lateral geniculate nucleus; NA = nucleus accumbens; OFC = orbitofrontal cortex; PAG = periaqueductal grey; Pulv = pulvinar; SC = superior colliculus; SI = substantia innominata; Th = thalamus; V1 = primary visual cortex [16].

Attention plays a central role in episodic memory (explicit, conscious) because it is necessary for lasting memory connections to be formed [7]. The role of attention in implicit memory has been more discussed. Implicit memory is a type of unconscious memory that is evaluated by the existence of repeat priming. Young and healthy people show implicit memory for the stimuli attended but the lack of this memory for the stimuli attended could be a marker of pathological aging.

Plasticity is defined as the ability of neurons to adapt to changes in the internal and external environment before any injury [10]. Neuroplasticity, adaptation and recruitment of brain areas in addition to those used by young people could be the brain's way to adapt to changes produced with age. One of the greatest experts in neuronal plasticity, Bruce Dobkin, divides the mechanism into two groups, these are the plasticity of neural networks and sympathetic plasticity [11].

There are electroencephalographic studies [8], they have shown the brain's ability to adapt to the changes produced during aging by recruiting additional areas to process the information and with more sustained neural processing. This ability to adapt and possibly to produce additional tissue is the basis of neuroplasticity [9].

When an individual has a new learning or a new experience, the brain establishes various neural connections. These neural circuits are constructed as routes for the communication of neurons.

These routes are created in the brain through learning and practice. Neurons communicate with each other through connections called synapses and these communication pathways can be regenerated throughout life. Whenever new knowledge is acquired, synaptic communication between the neurons in- volved is reinforced. A better communication between neurons means that the electric signals travel more efficiently along the new path.

At present, several technological developments have allowed us to study the brain anatomically and physiologically in a very detailed way. However, there are still many questions about the brain response during neurological stages. With technological advances, several alternatives have been proposed that allow studies to improve people's quality of life. Within these technologies is the electroencephalogram which allows us to collect a record of brain rhythmic activity that has several channels that represent the areas from which they were obtained [12].

The electroencephalogram comes from a technique that allows the sum of inhibitory postsynaptic potentials and neuronal excitations to be measured [13], the acquisition of these signals is carried out by means of surface electrodes that are positioned on the scalp according to several international standards [14].

Hans Berger was the one who developed the study of electroencephalography in 1929, thanks to this great contribution has been the subject of constant research leading to the EEG as a great area of interest in the research Unique.

This technique does not cease to have limitations as the amplitude is attenuated or contaminated with extra-cerebral activity or artifice; muscle, flickering, movement, sweat, poor contact etc. However, despite these limitations, it is the most widely used technique in BCIs because it is non-invasive, requires relatively simple and economical equipment, and has a good temporal resolution.

The EEG performs the analysis of the electric fields that are generated in the brain by amplifying the powers between the electrodes. There are different types of EEG that can be placed differently, for example, there are the basic EEGs that are placed on the scalp, the cortical EEGs that are placed on the cortical surface, and finally, the Depth EEGs that are placed intracerebrally.

The standard EEG is a non-invasive method, it is painless and inexpensive. This type of EEG is widely used in clinical practices because of its great utility and easy use. The electrodes are positioned on the scalp lubricated with a conductive gel, although there are some that are dry type where it is not necessary to use said gel [15]. The electroencephalogram has several recording channels and at least eight channels are accepted, however, in daily clinical practice, equipment between 8, 16, 32 and up to 64 channels is often used.

The assemblies are formed from the combination of pairs of electrodes. There are two basic types of assemblies: bipolar (transverse and longitudinal) and monopolar (or referential). The bipolar assembly is the one that records the voltage difference between two electrodes that are placed in areas of brain activity, while the monopolar assembly records the potential difference between an electrode located in an active brain zone and the other electrode placed over an area without activity or neutral (for example, the earlobe); or the difference of voltage between an electrode placed in an active zone and the average of all or some of the active electrodes.

Currently the devices that are used for the EEG signals use digital amplifiers since the cerebral rhythmic activities are of very small amplitudes. The analogue signal is completely disused, due to the great advantages that the digital EEG provides, among which the facilitation of some aspects stands out, for example:

- Acquisition of data collection.
- Signal analysis and storage.
- The possibility of modifying the recording during the test.
- Modify parameters such as filters and sensitivity.
- Registration time and assemblies.

2   Methodology

2.1   Participants

A sample of 10 undergraduate students with an age range of 17 to 20 years old was selected (Table 1). No one of them present any neurological, psychiatric or learning difficulties. All the participants who took the test went voluntarily.

Table 1. Population data

Age	Gender		Academic level
	Female	Male	
17	2	1	2
18	3	1	3
20	1	1	5
21	1	0	6

2.2   Materials

- **D2 Attention Test.** Is an instrument that allows measuring the basic processes of attention and concentration. The d2 test is a concise measure of selective attention and mental concentration. A good concentration requires an adequate functioning of motivation and attention control, these two aspects applied to the test are composed of three elements of the attentional behavior:

  • It focuses on the speed or amount of work; this refers to the number of stimuli that were enhanced in a given time.
  • The quality of work focuses on the degree of precision that is inversely related to the error rate.
  • Relationship between speed and precision that allows us to reach a conclusion about behavior and the degree of activity, stability and consistency.
      The d2 test is of a certain time, this to measure the selective attention and concentration, it is an improvement within the cancellation tests. The test measures the speed of processing, follow-up instructions and the execution time in selective tasks of visual stimuli, this allows an estimation of the attention and concentration of a person between 8 to 60 years old.
      It can be applied individually or collectively, establishing a total time, which varies between 8 and 10 min, including application instructions. The d2 has 14 lines each with 47 characters, that is, for a total of 658 elements, the characters are made up of the letters "d" or "p" that can be accompanied by 1 or 2 small lines, individually or in pairs, at the top or bottom of each letter.
      The objective of the person performing the test is to carefully review the contents of the line and mark all the letters "d" that contain two small lines (the two above,

the two below or one above and one below) these elements (correct stimuli) are known as relevant elements. The remaining combinations (the "p" with or without stripes and the "d" with one or no stripes) are considered "irrelevant", because they should not be marked. For each line the subject has 20 s.

The relevant scores are as follows:
- TR, total responses: number of items attempted in the 14 lines.
- TA, total successes: number of relevant elements correct.
- O, omissions: number of relevant elements attempted, but not marked.
- C, commissions: number of irrelevant elements marked.
- TOT, total effectiveness in the test, ie $TR - (O + C)$.
- CON, concentration index or $TA - C$.
- TR+, line with the largest number of items attempted.
- TR−, line with a smaller number of items attempted.
- VAR, index of variation or difference $(TR+) - (TR-)$.

- **EEG (Muse Band).** Muse headband is a powerful and compact EEG system. Its structure is seen in Fig. 2. By taking advantage of improvements in dry sensor technology, battery life and Bluetooth, as well as significant advances in digital signal processing Muse facilitates access and use of brain wave data, inside and outside the laboratory and in real-world environments.

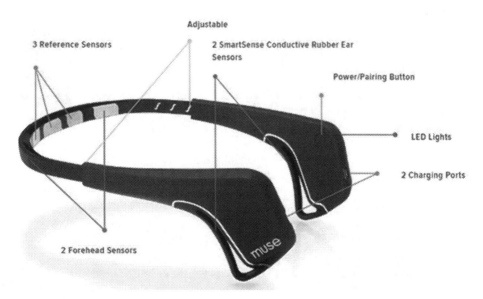

Fig. 2. Muse headband for the acquisition of EEG signals.

This headband has sensors in different positions, the headband is able to detect and classify 5 different waves in our brain: Delta, Theta, Alpha, Beta and Gamma, as shown in

Fig. 3. Delta waves are more present during deep sleep. Theta waves are associated with drowsiness, light, sleep and visualization. Alpha waves occur during awake relaxation. Beta waves occur when alert, actively thinking or solving problems. Gamma waves occur when you participate in a higher mental activity and in the consolidation of information.

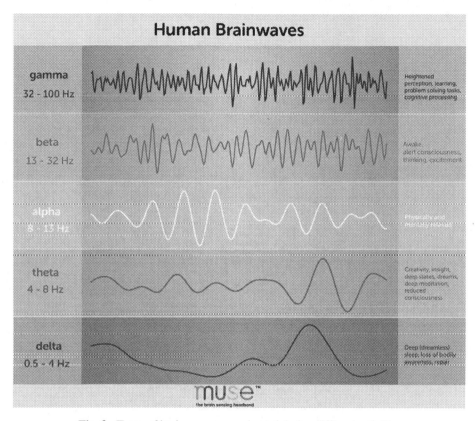

Fig. 3. Types of brain waves experienced during different activities

2.3   Experimental Procedure

The procedure for this study was as follows:

1. The participants arrived individually at the laboratory, signed the informed consent which was previously explained in detail, making known the purpose of the study and the tasks to be carried out.
2. The researchers placed the EEG equipment on the participant's head, checking before and during the experiment a good connection.
3. Subsequently, they were made aware of the d2 test of attention and how it is carried out by means of a test sheet.

4. Then the recording of EEG signals was started while the participants performed the test. At this time, the researchers indicated the time (15 s per line) with the intention that the only answer would be as far as the participant reached to finish. Given the operation of the EEG Muse Band, the signal was recorded with a sampling frequency of 50 Hz.
5. After 14 lines of evaluation, the EEG equipment was withdrawn.

2.4 Data Analysis

For each of the participants, the D2 test was reviewed, checking each of the parameters mentioned in the materials section. In this way, the progress per line and the total results of the test were checked, finding successes, failures, effectiveness, concentration, etc. In this way, it was possible to verify by means of the EEG signals the increase or decrease in the corresponding lines and whether or not this correlate in the result of the test carried out by hand.

The data analysis is a very important process to do in this kind of works. As the obtained signals are of a non-lineal form, the analysis of the resulted signals is quite complex to do. Previous works have shown different ways to process de data [17–21] and to take decisions after the process is done [22–24] but, without the use of artificial intelligent it will not be possible.

3 Results

Table 2 shows the results obtained from each of the participants who performed the D2 test of attention and concentration. The results are grouped by age to form small groups with similar characteristics, the tests were evaluated as indicated in the D2 test manual.

Table 2. Results of the test d2 attention

TR	TA	O	C	TR+	TR	TOT	CON	VAR
417	148	49	45	40	19	323	103	21
487	164	27	19	41	25	441	145	16
580	209	45	13	46	24	522	196	22
338	134	8	2	32	13	328	132	19
487	95	117	0	47	13	370	95	34
526	159	64	36	46	27	426	123	19
538	221	13	89	47	21	436	132	26
488	170	24	4	39	30	460	166	9
353	144	5	1	32	13	347	143	19
415	161	13	3	46	19	399	158	27

Where: TR: total responses, TA: total successes, O: omissions, C: commissions, CON: concentration index, TR+: line with the highest number of items attempted, TR–:

line with the lowest number of elements attempted, VAR: index of variation or difference
(TR+) − (TR −).

The obtained signals from this experiment are shown in Figs. 4 and 5. Notice that
the non-linearity, mentioned above, is observed.

The time over the x axis and the frequency over the y axis are the parameters that
define the success or not success of this experiment as a simple way to notice attention
without the use of the D2 test.

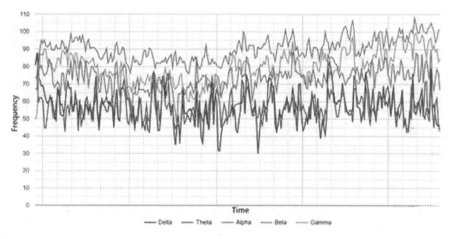

Fig. 4. EEG signals of a participant who showed good performance during the application of the
D2 test

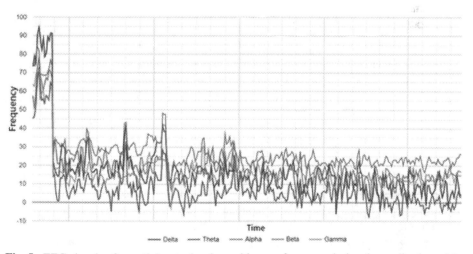

Fig. 5. EEG signals of a participant who showed low performance during the application of the
D2 test

With the electroencephalogram signals that were acquired during the attention test
application, an analysis was carried out to characterize the signals. When comparing

the results of the D2 test and of the EEG signals, a correlation was found, as shown in Fig. 4. The EEG signals observed in the graph remained stable within a frequency range throughout the test, this indicates that the level of attention remained constant over the period of time of the test in comparison with the graph shown in Fig. 5, in this graph, it is shown a decline in the level of attention of the participant at the time of the test, these results were observed within the evaluation of the D2 test.

4 Discussion

In this work, attention and concentration were analyzed through the Muse device, comparing the results obtained from an established test such as the d2 attention test. In the comparison made with the collected scores there is a small difference between the signals obtained. When using a digital signal, there will always be a loss of the information in this type of signals due to various adversities and difficulties suffered in the transmission compared to the analogue signals. However, these results demonstrate that the Muse device can be used to conduct focused, sustained and selective attention investigations. Today, portable EEG devices are developed that are easier to configure with mobile devices, are inexpensive and non-invasive, these changes have helped evolve EEG applications in both novel and established fields and al-lowed consumers to use without any particular expertise or preparations devices previously reserved for medical and scientific purposes only.

5 Conclusions

In this work, a simple option has been presented to identify whether the parameters of attention and concentration, measured in real time on a patient or test object, are adequate or not.

It is evident that the comparison that was carried out in this work made use of an element that senses the neurological activity of the patient while he/she answers a test that is well known and validated by the corresponding authorities and that is widely used for various applications that involve analyzing well the variables of attention and concentration.

Such is the case of the autism spectrum disorder (ASD or TEA in Spanish), where the patient is required to carry out tests of attention and concentration that validate that the therapy presented in them is or is not adequate, however, not all cases of autism present in patients is of the same type, some cases require more measurement criteria than others. Hence, this proposal could fit in an appropriate way in patients with autism spectrum disorder so that, while they carry out their specific cognitive activities and monitored by specialists, at the same time they can be measured, in a non-invasive way and without using paper, their neurological activity and, based on the graphs obtained, identify if the patient's neurological activity offers an acceptable frequency during the duration of the test and thereby verify whether this test is effective or not for the specific case of the patient under test.

6 Future Work

As work in the future, it is planned to increase the number of samples obtained to increase the database. In addition, the extraction of characteristics of the EEG signals and the implementation of the artificial intelligence technique for their classification. The principal interest of this work is to attend patients inside the ADS and offer them a non-invasive way to measure or identify the correct or most adequate therapy that will apport positively to the attention a concentration ability.

However, another area of interest to carry out future work is the application of this proposal for the training of high-performance athletes, who begin from an early age to develop their sports qualities, however, it has been observed that a limitation of their development Functional total many times falls on the lack of attention-concentration that the athlete in training can present due to many factors external to the sport and that in the Mexican population are usually very common.

References

1. García, J.: Psicología de la atención. Síntesis, Madrid (2008)
2. Cuesta, M., et al.: Psychometric properties of the d2 selective attention test in a sample of premature and bornatterm babies (2007)
3. Ballesteros, S., Manga, D.: The effects of variation of an irrelevant dimensión on same different visual judgments (1996)
4. Portellano, J., García, J.: Neuropsicología de la atención, las funciones ejecutivas y la memoria, Madrid (2014)
5. Pozuelos, J., Paz Alonso, P., Castillo, A., Fuentes, L., Rueda, R.: Development of attention networks and their interactions in child hood. Dev. Psychol **50**, 2405 (2014)
6. Parasuranam, R.: Sustained attention in detection and discrimination. In: Parasuranam, R., Davies, D.R. (eds) Varieties of Attention (1984)
7. Ballesteros, S., Reales, J.M., García, B.: The effects of selective attention on perceptual priming and explicit recognition in children with attention deficit and normal children. Eur. J. Cogn. Psychol. **19**, 607–627. (2007)
8. Osorio, A., Fay, S., Pouthas, V., Ballesteros, S.: Ageing affects brain activity in highly educated older adults: an ERP study using a wordstem priming task. Cortex **46**, 522–534 (2010)
9. Goh, J.O., An, Y., Resnick, S.M.: Differential trajectories of agerelated changes in components of executive and memory processes. Psychol. Aging **27**, 707 (2012)
10. Gispen, W.H.: Neuronal plasticity and function. Clin. Neuropharmacol. (1993)
11. Dobkin, B., Carmichael, T.: Principles of recovery after stroke (2005)
12. Sánchez de la Rosa, J.L.: Métodos para el procesamiento y análisis estadístico multivariante de señales multicanal: aplicación al estudio del EEG. España: Ph.D. thesis (1993)
13. Olejniczak, P.: Neurophysiological basis of EEG. In: Clinical Neurophysiology (2006)
14. Jasper, H.H.: The tentwenty electrode system of the International Federation. Electroencephalogr. Clin. Neurophysiol. **10**, 370–375 (1958)
15. Homan, R.W., Herman, J., Purdy, P.: Cerebral location of international 1020 system electrode placement. Electroencephalogr. Clin. Neurophysiol. **66**, 376–382 (1987)
16. Diederich, N.J., Stebbins, G., Schiltz, C., Goetz, C.G.: Are patients with Parkinson's disease blind to blindsight? Brain **137**(6), 1838–1849 (2014)
17. González, M.T. G., et al.: Analysis of pupillary response after a stimulus of light to generate characteristical groups. In: 2017 International Conference on Electronics, Communications and Computers (CONIELECOMP), pp. 1–6. IEEE, February 2017

18. Gómez-Díaz, M.S., Gutiérrez-Hernández, D.A., Ornelas-Rodriguez, M., Zamudio, V., Mancilla-Espinosa, L.E.: Analysis of non-linear behaviour through signal segmentation. Int. J. Appl. Eng. Res. **13**(10), 7267–7272 (2018)
19. Granados-Ruiz, J., et al.: Methodological approach for extraction of characteristics of biological signals. Compusoft **8**(2), 3011–3020 (2019)
20. Santiago Montero, R., et al.: A study of highest perfusion zones as biometric representation. Computación y Sistemas **24**(1) (2020)
21. Mendoza-Gámez, J.D., et al.: Recognition of characteristic patterns in human gait through computer vision techniques. Compusoft **7**(12), 2950 (2018)
22. Vera, M.D.L.Á.A., et al.: Design of a smart device with fuzzy multi-criteria group decision making system for the elderly. In: 2021 17th International Conference on Intelligent Environments (IE), pp. 1–8. IEEE, June 2021
23. López, S.U., et al.: Identification of parameters for the study of diabetes from light reflex with controlled stimulus. In: 2017 International Conference on Electronics, Communications and Computers (CONIELECOMP), pp. 1–6. IEEE, February 2017
24. Martínez, M.I.R., Ramírez, C.L., Rodríguez, V.M.Z., Hernández, D.A.G., Soberanes, H.J.P., Domínguez, A.R.: Fuzzy-regulated assistant based on mental engagement: a multi-agent approach to elderly care. In: 2021 17th International Conference on Intelligent Environments (IE), pp. 1–8. IEEE, June 2021

Laboratories of Public Innovation as a Methodology of Identification for Informal Settlements Actors in Duran City, Guayas, Ecuador

David Fernando Méndez-Areopaja[1] [ID], José Fernando Morán-Zambrano[2] [ID],
René Faruk Garzozi-Pincay[3]([✉]) [ID], José Luis Castillo-Burbano[4] [ID],
and Sara Rocía Correa-Soto[5] [ID]

[1] Universidad Católica Santiago de Guayaquil, Guayaquil, Ecuador
david_fermendez@hotmail.com
[2] Universidad de Guayaquil, Guayaquil, Ecuador
josfermor@gmail.com
[3] Universidad Estatal Península de Santa Elena, La Libertad, Ecuador
rgarzozi@upse.edu.ec
[4] Universidad Espíritu Santo, Guayaquil, Ecuador
castleman.jl@gmail.com
[5] Universidad Internacional del Ecuador, Guayaquil, Ecuador
sacorreaso@uide.edu.ec

Abstract. The phenomenon of Informal Settlements is a problem hardly ever discussed in Ecuador, notwithstanding the growth of this type of human settlements in large cities. This work describes the factors associated with increasing of dwellings on land without legalizing. Among the associated factors with the growth of housing on land without legalizing due to the fact that there is an inadequate supply for people who require it, usually, they do not have resources enough to get a house because prices are above their economic possibilities on the other hand, it was found that another factor that has increased the level of these settlements is that there is not an solid legal and regulatory framework, When the State intends to legalize land without an owner, there are people who promote the increase in land trafficking. From these factors we can identify the actor's role in this problem and we noticed the problem lies in the joint management of all sectors: private, public and citizens in general.

The work summarizes some academic, political and social considerations about the formal and informal real estate markets, and the Government of Duran city, and its relationship with the materialization of Informal Settlements. We highlight some evidences about the causes that promote this phenomenon from a systematic approach and design of public policies. Finally, it is presented to innovation laboratories as an alternative tool for public policy makers in the development of public innovation projects in the management of Informal Settlements.

Keywords: Informal settlements · Informal real estate markets ·
Materialization · Innovation laboratories · Public innovation

© Springer Nature Switzerland AG 2021
T. Guarda et al. (Eds.): ARTIIS 2021, CCIS 1485, pp. 559–572, 2021.
https://doi.org/10.1007/978-3-030-90241-4_43

1   Introduction

Informal settlements (IS) are a long-standing social phenomenon in the Latin American region. The displacement of people to cities has given way to the proliferation of these types of settlements. These spaces are fertile to harvest families in poverty and in deplorable conditions for human life. Not only the living conditions are worrying, but also the frustration of opportunities to build a hopeful future that guarantees healthy, inclusive cities and, in general, make cities better.

Among the main factors that generate the appearance of IS are: the cost of developable land, access to housing credit, conditions of supply that make inaccessible to land, the paperwork in legalization processes, political patronage within the legalization processes - which has become a challenge for local and national governments, as appropriate Among the main factors that generate the appearance of IS are: the cost of developable land, access to housing credit, conditions of supply which make inaccessible to land, the paperwork in the legalization processes, political patronage within the legalization processes - which has become a challenge for local and national governments, according to legal competences.

Policies appear are not enough to prevent or mitigate the perpetuation of IS and academic production on the treatment of IS is not abundant. The complexity in the treatment of these social phenomenon demands the use of techniques research focused on human being, since it takes into consideration the emotions, feelings, frustrations and expectations of the main actors: families. With this, we do not intend to have a definitive solution to the problem but rather to propose a methodology through which we can know the reality of the IS. The present work seeks, from the tools offered by the Chilean Innovation Laboratory, to contribute with some considerations in the formation of the IS, the identification of actors and their roles in the IS system in Duran city.

2   Theoretical Considerations

The concept of IS in urban planning studies and is related to political systems.

> In relation to capitalism, it was interpreted that these settlements were the effect of marginalizing the population that emigrated from rural areas to urban areas of Latin America and there is a difference between the structural exclusion of marginality and a "culture of poverty" (Castells 1973).

The IS are "places of decay, gangs and poverty for the people of the community" (Wacquant 2008). According to Brakarz (2002) the IS could "be interpreted as the effect caused by the deficient supply of formal housing" and consequently as market failure.

The Ministry of Urban Development and Housing (MIDUVI 2015), describes IS's as "households that are located on land that does not have formal deeds" it means land ownership deeds. Ruiz Hernández (2014) gives a legal focus to his definition and indicates that, it is "that housing that is located on ejido, communal, public, federal, state or municipal and private property; and also adds that an IS is housing that does not have a deed title".

There are divergences in the issue of ISs. Porter (2011) sums it up as the "class struggle". He indicates that formalization is important in economy, not only in the dynamization of agents, but also in the deconcentrating of resources from one group of people to another. Thus, formality in the settlements is considered "a way to create spaces, these arise from the resistance of the population to power groups and the lack of deregulation of basic services" (Roy 2009).

On the other hand, Brakarz (2002) and Mena (2010), agree that there is a direct relationship between the proliferation of IS and the income levels of the population in the area. This being so, the power relationship plays an important role in the proliferation of these settlements, so the issue includes a broad approach and a much more complex system involving social, political and economic actors.

2.1 The IS, Product of the Lack of Security of Land Ownership

These types of settlements are not regulated or supported by the Law. This category includes invasions and other land occupation mechanisms outside the regulatory sphere, a phenomenon that has been exacerbated by the informal market and land traffickers.

Security of tenure is an essential element in guaranteeing the right to housing. The lack of security of tenure makes protection against eviction impossible, leaving inhabitants of irregular settlements at imminent risk of suffering various violations of their human rights.

However, security of tenure would not be as important to IS residents. Settlers' preferences have changed over time and with the policies adopted; they have gradually become less concerned with security of tenure and the risk of forced eviction due to the force of human rights and their strict enforcement over the rest. The provision of basic services is the main concern of people in ISs, leading us to question whether titling is really the bottom line or whether housing and access to services are. On the other hand, even if they could not care about holding a title, it would be imprudent to provide the other services without the co-responsibility of inhabitants in terms of taxes. In other words, individual title is the first step in capturing capital gains and improvements and therefore the sustainability of municipal public finances.

The effect of individual regularization or titration on IS's is still uncertain. A review of the hypothesis that individual titles would raise the quality of life of the urban poor through access to mortgage credit concludes that there was little investment in the consolidation of the settlement and that living conditions remained virtually unchanged (Calderón 2004).

In addition to the tax benefits for municipal finances, individual legalization and titling per se is a strong tool for reducing the qualitative housing deficit.

2.2 IS, Consequence of Its Geographical Location

Although many of the IS's may be legally constituted, their geographical location on hillsides, riverbanks and even on the slopes of volcanoes makes them a problem for those who live there, both because of the risk of accidents and disease and because of government's cost interventions that become necessary in every emergency situation.

However, these communities show a strong attachment to their habitat to the point of rejecting relocation or resettlement projects in order to remain in their homes despite the obvious risks.

Previous studies about acceptance or rejection of relocation from communities in vulnerable sites used the contingent valuation method to predict how the probability of accepting or rejecting a relocation project changes with respect to demographic and socioeconomic variables (Bayrau 2007). The results of this study would contribute to the evaluation of the subsidy or compensation that the government should pay to the community member to occupy a new settlement in a risk-free zone.

ISs are the result of the qualitative deficit of housing. If within a settlement security of tenure predominates among its inhabitants and it is not in site risk, there is a third approach that can categorize it as informal: poor infrastructure in the materials part of housing.

In principle, the qualitative deficit does not imply the need to build more houses but rather to improve housing conditions.

These settlements, where land may be legalized and the risks of geographic failure is mitigated, still lack drinking water or sanitation services, connectivity and roads, public spaces, among other urban development services and safe habitat.

Poor sanitation systems and inadequate solid waste collection and disposal methods can multiply unhealthy rates; in turn, this prevalence of noncommunicable disease risk factors across all ages groups of IS suggests an increased likelihood of a high future disease burden (Anand et al. 2007).

Therefore, the qualitative housing deficit accentuates the incidence and magnitude of greater risk in the event of minor natural disasters, greater risk of disease and accidents due to poor and precarious infrastructure, access to more expensive basic services (travel costs, water per tanker, etc.) and a vicious circle of segregation and poverty that generates more poverty.

In terms of poverty levels, Table 1 shows the Duran city's data.

Table 1. Duran city's description

Description	2001	2010
Population	178714	243235
Poverty level	85227,9 (47,13%)	158588 (67,8%)
Number of homes	44579	72547

From the census information of 2001 and 2010; it can be seen that the population figures, poverty level and number of homes are increasing. However, the increase in number of homes is not sufficient compared to the increase of population.

IS's generate a charge of various types in public management of cities; insecurity of land tenure from the legal side, access to services and public spaces of communities from social side and from the urban-environmental side, inadequate sanitary conditions which generate pollution and negatively urban impact development; so it need to create urban agendas that allow or attempt to provide solutions to informality is imperative, however, the effects of regularization are uncertain and therefore determining general solutions to this problem would be erroneous.

The particular study by specific areas and the application of new methodological tools are required. For this reason, in this article we propose public innovation laboratories as a tool to determine possible solutions of Durán city's problems.

3 Contextualizing the Problem

According to the Organization for Economic Cooperation and Development OECD (2001), IS are defined as "areas consisting of a housing complex that were built in non-legalized land". A lack of urban planning, minimal building standards and the absence of urban regulations prevail in such settlements. (e.g., housing constructed in risk areas).

For UN-HABITAT (2016); this problem covers about 105 million people living in urban areas of Latin America. That is, approximately 25% of Latin American city dwellers live in ISs. The same document considers that IS is "a situation in which one fifth of the region's urban dwellers live".

In South America, by 2005 the countries with the highest percentages (over 20%) were Bolivia, Perú, Venezuela, Brazil, Argentina and Ecuador. Then countries like Argentina and Brazil decreased their percentages while in Ecuador the situation worsened. (UN 2014). In 2014, Ecuador and Bolivia had the highest percentages, 43.5% and 36%, respectively (Délano 2019).

ISs are a pending subject and Ecuador is not the exception. By (MIDUVI) 2015, 88% of the country's municipalities have some degree of informality in terms of land ownership. According to INEC, Population and Housing Census (2010), Durán city, with 38%, is among the five cantons with the highest percentage of households in precarious settlements. At the same time, it is the second with the highest percentage of households in IS with respect to the total number of households.

According to MIDUVI (2015), by 2013, 25% of households were living in precarious human settlements; in total, there would be 729,291 households that do not have access to safe habitat. Therefore, the housing conditions of these households have an impact on inequality, poverty, health risks, environmental deterioration and other social costs associated with informality.

Latin America (ECLAC), in a document called UN-HABITAT (2016), recognizes the growing inequality and prevalence of multiple dimensions of poverty, including the increase in the number of slum dwellers and informal settlements. The presence of informality promotes deficient urban planning that delays infrastructure works and the provision of basic services, being a manifestation of evidence of social inequalities and intensifying poverty levels.

The Inter-American Development Bank (IDB 2020) states that IS "are put in a situation of greater risk in the face of health emergencies and their impacts". The document states that "deplorable housing conditions, inadequate access to water, sanitation and other basic services, inadequate access to affordable and nutritious food, limited or no access to information technologies have negative impacts on public health management".

Similarly, these limitations have an impact on the access of the inhabitants to new technologies, which on the one hand prevents public policy actions, and on the other hand affects the guarantee of educational continuity in situations of health emergencies.

4   Analysis of the Situation of Duran's Informality

Duran city is one of 25 cantons that conform Guayas province. It was declared a city in 1986 after being a rural community of Guayaquil city. According to INEC, Census of Population and Housing (2010); it has a population of 235 769 inhabitants, with a projection for 2020 of 315 724 inhabitants; being the second most populated province's city after Guayaquil. It is organized by three urban communities: Eloy Alfaro, its city capital, Divino Niño and El Recreo. It has a territorial extension of approximately 340 km2; of these approximately 28% belong to the urban zone and near 72% to the rural sector (DURAN- MUNICIPALITY 2018). In Durán city, the industrial sector predominates as a source of production, it has a large industrial park as well as agricultural activities developed in rural sector near it.

According to DURAN City-Municipality (2018); the canton has about 40 IS identified. The geographical map of informality in the canton, with around 23,810 households living in precarious settlements (MIDUVI 2015).

In spite of the fact that precariousness prevails in these spaces, informality also appears in places called regular due to their urbanistic designs where even precariousness and qualitative housing deficit is not predominant.

The IS in Duran city are increasing, these spaces where precariousness predominates, restrict access to basic services and in some cases, there is no provision of services. Figure 1 below the map shows that informality has increased in Duran city. The map on the left side is from the year 2007, compared to the year 2018 (the map on the right side) has less areas painted in red.

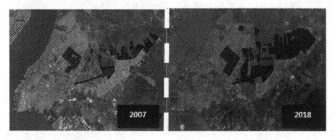

Fig. 1. The informality map in Duran city

5   Supply and Demand of IS

Under a market approach, the lack of supply of land used for low strata causes shortages and therefore people seek to satisfy their housing needs in informal market. High land prices, lack of housing programs and public budget, macroeconomic factors among others are the possible causes of proliferation and rapid informality's growth. In all cases the common effect is the informal production is numerically higher and faster than formal production.

According to Clichevsky (2000), the situation of urban informality is explained by macroeconomic conditions such as lack of employment, low wages and the consequent impoverishment of the population; by state policies; and, the functioning of urban land markets and different forms of housing.

5.1 Demand for IS

Among the main pillars of demand for this type of settlement are internal migrants, new family nucleus or socio-spatial integration; by asymmetry of information, giving way to the market of land traffickers; families who have income from non-formal work and by restrictions on access to credit.

The increase of migrants from rural cities to urban cities, in search of work, or a better life in general, generates unplanned overpopulation in Municipalities' urbanization plans. Because of this, migrants' resort to demanding housing from the informal sector, where they have easy access to housing that allows them to settle as soon as possible (Mitra 2010). On the other hand, families who have non-formal jobs do not have a secure source of income and therefore resort to settling in informal sectors where they find it easier to pay for housing. Additionally, another factor which increases the demand for these IS's is the asymmetry of information, it means that one of the parties has better or more information about housing in urban sectors. In order to solve the problems of informality, it is certainly necessary that everyone has the same and adequate information (Kohli 2013). Furthermore, access to credit to be able to buy a house also promotes the proliferation of IS. It is agreed that banks place restrictions on people from lower economic strata who are looking for housing but do not have enough resources to pay for it without the help of a financial institution (Ferguson 2003).

5.2 Offer from the IS

The offer of the IS is given for several reasons; the availability of land without services, the access to credit, the simple procedure, the support of in turn authorities and their predisposition to attend the problems and the prices of the land.

We understand the home as a 'special' good because its value of using is greater than its price. Since this price is directly associated with the supply of land for development, which is scarce, it generates a market failure in which excluded strata seek to meet their housing needs to an informal land market.

The difference between the prices of state and municipal programs lies in the geographic location of the properties and their quality of including or not the services of the land which is being served. Considering the research's observations in the informal markets of Durán city, a 90 m^2 plot of land can cost US$3,000, it means, about $34.00/m^2; the same plot of land being a municipal one, can be acquired for $1.00/m^2 without services and about $20.00/m^2 with the land server's services (MUNICIPALITY-DURAN 2018).

Similarly, the price of land from the private sector or developer is approximately $152.00/m^2; therefore, the cost of acquiring the land through informal market mechanisms is much higher than social housing market. Meanwhile, the prices of the private land market are higher than the informal market and the social market with services included; in THIS way it agrees with what was stated by (Smolka 2003) "the price of land in the informal market is higher than formal land without services, but lower than the sum of formal land plus the cost of providing habitat services".

In other words, on the one hand, it is possible to think that families invade the land because the cost is lower, but this is not always the case. In fact, in this section we have shown the cost can be higher but that families still decide to invade because it is the only option they have. Land prices (Table 2) vary depending on who the offer is. In the case of Duran city, the m2's price offered by the municipality is the most accessible. Below, in Table 2 you can see the different prices.

Table 2. Land prices in Duran city

Provider	Price of land/m^2 (in dollars)	Observation
Informal market	34.00	Land price per square meter according to informal suppliers
Duran city's Municipality	1.00	Land price per square meter according to municipal ordinance
Real Estate Developer	152.00	Price of land per square meter according to information from real estate developers (urbanizers)

6 Methodological Tools for Public Innovation.

For Cejudo (2016);

There is a new and relatively recent empirical approach that, from a multidisciplinary perspective, tries to respond to the purpose of improving the provision and quality of public services, from the experience of those who are its main protagonists (officials and citizens). These spaces are the Laboratories for Public Innovation (Lab-IP). For the author they have a hybrid nature, since not only do they depend on the public sector, but they are based on the idea on open innovation and are considered a matrix that articulates various capacities in a collaborative class, with the objective of solving problems and new challenges of public nature.

The LAB-IPs are not limited to a single concept, but "they have as a common denominator to work from citizen's perspective with an experimental approach trying and testing new approaches in the search for adaptable solutions" (Cejudo 2016). A laboratory is understood as "a central figure of innovation in public sector that requires being, at the same time, the one who connects and gives viability to the development of processes"

(Valdivia 2020). The author also indicates that a laboratory manages to progressively articulate a significant mass of mainly public and private actors, at same time he considers strategic actors who have managed to coordinate and collaborate. At this point, the LAB-IPs are presented as a tool that overcomes public sectors' paradigms and allows coordination among stakeholders. The laboratory is more than a space for discussion and agreement among actors.

LAB-IPs are playing an increasingly important role as spaces for innovation and, in the same way, banks of good practices and communities of innovative people in the public sector (Rodríguez 2018), for the author;

These spaces are known as laboratories of change, innovation teams or innovation laboratories; and their purpose is to formulate public policies and programs a much-needed injection of creativity and experimentation, bringing together different actors (stakeholders) to explore solutions to complex problems.

In reference to Acevedo (2016):

The laboratories carry out different activities such as; "making tests or prototypes; implementing random experiments; incorporating ideas from citizens and public servants; doing data analysis; implementing Design Thinking and People-Centered Design methodologies; developing mobile applications and software; training activities for public agencies; forming networks within the government; and forming external networks.

For Rodríguez (2018), the LAB-IPs have 5 fundamental challenges: "to incorporate the external visions to the government agencies; to form internal and external networks of an organization; to support leadership; to provide budgetary flexibility and human capital, and to manage risk". The author exemplifies the Chilean Government Laboratory, promoted by the Chilean Government itself; "MindLab, which was the Danish government innovation laboratory, jointly run by the Ministries of Business and Growth, Education and Employment and the City of Odense, and which incorporates people-centered designs and immersive research techniques, such as user days, journals and ethnographic studies, to radically transform the relationship between government and citizens; and the British Government's Behavioural Insights Team, a good example of a LAB-IP willing to undertake experimental approaches to public interventions and policy making" (Rodríguez 2018).

In his article Cejudo (2016), he also refers to the Government Laboratory (LabGob) in Chile; which is "mandated to create a new relationship between the Government and the citizens through developing, facilitating and promoting innovation processes in public services focused on people". The laboratory's mission is to facilitate the generation of better public services and seeks to change the innovation paradigm within the State, involving officials, users and the private world in improving public services.

Through workshops, LabGob develops tools for public innovation. The laboratory proposes four phases of the public innovation process; Challenge Discovery, Idea Generation, Prototyping and Testing, and Public Innovation Management. Each of the phases of the process presents six innovation tools as a work log.

The present work will focus on the Discovery of the Challenge, as a first phase to understand the problem of people in depth. The Discovery of the Innovation Challenge; presents the following tools; a research plan, Map of Actors, Cause-Effect Diagram, Qualitative research techniques, User Person and finally the User's Journey (Laboratory 2017).

6.1 A Research Plans

As mentioned in the first part, this research seeks to identify the problem of IS in Duran city, so the LAB-IP can be proposed as a methodological tool for the prevention and mitigation of IS.

It also defines the procedure to be carried out in order to obtain and analyze the information. Data will be obtained from primary and secondary sources. On the one hand, data will be obtained from censuses carried out by the Duran's Municipality. On the other hand, qualitative information will be obtained through focus groups and in-depth interviews. In the beginning, the mapping actors and description of the structure (system) of problems faced by actors will be obtained. In this way it will be possible to understand the problem in a holistic way.

6.2 Actor's Map

This process allows us to better understand the actors and their roles in the system, diagnose the levels of participation and connection among the actors, identify opportunities to create new relationships and explore the parts of the system, identify possible interventions, and discuss ideas and questions that arise from the evaluation and strategy development (Gopal and Clarke 2015).

The analysis of how actors in the system articulate, relate and develop in the context and territory of the exposed phenomenon. This is important not only in development projects but also in research projects such as this one, since they provide the position and idiosyncrasy of each one in front of problem to be solved in order to understand it (Gutiérrez 2007).

In Fig. 2, we identify the main actors in the system, analyses subgroups formed within each of them, and how they contribute to the unleashing of the system's forces.

The tool allows us to identify the actors of IS, it does not mean that we are involved in the treatment of the phenomenon. The study shows us the of actors' importance considered key, either by their power or their interest, their roles are decisive in the problem treatment. Similarly, it does not present the actors with whom work should be done, which because of their interest are support institutions in the comprehensive treatment of IS. In the case of less important ones, so called because of their current significance in the phenomenon rather than because of their importance, but which should be involved in order to be transcendental in the treatment. The potential actors could be considered as such since their active participation, due to their power, would make them key actors in the problem treatment.

Identification of power-interest

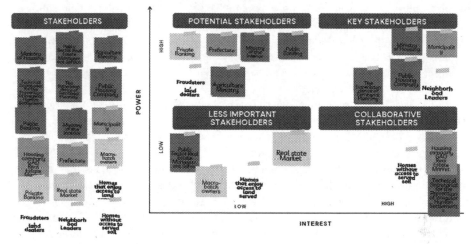

Fig. 2. Map of actors and the stakeholders.

7 Results

Using the tools of the Chile 2017 Laboratory, the Map of Actors and the Stakeholders' Map were created, which allows knowing the actors involved in the IS system and their respective roles within the system. Through the cause-and-effect diagram we have been able to identify the possible causes generated by these IS's and the effects on the community.

In addition, the number of IS is usually increasing because, first, the supply, from private companies dedicated to housing construction, is not adequate for the existing market. The price of these houses is very high compared to the income received by more than half of the citizens. There is no private urbanization plan with social interest, in other words, one that is suitable for low-income households, where sometimes only one in the family receives a basic salary.

Most of the people who buy this type of land are of scarce resources and have a very low level of education. Because of this, not everyone was aware that the land they were buying was owned by an IS. Land dealers easily deceive them by handing over papers which do not represent a real property deed: notarized receipts, purchase and sale documents, sales notes, "invoices", among others.

In short, some knew it was illegal, others didn't. However, they all decided to stay on the site because it was the only option they had. Then, they realize that illegality is very expensive, as they incur more expenses than they should. The reason this happens is because those areas are difficult to access. The police do not enter, there is no waste collection, there are not public infrastructure works, and in some areas the drinking water tankers do not enter. The IS, by not having basic services, appear in these micro-business sectors that claim to solve this lack of basic services but charge them more than what it really costs.

The municipality of Durán city launched a plan to legalize several of the IS. Most of those interviewed benefited from this plan. The legalization of these lands allowed them to feel more secure in their homes because it ensured that they would no longer be evacuated from their homes and also allowed them to improve their homes. However, it increased the insecurity of the neighborhood. This is considered to have happened because, from the legalization of land, not only did those who already lived their benefit, but also people from other places.

Most consider that they are disposed to pay the taxes as long as they increase public works in their sector. Few people said they should receive basic services whether their land is legal or not. All said they do believe they benefit from having the deeds to their land because they can improve their homes.

The previous authorities of the municipalities are convinced and agree that the problem of the IS requires the help of everyone, not only of them as a public entity but also from the other actors. On the other hand, they recognize that if a new census is not taken before the legalization plan is implemented, there will be many people who do not live in the area who will benefit from it without deserving it. In the case of Durán city, the interviewees said that for this reason insecurity in the sector has increased.

8   Conclusions

Public innovation laboratories appear as an alternative in the treatment of social phenomena. For Pascale (2020), citizen laboratories have been one of the most suggestive appearances: on the one hand, because they overcome the trinomial State-market-society and establish a new cooperative relationship in the three traditional instances of governance, putting, moreover -and above all- the citizenry at the center of the equation. The institutions are challenged to respond to communities' needs through transformative methodologies if they are to find solutions to the different social problems.

The research has allowed for the identification actors' map and their roles in the IS in Duran city; through personalized interviews and using the tools of focus groups with the IS persons, a demand was identified that generally lacks formal work, formal income and is not subject to credit, generating an opportunity for the informal market. The identification of actors, allowed to know the role of each actor within the system and therefore could be an input for the design of strategies to deal with the phenomenon (Molina-Betancur 2020).

Using the LAB-IP tools, the main causes of IS formation and its effects on the community were found. On the one hand, an offer with available land without services and without credit restrictions causes a proliferation of IS, on the other hand, a demand with credit restrictions, informal work and low income requires satisfying their housing needs and identifies as an alternative to take that offer from informal market (Ferguson 2003). The search for this balance in the market generates the problem that sets off social factors, it can be analyzed in future research.

It was found, based on the results of expert interviews, that in certain cities where are poles of development there is an increase in demand for housing due to population growth through migration, this causes an increase in demand for IS's if the city does not have an affordable housing supply (Nebot 2018). This is consistent with the findings of other studies which indicate that most migrants tend to demand housing in informal sectors, where they have easy access to housing that allows them to settle as soon as possible (Mitra 2010).

It was identified as part of the problem, local government authorities have been permissive with the informal offer (Arce 2018). In addition, it is added to the problem that the regularization processes take a long time to deal with and demand high budgets from local governments. Specialists suggest that urban development plans should be designed for the long term and not be subordinated to political authorities for the treatment of the problem.

Taking into consideration the causes of this problem, it is important to work on its treatment with all agents at different levels of government; the Central Government, in addition to housing programs, by promoting relevant regulations that could be a determining factor in the treatment of the phenomenon; Local Governments, which are the responsible for the regularization of settlements and are the way to implementation of public policy, private companies have the necessary conditions to provide an offer to unsatisfied demand in housing sector through housing solutions with social interest, with the citizens with whom they are the center of design and who must be involved in possible solutions, before, during and after the regularization processes.

To sum up, the treatment of the IS's problems must be given from a multidisciplinary approach, taking into consideration their main protagonists (Cejudo 2016), so the LAB-IP can become in this fertile space inviting all the actors, to propose solutions through innovation and to face the challenge of improving people's quality of life.

References

Acevedo, S.: Innovando para una mejor gestión. La Contribución de los laboratorios de Innovación Pública. Banco Interamericano de Desarrollo, Washington (2016)

Anand, K., et al.: Are the urban poor vulnerable to non-communicable diseases? A survey of risk factors for non-communicable diseases in urban slums of Faridabad. Natl Med. J. India **20**(3), 115 (2007)

Arce, A.: Asentamientos irregulares en el cantón Durán. (D. Méndez-Areopaja - J. Morán-Zambrano, Entrevistador) Durán, Guayas, Ecuador, 01 August 2018

Bayrau, A.: Households' willingness to resettle and preference to forms of compensation for improving slum areas in Addis Ababa City (2007)

Brakarz, J.R.: Ciudades para todos: La experiencia reciente en programas de mejoramiento de barrios Washington. DC. Inter-American Development Bank (2002)

Calderón, J.: The formalisation of property in Peru 2001–2002: the case of Lima, pp. 289–300 (2004)

Castells, M.: Imperialismo y urbanización en América Latina, vol. 12. Editorial Gustavo Gili (1973)

Cejudo, G.D.: La Innovación en el Sector Público: Tendencias internacionales y experiencias mexicanas. Cide, Ciudad de México (2016)

Clichevsky, N.: Informalidad y segregación urbana en América Latina: una aproximación. CEPAL (2000)

Délano, M. C.: Planificación multiescalar Las desigualdades territoriales Volumen II 92, Seminarios y Conferencias, No 92 (LC/TS.2019/54), Santiago, Comisión Económica Para América Latina y El Caribe (CEPAL) (2019)

Ferguson, B.: A financial framework for reducing slums: lessons from experience in Latin America. Environ. Urban. **15**(2), 201–216 (2003)

Field, E.: Property rights and investment in urban slums. J. Eur. Econ. Assoc. **3**(2–3), 279–290 (2005)

Gopal, S., Clarke, T.: FSG- Remaining Social Change. Obtenido de Guide to Actor Mapping (2015). https://www.fsg.org/tools-and-resources/guide-actor-mapping#download-area

Gutiérrez, P. M.: Mapas sociales: método y ejemplos prácticos (2007)

INEC: Instituto Nacional de Estadísticas y Censos. Censo de Población y Vivienda. Ecuador (2010)

Kohli, D.W.: Transferability of object-oriented image analysis methods for slum identification. Remote Sens. **5**(9), 4209–4228 (2013)

Laboratorio, L.D.: Herramienta para la innovación pública. Publicos, Innovadores, Santiago de Chile. Obtenido de (2017). www.innovadorespublicos.cl

Mena, A.: Asentamientos informales en el DMQ: Acceso al suelo urbano y políticas de legalización 1978–2008. FLACSO (2010)

MIDUVI: Informe Nacional del Ecuador. Habitat III, Quito (2015)

Mitra: Migration, livelihood and well-being: evidence from Indian city slums. Urban Stud. **47**(7), 1371–1390 (2010)

Molina-Betancur, J. C., Agudelo-Suárez, A. A., Martínez-Herrera, E.: Mapeo de activos comunitario para la salud en un asentamiento informal de Medellín (Colombia). Gaceta Sanitaria **35**(4), 333–338 (2021)

Nebot, J.: Asentamientos irregulares en la ciudad de Guayaquil. (D. Méndez-Areopaja, Entrevistador) Guayaquil, Guayas, Ecuador, 14 Agosto 2018

OECD: OECD-Glosario de términos estadísticos, Septiembre 2001. https://stats.oecd.org/glossary/detail.asp?ID=1351

Pascale, P.: Prototipando las instituciones del futuro: el caso de los laboratorios de innovación ciudadana (Labic). Revista Iberoamericana de Estudios de Desarrollo Iberoam. J. Dev. Stud. **9**(1), 6–27 (2020)

Porter, L.L.: Informality, the commons and the paradoxes for planning: concepts and debates for informality and planning self-made cities: ordinary informality? Plan. Theory Pract. (2011)

Rodríguez, E.: Laboratorios de Gobierno para la Innovación Pública: un estudio comparado de las experiencias americanas y europeas. Obtenido de Rosario: RedInnolabs (2018) http://www.cyted.org/sites/default/files/doc_goblabs_redinnolabs.pdf?utm_source=newsletter&utm_medium=email&utm_campaign=descarga_la_publicacion_laboratorios_de_gobierno_para_la_innovacion_publica&utm_term=2018-11-19

Roy, A.: The 21st-century metropolis: New geographies of theory **43**(6), 819–830 (2009)

Ruiz Hernández, I.E.: Identificación de asentamientos irregulares y diagnóstico de sus necesidades de infraestructura en Ciudad Juárez, Chihuahua, México. Investigaciones Geográficas, Boletín Del Instituto de Geografía **0**(0) (2014). https://doi.org/10.14350/rig.41793

Smolka, M.: Informalidad, pobreza urbana y precios de la tierra. Perspectivas Urbanas, 71–78 (2003)

Valdivia, V. A., Ramírez-Alujas, Á. V.: Innovación en el sector público chileno: la experiencia y aprendizajes del Laboratorio de Gobierno. Revista de Gestión Pública, **6**(1), 43–80 (2020)

Wacquant, L.: The militarization of urban marginality: lessons from the Brazilian metropolis. Int. Polit. Sociol., 56–74 (2008)

Sustainability

Design of Mobile Application for a Smart Home Nutrition System (SmartNS)

Carlos Carrisosa[1]($\boxtimes$), Arnulfo Alanis[2], and Javier Sotelo[3]

[1] Student of the Master's Program in Information Technology, Department of Systems and Computing, National Technology of Mexico, Campus Tijuana, Calzada del Tecnológico S/N, Fraccionamiento Tomas Aquino, 22414 Tijuana, B.C., México
carlos.carrisosa193@tectijuana.edu.mx
[2] Systems and Computer Department, National Technology of México, Campus Tijuana, Calzada del Tecnológico S/N, Fraccionamiento Tomas Aquino, 22414 Tijuana, B.C., México
alanis@tectijuana.edu.mx
[3] Computer Systems Student, Department of Systems and Computing, National Technology of Mexico, Campus Tijuana, Calzada del Tecnológico S/N, Fraccionamiento Tomas Aquino, 22414 Tijuana, B.C., México
javier.sotelo@tectijuana.edu.mx

Abstract. Every day there are more devices or objects that connect to the internet, these devices are found in different areas in the home, health, industry and others, this project is implemented in the internet of things for homes, it is a module called "nutrition", the which allows you to have a record of diets provided by a nutritionist, this allows reducing costs and food waste because with the mobile application called: Mobile application for smart appliances (EInt), you can obtain the products directly from a preferred provider. Given the situation current due to the COVID-19 pandemic, exits to non-essential situations have been reduced, this prototype pretends to be a support for users when making errand purchases and avoid going out as little as possible. The analysis and design of the device contains several agents, this article describes the nutrition agent, the food ontology, its semantic network.

Keywords: Nutrition · Intelligent agent · Internet of Things

1 Introduction

With the development of mobile technologies, many situations are at hand, such as a smartphone or a tablet and with these devices obtain applications that allow you to do a large number of things such as those proposed in this project, a mobile application installed on an Android operating system tablet [1], embedded in the refrigerator.

The nutrition system that is presented in this proposal is composed of a set of tasks, which will be in charge of several processes, such as: Shopping List, Orders, User Profile, Inventory, Supplier and a nutrition system, the latter being, where, the intelligent Agent, will be in charge of keeping a eating plan, designed by a nutritionist for which they take into account data such as: eating habits, weight, body mass index (BMI), This data is

© Springer Nature Switzerland AG 2021
T. Guarda et al. (Eds.): ARTIIS 2021, CCIS 1485, pp. 575–588, 2021.
https://doi.org/10.1007/978-3-030-90241-4_44

provided through the application and the expert, from this point decides what type of diet the user needs, for this, it assigns a meal plan to follow with a maximum of daily calories that you should consume; With the aforementioned meal plan, you get a list of products to consume with which the order is made from the Mobile application for smart appliances – Eint.

On the other hand, initially, the processes will be local, is mean, in each device, and as a second stage, cloud services will be used for database management.

This article presents the analysis and design of a prototype of a module of nutrition, which is intended to have frequent use in homes, This prototype will initially communicate with multiple applications with those obtained: food organization, supply record, nutritional plans and monitoring them together will generate satisfaction to the user who currently wants to have practicality and speed in each of the daily activities, such as: reminders of the products to be added to the order list, consult the inventory of products in the refrigerator and pantry, as well as keep in mind entertainment for children while the user cooks, to be able to review the weather, listening to music, etc.

2 Internet of Things

The internet of things is a network of devices and people where multiple platforms, different technologies and communication protocols can interact, with the aim of having an intelligent global infrastructure where the real, the digital and the virtual converge in various public or private sectors among other aspects of life [2, 3], which means that devices or objects can share information and specific data of the environment where they are, an example of this is sensors, which provide information on the weather or distance from a car to a one., etc. and this data can be read by people [4].

The internet of things is found in many places and with the interconnection with objects and devices, many tasks can be carried out within homes, industries and schools, etc.

It is an area of computing that aims to expand the technological spaces that support people in their day-to-day lives, it can detect information from the environment, analyze information and lead to make decisions for the benefit of users is one of the characteristics that they have these systems [5]. Among the areas of application of the Internet of Things architecture, the following stand out: smart homes, health services (hospitals, assistance, emergency services), work spaces and educational environments.

When the concept of IoT is introduced to the smart home application. This covers a much wider range of control. For example, smart home involves security, energy management, thermostat temperature control, family entertainment, and family businesses [6].

3 Nutrition

Nutrition involves processes by which the body transforms and incorporates nutrients obtained from food and fulfills the functions of supplying energy, providing materials for the formation, renewal and repair of body structures, and supplying substances to regulate metabolism, as well as supplying the necessary energy. For the maintenance of the body and its functions [7].

The study of the origin of diseases from the components of the diet and the state of health, provides knowledge with which eating plans can be made, however the eating habits of users do not allow such plans to be taken into account. food, all this due to the wide variety of foods available, especially in ultra-processed products (with high energy content, sugars, fat and salt) with a low purchasing value, and with abundant advertising to promote consumption [8].

Nutrition is essential for the vital functions of the body, it is necessary to supply components such as proteins, fats, carbohydrates, etc. for energy and for tissue repair.

Food is the basis of our health, it is important to have a good diet to prevent different diseases such as hypertension, diabetes, etc. in addition to combating obesity, which is one of the greatest evils in Mexican society [9].

As will be seen later in this article, the design of the intelligent nutrition agent is presented that will help the user with the records of their eating plans, initial weight, final weight and the generation of lists of items that they will have to buy to comply with the plan. Food prescribed by the specialist.

4 Intelligent Agent

They are programs that help users to perform certain actions, for example, fill in forms, choose products, find a certain thing, etc. They are also called softbot (robot software), there are also other chat applications that companies use to solve user doubts, intelligent agents use software tools and services based on people's behavior [10].

The agents are in a virtual environment where they act and these actions are capable of generating changes in the environment, they communicate and manage the actions with those of other agents in the same environment, the actions carried out by the agents are a consequence of the decisions made by the agent according to what is detected in his environment and according to the objectives he wants to achieve, with these decisions knowledge is obtained which generates the agent to acquire intelligence, said intelligence is obtained from aggregate knowledge or by some form of representation of knowledge [11].

5 Ontology

An ontology is a form of representation of knowledge that results from selecting a domain or field of knowledge, in which types, properties, and relationships between entities are defined.

Ontologies, through the semantic Web, allow information to be organized in such a way that it can be searched, extracted, processed and drawn conclusions, with terminology easy to understand by the actors involved: computers, users and companies [12].

Each time the use of ontologies has been implemented in the field of computational sciences and artificial intelligence, this is because, as mentioned above, knowledge is represented in a more efficient way, which allows it to be better understood.

Ontologies are composed of Classes, Subclasses, Properties and Restrictions, Classes are the concepts applied in the ontology such as the Food Class, Subclasses are the concepts that are part of the Classes for example: Fruits, Vegetables, Legumes, etc. are subclasses of the food class. The Properties are the described relationships of the classes and the restrictions that apply to the Properties [13].

6 Proposal

To stay healthy, human beings need to be nourished properly, it is very important to eat foods with certain characteristics, this will depend on each person since the requirements of each person are different. It also forms a fundamental pillar to prevent diseases, such as diabetes, hypertension and obesity. Eight out of ten patients who started a diet plan to lose weight, abandon it before reaching the goal [14].

In another order of ideas, according to figures from the UN Fund for Food and Agriculture (FAO) for October 2017, 1.3 billion tons of food produced for human consumption are lost, a third of total world production. While in America and the Caribbean it is estimated that 6% of the world's food loss is wasted [15], In Mexico, according to SEDESOL figures, 10,431,000 tons of food is wasted, 37% of the country's production [16].

Nutrition is one of the main determinants of chronic diseases, and if important changes were made in the diet style, there could be benefits in the health of the population [8].

For this particular article, a nutritional agent is presented and developed, which will help users to be able to have nutritional control.

The Nutrition Agent will have objectives and tasks to fulfill, and plan the meal plans, weight, body mass index, in addition to creating lists of products not only those included in their diet, but also household products for members of the family who are not on a diet to lose weight and later make the purchase from the mobile application, so the paper shopping list would be replaced by a digital list, the semantic network analysis will be carried out, then the ontology is based In the paradigm of intelligent agents, for its development, the ontologies carried out focuses on the foods required to define the concepts of the different domains and the relationships between them.

The design of the food ontology is built, taking into consideration the classes Nutrition (which is divided into the following categories: Diets, Nutritionist and User) and Food in which it is made up of the categories: Cereal seeds and derivatives, Seeds of legumes and derivatives, Other seeds, Algae and fungi, Fruits, Vegetables, Tubers, bulbs and roots, Milk and derivatives, Egg, Meats, organ meats and derivatives, Fish and shellfish, Sugars, honeys and sweets, Baby foods, Dressings, Drinks alcoholic and non-alcoholic and Various, data was collected from the document Tables of composition of food and food products (condensed version 2015), INCMNSZ [17].

For the analysis and design of the semantic nutrition network, it is contemplated that the user on the platform is registered and therefore has a file, in the latter the medical questionnaire applied to the user, initial weight, final weight and index will be recorded. For body mass, the nutrients required for the meal plan are selected, a type of diet is selected and the user is assigned the meal plan according to calories and portions for 21 days. The user uses the application to create shopping lists and generate orders as shown in Fig. 1.

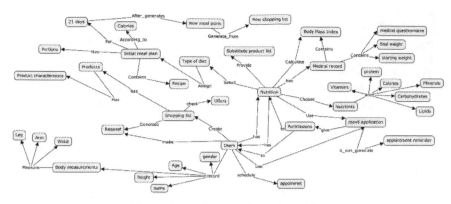

Fig. 1. Semantic network agent nutrition

Next, the pantry classification ontology designed in the Web Ontology Language (OWL) and the Protégé tool [18] is described, as shown in Fig. 2.

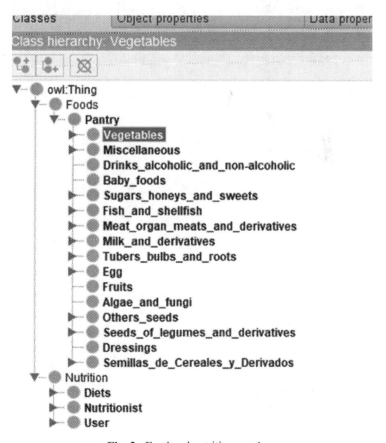

Fig. 2. Food and nutrition ontology

For the implementation of the agent, a module called, for mobile devices, said application allows the user to keep a record of the food in his home, which allows him to have control of what he consumes, since said records have information such as the expiration date of the food, the calories, the quantity, etc.

For this proposal, two methodologies were proposed, the first for the research approach, an exhaustive study of art was carried out, later the information was analyzed and from this point, the development of the system is proposed.

Which includes a module called nutrition and an intelligent agent that interact together. This article focuses on the nutrition module, the other methodology that was used was for the development of the system and for this the SCRUM [17] methodology was implemented.

6.1 Analysis

For the analysis, it was started by making the user's use cases (Fig. 3) as a basis, in which it is described how they will interact with the application and with the system in general. Later, the use case of a single user is described, which describes the logic of the program through sequence diagrams. Finally, the user interface is displayed. For all of the above, a requirements analysis was used where it is proposed to capture the idea through a graph or diagram.

For the nutrition module, the health use case and its derived cases are used.

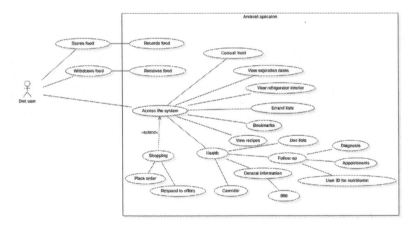

Fig. 3. A diagram of use cases that shows the user interaction with nutrition module

6.2 Developing

The application was developed in the Java programming language, using the Android Studio IDE. For this development, the analysis processes carried out through use cases, sequence diagrams, mockups and requirements analysis were taken into account.

During the development stage, the agile Scrum development methodology was used. It began with the main menu (Fig. 4), then each of the modules was developed, starting with the pantry (Fig. 5), continuing with the Shopping list (Fig. 6) and so on until reaching favorites.

Fig. 4. Screenshot of main menu nutrition module

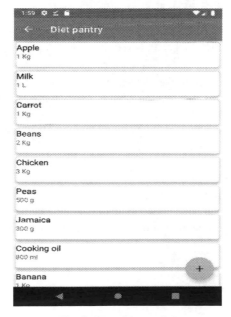

Fig. 5. User pantry view

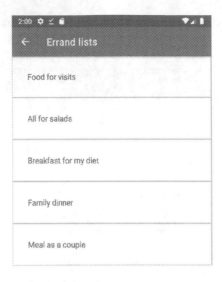

Fig. 6. Shopping list screen

Finally, the submodules are developed. In them we can register and delete products and display details.

The system model (SmartND) describes the operation of how the user uses an intelligent device, to access the system and obtain information about the products in the refrigerator, once this process has been carried out, the device called Raspberry Pi (sensor module) generates the Capture information elements (food) in two ways, first stored in a database that is hosted in the cloud, second Raspberry Pi device sends the data to the nutrition agent or vision agent, for identification, these data are classified by means of a neural network, and finally the food control module is responsible for keeping the food in the pantry with the requirements generated by the nutritional agent, for this process a list is generated, so that in the next task perform the purchase and payment, after all this process the Raspberry Pi returns the information to the database, as shown in Fig. 7.

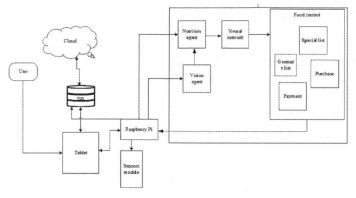

Fig. 7. System model (SmartND)

6.3 Database, Nutrition Module

The application data is stored in a device local database, developed with the database manager SQLite using DB Browser for SQLite.

It has the advantages of being compact and consuming little storage space.

The database file (db file) is an asset of the project; when the application first screen is opened (sign in) the app copies it and saves it to the device's internal storage.

The database structure is shown in Fig. 8.

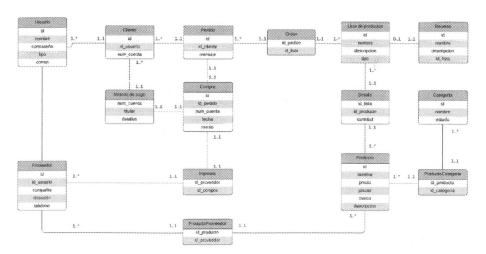

Fig. 8. Database entity model, represents the database tables and its relationships

7 Results

The analysis of the Nutrition Agent, intended to support the times of COVID-19, analyzed the elements to consider for its development and subsequent implementation, the tests were planned to be generated in a test environment (purchase process with non-real data), given the situation of COVID-19.

A design of the application was made, some views let the users interact with the system. An example of some application views as shown in Figs. 9, 10, 11, 12 and 13:

Fig. 9. A screenshot of new product view. User adds a new register of food

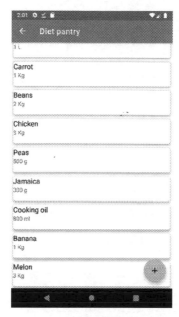

Fig. 10. Screenshot of Diet pantry view. The new product added by user is now in the pantry

When the product is consumed the user now edit the registry a set the amount to 0.

Fig. 11. User changes the amount of a register of food in the product information view.

Fig. 12. User changes the amount of a register of food in the product information view.

Finally, the food is consumed and the register is no show anymore.

Fig. 13. Product registered is gone because it's consumed

8 Conclusions

The development of an intelligent platform, with a nutritional approach allows users to have better control of their meal plans that could lead users not to abandon the nutritional program, in addition to being in communication with specialists, having healthy food options with the recipe repository and see how much progress has been made in the proposed objective.

It will also serve to support users to carry a shopping plan that can be the products of their meal plan or any other product for the other members of the family. This means that the design of this project is designed for the whole family, with all of the above described presents a scenario where some needs generated by the COVID-19 pandemic and after it are covered, for example, the user will be able to follow up on their nutritional treatment without having to leave home and expose themselves to the aforementioned virus.

References

1. Junestrand, S., Passaret, X., Vazquez Alvarez, D.: Domótica y Hogar Digital. Thomson Paraninfo, España (2005)
2. Gunturi, M., Kotha, H.D., Srinivasa Reddy, M.: An overview of internet of things. J. Adv. Res. Dyn. Control Syst. **10**(9), 659–665 (2018)
3. Lin, A., Vives, A., Bagula, A., Zennaro, M., Pietrosemoli, E.: Internet
4. Salazar, J., Silvestre, Y.S.: Internet de las Cosas
5. Cook, D.J., Augusto, J.C., Jakkula, V.R.: Ambient intelligence: technologies, applications, and opportunities. Pervasive Mob. Comput. **5**(4), 277–298 (2009)
6. Tania, L., Isabel, C.: IoT, El Internet de las Cosas y la Innovación de Sus Aplicaciones. UANL Sch. Business, FACPYA, México, pp. 2313–2340, May 2015
7. Castro Camacho, A.E.: Propuesta Didáctica Para Fomentar El Aprendizaje Significativo de los Conceptos Alimento y Nutrición. Universidad Del Norte (2017)
8. Pastor, A.C., Santamaría, M.: La nutrición desde la perspectiva comunitaria y de salud pública. Nutr. en Salud Pública, p. 222 (2017)
9. Guerrero, A., Joaquín J., Núñez, G., Jonathan, L., Laura, S.C., Artemio, S.O.: Sistema Nutricional Inteligente, pp. 206–209 (2007)
10. Bautista Vallejo, J.M.: Los Agentes de Software Inteligentes y la respuesta didáctica a la diversidad. Actual. Investig. en Educ. **7**(1), 67–78 (2011)
11. Coloma, J.A., Vargas, J.A., Sanaguano, C.A., Rochina, A.G.: Inteligencia artificial, sistemas inteligentes, agentes inteligentes Artificial intelligence, smart systems, smart agents Inteligência artificial, sistemas inteligentes, agentes inteligentes. Rev. Recimundo **4**(2), 16–30 (2020)
12. Rivera, E., Chavira, G., Ahumada, A., Ramírez, C.: Construcción y evaluación de un modelo ontológico nutricional (2018)
13. Montico, S., Di Leo, N.: Universidad Nacional de Rosario. Rev. Int. AI Argentina **IV**, 166–172 (2015)
14. Fernando, S.O.L.: Abandono del tratamiento dietético en pacientes diagnosticados con obesidad en un consultorio privado de nutrición. Nutr. Clin. y Diet. Hosp. **31**(1), 15–19 (2011)
15. Pérdidas y desperdicios de alimentos en América Latina y el Caribe | FAO. http://www.fao.org/americas/noticias/ver/es/c/239393/. Accessed 23 Mar 2020

16. Desperdicio de Alimentos en México. http://www.sedesol.gob.mx/boletinesSinHambre/Inf ormativo_02/infografia.html. Accessed 23 Mar 2020
17. ® Instituto Nacional de Ciencias Médicas y Nutrición Salvador Zubirán. Tablas de composición de alimentos y productos alimenticios (versión condensada 2015), Ciudad de México (2016)
18. protégé. https://protege.stanford.edu/. Accessed 12 Jan 2021

A Bibliometric Analysis About the Use of ICT in the Agricultural Sector

Maria I. B. Ribeiro[1] ⓘ, António J. G. Fernandes[1(✉)] ⓘ, Isabel M. Lopes[2] ⓘ, and António P. R. Fernandes[3]

[1] Centro de Investigação de Montanha, Instituto Politécnico de Bragança, Campus Santa Apolónia, 5300-253 Bragança, Portugal
{xilote,toze}@ipb.pt

[2] Instituto Politécnico de Bragança, Unidade de Pesquisa Aplicada em Gestão, Campus de Santa Apolónia, 5300-253 Bragança, Portugal
isalopes@ipb.pt

[3] Faculdade de Ciências da Universidade do Porto, Rua Campo Alegre, 4169-007 Porto, Portugal

Abstract. This work aims to identify the clusters of research thematic areas within the scope of the use of Information and Communication Technologies (ICT) in Agriculture. To achieve this objective, a search based on the words "Information", "Communication", "Technologies", "Challenges" and "Agriculture" was conducted in the Scopus database considering the period 2010 to May 2020. Later, the VOSviewer software version 1.6.14 and the word co-occurrence technique were used to carried out a bibliometric analysis based on 91 peer-reviewed publications. The results revealed the existence of two thematic areas. The first one emphasizes the importance of knowledge and the acquisition of skills by farmers. In this context, the use of ICT allows the development of a more sustainable, efficient and innovative Agriculture. The second thematic area refers to the "Internet of Things". In this context, Internet and other technologies are associated with Agriculture in order to minimize the risk of agricultural activities management, to achieve time and cost savings, to increase farms productivity and, to minimize the environmental impact of agricultural activities.

Keywords: Agriculture · Information and Communication Technologies · Bibliometric analysis

1 Introduction

Currently, the development of Agriculture is promoted by the idea that agricultural information is fundamental to transform and maintain an economic, solid and sustainable development [1] with the development of products/foods with less impact on the environment and nature. The generalized growth of Information and Communication Technologies (ICT) offers new opportunities in relation to the information services provided, which are more opportune and of low cost to farmers, in addition to being a great support in the management of agricultural activities [2]. ICT, if successfully implemented, can

T. Guarda et al. (Eds.): ARTIIS 2021, CCIS 1485, pp. 589–599, 2021.
https://doi.org/10.1007/978-3-030-90241-4_45

provide great benefits, with regard to the social and economic empowerment of people, especially those who live in rural and/or mountain areas [3].

ICT have contributed significantly to the growth and socio-economic development of countries and regions in which they are well adopted and integrated. The adoption and integration of ICT has enabled the reduction of information and transaction costs, the improvement of service provision, the creation of new jobs, the generation of new revenue flows and the more efficient use of scarce resources. Digital technologies have transformed the way companies, people and governments work, promoting efficiency and inclusion [4]. ICT have been responsible for the profound transformations in production models, providing more efficient production and exploration management, through the dissemination of information from the sector, better planning, monitoring and follow-up of agricultural activities [5].

The impact of the application of ICT in Agriculture can be assessed from two perspectives, namely, as a direct tool to improve the productivity of farms and as an indirect tool to enable farmers to make informed decisions that will have a positive impact in the way agricultural activities are conducted and developed [6].

In addition, the digitization of Agriculture has contributed to a greater attractiveness of the sector [7] that can be understood as a business opportunity [8], especially by the younger population with no professional occupation. Therefore, this research aimed to solidify the state of academic research developed within the scope of the use of ICT in Agriculture, from 2010 to May 2020.

This work is organized in four sections, the introduction, which presents the contextualization of the theme and its importance for the sustainable, efficient and innovative development of Agriculture. The second section describes the methodology used in this research. The third section presents the results. In the fourth and last section, the main conclusions of this research are drawn, the limitations of the study are identified and future lines of research are suggested.

2   Methods

This research focused on publications from the Scopus database. In this research, the words "Information", "Communication", "Technologies", "Challenges" and "Agriculture" were used.

In total, 268 publications were found. Subsequently, a filter was used that allowed to include publications from 2010 until May 2020 (112). The search was also limited to articles from peer-reviewed publications (91), as shown in Fig. 1.

Then, a bibliometric analysis was developed using the word co-occurrence technique. In this context, the unit of analysis was the article and the variables corresponded to the words included in the titles and abstracts of the 91 publications. The words were extracted using the VOSviewer version 1.6.14 software in order to build a map that showed the relations between the different words and their association into clusters of thematic areas. With this methodology, the distance between the various selected words is analysed, and the shorter the distance between two words, the stronger the relation between them [9]. On the map, the colours represent the various clusters of thematic areas, and the words with the same colour are part of the same cluster and, therefore, are more strongly related to each other when compared to words that have a different colour. In the analysis, the binary counting method was selected, which consists of verifying whether the word is present or absent in each document analysed.

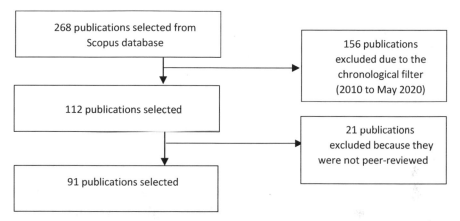

Fig. 1. Selection of the publications.

3   Results

The results are presented in two subsections. Initially, the results of the descriptive analysis are presented, such as the evolution of the articles published between 2010 and May 2020, the Top-10 of the sources, institutions, countries with the most publications, the Top-10 of the sub-areas with publications on ICT in agriculture, type of access to published articles and index h of the literature on ICT used in agriculture (h-12). Subsequently, the co-occurrence map of words for publications on the use of ICT in agriculture is presented.

3.1   Descriptive Analysis

It can be seen, through Fig. 2, that 2018 was the year that registered the largest number of published articles (19). In the period from 2010 to 2019, the average annual growth rate was 10.3%. In the year 2020, there were only 8 published articles, since it was considered, only the first four-month period of the year 2020.

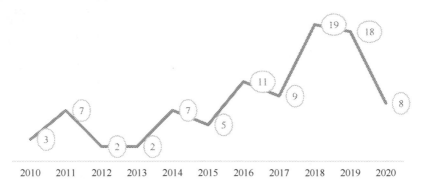

Fig. 2. Evolution of the number of published articles.

The literature on the use of ICT in Agriculture has been published in journals that focus on different scientific areas, namely, Agriculture and Extension, Economics, Technologies, Computing, Engineering, Biotechnology, among others. The journals "Journal of Cleaner Production", "Journal of Intellectual Property Rights" and "Library Philosophy and Practice" are the sources that register the most published articles (3 articles), as shown in Fig. 3.

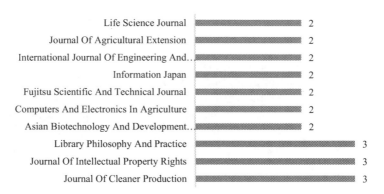

Fig. 3. Top-10 sources with the most publications.

At the institutional level, the "Sokoine University of Agriculture", located in Morogoro, Tanzania, a public university, specialized in agriculture, is the institution that occupies the first position in the Top-10 institutions with the most publications (4), as shown in Fig. 4.

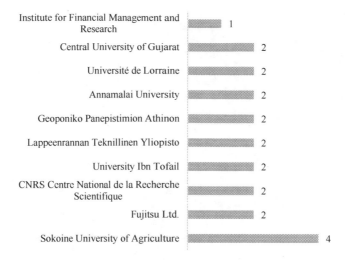

Fig. 4. Top-10 institutions with the most publications.

In Fig. 5, it is possible to observe that India (17%), followed by the United States of America (8%), constitute the countries with the most articles published in the Scopus database, followed by Japan (56%), Germany (4%), China (4%), Greece (4%), Tanzania (4%), among others (3%).

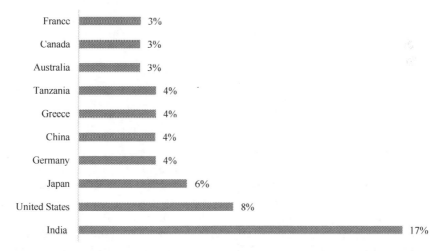

Fig. 5. Top-10 countries with the most publications.

The three sub-areas with the greatest representativeness are: Computer Science (18%), Engineering (15%) and Agricultural and Biological Sciences (13%), as shown in Fig. 6.

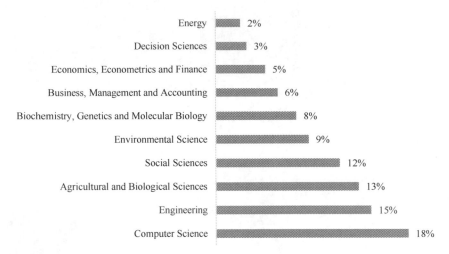

Fig. 6. Top-10 subareas with the most publications on the use of ICT in Agriculture.

As shown in Fig. 7, only 24% of the articles were accessible through open access. Most articles (76%) were available with other form of access.

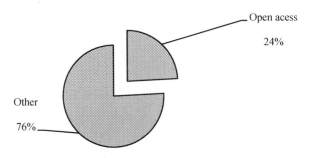

Fig. 7. Type of access to published articles.

Table 1 shows the researches included in the h-index, that is, the number of publications by a given author with, at least, the same number of citations [10], totalling 12 articles. The Hirsch Index, or h-index, as it is commonly known, quantifies a researcher's scientific production by measuring, together, the productivity of each researcher and their academic impact [11]. This method of calculating the scientific productivity of a researcher has been generally accepted by substituting other methods, namely, the total number of publications, the total number of citations or citations per article.

As shown in Table 1, taking into account the methodology used in the h-index publications, of the 12 articles, 6 are experimental researches and the remaining 6 are conceptual researches. Conceptual researches are, above all, review researches in which the authors propose models, structures and/or strategies to develop a greener, more sustainable and efficient use of ICT in Agriculture. The most cited article (445 citations), entitled "Sustainable Intensification In African Agriculture" [12], involves the description and summary of positive actions, processes and effective lessons, which resulted from projects, namely, the emergence of new crops, animals or fish that have been added to existing foods or vegetables and that are important to expand and disseminate to many other small farmers and herders across the African continent, namely: (1) inclusion of science, technologies and practices that combine animals and plants with agro-ecological and agronomic handling; (2) creating a new social infrastructure that builds trust between individuals and agencies; (3) improving farmers' digital knowledge and skills by attending local schools equipped with modern ICT; (4) commitment to the private sector to provide goods and services; (5) focus on educational, financing and agricultural technology needs for women; (6) guarantee the availability of microfinance and rural banks; and, (7) ensure public sector support to agriculture.

Table 1. H-index of the literature on the use of ICT in Agriculture (h-12).

Ref.	Method	Contributions	Cit.
[12]	Conceptual	Dissemination of positive practices and lessons learned from 50 projects developed at the African continent to disseminate, foster and expand rural and urban economic growth	445
[13]	Experimental	Presents the development of sustainable ICT systems using the interaction between humans and computers to create a user-centred design. In this way, it is possible to use ICT systems to their full potential	59
[14]	Conceptual	Presents a review of ICT and other devices, namely, underground Internet of Things, which consists of sensors and communication devices, partially or completely buried underground to detect and monitor, in real time, the soil. The adoption of these technologies arises from the need to develop precision agriculture to increase the amount of food in order to meet the arising needs resulting from the increase of the world population	47
[15]	Conceptual	Describes the development of an international program called "Computing and communications for sustainable development" by an international consortium, which aimed to combine advanced ICT with environmental, economic and social awareness. It concludes that the implementation of green ICT educational programs is important to ensure further development of ICT around sustainability concerns	46
[2]	Conceptual	Argues that the implementation of ICT in agriculture is only successful if the information and existing market failures in a given context are better understood. On the other hand, the information services provided, delivered through platforms based on local access and use of ICT, must be of high quality and from a reliable source. Finally, it is necessary to overcome the problem of digital literacy, in particular, the digital division between genders	45

(continued)

Table 1. (*continued*)

Ref.	Method	Contributions	Cit.
[16]	Experimental	Proposes a web-based decision support system, capable of supporting farmers in the process of selecting alternative crops that are more appropriate for land use. The system provides necessary information and supports the farmer throughout the growing period and process. The system also provides services through the use of mobile phones, since this technology has high adoption rates, even by farmers. The objective is to achieve a balanced and sustainable Agriculture, which responds to the new demands of the market	33
[17]	Experimental	Describes the experience and results of 11 researches that exemplify expansion strategies based on (1) value chains and private sector involvement, (2) ICT and agricultural consultancy services and (3) policy involvement. Effective expansion strategies that can contribute to achieve food and nutrition security under climate change in the coming decades	21
[18]	Experimental	Demonstrates, through the implementation of an experience, in a company, which is dedicated to the production of wine grapes, that electronic traceability data is a good basis to generate accurate and low-effort life cycles in Agriculture, especially when data is collected using efficient ICT	20
[19]	Experimental	Proposes a simulation structure, capable of predicting the behaviour and performance of the system as a whole, based on software to meet the challenges of designing, testing and evaluating the performance of the new automated precision feeding equipment for rural companies (exchange of information or requesting services using other software using a high-level communication language)	20
[20]	Conceptual	Discusses technologies, namely, Cloud Computing (CC) and Internet of Things (IoT) and how these technologies reduce energy consumption in Agriculture, allowing the development of Agriculture and a more sustainable World	19
[21]	Conceptual	Discusses the importance of the role of extension in the development of agriculture, namely, knowledge management, convergence of extension systems, the role of ICT and mass media, private sector initiatives, including public-private partnerships and extension systems led by farmers and the market	17
[3]	Experimental	Explores and compare the functioning of two ICT models, one in the public sector and the other in the private sector, in a rural region in India. Also, identifies the use of various services by farmers, namely, prices of agricultural raw materials, available products and market prices, meteorological information, State services, Health and Education. And, analyses farmers needs with regard to services and highlights restrictions and challenges in the implementation of these models	12

With regard to experimental researches, the most cited article (59 citations) highlights the importance of developing more sustainable precision agriculture [13]. However, the authors recognize that the majority of farmers, despite having the appropriate technologies to operate on site, do not use it or do not use it to the full. Recognizing this limitation, the authors propose the development of sustainable systems that include ICT and, using methodologies based on human-computer interaction, create a design for an agricultural system for nitrogen fertilization.

3.2 Thematic Areas Analysis

Taking into account the analysis of the thematic areas and using the VOSviewer software and the word co-occurrence technique, 3252 words were identified, of which only 49 had a minimum of 10 occurrences (minimum value defined by the software). For each of these words, the software calculated a relevance score. Based on this score, the most relevant words were selected. The standard choice was to select 60% of the most relevant words, accounting for 29 words. Finally, insignificant words (Examples: Case; Country, India, Research, Study, Tanzania, Paper, Survey and Concepts) were excluded, resulting in a total of 20 words distributed in two clusters of thematic areas.

The first cluster consists of 11 words, namely, Farmer, Health, Information and Communication Technologies (ICT), Impact, Innovation, Knowledge, Lack, Need, Process, Service and Use (colour red in Fig. 8). This cluster emphasizes the importance of knowledge and the acquisition of skills, by the farmer, in order to be able to take full advantage of the use of ICT in Agriculture. Its use allows the development of a more sustainable, efficient and innovative Agriculture.

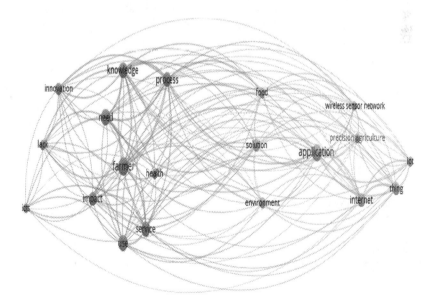

Fig. 8. Co-occurrence map of words for publications on the use of ICT in Agriculture.

The second cluster includes 9 words, namely, Application, Environment, Food, Internet, Internet of Things (IoT), Precision Agriculture, Solution, Thing and Wireless Sensor Network (colour green in Fig. 8). This cluster refers to the "Internet of Things" associating the use of the Internet and other technologies with Agriculture. The publications that are part of this cluster highlight the advantages of using the "Internet of Things" in Agriculture, with the following advantages: (1) the minimization of management risk of the agricultural activities; (2) the time and costs savings; (3) the increase of the productivity of lands and farms; and, (4) the reduction of the environmental impact.

4   Conclusion

The use of ICT in Agriculture is an issue that has originated an increasing number of publications, especially in the last decade. This study aimed to identify the main thematic areas of research in the field of ICT used in Agriculture. In this context, the Scopus database was used to do the search and the VoSviewer software, version 1.6.14, and the bibliometric technique of co-occurrence of words were used in order to group the literature into clusters of thematic areas.

Two clusters were identified. The first cluster emphasizes the importance of knowledge and the acquisition of skills, by farmers, for the full use of the advantages associated with the use of ICT in Agriculture. The use of ICT allows the development of a more sustainable, efficient and innovative Agriculture. The second cluster refers to the "Internet of Things" associating the use of the Internet and other technologies with Agriculture. This cluster highlights the advantages of using the "Internet of Things" in Agriculture, namely, minimizing the risk in the management of agricultural activities; time and cost savings; increasing productivity of farms; and, the reduction of the environmental impact.

The development of an innovative, efficient, smart and sustainable agriculture, with a reduced impact on the environment and nature, has been a reality, although not very significant, with the introduction of ICT in agricultural systems and practices. A challenging process that implies a joint effort by all, especially farmers, rural extension services, agricultural companies and policy makers.

One of the limitations of this research is due to the fact that it is limited to the Scopus database. In fact, other bibliometric databases, such as the Web of Science, are equally important regarding the number of publications, scientific areas, editors and miscellaneous documents; scope; frequency of use; easy to use; and, update.

Due to the enormous challenges that it will provide, in the near future, as well as the good results already proven, in the recent past, the use of ICT in Agriculture is a subject that deserves great interest and commitment by researchers, research units, policy makers and all who work and live in the agricultural sector.

Acknowledgments. The authors are grateful to the Foundation for Science and Technology (FCT, Portugal) for financial support by national funds FCT/MCTES to CIMO (UIDB/00690/2020).

References

1. Balamurugan, S., Divyabharathi, N., Jayashruthi, K., Bowiya, M., Shermy, R., Shanker, G.: Internet of agriculture: applying IoT to improve food and farming technology. Int. Res. J. Eng. Technol. (IRJET) **3**(10), 713–719 (2016)
2. Aker, J., Ghosh, I., Burrell, J.: The promise (and pitfalls) of ICT for agriculture initiatives. Agricultural Economics (United Kingdom) **47**, 35–48 (2016)
3. Narula, S., Arora, S.: Identifying stakeholders' needs and constraints in adoption of ICT services in rural areas: the case of India. Soc. Responsibil. J. **6**(2), 222–236 (2010)
4. FAO, IFPRI, OCDE: Information and Communication Technology (ICT) in Agriculture: A Report to the G20 Agricultural Deputie. Food and Agriculture Organization of the United Nations, Rome (2017)
5. Mendes, C., Buainain, A., Fasiaben, M.: Heterogeneidade da agricultura brasileira no acesso às tecnologias da informação. Espacios **35**(11), 1–11 (2014)
6. Patel, S., Sayyed, I.: Impact of information technology in agriculture sector. Int. J. Food Agric. Veterinary Sci. **4**(2), 17–22 (2014)
7. Irungu, K., Mbugua, D., Muia, J.: Information and Communication Technologies (ICTs) attract youth into profitable agriculture in Kenya. East Afr. Agric. For. J. **81**(1), 24–33 (2015)
8. Njenga, P., Frida, M. Opio, R.: Youth and women empowerment through agriculture in a Kenya. Voluntary Service-Overseas (VSO-Jitolee), Nairobi, Kenya (2012).
9. van Eck, N., Waltman, L.: Text mining and visualization using VOSviewer. ISSI Newsl. **7**(3), 238–260 (2011)
10. Costas, R., Bordons, M.: The h-index: advantages, limitations and its relation with other bibliometric indicators at the micro level. J. Informetr. **1**(3), 193–203 (2007)
11. Hirsch, J.E.: An index to quantify an individual's scientific research output. PNAS **102**(46), 16569–16572 (2005)
12. Pretty, J., Toulmin, C., Williams, S.: Sustainable intensification in African agriculture. Int. J. Agric. Sustain. **9**(1), 5–24 (2011)
13. Lindblom, J., Lundström, C., Ljung, M., Jonsson, A.: Promoting sustainable intensification in precision agriculture: review of decision support systems development and strategies. Precision Agric. **18**(3), 309–331 (2016). https://doi.org/10.1007/s11119-016-9491-4
14. Vuran, M., Salam, A., Wong, R., Irmak, S.: Internet of underground things in precision agriculture: architecture and technology aspects. Ad Hoc Netw. **81**, 160–173 (2018)
15. Klimova, A., Rondeau, E., Andersson, K., Porras, J., Rybin, A., Zaslavsky, A.: An international Master's program in green ICT as a contribution to sustainable development. J. Clean. Prod. **135**, 223–239 (2016)
16. Antonopoulou, E., Karetsos, S., Maliappis, M., Sideridis, A.: Web and mobile technologies in a prototype DSS for major field crops. Comput. Electron. Agric. **70**(2), 292–301 (2010)
17. Weswordann, O., Förch, W., Thornton, P., Körner, J., Cramer, L., Campbell, B.: Scaling up agricultural interventions: case researches of climate-smart agriculture. Agric. Syst. **165**, 283–293 (2018)
18. Bellon-Maurel, V., Peters, G., Clermidy, S., Schulz, M., Roux, P., Short, M.: Streamlining life cycle inventory data generation in agriculture using traceability data and information and communication technologies – Part II: application to viticulture. J. Clean. Prod. **87**(1), 119–129 (2015)
19. Pomar, J., López, V., Pomar, C.: Agent-based simulation framework for virtual prototyping of advanced livestock precision feeding systems. Comput. Electron. Agric. **78**(1), 88–97 (2011)
20. Nandyala, C., Kim, H.-K.: Green IoT agriculture and healthcare application (GAHA). Int. J. Smart Home **10**(4), 289–300 (2016)
21. Ferroni, M., Zhou, Y.: Achievements and challenges in agricultural extension in India. Glob. J. Emerg. Mark. Econ. **4**(3), 319–346 (2012)

Towards a More Sustainable E-commerce in the Post-COVID-19 Recovery of Portuguese Companies

Mónica Vieira[1], Tomás Malaquias[1], Valeriya Ketsmur[1], Viktoriya Ketsmur[1], and Manuel Au-Yong-Oliveira[1,2(✉)]

[1] Department of Economics, Management, Industrial Engineering and Tourism, University of Aveiro, 3810-193 Aveiro, Portugal
{monicavieira,tomas.malaquias,valeriya.ketsmur,viktoriya, mao}@ua.pt
[2] INESC TEC, Porto; GOVCOPP, Aveiro, Portugal

Abstract. Covid-19 is having a huge impact on Portuguese companies, causing a decrease in the revenue of many and the insolvency of some. To recuperate, e-commerce emerges as a viable solution for entrepreneurs to recover the reins of their business and move towards profit. However, e-commerce has harmful effects on the environment, generating large CO_2 emissions and an extraordinary volume of packaging and plastics. Hence, this study will provide: an action plan for companies to make e-commerce more sustainable; a detailed action plan for the electrification of a company's fleet; thus, proposing a circular business approach. Our solutions include the adjustment of the size of the packaging, using ecological transport (electric vehicles, cargo bicycles, drones, delivery droids), companies taking the initiative in the reuse and recycling of waste delivered to the consumer, the contribution to consumer awareness, and establishing direct communication with consumers through ICT. To support this research, fieldwork was carried out: an online survey with 409 responses to know the opinion of national residents on the environmental impact of e-commerce; an interview with the Director of Projects and Circular Economics of SONAE MC who added the vision of an expert in retail sustainability; and some purchases at online stores to observe the market practices in terms of packaging. The study follows a scientific methodology, which includes hypotheses tests (Chi-square) with a confidence margin of 95%. There is evidence that the Covid-19 pandemic is to have lasting effects on consumer preferences for sustainable companies. In an age where everything seems to be getting smarter, e-commerce firms will have to follow this trend. Hence, marketing and strategy will have to change for the better and for the long term. We hope, with our study, to have shown a way forward in that respect.

Keywords: Circular economy · E-commerce · Logistics effectiveness · Plastic · Sustainable development

T. Guarda et al. (Eds.): ARTIIS 2021, CCIS 1485, pp. 600–613, 2021.
https://doi.org/10.1007/978-3-030-90241-4_46

1   Introduction

Covid-19 has had an overwhelming impact on the Portuguese economy. The confinement led to the interruption of the activity of many companies, which decreased their income and caused the bankruptcy of many of them [1]. According to a study conducted by the INE (Instituto Nacional de Estatística – National Statistics Institute) between March and December 2020 there was a total contraction of companies' invoicing of 14.3%, compared to the same period of the previous year. More recent data from this same study show that 62% of participating companies said they had recorded a drop in their turnover in the first half of 2020 compared to the same period a year earlier [2]. In the third quarter of 2020, Portugal was the third country in the European Union with the largest increase in business insolvency [3].

Faced with this dark scenario, the question that arises is: How can companies rise from this serious economic crisis, which continues to worsen progressively, and which is already pointed out by the World Economic Forum as the most serious since the Great Depression of the 1930s [4]?

To survive the current economic situation, companies will have to show great resilience. This quality "is often understood as the degree to which a given system is able to tolerate financial, ecological, social and/or cultural changes - to reorganize itself around a new set of structures and processes" [5]. Thus, when resilience is indeed achieved, the system will be one step ahead of where it was before it suffered the impact [1].

However, e-commerce has a less luminous side. To avoid product damage, and the consequent displeasure of consumers, the goods come dipped in plastic [6]. This problem is added to the environmental pollution generated, due to a lack of transport efficiency.

Following a section on how we have plastic in excess, this study continues with the presentation of the methodology where the different fieldwork is addressed (survey, interview, and analysis of the sustainability of packaging and transportation practices through purchases in online stores). Next, the ecological problems raised by e-commerce, i.e., excess plastic and CO_2 emissions, are presented. Based on these, concrete solutions are developed to mitigate them. The positive impact of corporate responsibility on a brand's reputation was also analyzed. Environmentally conscious brands achieve consumer loyalty, which ultimately has a positive impact on profit. After that, a survey is conducted to listen to the opinion of residents in Portugal concerning the sustainability of e-commerce. The analysis of the results was performed using descriptive statistics and inferential statistics, through hypotheses tests (chi-square).

Finally, a case study was conducted on SONAE MC (the biggest Portuguese retail group), in which its environmental performance was analyzed. Finally, a detailed action plan is developed for the electrification of a company's fleet. This case study is also supported by an interview conducted with Pedro Lago, the Director of Projects and Circular Economy, at SONAE MC, whose contribution was valuable, demystifying common myths in this area and giving a concrete view of what is and can be done on the ground.

2 Background on Plastic in Excess

There are several characteristics of plastic that make it so desired and indispensable. These characteristics include flexibility, low cost, and durability [7].

However, these same features lead us to use it and discard it, and due to its durability, it will remain for many years in the environment [8], which raises serious ecological problems.

Some of the harmful effects of plastic are the contamination of marine food chains, soils, and oceans, which has an impact on the tourism sector and generates costs to requalify the affected spaces [8].

In terms of transportation, home deliveries associated with e-commerce allow the reduction of CO_2 emissions when associated with long-distance deliveries [9]. This happens since each customer's individual travel to the physical store is avoided. Instead, a single transport supplies an entire neighbourhood. The main problem lies in deliveries of "last kilometer" that generate congestion and high emissions in urban centres. In addition, fast deliveries, as well as subscription services that make the delivery free, "results in infrequent shipments of only one item, thus contributing to more carbon emissions and packaging waste" [10].

3 Methodology

This work required an extensive literary review at the level of the subjects addressed, to bring together the best solutions to the problems listed. In addition, it will fill a gap in the literature as it provides an action plan for companies to make e-commerce more sustainable. The survey addresses a current and still little addressed theme – sustainability of e-commerce in Portuguese companies. In addition, it is important to refer to the representativeness of our sample - 409 responses were obtained, leading to a 95% confidence margin. Inferential statistics were done namely hypotheses tests. Another contribution to the literature is the concrete action plan of how to implement measures to mitigate the problems presented.

Regarding fieldwork, first, some purchases were made at online stores to know the packaging and transport practices of the market, the most relevant ones having been selected. To make this analysis more enlightening, the respective act of unpacking was recorded on video. These videos were used to make a brief description of what was observed (packaging of products, materials used). To support this study, an online survey (Google Forms) was conducted aimed at the population living in Portugal, with the purpose of knowing their perception of sustainability in online purchases. This survey was open for 18 days, it included 21 questions and had 409 answers. It was divulged to the public using the authors' social networks. In addition, with the convenience sample an objective was to obtain a diversified sample in terms of location. Data analysis was not restricted to a mere description of the data (descriptive statistics), but we sought to follow a scientific approach with the execution of inferential statistics (the chi-square test).

Finally, an online interview was carried out on March 30, 2021, with a duration of 30 min, with the Director of Sustainability and Circular Economics Projects of SONAE

MC, Pedro Lago. The initial contact was established via email, which was answered with high brevity and promptness. The atmosphere of the interview was informal, with a great openness to the question-and-debate of ideas. This interview contributed significantly to the content of this study given the practical and theoretical knowledge of the interviewee regarding the theme under analysis.

4   Field Work Results

4.1   Results of the Analysis of Market Practices in Terms of Packaging

To evaluate this practice in e-commerce, we made some orders at different sites whose results are summarized in Table 1.

Table 1. Summary of the observed packaging practices in the experiment done

	The outer packaging was plastic
H&M	Inside these, each piece of clothing came inside a plastic bag
	Note that in the second outer package there was only one pair of socks that fit perfectly in the first one
Continente - "Home" Area	The bed linen came in a cardboard box, inside which the clothes came inside the traditional plastic bags used to accommodate this type of items
	The items came inside two plastic bags like the ones used in the store
Continente Store	It should be noted that inside the second bag came only a small package with a sample of a sauce that came as a gift
	This item fit perfectly inside the first bag which contained only a small frying pan, a lighter, and a small box of cream (also a gift)

4.2   Case Study

In 2001, Continente launched its e-commerce website, and at that time only about 2.1% of Portuguese people shopped online [11]. Continente is currently the leader in online food retail and has further consolidated more that position in 2020 when SONAE MC had an 80% increase in online sales [12].

SONAE MC is a business group with a strong focus on social responsibility, as communicated by the company itself: "Sonae believes that its businesses may contribute to the promotion of the social and cultural well-being of the communities where it operates, acting in six priority axes: Environmental awareness, social solidarity, science and innovation, education and culture" [13]. These sustainability efforts have not been in vain, since in 2020 Continente was elected as "Environmental Trust Mark" for the 11th consecutive time [14]. In 2019, Continente saved 3.9 thousand tons of plastic of fossil origin, committing to bring forward to 2025 the goal set by the European Union (EU) for 2030 of reducing, as much as possible, the use of this type of materials. Concerning e-commerce, the retailer has been taking several actions to make it more sustainable, having implemented measures such as bags that are 100% recyclable and made of 80% recycled plastic, a commitment to reduce the number of bags used in each delivery, since if people return the bags received, in the next delivery, their value is refunded" [15].

In face of this scenario, Continente is a true case study of corporate social responsibility. Nevertheless, we can identify some flaws.

4.3 Interview

Pedro Lago, Director of Sustainability Projects and the Circular Economy, at SONAE MC, was interviewed. The greatest contribution of this dialogue was the deconstruction of myths such as paper being the perfect substitute for plastic and the conclusion that there is no universal recipe to promote the sustainability of e-commerce but, instead, each company should act according to its reality. This interview led to a reformulation of the solutions presented in the study on the issue of substituting plastic for paper.

The following is a summary of the interview with Pedro Lago.

Continente has been trying to make the plastic bags used in e-commerce more sustainable by using 80% recycled plastic, which also means 20% of virgin plastic. Wouldn't paper bags be a more sustainable alternative, even taking into account that they already produce and sell them in the online store? "Many people assume that plastic is worse than paper, and this is highly debatable. Plastic has one big problem compared to paper - if it goes into the ocean it takes a long time to break down. But that is only part of the process. The most scientific analysis looks at the entire life cycle from production to end-of-life, thus analyzing the entire environmental footprint. In most cases, plastic beats paper. Although it comes from renewable sources, these sources are essential in the fight against climate change. Forests rescue carbon, paper production implies the wearing down of forests and this process is not always regenerative. From an energy consumption point of view, it takes much more energy to produce paper than to produce plastic. These are just a few points. It is not linear that it is a good move to replace plastic with paper. Such a replacement will depend on the situation. For example, Continente replaces plastic straws for its juices, widely consumed by children on beaches, with paper straws. In this case, we did not even do a life cycle analysis because we know that the probability of it ending up in the ocean is high. A plastic bag is not the same thing, since they are usually put in the ecopoints. In our view, the way forward is to decrease the consumption of virgin plastic and promote recyclability. We believe that if plastics are recycled, they are an excellent material".

Would it be possible, from a logistical point of view, to combine two orders with the same address, placed in different carts in the same delivery? "Ideally, yes. However, this is not always possible due to the ergonomics of the applications themselves. What Continente is trying to do is to make the routes more efficient and have the best possible consolidation of loads, to minimize transportation costs."

Why do orders have free shipping only from 30€? Don't you think that a higher value could motivate to reduce the frequency of consumption, but increase the quantity of each order? "First, it is important to realize that the amount paid for the delivery of a product does not fully cover the associated transportation costs. The vehicle itself must have refrigeration areas to keep the food fresh. In addition, it is necessary to combine these values with the business and the competition itself. Often, calculations are made to understand what the consumer's purchasing levels are, and in practical terms, there may be no difference between these two values (30€ and 50€). Therefore, this is a difficult balance to strike."

How was the bag take-back campaign received? "This type of implemented process has a double effect. On the one hand, it ensures that the bags are recycled and therefore not lost in such a lifecycle assessment, because by being reimbursed, people will more easily join this campaign. Another intangible advantage is the message conveyed to the consumer himself that there is a new life at the end of the use of his waste."

What do you intend to do in the future to make transportation greener? "We are looking to insert the "fleet electrification" movement. It is something that is still in the testing phase, as there are already several electric vehicles. The problem faced is that there are still quite a few limitations when it comes to the reach of this type of vehicle."

4.4 Survey Results - Inferential Statistics

In terms of descriptive statistics some interesting numbers may be communicated: 70% of young people (up to 30 years old) consider online shopping green compared to 40% of older people (over 50 years old); 76% of young people said they intend to decrease their online consumption post-pandemic; of those who consider that online orders come excessively packed in plastic, more than half do not reuse it; of those who consider that online orders come excessively wrapped in plastic, 38% still held the view that they are environmentally friendly at the end of the survey; people who shop less online are the ones who consider it most sustainable; among those who reuse plastic, some practices are: packaging products for sale, using large air bubbles to keep the shape of the bags, storing household products, school projects with children, rubbish bags, and handicrafts. As for the safety provided by plastic, opinions were divided. 48.6% stated that they had already received products ordered in the same cart on different days. Finally, some suggestions made to make online orders more sustainable were: replace plastic by paper or other biodegradable materials, adjust the size of packages, manage carts better and use eco-friendly vehicles.

To analyze whether there is an association between different variables, some chi-square tests were performed.

4.4.1 Frequency of Purchase and the Perceived Sustainability of Online Shopping

Null hypothesis: There is no association between purchase frequency and perceived sustainability of online shopping; Alternative Hypothesis: There is an association between purchase frequency and the perceived sustainability of online shopping.

The null hypothesis was verified. We verified the null hypothesis in some other chi-square tests, meaning that "There is no association between place of residence and perceived sustainability of online shopping" and "There is no association between Gross

Average Monthly Income and perceived sustainability of online shopping". Again, no statistically significant association was found in the following:

Null hypothesis: "There is no association between having already received, on different days, products ordered in the same cart and the perceived sustainability of online shopping". Alternative hypothesis: "There is an association between having already received, on different days, products ordered in the same cart and the perceived sustainability of online shopping" (Table 2).

Table 2. Chi-square statistic calculation

O	E	O-E	I(O-E) I-0,5	(IO-EI-0,5) ^2	(IO-EI-0,5) ^2/E
101	99,41	1,59	1,09	1,18	0,01
94	95,59	−1,59	1,09	1,18	0,01
107	108,59	−1,59	1,09	1,18	0,01
106	104,41	1,59	1,09	1,18	0,01
TOTAL					0,04

As the degree of freedom is equal to 1, the corresponding comparative value (for a margin of error of 5%) is 3.841. Thus, the null hypothesis is verified, which means that there does not seem to be a relationship between the variables analyzed, which are seen to be independent.

5   Solutions for a More Sustainable E-commerce

5.1   Better Plastic Life Cycle Management

It is common to assume that paper is a better material than plastic. However, according to Pedro Lago, with whom we conducted an interview, paper comes from a very useful renewable source in combating climate change - forests rescue CO_2 - and paper production is synonymous with their wear and tear. In addition, paper production requires a huge consumption of water, an increasingly scarce resource, and energy, being this higher than that required by plastic.

Having said that, the solution to the problems associated with plastic does not go through implementing a measure that will bring a huge problem behind it – deforestation. Instead, better management of the use of plastic is needed, based on a circular economy perspective, focusing on its reuse and recyclability, progressively reducing the consumption of virgin matter. An example of this is Continente that has renewed its bags, which now incorporate 80% recycled plastic and are 100% recyclable. For this measure to be feasible, it will be necessary to increase the recycling capacity of countries and adopt legal measures, such as the mandatory separation of waste.

5.2   Circular Economy

Generally, companies try to get rid of their responsibility for the management of packaging waste, claiming that this is a State responsibility [16]. In a circular economy approach, the company takes responsibility for the waste it produces, seeking to continuously reuse materials and prioritizes the use of renewable resources [17]. Furthermore, the company should seek to create durable products, slow the resource consumption cycle, and promote recycling at the end of a product's life.

5.3   Decrease/Replace the Use of Plastic

As the buying experiences already mentioned have shown, orders often incorporate plastics that can be eliminated, such as bags that separate different items of clothing, as these are also not used in physical shops.

However, for some items, such as jewelry, such a separation is necessary to avoid damage to products. Such a measure is appropriate. Additionally, because the plastics used for this purpose are single-use, paper, due to its biodegradability, presents itself as a better solution in this particular case. Other ways to eliminate plastic used in product packaging, namely air bubbles, include adjusting the size of packages to the volume of orders, which eliminates the need to fill empty spaces. However, it is not always possible to get a package the exact size of the order. In these cases, empty spaces can be filled using cardboard tubes and recycled paper.

5.4   Efficiency in Transport

Transport can be optimized in two main ways: better use of space, which is achieved by adjusting the size of packages so that they take up less space; renewal of fleets by less polluting vehicles such as electric cars, cargo bicycles, tricycles, drones, and delivery droids. The latter two, being unmanned, have a lower energy consumption. For the application of these measures to be feasible, parcels will have to be pre-sorted and then allocated to the most appropriate means of transport according to size and weight.

5.5   Conceptual Innovations

As regards urban deliveries, parcels are traditionally delivered to the customer's home, neighbors or workplace. Regarding the origin, a parcel can be shipped from traditional urban distribution centers or from alternative points within cities such as micro-hubs, which allows for a decreasing of the distance between the origin and destination of parcels and, consequently, CO_2 emissions diminish, contributing to the achieving of excellent customer service results with speed of delivery being the main reason for e-commerce success.

5.6   Innovation Associated with Information Systems

This strategy aims to take full advantage of available technologies, such as GPS, databases, and mobile applications, which allow consumers to receive real-time information about the delivery of their parcels and provide great flexibility. In addition, many apps allow consumers to turn their homes into local collection points for their neighbors' parcels.

6 Practical Application of the Suggested Measures

6.1 Action Timeline

Figure 1 synthesizes the measures mentioned above. For these measures to produce the desired result, proper planning is necessary. Figure 2 consists of an action plan that defines the person responsible, start and end date as well as the budget for the measures presented. This program can be adopted by any interested company.

The first measure to be taken is the transition to a circular business model, which is the basis for the application of all other sustainability measures, i.e., only after rethinking the business from a circular perspective can we move on to other measures. One of the ways to implement this business approach is through the recycling of the waste generated and delivered to the consumer, which will have a cost of 63€/tonne [18]. This task is left to the manager due to his global understanding of the business.

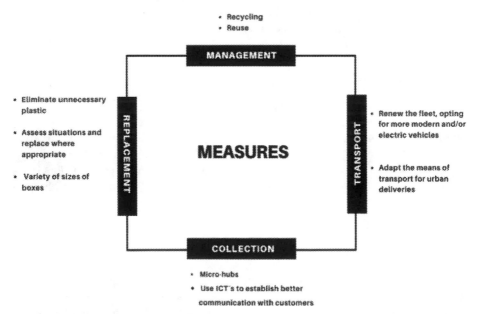

Fig. 1. Map summarizing the different sustainability strategies that companies can adopt (own elaboration)

Concerning packaging, the company should have different sized boxes so that each order can be assigned to the most suitable packaging according to its volume. A choice of eight models of different sizes gives an average of 22.59 euros [19]. However, it will never be possible to obtain a diversity of boxes in such a way as to always have a box of the exact size for each order. In this sense, to fill vacant spaces, companies can use cardboard cylinders, whose unit price is around 0.62€ unit [20]. Since it is a complementary measure to the previous one, it will start at the same time.

Measure	Responsible	Start date	End date	Estimated budget
Transition to a circular business model	Manager	1 June 2022	Continuous process (successive search for better alternatives)	63€/tone
Package size adjustment	Logistic Director	1 September 2022	Life sentence	22,59€/pack
Carton Cylinders	Director of Warehousing	1 Septemberr 2022	Life sentence	0,62€/unit.
New forms of transport-drone	Financial Manager	1 September2023	31 November 2023	690€ per week
New forms of transport-electric tricycle	Financial Manager	1 january 2024	Continuous process	300€/unit.
Micro-hub	Logistic Director	1 September 2024	Continuous process	2 700€/unit

Fig. 2. Action plan (own elaboration)

The adaptation of the means of transport to the type of cargo can be done using alternative means of transport such as tricycles, drones, and delivery droids. As this is an expensive technology, renting drones is more viable than purchasing them, although it is not within the reach of every company. The cost of renting a drone is, on average, €690 per week [21]. Since this is a rental contract, the person responsible for this task is the financial manager. The start date will be in September 2023, since, as it is a new technology, it is expected that prices will decrease over time. Additionally, taking into account this cost, the project should be re-evaluated after 3 months. In what concerns delivery droids, as they are a technology still under development and not very available, it should be something to study in the future. Another means of transport more accessible to Portuguese companies is the electric tricycle, which will have a base unit cost of 3000€ [22].

To optimize deliveries in city centres, the option of introducing micro hubs that enable people to pick up their orders during their daily commute was also presented. This measure will cost approximately 1700€ [23] per micro hub, should be borne by the logistics director and will start eight months after the start of the previous measure.

6.2 Fleet Electrification Plan

A plan will be presented for the electrification of a company fleet. Some assumptions: currently there are, on average, five vehicles in the 71 stores with online trading, which totals 355 vehicles; We get to sell each vehicle for 20,000€; On average, each new vehicle will be purchased for $40,000.

Plan 1: Purchase of Vehicles: The expected duration of this process is 10 years. During this period, 8 vehicles per quarter will be purchased, and there will be an adjustment in the following year, in which a total of 35 vehicles will be purchased. The distribution of the new vehicles will be done considering the stores' order flow.

During the first year we expect to sell quarterly, 8 vehicles at 20,000€ each, which totals 160,000€ per quarter. As for the projections of deliveries, during the first year, a value of 36,000€ is expected, considering 6000 orders at 6€ each. Therefore, the expected revenue totals 196,000€. As for the purchase of electric vehicles, a cost of

320,000€ per quarter is expected, considering that the 8 vehicles purchased will cost 40,000€ each. In short, the cash flow is negative by 124,000€.

Plan 2: Eight-year Lease: In the first 8 years, 11 vehicles will be acquired per quarter, and there will be an adjustment in the following year, in which 3 vehicles will be acquired.

As for plan 2, in which the financing modality is car leasing, the projected value of sales is 220,000€, assuming that 11 vehicles will be sold at 20,000€ each. Since the financing model is leasing, there will be an initial down payment of 1,278,000€.

Considering an anticipated quarterly rent of 85,657.51€, for the first year, the expected amount to be paid is 256,972.53€. Analyzing the results, it is possible to conclude that the quarterly value of revenues and expenses are respectively 220,000€ and 256,972.53€. In short, the quarterly cash flow is negative by 36,972.53€. Therefore, for the first year, based on these projections and based on SONAE MC Group profit in 2020 of 139M€ [13] considering the above-mentioned values, plan 1 and plan 2, will cause, in the first year, a profit contraction of 496,000€ and 147,890.12€, respectively.

Although this investment will cause a loss, companies must reduce their environmental footprint. Moreover, with the growing consumer attention, it becomes imperative that companies adopt a responsible attitude, which will have repercussions in the improvement of their reputation and, consequently, their brand becomes more valued and able to attract demanding consumers at this level. Hence, it is not, by far, a lost or bad investment.

The company should know its available resources well in order to adopt the best project that will allow it to directly and immediately bear the financial burden of the acquisitions (project 1) or resort to financing (project 2). To cover the losses presented, the company can adopt two strategies, such as entries from new partners (issue of shares) or resort to the value accumulated in free reserves, which by law can be mobilized at any time. According to the SONAE Group Report of Accounts 2021, in 2020, 3,763,264.75€ of net profit for the period was used to increase these reserves [24].

This plan can be adjusted and used by any company, adapting the number of vehicles, their cost, expected sales, and credit simulation.

7 Conclusions

This work highlighted the possibility of making e-commerce more sustainable by analyzing the market practices of some Portuguese companies regarding transportation and packaging. In this sense, several solutions were proposed, namely adjusting the size of the package to the volume of orders, eliminating the need to fill vacant spaces within them, and optimizing the space of transport vehicles.

A circular business approach was also proposed, with a focus on reusing and recycling the waste generated by companies. To make transportation environmentally effective, a detailed action plan for replacing fossil-fueled fleets with zero-emission vehicles was presented. To achieve this goal, companies should adopt the means of transport to the delivery location and the size and weight of the order. For example, tricycles can be used to transport light and small packages within cities. In this same context, companies will be able to use drones and delivery droids that have low energy consumption. Micro-hubs are an innovative alternative in terms of reception, allowing the customer to pick up their order, at a strategically chosen point in the city, avoiding purposeful travels to their home. This can also be achieved through the use of ICT that enables real-time communication between the company and the customer, which allows the customer to indicate an alternative delivery address, such as a neighbor's if he realizes that he will not be at home to receive it.

The solutions presented seek to align companies with the Sustainable Development Goals (SDGs). In this sense, this study presents solutions that should be adapted, with the utmost urgency, to each company's context.

The survey demonstrated a weak ability, by the sample, to identify sustainability issues in e-commerce since the hypothesis tests revealed that consumers who recognized the excess of plastic do not associate this issue with the lack of sustainability of the order. On the other hand, the same type of test also showed that shoppers do not relate the fact that they receive on different days products ordered in the same cart with a lack of sustainability.

In conclusion, it is important to emphasize that there are no miracle recipes to face the sustainability challenges raised by e-commerce. Each solution has its pros and cons, and it is up to each manager to search for the different alternatives and choose the most appropriate for his business model. However, there is evidence that the Covid-19 pandemic is to have lasting effects on consumer preferences for sustainable companies [25]. In an age where everything seems to be getting smarter [26], digital marketing [27] and e-commerce firms will have to follow this trend. Hence, marketing and strategy will have to change for the better and for the long term. We hope, with our study, to have shown a way forward in that respect.

References

1. Guimarães, P.: A preliminary assessment of the resilience of portugal's commercial fabric to the covid19 pandemic. Revista Brasileira de Gestão e Desenvolvimento Regional [Brazilian magazine of management and regional development] 16(4), 284–293 (2020). https://www.scopus.com/record/display.uri?eid=2-s2.0-85099416830&origin=resultslist&sort=plff&src=s&sid=d50d78fa8a474456c4ad58c2f73cfb4d&sot=b&sdt=b&sl=114&s=TITLE-ABS KEY%28A+preliminary+assessment+of+the+resilience+of+portugal%27s+commercial+fabric+to+the+covid-19+pandemic%29&relpos=0&citeCnt=0&searchTerm=
2. INE: Acompanhamento do impacto social e económico da pandemia - 48.° reporte semanal [follow-up of the social and economic impact of covid-19 – 48° weekly report]. Síntese INE @ Covid-19. [follow-up of the social and economic impact of covid-19 – 48° weekly report. Synthesis @ Covid-19]. Accessed 14 Mar 2021 (2021). https://www.ine.pt/xportal/xmain?xpid=INE&xpgid=ine_destaques&DESTAQUES dest_boui=486492317&DESTAQUESmodo=2&xlang=p
3. Eurostat: Quarterly registrations of new businesses and declarations of bankruptcies – statistics. Accessed 19 Mar 2021 (2021). https://ec.europa.eu/eurostat/statistics-explained/index.php?title=Quarterly_registrations_of_new_businesses_and_declaratons_of_bankruptcies_-statistics#Quarterly_comparison_in_EU_and_euro_area
4. Vince, A.: COVID-19, five months later. Hrvatski Lijecnicki Zbor 142(3–4), 55–63 (2020). https://translate.google.com/translate?hl=ptPT&sl=hr&tl=en&u=https%3A%2F%2Fhrcak.srce.hr%2F238504&prev=search&sandbox=1. https://doi.org/10.26800/LV-142-3-4-11

5. Kärrholm, M., Nylund, K., Prieto de la Fuente, P.: Spatial resilience and urban planning: Addressing the interdependence of urban retail areas. Cities **36**, 121–130 (2012). https://www.sciencedirect.com/science/article/pii/S0264275112001898. https://doi.org/10.1016/j.cities.2012.10.012
6. Lu, S., Yang, L., Liu, W., Jia, L.: User preference for electronic commerce overpackaging solutions: implications for cleaner production. J. Clean. Prod. **258**, 120936. (2020). https://www.sciencedirect.com/science/article/pii/S0959652620309835?via%3Dihub. https://doi.org/10.1016/j.jclepro.2020.120936
7. Heidbreder, L. M., Bablok, I., Drews, S., Menzel, C.: Tackling the plastic problem: a review on perceptions, behaviors, and interventions. Sci. Total Environ. **668**, 1077–1093 (2019). https://www.sciencedirect.com/science/article/pii/S0048969719309519?via%3Dihub. https://doi.org/10.1016/j.scitotenv.2019.02.437
8. Galloway, T., et al.: Science-based solutions to plastic pollution. One Earth **2**(1), 5–7 (2020). https://www.sciencedirect.com/science/article/pii/S259033222030004X. https://doi.org/10.1016/j.oneear.2020.01.004
9. Escursell, S., Llorach-Massana, P., Roncero, M.B.: Sustainability in e-commerce packaging: a review. J. Clean. Prod. **280**, 124314 (2021). https://www.sciencedirect.com/science/article/pii/S0959652620343596. https://doi.org/10.1016/j.jclepro.2020.124314
10. DHL: Rethinking packaging: DHL trend report discovers how e-commerce era drives wave of sustainability and efficiency [Press release]. 12 September 2019. https://www.dhl.com/global-en/home/press/press-archive/2019/rethinking-packaging-dhl-trend-report-discovers-how-e-commerce-era-drives-wave-of-sustainability-and-efficiency.html
11. Monteiro, A.C.: Continente turns 16 years of e-commerce. Three questions to ... Pedro Santos, Head of Ecommerce at Sonae MC. Hipersuper. 10 January 2017. https://www.hipersuper.pt/2017/01/10/continente-faz-16-anos-de-ecommerce-tres-perguntas-a-pedro-santos-head-of-ecommerce-da-sonae-mc/
12. Sonae, M.C.B.: Annual results 2020 (2021). Accessed 11 Apr 2021. from easonaemc4t20_pt_2641485896053059347cc7.pdf
13. Sonae: Institutional presentation 9 Mar 2019 (2019). https://www.sonae.pt/pt/sonae/media/publicacoes/click.php?id=66
14. Responsible Plastic Continente: Continente is an Environmentally Trusted Brand for the 11th time in a row (2020). Accessed 27 Mar 2021. https://plasticoresponsavel.continente.pt/continente-e-marca-de-confianca-ambiente-pela-11a-vez-consecutiva/
15. Sonae: Stronger, faster, better. Annual Report 2020 (2020). https://web3.cmvm.pt/sdi/emitentes/docs/PC78749.pdf
16. Ajwani-Ramchandani, R., Figueira, S., Torres de Oliveira, R., Jha, S., Ramchandani, A., Schuricht, L.: Towards a circular economy for packaging waste by using new technologies: The case of large multinationals in emerging economies. J. Clean. Prod. **281**, 125139 (2021). https://www.sciencedirect.com/science/article/pii/S0959652620351830. https://doi.org/10.1016/j.jclepro.2020.125139Resource-recycling (2021). Prices for most recycled plastics continue to rise. Accessed 5 May 2021 https://resource-recycling.com/recycling/2021/02/16/prices-for-most-recycled-plastics-continue-to-rise/
17. Bocken, N.M.P., de Pauw,I., Bakker,C., van der Grinten, B.: Product design and business model strategies for a circular economy. J. Ind. Product. Eng. **33**(5), 308–320 (2016). https://www.tandfonline.com/doi/full/10.1080/21681015.2016.1172124. https://doi.org/10.1080/21681015.2016.1172124
18. Resource-recycling: Prices for most recycled plastics continue to rise (2021). Accessed 5 May 2021. https://resource-recycling.com/recycling/2021/02/16/prices-for-most-recycled-plastics-continue-to-rise
19. Manutan: Cardboard box - Double fluted – Manutan (2021). Accessed 4 May 2021. https://www.manutan.pt/pt/map/caixa-em-cartao-canelado-duplo-manutan

20. Manutan: Cylindrical shipping pipe (2021). Accessed 4 May 2021. https://www.manutan.pt/pt/map/tubo-de-expedicao-cilindrico-a027105?shopping=true&gclid=Cj0KCQjw4cOEBhDMARIsAA3XDRi-KhAMfbvRkRd-mes0aq_LeIrH-9H_0L3hmQ-Xi40sbWNFjsI0xxUaAo6kEALw_wcB
21. Heliguy: Drone Rental (2021). Accessed May 2021. https://www.heliguy.com/collections/drone-hire#shopify-section-collection-template-rental
22. Alibaba: Auto rickshaw three-wheel electric (2021). Accessed 6 May 2021. https://portuguese.alibaba.com/product-detail/electric-auto-rickshaw-three-wheel50042087052.html?spm=a2700.7724857.normal_offer.d_title.10433c9bTXTgf1
23. Dancover: Storage Tent pro xl 4x10x3, 5x4, 59 m, pvc, cinza (2021). Accessed 9 May 2021. https://www.dancovershop.com/pt/product/tenda-de-armazenagem-pro-4x10x3 5x459m-pvc-cinza.aspx
24. Sonae, MC.C.: Proposal (2021). Accessed 5 May 2021. https://www.sonae.pt/fotos/ag/02.ag20212propostascasonaesgpsponto2_vce_18668604426064f9c17d511.pdf
25. He, H., Harris, L.: The impact of Covid-19 pandemic on corporate social responsibility and marketing philosophy. J. Bus. Res. **116**, 176–182 (2020)
26. Matos, A., Pinto, B., Barros, F., Martins, S., Martins, J., Au-Yong-Oliveira, M.: Smart cities and smart tourism: what future do they bring? In: Rocha, Á., Adeli, H., Reis, L.P., Costanzo, S. (eds.) WorldCIST'19 2019. AISC, vol. 932, pp. 358–370. Springer, Cham (2019). https://doi.org/10.1007/978-3-030-16187-3_35
27. Teixeira, S., Martins, J., Branco, F., Gonçalves, R., Au-Yong-Oliveira, M., Moreira, F.: A Theoretical analysis of digital marketing adoption by Startups. In: Proceedings of the CIMPS 2017. Mejia, J. et al. (eds.), Trends and Applications in Software Engineering, Advances in Intelligent Systems and Computing (Book of the AISC series), vol. 688, pp.94–105, Springer, Cham (2017). https://doi.org/10.1007/978-3-319-69341-5_9

Opportunities and Challenges for Becoming Montañita in a Smart City

Datzania Villao[1] ⓘ, Teresa Guarda[1](✉) ⓘ, Andrés Padilla[1] ⓘ, and Luis Mazón[2] ⓘ

[1] Universidad Estatal Península de Santa Elena, La Libertad, Ecuador
apadilla@upse.edu.ec
[2] BiTrum Research Group, León, Spain

Abstract. The rapid and disorganized growth of cities, generates urban expansion and produces a new urban aesthetic, which becomes the expression of economic, social and political transformations. In this current and future development scenario, the idea of smart cities is developed, cities capable of solving, or at least preventing, urban problems with the help of technological devices and platforms in order to improve the quality of life of its inhabitants. Montañita, one of the most visited communities in Ecuador by national and foreign tourists, aims to be a smart city as long as the opportunities that currently exist are taken into account and various challenges faced by the community are overcome. That is why the objective of the paper was to identify the opportunities and challenges that this community has to become in a digital city. A qualitative research was conducted aimed at identifying opportunities and challenges that Montañita has to become in a digital city. For which a documentary review and information gathering was carried out with local agents. As a result, several opportunities were identified, such as the regulations in the country, the projects for technological infrastructure that the local government will undertake in the coming months, and the economy of the community based on tourism. However, several challenges were also detected, such as conflicts among the different government levels, and lack of basic infrastructure, which must be overcome in order to convert Montañita into a digital city.

Keywords: Smart city · Technological transformation · Governance · Tourism · Opportunities · Challenges

1 Introduction

The strong urban growth and development in recent years, linked to important technological transformations, has put cities at the center of a multitude of proposals, projects and actions of all kinds, trying to respond to their needs. In this current and future development scenario, cities are going to be the main engines of change and the so-called smart cities emerge here as a new urban transformation necessary to achieve true sustainable, economic, environmental and social development [1].

© Springer Nature Switzerland AG 2021
T. Guarda et al. (Eds.): ARTIIS 2021, CCIS 1485, pp. 614–628, 2021.
https://doi.org/10.1007/978-3-030-90241-4_47

For the first time in human history, the population is concentrated in urban areas. Likewise, rural areas have the challenge of ensuring food sovereignty, as well as the opportunity to internationalize their production, with the urgent need to increase their productivity in all activities, especially agricultural ones; contributing towards the modernization of the agriculture. Given that cities have a great impact on economic and social development, they constitute true platforms where citizens develop their activities, the commercial and productive sectors carry out their tasks, in which numerous products and services are provided. [2].

Although there is no specific definition of what a smart city is, there are numerous studies on comprehensive theoretical frameworks that show the main elements that a smart city needs to have. Some definitions point out that a smart city monitoring and integrating infrastructure such as highways, tunnel bridges, airports, basic services, security, maximizing its resources to have an impact on the quality of life of citizens [3]. Several working definitions have been point out that a smart city uses computer technology to build its basic infrastructure, which includes city management, education, health, security, transportation, in a more connected, communicated and efficient way [4]. It is has also been denoted that a smart city combines ICT with the design and planning of bureaucratic processes and helps to identify innovative solutions for a complex management of a city in order to make a city more livable [5].

In almost all definitions ICT is the common element, which is linked with other dimensions to improve the quality of life for citizens. In fact, given the definition of different authors, some components have been identified that make a city be called smart.

According to Chourabi, a smart city needs eight components. They are administration and organization, technology, governance, political context, people and communities, economy, infrastructure and natural environment [6]. Sujeta also suggests dimensions such as the social part, management, economy, the legal part, technology and sustainability [7]. In the same way, Maccani emphasizes that a smart city needs technological infrastructure, social infrastructure, public and private fusion, governance, management and intelligent information services [8]. Dustart also points out that a smart city must have physical infrastructure, compounded by smart environment, smart mobility, innovation ecosystems compounded by people, smart economy and quality of life that include elements such as smart governance and smart life [9].

In Ecuador, although there is no specific definition about smart city, there is a clear idea of what a digital territory is. Digital Territory is any territorial unit that owns a series of services that are supported by the use and development of ICT, these include telecommunications, audio and video, internet, data or information transmission services and others. Any territorial unit, whether urban or rural, will be considered as digital territory. The purpose of a Digital Territory is to promote development of local governments by improving the quality of life of citizens. Given this definition, in the country, Telecommunications Ministry has developed a model called digital territory model, which is composed of three transversal components such as Infrastructure, Information Systems and Regulations and several fundamental components such as e-government, essential thematic elements and productive elements [10].

Among the most important cases of digital territories in Ecuador are; the city of Quito, Guayaquil, Cuenca and the Yachay project. In the case of Quito, capital of Ecuador, with QuitoTeConecta project, it provides free Wi-Fi internet access to citizens in non-residential or mixed areas such as public squares, parks and public transport stations. The content service generates the implementation of applications to public services at a cultural, social, tourist and economic level. In the case of Guayaquil, one of the largest cities in the country, Mayor of Guayaquil signed on October 7, 2014, the contract for the installation of 6,000 Wifi internet points, for the same number of sectors located in different areas of this city. Guayaquil Ciudad Digital project, has implemented various educational projects, with computer equipment to schools and colleges and the installation of free internet access points, which is another factor to position the city as a digital and inclusive city, improving the quality of life of the population. In the case of Cuenca, it is considered one of the cities with the highest quality of life in Ecuador according to levels of technology, mobility, security and tourism. Cuenca is considered an intermediate and sustainable city due to its size and density and because of its good economic and social development indicators as well [11].

In the case of Yachay Project, it is the first city that has been planned in Ecuador, aim to develop technological innovation to improve the quality of life of Ecuadorians. It is a universit research and industrial town located in the province of Imbabura, San Miguel de Urcuquí town, to north of Ecuador. It began its academic activities in March 2014, with 52 teachers and 415 students. It was created as a scientific and technology development university. The academic offer, the research lines and the training of the students are linked to the areas that the Ecuadorian government has detected as priorities for the change of the productive matrix in the country. It is an autonomous administrative and financial organization, whose operation ensures adequate infrastructure, operation and management. It has a services unit that provides all the services required for the normal operation of a high-tech smart city [12].

Montañita is located in Santa Elena Province in the coastal region of Ecuador. It is located three hours from Guayaquil, along the called Spondylus Route. Recognized as a Surf City because it meets all the requirements that a professional surfer needs and a range of possibilities, especially fun tourism that makes it recognized as one of the most fashionable destinations in South America. This city has grown in recent years, it is one of the most visited communities in Ecuador by national and foreign tourists. It has had a considerable growth in number of tourists in recent years. Regarding its economy, it is a city that has several businesses which are growing very fast, ranging from discos with international standards to gourmet food restaurants, luxury hotels and local handicraft stores. On the other hand, local governments want to undertake technological infrastructure projects in the coming years, added to positive current national regulations make that Montañita can become a digital territory, as long as it can overcome certain challenges as well. That is why, the objective of the research is to identify the opportunities and challenges that this community has to become smart.

The paper is organized as follows: The first section presents the literature review about components of a digital city. The next section shows the methodology to conduct the research, background of Montañita and the opportunities and challenges identified. The last section presents the conclusions, limitations and future research areas.

2   Literature Review

Taking into account the components identified in the Digital territory model developed by Telecommunication Ministry, transversal and fundamental components are the main part of the model. The transversal components are enabling elements that allow generating an ideal and stable scenario that facilitates the development and growth of each of the fundamental components. These components include technological infrastructure, information systems and regulations. On the other hand, fundamental components include e-government, essential thematic elements and productive elements.

2.1   Transversal Components

Technological Infrastructure

Infrastructure is the cornerstone of any digital territory development. The technological infrastructure, understood as the level of connectivity that a city has to access internet and the facilities that it provides to citizens. This will serve as a driver that allows the development of each one of fundamental components. This includes wireless infrastructure, fiber optic channels, and WI-FI networks [13]. This component is essential, since a city is taking the name of smart due to the rapid evolution and implementation of different technologies [14]. In fact, as a city applies more technology in its territory, it will improve the sustainability and quality of life of its inhabitants.

According to Gasson, there are 3 fundamental dimensions for the construction of the technological infrastructure in a city. One is the smart environment, the digital city, and the smart city [15]. The intelligent environment is related to create knowledge and labor force skills, citizenship and consumption. A digital city fundamentally needs a wireless infrastructure that at the moment it merges with the intelligent environment, makes it possible to access services mainly through cell phones. Thus, a smart city provides skills to solve problems.

Information Systems

Information systems are a set of elements oriented to the treatment and administration of data and information, organized and ready for later use, generated to meet a need or purpose [16]. Most of the systems in some cases seek to optimize management and strengthen ties with customers or citizens, and the optimization and modeling of processes in other cases, would be recommended in internal management and towards the citizen, in order to improve their internal processes based on the principle of transparency, to provide all information needed for citizens. Open data are usually in different formats and deal with different topics [17]. These data come usually from public administration and projects that have been financed with public sources or created by a public institution. The purpose of opening data to society is that it can take advantage of it, that is, any person or organization can build on it a new idea that results in new data, knowledge or even services. It is therefore about opening a door to innovation and knowledge as well as offering new business opportunities.

Regulations

Through legal and technical regulations, it seeks to standardize requirements, processes, services and activities that frame the development of digital territories. This regulatory aspect would allow to manage in an orderly and systemic way implications that a digital territory entails and to be able to transfer this concept to all local governments in a country. In the future, initiatives of digital territories would seek not only to be isolated entities but to achieve interaction. To get this, it is important to regulate, among other issues, interoperability [18].

According to Lynn this dimension is also known as governance, which is the entire set of laws, regulations, norms that prohibit or allow government activity for the production and delivery of goods and services [19]. Urban governance refers to the various groups in different territorial areas such as neighborhoods, cities and metropolitan areas.

2.2 Fundamental Components

E-government

E-government emphasizes the use of information technologies and knowledge in the internal processes of government, as well as in the delivery of State products and services to both citizens and companies [20].

E-government describes the use of technologies to facilitate the operation of government and the distribution of government information and services. It works with applications to help the task of the State powers and State institutions. This service is delivered through a large-scale use of technologies such as: telephone, fax, telecommunications networks, surveillance systems, identification by radio-frequency systems and even television and radio.

Essential Thematic Components

Education

The purpose of ICT is to serve as strategic allies to improve the quality of education and help students to develop in a new context of the Information and Communications Society. The equipment and digital content must facilitate learning and make services accessible to any potential recipient, either in person or remotely. It is important to highlight that education is a fundamental aspect of the competitive level of a country and companies. The use of information and communication technologies can improve the efficiency and effectiveness of education at all levels. On the one hand, improving connectivity and collaboration between students themselves and between students and schools, on the other, facilitating access to content and in general, providing unified communications. In fact, the importance of education has been mentioned as one of the factors of the component of people and communities. This factor seeks all smart city projects have more educated and intelligent citizens [21]. In the same way, ICTs in a smart city aim to foster more educated and participatory people in order they even can participate in the design and planning process of smart projects [22].

According to Nam, there are four important aspects in the relationship between humans and smart cities. These are the learning city, the creative city, the human city and the knowledge city, which create the basis for the creation of social infrastructure [23].

In this point, the learning city stands out, as it seeks to create a well-trained workforce, especially in ICTs. The ICTS in the same way, help people in rural areas to access information. For example, the tools that ICTs in education can provide are learning platforms, electronic books and other services.

It has been pointed out that human and social capital merge with the purpose of increasing productivity and innovation in a given place [24]. In addition, in large smart cities, higher-level educational institutions are key to training human capital which is necessary for economic growth of a city.

Mobility

Mobility in cities is an increasingly worrying problem. That is why, this element is one of the most important under the Digital Territory model. Mobility refers to the sustainability, safety and efficiency of transport infrastructure and systems that are essentially terrestrial, as well as local, national and international accessibility [25]. One of the biggest problems in the field of mobility is traffic congestion, which has a very considerable negative impact on the quality of life of citizens, both due to decrease in productivity and the deterioration of air quality, as well as noise pollution.

In general, mobility or sustainable transport refers to those actions of administrations to facilitate access to work, study, services and leisure through alternative mechanisms and means such as on foot, by bike, in ecological vehicles and in public transport. Intelligent mobility goes beyond having normal means of transport to be able to move around, but by using technology they can provide important information to user, such as schedules, traffic flow, this in turn can contribute to reduce accidents, improve public transport and make the parking system much easier [25]. It has also been pointed out that smart mobility is not only about transport infrastructure but also about improving quality of life of people. For example, cities like Paris have encouraged people to walk or use bicycle. There are also several models of intelligent mobility that use electric bikes, scooters that have even become a business alternative in various cities around the world [26].

Basic Services

Technologies such as smart grids, cloud systems, big-data technologies and social net works create opportunities for the launch of new products and services. At the same time, technology is key when it comes to drive operational improvements to reduce costs, generate competitive advantages, improve compliance with regulations, reinforce safety and promote an effective response to climate change and extreme weather conditions. In addition, as the world faces challenges of climate change, having services that do not affect the environment is essential in a smart city. In this sense, many cities are already deploying smart energy management grids as well as integrating renewable energy sources into current electricity grids. This concept is also known as smart energy grid and it is undoubtedly one of the start initiatives in the context of a digital territory model [27]. These ideas are combined with services that help save energy in buildings and infrastructures, or consumers themselves, as well as with intelligent transport systems, which also help optimize energy consumption.

It has been emphasized that to be a smart city it is not enough to provide or deliver a service, but it must have at least investments in infrastructure such as energy, gas, water, transportation, public recreational spaces, neighborhoods, public services, public facilities and others, which contemplate and promote a high quality of life. This idea has a strong link with basic services such as drinking water, sewerage and electricity. These services are directly or indirectly related to human development, social equality and quality of life [28]. The interruption of these services can generate problems in productive capacity of a city and alteration of public and family life. In particular, in drinking water supply, sewerage and sewage treatment, that are services linked to subsistence and quality of life that if lacking, can affect population health or, in extreme cases, compromise life.

Productive Components

The economy is one of the most important factors in smart city projects because it creates value to improve tourism, generate businesses and create jobs. Hence, it has been pointed out that within components for a city to be considered as smart, is the economy, which considers elements such as economic competitiveness, entrepreneurship and fusion of local and world markets [29]. Business is one of the key factors in a smart city. This implies that businesses use technology to improve their productive activities and at the same time have results such as creating more businesses, jobs and improving productivity in general.

The combination of people with skills, companies that innovate and government, can achieve a knowledge economy through social networks of trust and knowledge [30]. One of the best examples of this output is the Yachay project in Ecuador, which is the first city that has been planned in Ecuador and has a purpose technological innovation to improve quality of life of Ecuadorians. Here the efforts of national government, private companies and human resource prepared to carry out research and innovation projects merge [31].

The following Table gives a summary of dimensions of digital territory model created by Telecommunications Ministry of Ecuador.

Table 1. Digital territory model.

Transversal components	Fundamentals components
Technological infrastructure	Digital Government Essential components
	Education, Mobility, Basic Services
Information systems	Productive components
	Tourism, Businesses, Jobs
Legal regulations	

3 Methodology

It has been conducted a qualitative research aimed at identifying the opportunities and challenges that Montañita has to become in a digital city. For which, different processes have been designed and executed such as: documentary review, compilation of information through local agents and analysis and contrast of public government information.

3.1 Montañita Background

Montañita is located in the Santa Elena Province in the coastal region of Ecuador about 60 km northwest of Santa Elena city. Montañita is located in the called Spondylus Route. It is considered the City of Surf because it meets all requirements that a professional surfer needs. In addition, it has a range of possibilities, especially fun tourism that makes it recognized as one of the fashionable destinations in South America [32]. It has approximately 5000 inhabitants and is visited annually by 100,000 national and foreign tourists approximately, which is why it has become one of the most visited communities in Ecuador [33]. It has an extensive beach of 1,400 m. It also takes its name from having a location surrounded by hills and have vegetation at the foot of the sea. Its climate is dry, with temperature about 28 degrees Celsius. The climate is generally hot and temperate throughout the year. In summer, the days are very sunny, where a tourist can enjoy a beautiful sunset on the beach.

Montañita is a mostly peaceful place, with a bohemian touch that can be seen after walking through its streets where it can find all kinds of bars, restaurants, craft shops, ecological cabins, surf lessons, and foreigners. Its citizens live from fishing and crafts, but the main source of income is the tourism. Since 1960, the place became a meeting point for people, usually foreigners, linked or inspired by the hippie movement and other alternative movements, for fun, relax and contact with nature [34]. In those times there was some affinity between the alternative life of these visitors both nationals and foreigners and the community and autonomous structure and organization of the village. The buildings in Montañita continue having a rustic style of the coast, based on cane and straw, although currently, the community has beautiful and comfortable luxury hotels.

3.2 Opportunities and Challenges for Montañita

Technological Infrastructure
In recent years, Ecuador has experienced significant growth in the deployment of infrastructure and an increase in the number of subscriptions in all telecommunications services. The highest growth rate has been experienced by mobile phone service, with a total of 7.5 percentage points in terms of coverage since 2007, reaching 94.9% of population coverage by 2018 [35]. Additionally, between 2009 and 2018, there was a cumulative growth of more than 14% in the number of landlines, reaching more than 15.5 million users in September 2018 [36]. In this sense, Ecuador went from a level of 48% in 2017, to 60.7% of 4G technology coverage in 2021, benefiting almost 11 million of Ecuadorians [37].

This trend is also seen in internet services, particularly in the case of mobile internet, reaching 9.2 million users on September 2018, which means that only 54% of mobile lines have internet. Another emblematic project executed by Telecommunication Ministry, is Community Information Centers, which until May 2021, 886 of these Centers had been promoted nationwide, for which rural and border areas were prioritized, thus benefiting several residents of the country who are far from the cities [38]. One of the benefited communities in precisely Montañita, which has a center that has free internet for the community, where students mainly benefit.

On the other hand, the Ministry of Telecommunications has generated a project to repower current Wi-Fi sites and install 4,478 free Wi-Fi points nationwide until May 2021, in high concentration areas such as parks, squares, markets, commercial places, stadiums, coliseums, universities, nationwide. Only in the Province of Santa Elena there are 4 free points [39]. Regarding the National Fiber Optic Network, the Ministry reported that it grew by 294%. In fact, currently the Fiber Optic Network passes precisely through Spondylus Route where Montañita is located and it is expected that before the end of 2021, The Public Telecommunication Company (CNT) will provide residential internet service in the community [40]. However, there are several private providers that currently supply internet service to both homes and businesses. Moreover, the local Provincial Government has a project called Santa Elena Digital which has several stages and its main purpose is to provide free internet to various communities in the Province. The first stage of the project was to deliver 41,000 tablets to students from public schools in urban and rural sectors. Once the tablets are delivered, Local Provincial Government will install free internet points in several urban and rural communities [41].

Another project that the Municipality of Santa Elena has, is to modernize the electric system in the town. Currently, urban regeneration works are being carried out in the capital city Santa Elena, where the burying of the cables will already be applied and it is expected to extend to the communities in the north of the town, where Montañita is located. This community is expected to receive that benefit in the next years. However, despite the improvement in the technological infrastructure in the country, and the fact that the Fiber Optic Network passes through the Spondylus Route, Montañita still continues to receive internet through an old technology, where there are only 400 users with internet services supplied by CNT.

Regulations

Another opportunity is precisely current regulations in Ecuador. Ecuador has the following legal component that motivate local governments to undertake in smart projects. They are: Electronic Government Plan, which allows initially framing actions of a Digital Territory. Organic Law for the optimization and efficiency of administrative procedures, Organic Law of Transparency and Access to Public Information, Law of Electronic Commerce, Electronic Signatures and Data Messages, Executive Decree 1014 Free Software and Open Standards, Executive Decree 1384 Interoperability, Executive Decree 149 Electronic Government and Simplification of Procedures, Ministerial Agreement-No.-011–2018 National Electronic Government Plan, Ministerial Agreement 012–2016, Electronic Signature, Agreement 166 General Security Scheme of the Information and the National Development Plan [42]. All these regulations undoubtedly strengthen all projects of digital territories in the country. In fact, all these laws promote the active participation of local governments in the development of projects to convert cities into digital territories and there are even facilities through the State Development Bank, to ask for a credit for local governments to undertake in digital development projects. All these regulations aim to ensure local governments can guide institutional efforts towards the development of a community, for the right and efficient use of Information and Communication Technologies and have accessible, useful and timely services for citizens.

Regarding the level of Governance, it is important to highlight that Montañita has several levels of Governance. First, it is governed by the Law on the Organization and Regime of Communes. A commune in Ecuador is defined as any populated center that does not have the category of parish, that exists today or that will be established in the future, and that is known by the name of hamlet, annex, neighborhood, party, community, or any other designation. This level of government has as a purpose to promote community participation that leads to the management of productive, social and political projects that pursue the good life of its inhabitants. Every year the community members elect a president who is in charge of fulfilling the purpose described above.

Second, Montañita is subjected to the jurisdiction of the Manglaralto local Government, an institution that receives a budget from Central Government for projects in the communities. Third, Montañita is also subjected to the Cantonal Government of Santa Elena, since it is located in Santa Elena territory and it is one of the exclusive competence of the Cantonal local Government to plan, together with other public sector institutions and actors of society, the development plans. In addition, the cantonal local government work on issues of urban planning and land use, mobility system, public works, infrastructure, urban roads, provide public services of drinking water, sewerage, wastewater treatment, solid waste management, environmental sanitation, social inclusion, telecommunications and ICT programs. They preserve, maintain and disseminate the architectural, cultural and natural heritage of the territory. They have power to create, modify or suppress by ordinances, rates and special contributions for improvements. The province local Government is another level that cover all Santa Elena Province with the 3 cantons. Finally, on the part of the central government, Montañita administratively depends on the Ministry of Agriculture that supervise that the community follows the main regulations.

Taking into account that there are several levels of government, it has been stated by local actors that each level of government has different purposes and interests, and despite of there is a development community plan, in practice it is difficult to agree on all levels of government to undertake a development project. This is a great problem, since if one level of government has a technological project and does not have enough resources to execute it, it becomes difficult to have support of another level of government.

Essential Thematic elements
Education
Regarding the level of education, Montañita is a community that has a basic education school and a college. Its population on average has secondary studies. However, the number of tourists has a varied level of education. Despite CNT still does not provide residential internet through fiber optics, the majority of homes and economic establishments have internet, especially hotels and restaurants. This is important for the education of

children and young people who are currently receiving virtual classes due to the COVID 19 pandemic. On the other hand, Santa Elena digital project will benefit students from public schools in that community with tablets that the local Province Government will delivery, which will allow continuing closing the digital gap and strengthening ICT learning. In addition, Santa Elena University UPSE, the only public university in the Province, is currently working with the community on projects related to the use of ICTs and tourism development.

Basic Services

Basic services in Montañita have several problems. Regarding electric power, 100% of population have this service, which is provided by the National Electricity Corporation. However, there is still no system that provides drinking water in the community, since the water available comes from nearby wells, whose quality is not good. On the other hand, there are serious problems with the sewerage, since there have been several cases where it has collapsed and caused environmental pollution problems. Regarding mobility, despite the fact that the town is only reached by land, whether by private or public transport, there are still problems in some sections of the E 15 Road, which is a main State road, for which it must be passed to reach the community. However, the Municipality of Santa Elena has stated that projects have already been contracted to repower the sewerage of the community and the construction of a water purification plant and it is expected that in the coming months, work will begin to overcome these two problems.

Productive Components

Economy

Tourism represents a great opportunity for Montañita, since it is a community that has grown in this area in recent years. For instance, as part of the service sector, it offers more opportunities for the emergence of local businesses. Currently, according to the data provided by the President of the Commune, Montañita has 11 tour operators, 116 places of accommodation among hotels, hostels, community hotels, 41 restaurants and 17 bars and fun places, which boosts the economy of this community. Especially, it has a group of accommodation places that satisfies the demand it receives and perceives, in high season all these places are covered to their maximum capacity. Despite being a sector that requires strong investments in infrastructure and equipment, it also uses labor intensively, which is why it offers several jobs and business opportunities for women and young people.

There are a variety of tourist attractions in Montañita that have boosted tourism. Among them is the Montañita Center, which is a more charismatic and cheerful place, with only three blocks in which there are several bars, restaurants, hotels and more, which provide comfort and the best culinary art and cocktail. There is a variety of food from different parts of the world such as Argentine, Israelite, Peruvian, French, Tai and of course typical Ecuadorian food from the coast as well as Vegetarian food. El Tigrillo neighborhood is a unique sector that combines countryside and mountains on the coast. Nature is unspoiled and imperturbable, ideal to escape from the sea and enter another ecosystem and see the beginnings of a subtropical jungle. Surf Point Beach is a special beach for surfers. Here is the Surf Point with right-hand waves with a coral bottom of approximately 3 m, which is an ideal setting to see the best surfers in the world. Here international surf championships are organized every year as well.

The following Table 2 gives a summary of opportunities and challenges that Montañita has to become a smart city.

Table 2. Opportunities and Challenges for Montañita.

Opportunities	Challenges
Legal National regulations	Conflicts among local Governments
Future Technological Infrastructure from local Governments	Lack of Basic Services (Sewerage)
Economy (Tourism)	

4 Conclusions

Although there is no specific definition of what a smart city is, there are several common dimensions that the literature has provided for considering a smart city. Infrastructure one of the main components that includes wireless internet, fiber optic channels, Wi-Fi networks, information systems. Regulations understood as a set of laws, regulations that prohibit or allow governmental activity for production and delivery of goods and services. In the same way, with fundamental components, important areas such as education, mobility and basic services are included. Productive components, refers to the better management of economic resources, especially to improve tourism, trade and job creation.

Montañita, one of the communities most visited by national and foreign tourists, has several opportunities but also challenges to become in a smart city. First, there are technological infrastructure projects from the central and local governments to achieve the basic technological infrastructure in order to the city is considered as smart, and constitutes a fundamental pillar for the adoption of new technologies, expansion of telecommunications services and the development of smart cities. According to current regulations, it encourages the participation of local governments for technological projects. However, having different levels of local governments and taking into account that they have different priorities, there are no general agreements to undertake projects together, which would delay the aspirations of several institutions that, due to lack of budget, do not execute essential projects in the community. On the other hand, the sewerage and drinking water service is deficient, which threat sustainability or the desire to become the city smart. Nevertheless, economy of Montañita is based on tourism that has a wide potential and can be interpreted as an opportunity.

In conclusion, it is necessary for business and local governments to stop looking only at the technical and last line of financial statements and leave their state of comfort and technical-economic conformity that they have been in recent years, to join the changes that are taking place and take a long-term look at these services, more strategic with environmentally-friendly technology that takes care of population demands. The research have certain limitations given that the information was extracted from official documents from the central and local government and from the statements given by the president of the community. Moreover, a field study has not yet been carried out to verify the information from the documentary analysis. This would be an opportunity to carry out field research with the development of more structured data collection instruments. Furthermore, for future research it would be important to analyze the specific role of the actors to build the smart city in Montañita and evaluate the role of the citizen in this process. In relation to governance, it would be interesting to know the relationship between different actors, public and private, and how they would relate to each other.

References

1. Carrillo, F.: El nuevo rol delas ciudades, la smart city: el verdadero reto del S.XXI. Desarrollo y Planificación Estratégica de la Ciudad Inteligente. Instituto Universitario de Análisis Económico y Social, pp. 2–3 (2018)
2. Ministerio de Telecomunicaciones y de la Sociedad de la Información. https://www.telecomunicaciones.gob.ec/wp-content/uploads/2019/08/Libro-Blanco-Territorio-Digital-v3-30-Mayo-2018.pdf. Accessed 20 Jun 2021
3. Appio, F., Lima, M., Paroutis, S.: Understanding smart cities: innovation ecosystems, technological advancements, and societal challenges. Tech. Forecast. Soc. Change (142) 1–14 (2019)
4. Lazaroiu, G., Roscia, M.: Definition methodology for the smart cities model. Energy **47**, 326–332 (2012)
5. Dameri, R.: Searching for smart city definition: a comprehensive proposal. Int. J. Comput. Technol. **11**(5), 2544–2551 (2013)
6. Chourabi, H., et al.: Understanding smart cities: an integrative framework. In: 45th Hawaii International Conference on System Sciences. IEEE, pp. 2289–2294 (2012)
7. Sujata, J., Saxena, S., Godbole, T.: Developing smart cities: an integrated framework. Proc. Comput. Sci. **93**, 902–909 (2016)
8. Maccani, G., Donnellan, B., Helfert, M.: A comprehensive framework for smart cities. In: Proceeding of the 2nd International Conference on Smart Gridsand Green IT Systems SMARTGREENS, pp. 53–63 (2013)
9. Dustdar, S., Stefan, N., Ognjen, Š., Smart Cities. The Internet of Things, People and Systems. Springer, Cham (2017). https://doi.org/10.1007/978-3-319-60030-7
10. Ministerio de Telecomunicaciones y de la Sociedad de la Información. https://www.telecomunicaciones.gob.ec/wp-content/uloads/2019/11/LBTD_actualizado_25-11-2019_a.pdf. Accessed 20 Jun 2021
11. El Comercio. https://www.elcomercio.com/actualidad/ecuador/zonas-wifi-gratis-ecuador.html. Accessed 2 May 2021
12. Yachay. https://www.yachaytech.edu.ec/acerca-de/lugar-donde-estoy/. Accessed 6 May 2021
13. Mahmoud, A., Rodzi, A.: The smart city infrastructure development & monitoring. Theoret. Empiric. Res. Urban Manage. **4.2**(11), 87–94 (2009)
14. Serrano, W.: Digital systems in smart city and infrastructure: digital as a service. Smart Cities **1**(1), 134–154 (2018)
15. Gasson, M., Warwick, K.: D12. 2: study on emerging Am I technologies. FIDIS Deliverables **12**(2), 1–85 (2007)
16. Somjit, A., Dentcho, N.: Development of industrial information systems on the Web using business components. Comput. Ind. **50**(2), 231–250 (2003)

17. Kühn, E.: Reusable coordination components: reliable development of cooperative information systems. Int. J. Cooperat. Inf. Syst. **25**(04), 1740001 (2016)
18. Ministerio de Telecomunicaciones. https://www.telecomunicaciones.gob.ec/wp-content/uploads/2019/05/libro-blanco-de-la-sociedad-de-la-informacion-y-del-conocimiento..pdf. Accessed 03 May 2021
19. Lynn, J., Laurence, E., Carolyn, J., Hill, J.: Studying governance and public management: challenges and prospects. J. Publ. Admin. Res. Theory. **10**(2), 233–262 (2000)
20. Haldenwang, V.: Electronic government (e-government) and development. Eur. J. Dev. Res. **16**(2), 417–432 (2004)
21. Alawadhi, S., et al.: Building understanding of smart city initiatives. In: Scholl, H.J., Janssen, M., Wimmer, M.A., Moe, C.E., Flak, L.S. (eds.) EGOV 2012. LNCS, vol. 7443, pp. 40–53. Springer, Heidelberg (2012). https://doi.org/10.1007/978-3-642-33489-4_4
22. Przeybilovicz, E., Cunha, M., Souza, F.: The use of information and communication technology to characterize municipalities: who they are and what they need to develop e-government and smart city initiatives. Revista de Administração Pública **52**, 630–649 (2018)
23. Nam, T., Pardo, A.: Conceptualizing smart city with dimensions of technology, people, and institutions. In: Proceedings of the 12th Annual International Digital Government Research Conference: Digital Government Innovation in Challenging Times (2011)
24. Giffinger, R., Haindlmaier, G., Kramar, H.: The role of rankings in growing city competition. Urban Res. Pract. **3**(3), 299–312 (2010)
25. Benevolo, C., Dameri, R., D'auria, M.: Smart Mobility in Smart City Empowering Organizations, vol. 13, p. 28. Springer, Cham (2016). https://doi.org/10.1007/978-3-319-237 84-8_2
26. Mancebo, F.: Smart city strategies: time to involve people. comparing Amsterdam, Barcelona and Paris. J. Urban. Int. Res. Placemaking Urban Sustainabil. **13**(2) 133–152 (2020)
27. Pieroni, A.: Smarter city: smart energy grid based on blockchain technology. Inf. Technol. **8**(1), 298–306 (2018)
28. Rantakokko, M.: Smart city as an innovation engine: case Oulu. Elektrotehniski Vestnik **79**(5), 248 (2012)
29. Anttiroiko, A.-V., Valkama, P., Bailey, S.J.: Smart cities in the new service economy: building platforms for smart services. AI Soc. **29**(3), 323–334 (2013). https://doi.org/10.1007/s00146-013-0464-0
30. Vinod, K., Dahiya, B.: Smart economy in smart cities. Smart Economy in Smart Cities, pp. 3–76. Springer, Singapore (2017). https://doi.org/10.1007/978-981-10-1610-3
31. Presidencia de la República. https://www.presidencia.gob.cc/rafacl-correa-yachay-cambiara-la-historia-de-la-universidad-ecuatoriana/. Accessed 5 May 2021
32. Ministerio de Turismo. https://www.turismo.gob.ec/montanita-es-declarada-ciudad-de-surf-del-mundo/. Accessed 5 May 2021
33. BBC. https://www.bbc.com/mundo/noticias/2016/03/160308_montanita_lugar_argent inas_asesinadas_peligros_turismo_historias_bm#:~:text=Esta%20peque%C3%B1a%20l ocalidad%20de%20menos,Latina%2C%20Estados%20Unidos%20y%20Europa. Accessed 5 May 2021
34. Ecuador Turístico. https://www.ecuador-turistico.com/2012/05/playas-de-ecuador-montan ita-ecuador.html. Accessed 4 May 2021
35. Ministerio de Telecomunicaciones. https://www.telecomunicaciones.gob.ec/wp-content/upl oads/2016/08/Plan-de-Telecomunicaciones-y-TI..pdf. Accessed 4 May 2021
36. Ministerio de Telecomunicciones. https://www.telecomunicaciones.gob.ec/wp-content/upl oads/2020/01/LBTD-actualizado-14-01-2020.pdf. . Accessed 5 May 2021
37. El Universo. https://www.eluniverso.com/noticias/politica/vianna-maino-esperamos-tener-4817-puntos-wifi-instalados-para-finales-del-2021-en-ecuador-nota/. Accessed 4 May 2021

628   D. Villao et al.

38. Ministerio de Telecomunicaciones. https://www.telecomunicaciones.gob.ec/el-mintel-for talecio-las-bases-de-la-transformacion-y-modernizacion-digital-del-pais/. Accessed 7 May 2021
39. Ministerio de Telecomunicaciones. https://www.telecomunicaciones.gob.ec/gobierno-nac ional-entrega-100-puntos-de-acceso-gratuito-a-internet/. Accessed 4 May 2021
40. CELEC. https://www.celec.gob.ec/transelectric/index.php/produccion-3/red-de-fibra-optica. Accessed 8 May 2021
41. Revista Cool. https://www.planificacion.gob.ec/wp-content/uploads/downloads/2019/09/Agenda-Digital.pdf. Accessed 4 May 2021
42. Ministerio de Telecomunicaciones. https://www.planificacion.gob.ec/wp-content/uploads/downloads/2019/09/Agenda-Digital.pdf. Accessed 05 May 2021

Online Impulse Buying – Integrative Review of Social Factors and Marketing Stimuli

Daniel Costa Pacheco[1](✉), Ana Isabel Damião de Serpa Arruda Moniz[2],
Suzana Nunes Caldeira[3], and Osvaldo Dias Lopes Silva[3]

[1] FEG, University of the Azores, Ponta Delgada, Portugal
[2] CEEAplA, University of the Azores, Ponta Delgada, Portugal
ana.id.moniz@uac.pt
[3] CICS.UAc/CICS, NOVA.UAc, University of the Azores, Ponta Delgada, Portugal
{suzana.n.caldeira,osvaldo.dl.silva}@uac.pt

Abstract. Although the growth of e-commerce to the most distant areas of the world, the increasing orientation of civilisations towards consumption, new opportunities for impulsive buying, and considering that impulse buying has already been studied since the 1950s, its literature still seems to lack further details for a better validation and understanding. The intention of this paper is to make an integrative review on the impact of social factors and marketing stimuli on online impulse buying, specifically considering the following aspects: individualism and collectivism, power distance belief, parasocial interaction, social symbols and identity, the consumer's need for uniqueness, sales promotion, product diversity, product attractiveness, brand, color and hedonism, and credit card usage. This paper is also intended to encourage further studies about the impact of online impulse buying on environmental sustainability. Even though this review may help marketers tailor strategies to increase sales, it may also be a starting point to help consumers reduce their impulse buying behavior, and consequently, their environmental footprint. Apparently, all of the aforementioned factors impact online impulse buying.

Keywords: Online impulse buying · Social factors · Marketing stimuli

1 Introduction

Online impulse buying is defined as a purchase from a relatively extraordinary, exciting, emotional, often energetic and urgent behavior. It is mediated by tangible technological resources (e.g. computers, mobile phones, notebooks and tablets) and intangible technological resources (e.g. operating systems, application software, web browsers, etc.) with an internet connection. Online impulse buying happens on several digital platforms, such as amazon.com, ebay.com and flipkart.com. This behavior involves a quick experience and is more spontaneous than prudent. It tends to alter the consumer's routine, to be more emotional than rational and to be more likely to have a negative social connotation [1]. The consumer is even more likely to feel out of control [1]. Those who plan to buy

T. Guarda et al. (Eds.): ARTIIS 2021, CCIS 1485, pp. 629–640, 2021.
https://doi.org/10.1007/978-3-030-90241-4_48

a product, but have not yet chosen the brand, can also be impulsive [2]. The importance of this phenomenon has been highlighted by several studies. For instance, the market research company OnePoll noted that before the pandemic (January, 2020), the average American spent $155.03 monthly on impulse. During the pandemic (April, 2020), that number increased 18% to $182.98 [3]. In Europe an investigation by the market research portal Statista, in 2019, with 1001 Dutch people, found that when offered a big discount, the product categories most purchased on impulse were, in decreasing order of frequency: food products (37% bought on impulse regularly; 42% sometimes), clothing (27% bought on impulse regularly; 55% sometimes) and beauty products (20% bought on impulse regularly; 50% sometimes), [4]. In the United Kingdom, out of 10.000 respondents, more than a third in the 25 to 34 age group, confessed to often buying discounted products impulsively, which ended up being wasted [5]. Another study from 2016 [6] found that 39% of Danes interviewed, impulsively bought online clothes, shoes and jewelry.

The literature presents several social and marketing stimuli that can influence online impulse buying. In this paper, the following social factors are clarified: individualism and collectivism [7, 8], power distance belief [9], parasocial interaction [10], social symbols and identity [11, 12] and the consumer's need for uniqueness [11]. Four Marketing stimuli will also be analyzed: sales promotion [13–16], product diversity [17], product attractiveness, hedonism and brand [18–20], color [21] and credit card usage [15, 22].

2 Theoretical Framework

Throughout this section, social factors and marketing stimuli that may impact online impulse buying are presented.

2.1 Social Factors

Next, the possible influence of social factors on online impulse buying is examined. Specifically, individualism and collectivism, power distance belief, parasocial interaction, social symbols and identity, and the consumer's need for uniqueness.

2.1.1 Individualism and Collectivism

Culture, as defined by Hofstede [23], is the collective mental programming of the human mind that differentiates groups of individuals. This programming influences thought patterns, mirrored in the meaning that individuals attach to many aspects of life [23]. Culture has been recognized as one of the most influential factors of consumer behavior [24], shaping needs and desires and affecting consumer's behaviors, attitudes and preferences [25].

Being aspects of the Cultural Dimension Theory [26], individualism and collectivism are identified as influencing buying decisions [7], and are closely related to impulse buying [7].

Individualism is a social pattern where individuals see themselves as autonomous and independent. They are driven by their likings, needs and rights. They also prioritize their goals and highlight the rational inspection of their relationships [8].

In turn, collectivism is defined as the degree of interdependence among members of an audience, comprising those who see themselves as part of one or more groups, for example, the family and the work team [8, 23]. Collectivists are generally motivated by the norms, duties and goals of the group, being willing to sacrifice their personal goals for the purposes of the group, having greater control over their emotions than individualists [8].

It seems that we all have individualistic and collectivist tendencies. However, in some cultures, the likelihood of the ego, attitudes, norms, values and behaviors being revealed is higher than others [19]. Social standards are expected to influence impulsive buying behavior, affecting self-identity, the individual's ability to respond to normative influences and the need (or absence of it) to overpower beliefs [8, 19]. In collectivist cultures the predisposition to emphasis on group preferences and harmony leads to the repression of personal attributes [8, 19]. Consequently, collectivists often change their behavior relying on the context or what is "right" for the circumstances. For example, some studies indicate that members of Asian cultures (collectivists) are more likely to control negative emotions, presenting only positive emotions to known and unknown people [27]. Given that impulsivity involves the search for sensations and emotional excitement [1], it is expected that in collectivist societies people will learn to resist their impulsive propensities more than in individualist societies.

On the other hand, individualists are often expected to ignore possible negative outcomes of their impulsive buying behavior, tending to be moved by their own preferences, needs and rights, reaching personal goals [19]. For Mai et al. [28], the individualistic orientation is positively related to the impulsive buying behavior, while the collectivist orientation is negatively related to that behavior. According to Zhang and Shrum [29], individualists are more concerned with personal fulfillment, acting according to their thoughts, feelings and are more susceptible to impulsive buying behavior.

Culturally, individualistic Western societies are based on liberalism, with members being encouraged to be rational enjoying the right to set their goals and to choose freely [30].

East Asian collectivist cultures are grounded on Confucianism, which stimulates common goals and social cohesion under individual interests [19]. Within each culture, social cohesion is reinforced at the cultural level, through social institutions like schools, families and workplaces [19]. Even biologically ambitious people (that is, more individualistic) raised in China, are likely to control their impulses and emotions better than those very attentive on the family (i.e., more collectivists) of the U.S.A. [19]. In collectivist societies, people are inspired to overcome their hedonic wishes in favor of social welfare [19].

Some point out that collectivist Asians make less impulsive buying than individualist Caucasians, although the highly advanced consumer culture in East Asia [19]. Even if there may be collectivists and individualists with the same impulsive streak for buying, collectivists tend to suppress their impulse, acting in a way consistent with cultural standards [19].

However, Schaefer, Hermans and Parker [31] examined materialism among teenagers in China, Japan and the U.S.A., finding that Chinese teenagers endorsed a lower level of materialism than young Americans. Since then, the scenario seems to have changed.

In recent years, researchers have found that Chinese participants endorse higher levels of materialism than their American counterparts [32].

2.1.2 Power Distance Belief

Power distance belief is the dimension of Hofstede's Cultural Dimensions Theory [26] which regards how much a society considers and accepts power inequality, wealth and / or prestige as inevitable [23]. This belief is based on a measure of individual power and individuals' attitudes towards power disparity. Although inequalities exist in any society, they range in the degree of acceptance [9].

It is believed that when faced with buying opportunities, consumers with a low power distance belief make more impulse purchases than those with a high-power distance belief [9].

Power distance belief is associated with self-regulation, giving rise to behaviors such as impulse buying inhibition [9]. Usually, members of cultures with a high-power distance belief, since children, value obedience and conformity [33]. For example, students are expected to behave themselves in the presence of teachers [33], and adults to control and resist their impulses, adopting socially normative behaviors [33].

Over time, people from cultures with a high-power distance belief develop strong learning about containing socially prohibitive behaviors, such as impulse buying [9]. Members of cultures with a low power distance belief tend to be less likely to respond in a socially desired way, as they do not see the need to consent or demonstrate self-regulation [34]. They are more open to contesting authority or power. Students in these cultures are urged to talk, express differences publicly and even disagree with teachers. Western cultures, which normally have a low power distance belief, tend to value the present more than the future praising immediate gratification over delayed restriction or gratification [35]. Over time, this low belief can be associated with less self-regulation, even in situations that involve socially prohibitive temptations [9].

Zhang, Winterich & Mittal [9], through a series of studies, involving surveys to college students and North American consumers, proposed that the power distance belief influences impulse buying. According to the authors [9], (1) those with greater power distance belief make less impulse buying; (2) resistance to temptation can occur automatically in people who already have repeated practice (that is, chronically high, power distance beliefs); (3) countries with higher scores of power distance belief have lower unplanned buying trends (4) American consumers were more impulsive when their resources ran out.

2.1.3 Parasocial Interaction

Grant, Guthrie and Ball-Rokeach [36] defined parasocial interaction as a pseudo-intimate relationship between the public and the mass communicators. Parasocial relationships are not reciprocal. They are unidirectional, used to explain audience relations with a diversity of media personalities, including characters from soap operas, talk show hosts, active members of a community, vloggers, users of social commerce platforms, etc. [37]. The audience can foster a pseudo-intimacy or pseudo-friendship with some media personalities, who resort to many speech techniques to attract, keep an eye on and persuade the audience [10]. In other words, these personalities can instigate behavior in viewers, their followers, including impulse buying behavior.

Education can influence parasocial interaction. According to Park and Lennon [10], viewers with lower levels of education tend to develop more parasocial interactions, being more vulnerable to the influence of third parties, which tends to have an impact on impulse buying situations.

2.1.4 Social Symbols and Identity

Social image means the respect of others for the individual's moral and personal features, as well as the reputation for their efforts and success [38]. For Wang, Zhou and Huang [39] the concept of face involves the way in which individuals earn the reputation or admiration and obedience of others, through an impression or staging, in agreement with certain social standards. Individuals must consider two aspects of their social relationships: how to gain and maintain their image and how to take care of others' image [11]. Many consumers buy an iPhone due to the consumption of conformity, to gain face, as well as use a personalized phone case to express their uniqueness [11]. Face also seems to play a significant role on the choice of gifts, brand recognition and price sensitivity, word-of-mouth on social networks, luxury products consumption and impulse buying [11].

Geng, Yang and Xu [11] analyzed the relationship between the desire to win-lose face and its impact on consumer behavior. To this end, they collected data from 360 college students and university graduates. The results showed that personal identity-face and family identity-face obstruct consumers' need for uniqueness through encouraging interdependent self-construal and friend identity-face and occupational identity-face instigate consumers' need for uniqueness, through enhancing the consumer's susceptibility to normative influence.

Thus, products can have other purposes besides utilitarian and hedonic, representing lifestyles, social groups, statutes, classes, values, religions, identities and/or political positions [12]. Wicklund and Gollwitzer [40] suggest that the human being needs to define and confirm his identity, being able to do it through symbols. The buying of products is a means to this end, becoming more prominent when individuals feel doubts or threatened, or when their identity is compromised [12]. Impulse buying can be a way for a person to clarify, affirm, or express his or her identity. The consumer may consider that a product symbolizes a desired social position or a desired lifestyle [12].

2.1.5 Consumer's Need for Uniqueness

Consumer's need for uniqueness is defined as the search for differences in relation to others, through the purchase, use and disposal of consumer goods with the goal of improving self-image and social image [41]. Tian Bearden & Hunter [41] divided consumer's need for uniqueness into three dimensions: creative choice counter-conformity, unpopular choice counter-conformity and avoidance of similarity. Creative choice counterconformity reflects that consumers desire to differentiate themselves from others by making their own creative choices and they expect these choices to be approved by others [11]. Yet, their choices have a risk [11]. Unpopular choice counter-conformity reports to goods and brands that are opposed to the standards of the group. Consumers who make this choice run the risk of their preferences being rejected by third parties [11]. Avoidance of similarity applies to consumers who would never use trendy or ordinary goods, because they desire to break with the routine and difference themselves from others [11].

Geng, Yang and Xu [11] point consumer's need for uniqueness as a possible antecedent of impulse buying.

2.2 Marketing Stimuli

Below, the following marketing stimuli are considered: sales promotion, product diversity, product attractiveness, hedonism and brand, color and credit card usage.

2.2.1 Sales Promotion

In the last few decades, online sales, through various digital platforms - for example, amazon.com, ebay.com, flipkart.com and aliexpress.com - with effective marketing strategies, a wide range of products and good discounts for consumers, have encouraged impulse buying [42]. Behind many sales on these online platforms is marketing stimuli, that is, the impulsive buying behavior may be due to marketing strategies inside and outside the point of sale, such as advertised products and services, discounts and promotions [43].

Sales promotion reports to a range of motivational tools, intended to stimulate consumers to buy many goods, brands or services in short periods of time [44]. The goal is to instigate directly and immediately consumers' buying behavior [45]. Blattberg and Neslin [45] emphasized four fundamental goals in sales promotion: improving the store's image, generating traffic in the store, associating it with a certain price image and reducing excess inventory. Examples of sales promotion incentives are cash rebates, cash discounts, gift certificates, buy one get one free, markdown, clearance, purchase of newly arrived products, product bundling and one-stop shopping [14, 15, 46].

Sales promotion has a central role in online shopping, in which price, followed by shipping costs, is an attraction for online consumers [22, 47].

In the study by Sundström, Hjelm-Lidholm and Radon [48], when asked why they bought online, consumers pointed to marketing stimuli as the first option. The low price was considered an impressive trigger by all respondents, as well as free shipping and "on sale". Other stimuli reported were scarcity messages, "only available now" or "discount today", encouraging consumers to buy on impulse. Respondents also mentioned the emotional stimulus of impulse buying, as it is common to be in a hurry to buy products and/or services, due to the price: "...to find something you really want and to make a bargain is totally awesome!" (p.153). The price, as a marketing stimulus, is complex and, in some circumstances, the interviewees debated the feeling of not buying: "You do not think about the price in the same way online as when shopping in a physical store. When shopping online, the prices that would have seemed expensive in a physical store all of a sudden feel a bit cheaper. I do not know how to explain this but it seems that you have a totally different view on price when shopping online", said one respondent [48, p. 153).

Impulse buying is also linked to additional up-selling and cross-selling strategies [46]. Up-selling is seen as the retailer's efforts to update a customer's purchase to increase financial profitability, through recommendations, product highlights and other promotional offers, selling the consumer a better version of the product than initially intended [46]. In turn, cross-selling reports the retailers' attempts to make additional sales, often related to the product desired by the customer [49]. For example, in the study by Sundström, Hjelm-Lidholm and Radon [48], an interviewee described this scenario as follows: "On the website when I found my shoes, it popped up: you might like this too … I clicked there, browsed around there for a bit. It ended up with me buying three pairs of shoes and two shirts – on pure impulse!" (p. 153).

As for monetary gains, see the example of amazon.com, which after implementing promotional offers, such as cross-selling, and offering shipping costs for orders above US $25, their net sales grew 25% over the preceding year [50]. Thus, aiming to increase sales, marketers, in cooperation with suppliers, may periodically organize promotional activities with temporary and monthly price reductions and/or effective price reductions [51].

2.2.2 Product Diversity

Most online stores offer consumers a wider assortment of goods. The more opportunities for choosing products, the more time and energy consumers spend comparing and exchanging products [52], which can reduce their satisfaction, leading to greater regrets [53], and reducing buying desires and impulses [17].

Wu and Chen [17] explored the effect of online product diversity on consumers' impulse buying intentions. To validate their theoretical framework, the authors [17] conducted two studies, distributing surveys to young people aged 18 to 30 with experience in online shopping. The results indicate that product diversity has a noteworthy negative impact on consumers' online impulse buying intentions, with consumers more willing to buy online on impulse when there were not many options. Wu and Chen [17] also found that there is no substantial effect of product diversity on consumers' impulse buying intent, when consumers buy goods for third parties.

2.2.3 Product Attractiveness, Hedonism and Brand

The literature states that many consumers are attracted by the appearance/design of the product [18]. Other studies report that products/services whose advantages meet consumer expectations will be more attractive to its eyes, contributing to impulse buying [54, 55].

For some consumers, certain products, although not essential, have fun attributes, suddenly provoking the buying desire [20]. Some studies suggest that the displaying of the product, its color and font size have a relevant impact on impulse buying [56]. According to Hubert et al. [56], attractive packaging activates the brain regions of reward, while less attractive packaging activates the regions of negative emotions. Conforming to Reimann et al. [57], exposure to good-looking packaging leads to increased neural activity in the zones of the impulsive system and in specific zones of the reflexive system, such as the ventromedial prefrontal cortex. The patterns of neural activity observed propose that exposure to good-looking stimuli is linked to greater activity of the impulsive system and greater activity of the reflexive system. Consumers are more willing to pick goods that look more attractive than less attractive [13].

Regarding the brand, Qingyang, Yuxuan and Sijia [20] refer that when a consumer chooses a product, the reputation of the store and the brand have significant effects on the purchase, which may increase or decrease the buying impulse. Thus, the cultural identity of the brand is one of the contributors to the desire for a product or service.

2.2.4   Color

Color influences human perception, cognition and behavior [21]. With regard to the online context, Metha and Zhu [21] found that short exposure to red (versus blue) could improve the performance of detail-oriented (versus creative) cognitive tasks. Gorn et al. [58] indicated that their participants exposed to the blue background screen viewed the page download more quickly than those exposed to the red background screen. In the study by Elliot et al. [59], before an anagram test, participants who were momentarily exposed to red performed worse than those momentarily exposed to green. Wang, Pirouz and Zhang [60], through two experiments carried out with almost 200 participants, found that consistently the color (blue vs. red) influenced the individual's impulse buying behavior. Specifically, some participants completed an online survey on a red background while others on a blue background. Participants who completed the survey on a blue background showed greater impulsiveness in the buying intention than their peers.

2.2.5   Credit Card Usage

The development of plastic money, namely credit card and digital currency, has made online shopping more appealing [22]. Consumers feel more comfortable when they spend with a credit card. The use of a credit card reduces the perceived cost [61]. Feinberg [62] provides evidence that college students who use credit card buy more, compared to users of physical money [22]. For Soman and Gourville [63], regular credit card consumers always spend more. According to Badgaiyan and Verma [15], the use of credit card has a positive influence on impulse buying. As stated by Karbasivar and Yarahmadi [64], the use of credit card is positively related to impulse buying by consumers in the clothing trade. For Feinberg [62], the presence of credit card information increases the likelihood, speed and dimension of spending. Similarly, Roberts and Jones [61] refer to the use of credit card to encourage excessive spending, while Soman [63] suggest that regular credit card users make extra purchases and tend to spend beyond their means.

3   Final Remarks

As stated before, despite impulse buying has already been studied since the 1950s, its literature still seems to lack further details for a better validation and understanding, especially in the digital world. With this investigation, it was intended to (1) improve knowledge about the topic under consideration and to (2) encourage further studies about the impact of online impulse buying on environmental sustainability. Even though this review may help marketers tailor strategies to increase sales, it may also be a starting point to help consumers reduce their impulse buying behavior, and consequently, their environmental footprint.

The present investigation was delimited, focusing on the possible impact of certain social and marketing factors on the online impulse buying behavior. In this study, as a first delimitation, the following variables of the social dimension were considered: individualism, collectivism, power distance belief, parasocial interaction, social symbols and identity, and consumer's need for uniqueness. As a second delimitation, the next marketing variables were approached: sales promotion, product diversity, product attractiveness, hedonism and brand, color and credit card.

As far as the authors were able to find out, there are not many studies that allow consolidating the knowledge of the impact of the aforementioned factors on online impulse buying. Thus, the possible impact of social and marketing factors on impulse buying online is summarized below.

Starting with social factors, collectivism and individualism are identified as influencers of impulse buying [7, 19]. In turn, consumer's need for uniqueness with the buying, use and disposal of consumer goods, distinguishing himself from others, aiming to develop and improve his self-image and social image, may be a possible antecedent of impulse buying [11]. Nevertheless, parasocial interaction, that is, unidirectional pseudo intimate relationships between the public and mass communicators, can determine impulse buying, and these relationships are attenuated by the individual's increased education [10]. Furthermore, the desire/fear of consumers to gain/ lose face can lead to impulse buying of social symbols and identity, as a way of clarifying, affirming or expressing identity, as products/services can represent lifestyles, social groups, statutes, classes, values, religion or political positions [10, 12]. Likewise, many consumers with low power distance belief can make more impulse buying than those with a high-power distance belief [9].

Regarding Marketing stimuli, the impulsive buying behavior may be due to marketing strategies inside and outside the point of sale, such as advertised products and services, discounts and promotions [43]. Furthermore, product diversity seems to negatively and significantly impact consumers' online impulse buying intentions, who are more willing to do so when there is not much diversity [17]. Buying impulsiveness also seems to be triggered by the store's reputation, packaging and product brand [20, 56]. At the same time, color (blue vs. red) can influence the individual's impulse buying behavior [21]. Wang, Pirouz and Zhang [60], through experiences, found that individuals briefly exposed to blue had greater intention to impulse buying. Finally, studies suggest that the use of credit card positively influences impulse buying [15, 22].

References

1. Rook, D.W.: The buying impulse. J. Consum. Res. **14**(2), 189–199 (1987)
2. Hussain, M., Jan, F., Iqbal, K., Manzoor, S., Rahman, S.: Imran: do people consider self image in impulse buying behavior in peshawar, Pakistan? Interdisciplinary J. Contemp. Res. Busin. **2**(8), 674–687 (2011)

3. Slickdeals: Americans increased impulse spending by 18 percent during the COVID-19 Pandemic, according to new survey commissioned by Slickdeals, 8 May 2020. https://www.prnewswire.com/news-releases/americans-increased-impulse-spending-by-18-percent-during-the-covid-19-pandemic-according-to-new-survey-commissioned-by-slickdeals-301055530.html

4. Statista: Most frequently bought impulse purchases in the Netherlands 2019, by category 30 May 2020a. https://www.statista.com/statistics/1088692/most-frequently-bought-impulse-purchases-in-the-netherlands-by-category/

5. Statista: Impulse buying behavior on promotional items in the UK 2020, by age, 27 November 2020b. https://www.statista.com/statistics/1137668/uk-impulse-purchase-behaviour-by-age/

6. Statista: Impulse buying in Denmark 2016, by product category, 30 November 2020c. https://www.statista.com/statistics/699040/impulse-buying-in-denmark-by-product-category/

7. Badgaiyan, A.J., Verma, A.: Intrinsic factors affecting impulsive buying behavior—Evidence from India. J. Retail. Consum. Serv. 21(4), 537–549 (2014)

8. Jalees, T., Rahman, M.U.: Role of visual merchandizing, sensational seeking, and collectivism in consumers' impulsive buying behavior at shopping malls. Pakistan J. Psychol. Res. 33(1) (2018)

9. Zhang, Y., Winterich, K.P., Mittal, V.: Power distance belief and impulsive buying. J. Mark. Res. 47(5), 945–954 (2010)

10. Park, J., Lennon, S.J.: Psychological and environmental antecedents of impulse buying tendency in the multichannel shopping context. J. Consum. Market. Heckler, S.E., Childers, T.L., Arunachalam, R. (1989). Intergenerational influences in adult buying behaviors: an examination of moderating factors. ACR North American Advances (2006)

11. Geng, L., Yang, Y., Xu, Y.: To pursue personality or conformity: a study on the impact of face view on consumers' need for uniqueness. Psychol. Mark. 36(3), 188–197 (2019)

12. Verplanken, B., Sato, A.: The psychology of impulse buying: an integrative self-regulation approach. J. Consum. Policy 34(2), 197–210 (2011)

13. Kotler, P., Rath, G.A.: Design: a powerful but neglected strategic tool. J. Busin. Strategy (1984)

14. Dawson, S., Kim, M.: Cues on apparel web sites that trigger impulse purchases. J. Fashion Market. Manage. Int. J. (2010)

15. Badgaiyan, A.J., Verma, A.: Does urge to buy impulsively differ from impulsive buying behaviour? Assessing the impact of situational factors. J. Retail. Consum. Serv. 22, 145–157 (2015)

16. Chan, T.K., Cheung, C.M., Lee, Z.W.: The state of online impulse-buying research: a literature analysis. Inf. Manage. 54(2), 204–217 (2017)

17. Wu, Y., Chen, H.: The influence of product diversity on consumers' impulsive purchase in online shopping environment. Am. J. Ind. Bus. Manag. 9(3), 680–698 (2019)

18. Kotler, P., Armstrong, G.: Mercadotecnia. Prentice Hall Hispanoamericana (1996)

19. Kacen, J.J., Lee, J.A.: The influence of culture on consumer impulsive buying behavior. J. Consum. Psychol. 12(2), 163–176 (2002)

20. Qingyang, L., Yuxuan, X., Sijia, C.: Y-Generation digital natives' impulsive buying behavior. In 2018 3rd Technology Innovation Management and Engineering Science International Conference (TIMES-iCON), pp. 1–5. IEEE, December 2018

21. Metha, R., Zhu, R.J.: Blue or red? Exploring the effect of color on cognitive task performance. Science 323(5918), 1226–1229 (2009)

22. Akram, U., Hui, P., Khan, M. K., Tanveer, Y., Mehmood, K., Ahmad, W.: How website quality affects online impulse buying. Asia Pacific J. Market. Logist. (2018)

23. Hofstede, G.: Dimensionalizing cultures: the hofstede model in context. Online Readings in Psychol. Culture 2(1), 8 (2011)

24. Dameyasani, A.W., Abraham, J.: Impulsive buying, cultural values dimensions, and symbolic meaning of money: a study on college students in Indonesia's capital city and its surrounding. Int. J. Res. Stud. Psychol. **2**(4) (2013)
25. Mooij, M.: Consumer Behavior and Culture: Consequences for Global Marketing and Advertising. Sage, Thousand Oaks (2019)
26. Hofstede, G.: Dimensions of national cultures in fifty countries and three regions, in expiscations in cross-cultural psychology. In: Deregowski, J.B., Dziurawiec, S., Annis, R.C. (eds.) Lisse, Netherlands: Swets & Zeitlinger, pp. 335–355 (1983)
27. Gudykunst, W.B. (ed.): Communication in Japan and the United States. SUNY Press, Albany (1993)
28. Mai, N.T.T., Jung, K., Lantz, G., Loeb, S.G.: An exploratory investigation into impulse buying behavior in a transitional economy: a study of urban consumers in Vietnam. J. Int. Mark. **11**(2), 13–35 (2003)
29. Zhang, Y., Shrum, L.J.: The influence of self-construal on impulsive consumption. J. Consum. Res. **35**(5), 838–850 (2009)
30. Kim, U.E., Triandis, H.C., Kâğitçibaşi, Ç.E., Choi, S.C.E., Yoon, G.E.. Individualism and Collectivism: Theory, Method, and Applications. Sage Publications, Inc., Thousand Oaks (1994)
31. Schaefer, A.D., Hermans, C.M., Parker, R.S.: A cross-cultural exploration of materialism in adolescents. Int. J. Consum. Stud. **28**(4), 399–411 (2004)
32. Podoshen, J.S., Li, L., Zhang, J.: Materialism and conspicuous consumption in China: a cross-cultural examination. Int. J. Consum. Stud. **35**(1), 17–25 (2010)
33. Hofstede, G.: Culture's Consequences: International Differences in Work-Related Values, vol. 5. Sage, Thousand Oaks (1984)
34. Lalwani, A.K., Shavitt, S., Johnson, T.: What is the relation between cultural orientation and socially desirable responding? J. Personality Soc. Psychol. **90**(1), 165 (2006)
35. Chen, H., Ng, S., Rao, A.R.: Cultural differences in consumer impatience. J. Market. Res. **42**(3), 291–301 (2005). Chomvilailuk, R., Butcher, K.: Social effects on unplanned in-store buying. Proc. Soc. Behav. Sci. **148**, 127–136 (2014)
36. Grant, A.E., Guthrie, K.K., Ball-Rokeach, S.J.: Television shopping: a media system dependency perspective. Commun. Res. **18**(6), 773–798 (1991)
37. Hu, L., Min, Q., Han, S., Liu, Z.: Understanding followers' stickiness to digital influencers: the effect of psychological responses. Int. J. Inf. Manage. **54**, 102–169 (2020)
38. Hu, H.C.: The Chinese concepts of "Face." Am. Anthropol. **46**(1), 45–64 (1944)
39. Wang, C., Zhou, X., Huang, M.: Seeking similarity or reserving differences: How face facilitate or restrict consumer's need for uniqueness. J. Contemporary Market. Sci. (2019)
40. Wicklund, R.A., Gollwitzer, P.M.: Symbolic Self-Completion. Erlbaum, Hillsdale (1982)
41. Tian, K.T., Bearden, W.O., Hunter, G.L.: Consumers' need for uniqueness: scale development and validation. J. Consum. Res. **28**(1), 50–66 (2001)
42. Kumar, H., Garg, R., Kumar, P., Chhikara, R.: A qualitative insight into the personal factors impacting online impulse behavior. In Strategies and Tools for Managing Connected Consumers, pp. 279–291. IGI Global (2020)
43. Chomvilailuk, R., Butcher, K.: Social effects on unplanned in-store buying. Proc. Soc. Behav. Sci. **148**, 127–136 (2014)
44. Kotler, P.T.: Marketing Management. Pearson, London (2019)
45. Blattberg, R.C., Neslin, S.A.: Sales Promotion: Concepts, Methods, and Strategies. Prentice Hall, Hoboken (1990)
46. Dawson, S., Kim, M.: External and internal trigger cues of impulse buying online. Direct Market. Int. J. (2009)

47. Wadera, D., Sharma, V.: Impulsive buying behavior in online fashion apparel shopping: an investigation of the influence of the internal and external factors among indian shoppers. South Asian J. Manage. **25**(3), 55 (2018)
48. Sundström, M., Hjelm-Lidholm, S., Radon, A.: Clicking the boredom away–exploring impulse fashion buying behavior online. J. Retail. Consum. Serv. **47**, 150–156 (2019)
49. Levy, M., Weitz, B.: Retailing Management, 6th edn. McGraw-Hill/Irwin, Boston (2007)
50. Malester, J.: TWICE: this week in consumer electronics. Consum. Electron. **21**(10), 104 (2006)
51. Anić, I.D., Radas, S.: The relationships between shopping trip type, purchases made on promotion, and unplanned purchases for a high/low hypermarket retailer-evidence from the croatian market. Privredna kretanja i ekonomska politika **16**(107), 26–45 (2006)
52. Iyengar, S.S., Lepper, M.R.: When choice is demotivating: Can one desire too much of a good thing? J. Pers. Soc. Psychol. **79**(6), 995 (2000)
53. Madhavaram, S.R., Laverie, D.A.: Exploring impulse purchasing on the internet. ACR North American Advances (2004)
54. Gardner, M.P., Rook, D.W.: Effects of impulse purchases on consumers' affective states. ACR North American Advances (1988)
55. Surjaputra, Williem, R.: The effect of product attractiveness, word of mouth and product quality in elevating the impulsive buying behavior of Garuda Peanut in Surabaya. In: 2011 IEEE International Summer Conference of Asia Pacific Business Innovation and Technology Management, pp. 54–58. IEEE, July 2011
56. Hubert, M., Hubert, M., Florack, A., Linzmajer, M., Kenning, P.: Neural correlates of impulsive buying tendencies during perception of product packaging. Psychol. Mark. **30**(10), 861–873 (2013)
57. Reimann, M., Zaichkowsky, J., Neuhaus, C., Bender, T., Weber, B.: Aesthetic package design: a behavioral, neural, and psychological investigation. J. Consum. Psychol. **20**(4), 431–441 (2010)
58. Gorn, G.J., Chattopadhyay, A., Sengupta, J., Tripathi, S.: Waiting for the web: how screen color affects time perception. J. Mark. Res. **41**(2), 215–225 (2004)
59. Elliot, A.J., Maier, M.A., Moller, A.C., Friedman, R., Meinhardt, J.: Color and psychological functioning: the effect of red on performance attainment. J. Exp. Psychol. Gen. **136**(1), 154 (2007)
60. Wang, L., M Pirouz, D., Zhang, X.: Should santa still wear red? Investigating the effects of color on impulsive buying behavior. ACR North American Advances (2011)
61. Roberts, J.A., Jones, E.: Money attitudes, credit card use, and compulsive buying among American college students. J. Consum. Aff. **35**(2), 213–240 (2001)
62. Feinberg, R.A.: Credit cards as spending facilitating stimuli: a conditioning interpretation. J. Consum. Res. **13**(3), 348–356 (1986)
63. Soman, D., Gourville, J.T.: Transaction decoupling: how price bundling affects the decision to consume. J. Mark. Res. **38**(1), 30–44 (2001)
64. Karbasivar, A., Yarahmadi, H.: Evaluating effective factors on consumer impulse buying behavior. Asian J. Busin. Manage. Stud. **2**(4), 174–181 (2011)

Geographic Positioning and Flow Management for Electric and Electronic Equipment Waste (e-waste): Case of Chile and Generalizations for South-American Countries

Ximena Vargas[1] , Jesús González-Feliux[2] , William Sarache[3] ,
Alexis Olmedo[1] , Claudio Azat[1] , Romina Cayumil[1] , and Gustavo Gatica[1(✉)]

[1] Facultad de Ingeniería & Centro de Investigación Para La Sustentabilidad, Universidad Andres Bello, Santiago, Chile
{xi.vargas,aolmedo,claudio.azat,omina.cayumi,ggatica}@unab.cl
[2] Centre de Recherche en Innovation Et Intelligence Managériales (CERIIM), UMR 5600 Environnement, Excelia Business School, Ville et Société, La Rochelle, France
gonzalezfeliuj@excelia-group.com
[3] Universidad Nacional de Colombia, sede Manizales, Colombia
wasarachec@unal.edu.co

Abstract. Logistics is historically defined as the tool to provide the necessary commodities in a timely manner. Today, logistics is not only responsible for supplying, but also for the recovery and transformation of various products. In this context, electrical-electronic waste is toxic and pollutes the environment. Therefore, governments, under international regulations, must define public policies for its collection, collection and recovery. The proposed methodology is based on a quantitative case study and follows 5 steps: Analysis of the context and background, based on secondary data processing, data retrieval and processing, data geolocation, indicator construction and analysis and generalization. The positioning and flow management for these products by private companies in Chile is presented. The volumes and type of waste, allows to visualize how South America is 30 years behind Europe. The study highlights the role that governments and private companies should have to mitigate the environmental effects. The study generated showed that from 2014 to date the number of recycling points for plastic, glass, cans, cardboard and, above all, large and small electrical and electronic items, have increased satisfactorily. The study shows the need to collaborate directly with the central government authorities.

Keywords: E-waste · Best practices · E-recycling · Public policy

1 Introduction

Historically, logistics is one of the primary industrial activities to supply constant flows of resources [14]. In the last years, with the inclusion of sustainability and responsibility

© Springer Nature Switzerland AG 2021
T. Guarda et al. (Eds.): ARTIIS 2021, CCIS 1485, pp. 641–652, 2021.
https://doi.org/10.1007/978-3-030-90241-4_49

issues in corporate planning, new models of supply chain management have been developed [23], leading to the deployment of different green SCM. From them, eco-design (which includes also remanufacturing) and reverse logistics, aim at promoting circular economy practices to reduce waste production, and are popular in electronic device lifecycle management [11].

Due to technological evolution and increases in demands and economic restrictions, logistics must be adapted and modernized. In OECD countries, there are laws with effective recycling and product revaluation rates. In Europe, in particular oils, batteries, tires, among others, have been recycled since the 1980s [7].

In Chile, only in 2016 was the Law of Extended Producer Responsibility and promotion of recycling enacted [8]. The law seeks to reduce waste generation and promote revaluation [29]. The implementation of this has been developed gradually, however, there are no procedures for control, registration, and tax incentives for recycling. One of the most toxic products for the environment is e-waste, its volume is directly proportional to all the technological imports that countries receive. In Chile only in 2019, more than 186 ktons of electronic items were generated, therefore, the concern arises, where they are stored, transformed, or reused [3]. Unfortunately, the depicted by from the Ministry of the Environment, 89% of the waste generated by the population ends up with final disposal in garbage dumps or landfills [6]. Despite those issues, e-waste research remains mainly related to optimization and operations research issues with a small connection to spatial and territorial aspects.

This paper aims to propose a spatial analysis of e-waste production in Chile, on a demand and a space-driven approach. A five-step methodology has been used, to analyzing the context, recovering and processing the data of e-waste, geolocating recycling points, constructing indicators to finally analyze and generalize.

The paper in its second section presents a related literature, in a third section, it presents the Methodology used. Finally, the results and some recommendations generated from the study are presented with the scant information available at the governmental and public level.

2   Related Literature

In 1997, guidelines were established to manage return flows in the reuse of industrial production processes [21]. Since 2001, Taiwan has established a regulation for the recycling of household appliances and computer equipment, manufacturers and importers must take back their products [20]. The case of Taiwan is a good example of technology transfers as there are public private actors in the collection and collection of e-waste. For the Olympic games in Tokyo 2020, a large amount of electronic waste was used for the creation of the Olympic medals [17].

The literature presents optimization models based on mixed integer [1]. The models assign the discarded products, assembly, and parts to the actors of the treatment system [33]. However, depicted a classification method for Spanish municipalities to install recycling plants [26]. To classify the alternatives, the discrete multi-criteria decision method (Preference Classification Organization Method for Enrichment Assessments) is applied, combined with an expert survey.

Between 2009 and 2012, treatment plants are generated in Europe, due to high business volumes and growing demand. The home entertainment and electronics segment stand out [34]. The reverse logistics structure for e-waste is essential to minimize the impacts of its improper disposal [10]. It is necessary to measure the impact of legal incentives, by volume and the effective formalization of recyclers. To increase efficiency and responsiveness, technological solutions for waste monitoring are required. Thus, a strategic operational scheme can be generated focused on customer demand and maximizing e-waste collection [5].

The last research makes an interesting theoretical contribution by characterizing the behavior of young people with respect to e-waste, who are at the intersection of cross-cultural studies, sustainability, and reverse supply chain management areas [18]. Reverse logistics has been widely studied since 1994, in the OECD countries of the European continent. Currently, South America is just entering research on reverse logistics applied to e-waste, in Chile, Colombia, Bolivia, Brazil and Ecuador, they are implementing the REP law, public policy studies and new models to optimize costs monetary [24].

According to literature research, the main paths of action identified in reverse logistics research are the following:

- Methods and algorithms for optimized waste collection. These methods are mainly linked to the collection of household waste and hazardous wastes, though (more numerous) optimisation methods also exist for outbound logistics.
- Design of the reverse logistics chain. Many works have focused on the design of reverse logistics chains, but the integration of distribution and reverse logistics chains remain less explored. However, the fact that they remain interesting and have strong potential.
- Recycling management and waste electric and electronic equipment management. In both cases, the ideas and methods presented are similar and focus on optimising transport and storage. However, few authors have studied their integration in distribution logistics in detail.

In most cases, we observe that works are of computational nature, mainly related to supply issues. Moreover, the spatial characteristics of the application fields are considered as secondary. However, in this type of works territorial issues remain important, since environmental policies and actions need a spatial and territorial basis to be efficient [13]. For those reasons, we propose a systems thinking methodology based on demand quantification and geo-spatial analysis.

3   Metodology

The proposed methodology is based on a quantitative case study and follows 5 steps:

1. Analysis of the context and background, based on secondary data processing (national reports, press, national statistics).
2. Data retrieval and processing. Data is issued from 2014 and consists on the monthly collection of e-waste in a set of points located in all Chilean territory. Data is processed, categorized and geo-referenced.

3. Data geolocation: for each recycling company, each collection point geo-references are located using a GIS, integrated with Tableau [30].
4. Indicator construction: from the geo-location, a set of geo-spatial indicators (accessibility, centrality, connectivity, etc.) are defined.
5. Analysis and generalization. Data is compared and analysed to make conclusions on e-waste trends and evolutions, then generalization to South-America and comparison with Global, Worldwide trends, is made.

The methodology follows a systems thinking approach, in which each single collection point is geolocated and then processed first individually but then included on a larger system. Interactions among those points are considered. Moreover, a geo-spatial analysis is made to identify e-waste generation clusters and "regionalize" the territory in order to better understand the capabilities and strategies of e-waste collection in Chile.

4   Results

The global amount of electronic waste generated in 2019 stands at 53.6 million metric tons. The calculation corresponds to the collective sum of e-waste generated in a given year. It corresponds to the collective sum of discarded products in all previous years, multiplied by life expectancy. Its life expectancy distribution is obtained through consumer surveys, data models and the probability that a batch will be discarded in a given time [32].

E-waste is classified into at least 6 types, related to shape and composition: Temperature exchange devices, Monitors with screens with a surface area of more than 100 cm^2, Lamps, Large devices, Small devices and Small computer and telecommunications equipment [7].

Fig. 1. E-Waste generated in South America in 2014. Source: Own creation.

Since 2016, Chile has been subject to the REP law. Nevertheless, it fell from first place in Latin America to second place with 158.6 kilotonnes of e-waste [8].

In this way, it is possible to compare Fig. 1, with the new figures provided by United Nations University (UNU)/United Nations Institute for Training and Research (UNITAR) - co-hosted SCYCLE Program, International Telecommunication Union (ITU) & International Solid Waste Association (ISWA), Bonn/Geneva/Rotterdam in 2019. South America generated 9.1 kg of e-waste per person, as depicted in Table 1.

In this instance, Chile already belonged to the line of countries that made up the Organization for Economic Cooperation and Development (OECD), just as Brazil and Colombia already have a REP law [15].

Table 1. E-Waste generated in South America in 2019. Source: United Nations University (UNU).

Country	K/H	K/P	Country	K/H	K/P
Chile	9.9	186	Guyana	6.3	5
Uruguay	10.5	37	Colombia	6.3	318
Surinam	9.4	5.6	Paraguay	7.1	51
Venezuela	10.7	300	Perú	6.3	204
Brasil	10.2	2143	Ecuador	5.7	99
Argentina	10.3	465	Bolivia	3.6	41

In Chile, public policies on e-waste are incipient. However, there is knowledge and companies related to the recycling of other types of materials such as glass, plastic, cardboard, among others.

It is evident that the increase of e-waste recycling, require the generation of public policies and/or regulations. In this way, it is possible to keep track of the e-waste that enters the country (specify the imports records) and how much of it is recycled.

In the case of Chile, one of the main public entities that it has in terms of recycling, recycle large quantities of electronic items, such as computers, which are delivered together with the Ministry of Education to schools or neighborhood associations. In 2017, a total of 3,418 computers were delivered through donations from companies and thus generate social responsibility under the REP law.

The amount of CPU, Notebook, Screens, Servers and other e-waste that the foundation has collected over the years is presented in Fig. 2. It is identified that from 2012 to June 2014 the foundation received mostly only computer tools that allowed it to give a new useful life and thus be delivered to the Ministry of Education. These donations are subject to control by the foundation, where they identify the type of e-waste through donations. This does not have applications to identify its recycling points nationwide. There is a gap, both for companies and / or users, of when and where to deliver their waste and how to synchronize when they carry out campaigns with other institutions.

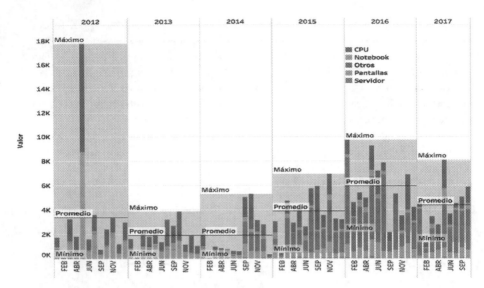

Fig. 2. Breakdown of donated artifacts between 2012–2017. Source: Private Foundation.

Another entity that generates large amounts of recycling, but of a private nature, contemplates the national distribution throughout 360-L depots for electronic waste. In Fig. 3, you can see the georeferencing of containers that certain entities have a national level to date.

In almost seven years since the first study in Chile, the rate of e-waste production per person has dropped by 12.1%. Almost six years after the enactment of the REP law, the goals are in the process of being drawn up, however are campaigns of private foundations and companies, in Chile and Latin America. The first goals will be established by a group of experts and the process that should end in mid-2020–2021, however the pandemic play negative.

In Fig. 4, a forecast is presented of how the amount in kilotons of e-waste will increase at a national, Latin American, and global level. This forecast was made based on real data studies delivered by the United Nations University in 2015 and 2017 of 2014 and 2016 respectively [7]. The forecasts are obtained via linear regressions, replying to the principles of the well-known Freight Trip Generation and Freight Generation models [16]. to e-waste. The study based on 2014 commented that world growth would be around 5% [8]. In which it did not exceed 3.5%, in the same way, that at the Latin American level it would rise 6%, and this did not exceed 4.5% annually. This was due to the fact that some Latin American countries joined the REP law and began the implementation and the first forms of communication to the population and the importance of the collaboration of public and private institutions and the population in general.

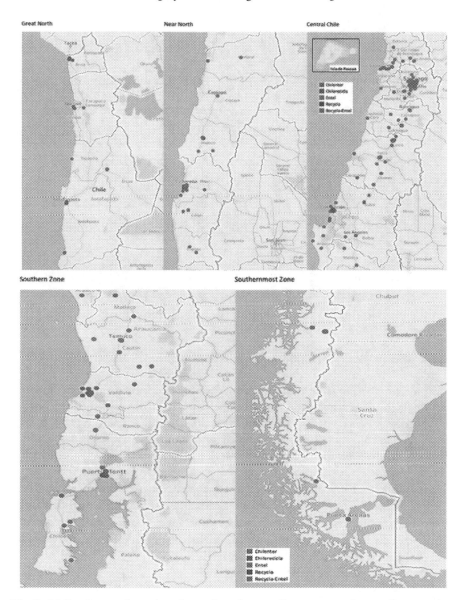

Fig. 3. National geo-referencing of containers by recycling company. Source: Own creation.

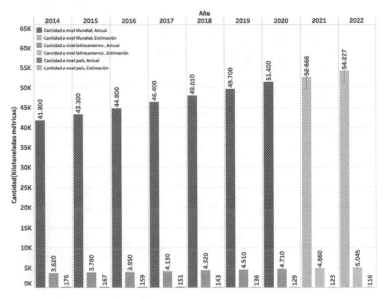

Fig. 4. Behavior and forecast of e-waste over time. Source: Own creation.

5   Discussion and Remarks

The territorial distribution of e-waste attractiveness seems, as shown in Fig. 3, homogenous. Although some zones present more collection points and there are disparities, it seems that e-waste generation follows population. Indeed, Fig. 4 shows an almost linear trend of e-waste collection that would be related to population. To go in-depth, further research on the determinants of e-waste generation would be made.

In any case, the increasing trends in e-waste generation are a fact. Therefore, if Chile continues to distribute information together with other entities, the levels of e-waste will drop as the forecast revealed, this without mentioning the new goals to be implemented. The best techniques and good environmental practices will be considered for this purpose; In addition, these goals will be established based on demographic, geographic and connectivity considerations, as required by the Producer's Extended Responsibility Law in paragraph 2 of article 12 [19].

Territorial implications are a key element for changing those trends. In a context in which several actors with different objectives are involved, as well as two main logics (one individual and one collective), the relationships between territorial development and logistics development can be represented through the interaction of three components (Fig. 5):

- the logistical performance of the companies and activities located in the territory, which follows an individual logic of economic profitability.
- Respect for the environment and the territory, both at an environmental level (conservation of resources and limitation of polluting emissions) and at a spatial level (conservation of the landscape and the territory) or socially.

- territorial development, be it urban, rural, social or economic.

Territorial development, combined with an increase in logistics performance (effectiveness, efficiency, flexibility and resilience, mainly) undoubtedly leads to an economic development of the territory. However, territorial development and logistics performance can be seen as opposing elements in some fields or complementary in others. Thus, the search for such complementarities and synergies can promote the economic development of a territory. At the same time, logistics performance is seen mostly in opposition to respect for the environment. In both relationships, logistics performance is seen as an individual (or company) logic, while both territorial development and respect for the environment follow collective logic. However, territorial development is seen as a contribution to individual development, so the complementarities between this sphere and logistics performance are easier to identify than in the latter case. Therefore, a logistics performance that wants to respect the environment must find a space for dialogue and consensus between economic activities (individual logic) and collective and territorial actors to carry out developments that allow both improving logistics performance and respecting the social equity and the territorial environment.

Finally, respect for the environment, which is viewed with a certain conservatism, may be in opposition to the development of the territory, since this development cannot always be carried out without destroying and / or transforming the areas considered, as well as impacting (not always in an acceptable way for the different groups) on their inhabitants. That is why the need to find a balance is imposed.

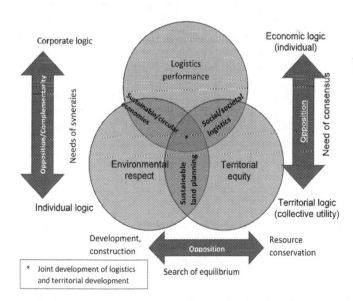

Fig. 5. Interaction issues between logistics and territorial planning. Source: Own creation.

The main lessons were identified before defining the R&D needs identified. To do this a synthesis of the main paths of research was performed on the basis of an analysis of all the experiments. The main lesson is that collaboration between territorial, governmental and corporation instances is necessary, not only for a better deployment of current laws but also for more sustainable collaboration in terms of e-waste and reverse logistics practices. The following measures have been identified as a priority to support that collaboration: 1) raise awareness to the society to extend the life of the products and at the end of their useful life they are delivered to recycling points or foundations and thus generate the manufacture of new products; 2) change the existing idea that products have a certain useful life and that after this time they work or should not be discarded; 3) control illegal landfills through stricter policies and better control by municipalities for the removal of these wastes so that they do not violate environmental regulations; 4) promote corporate social responsibility policies; and 5) create a research center on the matter, through the Ministry of the Environment or with external help, from universities or private centers specializing in the subject.

It is extremely important that society takes into account the following activities as the main focus for recycling e-waste: 1) Physical presence at points of sale (mall, specialized stores, distribution centers, among others); 2) Users who buy online, at the end of their purchase, the same information will be attached for a user described in the previous point.

Generate collection campaigns nationwide in different instances of time, with the help of foundations and / or specialized companies that are linked to recycling e-waste; 3) implement smart applications that allow the location of the closest recycling points and clear information on the days of collection of these points (such as the garbage truck); 4) new technologies from companies that manufacture bags that allow the collection of materials and that contribute to the ecology of the environmental system; and 5) economic and / or social incentives that allow society to contribute more actively to the collection of specific priority products.

6   Conclusion

This paper proposed a geo-spatial and territorial analysis of e-waste generation in Chile, comparing the context to South America and identifying main implications in territorial planning and policy making.

The study generated showed that from 2014 to date the number of recycling points for plastic, glass, cans, cardboard and, above all, large and small electrical and electronic items, have increased satisfactorily. This increase is due to the Law of Responsibility of the Producer and Promotion of Recycling (REP), which seeks that the country can recycle, reuse and become environmentally aware to continue preventing our cities from living together with garbage.

For this to be possible, it is necessary to have direct collaboration with the central government authorities, in this case the Ministry of the Environment, and for this it is necessary that the following measures begin to be implemented for a better development of this Law.

Further developments of the research include a more in-depth e-waste generation modelling, in both spatial and functional aggregations of data, the development of centrality and accessibility indicators to measure disparities and needs for territorial developments int terms of e-waste and reverse logistics promotions, and the proposal of location methods for improving the efficiency of current e-waste collection processes. However, the study considers disaggregated data available from various sources of information. The competent authority in Chile does not have the procedures to determine a correlation between imports of electronic equipment, its useful life and its final disposal. Therefore, what is collected and recycled may not be statistically significant.

Additionally, is possible use of heat maps to have a synthetic view of the scattering of the raised points.

1. References

1. Atabaki, M.S., Mohammadi, M., Naderi, B.: New robust optimization models for closed-loop supply chain of durable products: towards a circular economy. Comput. Ind. Eng. **146** (2020)
2. Chilenter: Obtenido de Fundación Chilenter (2017). http://www.chilenter.com/
3. Cesaro, A., Marra, A., Kuchta, K.,Belgiorno, V., Van Hullebusch, E.D.: WEEE management in a circular economy perspective: an overview. Global NEST J. **20**, 743–750 (2018)
4. Elia, V., Gnoni, M.G., Tornese, F.: Improving logistic efficiency of WEEE collection through dynamic scheduling using simulation modeling. Waste Manage. **72**, 78–86 (2018)
5. Esenduran, G., Atasu, A., Van Wassenhove, L.N.: Valuable e-waste: implications for extended producer responsibility. IISE Trans. **51**, 382–396 (2019)
6. European Commission – DG Environment: Development of Guidance on Extended Producer Responsibility (EPR). http://epr.eu-smr.eu/documents/BIObyDeloitte-GuidanceonEPR-Fin alReport.pdf?attredirects=0&d=1%5Cn. http://ec.europa.eu/environment/waste/pdf/target_ review/GuidanceonEPR-FinalReport.pdf
7. Forti, V., Baldé, C.P., Kuehr, R., Bel, G.: The Global E-waste Monitor 2020: Quantities, flows and the circular economy potential. United Nations University (UNU)/United Nations Institute for Training and Research (UNITAR) – co-hosted SCYCLE Programme, International Telecommunication Union (ITU) & International Solid Waste Association (ISWA), Bonn/Geneva/Rotterdam (2020)
8. Fundación Recyclapolis: Fundación Recyclapolis. Obtenido de Recyclapolis, 18 de Mayo de 2016. http://www.recyclapolis.cl/100-contenedodres-para-chile/
9. Ghisolfi, V., Chaves, G., Siman, R.R., Xavier, L.H.: System dynamics applied to closed loop supply chains of desktops and laptops in Brazil: a perspective for social inclusion of waste pickers. Waste Manage. **60**, 14–31 (2017)
10. Golinska, P., Romano, C.A. (eds.): Environmental Issues in Supply Chain Management: New Trends and Applications. Springer, Cham (2012). https://doi.org/10.1007/978-3-642-23562-7
11. González-Feliu, J., Cedillo-Campos, M.G.: Logística y desarrollo territorial. Revista Transporte y Territorio **17**, 1–9 (2017)
12. Gonzalez-Feliu, J., Sánchez-Díaz, I.: The influence of aggregation level and category construction on estimation quality for freight trip generation models. Transp. Res. Part E Logist. Transp. Rev. **121**, 134–148 (2019)
13. Govindan, K., Agarwal, V., Darbari, J.D., Jha, P.C.: An integrated decision making model for the selection of sustainable forward and reverse logistic providers. Ann. Oper. Res. **273**, 607–650 (2019)

14. Hafner, G.: Buenas Prácticas Internacionales en la Gestión de Residuos Sólidos Domiciliarios e Industriales con referencia específica al concepto de la Responsabilidad Extendida del Productor. Alemania, Stuttgart (2016)
15. Holguín-Veras, J., et al.: Transferability of freight trip generation models. Transp. Res. Rec. **2379**(1), 1–8 (2013)
16. Kamczyc, A.: Medals used in the Tokyo Olympics made from recycled materials (2021). Wastetodaymagaine.com
17. Kumar, A.: Exploring young adults' e-waste recycling behaviour using an extended theory of planned behaviour model: a cross-cultural study. Resour. Conserv. Recycl. **141**, 378–389 (2019)
18. Ley 20920: Biblioteca del Congreso Nacional. (M. D. AMBIENTE, Productor) Obtenido de, 12 de Mayo de 2016. https://www.leychile.cl/Navegar?idNorma=1090894&buscar=20920
19. Li-HsingShih.: Reverse logistics system planning for recycling electrical appliances and computers in Taiwan. Resour. Conserv. Recycl. **32**, 55–72 (2001)
20. Massari, F., Monier, V., Serouge, M., Gonzalez-Feliu, J.: The collection and transport of end-of-life products and wastes from the standpoint of reverse logistics. The state of knowledge and methodological proposals. English Synthesis. RECORD/ADEME, Paris (2014)
21. Massari, F., et al.: La collecte et le transport des produits usages et des déchets dans une optique de logistique inverse. Etat des connaissances et propositions méthodologiques. Final Report. RECORD/ADEME, Paris (2013)
22. Morana, J.: Sustainable Supply Chain Management. Wiley, Hoboken (2013)
23. Panepinto, D., Zanetti, M.: Technical and environmental comparison among different municipal solid waste management scenarios. Sustainability **13**, 1–11 (2021)
24. Puntos Limpios El Corte Inglés: Recuperado el 2017, de (2017). https://punto-limpio.info/elcorteingles/residuos-electronicos/
25. Queiruga, D., Walthera, G., González-Benito, J., Spengler, T.: Evaluation of sites for the location of WEEE recycling plants in Spain. Waste Manage. **28**, 181–190 (2008)
26. Recycla: Obtenido de (2004). https://www.recycla.cl/historia.html
27. Recycla: Residuos Electrónicos la nueva basura del siglo XXI. Santiago de Chile: Fundación Casa de la Paz (2007)
28. Resources, Conservation and Recycling: Xu, M. (ed.) Obtenido de (1994). https://www.journals.elsevier.com/resources-conservation-and-recycling
29. Tableau: Obtenido de (2018). https://www.tableau.com/es-es/products/desktop
30. Torricelli, G.P.: Algunas reflexiones sobre Logística y desarrollo territorial (RTT 17/2017). Revista Transporte y Territorio **18**, 372–376 (2018)
31. United Nations University: eWaste en América Latina. GSMA (2015)
32. Walther, G., Spengler, T.: Impact of WEEE-directive on reverse logistics in Germany. Int. J. Phys. Distribut. Logist. Manage. 337–361 (2006)
33. Waste Management: Cossu, R. (ed.) Obtenido de (1989). http://www.sciencedirect.com/science/journal/0956053X?sdc=1
34. Zoeteman, B.C., Venselaar, H.R.: Handling WEEE waste flows: on the effectiveness of producer responsibility in a globalizing world. Int. J. Adv. Manuf. Technol. **47**, 415–436 (2010)

Innovative Marketing Approaches as Triggers to Rural Tourism Sustainability: An In-Depth Analysis to Existing Literature

Sónia Rodrigues[1]([✉]) [ID], Ricardo Correia[1,4] [ID], Ramiro Gonçalves[2,3] [ID], and José Martins[1,2,3] [ID]

[1] Instituto Politécnico de Bragança, Campus de Santa Apolónia, 5300-253 Bragança, Portugal
{sonia.martins,ricardocorreia}@ipb.pt
[2] AquaValor – Centro de Valorização e Transferência de Tecnologia da Água, Chaves, Portugal
ramiro@utad.pt
[3] INESC TEC, Porto, Portugal
[4] CiTUR Guarda – Centro de Investigação, Desenvolvimento e Inovação em Turismo, Guarda, Portugal

Abstract. Rural tourism has become a truly relevant economic activity, with visible impacts (social and economic) to regional and national development and overall sustainability. The sole characteristics of rural destinations make them extremely attractive to tourists that search for experiences away from the massified and more urban areas. Despite this increase in the demand, in order to remain competitive and trigger its development and ensure sustainability, rural destinations need to ensure a twofold approach, first continuously create innovative and engaging tourism experiences, and secondly implement continuously innovative marketing approaches. Hence, to fully understand the state of the art in what concerns the incorporation of innovation by rural tourism marketeers, a systematic literature review focused on that same topic has been performed, the achieved set of 66 articles has been thoroughly analysed, and multiple results of this procedure are presented.

Keywords: Rural tourism · Innovation · Marketing · Sustainability · Systematic literature review

1 Introduction

Despite the United Nations World Tourism Organization' disclaimer on the concept of rural tourism as something very much related to experiences that take place in non-urban areas where tourists can interact with a "wide range of products generally linked to nature-based activities, agriculture, rural lifestyle / culture and sightseeing" [1], this type of tourism has been (re)defined by scholars throughout the time in order to further establish its boundaries [2]. If in the early 1900s authors claimed rural tourism was a difficult concept to define, Lane [3] endured on and established that in order for a tourism activity to be considered as rural tourism it had to assume a set of particularities such

T. Guarda et al. (Eds.): ARTIIS 2021, CCIS 1485, pp. 653–663, 2021.
https://doi.org/10.1007/978-3-030-90241-4_50

as being located in rural areas, built-upon these rural areas particular small-scale and traditional features and its natural resources, heritage and history.

As the world becomes increasingly digital, the relevance of incorporating Information and Communication Technologies (ICT) in all business trades has also become prominent. The tourism sector is no stranger to this evolution, as innovative tourism products and supporting solutions are being drawn by actively incorporating the referred technologies as their backbone [4, 5]. However, despite this willingness to innovate, there is still a digital divide that impales the tourism sector and that has its origin on both technical, social and motivational factors, to the point of being relatively easy to identify digital-related issues on both tourists and destinations [6].

In rural areas the digital divide is even significant as these territories tend to be, by nature, deprived of technological resources, human resources specialized in ICT-related areas, economic resources and, above all, a pro-innovation mindset. Despite this difficult context, according to Akca et al. [7], the yearly efforts of both (national and regional) governments and rural populations are paying off, and a novel set of opportunities is emerging, mainly due to the gradual adoption of ICT and to the implementation of a (wired and wireless) communication network that allows for rural regions to, literally, connect to the world [8, 9].

According to Richmond et al. [10] and Król [11], in order for rural destinations and businesses to fully battle against the existing digital divide as this will allow them to achieve development and growth through the incorporating of innovative and disruptive solutions/tools/technologies. One example of this innovative mindset is perceivable in the use of digital tools and technologies to define, plan and implement differentiating (digital) marketing initiatives.

From a conceptual perspective, the digital marketing concept is consensually accepted not only as the marketing of products and services through digital channels, but also as a social process through which individuals and organizations use digital technologies to attract customers, improve knowledge on current customers - thus triggering and personalizing the offer to their - needs, to promote brands, boost partnerships and increase sales [12, 13].

The main purpose of this paper is to present a Systematic Literature Review (SLR), supported by 66 papers, focused on both the innovative uses of marketing in the tourism sector, and on the issues that must be attained when planning and implementing marketing initiatives to the abovementioned sector. Considering that, to the best of our knowledge, there is no similar published research, this paper should be perceived as a contribute to both the scientific research community and the tourism sector stakeholders (organizations, regulators, governmental bodies, and tourists).

The remainder of the manuscript is composed by other four sections. While Sect. 2 presents the methodological approach associated to our research, the 3rd section of the paper presents the SLR results and achieved considerations. The fourth section reports on the conceptual framework that has been built as a consequence of the performed SLR. Finally, the 5th and final section of the paper debates on the reached conclusions, established implications, detected limitations and future research.

2 Methodological Approach

As argued by Paré et al. [14], the sheer creation of innovation and novel artefacts should always be drawn by previous theoretical and practical knowledge. The analysis of relevant literature will allow for a detailed understanding of both concepts and practical applications of those concepts, and also the basis for critically establishing novel theories and hypothesis. Drawing on Fernandes & Pires [15], by performing a systematic literature review (SLR) the bias that might arise from narrative analysis is deprecated and the achieve perception of the concepts is improved.

2.1 Research Strategy

According to Baptista et al. [16] and Ovčjak et al. [17], in order to accurately perform a SLR one must ensure a sequential set of tasks: i) establish the research question to which the literature review will aim at; ii) define the literature analysis and assessment procedure; and iii) systematization of the achieved results. Adding to this staging, Liberate et al. [18], also argue that to further improve the overall quality of a SLR, one must determine an assessment procedure that allows for a detailed analysis of all the information sources considered of value (i.e. what databases have been use, what was the date of the last research, triage, inclusion and exclusion criteria, quality evaluation, and extraction methods).

Hence, in order to undergo our research we have defined the following as the inherent research question: "How can innovative digital marketing approaches trigger rural tourism?" and, in parallel, we established the SCOPUS database as the one where we would exclusively focus our research efforts, mainly because it is currently considered the most reliable source of recent scientific literature [19, 20]. To formalize the search procedure, SCOPUS search form has been used with a combination of the following keywords applied to the title, keywords and abstract fields: i) "marketing"; ii) "rural"; iii) "tourism"; and "innovat". Considering our research main goal, we have filtered the set of results to only include journal articles published during the period comprised between 2016 and the first trimester of 2021 [21] and publications belonging to the research areas of "Business", "Computer Science" and "Decision Sciences". The search task has been performed during the beginning of the second trimester of 2021.

Drawing on Keele [22], we performed an initial analysis to each identified manuscript, that consisted of a simple validation of whether: i) it seemed relevant to our research; ii) it seemed possibly relevant but needed further analysis; or iii) it was not relevant to our research and ought to be discarded. After this initial procedure, we then applied Sepúlveda et al. [23] and Baptista et al. [16] evaluation procedure, that allowed us to fully perceived which articles represented relevant inputs to our research, and also to reach an answer to the posed research question.

3 Results Analysis

The performed literature analysis allowed to identify 65 journal articles that fitted the defined criteria and would allow to understand how innovative marketing approaches supported by digital technologies can trigger rural tourism development, and thus constitute the initial sample of our research. Drawing on the methodological procedure described above, a quality and adequacy assessment has been made to each of the articles from the initial sample, and this allowed to restrict the study sample to 40 valuable articles.

When analysing the source of the existing literature on the application of innovative approaches to rural tourism marketing, it was possible to perceive that the gross majority of the identified articles have been published in top SCOPUS quartile journals (Fig. 1). The journals that published the bigger number of (the identified) papers have been a) Journal of Place Management and Development; b) Tourism and Hospitality Research; and c) Journal of Travel Research.

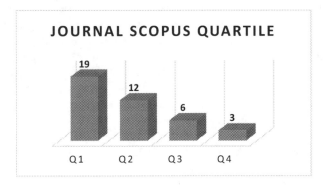

Fig. 1. SCOPUS quartile of the journals where the identified articles have been published.

To understand how the scientific community is addressing the incorporation of innovation and innovative approaches to rural tourism marketing, it was very relevant to analysis the inherent literature publication timeline (Fig. 2). From the performed analysis it was possible to perceive that this is a very up-to-date topic as the number of articles published during the last five years has increased.

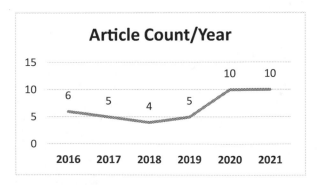

Fig. 2. Count of the identified articles per year from 2016 to 2021.

Aiming at perceiving the disparity in research topics, terms and words subjacent to the identified literature, an extraction of the author keywords as been performed to each of the analysed articles, thus reaching a set of key topics that represent the scope of the referred set of publications. The results of this activity are shown as a word cloud (Fig. 3), where the key topics that are most present in the analysed articles authors' keywords are highlighted through a dimension ratio (i.e., the topic dimension is directly related to the number of occurrences).

Fig. 3. Word cloud representing the overall presence of the identified research key topics on the existing literature.

Hence, the topics that have been identified has those with more direct relation to the incorporation of innovation in the rural tourism scope are: a) rural tourism [24–39]; b) destination marketing [25, 28, 37, 39, 40]; c) rural destination marketing [25, 31]; d) economic development [28, 41]; e) destination loyalty [27, 32, 42]; f) experience design [37, 43]; and g) push/pull/success factors [24, 44–46].

4   Conceptual Framework – What Future Holds

4.1   Rural Tourism

Rural tourism can be perceived as any tourism that takes place in the countryside, that is, in a territory marked by rurality, low population density, increased land use (Eg.: agriculture and forestry), traditional social structures and a community and heritage identity. According to Lane [3], rural tourism must be functionally rural (based on the characteristics of rural space, natural resources and traditional practices), small in scale and traditional in character, with slow growth and controlled by the local population.

Still, the concept of rural tourism is yet to be consensual. For instance, according to Paresishvili et al. [47] the essence of rural tourism is assumed to be living according to local customs and traditions, based on active tourism, rest and recreation and thus making the most of the natural and historical-cultural particularities of the destination.

Hence, by combining these previous conceptualizations with Lewis et al. [25], one can assume the concept of rural tourism as a tourism that takes place in low-density rural areas, that is contrary to the concept of mass tourism, that is typically characterized for a very individual and personalized service provision, and where nature, history and culture are closely bonded together.

Considering the existing migration movements from rural territories to more urban regions, rural tourism has gained additional relevance as it has the ability to trigger economic and social development, thus creating conditions for those that live in these regions to thrive and ensure regional sustainability.

4.2 Innovative Marketing Approaches to Promote Rural Tourism

From the performed SLR one was able to identify multiple topics that, if not innovative approaches themselves, are directly related to the establishment of innovation to rural tourism marketing initiatives. In Table 1 one can distinguish the innovation topics and approaches that were considered of utmost value to present and future research.

Table 1. Innovative approaches and Innovation topics that arise from the performed SLR.

Ref(s)	Innovative approaches and innovation topics
[24, 41]	By performing qualitative and quantitative studies, authors were able to establish that in order to implement efficient and effective marketing initiatives focused on rural tourism, it is critical the ensure a given alignment between those responsible for managing tourism (i.e., public sector) and those that have rural tourism related business (i.e., private sector). In fact, to be successful, it is critical that a novel management approach is applied, where stakeholders assume a decentralized management supported by community-based partnerships and oriented to ensure destinations' competitiveness
[30, 48–50]	Despite having followed the conventional approaches to the implementation of successful marketing initiatives, those who are focused on promoting (and developing) rural tourism must assume that a more detailed analysis has to be made to the population segments to whom they are directing their initiatives. According to the literature that has been analysed marketeers should not only define very narrow target-groups to their initiatives, but also consider the creation of population clusters (based on personality and behavioural traits) that are prone to be aligned to the rural destination features and characteristics. This innovative approach tends to not only allow for an easier communication but also to a more effective trigger to tourists' behavioural change. The existing literature also suggests the use of digital platforms and technologies (eg. Digital marketing), to foster the abovementioned approaches and initiatives

(continued)

Table 1. (*continued*)

Ref(s)	Innovative approaches and innovation topics
[27–29, 38, 51]	As tourists become increasingly aware and concerned with destinations sustainability, nature conservation and efficient resource management, marketers must indulge this mindset and, consequently, ensure alignment with their marketing initiatives. If, until very recently, when promoting rural tourism destinations, marketers would only slightly enclose these "green concerns" in their marketing initiatives, in order to ensure success in the near future, they must implement novel design and deployment tools (e.g.: eco-brand, eco-label, and environmental advertisement) and methodologies (e.g.: using sustainable marketing formats and content). This new and innovative approach, when properly defined, planned, and executed will, according to existing literature, trigger tourists behavioural change, thus ensuring they will engage with the rural destination
[35, 36, 39, 43]	As argued by the existing literature, not only the rural tourism related, but the majority of the "Tourism" related, as tourists become increasingly involved in the process of researching and analysing in detail the tourism destination before even arriving there, tourism operators must ensure that the provided experience is, at the very least, memorable. Hence, in order to continue competitive, rural destination marketeers must adopt innovative marketing approaches (mostly technology-based: e.g. virtual and augmented reality; featured mobile applications; digital marketing) that allow for the tourist to have an immersive experience that not only becomes memorable, but also trigger revisit and word-of-mouth behaviours

5 Conclusions, Limitations and Future Research

This paper aimed at describing and delivering the results of a systematic literature review centred on understanding what rural tourism innovation related topics and approaches are being focused by existing scientific literature published on Scopus database. To the best of our knowledge the presented SLR is a novel contribute to science and practice, as it has been possible to highlight present and future research innovative approaches and topics, some with a theoretical nature and others with a more managerial implication.

From the performed analysis it was possible to perceive that the majority of identified papers have been published in first and second quartile Scopus journals in a time period comprised by the last three years. From a content perspective, it was also possible to acknowledge that a good part of the identified papers authors considered that keywords such as "rural tourism", "destination marketing", "rural destination marketing", "economic development", "tourist loyalty", "experience design" and "push/pull/success factors", were the ones that most represented their research and the achieved results.

After thoroughly analysing all the articles from our final dataset it was possible to establish the existence of four main research directions that focus on the incorporation of innovation to rural tourism marketing: a) novel management approaches to rural tourism and rural destinations; b) improved, finer and feature-based segmentations of the target-population; c) rural tourism sustainability, green and eco-friendly rural destinations and marketing approaches; and d) adoption of (technological) innovation to the marketing process in order to deliver memorable experiences that trigger tourism behavioural change towards that destination.

Despite best efforts, the presented SLR is still limited to the search protocol that was established, hence does not cover the totality of existing literature addressing the incorporation of innovation to the rural tourism marketing processes. Even though this should be considered a limitation it is aligned with other similar works [15, 52]. Hence, a future work to be considered for this research is the widening of the search protocol in order for it to not only collect scientific contributes from other sources than Scopus journal list, but also to incorporate conference papers, Web of Science papers and also published/approved thesis [16, 53]. In order to establish, with an increased detail, the timeline associated with the innovative uses of marketing for promoting rural tourism, the search protocol should also consider articles published during the last decade [54].

References

1. UNWTO: Rural Tourism (2019). https://www.unwto.org/rural-tourism. Accessed 05 Jun 2021
2. Ayazlar, G., Ayazlar, R.: Rural tourism: a conceptual approach. In: Dinu, M., Hacıoğlu, N., Avcıkurt, C., Efe, R., Soykan, A. (eds.) Tourism, Environment and Sustainability, pp. 167–184. St. Kliment Ohridski University Press (2015)
3. Lane, B.: What is rural tourism? J. Sustain. Tour. **2**(1–2), 7–21 (1994)
4. Matos, A., et al.: Smart Cities and Smart Tourism: What Future Do They Bring? BT - New Knowledge in Information Systems and Technologies, pp. 358–370 (2019)
5. Martins, J., Gonçalves, R., Au-Yong-Oliveira, M., Moreira, F., Branco, F.: Qualitative analysis of virtual reality adoption by tourism operators in low-density regions. IET Softw. **14**(6), 684–692 (2020)
6. Minghetti, V., Buhalis, D.: Digital divide in tourism. J. Travel Res. **49**(3), 267–281 (2009). https://doi.org/10.1177/0047287509346843
7. Akca, H., Sayili, M., Esengun, K.: Challenge of rural people to reduce digital divide in the globalized world: theory and practice. Gov. Inf. Q. **24**(2), 404–413 (2007). https://doi.org/10.1016/j.giq.2006.04.012
8. Prieger, J.E.: The broadband digital divide and the economic benefits of mobile broadband for rural areas. Telecomm. Policy **37**(6), 483–502 (2013). https://doi.org/10.1016/j.telpol.2012.11.003
9. Philip, L., Williams, F.: Remote rural home based businesses and digital inequalities: understanding needs and expectations in a digitally underserved community. J. Rural Stud. **68**, 306–318 (2019)
10. Richmond, W., Rader, S., Lanier, C.: The 'digital divide' for rural small businesses. J. Res. Mark. Entrep. **19**(2), 94–104 (2017). https://doi.org/10.1108/JRME-02-2017-0006
11. Król, K.: Forgotten agritourism: abandoned websites in the promotion of rural tourism in Poland. J. Hosp. Tour. Technol. **10**(3), 431–442 (2019)
12. Chaffey, D., Smith, P.R., Smith, P R.: eMarketing eXcellence: Planning and Optimizing your Digital Marketing. Routledge, London (2013)
13. Kannan, P.K., Alice Li, H.: Digital marketing: a framework, review and research agenda. Int. J. Res. Mark. **34**(1), 22–45 (2017). https://doi.org/10.1016/j.ijresmar.2016.11.006
14. Paré, G., Trudel, M.-C., Jaana, M., Kitsiou, S.: Synthesizing information systems knowledge: a typology of literature reviews. Inf. Manag. **52**(2), 183–199 (2015). https://doi.org/10.1016/j.im.2014.08.008

15. Fernandes, C., Pires, R.: Technological innovation in hotels: open the 'Black Box' using a systematic literature review. In: Education Excellence and Innovation Management: A 2025 Vision to Sustain Economic Development during Global Challenges, pp. 6770–6779 (2020). https://ibima.org/accepted-paper/technological-innovation-in-hotels-open-the-black-box-using-a-systematic-literature-review/
16. Baptista, A., Martins, J., Goncalves, R., Branco, F., Rocha, T.: Web accessibility challenges and perspectives: a systematic literature review. In: 2016 11th Iberian Conference on Information Systems and Technologies (CISTI), pp. 1–6 (2016)
17. Ovčjak, B., Heričko, M., Polančič, G.: Factors impacting the acceptance of mobile data services–a systematic literature review. Comput. Human Behav. **53**, 24–47 (2015)
18. Liberati, A., et al.: The PRISMA statement for reporting systematic reviews and meta-analyses of studies that evaluate health care interventions: explanation and elaboration. J. Clin. Epidemiol. **62**(10), e1–e34 (2009)
19. Aghaei Chadegani, A., et al.: A comparison between two main academic literature collections: web of Science and Scopus databases. Asian Soc. Sci. **9**(5), 18–26 (2013)
20. Durán-Sánchez, A., Álvarez-García, J., de la, M., del Río-Rama, C., Rosado-Cebrián, B.: Science mapping of the knowledge base on tourism innovation. Sustainability **11**(12), 3352 (2019)
21. Ahmad, S., Miskon, S., Alkanhal, T.A., Tlili, I.: Modeling of business intelligence systems using the potential determinants and theories with the lens of individual, technological, organizational, and environmental contexts-a systematic literature review. Appl. Sci. **10**(9), 3208 (2020)
22. Keele, S.: Guidelines for performing systematic literature reviews in software engineering, Technical report, Ver. 2.3 EBSE Technical Report. EBSE (2007)
23. Sepúlveda, S., Cravero, A., Cachero, C.: Requirements modeling languages for software product lines: a systematic literature review. Inf. Softw. Technol. **69**, 16–36 (2016)
24. Tirado Ballesteros, J.G., Hernández Hernández, M.: Challenges facing rural tourism management: a supply-based perspective in Castilla-La Mancha (Spain). Tour. Hosp. Res. **21**(2), 216–228 (2021)
25. Lewis, C., Nelson, K., Black, R.: Moving Millennials out of the too hard basket: exploring the challenges of attracting Millennial tourists to rural destinations. J. Hosp. Tour. Manag. **46**, 96–103 (2021)
26. Cheuk, S., Atang, A., Chiun, L.M., Ramayah, T.: Barriers to digital marketing adoption at remote rural tourism destinations in Sarawak: an exploratory study. Int. J. Eng. Technol. **7**(2), 86–90 (2018). https://doi.org/10.14419/ijet.v7i2.29.13135
27. Campón-Cerro, A.M., Hernández-Mogollón, J.M., Alves, H.: Sustainable improvement of competitiveness in rural tourism destinations: the quest for tourist loyalty in Spain. J. Destin. Mark. Manag. **6**(3), 252–266 (2017)
28. Peroff, D.M., Deason, G.G., Seekamp, E., Iyengar, J.: Integrating frameworks for evaluating tourism partnerships: an exploration of success within the life cycle of a collaborative ecotourism development effort. J. Outdoor Recreat. Tour. **17**, 100–111 (2017)
29. Gronau, W.: Encouraging behavioural change towards sustainable tourism: a German approach to free public transport for tourists. J. Sustain. Tour. **25**(2), 265–275 (2017)
30. Polo Peña, A.I., Frías Jamilena, D.M., Rodríguez Molina, M.Á., Rey Pino, J.M.: Online marketing strategy and market segmentation in the Spanish rural accommodation sector. J. Travel Res. **55**(3), 362–379 (2016)
31. Sykes, D., Kelly, K.G.: Motorcycle drive tourism leading to rural tourism opportunities. Tour. Econ. **22**(3), 543–557 (2016)

32. Hernández-Mogollón, J.M., Alves, H., Campón-Cerro, A.M., Di-Clemente, E.: Integrating transactional and relationship marketing: a new approach to understanding destination loyalty. Int. Rev. Publ. Nonprofit Market. **18**(1), 3–26 (2020). https://doi.org/10.1007/s12208-020-00258-z
33. Martínez, J., Martín, J., Fernández, J., Mogorrón-Guerrero, H.: An analysis of the stability of rural tourism as a desired condition for sustainable tourism. J. Bus. Res. **100**, 165–174 (2019). https://doi.org/10.1016/j.jbusres.2019.03.033
34. Chang, K.C.: The affecting tourism development attitudes based on the social exchange theory and the social network theory. Asia Pacific J. Tour. Res. **26**(2), 167–182 (2021)
35. Ye, S., Wei, W., Wen, J., Ying, T., Tan, X.: Creating memorable experience in rural tourism: a comparison between domestic and outbound tourists. J. Travel Res. 0047287520951641 (2020)
36. Oriade, A., Broad, R., Gelder, S.: Alternative use of farmlands as tourism and leisure resources: diversification, innovations and competitiveness. Int. J. Manag. Pract. **13**(5), 565–586 (2020)
37. Wang, M., Chen, L.-H., Su, P., Morrison, A.M.: The right brew? An analysis of the tourism experiences in rural Taiwan's coffee estates. Tour. Manag. Perspect. **30**, 147–158 (2019)
38. Chin, C.-H., Chin, C.-L., Wong, W.P.-M.: The implementation of green marketing tools in rural tourism: the readiness of tourists? J. Hosp. Mark. Manag. **27**(3), 261–280 (2018)
39. Kastenholz, E., Carneiro, M.J., Marques, C.P., Loureiro, S.M.C.: The dimensions of rural tourism experience: impacts on arousal, memory, and satisfaction. J. Travel Tour. Mark. **35**(2), 189–201 (2018)
40. Stylidis, D., Cherifi, B.: Characteristics of destination image: visitors and non-visitors' images of London. Tour. Rev. (2018)
41. Clark, J., Rice, G.: Revitalising rural Scotland: loch Fyne, branding and belonging. J. Place Manag. Dev. (2019)
42. Alves, H., Campón-Cerro, A.M., Hernández-Mogollón, J.M.: Enhancing rural destinations' loyalty through relationship quality. Spanish J. Mark. (2019)
43. Agapito, D., Pinto, P., Ascenção, M.P., Tuominen, P.: Designing compelling accommodationscapes: testing a framework in a rural context. Tour. Hosp. Res. 1467358420972753 (2020)
44. Al Adwan, A.: The impact of motivation factors and intention to adopt Jordan as a destination for medical tourism in the middle east. Marketing **16**(2), 146–158 (2020)
45. Marchini, A., Riganelli, C., Diotallevi, F.: The success factors of food events: the case study of umbrian extra virgin olive oil. J. Food Prod. Mark. **22**(2), 147–167 (2016)
46. Pashkus, V.Y., Pashkus, N.A., Krasnikova, T.S., Pashkus, M.V.: Realization of breakthrough positioning strategy for agritourist objects. J. Environ. Manag. Tour. **7**(3)(15), 439–448 (2016)
47. Paresishvili, O., Kvaratskhelia, L., Mirzaeva, V.: Rural tourism as a promising trend of small business in Georgia: topicality, capabilities, peculiarities. Ann. Agrar. Sci. **15**(3), 344–348 (2017)
48. Alavion, S.J., Taghdisi, A.: Rural E-marketing in Iran; modeling villagers' intention and clustering rural regions. Inf. Process. Agric. **8**(1), 105–133 (2021). https://doi.org/10.1016/j.inpa.2020.02.008
49. Chowdhary, N., Kaurav, R.P.S., Sharma, S.: Segmenting the domestic rural tourists in India. Tour. Rev. Int. **24**(1), 23–36 (2020)
50. Rodrigues, S., Correia, R.F., Martins, J.: Digital marketing impact on rural destinations promotion : a conceptual model proposal. In: 2021 16th Iberian Conference on Information Systems and Technologies (CISTI), pp. 1–8 (2021) https://doi.org/10.23919/CISTI52073.2021.9476533
51. Hultman, J., Säwe, F.: Absence and presence of social complexity in the marketization of sustainable tourism. J. Clean. Prod. **111**, 327–335 (2016)

52. Følstad, A., Kvale, K.: Customer journeys: a systematic literature review. J. Serv. Theory Pract. **28**(2), 196–227 (2018). https://doi.org/10.1108/JSTP-11-2014-0261
53. Martins, J., Gonçalves, R., Pereira, J., Oliveira, T., Cota, M.P.: Social networks sites adoption at firm level: a literature review. In: 2014 9th Iberian Conference on Information Systems and Technologies (CISTI), pp. 1–6 (2014). https://doi.org/10.1109/CISTI.2014.6876910
54. Amrollahi, A., Ghapanchi, A.H., Talaei-Khoei, A.: A systematic literature review on strategic information systems planning: insights from the past decade. Pacific Asia J. Assoc. Inf. Syst. **5**(2), 39–66 (2013)

Smart Tourism Destinations: A Content Analysis Based on the View of the Experts

Adalberto Santos-Júnior[1]([✉]) [ID], Sofia Almeida[2,4] [ID], Fernando Almeida-García[3] [ID],
and José Manuel Simões[4] [ID]

[1] Mercosur Integration Center, Federal University of Pelotas, Pelotas 96020-080, Brazil
adalberto.santos@ufpel.edu.br
[2] Universidade Europeia, 1500-210 Lisboa, Portugal
salmeida@universidadeeuropeia.pt
[3] Department of Geography, University of Málaga, 29071 Málaga, Spain
falmeida@uma.es
[4] Centre of Geographical Studies, IGOT, Universidade de Lisboa, 1600-276 Lisboa, Portugal
jmsimoes@campus.ul.pt

Abstract. The objectives of this research are to identify and to analyse the view of experts in tourism, geographic information system and spatial planning regarding smart tourism destinations, using the case of the city of Lisbon, the capital of Portugal. Therefore, focusing on the convergence of the concepts of smart tourism destinations and smart cities, a qualitative research was conducted based on semi-structured interviews and content analysis. According to the theoretical-conceptual perspective and the opinion of the experts, Lisbon is recognized as a very attractive and competitive tourist destination but is still in the process of establishing itself as a smart destination. Considering the factors that constitute smart cities and smart tourist destinations, the results show that Lisbon stands out especially in relation to culture and creativity, innovation, information and communication technologies, sustainability, and governance. Although the city of Lisbon has a consolidated strategic plan for tourism and a strong public-private relationship, to become a smart tourism destination, it is essential that there is greater investment in technological infrastructure, greater involvement of citizens in the process of tourism governance and better information management as a strategic tool for tourism.

Keywords: Smart tourism destination · Smart city · Information and communication technologies · Lisbon · Experts

1 Introduction

Faced with the challenges of the contemporary world, it is essential that tourist destinations decision makers establish new tourism development strategies, based above all on sustainability, new technologies and innovation, in order to preserve the resources of the destinations (natural and cultural) and to generate value for tourists (tourist experiences) and local communities (quality of life). Considering the serious global health

© Springer Nature Switzerland AG 2021
T. Guarda et al. (Eds.): ARTIIS 2021, CCIS 1485, pp. 664–683, 2021.
https://doi.org/10.1007/978-3-030-90241-4_51

crisis that the COVID19 pandemic generated in 2020, it is observed that the tourism sector is rethinking issues that have been known and debated for a long time, mainly about the influence of the macro-environment and the impacts of tourism [1], so that it can reinvent, reorganize, and develop.

With the advancement of information and communication technologies (ICT), which include a range of technological tools [2, 3], it is assumed that both tourism companies and the tourism destinations management would be driven to develop new processes, new products, and new forms of organization, in order to increase competitiveness and meet the new market and the local community needs. Thus, from the extension of the definition of smart cities [4, 5], in the 2010s the concept of smart tourism destinations (STD) emerged, to mention those territories based essentially on a cutting-edge technological infrastructure [6] that they are able to improve tourist satisfaction and increase the residents quality of life [7–9].

Based on the intensive use of ICT, the smart tourism destinations, together with the smart business ecosystem and smart experiences, constitute the components of smart tourism [10, 11], which is a topic that is highlighted in the academic and professional world, but in the initial phase of research development [12, 13]. Because it is a recent research, there are still few publications on STD in the literature, mainly in relation to their dimensions or factors [14, 15]. In much of the research, the technological factor is highlighted, however, the combination with other factors is essential to convert a STD, taking into consideration its complex and dynamic ecosystem [16, 17].

Based on the above, this study is an empirical analysis of a case study of the city of Lisbon, the capital of Portugal, which is recognized for its vocation to tourism and is characterized as an European smart city. Therefore, we sought to answer the following questions: What is the perception of the experts about Lisbon as a smart tourism destination? In this way, the objectives of this research are to identify and to analyze the vision of the experts in tourism, geographic information system and spatial planning on the city of Lisbon, taking into consideration the dimensions of the smart tourism destination.

Through the content analysis of the perception of the experts, the analysis of the Lisbon tourism situation is identified and the main aspects of improvement to transform the city into a STD are determined. The results of this study can offer theoretical contributions, as well as contribute with information about the tourism industry and help decision makers to develop STD.

2   Literature Review

The concept of smart tourism emerged in the early 2010s from the integration of the tourism phenomenon with ICT [10, 18]. Through the literature review, it is perceived that the idea of "smart" is essentially linked to the intensive use of ICT [11–13] or smart technologies and smart solutions [19], which can promote the tourist experience, increase the quality of life of the local community, boost sustainability and competitiveness of tourist destinations, promote knowledge and open innovation, and increase the competitiveness of tourism companies. Among the new technologies, the following stand out: mobile technology, real-time information [20], cloud services and internet services available to end users, internet of things (IoT) [6], applications, virtual reality

(VR) and augmented reality (AR), artificial intelligence (AI), near field communication (NFC) and radio frequency identification (RFID) [19] and big data [18, 21].

Taking into account the scarcity of theoretical-conceptual works [11–13], smart tourism is defined as tourism that relies on integrated efforts in a tourist destination to collect and aggregate data derived from public-private exchange – consumer in combination with the use of ICT, in order to "to transform that data into on-site experiences and business value-propositions with a clear focus on efficiency, sustainability and experience enrichment" [10] (p. 181). Reinforcing this thought, it is inferred that smart tourism is based on a ubiquitous and efficient tourist information service, which is based on the use of big data, which favors the development of innovative e-commerce models and the promotion of consumption of tourist information [18].

Smart tourism is considered to be made up of three components [10, 11]: the smart tourism destination, the smart experience, and the smart business ecosystem. Smart experiences occur throughout the trip in the tourist destination [10], which through the intensive use of smart technologies would allow the enrichment [22], the co-creation of value [19] and satisfaction/happiness of tourists [23, 24]. Smart business ecosystems refer to a network of multiple agents that, through the effective use of information flow and technological platforms, are capable of creating value for tourism companies and tourism experiences [25, 26].

On the other hand, based on the SEGITTUR report [8] (p. 32), the smart tourism destination is defined as "an innovative tourist space, accessible to all, consolidated on a cutting-edge technological infrastructure that guarantees the sustainable development of the territory, facilitates the interaction and integration of the visitor with the environment and increases the quality of their experience in the destination and the quality of life of the residents". In addition to this definition, it is also understood that STDs, through the technological infrastructure provided by the smart city, improves the tourist experience and empowers the destination marketing organizations (DMOs), local institutions and tourism companies to make decisions based on the produced data collected, managed, and processed at destination [20]. From a marketing perspective, STDs, using technological tools, allows demand and supply to co-create value, which produces experiences for tourists and profits and benefits for companies and the destination [14].

In addition to the technological factor, it is observed that few studies indicate other relevant factors that could constitute a STD [8, 14, 25, 27, 28], which have a strong relationship with the economic, sociocultural, environmental, and political dimensions [9] (see Table 1). It is noted that governance, innovation, sustainability and accessibility are the dimensions most cited in the studies. However, the creativity and culture dimension are still little explored. It is important to highlight that each of the dimensions presented and described in Table 1 can be made up with other sub-dimensions, variables and indicators of smart cities models [9, 29, 30].

The relevance of the role of smart technologies in STDs is evident, however, a tourist destination is made up of people, resources and tourist attractions, infrastructure, government, and many stakeholders. Therefore, these other dimensions must be considered when talking about smart places [9]. It is inferred that all these factors are interdependent and interrelated and are influenced by the effects of ICT.

Table 1. Dimensions of the smart tourism destinations

Dimension	Description	References
Governance and leadership	It refers to the stakeholders of tourism: public-private partnerships, government, DMO, and community. In relation to the variables that can be analyzed, transparency, communication, leadership, decision-making, planning and management, strategy, and data protection stands out	[8, 14, 25, 27]
Sustainability	Although the concept of sustainability includes economic, environmental, and socio-cultural factors, this dimension is perceived to be more related to the environmental issues of STDs. E.g., energy efficiency, green areas, waste management, pollution control, carrying capacity	[8, 27]
Accessibility	It relates to the efforts of the STD to include and adapt tourism infrastructure to the needs of people with disabilities, the elderly, pregnant women, and children. It encompasses both public services and business services	[8, 27, 28]
Innovation and entrepreneurship	It refers to the creation of new businesses, the modernization of companies, efficiency of processes, creation of new products and services, startups, open innovation, clusters, entrepreneurial "spirit". Innovation is a very important process to the competitiveness of tourist destinations	[8, 14, 25, 27]
Human capital	It is understood as the set of knowledge, skills and attitudes generated in the tourist destination. This being the case, the professional training of residents, adaptation to new technologies, language skills and access to information could be considered	[14, 25]
Social capital	It refers to the connections, interactions, and networks of relationships of people in STD, which can be intensified with the use of ICT. In that sense, we consider, for example, interactions on social networks, cultural exchange	[14, 25]

(continued)

Table 1. (*continued*)

Dimension	Description	References
Culture and creativity	It refers to the cultural heritage (tangible and intangible) of the tourist destination. Cultural identity, history, creative industry, creative economy, entertainment offerings, modernization and preservation of cultural heritage can be considered	[25, 28]

Thus, ICTs are characterized as cross-cutting factors that affect all dimensions of STD [9], either more intensively (hard effect) or less intensively (soft effect), in relation to their importance as key technologies [30]. In the case of the sustainability factor, ICT systems play a very relevant role in STD planning, using technological infrastructure – information systems, sensors, big data. On the other hand, governance, social capital, human capital, culture and creativity, innovation and entrepreneurship, ICT, play a more limited role.

3   Methodology

3.1   Characterization of the Study

This article is characterized, regarding the approach to the problem, as a qualitative investigation, and as for the objectives, it refers to an exploratory and descriptive study, for which the integration of theoretical and practical knowledge is sought. Regarding the procedures, the bibliographic research methods, documentary research, case studies and content analysis were used. Therefore, taking Lisbon as a case study, interviews were conducted with experts to find out their perceptions on the configuration of the city as a STD. It is noteworthy that the results presented in this paper are preliminary, since this research is under development.

Thus, in the first part of this paper, an exploratory study was developed to delve into the subject of STDs, through bibliographic and documentary research. For bibliographic research, 27 relevant papers published, of a theoretical-conceptual nature and case studies, available on the Scopus and Google Scholar platforms, were selected and analyzed, regarding the topic smart tourism. In the continuation, the documentary research included reference documents on STD, considering the case of Spain, such as the SEGITTUR [8] and IVAT.TUR [27] reports, and the European Commission program "European Capitals of Smart Tourism" [28], which corroborated the definition of the categories of this research. In addition, visits were made to official websites of government institutions and associations in Lisbon and Portugal, and consultations on documents related to tourism and new technologies, such as the plans: "Plano Estratégico de Turismo para Região de Lisboa 2020–2024" [31] and "Estratégia Turismo 2027" [32], and the programme: "Programa Turismo 4.0" [33].

The second part of this paper comprises the descriptive study, which is made up of the case study methods and content analysis. Therefore, taking the city of Lisbon as a case study, intentional sampling of experts in tourism, geographic information system and territorial planning of the renowned University of Lisbon (ULISBOA) was defined, for data collection through in-depth interviews. As is known, the purpose of intentional sampling is to select the specific units of study that generate the most relevant and abundant data in relation to the subject of study [34]. Based on the indication of ULISBOA experts, other experts from other teaching centers around Lisbon have been included: Estoril Higher School of Hospitality and Tourism (ESHTE), and Universidade Europeia (UE). Academic experts are considered one of the agents of tourism, who have a relevant contribution to the exploration of the topic. Due to the certain redundancy or repetition in the responses of the interviewees, the sampling has been determined by saturation, which resulted in interviews carried out with 9 experts in the city of Lisbon, in 2019 (see Table 2). It is observed that a large part of the experts has a doctorate and occupy positions of professor and researcher in recognized universities.

Table 2. Experts interviewed

Gender	Degree	Institution	Position	Interview duration
Female	PhD in geography-spatial planning	ULISBOA	Professor/researcher	0:22:29
Male	PhD in geography-regional and urban planning	ULISBOA	Professor/researcher	0:45:17
Male	PhD in geography-regional and urban planning	ESHTE	Professor/researcher	1:06:26
Male	PhD in human geography	ULISBOA	Professor/researcher	0:36:46
Male	PhD in geography-geographic information science	ULISBOA	Professor/researcher	0:45:02
Male	PhD in geography-regional planning	ESHTE	Professor/researcher	0:52:04
Male	PhD candidate in geography-geographic information science	ULISBOA	Researcher	0:33:23
Female	PhD in Tourism	UE	Professor/researcher	0:59:22
Male	Consultant in innovation and entrepreneurship	UE	Professor/researcher	0:55:06

To carry out the in-depth interviews, a semi-structured script was used with the main points to be discussed, allowing total flexibility in the discussion. The corresponding questions in this script were open-ended and based on the dimensions of the STDs identified in the literature review (see Table 1).

Finally, after transcribing the interview recordings, the data were analyzed using the content analysis method. Content analysis refers to the systematic procedures for describing the content of communications messages, to make inferences of knowledge related to production conditions using quantitative indicators or not [17, 35]. Through content analysis, the segments of the content of the communications that are characterized for categorization are indicated, allowing the establishment of relationships and inferences from them [35].

To develop the content analysis, the data from the interviews were triangulated with the literature review and documentary research, which, through the deductive and inductive approach, allowed to establish the categories/dimensions [8, 9, 14, 25, 27, 28] and subcategories [9, 30, 31] of Lisbon STD, as well as the establishment of the recording units and context (textual fragments of the interviews), respectively. Data was processed using NVIVO 11 for Mac and Excel 16.51 for Mac software.

3.2 Lisbon City Characterization

The case study refers to Lisbon, which is the largest city and municipality in Portugal, made up of a territorial area of approximately 100 km^2. Lisbon is the Capital of the country, the Lisbon Region, the Lisbon District, and the Lisbon Metropolitan Area, having an approximate population of 547,773 inhabitants. The city is located at the mouth of the Tejo River, in the Lisbon Region, which is a region in the center-west of Portugal also known as Estremadura. It has a maximum altitude of 227 m and has an average annual temperature of 17.8 °C, which is very favorable to tourism.

According to data from the Lisbon City Council [36], Lisbon constitutes the Lisbon Metropolitan Area together with more than 17 municipalities, which is an area of relevant economic development in Portugal, where a significant number of companies with a high degree of technology and innovation, being the territorial space where approximately 323,000 companies are installed, which corresponds to a GDP of 66,521 million euros and a GDP per capita of 23.6 thousand euros. Tourism is a very relevant economic activity for the city of Lisbon, which generates approximately 80 thousand jobs. Among the main strengths of Lisbon as a tourist destination, the following stand out: the climate, cultural heritage, hospitality, gastronomy, nightlife, tourist infrastructures, events, business and technological innovation.

Recognized as the green capital of Europe in 2020, Lisbon is a city that develops many initiatives of smart cities and smart tourism destinations, through plans, programs and projects in the field of innovation, technology, sustainability and tourism, developed by government institutions, public-private associations and agencies, such as: "Turismo de Portugal", Lisbon City Council, "Turismo de Lisboa", and "Lisboa E-Nova".

"Turismo de Portugal" is the national tourism authority, linked to the Ministry of the Economy and Digital Transition, whose main objective is the promotion, valuation, and sustainability of tourism activity in Portugal. Among the main innovation initiatives in tourism, the following stand out:

- "Estratégia Turismo 2027" [32]: Portugal's national tourism plan, which has 5 strategic axes: valuing the territory, boosting the economy, promoting knowledge, generating networks and connectivity, and projecting Portugal. Regarding the subject of STDs, the promoting knowledge axis proposes, in one of its lines of action, affirming Portugal as a smart destination.
- "Programa Turismo 4.0" [33]: national initiative whose focus is to promote the transition of tourism activity to the digital economy.

Among the initiatives developed by the Lisbon City Council, the "Smart Open Lisbon" program can be highlighted, which aims to launch projects for the development of innovative solutions to improve tourist satisfaction and the quality of life of tourists. citizens, such as the area of transport, energy, and logistics.

In relation to public-private partnerships and agencies, it is worth highlighting the public-private partnership "Turismo de Lisboa – Visitors & Convention Bureau" and the agency "Lisboa E-Nova – Agência de Energia e Ambiente de Lisboa". The "Turismo de Lisboa" public-private association was created in the 90s, and focuses on the development of sustainable tourism, the promotion of Lisbon as a leisure and MICE (Meetings, Incentives, Conferences and Exhibitions) tourist destination, and the information and support to tourists. One of the most relevant instruments of "Turismo de Lisboa" is the "Plano Estratégico do Turismo para Região de Lisboa 2020–2024" [31], which was developed together with the "ERT-RL – Entidade Regional de Turismo da Região de Lisboa", which has as lines of action: improve accessibility, improve the conditions of tourist attractions, intensify the offer, increase innovation and digitization, adapt the promotion strategy to tourism segments, develop intra-regional and urban mobility, improve management quality of tourism, and guarantee financial and human resources. On the other hand, the "Lisboa E-Nova" agency aims to promote the sustainable development of Lisbon and the respective metropolitan area, with three main axes: energy, water and materials, and four horizontal axes: circular economy, education, communication and data science.

4   Results and Discussion

From the content analysis of the interviews with academic experts, it appears that Lisbon is still at a very early stage in the process of shaping a STD. A set of actions implemented in the city is perceived that are related to the STD dimensions [8, 9, 14, 25, 27, 28]: ICT, innovation, sustainability, accessibility, governance, culture and creativity, human capital, and social capital. From the deductive and inductive approach, the content analysis structure is presented, through its respective categories (dimensions) and subcategories, and registration units and context units (text fragments), with respect to the Lisbon configuration as STD (see Table 3).

Table 3. Structure of the content analysis of the experts' vision of Lisbon as a smart tourism destination.

Categories	Subcategories	Registration unit	Context unit
ICT	Apps		"[…] Geo Estrela, which is in the parish council of Campo de Ourique, I believe, is a Parish here in Lisbon, where there is a team that is constantly monitoring what are the indications of the customers, the people who live in the Parish."
	Big data and information systems		"[…] The way in which this information is managed and how this information can serve to improve the quality of life of citizens is what can be an smart management and then transform the city into an smart one. Otherwise it's just a digital city."
	Investment		"[…] I also think that investment has still been made essentially in areas other than tourism."
	Digitalization		"[…] What I think we obviously live today in a city that is a much more, much more digitized city, I don't know if it is smart but it is much more digitized."
Innovation	Startups		"[…] There is a technology center in Lisbon where companies incubate, Lisbon E-nova itself was born…"

(*continued*)

Table 3. (*continued*)

Categories	Subcategories	Registration unit	Context unit
	Sharing economy		"[…] I think there has been a set of technological innovations in recent years, from the outset the appearance of all these shared economy platforms, this completely transformed the city of Lisbon."
	MICE Tourism		"[…] so here it is the second year and I think that in the next two years the Web Summit, which is the biggest technology event in the world."
	Entrepreneurship		"[…] and a process of creativity of economic agents that has created, both in the area of restaurants and tourist entertainment, as in the area of hotels, new contexts."
	Economic exploitation		"[…] Who are very interested in tourist activity as an economic activity, nothing more"
	Cost of living		"[…] Only those who have money will live here and I will receive people and give the best services I have to receive people."

(*continued*)

Table 3. (*continued*)

Categories	Subcategories	Registration unit	Context unit
Sustainability	Mobility	Public transport	"[…] Some programs including the incorporation of electric buses, there is also a perspective of extending the electric network, which in Portugal, for many years, was destroyed, destroying the tram."
		Alternative transports	"[…] For example, we can see nowadays people riding electric scooters everywhere, or bicycles, or sharing motorbikes, or taxis or whatever, right? So this was absolutely unthinkable."
		Bike lanes	"[…] Well, in recent years in Lisbon, the issue of creating and expanding the network of cycle paths has come to the fore."
		Airport	"[…] There is an infrastructure component that is very strong, which is that the airport is practically inside the city, although it is a danger in another context."
		Pedestrian areas/sidewalk	"[…] on the one hand the reduction of car traffic lanes, isn't it, and there is a certain, therefore, of reducing the lanes of car traffic lanes to these spaces, to give these spaces, to return these spaces to pedestrians, right?"

(*continued*)

Table 3. (*continued*)

Categories	Subcategories	Registration unit	Context unit
	Green areas		"[…] New green spaces, green spaces where I notice that there is already a concern with the type of species that are planted and with their needs, for example, for water."
	Energy efficiency		"[…] I think that a lot of progress has also been made in the field of energy efficiency, in public institutions, in hotels, I think this is very visible"
	Pollution	Noise	"[…] If the opposite is true, that is, if the resident population begins to think that tourists are really just making noise, that they arrive at bad times, that they consume little, that, in other words, they begin to think that the costs are much more than benefits."
		Garbage	"[…] where the garbage trucks should go to pick up first, what are the types of route, by the way, the route is not always the same, therefore the routes are according to whether the equipment is crowded or not, therefore, that's where we start to have smart management."

(*continued*)

Table 3. (*continued*)

Categories	Subcategories	Registration unit	Context unit
	Overtourism		"[…] Heavy in the sense of being very structural in the management of the tourist territory, in the tourist destination, namely in metropolitan dimensions such as Lisbon, which is not yet being achieved, which is the question of the territorial balance of the supply and demand."
Accessibility	Inclusive spaces		"[…] And therefore, restaurants that have to have access roads, spaces for children, access roads for the disabled, etc., so there are still things to be done."
	Legislation		"[…] There is an accessibility standard, which in general is respected and is implemented, it is not, at the level of hotel establishments and which, I think it is, especially for hotel establishments, then there is local accommodation, there may eventually be some."
Governance	ATL		"[…] Then there is a dynamic that is very much in the domain of those of the DMO, which is the "Associação Turismo de Lisboa", and which I think is still a little distant from these innovation dynamics."

(*continued*)

Table 3. (*continued*)

Categories	Subcategories	Registration unit	Context unit
	Private associations	National associations	"[…] but there are also national associations, such as APAVT, APECATE, that's why associations that generate hotels, for example, AHRESP, all these tourism associations…"
		Local associations	"[…] local hosting associations, interest associations… catering…"
	ICT companies		"[…] NOS has the NOS portal, which is a mobile phone operator… One of the mobile phone operators in Portugal, it has a portal dedicated to tourism."
	Government	Turismo de Portugal	"[…] It would have to be Turismo de Portugal."
		Lisbon City Council	"[…] It would have to be the City Council of Lisbon, it is not, therefore, the public entity responsible for the management of the city."
		National government	"[…] The articulation between the local and the regional, whether it exists or not, and the national in a different way."
	Community participation		"[…] Very bad. I think the community is not called to participate, nor to share or discuss and so…"
	Research centers		"[…] should be called a lot, universities, I think they should be called…"

(*continued*)

Table 3. (*continued*)

Categories	Subcategories	Registration unit	Context unit
	Lobby		"[…] it is clear that there was someone who managed to have a lobby, no, to managed to gather friends who had more access to the internet and who voted more for it. And we know that, as interesting as a rugby field is, it won't be one of the things Lisbon needs the most."
Culture and creativity	Tourist attractions		"[…] there is innovation in products by companies or in equipment, for example, something that I defended for many years and that I used to gather, it was made very recently, a museum and the possibility of climbing the 25 de Abril Bridge"
	Requalification of spaces		"[…] There is an intense innovation very, very oriented to the requalification of spaces, that is, old industrial spaces, there is a completely new dynamic in the line that connects the center of Lisbon with the Parque das Nações."
	Abandoned spaces		"[…] there was a whole area of Lisbon that began to be recovered, all the containers were removed from the site, they were industrial warehouse spaces, right, container spaces, really"

(*continued*)

Table 3. (*continued*)

Categories	Subcategories	Registration unit	Context unit
	Experiential city		"[…] In other words, we discover, we rediscover the experience of the river, we rediscover the experience of the night."
Human capital			"[…] I think we grew up. And I think, I'm talking here and a kind of collective intellectual, cultural growth, let's say."
Social capital			"[…] I think the city has become more agile, more resident friendly, despite everything"

The results showed a total of 487 inferences in relation to the established dimensions of a STD, being that 318 (65.30%) inferences represent the good practices of Lisbon as STD, and 169 inferences refer to the negative aspects or weaknesses (34.70%). The factors that have been most prominent are governance, sustainability, culture and creativity, innovation, and ICT. On the other hand, the dimensions of accessibility, social capital and human capital were the ones that received the least inferences (see Fig. 1).

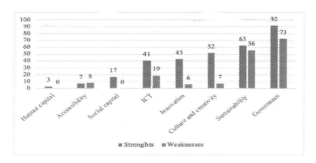

Fig. 1. Number of inferences per dimension

The governance of Lisbon was the dimension that received the most inferences, both positive and negative. Thus, it is understood that governance plays a very relevant role for the implementation and operation of STDs [6]. The experts recognize the importance of the public-private partnership "Associação Turismo de Lisboa (ATL)" for the configuration of Lisbon as STD; however they emphasize that the association should act more in the development of smart actions, and include the community in the governance process of the tourism [9]. According to the interviewees, governance management should encourage the participation of residents, either directly, through digital platforms, or indirectly, through social representations – associations. On the other hand, another aspect observed is that the Lisbon City Council would be the main institution to plan and manage STD programs, projects, and plans, and solve the problems generated by tourist activity, such as overtourism and gentrification.

Regarding the sustainability category, the improvement of the city's public transport service was identified [9, 30, 31], as well as the incentive to use alternative transport, such as scooters and bicycles. The interviewees highlight the creation of the integrated public transport card "Viva Viagem", which allows the user to use different modes of transport within the metropolitan area of Lisbon. In addition, they also commented on the creation of green spaces, and the better use of energy in public buildings [9, 30]. However, the problem of noise and environmental pollution is mentioned due to the increase in tourist flow.

In relation to the dimension of culture and creativity, there is a dynamic in the city that favors night tourism, cultural tourism, urban tourism. It was commented that Lisbon is an experiential city, with a diverse gastronomy, and a very relevant cultural heritage. In addition, he was also informed about the programs of the Lisbon City Council for the requalification of heritage and the modernization of tourist products and attractions [9, 25, 28]. One of the problems identified would be the concentration of tourist attractions in certain areas of the city, which can cause a large flow of people and annoy residents. It should be noted that cultural heritage and the creative economy associated with smart technologies could stimulate the creation of new businesses and complement the tourist offer [30], create value for tourist experiences and increase tourists' satisfaction [23, 24].

Regarding the innovation dimension, the interviewees recognize Lisbon as a favorable region for the development of startups and new ventures. Among the technology and innovation programs, the "Smart Open Lisboa" program was mentioned. Another factor driving tourism in the city is the MICE segment, which includes, for example, the great Web Summit technology event. Another event mentioned, which was a milestone in the transformation of tourism in the city, is Expo98. In the technology category, the award-winning App Geo Estrela stands out, which was developed by the Parish of Estrela of the city of Lisbon, by allowing residents to make directions to solve problems in the neighborhood, including problems generated by tourism. However, all these actions could be intensified and expanded to other parts of the city, in order to have a smart and more integrated management of the destination.

Finally, in relation to the dimensions of social capital, accessibility and human capital, the interviewees indicated, respectively: the characteristic of the Lisbon population to be friendly and hospitable; the compliance with municipal legislation on accessibility by tourism companies, especially by hotel companies; and the intellectual development of society and the strengthening of culture.

Therefore, based on the results and considering the literature review, it is believed that through the coordination and integration of the dimensions of the STD, satisfaction can be generated for both tourists and residents. Through good management and governance, and the use of new technologies, it is possible to generate valuable tourist experiences [19] and improve the quality of life of the community [8, 9].

5   Conclusion

This study sought to analyze the perception of academic experts, to explore the theme of Lisbon as a smart tourism destination. It has been observed in recent years that Lisbon has consolidated itself in the touristic panorama, essentially because it is characterized as an innovative, sustainable, and experiential city.

The results show that Lisbon is still in the early stages of establishing itself as a STD. It is concluded that ICTs are key and cross-cutting factors of STD [9], however, it is also necessary to invest in human and social capital, have good governance, develop actions for sustainability, innovation, and accessibility, and preserve and modernize cultural heritage.

Governance was perceived to play a very relevant role in the STD implementation and operation [6, 17]. In this way, one of the aspects observed is the existence of a public-private tourism association, named "Associação Turismo de Lisboa (ATL)", which, through the increasing implementation of smart actions and solutions, could develop Lisbon as a STD. Another very important factor is the existence of strategic plans and programs that favor the transformation of Lisbon as STD. On the other hand, it is highlighted that the participation of the community and the debate with the research centers is essential for the conformation of Lisbon as a more inclusive, accessible, and sustainable tourist destination.

In the tourism literature, the topic of STD is still in the early stages of research. Therefore, this article corroborates with theoretical and practical contributions, by indicating the main dimensions or factors that constitute the STD. Through content analysis, it was possible to frame the inferences in the context of the dimensions of the STDs, which were identified in the bibliographic analysis. These dimensions could help decision makers in the STD implementation and development process.

Regarding the limitations of this research, it should be considered that the interviews were directed only to representatives of three universities. As it is an investigation in the development stage, it is intended to include other stakeholders: representatives of tourism and ICT companies, residents, the government, and public institutions, with the aim of having a vision more comprehensive and consolidated on the smart tourism process. On the other hand, as proposals for future lines of research, it would be interesting to carry out a quantitative study on the perception of residents (social capital) and tourism workers (human capital) of Lisbon as a smart tourism destination. This triangulation will allow for the confrontation of perspectives and will help decision makers to make more informed decisions, which will contribute to the creation of sustainable STD.

Funding. This research was supported by Portuguese national funds through the Fundação para a Ciência e a Tecnologia (FCT, I.P.), under the grants «UIDB/GEO/00295/2020» and «UIDP/GEO/00295/2020».

References

1. Almeida-García, F., Peláez-Fernández, M.Á., Balbuena-Vazquez, A., Cortes-Macias, R.: Residents' perceptions of tourism development in Benalmádena (Spain). Tour. Manage. **54**, 259–274 (2016)

2. Buhalis, D., Law, R.: Progress in information technology and tourism management: 20 years on and 10 years after the internet – the state of eTourism research. Tour. Manage. **29**(4), 609–623 (2008)
3. Buhalis, D.: Technology in tourism-from information communication technologies to eTourism and smart tourism towards ambient intelligence tourism: a perspective article. Tour. Rev. **75**(1), 267–272 (2019)
4. Zhu, W., Zhang, L., Li, N.: Challenges, function changing of government and enterprises in Chinese smart tourism. Inf. Commun. Technol. Tour. **10**, 553–564 (2014)
5. Guo, Y., Liu, H., Chai, Y.: The embedding convergence of smart cities and tourism internet of things in China: an advance perspective. Adv. Hosp. Tour. Res. **2**(1), 54–69 (2014)
6. Buhalis, D., Amaranggana, A.: Smart tourism destinations. In: Xiang, Z., Tussyadiah, I. (eds.) Information and Communication Technologies in Tourism 2014, pp. 553–564. Springer, Cham (2013)
7. López de Ávila, A., García, S.: Destinos Turísticos Inteligentes. Economía Industrial. **395**, 61–69 (2015)
8. SEGITTUR (Secretaría de Estado de Telecomunicaciones y para la Sociedad de la Información a la Sociedad Estatal para la Gestión de la Innovación y las Tecnologías Turísticas, S.A.): Informe destinos turísticos inteligentes: construyendo el futuro. https://www.seg ittur.es/wp-content/uploads/2019/11/Libro-Blanco-Destinos-Tursticos-Inteligentes.pdf. Last Accessed 05 July 2021
9. Santos-Júnior, A., Almeida-García, F., Morgado, P., Mendes-Filho, L.: Residents' quality of life in smart tourism destinations: a theoretical approach. Sustainability **12**(20), 8445 (2020)
10. Gretzel, U., Sigala, M., Xiang, Z., Koo, C.: Smart tourism: foundations and developments. Electron. Mark. **25**(3), 179–188 (2015). https://doi.org/10.1007/s12525-015-0196-8
11. Celdrán-Bernabeu, M.A., Mazón, J.N., Ivars-Baidal, J.A., Vera-Rebollo, J.F.: Smart Tourism.: un estudio de mapeo sistemático. Cuad. Tur. (41) (2018)
12. Mehraliyev, F., Chan, I.C.C., Choi, Y., Koseoglu, M.A., Law, R.: A state-of-the-art review of smart tourism research. J. Travel Tour. Mark. **37**(1), 78–91 (2020)
13. Ye, B.H., Ye, H., Law, R.: Systematic review of smart tourism research. Sustainability **12**(8), 3401 (2020)
14. Boes, K., Buhalis, D., Inversini, A.: Conceptualising smart tourism destination dimensions. In: Tussyadiah, I., Inversini, A. (eds.) Information and Communication Technologies in Tourism 2015, pp. 391–403. Springer, Cham (2015)
15. Ivars-Baidal, J.A., Celdrán-Bernabeu, M.A., Mazón, J.-N., Perles-Ivars, Á.F.: Smart destinations and the evolution of ICTs: a new scenario for destination management? Curr. Issue Tour. **22**(13), 1581–1600 (2019)
16. Baggio, R., Micera, R., Del Chiappa, G.: Smart tourism destinations: a critical reflection. J. Hosp. Tour. Technol. (2020)
17. Santos-Júnior, A., Mendes-Filho, L., Almeida-García, F., Manuel-Simões, J.: Smart tourism destinations: a study based on the view of the stakeholders. Rev. Turismo Análise **28**(3), 358–379 (2017)
18. Li, Y., Hu, C., Huang, C., Duan, L.: The concept of smart tourism in the context of tourism information services. Tour. Manage. **58**, 293–300 (2017)
19. Femenia-Serra, F., Neuhofer, B.: Smart tourism experiences: conceptualisation, key dimensions and research agenda. J. Reg. Res. **42**, 129–150 (2018)
20. Lamsfus, C., Wang, D., Alzua-Sorzabal, A., Xiang, Z.: Going mobile: defining context for on-the-go travelers. J. Travel Res. **54**(6), 691–701 (2015)
21. Del Vecchio, P., Mele, G., Ndou, V., Secundo, G.: Creating value from social big data: implications for smart tourism destinations. Inf. Process. Manage. **54**(5), 847–860 (2018)
22. Huang, C.D., Goo, J., Nam, K., Yoo, C.W.: Smart tourism technologies in travel planning: the role of exploration and exploitation. Inf. Manag. **54**(6), 757–770 (2017)

23. Pai, C.K., Liu, Y., Kang, S., Dai, A.: The role of perceived smart tourism technology experience for tourist satisfaction, happiness and revisit intention. Sustainability **12**(16), 6592 (2020)

24. Lee, H., Lee, J., Chung, N., Koo, C.: Tourists' happiness: are there smart tourism technology effects? Asia Pac. J. Tour. Res. **23**(5), 486–501 (2018)

25. Boes, K., Buhalis, D., Inversini, A.: Smart tourism destinations: ecosystems for tourism destination competitiveness. Int. J. Tour. Cities **2**(2), 108–124 (2016)

26. Gretzel, U., Werthner, H., Koo, C., Lamsfus, C.: Conceptual foundations for understanding smart tourism ecosystems. Comput. Hum. Behav. **50**, 558–563 (2015)

27. Invat.tur (Instituto Valenciano de Tecnologías Turísticas): http://www.thinktur.org/media/ Manual-dedestinos-tur%C3%ADsticos-inteligentes.pdf. Last Accessed 05 July 2021

28. European Commission: European capital of smart tourism. https://smarttourismcapital.eu. Last Accessed 05 Nov 2019

29. Giffinger, R., Fertner, C., Kramar, H., Kalasek, R., Pichler-Milanović, N., Meijers, E.: Smart Cities: Ranking of European Medium-Sized Cities. Centre of Regional Science. Vienna University of Technology, Vienna, Austria. http://www.smart-cities.eu/download/smart_cities_ final_report.pdf (2007). Last Accessed 09 Sep 2019

30. Neirotti, P., De Marco, A., Cagliano, A.C., Mangano, G., Scorrano, F.: Current trends in smart city initiatives: some stylised facts. Cities **38**, 25–36 (2014)

31. Plano Estratégico de Turismo para Região de Lisboa 2020–2024: https://www.lisboa.pt/fil eadmin/atualidade/noticias/user_upload/Relatorio_Final_Plano_Estrategico-2020-2024_c ompressed.pdf. Last Accessed 06 May 2021

32. Estratégia Turismo 2027 (ET2027): http://www.turismodeportugal.pt/pt/Turismo_Portugal/ Estrategia/Estrategia_2027/Paginas/default.aspx. Last Accessed 06 May 2021

33. Programa Turismo 4.0: http://business.turismodeportugal.pt/pt/Conhecer/Inovacao/turismo-4-0/Documents/Turismo40-apresentacao-LA-2017.pdf

34. Yin, R.K.: Pesquisa qualitativa do início ao fim. Penso Editora, Porto Alegre (2016)

35. Bardin, L.: Análisis de contenido. Akal Ediciones, Madrid (1996)

36. Lisbon City Council: https://www.lisboa.pt. Last Accessed 05 May 2021

Assessing Buyer's Energy Consumed in the Purchase Process

Andrii Galkin[1]([✉]) [ID], Paula Bajdor[2] [ID], Dmytro Prunenko[1] [ID], Iryna Balandina[3] [ID],
Iryna Polchaninova[3] [ID], Mykola Pysarevskyi[4,5], Iryna Pysareva[3] [ID],
and Olha Radionova[3]

[1] Department of Transport System and Logistics, O. M. Beketov National University of Urban
Economy in Kharkiv, Kharkiv, Ukraine
[2] Czestochowa University of Technology, Dabrowskiego 69, 42-201 Czestochowa, Poland
[3] Department of Tourism and Hospitality, O. M. Beketov National University of Urban
Economy in Kharkiv, Kharkiv, Ukraine
[4] Faculty of International Economic Relations and Tourism Business, V. N. Karazin Kharkiv
National University, Kharkiv, Ukraine
pisarevskiy@karazin.ua
[5] O. M. Beketov National University of Urban Economy in Kharkiv, Kharkiv, Ukraine
irinapisareva@kname.edu.ua

Abstract. Buyers within the process of purchases require new system approaches
to assess their fatigue for in-store service improvement. The buyer's fatigue can be
assessed by examining energy consumed during the purchase process. The neuromarketing concept is an innovative direction which can boost the effectiveness of
end-consumers feedback for retailer. The research is geared toward assessing the
impact of the surrounding of the method of purchases on buyer fatigue at urban
retailers. The set of recommendations for reducing the fatigue of buyers, improving the in-store service and comparison of different store surrounding via energy
consumed was presented. The result can improve the standard of in-store services
by decreasing average fatigue level (energy consumed) during purchase.

Keywords: Buyer · Total energy expenditure · Marketing · Energy · Behavior

1 Introduction

In contemporary conditions person interacts with various systems in which he lives,
works and rests. The consumption of goods system is one of such systems. The purchases
process consist of following elements: a buyer, a store, surrounding, and management
system [12].

Specific features and problems arising during purchases, from the standpoint of
ergonomics, can be caused as well by the system: "Person – Tool – Work Piece – Industrial
Environment" [10]. Designing and functioning of the system "End-consumer – Retailer –
Resource Management System – Surrounding" (CRIS) is connected with the efficiency
increase for the society, in general, at purchasing.

© Springer Nature Switzerland AG 2021
T. Guarda et al. (Eds.): ARTIIS 2021, CCIS 1485, pp. 684–694, 2021.
https://doi.org/10.1007/978-3-030-90241-4_52

The purchases process is interacting a few systems [19]: marketing (product, price, advancing and place), surrounding (politics, economy, technology, retailers, goods substitutes etc.) and person – buyer. Exploring factors affecting requires new methods evaluation efficiency, boost sales, diminish buyers' fatigue (energy), and increase utility from purchases in particular retailer.

The increase of efficiency and reliability of complex systems activity with the participation of the person is possible on the basis of improvement of the system "person – tools – work place – industrial environment" [15]. Modern ergonomic systems are directed to studying of the operator and reliability of all system spanned with that. Distribution of functions between operators during functioning of modern systems is presented by Lyubchak [28]. Criterion function of efficiency at the organization of routing bus transportations described with society value expression expenditures in transportation process.

The quality of shopping services problem constantly worries buyers and merchants because of quite natural reasons [4]. The growth of welfare of people causes the raise of their cultural level, which leads to the desire to purchase quality goods at a high level of service, which constantly follow to sustainable development. Various factors influence consumer in the shopping, each of which may have a decisive influence on the magnitude and timing of fatigue [25] and as a result the buyer will make a purchase or not. But those methods provide not full information on consumer's fatigue [26]. The consumer requires new method in the online purchases process to assess the fatigue or energy spent. Neuromarketing is an innovative direction to improve the effectiveness of the company's marketing communications (primarily merchandising and advertising), by influencing the behaviour of a person as a potential buyer, taking into account the neurophysiological features of the process of making a purchase decision [14]. The aim of the research is to developed method to assess the fatigue of the buyer visiting any retailer according calories spend in purchase process.

2 Methods of Research

2.1 Interrelation of the Elements of the System "CRIS"

The most known outline of the process of acceptance by the consumer of the decision of goods purchase is the conception of F. Kotler (Kotler & Armstrong, 2010). In the case of positive purchase experience, it is possible to expect to repeat of purchases, in the case of negative – isn't. Actions of buyers substantially differ on their needs and purchases purposes, demand, behavior motivation and actions on the market [10]. In case, for system operation efficiency increasing its necessary to solve this task according to system and integrated analysis principles, as process links person's interaction – a end-consumers in the shop with environment influence. The efficiency of the interaction of system elements can be presented as the following function.

The system can be presented as "CRIS", Fig. 1.

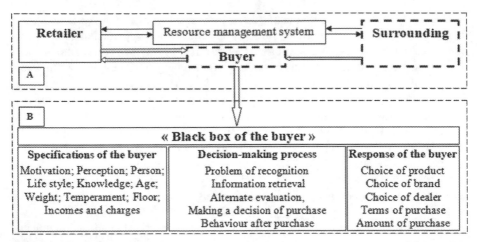

Fig. 1. Interrelation of the elements of the system "CRIS" (A) and subsystem "Buyer" (B) (Source: own developed)

We will consider system elements in more detail.

Surrounding
The market is based at present on the competition. Among themselves, the manufacturers of goods and services, shops, shopping centers, cities and countries, as well as consumers compete, due to it, the consumer receives a wide choice of qualitative of the same type goods, at different price [19]. The competitive environment is a temporary category, to which the participants of struggle have influence, the substance of which is in rivalry supplying mechanism.

Evaluating retailer's competitors and forecast their actions is allows analyzing the competitive threat level. In connection with that analysis of competitive environment puts following main purposes and tasks (Kotler & Armstrong, 2010): identification of the competitive market type; revealing of actual and potential competitors, quantifying, type and size of challengers; market share estimate occupied by the competitors; specification of rate and competition directivity; revealing of strong and weak parties, strategies and the goods' competitors evaluation; analysis and behavior forecasting of the competitor on the market, his/her reaction to different marketing actions [40].

The level of the organization of competitive environment can facilitate or to make difficult a purchasing process, to influence fatigue and emotional condition of buyers. The environment is characterized by economic, technological, political, demography, natural processes in it. In purchasing process environment takes into account influence of factors not dependent on a particular buyer, but affecting it (Halkin, 2016). News about the deficiency of some goods cans growth of its demand purchases.

Specification of Retailers
Demand for qualitative TS is constantly growing. With society evolution increase of cultural level takes place, resulting in intention to purchase qualitative goods with high service level. On the other hand, high service level of retailer allows them to increase the

quantity of steady customers [40], and by that to raise their economic efficiency [31]. Researchers confirm that in a long-term perspective, high service level diminishes the retail charges [8].

TS includes such concepts, as "TS quality", "trade culture", "service culture", "service level", in the base of which care of buyer [16]. The buyer, evaluating TS quality, based on the expenditures of the time to acquisition of goods and conditions, in which the buyer commits purchase [17].

To important parameters of retailers affecting frequency of their visiting and the amount of purchases in them is possible to attribute [30]: the area of trade hall; the amount of calculated-cash knots; the area of storage, auxiliary, office premises; the amount of the personnel; product range; presence and absence of different goods; presence of own production; additional services (delivery, repair service etc.); the amount of purchases in day; "average" check; etc.

The aggregate of these parameters characterizes the retail format: pulsing and scheduled; booth, retail shop, supermarket, shopping center etc. and as well characterizes nature of purchases, the strategy of functioning and positioning, the level of retail interaction with consumer and suppliers.

Resource Management System

Resource management system is a complex, multiplane concept, to which, however, the customary approach has not been generated yet. Some specialists consider him as control issue, and first of all by the people who engage in sales (including a selection of the personnel, his motivation, training etc.) (Waters, 2003). Various approaches believe that control system of sales is a primary control of sales channels [29]. In wide sense approaches, the control system of resources considering are people and processes control in the sales area (deliveries, reserves, merchandising and other).

To controlled management system parameters by sales it is possible to attribute: product, price, advancing, place and other. To controlled logistics parameters it is possible to attribute: standard item and storage, the order time, the material flow rate in the logistical system. These parameters influence the behavior of the buyer. Therefore, e.g., if the buyer is not suitable for price, quality or the service level he/she can go to another retailer. Factors characterizing control system, the basis on held analysis of the sources [30].

Control systems of resources ("Planning of enterprise resources" is ERP, "ERP+", "Consumer-driven supply chain" and other) are development of the strategy which, as opposed to the initial takes into account not only "obvious" resources (finances, personnel, operation), but also "hidden", which in himself are allocated by consumer behavior. Application of given conceptions allows proceeding to the production of goods, ready for "consumer", instead of for shop [6]. The control system is a link between the elements of the system "CRIS", and it defines efficiency of their interaction among themselves, as a system.

The End-Consumer

Saying of the buyer, it is necessary to consider him first of all as a person. Each person has his/her psychophysiological features [38]. It is important to consider his/her floor, age, weight, growth, state of health. As well important is the rating of his/her physiological expenditures, fatigues, incomes, expenditures and their structure, way of life and others [8]. Scientists in their paper consider a person on his/her time value, which has a cost estimate, customer expenditure to achieve to the item, where the product is acquired, to TS, and to deliver product to consumption place.

The main part of purchases by the customers, is implemented to time off, that is, free, in such a manner, its value has a direct influence to the size, radius, client's service. Imagining in money form temporary expenditures of the customer it becomes possible to define an optimum value of the radius of service of consumers. Understanding of interaction of the participants of the system is an important factor at planning and demand management and resources. At the same time, losses of the enterprise from a modest service level turn out to decrease of products sales volumes, and, as examination, the incomes of the enterprise.

2.2 Methods for Determining the Number of Calories Consumed

The number of calories a person spends in different activities is a function that depends on the gender, age, weight and type of activity performed by the person (Lincoln, 1972). The consuming of goods is associated to process of purchase [20]:

$$E^{cn} = \sum_{p=1}^{P} E_p = E_\omega^{prep} + E_{\omega j}^{\prime movm} + E_j^{TS} + E_{j\omega}^{\prime\prime movm} + E_\omega^{aftsell} \qquad (1)$$

where E_ω^{prep} – energy value consumption of the end-consumer at the preparatory stage of consumption, preceding the purchase, kJ (kcal); $E_{\omega j}^{\prime movm}$ – the energy value consumption of the end-consumer when travelling from the zone ω to the retailer j, kJ (kcal); E_j^{TS} – the energy value consumption of the consumer during the shopping service in the j-th retailer, kJ (kcal); $E_{j\omega}^{\prime\prime movm}$ – the energy value in the delivery of goods from the j-th retailer to zones ω destination, kJ (kcal); $E_\omega^{aftsell}$ – the energy value consumption after-sales purchase, kJ (kcal).

The preliminary stage of consumption, which precedes the purchase itself, includes the following elements: awareness of product needs, information seeking and alternative valuation. In practice, this stage is related to the list of goods and their quantity, possible places of purchase, possible ways of purchase (store, Internet, etc.). Choice of product depends on time spent on the buying. Choosing a purchase method determines the following elements of the process of consumption of material flow. So, when choosing shopping through a store, the consumer in the first stage needs to go or get to him. The consumer spends some time in a store, which is spent on the choice and purchase of goods (trade service) after arriving at the store. After, end-consumer desires to return to his/her main destination (home, work, etc.). When choosing an online purchase, such element is missing. The final stage is after-sales consumption, which may include the assessment of the results of the purchase, direct use or consumption (eg, cooking) and deprivation of the used goods.

To estimate consumption of end users, it is advisable to use experimental methods based on the collection of real-time information. These include the use of electronic watch Smart [12], which calculates the number of meters travelled, time spent, and calories at different stages of the purchase process. This will make it possible to more accurately assess these parameters, comparing them with theoretical methods.

2.3   Estimation of the Monetary Costs of End-Consumer Fatigue

Estimation of fatigue is carried out on the indicator of energy cost of movement. This value characterizes the direction of the energy regulation channels in the human body [9]. For any consumer activity, energy is consumed [24]. The amount of energy expended depends on the amount of effort spent on one or another element of the consumption process. Estimation of the amount of energy expended is carried out in various ways, among which one can distinguish: cost of action [23], pulse based on built-in sensors [3], etc.

The value of 1 kcal is determined based on different incomes of citizens, the structure of expenditures of one person's budget and households' budget, as well as the different cost of the products themselves and their usefulness to humans. American and British scientists in medicine have achieved great success in these studies in creating diets and proper healthy eating. Their research indicates that «healthy» food costs three times more than «unhealthy» food, as a result of which the price gap between them increases. The study looked at nearly 100 popular food items, which were determined according to government criteria as healthy or not. The results indicate that 1,000 cal of «healthy» food, such as meat, salmon, yogurt and tomatoes, cost an average of £ 7.49 in 2012 [9]. Calorie intake of less healthy foods, such as pizza, beef cutlets, and donuts, was cheaper by an average of £ 2.50. The gap between the two categories of food is £ 4.99. In 2002, this gap was £ 3.88. The average increase in the cost of «healthy» food was £ 1.84 per 1,000 cal over the decade, while the cost of «unhealthy» food increased by only 73 pennies [32].

The choice of food is based on taste, cost and convenience, and, to a lesser extent, health and variety. Taste refers to the sensory appeal of products such as taste, aroma and texture. The energy density of products is defined as energy per unit mass or volume (kcal/100 g or MJ/kg) [1].

The choice of goods, shop, etc. affects the calories consumed [2]. Existing methods for determining the required number of calories are based on diets and human consumption [5]. High developed countries (USA, UK) have higher absolute food expenditures, but the share of household consumption spent on home-cooked food is low – less than 10%. In Kenya and other low-income countries, the share of consumer spending devoted to homemade food can be as high as 50%. Per capita calorie consumption data show an inverse relationship. In 2015, per capita calorie consumption in the United States was at a high level of 3,639 cal per day, while Kenya had only 2,189 cal [7].

The value of energy consumed is proposed in dependence:

$$S_{KCal}^{cn} = \frac{\sum_{1}^{M}(Q_{\omega} \cdot P_{yina})}{ALF \cdot T_{cons}} \qquad (2)$$

where Q_{ω} – an individual consumption of 1 resident for a period of time living ω-th district for the analysed period, for normal functioning of the organism, kg/inhabitant (unit/inhabitant); $P_{\text{ціна}}$ – good's price, UAH/kg (unit/inhabitant); ALF – daily energy norm of the consumer, kcal; $_{cons}$ – time good's consumption, days.

Determination of the monetary value of energy costs can be found by the formula:

$$\Theta_3^{ij} = E_{\omega j}^{cn} \cdot S_{KCal}^{cn} \tag{3}$$

where $E_{\omega j}^{cn}$ – energy consumption in the process of purchase, kcal; S_{KCal}^{cn} – cost of one calorie, UAH/kcal.

People with different incomes and cost structure may have completely different monetary value of energy costs, which have impact on their behaviour in choosing a store.

3   Results

In order to find the initial values of the parameters of end-consumers and retailer, natural studies were conducted. The studies use a two-stage methodology for determining the relevant geographic retail market [20]: distance, the non-linearity factor, slope factor, etc. (Fig. 1).

The research was in visiting retailer via end-consumers in the service area and monitoring the selected indicator: the number of calories consumed for a one-time visit to

Fig. 2. Trading area: 1,..,11 – zones; A,..,O – stores.

a retailer. For all consumers, a single set of goods (consumer basket) was selected. In general, 27 people (women and men) aged 19–65 participated in the study. The received data are presented in the Table 1 (Fig. 2).

Table 1. Total energy costs when walking from the store

Grocery	District, kcal										
	1	2	3	4	5	6	7	8	9	10	11
A	198.9	65.1	84.8	198.3	230.8	162.2	155.5	281.9	374.5	357.5	374.5
B	183.2	135.2	165.2	253.2	200.4	159.3	186.4	282.1	390.7	373.9	396.6
C	111.3	138.1	183.4	260.8	189.7	111.9	175.0	221.7	339.0	335.2	370.3
D	216.0	175.5	163.8	178.6	172.9	81.3	53.7	173.5	264.4	232.4	253.5
E	306.3	221.4	160.7	98.5	281.0	191.2	102.7	267.8	344.5	278.0	256.3
F	254.2	226.1	213.0	212.2	184.7	111.1	106.1	141.5	225.9	191.3	221.7
G	231.1	259.6	272.0	284.8	128.5	117.7	146.0	124.6	232.1	214.1	254.2
H	247.6	268.9	280.2	285.6	161.6	132.5	174.8	60.7	185.2	196.2	241.4
I	219.9	285.8	311.0	317.7	133.5	154.7	205.7	26.4	151.8	193.1	244.6
J	395.0	425.4	424.7	391.6	278.2	287.0	312.5	178.2	56.8	125.9	201.7

The utility of retailer assessed in O-D matrix using generalized cost of end-consumers. Monetary value of the energy spent on on (off)-line shopping are given in Table 2.

Table 2. Monetary value of the energy spent on on (off)-line shopping, UAH

Grocery	District, UAH										
	1	2	3	4	5	6	7	8	9	10	11
A	2.97	0.97	1.27	2.96	3.45	2.42	2.32	4.21	5.59	5.34	5.60
B	2.61	1.92	2.35	3.60	2.85	2.27	2.65	4.01	5.56	5.32	5.64
C	1.59	1.98	2.63	3.74	2.72	1.60	2.51	3.18	4.86	4.80	5.31
D	3.23	2.62	2.45	2.67	2.58	1.22	0.80	2.59	3.95	3.47	3.79
E	3.96	2.86	2.08	1.27	3.63	2.47	1.33	3.46	4.45	3.59	3.31
F	3.62	3.22	3.03	3.02	2.63	1.58	1.51	2.01	3.21	2.72	3.15
G	3.40	3.82	4.00	4.19	1.89	1.73	2.15	1.83	3.41	3.15	3.74
H	3.20	3.48	3.62	3.69	2.09	1.71	2.26	0.78	2.39	2.54	3.12
I	3.13	4.07	4.42	4.52	1.90	2.20	2.93	0.37	2.16	2.75	3.48
J	5.62	6.05	6.04	5.57	3.96	4.08	4.44	2.53	0.81	1.79	2.87

Attractiveness of visiting retailer:

- A higher size of retailer, slope factor, none linearity factor, distance to retailer, higher income of the end-consumers causes a higher value of cost associated with purchase;
- Lower level of fatigue (calorie spend) of the end-consumers ensure small size of retailer, slope factor, none linearity factor, distance to retailer and low income of end-consumers. Therefore, if the end-consumers what to lose they should choose vice versa retailers with higher value of named parameters;
- The presence of a large number of end-consumers increase attractiveness of any retailers in this zone;
- Retailer D and G will have the highest value of probability of visiting, retailer B – the lowest, due to high generalized costs in them;
- Number and assortment of goods and prices, ultimately the choice of retailer.

Market relations in Ukraine are constantly evolving, which greatly contributes to the development of trade services [11]. On the other hand, competition between trade organizations and supply systems is growing. The sharp increase in the number of retail outlets with different quality of service and price ranking means that supply systems must adapt to changing demand conditions [22]. In such conditions, the analysis of the consumer market and the identification of the service area of the trading company is one of the forms of improving the efficiency of trade organizations.

The problem of distribution of demand between retail has been considered by many scholars from different points of view. The growing competition between logistics systems and technologies for the promotion of goods forces to look for new opportunities to improve their operation, taking into consideration buyers [18]. Consideration of the functioning of the system at the stage "Shop" – "Household" allows you to take into attention factors that have not been considered in the current models and methods.

4 Conclusions

The proposed method estimate energy value of end-consumers while visiting the physical store and online shopping for the first time. For the first, the energy value was determined. Developed models can be used for simulation of purchase process, founding costs associated to shopping and assessing probability of visiting stores.

The calculated and experimental value of energy costs can be found to any retailer. According to it level of fatigue can be assumed and compare to the competitors in trading zone. Existing retailer selection methods rarely explore online monitoring of energies of purchase process and have never used energy consumption. The proposed method can stand like additional factor in Scott [39], Oruc [36], and Nakaya [34]. The buyer compensates for the low value of one factor (attribute) by a higher value of another. Applying real-time monitoring of buyer energy provides bigger opportunities for assessing the quality of shopping services with more accurate results.

The result can improve the quality of trade services by creating conditions conducive to a more favourable environment for shopping, planning sales areas, retailer, sales analysis, advertising and analysis customer behaviour. A method can estimate the level of fatigue of the buyer during its visit to any retailer. Also, the average fatigue level of retailer can be found.

References

1. Ainsworth, B.E., et al.: 2011 Compendium of physical activities: a second update of codes and MET values. Med. Sci. Sports Exerc. **43**(8), 1575–1581 (2011)
2. Ainsworth, B., Haskell, W., Herrmann, S., Meckes, N., Bassett, D.R., Tudor-Locke, C.: The compendium of physical activities tracking guide. 2011. Beschikbaar via: http://prevention. sph.sc.edu/tools/docs/documents_compendium.pdf. Geraadpleegd (2013)
3. Baevskii, R.M.: Analysis of heart rate variability in space medicine. Hum. Physiol. **28**(2), 202–213 (2002)
4. Birkin, M., Clarke, G., Clarke, M.: Retail Location Planning in an Era of Multi-Channel Growth. Routledge (2017)
5. Blaydes, L., Kayser, M.A.: Counting calories: democracy and distribution in the developing world. Int. Stud. Quart. **55**(4), 887–908 (2011)
6. Cooper, M.C., Lambert, D.M., Pagh, J.D.: Supply chain management: more than a new name for logistics. Int. J. Logist. Manag. **8**(1), 1–14 (1997)
7. Dąbrowska, A.: Consumer behaviour in the market of catering services in selected countries of Central-Eastern Europe. Br. Food J. **113**(1), 96–108 (2011)
8. Dev, C.S., Schultz, D.E.: A customer-focused approach can bring the current marketing mix into the 21st century. Mark. Manag. **14**(1), 18–24 (2005)
9. Drewnowski, A., Darmon, N.: The economics of obesity: dietary energy density and energy cost. Am. J. Clin. Nutr. **82**(1), 265S–273S (2005)
10. Engel, J.F., Blackwell, R.D., Miniard, P.W.: Consumer Behavior, 8th edn. Dryder, New York (1995)
11. Galkin, A., Dolia, C., Davidich, N.: The role of consumers in logistics systems. Transp. Res. Procedia **27**, 1187–1194 (2017)
12. Galkin, A., Prasolenko, O., Chebanyuk, K., Balandina, I., Atynian, A., Obolentseva, L.: The neuromarketing ICT technique for assessing buyer emotional fatigue. In: ICTERI, pp. 243–253 (2018)
13. Galkin, A., Obolentseva, L., Balandina, I., Kush, E., Karpenko, V., Bajdor, P.: Last-mile delivery for consumer driven logistics. Transp. Res. Procedia **39**, 74–83 (2019)
14. Galkin, A., et al.: Assessing the impact of population mobility on consumer expenditures while shopping. Transp. Res. Procedia **48**, 2187–2196 (2020)
15. Gašová, M., Gašo, M., Štefánik, A.: Advanced industrial tools of ergonomics based on industry 4.0 concept. Procedia Eng. **192**, 219–224 (2017)
16. Ghobadian, A.: Service quality: concepts and models. Int. J. Qual. Reliab. Manag. **11**(9), 43–66 (1994)
17. Grönroos, C.: A service quality model and its marketing implications. Eur. J. Mark. **18**(4), 36–44 (1984)
18. Halkin, A.: Emotional state of consumer in the urban purchase: processing data. Found. Manag. **10**(1), 99–112 (2018)
19. Halkin, A., Bliumska-Danko, K., Smihunova, O., Dudnyk, E., Balandina, I.: Investigation influence of store type on emotional state of consumer in the urban purchase. Found. Manag. **11**(1), 7–22 (2019)
20. Halkin, A.: Assessing the utility of retailer based on generalized costs of end-consumers. Found. Manag. **12**(1), 31–42 (2020)

21. Hernandez, T., Biasiotto, M.: Retail location decision-making and store portfolio management. Can. J. Reg. Sci. **24**(3), 399–421 (2001)
22. Ibrahim, M.F., McGoldrick, P.J.: Shopping Choices with Public Transport Options: An Agenda for the 21st Century. Routledge (2017)
23. Keytel, L.R., et al.: Prediction of energy expenditure from heart rate monitoring during submaximal exercise. J. Sports Sci. **23**(3), 289–297 (2005)
24. Kidwell, B., Hardesty, D.M., Childers, T.L.: Consumer emotional intelligence: conceptualization, measurement, and the prediction of consumer decision making. J. Consum. Res. **35**(1), 154–166 (2008)
25. Kotler, P., Dubois, B.: Marketing Management. 13e Editions, Paris (2009)
26. Lemon, K.N., Verhoef, P.C.: Understanding customer experience throughout the customer journey. J. Mark. **80**(6), 69–96 (2016)
27. Lincoln, J.E.: Calorie intake, obesity, and physical activity. Am. J. Clin. Nutr. **25**(4), 390–394 (1972)
28. Lyubchak, V., Lavrov, E., Pasko, N.: Ergonomic support of man-machine interaction: approach to designing of operators' group activities (<special issue> variational inequality and combinatorial problems). Int. J. Biomed. Soft Comput. Hum. Sci.: Off. J. Biomed. Fuzzy Syst. Assoc., **17**(2), 53–58 (2012)
29. Mallik, S.: Customer service in supply chain management. In: H. Bidgoil (ed.), The Handbook of Technology Management: Supply Chain Management, Marketing and Advertising, and Global Management, vol 2 (1st ed.), p. 104. John Wiley & Sons, Hoboken, New Jersey, ISBN 978-0-470-24948-2 (2010)
30. Makarova, I., Khabibullin, R., Belyaev, E., Mavrin, V., Verkin, E.: Creating a safe working environment via analyzing the ergonomic parameters of workplaces on an assembly conveyor. In: 2015 International Conference on Industrial Engineering and Systems Management (IESM), pp. 947–954. IEEE (2015 October)
31. Makarova, I., Shubenkova, K., Pashkevich, A.: Development of an intelligent human resource management system in the era of digitalization and talentism. In: 2018 18th International Conference on Mechatronics-Mechatronika (ME), pp. 1–6. IEEE (2018, December)
32. Monsivais, P., Drewnowski, A.: The rising cost of low-energy-density foods. J. Am. Diet. Assoc. **107**(12), 2071–2076 (2007)
33. Nakaya, T., Fotheringham, A.S., Hanaoka, K., Clarke, G., Ballas, D., Yano, K.: Combining microsimulation and spatial interaction models for retail location analysis. J. Geogr. Syst. **9**(4), 345–369 (2007)
34. Oruc, N., Tihi, B.: Competitive location assessment – the MCI approach, south east European. J. Econ. Bus. **7**(2), 35–49 (2012). https://doi.org/10.2478/v10033-012-0013-7
35. Popa, V., Duică, M., Gonzalez, A.: Supply chain information alignment in the consumer goods and retail industry: global standards and best practices. Electron. J. Inf. Syst. Eval. **14**(1), 134–149 (2011)
36. Scott, P.: Geography and Retailing, vol. 137. Transaction Publishers (2017)
37. Solomon, M.R.: Consumer Behavior: Buying, Having, and Being, vol. 10. Prentice Hall, Upper Saddle River, NJ (2014)

The Potential of Digital Marketing in the Promotion of Low-Density Territories: The Case Study of Mirandela Municipality

Manuela Cunha[1], Ricardo Correia[1,2]($\boxtimes$) (iD), and Aida Carvalho[1,2] (iD)

[1] Instituto Politécnico de Bragança, Campus Santa Apolónia, 5300-253 Bragança, Portugal
a37278@alunos.ipb.pt, {ricardocorreia,acarvalho}@ipb.pt
[2] CiTUR Guarda – Centro de Investigação, Desenvolvimento e Inovação em Turismo, Guarda, Portugal

Abstract. Information and communication technologies (ICT'S) have introduced a new form of society, the network society, with the paradigm based on digital marketing. This form of communication has constantly evolved due to its intensive study and the exponential increase in its use. The imposition of digital communication, together with social networks, becomes imperative for both organisations and territories to adjust their communication strategies in order to ensure the effectiveness of the messages conveyed. It is a very useful tool for tourist destinations marketing since it is able to materialize in itself many of the communication objectives: it stimulates the consumer's relationship with the brand, generates buzz, attracts potential visitors, energizes the territories around an idea, encourages participation and promotes recommendation. Due to the specificity of low-density territories, digital marketing involves the consumer through instant messaging tools, facilitating the interaction between individuals, allowing the share of information (with great ease and speed) and encourage other visitors. In this work the digital presence of Mirandela (a small municipality located in the Northeast of Portugal), is analysed as well as its positioning and contents. For that purpose, data were collected in several digital channels of public and private entities. In this context and according the obtained results, it was clear that Mirandela does not prioritize the digital communication, being therefore important to reformulate its communication strategies.

Keywords: Tourism · Digital marketing · Low-density territories · Mirandela

1 Introduction

In recent years, Internet and social media have achieved significant growth, particularly with the emergence of Web 2.0, which has considerably increased the information available online that can be easily accessed. In the tourism context, these developments have had a considerable effect, as they have changed the way tourists' research information, plan trips and share experiences [19, 28]. All this, has led tourism organizations

T. Guarda et al. (Eds.): ARTIIS 2021, CCIS 1485, pp. 695–708, 2021.
https://doi.org/10.1007/978-3-030-90241-4_53

to reformulate their management and marketing plans, making them compulsorily more technological and digital [26].

In a post-COVID-19 world, the innovative use of technologies to engage visitors online through virtual information has gained increasing importance as it has the ability to provide alternative destination experiences, thereby attracting consumer interest in tourist attractions [43].

Pandemic has also highlighted less mass tourism proposals and the so-called low density territories. These territories can be understood as those with a small population and a set of characteristics that hinder the development of economic activities, since they have great tendencies to relocate, ageing population, low levels of education and purchasing power [4, 34]. Low-density territories are faced with numerous adversities, thus requiring not only a more efficient and effective use of available resources, but also promotion policies and practices, particularly at the digital level, capable of promoting and disseminating their identity resources, capturing the interest of potential visitors.

Tourism, when developed in these territories can constitute a method of invigorate and changing the space, implementing new social and consumption patterns, generating new practices and multiple impacts and a way of promoting local tourism resources (natural, heritage and cultural), contributing beneficially to the local economy [1, 10]. Simultaneously low-density territories characteristics reveal a virtuous side [8]. (Covas, 2019), which has reinforced by the Pandemic that could be a generator of opportunities and attractiveness. Post-pandemic tourists value nature, authenticity, silence [37] characteristics that are generally present in these territories. However, these characteristics alone are not enough to generate dynamics and value. It is necessary for these territories to organise, position and communicate their positioning effectively and in an integrated manner.

In this sense, digital presence becomes a great opportunity for any tourism business [2, 27]. Jansson [20] states that communication influences in a determinant way the perceptions of place, distance, sociability, authenticity and other previous knowledge that configure the tourism activity, becoming a great advantage for low-density territories. Digital communication is also an alternative to communicate at low cost and, at the same time that it allows reaching distant markets and has the ability to reach the target audiences highly interested in the particularities of their touristic product. In other words, the communicational power is amplified and the physical barriers of communication are eliminated.

This research aims to analyse the online presence (websites and social networks) of both public and private entities in Mirandela municipality (a low-density territory located in the Northeast of Portugal), in order to understand if this presence is efficiently taking advantage of the potential of digital marketing to generate attractiveness for the territory.

In this sense, the research is divided into several stages, having started with a literature review which addressed aspects related to digital marketing and communication applied to the tourism sector. Subsequently, it was carried out a content analysis of the diverse digital platforms of Mirandela municipality. Then, the results were discussed and the main conclusions were drawn and, finally, the limitations of the study were presented and future lines of research were suggested.

2 Literature Review

The technological advances experienced with the onset of the internet and social media, as well as the proliferation of new media, have significantly impacted the way information is disseminated having become the most common form of research [25, 42]. Given this reality, consumers are now "constantly connected", researching and communicating, increasingly, through digital means, becoming therefore a more intervenient, informed and aware audience. Thus, it is extremely important that companies and organisations adapt to this new digital era [39].

Due to the increasing use of online technologies and devices, digital marketing has become a powerful tool, both for companies and destinations. According to Morrison [30], digital marketing is the largest communication tool and the most important form of marketing. Roughly speaking, digital marketing is based on a business model where the main resource to carry out promotional actions in order to promote products, services or brands, it is the Internet and the digital media exploited from it [36]. Kannan and Li [22] refer that this type of marketing should be based on adding value for the consumer and for the different stakeholders.

In the tourism sector, these digital platforms have had a considerable effect. Due to its intrinsic characteristics, and since, as a service sector, it markets intangible, inseparable, perishable and heterogeneous products, the communication process becomes a core element of the offer [5]. In other words, the Internet and information and communication technologies (ICTs) have considerably reshaped the way tourism information is distributed and the way people research, plan and consume their trips [3]. In this sense, both marketing and ICT have eventually become indispensable tools for effective management of tourism organizations.

The emergence of web 2.0 was the milestone that started two major trends, namely the rise of social media and the increase in the amount of information available online that can be easily consulted. Nowadays, tourists essentially search for information that will help them make the best decision when choosing a holiday destination, an establishment to stay in, a restaurant or any other subject of their interest. These searches are carried out through different channels that have been developing over time [42]. According to Kemp [23], about 4.66 billion people use the Internet, and 4.2 billion of these users, actively use social media these users spend approximately seven hours daily on these tools and their main motivation is the search for information. In this context, investments in new techniques of persuasion, dissemination and communication have become the rule, leaving behind traditional media, to bet on a digital strategy [40].

There are several technological devices that provide a wide variety of tools capable of leveraging the growth process of any organisation or brand [38]. In this context Ryan [35], states that the institutional website is assumed as one of the most important tools of digital marketing, since it is the main frontage of any business. It is a virtual and exclusive web space, which aims to disseminate the information of a particular business, in addition to its services, products and mission. This platform allows total control of its content, and should therefore be the main means of communication for any company and to be positioned at the centre of any online strategy [13].

On the other hand, social networks are a trend that today occupies an unprecedented centrality in modern societies, having conquered over the years a enthusiastic space in people's lives, thus becoming one of the most important tools in digital marketing. As sharing platforms, they have several tools that enable their users to exchange opinions, expectations, experiences, interests and a multitude of flows among themselves. For this reason, these platforms assume themselves as one of the most important components in the constitution of social relationships between people and organizations [12, 17]. In this sense, communication carried out through social media is an essential component for the success of organisations, since it offers a short-term return and allows not only the creation of a closer relationship between the entity and its target, but also enables faster feedback from users [9].

Despite the continuous emergence of new social networks, Facebook is the world leader, with about 2.8 billion monthly active users (MAUs) and 1.84 billion daily active users (DAUs) [15]. On the other hand, Instagram contains approximately 1 billion MAUs and about 500 million DAUs against 340 million MAUs present on Twitter and 152 million DAUs [41].

In this vein, all these tools, when properly used, i.e. based on a strategy and a marketing plan, allow achieving greater visibility, customising and directing the offer according to the intended audience, attracting and building customer loyalty with very low costs, compared to advertising carried out by traditional means [11, 18, 21].

In summary, the optimization of digital platforms should be seen as an asset to the sector, as it provides advantages both from the perspective of those who use the services, since it facilitates the process of obtaining information on products, services or destinations, and from the perspective of tourism organizations themselves, since it allows to increase the effectiveness of management processes and marketing strategies [44].

2.1 Digital Marketing in the Promotion of a Touristic Destination

Information and communication technologies have completely transformed the way tourist destinations are promoted. Destination marketing has evolved from passive to active promotion, from one-sided to interactive marketing, and from collateral to user-generated content [29]. According to Fan, Buhalis, and Lin [16], digital empowerment has offered the possibility of combining the tourists' network "at home" with the destination's network, thus enabling the emergence of hybrid social networks, where tourists have simultaneous access to online and physical networks. This presents tourists with a complex, functional and connected world.

Tourism destinations are difficult spaces to manage, due to the complexity that the interdependence of the various stakeholders adds [29]. In other words, tourism activity involves a wide range of institutions with different legal characteristics (in the public and private sectors). In addition to this, tourism also involves other service businesses and industries, which although not specifically dedicated to the sector, such as restaurants, part of their revenue is based on the performance of tourism activity [24]. Each of these entities acts autonomously and individually in a destination, thus contributing to its supply and production. Thus, and since a territory generates a wide range of products, all parts are interdependent, having the ability to influence the value of the others. In this context, and given this dependence between multiple agents, the communication of a territory depends on any individual performance [7].

In this sense, the success of the brand of a destination comes from the creation of relationships and synergies between the different stakeholders, as well as, their contributions to the creation of strategies in order to communicate a final, integrated and complex product [31].

3 Methodology

This article aims to analyse the online presence (websites and social networks) of both public and private entities in Mirandela municipality, in order to understand if this presence is efficiently taking advantage of the potential of digital marketing to generate attractiveness for the territory.

Mirandela is a low-density territory, with a vast archaeological, architectural, historical, religious, natural and gastronomic heritage. The destination is well known for 2 important gastronomic references, the "alheira" (a traditional smoked sausage famous all around Portugal) and the olive oil. It is also parte of the recently formed Regional Natural Park of the Tua Valley, and of the International Biosphere Reserve of the Iberian Meseta. Although all this resources the municipality only have 4 hotels [33]. In territorial terms presents itself as a medium-sized county with an area of about 674 km^2, covering 30 parishes [6]. In demographic terms, the county contains 21,781 inhabitants and a population density of 33.1 inhabitants/km^2 [32].

Considering the purpose of the article a qualitative methodology was followed, based on a content analysis of secondary data collected in various digital channels, i.e. social networks (Facebook, Instagram, Twitter, Linkedin and Youtube) and institutional websites of public and private entities of the Mirandela municipality as shown in Table 1.

Table 1. Sample

Domain	Entity	
Public	Municipality	Mirandela Town Council
	Museums	Museu Armindo Teixeira Lopes
		Olive Oil and Olive Museum
Private	Touristic accommodation	Hotel Jorge V
		Dona Fina Guest House
		Grande Hotel Dom Dinis
		Hotel Globo
	Restaurants	Flor de Sal
		Bem Bô
		A Taberna
		A Adega

Three entities of public domain were selected, namely the municipality of Mirandela, since it is the main promotional actor of the territory and 2 major museums that represent the cultural offer. On the other hand, eight private entities were identified, subdivided between tourist accommodation and restaurants, since these facilities represent the main amenities of the destination, having therefore the ability to influence the perception of it.

The data were collected from the various official platforms of each entity, between 19 March and 5 April 2021. While the analysis criteria of the websites were based essentially on the observation of their structure and content, the analysis criteria of the social networks were based mainly on the number of followers, likes, average weekly posts, average number of comments, shares per post and content. In order to obtain consistent data, the averages were calculated for the months of January, February and March 2021.

4   Presentation and Discussion of Results

4.1   Public Entities

The provision of clear and precise information about tourist attractions, activities, accommodation, gastronomy, restaurants and heritage in its different aspects by the municipalities websites, allows the tourist a greater assimilation of the destination, facilitating the decision making process [14]. In this sense, and from the analysis of the official Mirandela municipality website, it was firstly found that it is available in ten languages, depending on an initial menu with five tabs (Municipality, Living, Investing, Visiting and Covid-19). However and taking into account that the focus of the research is on the tourism sector only the tab "Visit" was analysed, which in turn is subdivided into six options (Arrive, See, Do, Eat, Sleep and Buy) that together compile all the information needed for tourism activity. It should be noted that this section is presented as a kind of individual site dedicated exclusively to the visitor.

From the carried out analysis it was clear that Mirandela is a municipality with a vast natural and cultural heritage, and where gastronomy stands out at all times, since it is the aspect most highlighted throughout the various tabs and where the "Alheira" sausage stands out as a national brand.

However, and although the website provides a wide and varied set of relevant information in tourism terms, it is undeniable that its structure is more informative than appealing. This aspect is highlighted not only by the layout itself that is more descriptive than imagistic, but also by the lack of concrete examples of itineraries and activities. It should also be noted that there are some inconsistencies related to the outdating of some relevant information, such as the number of local accommodation and the date of the exhibitions.

Communication through social media is an essential component for the success of any company or destination, since it allows not only the creation of a closer relationship between the entity and its target, but also allows a faster feedback from users [9]. In this path, we proceeded to the analysis of the social networks of the municipality, more specifically, Facebook, Instagram, Linkedin, Twitter and Youtube.

Thus, from the data collected and represented in Table 2, it was possible to realize that the Facebook platform has a significant number of likes and followers compared with Instagram, recording an average of 10 weekly publications, which translates approximately into a daily publication. This platform also registers about 16 comments per publication and 240 shares per publication, which contrasts with Instagram that only has about 5000 followers, 3 weekly publications and 3 comments per publication. It should be noted that the high number of comments and shares per publication registered on Facebook was largely due to the Jerusalem challenge, a video made by the municipality, which went viral in February, with more than 5,000 shares and 500 comments.

In addition, it was also found that the municipality uses these platforms to disseminate in the form of photographs, videos and digital flyers, the events, landscapes, gastronomy, news (aimed both to the locals and the tourists), future projects and webinars. The quality, in turn, is an aspect that is maintained in all publications and all posts are accompanied by a descriptive text using formal language. Although the content of the two platforms is almost identical, it is clear that the publications on Instagram are less frequent and more graphic and visual, than on Facebook, presenting more photographs and videos than processed texts, conveying the idea that the municipality gives more importance to Facebook as a communication and promotion tool.

Table 2. Analysis of the municipality's official social networks

Digital platforms	Followers	Likes	Average weekly posts	Average comments per post	Average shares per post
Facebook	27 518	25 191	9,91	15,50	239,49
Instagram	4 923	...	2,75	3,42	...
Linkedin	1 026	0	0	0	0
Twitter	2 216	...	0	0	0

In addition to these platforms, it was found that the municipality also has an account on Linkedin, Twitter and Youtube. However, the Linkedin page does not present any type of content/publication, although it was already created in March 2019 and the Twitter page has not been active for over two years. Finally, the Youtube account is quite recent, having been created less than a year ago, presenting only 39 subscribers and a total of 15 videos that revolve essentially, around gastronomy and endogenous products of the region.

In general, it was found that although the municipality has an account in several digital platforms, the Facebook page is undoubtedly the one in which the municipality invests more, being quite notorious the lack of commitment and dedication in the creation of content and communication and dissemination strategies in the remaining social networks. Still, it was evident that the municipality communicates Mirandela essentially as a gastronomic destination, since most of the promoted events and promotional videos revolve around this aspect, more specifically the "alheira" sausage and olive oil, from show cooking and webinars to gastronomic festivals and fairs.

In addition to the analysis of the municipality, some museums of Mirandela, were studied since they are public spaces that directly and indirectly preserve, promote and disseminate the memory and identity of the municipality. Thus, in a first phase was sought for the existence of the official websites of each of the spaces, however it was found that only the Armindo Teixeira Lopes museum provides an official website. That said, and although it is not considered an interactive and dynamic digital space, this page provides a set of very descriptive and informative information about the space itself, the patron and the collections. There is also a gallery where photographs of some exhibitions are displayed, some news, activities and the contacts and timetables of the museum. However, it should be noted that this web platform is a page created in the Weebly tool (service for website development and eCommerce) and for this reason it does not stand out when searched in a search engine.

Subsequently, the social networks of the selected cultural sample were explored. However, only pages on the Facebook platform were found, as can be seen from Table 3.

Table 3. Analysis of the museums on the facebook platform

Museums	Followers	Likes	Average weekly posts	Average comments per post	Average shares per post
Armindo Teixeira Lopes	1 001	993	1,41	0	0,87
Olive Tree and Olive Oil	2 815	2 750	2,58	0	2,84

In this context, the research allowed to verify that among the 2 spaces analysed, the Olive Tree and Olive Oil Museum is the one that stands out in terms of likes and followers. Moreover, it is also the one that carries out the largest number of publications per week and the one that has the most shares per publication. Although its content revolves around olive oil, through images, videos, showcooking's and webinars, some photographs of the municipality are also published.

Broadly speaking, after this observation it was found that the online presence of these entities is quite rudimentary, with only one of the museums having a website and Facebook being the only social network where there is any presence, which is still not active or regular. All of this results in a lack of communication and promotion.

4.2 Private Entities

Both restaurants and tourist accommodations are an essential component for the tourism development of a destination, since they are the basic facilities that sustain the stay of visitors. For this reason, it is important that companies exploit the communication, promotion and distribution potential that digital platforms offer.

Therefore, it was decided to analyse at first the websites corresponding to each of the different categories of accommodation of the sample under study. However, it was found that of the four entities, only two (Hotel Dom Dinis and Hotel Globo) have a website. In this sense, regarding the Hotel Dom Dinis, and although it was found that the website presents a set of tabs that allow the user to know the facilities and services provided, several gaps were identified both aesthetically and technically. Thus, in addition to an obsolete and out-dated layout, the reservation system, although incorporated, is not highlighted. The presence in social networks is not referenced and the attractive and interesting elements of the municipality of Mirandela are not addressed. On the other hand, the Globo Hotel already presents a website with a more updated layout, with a highlighted reservation system and a set of information that allows not only to explore the facilities and services available, but also the points and activities of interest in Mirandela.

After the analysis of the websites, we proceeded to the observation of the social networks of the sample under study. Therefore, and since no accounts were found on the Twitter, Linkedin and Youtube platforms, Table 4 refers only to the analysis of the Facebook platform.

Table 4. Analysis of the online presence of tourist accommodation on facebook

Touristic accommodation	Followers	Likes	Average weekly posts	Average comments per post	Average shares per post
Hotel Jorge V	484	478	Irregular	Irregular	Irregular
Dona Fina Guest House	2 470	2 423	1,75	2,17	1,07
Hotel Dom Dinis	756	744	Irregular	Irregular	Irregular
Hotel Globo	527	523	Irregular	Irregular	Irregular

Among the various tourist accommodations analysed, it was found that Dona Fina Guest House, besides being undoubtedly the one that stands out in terms of followers and likes, is the only one that has an active and regular presence, making an average of two publications per week sharing essentially pictures of the facilities, as well as of the municipality itself. The Jorge V Hotel is out of activity since December 2020, the Globo Hotel, in turn, is also out of activity since 2018 and the Grande Hotel Dom Dinis has not updated its page since 2015. It should be noted, that of the four accommodations, the Hotel Dom Dinis is the only one that does not present an account on the Instagram platform. However, and once again, only the Dona Fina Guest House maintains an active presence in this social network, with an average of two weekly publications and a content quite similar to that published on Facebook. The Hotel Globo, has only two publications made in August 2020 and the Hotel Jorge V, besides presenting a private account, does not contain any publication so far.

Following on from this, and despite these tools being considered relevant for digital marketing, according to the literature review, the results show that tourist accommodation does not take advantage on it as a communication tool.

In the second moment of analysis to private entities, the restaurants in the municipality of Mirandela were analysed. A pattern in all restaurants was noticed i.e., all publications stagnated to January 2021. This situation was due to the fact that on January 13, 2021 a new general confinement was decreed motivated by the worsening of the Covid-19 pandemic in the country, because of that the restaurants could only operate in take-away or home delivery regime. Thus, it was considered relevant to analyse the three months prior to the closure, i.e. October, November and December 2020, in order to understand whether or not this digital stagnation was due only to the closure imposed by government authorities.

After verifying that none of the restaurants of the sample has a website, the study proceeded with the analysis of the Facebook platform. From the data in Table 5, it was possible to realize that among the different establishments, the restaurant Flor de Sal is undoubtedly the one that stands out most in terms of likes and followers, being also the one that expresses a higher average of shares per publication. However, it is surpassed by the restaurant A Taberna in the number of weekly publications and in the average number of comments per publication. It should be noted, that the content varies according to the restaurants, i.e., while Flor de Sal uses this platform to disclose their menus, the facilities and the landscapes of the municipality, the A Adega and A Taberna only make reference to their daily menus and information about the opening hours.

Table 5. Analysis of the online presence of restaurants on the facebook platform

Restaurants	Followers	Likes	Average weekly posts	Average comments per post	Average shares per post
Flor de Sal	7 846	7 757	1,5	0,66	3,05
Bem Bô	2 604	2 606	1,25	0,80	3
A Taberna	4 217	4 181	4,66	1,17	2,35
A Adega	2 858	2 801	2,5	1,56	2,76

Due to the absence of Twitter, Linkedin and Youtube, accounts it was analysed lastly the online presence of each of the restaurants on the Instagram platform, which is represented in Table 6. The data obtained shows that, in general, the restaurants are less active and assiduous on this platform, since, in addition to the number of followers being much lower than on Facebook, there was a significant decrease in the average number of weekly publications. This aspect was particularly evident in the restaurant A Taberna that from an average of five weekly publications on Facebook reduced to one publication per week on Instagram. The A Adega is also another example of this situation, since the three weekly publications made on Facebook went to one monthly on Instagram. It looks clear that the restaurants, do not attach so much importance to this platform as a tool of communication and promotion of their products and services.

Table 6. Analysis of restaurants online presence on the instagram platform

Restaurants	Followers	Average weekly posts	Average comments per post
Flor de Sal	…	…	…
Bem Bô	1 112	1,16	0,42
A Taberna	1 058	0,75	0,67
A Adega	566	Irregular	Irregular

In this context, it has become quite visible the lack of commitment in the creation of content and communication strategies and dissemination in the digital universe on the part of private entities. The COVID-19 pandemic has become one of the biggest catalysts of digital transformation in recent decades, demonstrating that many everyday activities, including catering, can continue to be carried out without physical contact. However, these establishments have shown inertia in the face of the adversities caused by the health crisis. These businesses did not use digital technology to reinvent and reposition themselves in the market or to make their presence felt. The same happened with the tourist accommodation, which, with the exception of the local accommodation Dona Fina Guest House, showed no interest in digital promotion.

5 Conclusion

In view of the results obtained from the methodology applied, it was perceived that although public entities have a greater online presence and show greater commitment and dedication in the creation of digital content, it was noticeable that there are gaps both at the level of public and private entities.

The permanent updating of institutional websites and social networks adds intangible and essential values to any organisation or business, since it conveys an image of commitment, dedication and interest. However, the analysis carried out showed that the few websites registered, besides being outdated, do not present an appealing layout, therefore deducing that they are not recognized as essential tools for promotion, dissemination and communication. Regarding social networks, with the exception of the tourist accommodation, it was perceived that Facebook is clearly the platform where there is greater investment. Twitter and Linkedin are totally neglected tools and the potential of Youtube is only acknowledged by the municipality.

The analysis of the content of all these platforms allowed us to deduce that the municipality, positioned Mirandela as a mainly gastronomic destination, since this tourist product seems to be the main focus of most of its communication actions, overlapping with natural beauty, heritage and hospitality. The private entities, in turn, in the little use they make of these platforms, disseminate predominantly aspects related to their business, disregarding the resources of the territory, even though the tourism activity is responsible for part of their revenues.

It was also clear that the municipality does not prioritize digital communication, since these tools are used irregularly and unevenly between public and private entities, denoting a lack of synergies and a misalignment in the focus of communication. The municipality of Mirandela does not maximize the potential that digital tools offer to communicate and promote tourism activity, which in turn reflects in a weak and unstable online positioning. Thus, it is necessary a redoubled effort by the various stakeholders of the municipality in the investment of promotion and communication actions that give them attractiveness and inseparable characteristics, able to attract and retain the largest possible number of visitors at a reduced cost. It is also crucial to develop a congruent strategy that favours the creation of a clear image of the destination.

As in any research work, there were limitations during the course of this study. The main constraint was essentially due to the COVID-19 pandemic, which prevented the normal functioning of the tourism sector, which may have influenced the online presence of the sample under study, consequently affecting the results obtained. The short period of analysis was also a limitation of the study. To conclude and as future lines of research, it is suggested that other municipalities with the same characteristics be analysed so as to verify whether the incidences of this particular case are repeated. On the other hand, extending the period of analysis to one year could be another future line of research so as to understand whether seasonality influences online presence.

References

1. Abella, O.M.: Turismo y desarrollo territorial: los planes de dinamización turística en la interpretación y puesta en valor del territorio. Facultad de Geografía e Historia. Universitad Complutense de Madrid, Madrid (2007)
2. Amirou, R., Pauget, B., Lenglet, M., Dammak, A.: De l'image à l'imagerie en passant par l'imaginaire: une interprétation du tourisme à partir des représentations proposées par dix villes européennes. Recherches en Sci. de Gestion 86(5), 87–102 (2011)
3. Buhalis, D., Law, R.: Progress in information technology and tourism management: 20 years on and 10 years after the Internet—the state of eTourism research. Tour. Manage. 29(4), 609–623 (2008)
4. Carmo, A., Rêgo, P.: Covid-19 No Alentejo: Breves Notas Sobre Territórios De Baixa Densidade E O Seu Futuro. Finisterra 55(115), 163–168 (2020)
5. Chen, Y.S., Wu, S.T.: Social networking practices of Viennese coffeehouse culture and intangible heritage tourism. J. Tour. Cult. Change 17(2), 186–207 (2019)
6. CMM: Visit Mirandela. Município de Mirandela. http://www.visitmirandela.com/pages/1000 (2021). Accessed 7 April 2021
7. Correia, R., Brito, C.: Envolvimento da Comunidade – a condição necessária para o sucesso da marca regional. Revista Turismo Desenvolvimento 1(27/28), 815–824 (2017)
8. Covas, A.: O lado virtuoso dos territórios de baixa densidade retrieved from HYPERLINK https://alentejo.sulinformacao.pt/2019/11/o-lado-virtuoso-dos-territorios-de-baixa-densidade/ (2019)
9. Costa, I., Alturas, B.: Líderes de opinião digital portugueses, e o seu impacto, na promoção de produtos, serviços e eventos nas redes sociais. In: Iberian Conference on Information Systems and Technologies. Lisboa, ISCTE-IUL (2018)
10. Cunha, L.: Economia e Política do Turismo. LIDEL, Lisboa (2013)
11. Danias, K., Kavoura, A.: The role of social media as a tool of a company's innovative communication activities. Zeszyty Naukowe Małopolskiej Wyższej Szkoły Ekonomicznej w Tarnowie 23(2), 75–83 (2013)

12. Dehghani, M., Niaki, M.K., Ramezani, I., Sali, R.: Evaluating the influence of youtube advertising for attraction of young customers. Comput. Hum. Behav. **59**, 165–172 (2016)
13. Dias, H.: Marketing Digital e Redes Sociais para o Turismo. Retrieved from Community Manager: https://www.communitymanager.pt/marketing-digital-e-redes-sociais-para-o-turismo/ (2014)
14. Dotto, D., Pons, M., Denardin, A., Ruiz, L.: Marketing Digital e Turismo: Uso de Websites para Atração de Turistas nos Municípios do Rio Grande Do Sul/ Brasil. Revista de Linguagens, Artes e Estudos em Cultura **1**(2), 214–216 (2015)
15. Facebook: Quarterly earnings. Facebook Invester Relations: https://investor.fb.com/financials/default.aspx (2021). Accessed 2 April 2021
16. Fan, D., Buhalis, D., Lin, B.: A tourist typology of online and face-to-face social contact: destination immersion and tourism encapsulation/decapsulation. Ann. Tour. Res. **78**, 1–16 (2019)
17. Fialho, J., Baltazar, M., Saragoça, J., Santos, M.: Redes Sociais: Perspetivas E Desafios Emergentes Nas Sociedades Contemporâneas. CICS.NOVA, Évora (2018)
18. Gomes, B., Mondo, T.: A contribuição das redes sociais na captação de clientes sob a perceção dos gestores hoteleiros. Rev. Bras. Market. **15**(2), 195–206 (2016)
19. Hays, S., Page, J., Buhalis, D.: Social media as a destination marketing tool: its use by national tourism organisations. Curr. Issues Tour. **16**(3), 211–239 (2013)
20. Jansson, A.: A sense of tourism: new media and the dialectic of encapsulation/decapsulation. Tour. Stud. **7**(1), 5–24 (2007)
21. Jiménez, M., Alles, M., Franco, J.: El uso y la importancia de las redes sociales en el sector hotelero desde la perspectiva de los responsables de su gestión. Rev. Investigaciones Turísticas **20**, 50–78 (2021)
22. Kannan, P.K., Li, A.: Digital marketing: a framework, review and research agenda. Int. J. Res. Market. **34**(1), 22–45 (2017)
23. Kemp, S.: Digital 2021: the latest insights into the 'state of digital'. We are Social: https://wearesocial.com/us/blog/2021/01/digital-2021-the-latest-insights-into-the-state-of-digital (2021). Accessed 1 April 2021
24. Kimbu, A.N., Ngoasong, M.Z.: Centralised decentralisation of tourism development: a network perspective. Ann. Tour. Res. **40**, 235–259 (2013)
25. Kotler, P., Setiawan, I., Kartajaya, H.: Marketing 4.0: Mudança do tradicional para o digital, Actual Editora (2017)
26. Leite, R.: Papel do marketing digital na estratégia de comunicação e marketing dos estabelecimentos hoteleiros do porto. Universidade do Minho (2017)
27. Losada, N., Mota, G.: 'Slow down, your movie is too fast': slow tourism representations in the promotional videos of the Douro region (Northern Portugal). J. Destin. Market. Manage. **11**, 140–149 (2019)
28. Mirzaalian, F., Halpenny, E.: Exploring destination loyalty: application of social media analytics in a nature-based tourism setting. J. Destin. Market. Manage. **20**, 100598 (2021)
29. Mistilis, N., Buhalis, D., Gretzel, U.: Future eDestination marketing: perspective of an Australian tourism stakeholder network. J. Travel Res. **53**(6), 778–790 (2014)
30. Morrison, A.M.: Marketing and Managing Tourism Destinations. Routledge (2013)
31. Peres, R., Rita, P.: Marketing e Comunicação Dos Destinos. In: Silva, F., Umbelino, J. (eds.) Planeamento e desenvolvimento turístico, pp. 173–182. Lisboa, LIDEL (2017)
32. Pordata: População. Pordata. https://www.pordata.pt/Municipios/Popula%c3%a7%c3%a3o+residente++m%c3%a9dia+anual-359 (2021). Accessed 7 April 2021
33. RNAT: Registo Nacional da Atividade Turística. https://registos.turismodeportugal.pt/ (2021). Accessed 4 June 2021

34. Rodrigues, S., Gonçalves, R., Teixeira, M.S., Martins, J., Branco, F.: Bidirectional e-commerce platform for tourism in low-density regions: the Douro Valley case study. In: 13th Iberian Conference on Information Systems and Technologies (CISTI). Instituto Politecnico de Braganca (2018)
35. Ryan, D.: Understanding Digital Marketing: Marketing Strategies for Engaging the Digital Generation, Kogan Page, vol. 3 ed. (2014)
36. Sabbag, K.: Marketing Tradicional e Marketing Digital: Evolução ou Mudança? Universidade Federal do Paraná, Curitiba (2014)
37. Sigala, M.: Tourism and COVID-19: impacts and implications for advancing and resetting industry and research. J. Bus. Res. **117**, 312–321 (2020)
38. Silva, A.: A Utilização das Ferramentas de Marketing Digital nas empresas B2B no Setor das Tecnologias de Informação em Portugal. Faculdade de Economia da Universidade do Porto (2015)
39. Stone, M., Woodcock, N.: Interactive, direct and digital marketing: a future that depends on better use of business intelligence. J. Res. Interact. Mark. **8**(1), 4–17 (2014)
40. Teixeira, Sérgio., Martins, J., Branco, F., Gonçalves, R., Au-Yong-Oliveira, M., Moreira, F.: A Theoretical Analysis of Digital Marketing Adoption by Startups. Presented at the (2018). https://doi.org/10.1007/978-3-319-69341-5_9
41. Twitter: Quarterly earnings. de Invester Relations. https://investor.twitterinc.com/home/default.aspx (2020). Accessed 2 April 2021
42. Xiang, Z., Gretzel, U.: Role of social media in online travel information search. Tour. Manage. **31**(2), 179–188 (2010)
43. Yung, R., Khoo-Lattimore, C., Potter, L.: Virtual reality and tourism marketing: conceptualising a framework on presence, emotion, and intention. Curr. Issues Tour. **1–21** (2020). https://doi.org/10.1080/13683500.2020.1820454
44. Teixeira, A., Fonseca, M., Castro, L., Garcia, J., Igreja, C., Costa-Santos, C.: Escala Webqual na avaliação de websites de hotéis do Porto. Eur. J. Appl. Bus. Manage. 55–72 (2018)

Towards a Noise Pollution Public Policy for Sustainable Kindergartens

Marco Bustamante[1] (ID), Ramón Hernández[1], Alexis Olmedo[1], Héctor Reyes[1], David Ruete[1], Diego Fuentealba[2] (ID), and Gustavo Gatica[1](✉) (ID)

[1] Faculty of Engineering, Universidad Andres Bello, Santiago, Chile
{m.bustamanteferrada,r.hernandezriquelme}@uandresbello.edu,
{rhernandez,aolmedo,hreyes,druete,ggatica}@unab.cl
[2] Departamento de Informática y Computación, Universidad Tecnológica Metropolitana, Santiago, Chile
d.fuentealba@utem.cl

Abstract. Noise affects people's health, but there is a lack of public policies on noise control in Chile, applicable to kindergartens and nursing homes. A noise policy contributes to a sustainable environment because it can reduce noise pollution and health problems. The research demonstrates this lack through a quantitative measurement, analysis of legal documentation, local and foreign regulations. In Chile, the national legislation considers protection to workers from the point of view of occupational health and industrial hygiene. However, no legislation can be categorical against the exposure of this physical agent and its consequences on the cognitive and developmental abilities of children and the elderly. A low-cost technological infrastructure is presented, which allows monitoring noise in this type of environment. According to the literature review, Santiago's noise map is insufficient compared to Milan, Curitiba, Konya, and Tehran. This work demonstrates that the ten noise measurement points are insufficient to construct a noise map of the city of Santiago.

Keywords: Public policy · Physical agent · Noise · Regulation · Occupational health

1 Introduction

Noise is defined as any pressure variation that a human being can perceive. Its intensity is quantified in decibels (dB), frequency in Hertz (Hz), and noise can become an invisible enemy that threatens people's health, which does not contribute to a sustainable environment [1]. The Organization for Economic Cooperation and Development (OECD) indicates that Santiago de Chile presents [2]:

- 71% of Educational Establishments are built in areas of unacceptable noise (67,677 students).
- 3.7% of ischemic heart diseases are attributable to exposure to high noise levels.

© Springer Nature Switzerland AG 2021
T. Guarda et al. (Eds.): ARTIIS 2021, CCIS 1485, pp. 709–723, 2021.
https://doi.org/10.1007/978-3-030-90241-4_54

- 6% (approx. 400,000) of the population suffers from high sleep disturbance.
- There are 1,880,000 people exposed to high noise levels during the night.
- 85 health facilities are in areas with non-recommended noise levels.
- Vehicular traffic contributes 70% of the environmental noise.

These data show the need to analyze and identify public policies that promote a healthy life in early childhood education establishments. The methodology contemplates a mixed approach in two phases. The first phase uses a qualitative approach to analyze Chile's regulations and compare them with other countries. The second phase measures noise to obtain a data sample to focus the discussion at a strategic level.

Chilean noise regulation is approached from the occupational health point of view. There are statutes and regulations focused on the workers' health who are exposed to noise sources. However, Chilean regulations do not contemplate noise measurement, mitigation, and potential sources to enable kindergartens, or nursing homes. Although exposure to noise sources with high decibels is harmful to health, there is no data or public references on the matter.

On the other hand, noise measurements can enable new business opportunities when an enterprise can advise on suitable places to install noise-sensitive businesses.

This paper first analyzes the regulatory context in Chile and its comparison with the European reference. The second part shows the details of the measurement experiment conducted outside a kindergarten. Subsequently, the results of the measurements and the conclusions are shown.

2   Background

The problem is analyzed in the following steps. First, the definitions of noise are reviewed, and its sources are identified. Then, some of the known effects of noise on people's health and the occupational health perspective are identified. Also, available technological tools are discussed, and, finally, the regulations in force in Chile and other countries are compiled.

2.1   Noise: Definition

Noise is an inarticulate sound, usually unpleasant. By contrast, acoustic comfort is defined as "that situation where the noise level caused by human activities is adequate for people's rest, communication and health" [3].

The Chilean Institute of Public Health (ISP) defines *noise* as "any pressure variation that the human being can perceive, quantifiable according to intensity (dB) and frequency (Hertz)" [1]. This physical agent (noise) is present in every activity or production process, whether commercial or recreational. Therefore, any worker exposed to high noise levels can suffer hearing loss, regardless of the area of performance [1].

2.2   Noise Sources

Noise exists inherently with nature. It is possible to hear the noise of the sea on the beach, a river, or a bark. Human activity adds amounts of noise due to the use of machinery and tools. Within urban areas, the main responsible for noise are the means of transportation. In airports and airfields, air traffic is the agent of noise [4].

2.3 Health Effects of Noise

The WHO has characterized the groups vulnerable to noise as follows:

Table 1. Vulnerable groups to noise [5].

Group	Risks
Children	Cognitive development problems decreased motivation and reduced speech, intelligibility, listening comprehension, and concentration, resulting in annoyance, disturbance, and increased restlessness. Children may experience poorer reading, poorer memory capacity, and performance
	Cognitive impairment may also be related to noise exposure in the home during sleeping hours, which can cause low mood, fatigue, and poor performance the next day
	Noise in the home may also be related to problems with hyperactivity and inattention. It can cause poorer academic performance and concentration
Elderly	Older adults are more vulnerable to sleep disturbance, more prone to cardiovascular effects than noise
Shift workers	Shift workers show a higher risk of adverse impacts with exposure to environmental noise because their sleep structure is under stress
Pre-existing health	People with chronic diseases may be at greater cardiovascular risk from noise than those without such pre-existing conditions
Noise-sensitive individuals	People with autism or Asperger's may consider noise a threat, and it throws them off. They are more susceptible to sleep disturbances and psychological effects due to noise
Pregnant women	The sleep structure of pregnant women becomes fragmented. Environmental noise may also increase the risk of preterm delivery and low birth

According to Table 1, noise is a risk factor for children's health and negatively repercussions their learning. Children immersed in noisy environments are less susceptible to the acoustic signals around them, and their ability to listen is disturbed [6].

Children present a delay in learning to read in schools more exposed to noise. In addition, noise hinders spoken communication, can favor a feeling of isolation, hinder children's sociability and disturb their way of relating to others [6].

It is necessary to contemplate the relationship between space and functionality inside kindergartens to obtain acoustic comfort, where each of the spaces obtains sufficient conditions of isolation and acoustical conditioning.

The World Health Organization (WHO) establishes that exposure to certain sound pressure levels could negatively affect health. Table 2 shows this relationship.

Table 2. Negative health effects of noise exposure [7]

Adverse effects	Threshold (dB)
Loss of sleep quality and difficulty falling asleep	30
Difficulty in verbal communication	40
Probable sleep interruption	45
Moderate daytime discomfort	50
Severe daytime discomfort	55
Extremely difficult verbal communication	65
Long-term hearing loss	75
Short-term hearing loss	110–140

2.4 Occupational Health Perspectives

Chile has a protocol for surveillance workers' hearing health, and its acronym is PREXOR [8]. This protocol involves environmental surveillance processes, technical recommendations to companies, continuous audiological evaluations, and hearing prevention to mitigate damage due to noise exposure of exposed subjects [9].

Supreme Decree 594 [10] establishes standards regarding noise exposure in the workplace. This decree sets a maximum daily exposure period of 8 h at 85 dBA (Table 3) for a person without hearing protection. According to Chilean regulations [9], a noise dose unit represents the exposure for 8 h to noise at 85 dBA SPL average intensity and means the maximum recommended exposure.

Table 3. Noise dose equivalents [9]

Sound pressure	Noise dosage time
85 dB	8 h
88 dB	4 h
91 dB	2 h
94 dB	1 h
97 dB	30 min
100 dB	15 min
103 dB	7.5 min
106 dB	3.75 min

2.5   Information Technologies for Monitoring and Control

According to the Environmental Noise Directive (END), on 5 June 2019, the E.U. required the Member States to report noise data to the European Environmental Information and Observation Network (Eionet). The data is managed by the European Environment Agency (EEA) to have control of the measurements [11, 12].

There are only 14 permanent noise measurement points in Chile, 10 of them in Santiago de Chile. Noise measurements are not binding with any action plan in comparison with environmental pre-emergencies for air pollution. In addition, there are stations installed in Concepción (2), Valparaíso (1) and Viña del Mar (1) [13].

New information technologies such as IoT enable measuring in more places through low power consumption and comprehensive coverage communication architectures [14]. Even open-source electronics such as Arduino and low-cost sensors can be used [15].

Figure 1 shows a distant sound and gas measurement system based on the Arduino microcontroller and a ZigBee unit as a communications gateway [16]. Arduino-compatible sound sensors cost between USD 2 and USD 5.

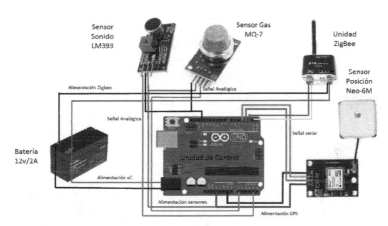

Fig. 1. IoT-based noise detector device [17].

2.6   Chilean Regulations

The Chilean General Regulations for Urbanism and Construction (GRUC) classifies schools in group 1. That is, "premises that by their nature must be isolated from exterior sound waves and internal sounds must be extinguished inside the rooms in which they are produced". Therefore, they must be subject to the requirements established in the Official Standards on acoustic conditions of premises (NCh354. Of61: Acoustic conditions to be met by buildings) [18].

This regulation raises the need for acoustic quality standards in educational spaces, but an opposing argument is the economic costs of implementing these measures. Not only to build new educational establishments but also to refurbish existing schools. The OECD recommends investing in quality educational spaces to improve students' academic performance and translate into increases in the nation's GDP [8, 19].

The main regulations in Chile that regulate noise exposure in work areas are summarized in Table 4:

Table 4. Regulations that regulate noise exposure in Chile

Regulation name	Scope
Constitución Política del Estado (Art. N° 19, inciso N° 9)	Establishes the right to health protection
Código Sanitario (Art. 67 y 68)	Hygiene and safety of the environment and workplaces
Código del Trabajo (art. 12, 153, 183-A, 183-B, 183-E, 183-AB, 184a, 193, 209 – 2011, 506	It governs labor relations between employers and workers
Law N° 16.744, Ministerio del Trabajo y Previsión Social (Art. 65, 68, 71)	Prevention of occupational risks
Law N° 20.123, Ministerio Del Trabajo Y Previsión Social	Regulates subcontracting work and temporary service companies
Law N° 19.937, Ministerio de Salud	Regulates new concession of sanitary authority, management modalities and citizen participation
D.S. N° 594/99, Ministerio de Salud (Art. 3, 37, 70–82 y 117)	Regulation on basic sanitary and environmental conditions in workplaces
D.S. N° 101/68, Ministerio del Trabajo y Previsión Social (art. 72)	Regulation for the application of Law No. 16,744
D.S. N° 109/68, Ministerio del Trabajo y Previsión Social (art. 21)	Regulation for the qualification and evaluation of work accidents and occupational diseases
D.S. N° 73/05, Ministerio del Trabajo y Previsión Social	Introduces amendments to the regulation for the application of Law No. 16,744
D.S. N° 40/69, Ministerio del Trabajo Y Previsión Social (Art. 2, 3, 21, 22)	Regulation on prevention of occupational hazards
D.S. N.° 18/82, Ministerio de Salud	Quality certification of PPE against occupational risks
D.S. N° 76/06, Ministerio del Trabajo y Previsión Social	Regulation for the application of Article 66 Bis of Law No. 16.744
D.S. N° 168/96, Ministerio del Trabajo y Previsión Social	Regulation for the constitution and operation of the joint health and safety committees, public sector
D.S. N° 1222/96, Ministerio de Salud	Regulation of the institute of public health of Chile
Circular 3G/40, del 14 de marzo de 1983 y sus modificaciones, Ministerio de Salud	Instructions for the qualification and evaluation of occupational diseases of the regulation D.S. No. 109/68 of Law 16.744

2.7   Regulations in Other Countries

Regulations at the international level are summarized, particularly from the European Union. Table 5 consolidates some of the regulations identified and their thematic scope.

Table 5. Regulations governing noise exposure in other countries.

Location	Regulation name	Scope
Europe	Regulation (EU) No. 540 (2014)	Motor vehicle regulation
Europe	Regulation (E.U.) No. 168 (2013), Commission Delegated Regulation (E.U.) No. 134 (2014)	Motor vehicle regulation
Europe	Directive 2001/43/E.C. (2001)	Motorcycle Regulation: tires for motor vehicles and their trailers
Europe	Regulation (EC) No. 216 (2018). Commission Regulation (EU) No. 748 (2012)	Aircraft noise limitations
Europe	Regulation (EU) No. 598 (2014)	Operating restrictions at community airports
Europe	Directive 2006/93/E.C. (2006)	Regulation of subsonic civil aircraft in Chapter 3
Europe	Directive 2008/57/E.C. (2008)	Railway interoperability
Europe	Commission regulation (E.U.) No. 1304 (2014)	Technical specifications for interoperability (TSI) on railway noise
Europe	Commission implementing regulation (EU) 2015/429 (2015)	Rail noise levy
Europe	Regulation (E.U.) No. 1316 (2013)	Connecting Europe mechanism
Europe	Directive 2000/14/E.C. (2000)	Environmental noise emission for outdoor use
Spain	Royal Decree 1513 (2005)	Application in all areas
Spain	Directive 2002/49/CED (2002)	Application in all areas
Colombia	Resolution 0627 (2006)	Maximum permissible standards for noise emission levels
Colombia	Resolution 1034 (2015)	Air traffic regulation

European legislation on the assessment and management of environmental noise states that: "A high level of environmental and health protection must be achieved within the framework of Community policy, and one of the objectives to be pursued is protection against noise. In the Green Paper on future noise policy, the Commission refers to environmental noise as one of the major environmental problems in Europe" [20].

If it compares the regulations in Chile with the European regulations, it can see that in Europe there is a clear projection in terms of reducing by 30% the number of people affected by transport noise. In Chile, the regulations are more static in establishing maximum permitted levels and reducing noise exposure from the occupational health point of view.

2.8 Noise Maps

Noise maps contain points used to measure the noise level and are used for mitigation measures. Table 6 shows the measurement points for the noise maps implemented in Curitiba, Konya, Tehran, and Milan. Kirrian and Trombetta (2014) used 232 measurement points to construct a noise map for Curitiba in Brazil, considering four measurement areas with a total area of approximately 13 km^2 [21]. In Konya in Turkey, a noise pollution map was constructed using 366 measurement points [22]. In a case study conducted in the 14th district of Tehran city (Iran), 88 measurement points on streets with high vehicular traffic and highways were considered for 9.5 hectares of the surface area [23]. In Milan (Italy), a map with 93 measurement points was constructed for the Lyfe DynaMap project within a surface of 181.67 km^2 [24].

Table 6. Measurement points per km^2 in several cities.

Country	City	Measurement points number	Area (km^2)	Points per km^2
Italia	Milán	93	181.67	0.5
Brasil	Curitiba	232	13.00	17.8
Turquía	Konya	366	38.87	9.4
Irán	Tehran	88	0.10	880.0
Chile	Santiago	10	641.00	0.0

3   Material and Methods

This work measures noise quantitatively to identify harmful levels to the health of members of a given community, whether residents or workers. This work considered two factors to find a proper location for a measurement point. The first criteria is a zone with several kindergarten schools because children are a risk group for noise pollution [5]. Additionally, the Chilean government does not have regulations that protect children in kindergarten schools. The second criteria are the proximity to a polluted noise area such as avenues or streets with high traffic. Figure 2 shows 89 kindergarten schools located in downtown Santiago [25]. A red circle highlights the chosen location for the measurements. The map shows that several establishments are located near Alameda Avenue, with permanent daytime noise levels. In this scenario, it is necessary to know if the kindergarten schools have any mitigation infrastructure for external and internal noise levels.

Fig. 2. Private kindergarten schools located in downtown Santiago (Chile) [25]

The measurement site is located at coordinates −33.4465064, −70.6460539, located on Tarapacá Street, Santiago, Metropolitan Region. Tarapacá Street has direct exposure to the street and is in a sector with high vehicular traffic. In addition, this street is close to two significant avenues (67 m to Santa Rosa Avenue and 90 m to San Francisco Avenue), where multiple routes of public transportation and private vehicles converge.

Figure 3 shows the target location and highlights the sources of major vehicular flow in the area in red.

Fig. 3. Map with traffic flow [26] (Color figure online)

Table 7 shows that more than two million vehicles travel along Santa Rosa Street every month, of which 7.5% are buses [27].

Table 7. Accumulated monthly vehicular flow through Santa Rosa avenue between 2017–2021 (millions) [27].

Month	Year				
	2017	2018	2019	2020	2021
Jan	2.07	2.11	2.18	2.26	1.92
Feb	1.80	1.82	1.86	2.04	1.83
Mar	2.30	2.28	2.28	2.05	1.93
Apr	2.10	2.28	2.21	1.52	
May	2.24	2.24	2.24	1.22	
Jun	2.12	2.19	2.15	1.23	
Jul	2.18	2.14	2.20	1.48	
Aug	2.26	2.29	2.33	1.78	
Sep	2.13	2.09	2.13	1.96	
Oct	2.24	2.26	2.22	2.19	
Nov	2.25	2.23	2.23	2.15	
Dec	2.29	2.33	2.43	2.10	
Total	25.97	24.19	26.45	21.97	5.68

A sound level meter was used that includes two virtual noise level meters for real-time measurement of a full band or third octave and broadband sound simultaneously. In addition, historical data is recorded with intervals from 1 s to 60 min.

Measurement is performed for 30 days from Tuesday 08/05/2019 between 05:00 h to 20:00 h. A "QUEST" model 2900 sound level meter is used, allowing measurements every 10 min, taking a sample window every 15 s for 15 h.

The experimental measurement needs a diagnostic assessment of the site and its surroundings. According to Chilean legislation [10], this assessment must identify the noise peak points. The measurement records the peak sound pressure level (NPS peak) in dB(c) for at least one minute during the highest noise time.

In cases of variable noise, the measurement should record at the precise time when the noise is heard, considering the worst condition for the measure. Measurements was saved on a platform that mitigates the technical risks associated with infrastructure management proposed by [28]. This platform guarantees requirement scalability, allowing data growth and complexity.

4   Results

Figure 4 shows the average daytime noise levels for a one-day sample, where the noise exceeds 70 dBA from 09:00 h and maintains the same behavior until the end of the measurements at 20:00 h.

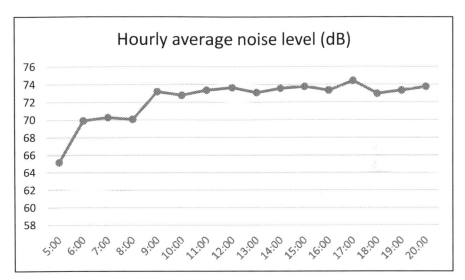

Fig. 4. Average hourly noise over one day of measurement.

Figure 5 shows the 30-day measurements separated into weekdays (Blue) and weekends (Orange). It is observed that there is a similar hourly behavior, but the weekend shows a lower amount of noise. The lower flow of private vehicles could explain this difference.

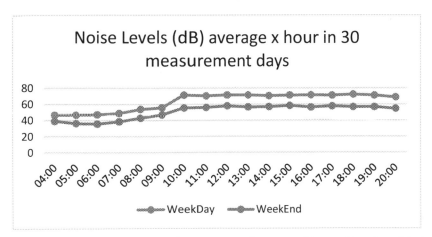

Fig. 5. Average noise over 30 days of measurement is separated by working days (blue) and weekends (orange) (Color figure online).

According to the Chilean Environmental Ministry [29], noise can be classified into four categories "good", "acceptable", "unacceptable" and "risky". Table 8 shows the number of measurements in each class.

Table 8. Measurements are classified according to MMA scale.

Hour	Classification			
	Good	Acceptable	Unacceptable	Risky
5:00	231	128	120	241
6:00	154	140	129	297
7:00	145	127	150	298
8:00	149	132	145	294
9:00	62	148	180	330
10:00	54	177	174	315
11:00	58	154	175	333
12:00	50	152	165	353
13:00	71	156	163	330
14:00	67	159	149	345
15:00	51	166	147	356
16:00	57	159	158	346
17:00	56	145	163	356
18:00	50	179	168	323
19:00	57	149	184	330
20:00	52	163	158	347

Figure 6 plots the acceptable and unacceptable categories for the period 09:00 to 20:00. 70% of the measurements are in the "unacceptable" range.

The results shows that several measurements are classified as risky, which is threatened for kindergartens. Thus, this work suggests that a public policy to decrease noise pollution is needed in Chile. On another hand, the proposed architecture achieves complexity criterion because it is based on a container-based architecture and microservices.

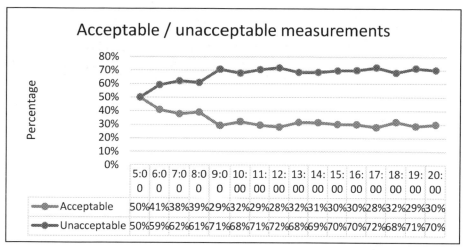

Fig. 6. Noise measurements are grouped into acceptable/unacceptable over one day of measurement.

5   Conclusions

The results show that vehicular noise is a fixed source of noise emanation to be considered in Chilean legislation. Thus, noise mitigation works could be required in kindergartens.

From the normative point of view, there is legal multidimensionality concerning the leading authority in noise pollution. From this perspective, four main areas can be identified as a source of legal regulations against noise in daycare centers.

The first perspective concerns the building zone because the results showed that noise measurements exceed the threshold for schools located in residential areas. The second perspective examines occupational hazards because workers in the noise area are exposed to a potential health problem. Thirdly, a regulatory problem allows vehicles to exceed the maximum permitted limits when they are in operation.

Finally, from the point of view of operating authorization, internal/external noise mitigation measures to ensure the protection of people are not observed.

A comparison of current regulations shows that In Europe, there is a binding initiative for the generation of noise maps to monitor compliance with the standard.

In contrast, and as mentioned above, there are only 14 measurement points in Chile, which is insufficient to achieve the construction of noise maps, even only for the city of Santiago.

Several areas for future work can be identified. Firstly, to research the effectiveness of the mitigation measures applied in the gardens, contrasting measurements outside/inside the classrooms. Secondly, to determine the optimal number of measurement stations for mapping. Thirdly, to propose and evaluate noise mitigation measures mandated by legal regulations. Fourthly, to build visual sound level meter prototypes to record and display noise levels inside classrooms. Finally, to create dynamic and collaborative noise maps using smartphones and 3G/4G data networks.

References

1. Instituto de Salud Pública de Chile: Manual de la Ficha de Evaluación Cualitativa de Exposición a Ruido. http://www.ispch.cl/saludocupacional (2015). Accessed: 12 July 2021
2. Valdebenito: Avance en la Gestión de Control de ruido Ambientall. In: XX Seminario de Ruido Ambienta, p. 10 (2020)
3. Proaño, C.: Ruido y silencio en el paisaje sonoro de un barrio de clase alta quiteño, intersecciones en el continuum. Flacso sede Ecuador, Quito (2012)
4. Comisión Europea: INFORME DE LA COMISIÓN AL PARLAMENTO EUROPEO Y AL CONSEJO. http://ec.europa.eu/environment/noise/evaluation_en.htm (2015). Accessed 15 July 2021
5. Stansfeld, S.A.: Environmental noise guidelines for the European region. In: Proceedings of the Institute of Acoustics, vol. 41, pp. 17–20. https://www.euro.who.int/en/health-topics/environment-and-health/noise/publications/2018/environmental-noise-guidelines-for-the-european-region-2018 (2019). Accessed 13 July 2021
6. Conama: Campaña de Sensibilización sobre el Ruido Ambiental Baja el Volumen. http://www.socha.cl/wp-content/uploads/2013/06/1-Gestión-del-Control-de-Ruido-Ambiental-a-nivel-local-Seminario-Ruido-2009.pdf (2009). Accessed 13 July 2021
7. de la Salud, M.: MAKE LISTENING SAFE Escuchar sin riesgos (2015)
8. Minsal, Protocolo sobre normas mínimas para el desarrollo de programas de vigilancia de la perdida auditiva por exposición a ruido en los lugares de trabajo, p. 55 (2013)
9. Aedo, C., Cuellar, G.: Exposure to non-occupational noise from physiology to Chile auditory evaluation and normative in Chile. J. Heal. Med. Sci. **5**(3), 141–147 (2019)
10. Ministerio de Salud: Decreto supremo n° 594, p. 44 (1999)
11. The European Parliament and the Council of the European Union, Commission Regulation (EU) No 748/2012 of 3 August 2012 laying down implementing rules for the airworthiness and environmental certification of aircraft and related products, parts and appliances, as well as for the certification of design and production, p. 85 (2012)
12. European Environmental Agency: Environmental noise in Europe. https://www.eea.europa.eu/publications/environmental-noise-in-europe (2020). Accessed 14 July 2021
13. Ministerio del Medio Ambiente: Nivel Equivalente Minuto a Minuto – Ruido Ambiental. https://ruido.mma.gob.cl/red-de-monitoreo-de-ruido/minuto-a-minuto/ (2021). Accessed 14 July 2021
14. LoRa Alliance: What is LoRaWAN® Specification, LoRa Alliance®. https://lora-alliance.org/about-lorawan/ (2018). Accessed 14 July 2021
15. Segura-Garcia, J., Felici-Castell, S., Perez-Solano, J.J., Cobos, M., Navarro, J.M.: Low-cost alternatives for urban noise nuisance monitoring using wireless sensor networks. IEEE Sens. J. **15**(2), 836–844 (2015). https://doi.org/10.1109/JSEN.2014.2356342
16. Zigbee Alliance: Zigbee specification, pp. 1–378 (2015)
17. Reyes Díaz, H.E.: Observatorio medioambiental georreferenciado para monitoreo de jardines infantiles basado en internet de las cosas y websockets. Universidad Andrés Bello (2018)
18. Agencia Chilena de Eficiencia Energética (AChEE): Guía de Eficiencia Energética en Establecimientos ducacionales. https://drive.google.com/file/d/1ObfW9kMnBrC_IorbUb7kBoXAVyeUHOdm/view (2012). Accessed 14 July 2021
19. Aguilar, J.R.: A review of acoustic design criteria for school infrastructure in Chile. Rev. Ing. Constr. **34**(2), 115–123 (2019). https://doi.org/10.4067/S0718-50732019000200115
20. Parlamento Europeo y del Consejo: Evaluación y Gestión del Ruido Ambiental. [Directiva 2002/49/CE del 25 de junio de 2002], D. Of. las Comundades Eur., vol. 189, pp. 12–25. http://sicaweb.cedex.es/docs/leyes/Directiva-2002-49-CE-Evaluacion-gestion-ruido-ambiental.pdf (2002). Accessed 14 July 2021

21. Kirrian, P., Trombetta, P.: Evaluation of noise pollution in urban traffic hubs-noise maps and measurements. Environ. Impact Assess. Rev. **51**, 1–9 (2015). https://doi.org/10.1016/j.eiar.2014.09.014

22. Dursun, Ş, Özdemir, C., Karabörk, H., Koçak, S.: Noise pollution and map of Konya city in Turkey. J. Int. Environ. Appl. Sci. **1**(2), 63–72 (2006)

23. Abbaspour, M., Karimi, E., Nassiri, P., Monazzam, M.R., Taghavi, L.: Hierarchal assessment of noise pollution in urban areas – a case study. Transp. Res. Part D Transp. Environ. **34**, 95–103 (2015). https://doi.org/10.1016/J.TRD.2014.10.002

24. Zambon, G., Benocci, R., Bisceglie, A., Roman, H.E., Bellucci, P.: The LIFE DYNAMAP project: towards a procedure for dynamic noise mapping in urban areas. Appl. Acoust. **124**, 52–60 (2017). https://doi.org/10.1016/J.APACOUST.2016.10.022

25. Mi Jardín Infantil.cl: Mi Jardín Infantil – ¡La Guía de Jardines Infantiles de Santiago y de Chile!. https://www.mijardininfantil.cl/ (2021). Accessed 14 July 2021

26. Google: Google Maps. https://www.google.cl/maps/ (2021). Accessed 14 July 2021

27. MOP Concesión: Informacion de Flujo Vehicular. http://www.concesiones.cl/proyectos/Documents/CorredorSantaRosa/2021/Diptico_StaRosa_2021_03.pdf (2021). Accessed 14 July 2021

28. Araya, S. et al.: Design of a system to support certification management with an adaptive architecture. In: 2021 16th Iberian Conference on Information Systems and Technologies (CISTI), June, pp. 1–6 (2021). https://doi.org/10.23919/CISTI52073.2021.9476390

29. Ministerio del Medio Ambiente: Red de Monitoreo de Ruido – Ruido Ambiental. https://ruido.mma.gob.cl/red-de-monitoreo-de-ruido/red-de-monitoreo-de-ruido-ambiental/ (2021). Accessed 15 July 2021

Exploration of 3 W's of Web Marketing in the Hotel Sector – A Study Conducted at the Casa da Calçada Hotel

João Marinho[1]([⊠]), Sofia Almeida[2] [iD], and Catarina Neto[1]

[1] Universidade Europeia, Lisbon, Portugal
[2] Universidade Europeia e CEG/Territur, Universidade de Lisboa, Lisbon, Portugal

Abstract. Hotels should implement new digital strategies, to become more competitive and guarantee confidence and security for their guests. In a more technological world, it is possible for hotels to gain a competitive advantage through digital and internet marketing strategies to capture potential customers. The purpose of this study is to explore the importance of webmarketing strategies in the hotel sector, namely, webdesign, webpromotion and webperfomance, using the Casa da Calçada hotel, as a case study. For this, three objectives were defined: i) to analyze the current digital marketing strategy; ii) to identify the most effective tools in the Web Marketing strategy and iii) to explore web marketing opportunities to improve the hotel's performance on the internet. To achieve these objectives, various data collection methods were used, such as semi-structed interviews and netnography. Also, an analysis of the digital marketing strategies implemented by the hotel was carried out. Results show that the global classification achieved was 60%. Of the five categories analyzed, the criteria's usability and promotion presented the best rating, followed by customer relationship and point of sale and price and product. At the end, limitations are identified and theoretical and practical recommendations in the hotel sector are presented, also future research is pinpointed.

Keywords: Web marketing · Webdesign · Webpromotion · Webperformance · Casa da Calçada hotel · Hotel sector

1 Introduction

Before COVID-19 in 2019, the World Tourism Organization (UNWTO's) report [60] revealed a total of 1460 million international arrivals and 1481 trillion USD receipts worldwide, as for 2020, the UNWTO's [60] report registered 381 million international arrivals worldwide (−74%) and estimated a loss of 1.3 trillion USD international tourism receipts. Regarding Portugal, TravelBI's [57] reports indicate that Portugal, in 2019, counted 29 million international arrivals and 22 million USD receipts, as for 2020 TravelBI's [58, 59] reports showed that Portugal counted 12 million international arrivals (−58.3%) and 9 million USD receipts (−40.9%). Industries across the world are trying to maintain consumer confidence and keep the economy moving [47].

T. Guarda et al. (Eds.): ARTIIS 2021, CCIS 1485, pp. 724–738, 2021.
https://doi.org/10.1007/978-3-030-90241-4_55

One of the ways to gain competitive advantage is through digital strategies. Hospitality and marketing research is an important topic in both fields and has grown continuously over the past three decades [66]. Internet technology, as an important information technology is replacing traditional marketing tools and leading to fundamental changes in the principles and operations of marketing practice [44]. As internet technology continues to develop, internet marketing, or e-marketing, has been considered one of the influential trends in the hotel and tourism industry [44, 66]. The significant role of internet technology in tourism and hotel sector leads to an emerging research direction in Internet marketing [35]. Hereupon, the purpose of this study is to explore the 3 W's of webmarketing in the hotel sector, and how hoteliers can find ways to gain competitive advantage, namely in a post-COVID-19 era.

This study is structured as follows: literature review on the consumer behaviour trends after COVID-19 focusing on hospitality, followed by the influence of webmarketing in hotel sector and the 3 W's of Webmarketing. Secondly, the methodological approach, the netnography technique to collect information and to analyse the collect data and semi-structured interviews planning are described. Lastly, the results are presented and discussed followed by conclusion, contributions, limitations, and future research.

2   Literature Review

2.1   Consumer Behavior Trends in Hospitality After COVID-19

In the space of a few months, in the first semester of 2020, the world changed due COVID-19 pandemic. "The COVID-19 pandemic, also known as the coronavirus pandemic, caused by the acute respiratory syndrome coronavirus 2 (SARS-CoV-2)" [17, p.2]. COVID-19 effectively changed behaviors at different levels as economic, political, socio-cultural [3, 51]. According to [41] trends in consumer behavior are influenced by socioeconomic and technological changes that emphasize the importance of innovative and alternative products and services. Regarding travel sector, has been hardest hit by COVID-19, the travel spending has decreased significantly, and the sector has not recovered yet [25]. Tourists choose between hospitality products and destinations bases on their personal experience or the perceived service experience (functional quality) of a product or service provided [19]. [18] stated that in an uncertain era, almost all the tourism sectors will face the likelihood of experiencing some form of crisis. Under that thought, academics started and conducted investigations on the bases of crises and how to manage unexpected crisis [1, 24, 62]. Due to the fragility of tourist sectors (regarding worldwide pandemics), studies on crisis management, effects of crises on organizations also on the system and consumer behavior, containing countries, sectors, and initiatives, as well as the influence of crises on tourist behavior, are very essential and vital [22, 39]. [25] concluded that amounts in credit and debit card transactions for online purchases increased gradually since the beginning of COVID-19. [61], pointed out one characteristic behavior of tourists is that the people did not stop travelling completely, instead, they condense their expenses, like choosing cheap places, shortening the vacation distance, and tending to use low-cost services. [6] reported that tourists will depend more on the internet to obtain data as well as service.

Before making a reservation, consumers try to collect all information for reducing uncertainty regarding inexperienced product or service. To avoid this uncertainty, hotels need to present a trustworthy image on booking websites by providing detailed information, which should be consistent with the website's promises [27].

There is a need for hotels to pay attention to provide complete, useful, and reliable information about their products and services, so the managers must take this into consideration when designing/maintaining their websites [42]. COVID-19 has indeed accelerated the immersion of new technologies and applications in tourism and hospitality operations [47]. At a time when people are afraid to travel, technological innovations that may have been primarily designed to be launched as extra innovations or services are suddenly becoming obligations [21]. Recognizing and employing technology trends can increase the efficiency of operations and further improve the customer experience [47]. [24] Piloted a study on the impacts of the COVID-19 pandemic on the Consumer Behavior of Turkish Tourists. In a study conducted in a hill station in Northern India, [50] find out factors leading to hotel choice: i) perception of personal space; ii) safety and security; iii) value for money experience; iv) convenience; v) homely atmosphere.

Hotels must keep pace with emerging travel technology trends, so they are not overtaken by the competition [47]. In that regard, hotel managers and their marketing team must highlight these previous characteristics when promoting their hotels on digital platforms, namely: safety and security, hygiene, the experience in the hotel and the accommodation with homely atmosphere.

2.2 Webmarketing Influence on the Hotel Sector

With the advance of Internet technologies, more travelers are using internet to seek destination information [2, 36].Guest engagement behavior has led to a chance in the management and marketing strategies of companies in the hotel sector, leading them to augment the use of digital marketing tools [2, 33]. In this "digital era" hotel managers, should establish a digital marketing plan, and it is important to actively manage the hotel online presence [34, 40]. "Digital marketing, as the term says, refers to a marketing through digital technologies" [2, p.29]. According to [2] some of the channels associated with the digital marketing are: SMS marketing, digital print ads, television marketing, radio advertising, internet marketing (web marketing), among others.

Web marketing is a subset of digital marketing and can be defined as the act of promoting good and services through the internet and involve search engine marketing, email marketing, social media marketing and types of display advertising, including web banner advertising [2]. The digital platforms can be classified in two categories: informational and revenue generating [36]. According to [36], regarding informational digital platforms, it is important to hospitality and tourism marketers establish procedures that allow to collect discussion and feedback created online. As for the revenue generating digital platforms, is no less important the need to manage electronic word of mouth (E-WOM) with revenue purposes [28]. Tourism and hospitality marketeers should direct the efforts to spreading a good E-WOM about the property and destination, helping potential information-seeking tourists by providing images and reinforcing opinions [36]. In a hotel digital marketing strategies, two main components can be distinguished: first, a hotel may actively use digital information in its marketing efforts such as using information and metrics from review sites, providing a link to/or integrating third-party reviews on its site, using tracking software to analyze reviews over Online Travel Agents (OTA) or using OTA management reports; second, a hotel could have a strategy for managing conversations with its customers, for example, responses to guests comments and encouraging guests to post comments [9]. Worldwide, tourists browse OTA websites first and visit the hotel websites later, looking for more specific information [54].

Managers who value customer-generated feedback more are more likely to improve the hotel's perceived quality [56]. Furthermore, some authors argue that hoteliers should try to increase the number of reviews they receive and therefore should facilitate access to customer review site [9, 36, 39]. The number of reviews that a product or service receives from customers is one of the most critical review attributes [14]. Also, hotels are increasingly changing from passive listening to active engagement through management response [9]. To [16] online management responses are a form of customer relationship management.

Notwithstanding, digital marketing keeps a record of the number and duration of views of any ad, post, etc. and the effect of it on the sales, thus measuring the total impact of it [2]. Hereupon, hotel managers, in addition to the need of guarantee a quality service [32], also should be concern in spread those experiences to other potential tourists collecting information about the destination and hotel. So, it is not only important the quality offline service during the guest stay, but also the digital online experience to captivate the guest to choose that hotel among a variety of possible choices. Research based on 50 articles about hospitality and tourism E-WOM concludes that "online reviews appear to be a strategic tool that plays an important role in hospitality and tourism management, especially in promotion, online sales, and reputation management" [49, p.618].

The hotel sector is witnessing greater transparency in access to information, which enables comparison between alternative products, as well as a reduction in the distance between the company and the customer in geographical and time terms.

2.3 The 3W (Web Design, Web Promotion and Web Performance)

It is in this context that web marketing emerges as a fundamental activity that allows the company to create competitive advantages over its competitors, which requires a 3W approach from a management point of view: the creation of sites suitable to its profile (web design), its dissemination to target customers (web promotion) and the measurement of the results achieved (web performance) [48]. Web design plays an important role for website users, and it usually includes the interactive and security aspect with user interface. A good web design can influence the observation of user's and their understanding of functions of the system [11]. The three characteristics of website design were navigation, information, and visual design [43]. The World Wide Web Consortium (W3C), the main international standards organization for the World Wide Web, developed the WCAG 2.1 (Web Content Accessibility Guidelines) in cooperation with individuals and organizations around the world, with a goal of providing a shared standard for Web content accessibility that meets the needs of individuals, organizations, and governments internationally [63]. To ensure that the organization meets the WCAG standard, it must follow four design principles: perceivable, operable, understandable and robust [63].

Website promotion is the continuing process used by webmasters to improve content and increase exposure of a website to bring more visitors. Many techniques such as search engine optimization and search engine advertisement are used to increase a site's traffic once content is developed [38]. Web performance has been used to refer to a subjective judgement of web users' evaluation of a particular site and is the criterion for evaluating the success of failure of the website [20]. Furthermore, [20] stated that web performance is the main outcome variable in the web experiences that the site can offer consumers. According to [26], web performance measures how quickly a page on a website load and display in the browser also is the process of improving website performance using various methods and techniques. Faster websites perform better [26].

3   Methodology

3.1   Sample Characterization

The purpose of this study is to understand the importance of digital marketing strategies to hotel sector and how these strategies contribute to gain competitive advantages by means of a case study at Casa da Calçada hotel. A case study approach is used when the authors desire to cover some research, using qualitative research methods, that they qualify as relevant phenomenon and context [15, 64]. A case study should be considered when the focus of the study is to answer "how" and "why" question [64]. Case study is also known as triangulation research strategy [55]. As [53] affirmed that triangulation consists in ensure precision and different explanations, and to confirm the veracity of the processes the need of triangulations emerge. In this research were identified four types of triangulations: i) method triangulation, ii) investigator triangulation, iii) theory triangulation, and iv) data source triangulation [10, 13, 45]. In this specific case study methodological, investigator and data triangulation were applied. Methodological triangulation involves the use of several methods of data collection about the same phenomenon [46], and is frequently used in qualitative studies, that may include interviews, observation, and field notes [7]. Investigator triangulations occurs when involves two or more searchers in the same study to provide different observations and conclusions [7]. Lastly, "Data triangulation, which entails gathering data through several sampling strategies, so that slices of data at different times and social situations, as well as on a variety of people, are gathered" [12] as cited in [4].

A qualitative research design tests the fidelity of the research through credibility, transferability, reliability, and confirmability [23].

In this specific study, qualitative research design was used to molding the study, and data, investigator and method triangulation was used as strategy to reach the study's objectives, namely: i) to analyze the current digital marketing strategy of Casa da Calçada hotel; ii) to identify the most effective tools in the Web Marketing strategy and iii) to explore web marketing opportunities to improve Casa da Calçada hotel's performance on the internet. Set in a 16th century manor, this boutique hotel situates in the central Amarante with views over the Tâmega River. It offers an outdoor pool, nearby golf facilities and free parking. The guestrooms of the Casa da Calçada Relais & Châteaux feature antique furnishings and features. The hotel is a member of Relais & Châteaux. This hotel marketing consortium established in 1954, it is an association of more than

580 landmark hotels and restaurants operated by independent innkeepers, chefs, and owners who share a passion for their businesses and a desire for authenticity in their relationships with their clientele. Their members have a driving desire to protect and promote the richness and diversity of the world's cuisine and traditions of hospitality. They are committed to preserving local heritage and the environment, as encompassed in the Charter presented to UNESCO in November 2014.

The following criteria were considered to choose this specific hotel as the unit of analysis: data accessibility, author with good connections with the hotel. According to [5] data accessibility is a consideration at all stages of the research process in other to bench scientists who make data accessible to informatics, teams who share data across departments and researchers who make data accessible to the public. [5] also explained that data accessibility is essential for minimizing data redundancy of research efforts; to draw more reliable conclusions from more data and to inspire novel questions from different approaches and to be of an international hotel chain; and its potential to grow in the digital world [5].

3.2 Data Collection and Analysis Methods

In this case study, different data collection techniques were used, as suggested for the case study approach [65], namely: i) netnography and ii) semi-structed interviews. Netnography is recognized as a useful research tool for collecting and analyzing information online [30]. It is based on an ethnographic approach to studying and understanding consumption-related aspects of customers' lives online [31]. With the digitalization, netnography became now more relevant than ever before [52]. According to [29] semi-structured interviews are probably one of the most used qualitative methods. Semi-structured interviews are useful for investigating complex behaviors, opinions, and emotions and for collecting a diversity of experiences [37]. Furthermore, semi-structured interviews have a colloquial and informal tone and allow for an open answer in the participants' own words, rather than "yes or no" answer [37].

To fulfil the first objective of this study, it was carried out a descriptive/exploratory analysis of the website. In a second phase were analyzed the social networks and online booking platforms in which the Hotel Casa da Calçada is present on. To identify the features and evaluate the website from the marketing point of view, was used an adaptation of a model proposed by [8]. The thirty-one indicators were analyzed and distributed across five criteria: promotion, point of sale, price and product, customer relationship and usability.

Regarding the measures adopted, two types were used: Binary (Yes/No) and Traffic Light. For the first type, verification of the indicator contributes with 100%, and failure to verify the indicator will be classified as 0. In the case of Traffic Light type indicators, the green light contributes to 100%, the yellow light indicator contributes half (50%) and red, zero (0%). Tools used for test website performance were responsive website, website loading, absence of invalid links and plug-ins and legible letter. The second first-hand data was gathered through online interviews with the hotel's sales manager and its communication outsourcing company *Nomore*. *This company* partner´s helps the hotel, managing digital content. Both interviews were made with the help of *Zoom* software and took 30 min each. Also, the interview was taped, and some important notes were taken by one of the researchers.

It was prepared an interview to gather the necessary information divided into 5 questions. The first two questions were open-ended and aimed to understand the assumptions of the web marketing strategy and how do the hotel measure the impact of web marketing actions on the consumer. To the following three questions was used a Likert scale from 1 to 5, (1 = "not at all important" and 5 = "extremely important") to analyze the most effective tools in each of the 3 w's of Web Marketing (Web Design, Web Performance, Web Promotion). Regarding the third research question, based on the interviews and literature review was made possible suggestion to hotel improve their digital performance. Lastly, a descriptive analysis was conducted to the website, social media platforms and extranets.

3.3 Interviews

The interviews were made with the purpose of the hotel explained what strategies this specific hotel consider more important regarding web design, web promotion and web performance. Furthermore, with the interviews was possible to find some suggestions to improve the hotel efficiency in digital performance. According to the Sales Manager the all the tools are extremely important for their strategy, except the Website navigability that is not extremely, but very important.

4 Data Findings and Analysis

According to the first research objective, namely, to analyze, at Casa da Calçada hotel, the current digital marketing strategies, social media and extranets presence and what objectives they intend to achieve, to be able to fulfil this objective, an analysis of the website, social networks and extranets was carried out. As explained on the methodology, to explore the capacity of the Casa da Calçada website, the model of [8] was used. Regarding social networks, a survey was carried out on the accounts that the hotel has on each of these social networks to explore their presence. As for Review pages/Partner channels/extranets, an in-deep exploratory survey was carried to identify which extranet platforms the hotel is present on.

4.1 Website Analysis

Regarding the results obtained, the global classification achieved was 60% (Table 1). Of the five categories analyzed, the criteria's Usability and Promotion presented the best rating (70%), followed by Customer Relationship (60%) and Point of Sale and Price and Product (50%).

As for the Promotion criteria, the hotel presents all the necessary information that is fundamental. However, despite providing a tourist guide on the website it is not connected to any link. Also, it does not have a price comparison engine or a search engine.

Regarding the Point-of-Sale Criteria the website has a reservation system, where there is information about the booking conditions (commercial policy). The Security

Policy is not accessible through the website. Nevertheless, if it is searched on Google (seen on July 5th, 2021) "Casa da Calçada Terms and Conditions" the link of that page appears and contains the security and privacy policy. As the payment is at the hotel, the website does not have information about secure online payment.

It is also possible for guests to add comments in the reservation, which can make the service more personalized (Indicator 3.2 – Personalized and Customized Service, Table 1). As for the Customer Relationship criterium, the website does not have a Questions and Answers (Q&A) section, and although it as reference to the Relais & Chatêaux because of the logo in the bottom of the page, there is no information about membership or the benefits.

The Usability criteria (Table 1) presents 9 indicators on the user experience when navigating the hotel's website. There are only two indicators that have the score 0, since were found invalid links and they do not change color when visited. The authors considered the website has a consistent design and innovation and thus it has a score of 100%. According to the tools of Table 1 the website has a responsive design and absence of plug-ins (score of 100%), but the load time of the website is higher than 2 s (3.12 s) and there are letters that are not legible and that's why these last two indicators have half score. Whey the authors analyzed the website found that it has unique URLs, has the back button functionality and it is possible to access with or without www.

Table 1. Casa da Calçada website performance (adapted [10]).

Criteria		Indicators	Weight	Measure	Score	Criteria Score
Promotion (20%)	1.1	Basic Information of the Hotel	10%	Yes	100%	70%
	1.2	Information about the Services	10%	Yes	100%	
	1.3	Information about the Rooms	10%	Yes	100%	
	1.4	Information about the prices	10%	Yes	100%	
	1.5	Price Comparison Engine	10%	No	0%	
	1.6	Information about Promotions/Offers	10%	Yes	100%	
	1.7	Information about the destination	10%	Yes	100%	
	1.8	Links to tourist attractions	10%	No	0%	
	1.9	Information about guest reviews	10%	Yes	100%	
	1.10	Search Engine	10%	No	0%	
Point of Sale (20%)	2.1	Reservation System	25%	Yes	100%	50%
	2.2	Commercial Policy (Cancellation)	25%	Yes	100%	
	2.3	Security Policy	25%	No	0%	
	2.4	Information about secure online payment	25%	No	0%	
Price & Product (20%)	3.1	User identification for access to different prices	50%	No	0%	50%
	3.2	Personalized and Customized Service (special requests)	50%	Yes	100%	
Customer Relationship (20%)	4.1	User Registration	20%	Yes	100%	60%
	4.2	Membership	20%	No	0%	
	4.3	Q&A	20%	No	0%	
	4.4	Privacy Policy	20%	Yes	100%	
	4.5	Customer Service	20%	Yes	100%	
Usability (20%)	5.1	Consistent Design and Navigation	10%	⊛	100%	70%
	5.2	Responsive Design	10%	⊛	100%	
	5.3	Website Loading until 2 seconds	10%	⊛	50%	
	5.4	Unique URLs	10%	⊛	100%	
	5.5	Back button functionality	10%	Yes	100%	
	5.6	Absense of invalid links	10%	No	0%	
	5.7	Links change color when visited	10%	No	0%	
	5.8	Absense of plug-ins	10%	Yes	100%	
	5.9	Letter legible	10%	⊛	50%	
	5.10	Access with or without www (or https)	10%	Yes	100%	
Total Score						60%

Source: Author's own elaboration, based on [10] model

Concerning the analyses of the website, the customer does not need to leave the homepage to get an overview of all the services offered by the hotel. There are two buttons that are always visible: the menu and "book now" and therefore the customer can access it or make a reservation at any point of the site.

In the upper right corner, the customer can select one of four languages available, namely French, Spanish, Portuguese, and English. Scrolling down the page, after the slideshow, an option to book appears, followed by a video with the hashtag #itstime-tomakememories with the intention of creating a need in the customers. A brief description of the city is also present, with an image that translates its history, followed by an overview of the rooms offered by the hotel. Next, there is a presentation of the Michelin-starred restaurant present in the hotel, where some representative pictures of dishes belonging to the menu are highlighted. Therefore, are presented special offers for bookings, events inside the hotel, news about the destination and TripAdvisor comments, where clients report their experiences. At the bottom of the page there is contact information, such as telephone, email, location, and a blank space where the customer enters his email address to have access to the newsletter. On the left there is a space nominated "follow us" that has the logo of Facebook, Instagram, and TripAdvisor. Each one with a direct link to the social media page of the hotel.

In the menu it is possible to explore more about the hotel, as well as the city, the awards and distinctions, the rooms and details, gastronomy, events, offers, experiences, and a gallery with high quality and inspirational images.

4.2 Webdesign

According to the interviews having a Website Responsive is the key because as stated by both interviewers "Nowadays if we want to capture all customers, the website has to be as adapted as possible in terms of visibility and it is extremely important to have the same ease of access to the website on all platforms". In relation to their web content communication must be clear, direct, directed to the target and in coherence with the team to be uniform. Not only the way they communicate with the client (images, text) but the truthfulness because "if the client reads something that is not explicit, he can complain, ask or demand, which is very common in communication agencies that sometimes change words." It is very important to have all platforms in conformity at information level. They must be appealing, real, since clients create images in their minds. They have maximum importance at communication level but can be a great risk if the image does not reflect reality. Videos are more advantageous on platforms like Instagram because if customers see movement they stop. On the website they can distract the customer and increase the time it takes to book. Regarding Usability, the website should be accessible and self-driven.

The Website Navigability is quite important for the Sales Manager but for the hotel management it is less of a priority because they have little autonomy to change the site. There is another company that manages the site and so the hotel tries as little as possible to change the hyperlinks and pages because it is very expensive. Only the images and information can be changed more easily.

4.3 Webpromotion

For the hotel the most important tools of Web promotion are the website, social media and Search Engine Optimization Strategy which are important. For the Sales Manager the website is "the second house: the client has to be absorbed right from moment zero, at the beginning of his research and journey and so a website presence, appealing images and adequate and coherent information are extremely essential to retain the client". Regarding social media, in her opinion, in today's world who is not on Facebook and Instagram does not exist. The challenge is to generate sales through this presence on social networks. Many times, it gives the hotel status and visibility but does not necessarily convert into reservations and sales. For what they see, clients know Casa da Calçada by name but the presence on social networks has an impact on the level of web presence. The SEO strategy is also extremely important because it is a holistic way to analyze data and see where they can improve, grow and highlight.

The Web Promotion tools are the newsletters, User Generated Content (UGC), Videos, Banners and Influencers. There is a space to subscribe to their newsletter in their website which is for the hotel one of the best ways to communicate with their guests and build loyalty. It encourages them to visit the hotel again. In relation to the reviews and comments (UGC) it is essential to know where they can improve and where we their weaker and stronger, according to the Sales Manager, the opinion of their guests is a key for success. The videos are more dynamic and therefore more appealing, and the banners are very important to promote the hotel. The influencers are also important because they a very quick way to increase followers and in turn bring visibility to the hotel. The blog is moderately important because for the Sales Manager it does not have much expression.

4.4 Webperformance

Regarding the Web Performance the analyzed criteria, Web analytics, the Google AdSense (Search Engine) and the Web analytics. In relation to the tracking tools and Web analytics, monitoring web-performance through Google Analytics is one of the most important practices in the communication planning of Casa da Calçada. Besides measuring its performance, it allows them to identify not only practices with a greater potential for return, but also the new behaviors and trends of the consumer public. In addition, it allows the hotel to understand if the set of campaigns and communication that has been carried out is reaching the public and if the objectives are, or are not, being achieved.

Google search engine is extremely important, and its fruitful potential is worked on from two different angles. The first – the most important – is the organic one, which focuses on the good natural positioning of Casa da Calçada's website and its communication objects in search results. Here, they bet on the development of the site's SEO, regular press advisory services (external to this company) and quality content in the social networks. On the other hand, we credit Google results sponsorship with a lot of relevance, but they place this practice in the wake of the previous one and that's why they gave a level of importance of 4 to Search Engine Advertising (SEA) Campaigns. This is because, despite its importance, and in order not to compromise the solidity of the hotel's premium positioning, paid content should not overly surpass Casa da Calçada's organic communication. In other words, it is the function of organic communication to be "one step ahead" of sponsored contents, reducing their function not to the responsibility of a first contact, but to a healthy position of complementarity. In relation to the Webrankings they are extremely important and place Casa da Calçada's communication media at the top of search results is an integrated objective in all digital campaigns, to guarantee the greatest reach and consumption of these contents.

5 Conclusion

The purpose of this study was to identify the importance of webmarketing strategies, namely, webdesign, webpromotion and webperformance in the hotel sector. In this exploratory case, was perceived the importance of the usage of all these strategies and digital techniques to increase the digital footprint, also to improve the guest satisfaction. Regarding the first objective analyze, at Casa da Calçada hotel, the current digital marketing strategies, social media, and extranets presence, first, according to Carvalho et al. (2018) model, the results obtained, the global classification of the website was 60% (Table 1). Of the five categories analyzed, the criteria's Usability and Promotion presented the best rating (70%), followed by Customer Relationship (60%) and Point of Sale and Price and Product (50%). Second, the hotel is present in three social media platforms: Facebook, Instagram, and YouTube (Fig. 1). Facebook and Instagram are the most used by the hotel and there are new publications every day or in maximum every three days in each platform. YouTube was created in 2014, and it is by far the one that has less expression with only 1 subscriber and 3 videos. Thirdly, the OTA's, Fig. 3 shows a brief analysis of the performance of the hotel Casa da Calçada in the main booking channels (OTA's). Based on interactions by clients (Fig. 3), it was found that the most used platform is Booking (754 reviews) followed by Trivago (395 reviews), Expedia (175 reviews), Hotels.com (85 reviews), Relais & Chateaux (68 reviews), Trip.com or Ctrip (12 reviews), Agoda and Destinia (7 reviews). Despite the platforms have different score ratings, it was perceived that the hotel has an excellent global score in all.

Concerning the second objective of the paper, to identify the most effective tools in the web design, web promotion and web performance (3 W's of Web Marketing) of the hotel. First, according to the interviews the main factors are considered as truly important: Webdesign – website responsive, web content, photos, videos, and usability (5 = extremely important) and website navigability (4 = important); Webpromotion – website, social media, SEO Strategy (5 = extremely important), newsletters, UGC, videos, banners, influencers (4 = important) and blog (3 = more or less important); Webperformance – tracking tools, webanalytics, search engine – google adsense and webrankings (5 = Very important), SEA campaigns (4 = Important), GDS (Not applicable). Lastly, to improve the hotel digital performance, based on the interviews and literature reviews the suggestions are: i) creating a section about the services provided by the hotel can make guests more interested in the hotel; ii) more pictures on the website otherwise, can run serious risks of losing potential direct customers and become more dependent on OTA's; iii) solve the problem of links going to blank pages, as the digital world is measured by click, it is very important to correct these errors on the website, as it can lead to the purchase being abandoned on because the website does not convey confidence and do not provide a pleasant digital experience; iv) a chat-bot could be creative, thus, the experience at Casa da Calçada, starts from the moment the guest access the website; v) regarding the social networks, the hotel should explore other hotel's accounts with success examples to understand what they are doing, and some explore techniques to increase the engagement with customers; vi) through the analysis of the OTA's where the hotel has presence was perceived that all channels have information about the services of the hotel but some OTA's present wrong information, compromising the service provided to meet and exceed customer expectations, in that case, the hotel should solve this problem.

Regarding the theorical contributions, this research discussed the usage of the 3 W's of Webmarketing (Webdesign, Webpromotion and Webperformance) and the importance of them on hotel digital performance. Also, this research intends to contribute in a theoretical way by providing inputs to the body of literature on digital marketing applied to the hotel sector. As for managerial contributions, this research intends to help hotel managers who want to improve hotel performance by implementing digital strategies. It also shows suggestions for improvements regarding digital performance, useful for hoteliers. There is lots of potential to the grew of digital on the hotel sector and this case study helps other hoteliers to develop digital good practices to the hotel sector.

This study has also two limitations: each OTA have their special criteria to receive comments from guests. It was not possible to collect information about the reviews, to better understand, if what the content online offers is attended on the experience Regarding future research, more exploratory research may also be useful o the hotel sector, specially to those who are investing in digital strategies and platforms applied to the hotel sector.

References

1. Alan, B., So, S., Sin, L.: Crisis management and recovery: how restaurants in Hong Kong responded to SARS. Int. J. Hosp. Manage. 25(1), 3–11 (2006)
2. Atshaya, S., Rungta, S.: Digital marketing vs. internet marketing: a detailed study. Int. J. Novel Res. Market. Manage. Econ. 3(1), 29–33 (2016)
3. Baum, T., Hai, T.: Hospitality, tourism, human rights and the impact of COVID-19. Int. J. Contemp. Hosp. Manage. (2020)
4. Bryman, A.: Triangulation and measurement. Department of Social Sciences, Loughborough University, Loughborough, Leicestershire (2004). www.referenceworld.com/sage/socialsci ence/triangulation.Pdf
5. Bozoki, W.: 3 Key Reasons data accessibility is essential in research. https://www.labkey. com/3-key-reasons-data-accessibility-essential-research/ (2018). Accessed 24 July 2021
6. Cai, J.: Pay attention to the influences of SARS on tourists' psychological changes. China Tourism News (2003)
7. Carter, N., Bryant-Lukosius, D., DiCenso, A., Blythe, J., Neville, J.: The use of triangulation in qualitative research. Oncol. Nurs. Forum 41(5), 545–547 (2014)
8. Carvalho, D., Lopes, F., Alexandre, I., Alturas, B.: Qualidade dos sítios web da administração pública portuguesa. RISTI-Revista Ibérica de Sistemas e Tecnologias de Informação 20, 78–98 (2016)
9. De Pelsmacker, P., van Tilburg, S., Holthof, C.: Digital marketing strategies, online reviews and hotel performance. Int. J. Hosp. Manage. 72, 47–55 (2018)
10. Decrop, A.: Triangulation in qualitative tourism research. Tour. Manage. 20(1), 157–161 (1999). https://doi.org/10.1016/S0261-5177(98)00102-2
11. DeLone, H., McLean, R.: Information systems success: the quest for the dependent variable. Inf. Syst. Res. 3(1), 60–95 (1992)

12. Denzin, K.: The Research Act in Sociology. Aldine, Chicago (1970)
13. Denzin, K.: Sociological Methods: A Sourcebook. McGraw-Hill, New York, NY (1978)
14. Duan, W., Gu, B., Whinston, B.: The dynamics of online word of mouth and product sales: an empirical investigation of the movie industry. J. Retail **84**(2), 233–242 (2008)
15. Feagin, R., Orum, M., Sjoberg, G. (eds.): A Case for the Case Study. UNC Press Books (1991)
16. Gu, B., Ye, Q.: First step in social media: measuring the influence of online management responses on customer satisfaction. Prod. Oper. Manage. **23**(4), 570–582 (2014)
17. Haryanto, T.: COVID-19 pandemic and international tourism demand. J. Dev. Econ. **5**(1), 1–5 (2020)
18. Henderson, J.C., Ng, A.: Responding to crisis: severe acute respiratory syndrome (SARS) and hotels in Singapore. Int. J. Tour. Res. **6**(6), 411–419 (2004)
19. Heung, S.: Satisfaction levels of mainland Chinese travelers with Hong Kong hotel services. Int. J. Contemp. Hosp. Manage. **12**(5), 308–315 (2000). https://doi.org/10.1108/09596110010339689
20. Huang, H.: Web performance scale. Inf. Manage. **42**(6), 841–852 (2005)
21. Ivanov, S.H., Webster, C., Stoilova, E., Slobodskoy, D.: Biosecurity, crisis management, automation technologies and economic performance of travel, tourism and hospitality companies – a conceptual framework. Tour. Econ. (2020). https://doi.org/10.1177/1354816620946541
22. Ivanova, M., Ivanov, I.K., Ivanov, S.: Travel behaviour after the pandemic: the case of Bulgaria. Anatolia **32**(1), 1–11 (2020)
23. Jackson, L., Drummond, K., Camara, S.: What is qualitative research? Qual. Res. Rep. Commun. **8**(1), 21–28 (2007)
24. Jafari, K., Saydam, B., Erkanlı, E., Olorunsola, O.: The impacts of the COVID-19 pandemic on the consumer behavior of Turkish tourists. Revista TURISMO: Estudos e Práticas, p. 5 (2020)
25. Jo, H., Shin, E., Kim, H.: Changes in consumer behaviour in the post-COVID-19 era in Seoul South Korea. Sustainability **13**(1), 136 (2021)
26. Juliver, J.: The ultimate guide to website performance. https://blog.hubspot.com/website/website-performance. Accessed 21 July 2021
27. Kim, Y., Kim, U., Park, C.: The effects of perceived value, website trust and hotel trust on online hotel booking intention. Sustainability **9**(12), 2262 (2017)
28. Kirkpatrick, D., Roth, D.: Why there's no escaping the blog. Fortune **10**, 44–50 (2005)
29. Kitchin, R., Tate, N.J.: Conducting Research into Human Geography. Edinburgh Gate, Pearson (2000)
30. Kozinets, R.V.: E-tribalized marketing? The strategic implications of virtual communities of consumption. Eur. Manage. J. **17**(3), 252–264 (1999)
31. Kozinets, R.V.: Click to connect: netnography and tribal advertising. J. Advert. Res. **46**(3), 279–288 (2006)
32. Lebe, S., Mulej, M., Zupan, S., Milfelner, B.: Social responsibility, motivation and satisfaction: small hotels guests' perspective. Kybernetes (2014)
33. Leite, R.A., Azevedo, A.: The role of digital marketing: a perspective from porto hotels' managers. Int. J. Mark. Commun. New Media **2** (2017)
34. Levy, E., Duan, W., Boo, S.: An analysis of one-star online reviews and responses in the Washington, DC, lodging market. Cornell Hosp. Q. **54**(1), 49–63 (2013)
35. Leung, X.Y., Xue, L., Bai, B.: Internet marketing research in hospitality and tourism: a review and journal preferences. Int. J. Contemp. Hosp. Manage. **27**(7), 1556–1572 (2015)
36. Litvin, W., Goldsmith, E., Pan, B.: Electronic word-of-mouth in hospitality and tourism management. Tour. Manage. **29**(3), 458–468 (2008)
37. Longhurst, R.: Semi-structured interviews and focus groups. Key Methods Geogr. **3**(2), 143–156 (2003)

38. MacDonald, M.: Creating a Website: The Missing Manual. O'Reilly Media, ISBN 978-1-4493-7454-9 (2015)
39. Masiero, L., Viglia, G., Nieto-Garcia, M.: Strategic consumer behavior in online hotel booking. Ann. Tour. Res. **83**, 102947 (2020)
40. Melo, J., Hernández-Maestro, M., Muñoz-Gallego, A.: Service quality perceptions, online visibility, and business performance in rural lodging establishments. J. Travel Res. **56**(2), 250–262 (2017)
41. Mihajlović, I., Koncul, N.: Changes in consumer behaviour – the challenges for providers of tourist services in the destination. Econ. Res. Ekonomska Istraživanja **29**(1), 914–937 (2016). https://doi.org/10.1080/1331677X.2016.1206683
42. Morosan, C., Jeong, M.: Users' perceptions of two types of hotel reservation web sites. Int. J. Hosp. Manage. **27**(2), 284–292 (2008)
43. Newman, W., Landay, A.: Sitemaps, storyboards, and specifications: a sketch of web site design practice. In: Proceedings of the 3rd Conference on Designing Interactive Systems: Processes, Practices, Methods, and Techniques, pp. 263–274 (2000)
44. Oh, H., Kim, B., Shin, J.: Hospitality and tourism marketing: recent developments in research and future directions. Int. J. Hosp. Manage. **23**(5), 425–447 (2004)
45. Patton, Q.: Enhancing the quality and credibility of qualitative analysis. Health Sci. Res. **34**, 1189–1208 (1999)
46. Polit, F., Beck, T.: Gender bias undermines evidence on gender and health. Qual. Health Res. **22**(9), 1298 (2012)
47. Relais & Châteaux Linkedin Page. https://www.linkedin.com/company/relais-&-chateaux/?originalSubdomain=pt. Accessed 08 July 2021
48. Rita, P., Oliveira, C.: O Marketing no Comércio Eletrónico, 1st edn. Sociedade Portuguesa de Inovação, Porto (2006)
49. Schuckert, M., Liu, X., Law, R.: Hospitality and tourism online reviews: recent trends and future directions. J. Travel Tour. Mark. **32**(5), 608–621 (2015)
50. Shah, C., Trupp, A.: Trends in consumer behaviour and accommodation choice: perspectives from India. Anatolia **31**(2), 244–259 (2020)
51. Sigala, M.: Tourism and COVID-19: impacts and implications for advancing and resetting industry and research. J. Bus. Res. **117**, 312–321 (2020)
52. Simmons, G.: Marketing to postmodern consumers: introducing the internet chameleon. Eur. J. Mark. **42**(3/4), 299–310 (2008)
53. Stake, R.: The Art of Case Research. Sage Publications, Newbury Park, CA (1995)
54. Teng, M., Wu, S., Chou, Y.: Price or convenience: What is more important for online and offline bookings? A study of a five-star resort hotel in Taiwan. Sustainability **12**(10), 3972 (2020)
55. Tellis, W.: Application of a case study methodology. The Qual. Rep. **3**(3), 1–19 (1997)
56. Torres, N., Singh, D., Robertson-Ring, A.: Consumer reviews and the creation of booking transaction value: lessons from the hotel industry. Int. J. Hosp. Manage. **50**, 77–83 (2015)
57. TravelBi.: Turismo em Portugal. https://travelbi.turismodeportugal.pt/pt-pt/Documents/Turismo%20em%20Portugal/Turismo%20em%20Portugal%20e%20NUTS%20II%20-%202019.pdf (2021). Accessed 03 July 2021
58. TravelBi: Receitas do Turismo: Viagens e Turismo na Balança de Pagamentos. https://travelbi.turismodeportugal.pt/pt-pt/Paginas/PowerBI/balanca-de-pagamentos.aspx (2021). Accessed 03 July 2021
59. TravelBi: Impacto do COVID-19 nas chegas de turistas com origem nos principais mercados long-haul (AU, BR, CA, CN, IN, JP, KR e US) e mercardos Europa (BE, DE, ES, FR, GB, IE, IT, NL). https://travelbi.turismodeportugal.pt/pt-pt/Paginas/PowerBI/chegadas-internacionais.aspx (2021). Accessed 03 July 2021

60. World Tourism Organization (UNWTO): 2020: A year in review (2021). https://www.unwto. org/covid-19-and-tourism-2020/. Accessed 03 July 2021
61. Wen, Z., Huimin, G., Kavanaugh, R.: The impacts of SARS on the consumer behaviour of Chinese domestic tourists. Curr. Issue Tour. **8**(1), 22–38 (2005)
62. Wishnick, E.: Dilemmas of securitization and health risk management in the People's Republic of China: the cases of SARS and avian influenza. Health Policy Plan. **25**(6), 454–466 (2010)
63. World Wide Web Consortium (W3C): Web Content Accessibility Guidelines (WCAG) 2.1. https://www.w3.org/TR/WCAG21/. Accessed 05 Aug 2021
64. Yin, R.K.: Case Study Research: Design and Methods, 3rd edn. Sage, Thousand Oaks, CA (2003)
65. Yin, R.: Case Study Research: Design and Methods, 2nd edn. Sage Publishing, Thousand Oasks, CA (1994)
66. Yoo, M., Lee, S., Bai, B.: Hospitality marketing research from 2000 to 2009: topics, methods, and trends. Int. J. Contemp. Hosp. Manage. **23**(4), 517–532 (2011)

Author Index

Printed in the United States
by Baker & Taylor Publisher Services